The emergence of the evangelical community is a remarkable story within the Christian church. Embodying a heartfelt love for Christ, His church, and the Scriptures, its radiating effect is to bring life transformation to people and society. *Evangelicals Around the World* paints with a broad brush, but also with sufficient detail to provide a picture of Evangelicals. This handbook will help Evangelicals better understand themselves and enable other religions, communities, media, and the academy in knowing about our development, prime influencers, essential ideas which shape our vision, and a compelling faith, that God was in Christ, reconciling the world.

Bishop Efraim Tendero, Secretary General of the World Evangelical Alliance

This book is like a rich biography, full of kaleidoscopic insights, backgrounds, and narratives of the real life and multi-cultural diversity of evangelical presence, life, witness, and activity around the world today. It is remarkably comprehensive as a resource and wonderfully revealing as a panorama.

Rev. Dr. Christopher J. H. Wright, International Ministries Director, Langham Partnership

The handbook is an incredible source to know how God's people faithfully fulfilled the purposes of God for this world as they journeyed with God and one another. Its stories motivate us to engage in God's redemptive mission.

Rev. Dr. Richard Howell, General Secretary, Asia Evangelical Alliance

This singular handbook gives the most comprehensive, factual account of connected Evangelicals to date, and the most complete understanding of our goals and identity. It is a must read for anyone who wants to understand the nature and impact of today's Christianity.

Rev. Dr. Joel C. Hunter, Senior Pastor, Northland—A Church Distributed

Evangelicals Around the World is an invaluable resource for all Christians. This book will help build bridges among Evangelicals of all denominations, help us understand the opportunities and challenges that we face as the Body of Christ, and will help to clarify our distinctiveness as Evangelicals.

Rev. Dr. Wirachai Kowae, Chairman, Evangelical Fellowship of Thailand

An era of increased access to information has also yielded misperceptions about who Evangelicals are globally. We now have a comprehensive resource to dispel misinformation, serving both the skeptic and serious inquirer. This clearly written volume allows Evangelicals to confidently describe themselves, demonstrating the breadth, vitality, and texture of this significant segment of World Christianity.

Byron D. Klaus, President, Assemblies of God Theological Seminary, Springfield, Missouri

This handbook is a footprint of gospel exploits that transform Evangelicals while turning the world upside down. The volume of faithfulness will inspire the most timid to exercise their Evangelical capacity with a contextual mandate.

Commissioner M. Christine MacMillan, The Salvation Army; Chair, WEA Global Human Trafficking Taskforce

This handbook is a great resource for all Evangelicals who want an in-depth knowledge about this global movement and for others who want to understand this growing movement. Since the authors are as diverse as the movement they describe, this wider approach captures the DNA of the global evangelical movement. A great and timely resource for those who want to look behind the scenes.

Prof. Dr. theol. Dr. phil. Thomas Schirrmacher, President, International Council, International Society of Human Rights (Geneva); President, Martin Bucer European Seminary and Research Institutes

This handbook is a seminal work on the whole question of Evangelical identity and a corrective of the popular stereotypes of what the 21st century world makes of Evangelicals. It is a welcome resource for Evangelicals around the world, and a witness of how God continues to work out His purposes.

Aiah Foday-Khabenje, General Secretary, Association of Evangelicals in Africa (AEA)

The reader will find a wealth of information that will serve to view Evangelicalism in its diversity and richness. It will become obvious that the Latin American Evangelical world is as Joseph's coat, a beautifully embroidered gathering of colors, which changes its hues continually as it finds its own identity and expresses the Body of Christ. And that the Evangelicals, while not beholden to any one line of thought, are taking their place in the Christian world.

Rev. Samuel Olson, Pastor, Venezuela

EDITORS:

BRIAN C. STILLER, TODD M. JOHNSON,
KAREN STILLER, MARK HUTCHINSON

EVANGELICALS AROUND THE WORLD

A GLOBAL HANDBOOK

FOR THE 21ST CENTURY

Published in Nashville, Tennessee, by Thomas Nelson. Thomas Nelson is a registered trademark of HarperCollins Christian Publishing, Inc.

Thomas Nelson titles may be purchased in bulk for educational, business, fund-raising, or sales promotional use. For information, please e-mail SpecialMarkets@ThomasNelson.com.

ISBN 978-1-4016-7853-1

Printed in China
15 16 17 18 19 20 DSC 6 5 4 3 2 1

CONTENTS

FOREWORD TO A MASSIVE UNDERTAKING

It is no small challenge to define and outline the life and history of any of the three major Christian communities in the world. Evangelicals, who some estimate make up 600 million of Christians around the world, Roman Catholics who are estimated at 1.2 billion and the World Council of Churches (including Orthodox Churches) numbered at 550 million—are all varied in history and their make up.

Evangelicals Around the World: A Global Handbook for the 21st Century attempts to blaze a trail: to set out to provide definition as to who Evangelicals are.

Over the past decades many others have defined our particular community in its various forms. Our team decided it was time to provide our own definition.

As the Evangelical community has grown, especially in the past few decades, its influence in some places is significant, and in other countries and regions, Evangelical influence is much smaller.

This book is a beginning. It is an imperfect book for an imperfect community. Each of us will find articles or data with which we may not agree. There will be places, people, and events that you would have included that we did not.

As we outlined the book, we consulted far and wide. With our finite amount of space, we chose how much we could devote to various topics. Our team then asked scholars and practicioners around the world—those researchers and writers with specialized knowledge—to put their fingers to the keyboard. It was not a simple task to match the right writer with the best topic. Each writer presents his or her own understanding of what are often complex subjects, full of nuance and potential debate. You won't be surprised to learn that the editorial committee doesn't always agree with everything written. Such is the reality of a complex community. We stand by the integrity of the writer's scholarship, as they reflected on this wide and varied Christian community past, present, and future.

We invite you to join the journey as this edition inevitably leads into a second edition. Please send your thoughts, suggestions, and additions to handbook@worldea.org. These will be used for future considerations.

I'm grateful for my colleagues who served on the editorial team: Todd Johnson, as Associate Editor, Karen Stiller as Managing Editor, and Mark Hutchinson as Regions Editor. They poured their expertise and time into making this a reality. As well we are so thankful for others who served us at the very right times with their immense skills in writing, editing, and research: Debra Fieguth, Albert W. Hickman, and Rob Robotham. Please read through the list of contributing writers. Their time and effort made this a reality. Our heartfelt thanks to Alee Anderson and Frank Couch at Thomas Nelson for their hard work on this project.

On the following page we note our thanks to those people, foundations, churches, and agencies that provided the development funds to get this up and running. Your vision and support has made this a reality, and for you I again express my thanks.

This book is about a part of Christ's church that is growing in new and wonderful and at times troubling ways. I noted it is imperfect, wrestling with issues and challenges which inevitably face those who have the temerity to believe that Jesus Christ came to our world as God, dying and rising again so we might live eternally.

May you thrill to the stories, histories, and issues, knowing that the Spirit of God is leading, empowering, and pouring into his people the very life of our risen Lord.

When I am asked, "What is an Evangelical?" my answer is: "Enthusiastic Christians." That is, Christians who believe the Bible to be true, and that it is God's message of love and his plan for life, peace and reconciliation. We are a community of Christians who want the world to know this very good news story.

Brian C. Stiller, General Editor

A WARM THANK-YOU TO BENEFACTORS AND SPONSORS

We wish to express our thanks to those whose vision and generosity provided the development funds to make this first-of-its-kind publication a reality.

Benefactors

First, the editorial team expresses its sincere thanks and appreciation to benefactors who invested considerable funds right from the beginning of this vision. In explaining the importance of this handbook, these families and individuals saw how important this publication would be to the fostering of understanding among the Evangelical community and the wider Christian community and beyond. They also saw the value it would have within the media, providing a single source for articles, documentaries, and publications.

To these our friends and benefactors, on behalf of the World Evangelical Alliance, we offer our hearty, ongoing thanks and appreciation.

Herb and Erna Buller

The Falle Family Foundation

Timothy J. Hearn

Arnold and Ruth Heron

Paul and Heather Hogeboom

Hugh and Sharon Little

Archie and Kay McLean

Ralph and Melanie Moulton

Dr. Donald S. Reimer

Brian and Ellen Relph

Ian and Alice Van Norman

Harry Voortman

Prem Watsa

Sponsors

Our thanks go to you, the churches and organizations who saw the potential within this initiative to serve the body of Christ and provide information that often is obscure or hard to find. You understand the importance of others getting the facts straight. You are aware of how valuable it is for media to have information ready in the development of their material. As an editorial team and on behalf of our worldwide Christian community, we thank you for your vision and generosity.

Bakerview Mennonite Brethren Church, Abbotsford, Canada

Centre Street Church, Calgary, Canada

Church on the Queensway, Toronto, Canada

Evangel Church, Toronto, Canada

Millwoods Assembly, Edmonton, Canada

Pentecostal Assemblies of Canada

Pentecostal Assemblies of Newfoundland and Labrador, Canada

Toronto Chinese Community Church, Toronto, Canada

World Vision Canada

AN INTRODUCTION TO THE WORLD EVANGELICAL ALLIANCE

By Brian C. Stiller

The World Evangelical Alliance (WEA) is the global association that serves six hundred million Evangelicals worldwide. In 1846 Christian leaders from ten countries met in London for the purpose of launching something entirely new: an organization that would express unity among Christians who belonged to different churches. On the basis of a statement of faith and with the vision of Jesus' prayer for the unity of believers recorded in John 17, the WEA[1] operated for more than one hundred years as an informal structure and platform for evangelical unity in prayer and action, holding regular conferences for fellowship and unity in different cities of Europe and in North America.

Two world wars decimated hopes for greater unity.

In 1951, some ninety-one men and women from twenty-one nations met in Holland as the International Convention of Evangelicals to reenvision the old Evangelical Alliance into a global fellowship. Renamed the World Evangelical Fellowship, it established this threefold purpose: the furtherance of the gospel, the defense and confirmation of the gospel, and fellowship in the gospel (Phil. 1). Since then, the WEA has grown worldwide, with its international office located in the United Kingdom, Singapore, the Philippines, and now the United States. David Howard, WEA's International Director from 1982–92 pointedly titled his book *The World Evangelical Fellowship: A Dream that Would Not Die*. A growing membership, new partnerships, and newly established initiatives and task forces are core to the work of the WEA in its task to serve its worldwide constituency.

Today the WEA is comprised of evangelical alliances in seven regions and 129 nations with 150 member organizations. WEA's specialized commissions, initiatives, and task forces, together with global partner organizations, engage in areas ranging from mission, theology and religious liberty, to social justice issues including human trafficking, poverty, peace building, creation care, and nuclear weapons disarmament.

The WEA's mission is threefold:

- Representing over six hundred million Evangelicals worldwide, the WEA as a voice, speaks through its national alliances and regional offices. On the global stage the WEA speaks for the wider evangelical constituency to governments and media, raising awareness about religious liberty and human rights. The WEA serves to answer queries about Evangelicals and their vision and various ministries in the world from other religions, media, and students. Holding consultative status at the Economic and Social Council

> **Today the WEA is comprised of evangelical alliances in seven regions and 129 nations with 150 member organizations.**

---

1. The WEA was called the World Evangelical Fellowship (WEF) until 2002 when its name was changed to the World Evangelical Alliance.

(ECOSOC), the WEA is also present at the United Nations in New York and Geneva. Working together with its regional and national alliances and partner organizations, the WEA submits national human rights reports and engages in issues such as refugee crises, small arms disarmament, and conflict resolution.

- The WEA equips its regional and national Evangelical Alliances to serve their communities through leadership and advocacy training, regular research and analysis reports on religious liberty situations, and theological, missiological, and practical books and publications that address critical issues that matter for the church today.
- The WEA serves as a platform to connect globally minded organizations with regional and national alliances to foster partnerships and collaboration. It seeks to bring people together to address those challenges that go beyond single countries and organizations and deliver practical outcomes to issues that are faced daily by pastors and leaders in local churches and communities worldwide.

Led by and inspired by Jesus' call to unity (John 17), the WEA's overall vision and call is to foster understanding and faith among its membership, so that the witness of Jesus Christ and Savior and Lord resonates throughout the world.

"The world Evangelical family has expanded significantly during this last century, and this we receive as a gift from God. As we move into the future, let's keep in mind that our significance and faithfulness to our call depends on the willingness to stress and recover the principles of this journey: solus Christus, sola gratia, sola scriptura, sola fide. It is all an effort to say Soli Deo Gloria."

—Dr. Valdir Steuernagel, Pastor, Comunidade do Redentor, Brazilian Lutheran Church; Coordinator of the Evangelical Alliance of Brazil, World Vision International Theologian at Large

200 EVENTS IN EVANGELICAL HISTORY

By Albert W. Hickman

The *Oxford Dictionary of English* defines history as "the whole series of past events connected with a person or thing . . . a continuous, typically chronological, record of important or public events or of a particular trend or institution."[1]

The following listing attempts to set forth just such a record of evangelical history. Some of the events occurred at an instant in time, while others spanned years or even decades. Some remain well known (even by non-Evangelicals), while others are more obscure. The importance of some was apparent at the time, while the significance of others has become obvious only in hindsight.

Most events in this listing were taken from David B. Barrett's "World Christian Chronology" contained in the *World Christian Database*.[2] Events fall mainly into one of four categories:

- Revivals, evangelical awakenings, and evangelistic crusades
- Founding of Bible societies, mission societies, denominations, and other organizations that were evangelical at the time, even if they are not so now
- Sending of missionaries
- Conferences, mostly related to missions and/or evangelism

The remaining entries span a variety of genres, including the production of Scripture translations and the development of movements such as Fundamentalism and Neo-Evangelicalism.

Multiple similar events, often spanning years or even decades, frequently were merged into a single entry with the relevant years noted. In the case of conferences, only the first of a series was chosen for the final list, unless a subsequent meeting provided a notable contribution to evangelical history. Due to space constraints, not every World Christian Chronology entry of a given type could be included in the final list. Effort was made to include those events that had the greatest impact on Evangelicalism as well as to balance the list geographically. Given the movement's roots in the United Kingdom, the United States, and Western Europe, the events are inevitably heavily weighted toward those areas. Despite its limitations, however, this chronology does offer insight into the events that have shaped (and continue to shape) twenty-first-century Evangelicalism.

1521: Erfurt University rector Johannes Crotus Rubianus, friend of Martin Luther, is the first to call Luther and his followers "Evangelicals" (Evangelische); the term rapidly gains widespread usage, and a variant is used to mean "Protestant" in most non-English European languages today.

Martin Luther.
Image: North Wind Picture Archives

1705: The Danish-Halle Mission (Lutheran), forerunner of Protestant missionary societies, is formed. Its first workers include Protestant pioneers to Tranquebar (India) Bartholomew Ziegenbalg, Heinrich Plutschau, and, later, Christian Schwartz.

1716: Irish Presbyterian educator William Tennent begins evangelizing in Britain's American colonies. In 1735 he will form his "Log College" to train men for revivalist ministry.

1720: German Pietist evangelist Theodorus Jacobus Freylinghuysen arrives among the Dutch Reformed churches in New Jersey, laying the foundation for the (First) Great Awakening in America. Beginning in 1726 he guides Irish Presbyterian minister and revivalist Gilbert

---

1. Angus Stevenson, ed., *Oxford Dictionary of English,* 3rd ed. (Oxford: Oxford University Press, 2010), 831.

2. Todd M. Johnson, ed., *World Christian Database* (Leiden/Boston: Brill, accessed November 2013).

Tennent (son of William) and others in a revival ministry, evangelizing among Scottish and Irish in Philadelphia, in New Jersey, and beyond.

1721: Norwegian pastor Hans Egede arrives in Greenland with his wife and family to begin Lutheran mission to the Inuit. His son Poul will translate the Gospels (1744) and entire New Testament (1766) into Inuktitut.

1722: Moravian (Herrnhut) Pietism begins in what is today Germany, led by Count Nicholas von Zinzendorf.

1725: The (First) Great Awakening, which was initiated under Freylinghuysen in New Jersey, spreads to New England under the leadership of revivalist Jonathan Edwards. From there it spreads throughout the British colonies in North America, lasting until 1770.

1730: Welsh Anglican vicar Griffith Jones starts the Circulating Charity School Movement, teaching up to 250,000 people basic Welsh literacy skills by the time of his death and paving the way for local and national revivals that will sweep the country for the remainder of the century.

1732: The Moravian Church organizes foreign missions under Bishop Zinzendorf and others, sending its first missionaries to St. Thomas, Danish West Indies. In 1787 the Society of the United Brethren for Propagating the Gospel among the Heathen is formed in Pennsylvania, United States. Between 1732 and 1862, the Moravians send abroad 2,000 missionaries.

1733: Welsh lay preacher Howell Harris adopts itinerant evangelism and open-air preaching; his method is later adopted by George Whitefield and John Wesley.

1735: George Whitefield undergoes a conversion experience in England. In 1736 he begins evangelistic travels in Britain and North America that will continue for the rest of his life.

1735: Moravians, the first evangelical missionaries to South America, arrive in Suriname to begin work among the African slaves and the native population.

George Whitefield.
Image: North Wind Picture Archives

1738: Charles Wesley and his brother John—who later become agents of the eighteenth-century Evangelical Revival and founders of Methodism—are converted in England.

1743: Missionaries from the (British) Society for the Propagation of the Gospel in Foreign Parts arrive in Nicaragua to work among the Miskito Indians. In the 1850s most Miskitos will join the Moravian Church, which continues to be influential on the country's Caribbean coast.

1750s: Revivals sweep Wales under Howell Harris, Daniel Rowland, and William Williams.

1773: The first instance of a Pentecostal-type religious revival in North America breaks out in Virginia. A recurrence follows in 1787.

1776: Nova Scotia, Canada, experiences an extensive revival awakening under the preaching of Henry Alline.

1780: German Lutherans begin the Deutsche Christentumsgesellschaft (Christendom Society) to build the Kingdom of God on an ecumenical basis. In 1815, members found the Evangelische Missionsgesellschaft in Basel (Basel Mission).

1780: Robert Raikes organizes the first Sunday school in Gloucester, England. By 1786, 200,000 children are enrolled in England, and by 1789, the movement has spread to Wales, Scotland, Ireland, and North America.

Henry Alline.
Image: Public Domain

1782: Concerts of Prayer (for revival and world mission), as envisaged by Jonathan Edwards, begin and spread in Britain; the same type of movement spreads in the United States from 1790. They serve as the basis for the subsequent worldwide missionary advance.

1782: Former slave George Liele (Lisle), designated by some as "the first foreign missionary from America," arrives in Jamaica from Georgia, United States. In 1783, he establishes the precursor to the Native Baptist Church, which will play a significant political role some eighty years later.

Charles Simeon.
Image: Public Domain

1783: Anglican vicar Charles Simeon starts an evangelical student movement in Cambridge, England.

1783: The Eclectic Society is formed in England. Members of the Eclectic Society and the Clapham Sect (formed 1790) would found the Anglican Church Missionary Society (1799) and play a large role in such moral reforms as ending the British slave trade (1807).

1784: At the Christmas Conference in Baltimore, the American Methodist Society breaks from the Church of England, taking the name Methodist Episcopal Church and electing Francis Asbury as its bishop.

1785: Evangelical awakenings (revivals) are rekindled in Wales. They recur repeatedly into and throughout the nineteenth century.

1787: Moravians in North America form the Society for Propagating the Gospel among the Heathen. Since 1949 it has been known as the Board of World Mission of the Moravian Church. In 1800, Moravians in Germany will found the Institute of Missions to promote foreign mission.

1792: The Second Great Awakening begins among Congregational and other churches in New England. It expands to other parts of the United States and continues until the 1820s.

William Carey.
Image: Public Domain

1792: William Carey publishes *An Enquiry into the Obligations of Christians, to Use Means for the Conversion of the Heathens*, the first statistical global survey of foreign missions. The next year he sails to India under the sponsorship of the newly formed Particular Baptist Society for Propagating the Gospel among the Heathen, initiating the modern era of Protestant world missions.

1793: The Tract and Colportage Society of Scotland is founded to distribute inexpensive Bibles and Christian literature. It is followed by others, including the Edinburgh Tract Society (1796), the London Religious Tract Society (1799), the Christlicher Verein im Nördlichen Deutschland (1811), the Wupperthaler Traktatgesellschaft (1814), the American Tract Society (1825), and the Tract Society of Lausanne and Eszlingen (1832).

1795: A mass movement to Christ begins among Nadars (Shanars) in Cape Comorin (South India), with 5,000 being baptized by missionaries of the Society for the Propagation of Christian Knowledge over ten years.

1795: The London Missionary Society (LMS)—originally interdenominational, later Congregationalist—is founded. It opens work in the South Pacific in 1796 and sees its first converts in 1814 in New Zealand.

1796: Norwegian Revival occurs under Hans Nielsen Hauge.

1796: The Edinburgh Missionary Society (later Scottish Missionary Society) and the Glasgow Missionary Society are founded. By 1848 their work is transferred to Scottish Presbyterian denominations and the two independent societies cease to exist.

1797: The Netherlands Missionary Society (NZG) is founded in Rotterdam.

1800: Local awakenings (revivals) begin in Scotland: Lewis, Harris, Perthshire.

1800: The first camp meeting (Presbyterian/Methodist) is held in Kentucky, United States. Others then rapidly increase across North America and spread to Britain.

1802: The Massachusetts Baptist Mission Society, founded by Hezekiah Smith, is formed "for the evangelization of frontier communities."

1804: The British and Foreign Bible Society is founded in London with the vision of providing the Scriptures to the whole world. By 1817, local or national Bible societies have been founded in what is today's Denmark, Estonia, Finland, Germany, Hungary, Iceland, Ireland, Latvia, the Netherlands, Norway, Poland, Russia, Scotland, Sweden, Switzerland, and the United States.

1806: The Haystack Prayer Meeting, Williams College, Massachusetts, launches the North American foreign missions movement. In 1810, at the urging of Williams College students, Congregationalists in Massachusetts organize the first North American mission society, the American Board of Commissioners for Foreign Missions (ABCFM), predecessor to today's Common Global Ministries Church and United Church of Christ.

1807: Robert Morrison, the first Protestant missionary (LMS) to China, arrives in Macao. He translates the Bible into Chinese (1818) and compiles a dictionary (1821), but dies in 1834 having seen only ten Chinese baptisms.

1809: The Aberdeen Female Servant Society, for Promoting the Diffusion of the Scriptures—the first known women's organization dedicated to raising funds for Bible translation and distribution—is founded by domestic workers in Scotland. Similar societies are formed elsewhere in Scotland as well as in England, Ireland, the United States, and Canada over the following decade.

1809: British Evangelicals form the London Society for Promoting Christianity Amongst the Jews, an Anglican society that is today known as the Church's Ministry Among Jewish People. Both Benei Abraham in London (the first recorded congregation of Jewish believers in Jesus, 1813, and Christ Church, Jerusalem (the oldest Protestant church in the Middle East, 1849), resulted from its work. Its Presbyterian counterpart, the British Society for the Propagation of the Gospel Among the Jews, is founded in 1842.

1812: The ABCFM ordains its first five male missionary candidates, who sail for India in two separate ships. Adoniram and Ann Judson, refused permission to stay, arrive in Burma in 1813. In 1814, Baptists in the United States form the American Baptist Missionary Union (later American Baptist Foreign Mission Society) to support the Judsons, who had become convinced of Baptist doctrine en route to India.

1813: The Charter Act signed in 1813 requires the British East India Company to allow Christian missionaries to enter and preach in the territory it controls.

1816: The first Bible translation into a sub-Saharan African language, Bullom (Sierra Leone), is completed.

1816: The first Elberfeld revival breaks out in western Germany. A second follows in 1820.

1817: The London Missionary Society undertakes organized evangelization among Buryats around Lake Baikal in Siberia. By 1840 missionaries translate the Bible into Mongolian, but in 1841 they are ordered to leave by the Russian holy synod and the tsar.

1818: James Thompson, a Scottish colporteur, becomes the first Protestant missionary to Spanish-speaking Latin America. On three journeys through Latin America (1818–1825, 1827–1834, and 1842–1844) he sells Bibles in Argentina, Chile, Colombia, Mexico, Peru, Venezuela, and many islands in the Caribbean.

1818: The Wesleyan Methodist Missionary Society (later MMS) is organized in London. In 1819 the Missionary Society of the Methodist Episcopal Church is formed in the United States.

1819: The Genevan Revival (Réveil Génévois) sweeps that city under the leadership of Merle d'Aunigne, Robert Haldanes, and a band of Moravians. Henriette Feller, one of its converts, later becomes the first Protestant missionary to French-speaking Canada.

1820s: The American Board of Commissioners for Foreign Missions and the London Missionary Society begin sending Polynesian converts as missionaries among the Pacific islands.

1820s: The Österbottniska Väckelse (Ostrobothnian Revival) begins among Lutherans in Swedish-speaking areas of Western Finland, and continues into the 1840s. Another Lutheran revival, one among the Sami of northern Finland, begins in 1844 with the evangelical conversion of Swedish-speaking Sami Lutheran pastor L. L. Laestadius.

1821: The Danish Missionary Society is founded, but initially it supports only existing work, not sending its own missionaries to India until 1864. In 2000 it merges with the Danish Santal Mission (founded 1867) to form Danmission.

1822: Lott Carey, a former slave from Virginia and first missionary from the United States to Africa, establishes Providence Baptist Church in Monrovia, Liberia, the oldest Baptist congregation in Africa.

1822: The Paris Evangelical Missionary Society, serving all Protestants but supported mainly by Reformed churches, is founded in France. In 1971 it dissolves, forming the Département Français d'Action Apostolique (a missions agency serving French Protestant denominations) and the Communauté Evangélique d'Action Apostolique (an international communion of churches in French-speaking areas).

1822: Missionaries of the ABCFM establish the American Mission Press on the island of Malta; in 1834 the work is relocated to Beirut (Arabic) and Izmir (Turkish, Armenian, Greek). Its publications include an Arabic translation (the Van Dyke Bible, completed in 1865) that remains widely used and an Armenian translation that standardized the written form of that language.

1824: The Berlin Missionary Society is formed by Lutherans in Germany.

1825: David Nasmith establishes the Glasgow City Mission, the first of fifty city missions begun in Britain's largest cities. Over the ensuing decades, city missions open in North America and continental Europe as well.

1825: The Bombay Missionary Union is formed for prayer and discussion among missionaries from different denominations. Eventually it produces both the principle of comity (dividing a geographical area among mission agencies to avoid duplication of work) and interdenominational regional conferences among missionaries, first in India (1855) and then in other countries.

1826: Rufus Anderson is ordained as an evangelist and Assistant Secretary of the American Board of Commissioners for Foreign Missions. In 1832 he is named Foreign Secretary, serving for forty-eight years as the acknowledged theoretician of the American missionary enterprise.

1827: John Nelson Darby, an Anglican clergyman, joins the Christian Brethren movement in Dublin. The premillennial dispensational theology he subsequently develops is still widely taught in conservative Evangelical and Fundamentalist churches and seminaries.

1828: The Rhenish Missionary Society (RMG) is formed in Germany. Beginning work among the Dayaks of Borneo, it sees its first Dayak baptism in 1839.

1829: Anthony N. Groves, the "father of faith missions" (those not supported by denominations), launches the first Protestant mission to Arabic-speaking Muslims in Baghdad.

1830s: Revivals sweep Reformed churches in the Netherlands, Switzerland, and France.

1835: The Swedish Missionary Society (Svenska Missionssällskapet) is founded to work among the Sami in Lappland. Its later work in Asia is taken over by the Church of Sweden Mission in 1874; the Society ceases to exist in 2001.

1836: The Dresden Evangelical Lutheran Mission, founded in Germany in 1819 to support missionaries of the Basel Mission Society, becomes an independent mission society in its own right. Its name is changed and its headquarters are moved to Leipzig in 1848.

1837: The Great Awakening starts in Hawaii, a remarkable revival with mass conversions (27,000 Protestant adult converts, or 20% of the population) that lasts until 1843.

1837: The Presbyterian Church in the USA (Old School) adopts the Western Foreign Missionary Society (established 1831) as its denominational Board of Foreign Missions. Following several mergers during the nineteenth and twentieth centuries, the denomination and mission agency are today known as the Presbyterian Church (USA) and Presbyterian World Missions.

1841: The Edinburgh Association for Sending Medical Aid to Foreign Countries is founded. It becomes the Edinburgh Medical Missionary Society in 1843 and divides into EMMS International and The Nazareth Trust in 2001.

1842: Revival spreads through the state church of Norway, leading to the creation of the Norwegian Mission Society in Stavanger. H.P.S. Schreuder, author of the treatise "A Few Words to the Church of Norway on Christian Obligation to be Concerned about the Salvation of Non-Christian Fellow Men" while a theology student, is appointed its first missionary to Zululand.

1843: Samuel Ajayi Crowther arrives in his native Nigeria as a Church Missionary Society missionary. In 1846 he is consecrated as the first non-European Anglican bishop.

1843: The Disruption takes place in the Church of Scotland as Evangelicals (40% of church members) secede and form the Free Church of Scotland.

1844: The first Young Men's Christian Association (YMCA) is founded by George Williams in London to serve spiritual and social needs of young men moving to the city from rural areas.

1845: The Southern Baptist Convention is formed in Augusta, Georgia, in reaction against ABFMS refusal to accept slave owners as missionaries. Two of its first agencies are the Board of Domestic Missions (now North American Mission Board) and the Foreign (now International) Mission Board.

1846: The Evangelical Alliance is formed in London to further unity among Evangelicals worldwide. Intended as an international body, the Alliance instead emerges as the British member of a loose network of national and regional evangelical alliances. The Evangelical Alliance becomes a founding member of the World Evangelical Fellowship (now Alliance) in 1951.

1848: The Evangelische Gesellschaft für Deutschland is founded in Germany as the first of many evangelistic societies. Others to follow include the Evangelical Brotherhood (1850), the Society for Itinerant Preachers (1852), the Society for Home Missions (1857), the Herborn-Dillenburg Society (1863), the Nassau Colporteur Society (1864), the Evangelical Brotherhood of the Reich for Furthering Evangelism and Evangelical Fellowship (1878), and the Home Mission Society of Hesse (1886).

1850s: CMS Secretary Henry Venn and ABCFM Secretary Rufus Anderson independently develop the "three-self" theory of missions stating that churches founded by missionaries should be indigenous and self-supporting, self-governing, and self-propagating. John L. Nevius, an American Presbyterian missionary to China, refines their ideas in the 1880s and has a profound influence on missions in Korea after he addresses missionaries there in 1890.

1853: The first home mission society in Norway (Indremisjon) begins within the state Lutheran church by Gustav Adolph Lammers, in Skien. Similar societies follow in other parts of Norway, as well as in Sweden (beginning 1856) and Denmark (beginning 1861).

1854: Charles Haddon Spurgeon, who will become a prolific author and be deemed "the Prince of Preachers," is named pastor of New Park Street Chapel in London at age 20, a position he holds until his death in 1892. The church's Metropolitan Tabernacle, opened in 1861, is the largest non-Anglican church in Britain at the time.

Charles Haddon Spurgeon.
Image: Public Domain

1854: The First Union Missionary Convention (First International Missionary Conference) convenes in New York, guided by Alexander Duff; a similar conference is held in London, England. In 1867 Duff is appointed to the first chair of evangelism and evangelical theology at New College, Edinburgh.

1854: The Canada Presbyterian Synod augurates its Foreign Mission Committee. As the result of denominational mergers, its work is today part of the Division of World Outreach of the United Church of Canada.

1855: Emma Roberts initiates a "prayer union" in Britain and Ireland; that same year, The Honorable Mrs. Arthur Kinnaird opens a hostel in London for Florence Nightingale's nurses who are traveling to and from the Crimean War theater. The two organizations eventually combine to form the Young Women's Christian Association (YWCA).

1857: An Evangelical Awakening under C. G. Finney and others in the northern United States sees a million converts in two years. From there it spreads to Europe and then parts of the other continents, including India (1859) and China (1860).

1857: Evangelist D. L. Moody evolves organized mass evangelism in Chicago, including perfecting methods of preparation and publicity in cooperative city campaigns, the use of theaters and tents, and finance committees. He is estimated to have preached to 100 million

D. L. Moody.
Image: North Wind Picture Archives

Billy Sunday.
Photo: Public Domain

during his lifetime and to have had individual evangelistic personal dealings with 750,000 persons. Moody's methods mark the beginnings of large-scale lay-centered evangelism that will be employed by other evangelists, including R.A. Torrey, Billy Sunday, and Robert P. Wilder.

1858: Two events—the Second Evangelical Awakening in the United Kingdom (in which 1.1 million people are converted) and the opening of the world east of the Suez Canal to Western missionaries (who then pour into China, Japan, and India)—lead to the year being deemed the *"annus mirabilis* of foreign missions." The 1860 Liverpool Conference on Missions, the first major world missionary conference, is held as a direct result.

1859: Lutherans in Finland form the Finnish Missionary Society for work in Africa.

1860: Revival occurs in Ukraine, only to be followed a generation later by persecution of Evangelicals (1884–1904).

1861: The Woman's Union Missionary Society of America for Heathen Lands (WUMSA) is formed in New York as the pioneer women's sending society, with forty other women's societies arising subsequently.

1865: J. Hudson Taylor founds the China Inland Mission (CIM) as a faith mission for evangelizing the interior provinces of China. Expanding its focus elsewhere in East Asia following the expulsion of missionaries from China in 1950, CIM is renamed Overseas Missionary Fellowship and later simply OMF International.

William Booth.
Photo: Public Domain

1865: Methodist evangelist William Booth founds the Christian Revival Association for urban social outreach and street evangelism in England. It receives its present name, the Salvation Army, in 1878 and spreads worldwide.

1866: The Continental European Missions Conference, also named the Ausschuss, holds its first meeting in Bremen (Germany); eleven more Bremen conferences take place before it merges with the Edinburgh world missionary conference in 1910.

1866: Cuban immigrant Joaquin de Palma organizes a Spanish-speaking Anglican congregation in New York City. Cuban Anglicans return to the island in 1878 to found the first locally-led Spanish-speaking Protestant churches in Latin America.

1870: A mass movement begins of 50% of Hindu Chuhras in Sialkot, Punjab, to the American Presbyterian mission, with continuing revival up to 1912.

1870s: This decade is the heyday of British evangelists, typified by the preaching of William Booth, C. H. Spurgeon, Henry Drummond, Wilson Carlile, and Gipsy Smith.

1872: The first great wave of indigenous evangelization sweeps Japan, as young samurai bands of converted students form chiefly at Yokohama, Kumamoto, and Sapporo, carrying the gospel far and wide in the interior where foreign missionaries are prohibited. In 1896, Kumamoto descendants organize a YMCA branch and invite J. R. Mott to hold meetings with students.

1873: Dwight L. Moody begins his first evangelistic campaign in England. It lasts until 1875 (including a five-month London Crusade with 2.5 million attendees) and is followed by two more (1882–1884 and 1891–1892).

1878: The first National Christian Conference is held in Japan.

1878: The General Conference on Foreign Missions is held in London as successor to the 1860 Liverpool conference, with more than 160 delegates from thirty-four societies (six American, five Continental) but only one non-Western pastor, a Burmese.

1882: Church Army, a society dedicated to the vocation of evangelists, is formed within the Church of England by Wilson Carlile. By 2007 it has 458 British and Irish evangelists (35% women) and eight sister societies operating internationally.

1883: The Fourth Evangelical Awakening of the century breaks out in Norway, especially in Skien.

1884: Several evangelists (including Samuel Porter Jones & E.O. Excell; B. Fay Mills; and J. Wilbur Chapman) begin citywide evangelistic campaigns in the United States. By 1906 Jones and Excell attract some 25 million attenders, resulting in 500,000 converts.

1885: The "Cambridge Seven" (M. Beauchamp, W. W. Cassels, D. E. Hoste, A. T. Polhill-Turner, C. H. Polhill-Turner, S. P. Smith, and C. T. Studd) leave Britain as missionaries to China. The story of privileged young men leaving behind everything captures the nation's attention and catapults the China Inland Mission from obscurity.

1885: The Wesleyan Forward Movement in British Methodism begins under Hugh Price Hughes of West London Mission, founding central halls in cities and stressing social evangelism. In 1896 Hughes founds the National Council of Evangelical Free Churches.

1886: The first of D. L. Moody's International Student Conferences convenes at Mount Hermon, Massachusetts. In 1888 it gives birth to the Student Volunteer Movement for Foreign Missions (SVM), organized with 2,200 initial volunteers and based on the Watchword "The Evangelization of the World in This Generation." The Student Volunteer Missionary Union (SVMU) follows in Britain in 1892. By 1945, as a result of SVM, a total of 25,000 university graduates have gone overseas as foreign missionaries.

1887: Canadian evangelists John Edwin Hunter and Hugh Thomas Crossley begin a partnership that lasts until 1909 and takes them to every major Canadian city except Quebec City.

1887: The Christian and Missionary Alliance is established in the United States by Canadian Presbyterian pastor A.B. Simpson as an interdenominational missionary society. Over time its branches come to be more like local churches, and as a denomination (still with a strong focus on missions and church planting) in 1974.

1888: Italian Bible colporteur F. G. Penzotti begins the first Spanish-speaking evangelical church in Peru, in Callao.

A. B. Simpson.
Photo: The Christian
and Missionary
Alliance Archives

1888: Southern Baptist women organize Woman's Missionary Union (WMU), which becomes the largest mission-support body in the world organized by women. By 1988 it has 1.2 million members supporting 7,000 missionaries and has raised a cumulative 1 billion dollars.

1888: The First General Assembly of Evangelical Missionaries meets in Mexico City with ninety-five missionaries from twelve denominations and one Mexican pastor. The Second General Assembly (1897) includes only fifty missionaries but 150 native workers.

1888: The German Association for Evangelism and Christian Fellowship (Gnadauer Band) is formed at Gnadau. By 1920 the Association has 6,000 organizations and 225,000 registered members.

1888: The Mar Thoma Syrian Christian Evangelistic Association of Malabar is formed in India for non-Syrian outcaste converts. Their annual Maramon Convention, an eight-day preaching event, grows so much that the centennial meeting in 1988 attracts two million attenders.

1889: British Salvation Army evangelist Gipsy Smith holds large meetings in major cities in the United States. His ministry over fifty years will see vast numbers come to Christ in the United Kingdom, United States, and Australia.

1890: Church of Scotland converts among the Nepali and Lepcha go as Indian missionaries to Bhutan; many meet early deaths.

1890: The Scandinavian Alliance Mission of North America is founded for worldwide evangelism and church planting. In 1949 it is renamed TEAM (The Evangelical Alliance Mission).

1890: Cyrus I. Scofield founds the Central America Mission, the first faith mission focused on that region. In 1981 CAM-related churches in Central America establish the Evangelical Missionary Agency for evangelism and church planting in Africa.

1892: Evangelist W. A. "Billy" Sunday begins evangelistic campaigns in the Midwestern United States. By 1900 his focus shifts to major cities.

1892: The Free Church Congress meets in Manchester, England. Soon after, the National Council of the Evangelical Free Churches is formed in Britain, along with numerous local councils of churches.

1893: Founders of Soudan Interior Mission (renamed SIM International in 1980) arrive in Nigeria to evangelize inland Africa south of the Sahara and between the Atlantic and the Red Sea (the world's largest single totally unevangelized area with no resident missionary). The scope of mission expands to Asia and Latin America through later mergers with other agencies.

1895: The Association of Pentecostal Churches in America is formed, sending its first foreign missionaries in 1897. It takes its present name, the Church of the Nazarene, in 1919.

1895: The World's Student Christian Federation, with the aim "to claim students—the future leaders of their nations—for Christ and for the evangelization of the world," is founded at a meeting in Sweden. Chapters in Britain, Germany, Scandinavia, and Canada and the United States are joined by the Australasian Student Christian Union (Australia and New Zealand) the next year. After 1914, nonevangelistic interests predominate.

1896: The College Young Men's Christian Association of China (CYMCAC) is founded during a national conference in Shanghai with J.R. Mott and twenty-two new China associations in the same year a Student Volunteer Movement for foreign missions is organized.

1897: African-Americans organize the Lott Carey Baptist Foreign Mission Convention as a missionary-sending body.

1899: CMS missionary W. H. Temple Gairdner arrives in Egypt. He becomes one of the most influential advocates for mission to Muslims, and his writings influence both local Christians and future missionaries.

1902: An evangelistic partnership is initiated between R. A. Torrey and C. M. Alexander; it lasts until 1908 and takes them around the world, resulting in 130,000 converts.

1902: The German Tent Mission begins evangelistic tent campaigns in Germany. Others follow, including Christian Endeavor (1924), Baptist Tent Mission (1926), Methodists (1926), and the Evangelical Free Church Tent Mission (1951).

1904: The Welsh Revival begins through the ministry of Evan Roberts in Glamorganshire, Anglesey, and Caernarvonshire, with 100,000 converts in Wales in six months. It lasts until 1906 and, publicized by the press, literally sweeps the world, leading into the worldwide Pentecostal movement.

1905: A year of evangelical awakenings includes revivals in London (under Torrey and Alexander) and at Mukti Mission, India (under Pandita Ramabai), as well as elsewhere in India (Assam, Kerala, Sialkot through Praying Hyde) and in Denmark, Finland, Sweden, Germany, Russia, Madagascar, Korea, and China.

1906: American Reformed missionary Samuel Zwemer convenes the First General Conference of Missionaries to the World of Islam in Cairo, Egypt, with sixty-two missionaries from twenty-nine societies.

1906: Laymen's Missionary Movement (LMM) is launched in the United States as a foreign missions auxiliary agency via SVM and seventeen major North American Protestant denominations. By 1916, one million men have attended its 3,000 conferences.

1906: The Azusa Street Revival in Los Angeles, California, under W. J. Seymour brings national, then global, attention to Pentecostalism. Lasting until 1909, it results in the birth of new Pentecostal denominations and in the "Pentecostalization" of several existing Holiness denominations.

1909: German Evangelicals release the Berlin Declaration condemning Pentecostalism, effectively marginalizing Pentecostalism from Evangelicalism. Efforts at reconciliation result in the joint issuance by Evangelicals and Pentecostals of the "Kassel Declaration" (1996) acknowledging what they hold in common and urging cooperation rather than antagonism.

1909: USA Methodist missionaries to Chile Mary Louise and Willis Hoover are excommunicated, along with thirty-seven Charismatic Chileans. They then form the Iglesia Metodista Pentecostal, marking the organization of the Pentecostal movement in Chile.

1910s: The rise of organized Fundamentalism begins with the publication of I. Scofield's *Scofield Reference Bible* in 1909 and is propelled forward by the widely distributed twelve-volume paperback anti-modernist series *The Fundamentals*, containing defenses of fundamental doctrines by conservative writers.

1910: Evangelist Billy Sunday and musician Homer Rodeheaver embark on a twenty-year series of evangelistic meetings across the United States, in which Sunday preaches to 100 million people.

1910: The World Missionary Conference convenes in Edinburgh, Scotland, with 1,355 delegates, marking the beginning of the twentieth-century ecumenical movement. Only seventeen of the delegates are non-Western, however, and none are from Africa or Latin America.

1911: Shukri Musa, an Arab from Galilee who experienced an evangelical conversion in the United States in 1910, returns to Mandate Palestine, beginning work in Safar. Later that year he moves to Nazareth, where he establishes a Baptist church. Baptists will go on to become the largest group of Evangelicals in Israel.

1912: The Oriental Missionary Society undertakes the first attempt by a mission body to reach systematically every home in an entire nation. By 1917 it reaches some 10.3 million households in Japan, and the concept is later extended to other countries and then to the world.

1913: English missionary C. T. Studd (one of the "Cambridge Seven") founds Christ's Etceteras (later renamed Worldwide Evangelization Crusade and today known as WEC International) to focus on evangelizing "the remaining unevangelized parts (peoples) of the world."

1915: The Conference of Missionary Translators, with six missionary couples, meets in Chichicastenango, Guatemala, to set the foundation for the modern Bible translation movement. By 1997, now known as Wycliffe Bible Translators/SIL, it has 6,000 missionaries worldwide at work in over 1,500 languages.

C. T. Studd.
Photo: Public Domain

1916: The Congress on Christian Work in Latin America convenes in Panama City, Panama, as the first Protestant missionary conference to be held in that region. From it comes the Committee on Cooperation in Latin America, organized to promote stronger links between missions and national churches.

1917: The Interdenominational Foreign Mission Association of North America (IFMA) is founded by nondenominational Protestant "faith" missions "to make possible a united testimony concerning the existing need for a speedy and complete evangelization of the world." In 2007 it becomes CrossGlobal Link and in 2012 merges with The Mission Exchange (1945) to form Missio Nexus.

1920: The General Council of Cooperating Baptist Missions of North America is organized in the United States; in 1953 it is renamed Baptist Mid-Missions.

1920: The term "Fundamentalist" is elaborated in the United States to mean a militant or angry conservative Evangelical, mostly dispensationist-premillennialist. After 1925, Fundamentalists have difficulty gaining national attention, and by 1930 Fundamentalism has lost its initial national prominence within mainline Protestant churches and begins to fragment into small denominations. The term has now come to mean ecclesiastical separatists, almost all of whom are separate Baptist dispensationalists.

1921: Latin American Evangelization Campaign conducts citywide united campaigns; later it becomes Latin America Mission.

1925: The era of large evangelistic healing campaigns is launched in Europe and the United States under the first generation of Pentecostal evangelists, including Smith Wigglesworth, who preaches to large crowds in most of the world's largest capitals.

1926: The German Association for Mass Evangelism (Deutscher Verband für Volksmission) begins, uniting many state-church evangelists and evangelistic programs started over the previous decade.

1927: InterVarsity Fellowship (IVF), known today as Universities and Colleges Christian Fellowship (UCCF in Great Britain), is founded to further cooperation between evangelical Christian unions in Britain's universities and colleges. By 1946 the movement has spread to nine more countries, including China.

1927: The Association of Baptists for Evangelism in the Orient is formed. In 1939 it becomes the Association of Baptists for World Evangelism.

1928: The Kingdom of God Movement is begun in Japan by evangelist and social activist Toyohiko Kagawa. Supported by most Protestants, it is a comprehensive Japanese-led plan with the stated aim of winning one million Japanese to Christ and thence to reaching the entire nation with the Christian message.

1929: American Congregationalist missionary Frank C. Laubach begins his "Each one teach one" method in the Philippines, subsequently developing literacy primers for 300 languages worldwide. In 1950 he publishes *Literacy as Evangelism*.

1929: China Inland Mission director D. E. Hoste issues a call to Europe and America for "Two Hundred Evangelists" to China's remaining unreached peoples, with the goal "to reach China within 2 years"; more than a dozen are martyred.

1929: Chinese evangelist Cheng Ching-yi, a colleague of J. R. Mott since Edinburgh 1910, makes his famed appeal for an evangelistic campaign to double church membership in China in the next five years. Mott supports Cheng with his strategy of "A Larger Evangelism," and the challenge is then taken up by the seventh meeting of the National Christian Council of China, held in Hangchow.

1929: HCJB ("The Voice of the Andes") is founded in Quito, Ecuador, as the world's first missionary radio station, with its first broadcast on Christmas Day 1931. HCJB Global, which grew out of the station, has expanded to broadcasting through a variety of media and offering medical and community-development ministries.

1929: The seeds of the East Africa Revival are sown when Joe Church, a missionary doctor in Rwanda, meets Anglican churchman Simeoni Nsibambi in Uganda. The Revival breaks out in Rwanda in the early 1930s, spreading to Uganda in 1935 (where its effects continue to be felt more than a half-century later) and across Eastern Africa by the 1940s.

1930: The Movement for World Evangelization (Mildmay Movement) begins in London. Its on-the-spot surveys of every mission field on earth were intended to prevent duplication of missionary work and promote evangelization where there was none.

1930: The Shantung Revival begins in the Southern Baptist mission in China, eventually spreading to the Chinese as well.

1930s: Numerous independent evangelists emerge in China, including Wang Mingdao and Song Shanjie (John Sung), with huge followings.

1932: The Indian National Council of Churches launches the All-India Forward Movement in Evangelism in Nagpur to promote cooperative evangelism among Protestant churches.

1933: Dawson Trotman, a California lumberyard worker and Sunday school teacher, begins teaching basic Christian discipleship to sailors in the US Navy. His work gives rise to The Navigators, a one-by-one disciple-making agency based on multiplication theory.

1935: World Intercessors (Prayer Circle Department of the Oriental Missionary Society) begins as a worldwide prayer movement for world evangelization.

1937: Child Evangelism Fellowship is founded, based on the belief that "Before Christ's return a mighty work among children will encircle the globe." By 1985, 160 foreign missionaries are working in sixty countries.

1937: The China: Forward Evangelistic Campaign, under Methodist evangelist E. Stanley Jones, is held in Mokanshan and other centers despite Japanese bombing attacks.

1938: The Nation-Wide United Evangelistic Campaign 1938–1940 is launched by the All-Japan Christian Conference, with T. Kagawa prominent as speaker.

1940: The rise of Neo-Evangelicals, reformers of Fundamentalism in the United States anticipating a broad evangelical resurgence, begins under C. F. H. Henry, H. J. Ockenga, and faculty of Fuller Theological Seminary, delineating secular humanism as a religious ideology and major enemy of Evangelicalism. The movement flourishes and expands greatly, peaking by 1970, then declines, though a wider definition of "Evangelicalism" mushrooms.

1942: The Ling Liang World-Wide Evangelistic Mission is founded in Shanghai, China, "to send Chinese missionaries to the uttermost part of the world."

1943: Conservatives concerned by theological liberalism within the Northern Baptist Convention meet in Wheaton, Illinois, to form the Conservative Baptist Foreign Mission Society (later CBInternational; now WorldVenture), dedicated to sending only evangelical missionaries. In 1948 the Conservative Baptist Association of America (today CB America) is founded as an alternative to the NBC for similar reasons.

1943: The first Youth for Christ rally is held in Brantford, Ontario, Canada, under Paul Guiness. In 1944 YFC International begins, first in USA cities, as a worldwide evangelistic movement "specializing in aggressive teenage evangelism."

1944: The Dutch East Indies sees the rise of Third-World missionaries. Chinese evangelist John Sung trains 5,000 three-man evangelistic teams who make a major impact across the archipelago. Subsequent outreaches include those by Japanese and Pakistani evangelistic teams (1969) and by the Asian Evangelists Commission (1975).

1945: The end of World War II inaugurates a massive surge in new Christian parachurch ministries (independent of the churches), increasing by 1980 to 17,500 distinct and separate agencies, most of them evangelical.

1945: The Evangelical Foreign Missions Association (EFMA) is organized in Washington, DC, United States, consisting primarily of denominational mission agencies. In 2007 it becomes The Mission Exchange, merging in 2012 with CrossGlobal Link (1917) to form Missio Nexus.

1946: A series of massive student conferences is launched in North America with the first InterVarsity Student Foreign Missions Conference in Toronto, followed in 1948 by the first Urbana Conference at the University of Illinois. Urbana meets there every three years through 2003, when its continued growth necessitates a move to St. Louis, Missouri, for the 2006 and subsequent conferences.

1946: Asociación Misionera Evangélica Nacional (AMEN; National Evangelical Missionary Association) begins as a home mission in Peru. In 1979 it is reorganized (with Methodist personnel) as a home and foreign missionary society with a global vision and renamed Asociación Misionera Evangélica a las Naciones.

1947: Representatives from InterVarsity student movements in ten countries meet at Harvard University to form the International Federation of Evangelical Students (IFES), which today has member movements in more than 150 countries.

1947: Southern Baptist evangelist Billy Graham begins his global ministry, preaching face-to-face to more than 200 million attendees by 2007.

1948: The Gossner Mission's Church on Wheels (Rollende Kirche) and The Mobile Church (Die Kirche Unterwegs) evangelize in Westphalia, Schleswig-Holstein, and Baden in Germany. By 1960, sixteen tent missions are at work, with 235 tent facilities in operation.

1949: The First Latin American Evangelical Conference (CELA-1) convenes in Buenos Aires, Argentina. It gives rise to additional CELA meetings as well as (in 1964) the Provisional Commission for Latin American Evangelical Unity (UNELAM, Movimiento pro Unidad Evangelica Latinoamericana), founded at Montevideo, Uruguay.

Billy Graham.
Photo: Courtesy of
Billy Graham
Center Archives,
Wheaton, Ill.

1949: The Japanese Evangelical Missionary Society is formed (United States, Tokyo) to send Japanese abroad.

1951: The International Convention of Evangelicals is held at Woudschoten, Netherlands, with ninety-one delegates and observers from twenty-one countries. The World Evangelical Fellowship (from 2004, Alliance) is inaugurated at the first General Assembly.

1953: Methodists launch Australian Mission to the Nation, a three-year mass evangelism and media campaign and the largest ever held in Australia, with more than one million attenders. It also marks the start of the thirty-five-year mass evangelism ministry of evangelist Alan Walker.

1953: Worldwide Evangelization Crusade begins work on Java, founding the Batu Bible School. In 1961 it gives rise to the indigenous Indonesian Missionary Fellowship, with its own plan for world evangelization.

1956: The killing of five American missionaries in the Ecuadorean jungle by members of the Huaorani tribe galvanizes support for international missions, especially in the United States and in Latin America.

1957: Send the Light (later Operation Mobilization) is incorporated in the United States, in Mexico, then in more than fifty countries as an interdenominational youth agency sending short-term mission workers abroad for evangelism and literature distribution.

1959: The first nationwide Evangelism-in-Depth campaign is organized, in Nicaragua, with 125 local churches, 65,000 homes visited, 126,000 attendees in fourteen local crusades, 2,604 professions of faith, and 500 prayer cells formed. Upon its successful conclusion, the Latin America Mission sponsors similar campaigns in eleven other Latin American countries by 1971. After 1975 it fades out as a movement, however, because it has largely been accepted and incorporated into church programs.

1960: Youth With A Mission (YWAM) begins as an Evangelical-Charismatic sending agency, expanding as an outgrowth of the Jesus Movement in the United States. It remains relatively unknown until 1977, when it outfits the 10,000-ton evangelistic ship M.V. *Anastasis* for discipleship and mercy ministries; by 1983 it is the world's largest evangelistic agency, with 14,000 short-term young people sent overseas each year.

1963: The TEE (Theological Education by Extension) movement originates at Evangelical Presbyterian Seminary in Guatemala. By 1980, more than 200 major TEE organizations are at work worldwide, with 400 programs and 60,000 current extension students in 90 countries.

1965: Beginning that year, revival among the Javanese in Indonesia results in the conversion of hundreds of thousands of Muslims to evangelical Christianity over the next two decades. By the year 2000, Muslim converts are estimated to number more than 10 million.

1970: Operation Mobilization purchases the 2,500-ton evangelistic ship M.V. *Logos* for UK£80,000 to visit large-city ports in difficult countries around world, with literature, evangelism, book sales, and missionary conferences. It runs aground and is lost off Tierra del Fuego in 1988. In 1977 its sister ship M.V. *Doulos* (6,000 tons) begins travels.

1971: A nationwide Evangelism-in-Depth campaign in Mexico involving more than half of the country's 10,000 evangelical churches results in 13,000 prayer cells and one million Scriptures distributed.

1972: Taiwanese educator Shoki Coe introduces the term "contextualization" at a meeting of the World Council of Churches' Theological Education Fund. Evangelicals at first reject it, but eventually they come to embrace the term and concept, even if not Coe's definition.

1973: The Presbyterian Church in America launches its foreign missions agency, Mission to the World. By 1987 it has 50 missionaries in forty countries, with the goal of evangelizing twenty-five world-class cities by 1993.

1974: A prayer group in a Bible school in Cianorte, Brazil, organizes the Antioch Mission (Missão Antioquia) to inspire the Brazilian church to send and support missionaries, particularly to the most neglected areas of the world.

1974: At a DAWN (Discipling A Whole Nation) conference in the Philippines, seventy-five leaders of 4,000 evangelical churches plan to have 50,000 churches planted by AD 2000, one in every barrio in the country. A National Church Growth Strategy Congress with 300 leaders of 12,000 evangelical churches reaffirms this goal in 1985. After 1981 it becomes a world plan, with the goal to begin by AD 2000 a DAWN project in every country of the world.

1974: German Evangelicals within the Lutheran church, led by theologian Peter Beyerhaus, issue the Berlin Declaration critiquing ecumenism.

1974: The International Congress on World Evangelization (ICOWE, Lausanne I) meets in Lausanne, Switzerland, with 2,473 delegates from 150 countries (50% from the Global South). From it comes the Lausanne Covenant, stating "Evangelism itself is the proclamation of the historical, biblical Christ"; a shift in mission strategy from geographic areas to people groups; and, by 1980, the vast network known as the Lausanne Movement, directed by the Lausanne Committee for World Evangelization.

1974: *Operation World*, a prayer guide, is published by Patrick Johnstone, emphasizing world evangelization through daily intercession, the centrality of local churches and the call to "mobilize the churches of the whole world to finish the task"; 2010 marks the release of its seventh edition.

1975: Continente-75, a Latin American mass-media campaign under Argentinian evangelist Luis Palau utilizing fifty-six radio and 100 TV stations in twenty-three countries, is heard or seen by seventy-five million in all Latin America. In 1978 Palau preaches to more than two million persons face-to-face and holds that every city should have a citywide crusade three times in a generation (once every ten years).

1975: The World Evangelical Fellowship Missions Commission is inaugurated in Seoul, dedicated to development of the non-Western missionary movement utilizing a network of agencies and evangelical fellowships across the world. Its most recent meeting is in 2014 in Izmir, Turkey.

1976: The First Chinese Congress on World Evangelization (CCOWE) meets in Hong Kong with 1,600 participants from more than twenty countries. From it the Chinese Coordination Centre of World Evangelism (CCCOWE) is set up in Hong Kong.

1978: "The Glen Eyrie Report: Muslim Evangelization" helps inspire a new generation of evangelical missionaries to Muslims.

1979: The JESUS Film Project of Campus Crusade for Christ releases *Jesus*, a two-hour dramatization of the life of Christ based on the Gospel of Luke. As of 2013 it is available in approximately 1,200 languages and has had more than six billion viewings.

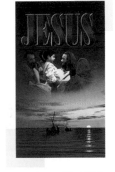

Jesus Film 1979.
Image: Public Domain

1980: The First World Consultation on Frontier Missions (WCFM) meets in Edinburgh, organized by the US Center for World Mission with the theme "A Church for every People by the Year 2000."

1982: The Latin American Council of Churches (CLAI), an ecumenical group with 110 denominations and agencies (some Pentecostal), is formed in Lima, Peru, following a UNELAM proposal at CELA-IV in 1978. Conservative evangelical opponents organize the rival CONELA (Confraternity of Latin American Evangelicals), claiming 20 million Evangelicals in ninety-eight founding denominations.

1982: Three hundred delegates from Korean churches on five continents meet at the first Korean World Mission Congress, in Pasadena, California (United States), "to unite Koreans worldwide for the Great Commission of Christ" and "to establish a Korean World Mission Coordinating Center."

1982: Participants in the Lausanne Movement from the Global South who feel their concerns are not being addressed by its largely Northern leadership found the International Fellowship of Evangelical Mission Theologians from the Two-Thirds World (INFEMIT) in Bangkok.

1982: The Asian Conference on Church Renewal, in Seoul, Korea, results in the inauguration at Hong Kong in 1983 of the Evangelical Fellowship of Asia (EFA) with twelve member bodies (eight being national fellowships).

1982: General Efraín Ríos Montt becomes president of Guatemala in a coup d'état, the first Evangelical to lead a Central or South American country. He is ousted in another coup the following year and has been accused of genocide and crimes against humanity during his rule. Jorge Serrano Elías, also an Evangelical and President of Guatemala 1991–1993, is forced to resign when he attempts to suspend the country's constitution; he lives in exile, facing charges of corruption.

1984: Fourteen Costa Rican denominations start an interdenominational missions society, formalized in 1986 as the Federación Misionera Evangélica Costarricense (FEDEMEC). Its campaign "Unidos en Cristo Evangelizando las Naciones" aims to mobilize 10,000 world prayer missionaries and to send out 500 missionaries to twenty-five unreached peoples "From Costa Rica to the Uttermost Parts of the Earth" by AD 2000.

1984: The DAWN Congress is held in Guatemala as a new wave of evangelism and church planting sweeps that nation, with a goal to double evangelical churches from 7,500 to 15,000 by 1990.

1985: The first Venezuelan Congress of World Missions convenes in Maracay with the aim of appointing 500 missionaries by 1987.

1985: The Nigeria Evangelical Missions Association and the World Evangelical Fellowship convene the International Consultation on Missions (ICOM) in Jos under the theme "Mobilizing Indigenous Missions for the Final Harvest," attracting eighty-three mission executives (mainly Nigerians).

1987: The First Ibero-American Missions Congress (Congreso Misionero Ibero-Americano, COMIBAM) meets in São Paulo with 3,500 evangelical representatives (70% Pentecostal/Charismatic) from across Latin America as well as Spain, Portugal, and North America. Subsequent congresses will be held in 1997 and 2006.

1988: Thirty-five church and mission leaders from twenty-one (mostly non-Western) countries meet in Portland, Oregon, for a Consultation on Third World Missions Advance. From it comes the Third-World Missions Association to promote mission among and by people from the Global South, along with an International Mutual Fund to finance such activities.

1988: The first Korean World Mission Conference, sponsored by the Billy Graham Evangelistic Association and supporting Korean missionaries and mission agencies worldwide, is convened. In 2013 the 26th KWMC meets in Flushing, New York.

1989: The Global Consultation on World Evangelization by AD 2000 and Beyond is convened in Singapore, inviting two representatives of each of the seventy-eight major current plans for world evangelization and "open to all leaders of Great Commission groups within the worldwide body of Christ."

1990s: Tens of thousands of Muslim Kabyle Berbers in Algeria convert to Evangelical/Charismatic Christianity.

1994: Haik Hovsepian, Assemblies of God bishop and national evangelical leader in Iran, is martyred. He had been both an outspoken advocate of religious freedom and a key figure in the movement of thousands of Iranian Muslims to embrace Christianity since 1979.

2000: Following meetings in 1983 and 1986, 10,000 evangelists from 200 countries gather in Amsterdam for the third International Conference for Itinerant Evangelists, sponsored by the Billy Graham Evangelistic Association.

2000: Evangelical Anglican archbishops Emmanuel Kolini of Rwanda and Moses Tay of South East Asia consecrate North America's Chuck Murphy and John Rodgers as bishops, in effect declaring The Episcopal Church (USA) and the Anglican Church of Canada to be heretical. Anglicans from the Global South become increasingly critical of Northern Anglicans over the decade.

2005: Leaders from twenty-eight evangelical mission agencies inaugurate the Global Network of Mission Structures to allow for networking and cooperation among member agencies on an equal basis regardless of size, age, or geographic location.

2010: The Third International Congress on World Evangelization (Lausanne III, sponsored by the Lausanne Committee on World Evangelization) is held in Cape Town. Its 5,000 participants include church and mission leaders from 200 countries.

WHO ARE EVANGELICALS? A HISTORY

By John Wolffe

"In the beginning was the Word." The opening sentence of John's Gospel evokes a central, recurrent emphasis of Evangelicals: the Word of God as revealed in the Bible. Indeed, the word *Evangelical* itself derives closely from the Greek *evangelion*, the good news of the gospel of Jesus Christ. Its specific meaning and usage have not, however, been constant across time. Until the nineteenth century *Evangelical* was used almost exclusively as an adjective to denote ideas and practices that related closely to the teaching of the gospels. In 1531 William Tyndale wrote of evangelical truth. Only during the last two hundred years or so has the word been widely used as a noun to designate particular people as *Evangelicals*, along with their associated framework of belief, *Evangelicalism*.

Evangelicals Are a Noun

This change from adjective to noun reflects an underlying historical transition that had occurred by 1800, the emergence of Evangelicalism as a distinctive movement of identifiable people, whereas in earlier periods it had been possible to talk of evangelical ideas and emphases only within the wider framework of Christianity. Joseph Milner, a schoolmaster and Church of England clergyman, made one of the most sustained attempts to trace an evangelical presence, in the adjectival sense of the word, across the whole canvas of earlier Christian history in his book *The History of the Church of Christ*, first published between 1794 and 1809. In the introduction Milner wrote,

> It is certain, that from our Saviour's time to the present, there have ever been persons whose dispositions and lives have been formed by the rules of the New Testament: men who have been *real*, not merely *nominal* Christians: who believed the doctrines of the Gospel, loved them because of their divine excellency, and suffered gladly the *loss of all things, that they might win Christ and be found in him*. It is the history of these men which I propose to write. It is of no consequence, with respect to my plan, not of much importance, I believe, in its own nature, to what EXTERNAL Church they belonged.[1]

Milner's examples of such "real" Christians included the Jerusalem church in the book of Acts; Saint Augustine of Hippo, "the great instrument of reviving the knowledge of evangelical truth" in the fifth century;[2] the Venerable Bede, the early eighth-century English scholar-monk; and Saint Bernard of Clairvaux, the founder of the reforming Cistercian monastic order in the twelfth century. Milner particularly admired the later medieval Waldensian movement in what is now southeast France and northwest Italy, which asserted its understanding of the truths of Scripture against the perceived corruptions of the Catholic Church. He hailed it as "a spectacle . . . both of the power of divine grace, and the malice and enmity of the world against the real Gospel of Jesus Christ."[3] His book concluded with Martin Luther and the early stages of the sixteenth-century Reformation, which Milner saw as "an attempt to restore the light of the gospel, more evangelically judicious, more simply

---

1. Joseph Milner and Isaac Milner, *The History of the Church of Christ* (London: Thomas Nelson, 1849), iii.

2. Ibid., 297.

3. Ibid., 533.

founded on the word of God, and more ably and more successfully conducted than any which had ever been seen since the days of Augustine."[4]

Present-day historians, mindful of the more specific meaning the word *Evangelical* has acquired since the eighteenth century, are reluctant to use it, even as an adjective, to describe Christians in the centuries before the Reformation. However, Evangelicals continue to see themselves as inheritors of a tradition of authentic Christianity that can be traced back to the early church, although often operating outside formal ecclesiastical structures and sometimes in open revolt against them.

Evangelicals Are United by the Reformation and in Their Diversity

The Reformation gave the word *Evangelical* greater currency, though it was often used in a rather vague sense and interchangeably with *Protestant*. Such use of the equivalent word in German, *evangelisch*, is especially widespread in historically Lutheran continental European countries. However, by no means all Evangelicals—that is, Protestants, or Christians, in this general sense of the word—were associated with the evangelical movement as it developed from the mid-eighteenth century onward. This movement began in the 1730s, with near simultaneous revival outbreaks from central Europe to the American frontier. Count Nikolaus von Zinzendorf at Herrnhut in Saxony (southeast Germany), John and Charles Wesley in England, Howel Harris in Wales, John Cennick in Ireland, and Jonathan Edwards in Massachusetts were key leaders. The most energetic of the revivalists was George Whitefield, the Englishman who crisscrossed the Atlantic numerous times between the late 1730s and his death in 1770, preaching the gospel and encouraging believers.

It is possible to trace most, if not all, of the specific ideas of the early Evangelicals back to the sixteenth-century Protestant Reformation through, in particular, the seventeenth-century movements of Puritanism in England and Pietism in Germany. In the 1730s, however, these old ideas came together in new and dynamic ways, which led participants like Edwards to believe they were experiencing "a surprising work of God."[5] It led them to challenge what they saw as merely nominal Christianity in the institutional Protestant churches of their day, calling their hearers to sincere repentance for their past sins, to a personal conversion to Christ, and to a subsequent life of authentic Christian living and zealous proclamation of the gospel to others.

Right from the outset, Evangelicalism was a theologically diverse movement. The early Evangelicals included both Calvinists—such as Edwards and Whitefield, who believed God in his absolute sovereignty and wisdom had preordained those whom he would save—and Arminians—such as the Wesleys, who held that salvation was potentially open to all human beings who responded to the call of the gospel. Subsequent key areas of disagreement have included the specific nature of the Bible, held by all Evangelicals to be authoritative and divinely inspired, but only by some as verbally inerrant, and whether the active manifestation of the "baptism of the Holy Spirit" and the "gifts of the Spirit" is to be expected and affirmed in the present-day church or should be seen as a divine privilege uniquely accorded to the early church in the book of Acts.

Moreover, the typical Evangelical has not been a sophisticated theologian preoccupied with articulating a specific system of belief but rather a convinced but poorly educated believer, who, for example, labors in the textile mills of early industrial England or lives in the favelas of present-day Latin America. Such believers have had little or no abstract theological knowledge or training. They have had, however, a powerful personal experience of encounter with Jesus and of being released from a sense of sin and guilt. Amid earthly lives that are

---

4. Ibid., 660.

5. Jonathan Edwards, *A Faithful Narrative of the Surprising Work of God in the Conversion of many Hundred Souls in Northampton, and the Neighbouring Towns and Villages of New-Hampshire and New-England. In a letter to the Rev. Dr. Benjamin Colman of Boston. By the Rev. Mr. Edwards, Minister of Northampton* (Elizabeth-Town, NJ: Shepard Kollock, 1790).

at best humdrum and at worst permeated by suffering, loss, and violence, they have found a sense of Christ's abiding presence, mediated through the words of Scripture, to be a continuing guide and inspiration.

Thus, historians have preferred to see Evangelicalism not as a hard-edged theological system but rather, in more imprecise terms, as a distinctive style of Protestant religious practice. One widely utilized characterization was offered by David Bebbington: "*conversionism*, the belief that lives need to be changed; *activism*, the expression of the gospel in effort; *biblicism*, a particular regard to the Bible, and . . . *crucicentrism*, a stress on the sacrifice of Christ on the cross."[6]

Bebbington's summary is sufficiently flexible to encompass the wide internal variety that became apparent even in the early years of the movement and has increased over the years as Evangelicalism has moved out from its original North Atlantic heartland to become a truly global movement. This very diversity reflects a central tension within Evangelicalism: on the one hand, it is an intensely individualistic movement, rooted in manifold distinctive personal encounters with God; on the other hand, Evangelicals have a sense of themselves as members of a united, global body of true Christian believers.

Evangelicals Grow through Revivalism

Throughout the history of Evangelicalism, its advance has been closely associated with revivalism, movements of intense, shared spiritual experience in which many people, and sometimes whole communities, profess conversion. Famous examples occurred in Cambuslang, Scotland in 1742; Cane Ridge, Kentucky in 1801; Rochester, New York in 1830; Ulster, Northern Ireland in 1859; and East Africa in 1936. There have been countless other occurrences, sometimes stimulated by prominent itinerant preachers, such as George Whitefield in the eighteenth century, Charles Finney and Dwight Moody in the nineteenth, and Billy Graham, Luis Palau, and Reinhard Bonnke in the twentieth.

The initial wave of revivals in the 1730s and 1740s—subsequently seen as the First Great Awakening—was followed, from the 1790s onward, by an upsurge that has been termed the Second Great Awakening, though, in fact, localized revivalistic activity had continued in the intervening decades. From the late nineteenth century onward, revivalism in the original North Atlantic heartland of Evangelicalism became less widespread, though there were still significant instances of revivalism, for example, the Welsh revival of 1904–5 and the missions of Billy Graham in Great Britain and the United States in the 1950s. Nevertheless, in the twentieth century the dynamic of revival increasingly shifted toward Africa, Asia, and Latin America (the Global South), where numbers of Evangelicals increased spectacularly while they stagnated or declined in the West.

Evangelicals Have Institutional Flexibility

The theological imprecision of Evangelicals has been paralleled by the fluidity of their institutional structures. Evangelicals have always been energetic planters of new local churches, but they seldom deliberately set out to found new denominations at a regional or national level. Rather, they seek to bring spiritual renewal within their existing churches, and only when their "new wine" cannot be contained within these "old wineskins" (Mark 2:22) do they break away. Thus, during the eighteenth and early nineteenth centuries Evangelicals developed a substantial presence in all the major orthodox Protestant denominations in the English-speaking world. John Wesley founded the Methodist movement in order to change the Church of England rather than to break away from it, and well into the nineteenth century many English Methodists continued to attend their parish churches.

Nevertheless, the institutional inflexibility of the Church of England and the internal dynamics of Methodism generated tensions and incompatibilities that ultimately made separation inevitable, though at the same

---

6. D. W. Bebbington, *Evangelicalism in Modern Britain: A History from the 1730s to the 1980s* (London: Unwin Hyman, 1989), 2–3.

time a substantial number of Evangelicals continued within the Church of England. At the local level, denominational loyalties were by no means fixed. Evangelical ministers in the Church of England could build up a substantial following and keep it within the national church, but such congregations would readily turn to the Methodism if a subsequent clergyman was less sympathetic to their views.

Similarly, in the second quarter of the nineteenth century, Evangelicals sought to promote widespread renewal and evangelism within the Church of Scotland. In the end, however, after a series of high-profile legal disputes, they decided their aspirations for a purified and evangelical church could only be met by seceding in 1843 to form the Free Church of Scotland. A comparable pattern of evangelical growth within existing church structures was apparent in North America, though institutional tensions eventually manifested themselves. An example can be found in the split in the 1830s in the United States between New School Presbyterians, who supported revivalism, and Old School Presbyterians, who regarded it with suspicion.

Evangelicals Form Societies

The distinctive organizational expression of Evangelicalism, however, has been societies rather than churches. Starting at the turn of the nineteenth century and continuing until the present day, Evangelicals in Great Britain and the United States have set up organizations for a wide range of missionary, moral, and social purposes. Sunday schools, which combined rudimentary general education with the Christian nurture of children and young people, were an early priority. Initially, they were promoted from 1785 by the Society Established in London for the Support and Encouragement of Sunday Schools, and then subsequently by the London Sunday School Union (1803) and the American Sunday School Union (1824). The British and Foreign Bible Society (1804) and the American Bible Society (1816) advanced the publication and widespread distribution of the Scriptures, while the Religious Tract Society (1799) and the American Tract Society (1825) focused on other Christian literature.

Numerous societies pursued aspects of home mission, both to particular groups like seamen, Roman Catholics, slaves, and native Americans (who were perceived as being in particular need of evangelization) and in specific localities through numerous city and town missions set up in centers like Glasgow (1826), Belfast (1828), New York (1830), and London (1835). Other societies sought to advance particular evangelical moral and behavioral preoccupations, including the Society for the Suppression of Vice (1802), the Lord's Day Observance Society (1831), and the American Temperance Union (1836).

Societies for foreign missions were an integral part of this movement. In its first half century evangelical horizons had not, in practice, moved far beyond Europe and North America, apart from some Methodist activity in the West Indies. In 1792, however, William Carey published his book *Enquiry into the Obligations of Christians to Use Mean(s) for the Conversion of the Heathen(s)*, inspiring the formation of the Baptist Missionary Society in the same year. The London Missionary Society followed in 1795, the Society for Missions to Africa and the East (later called the Church Missionary Society) in 1799, and the American Board for Foreign Missions in 1810.

George Whitefield: prominent itinerant preacher of the eighteenth century.
Image: North Wind Picture Archives

Western evangelical missionaries to the East and South have received a mixed press. Although some peoples, notably in the Pacific Islands, proved receptive, specifically evangelistic successes were initially limited. William Carey and his associates worked for many years at Serampore near Calcutta, for example, but converted few Indians to Christianity. David Livingstone, the most famous of the nineteenth-century missionaries to Africa, reportedly made only one convert during his entire career. Nineteenth-century missionaries had a greater impact in spreading Western culture and education, but later generations have had a decidedly ambivalent view of that achievement. In the later nineteenth century, however, James Hudson Taylor's China Inland Mission pioneered the concept of faith missions, operating without Western denominational support and thus better placed to communicate the gospel in the framework of the receiving culture.

Evangelicals Are Socially Active

Meanwhile in the West during the early to midnineteenth century, Evangelicals secured considerable social and political influence. The foundations of this ascendancy were laid by the work of the so-called Clapham Sect, led by William Wilberforce, which was instrumental in securing the abolition of the British slave trade in 1807. Alongside this specific achievement, Wilberforce and his associates gave Evangelicalism a wider social respectability and political credibility, which was consolidated by subsequent leaders like Thomas Chalmers, who strongly influenced public policy toward poverty, and Lord Ashley (later the Earl of Shaftesbury), who spearheaded campaigns for the improvement of working conditions in factories and mines.

William Wilberforce was instrumental in securing the abolition of the British slave trade.
Image: North Wind Picture Archives

Indeed, such was the prominence of evangelical ideas in early Victorian Britain that one historian, Boyd Hilton, has characterized the period between 1785 and 1865 as "the age of atonement."[7] A similar description can be applied to the United States, where Evangelicals came to dominate most Protestant denominations. Although opportunities for direct political influence were limited in the United States, religion, in the words of the French observer Alexis de Tocqueville, "directs the customs of the community, and, by regulating domestic life, regulates the state."[8] In such a context the challenge of defining Evangelicals becomes even more acute, as Evangelicals influence people in various ways, but those people do not thereby subscribe to all their beliefs or share in their spiritual commitment and experience.

Inevitably, nineteenth-century Evangelicals became victims of their own success and provoked criticism. Some of their most trenchant critics were novelists, such as Charles Dickens, who satirized evangelical mores through the creation of such memorable characters as Mrs. Jellyby in *Bleak House* (first published in 1853), a woman obsessed with the "telescopic philanthropy" of educating the natives of Borrioboola-Gha on the banks of the Niger.[9] A wider anti-Evangelical reaction began to set in from the 1860s. This was engendered in part by a more hostile intellectual climate shaped by Darwinian biology and liberal approaches to the Bible. It was also a result of the shocks of the Indian rebellion of 1857–58 and the American Civil War of 1861–65, which challenged implicit evangelical assumptions about the inexorable interlinked advances of the gospel and social improvement.

---

7. Boyd Hilton, *The Age of Atonement: The Influence of Evangelicalism in Social and Economic Thought*, 1785–1865 (Oxford: Clarendon Press, 1988).

8. Alexis de Tocqueville, *Democracy in America* (London: Everyman's Library, 1994), 1:304.

9. Charles Dickens, *Bleak House* (London: Penguin, 1985), 82–86.

Evangelicals Regroup

A worship band performs at Keswick 2013. *Photo: Keswick Ministries*

The late nineteenth and early twentieth centuries saw substantial Evangelical regrouping and restatement. Central to this process was the movement to promote a transformed "higher" spiritual life, stimulated by the annual conventions held from 1875 onward in the English Lake District town of Keswick. These continue today. For many Evangelicals, influenced in particular by Henry Grattan Guinness's book *The Approaching End of the Age* (1879), increased pessimism regarding the future prospects of unredeemed humanity was a spur to redoubled missionary efforts. It is to this period that the roots of indigenous evangelical churches in Asia, Africa, and Latin America can be traced.

The Pentecostal movement in the first decade of the twentieth century gave further impetus to these trends. While the origins of Pentecostalism are conventionally associated with the revival at the Asuza Street Church in Los Angeles in 1906, in reality the movement, like other significant revival movements in evangelical history, was a polycentric one. For example, the outpouring of the Spirit at the Asuza Street Revival was *preceded* by a 1905 revival at the Mukti mission led by Pandita Ramabai in India and rapidly succeeded by the 1907 revival at Pyongyang, which stimulated the subsequent growth of Evangelicalism in Korea. Thus, whereas in the nineteenth century the predominance of Evangelical numbers lay in Great Britain, Ireland, and the United States, and to a lesser extent in continental Europe, the twentieth century saw a decisive shift toward the non-Western world. This trend began to gather momentum in the 1920s and 1930s.

In the meantime, Western Evangelicals were divided on the best way to respond to liberal intellectual trends. Fundamentalists, such as those who prosecuted John Scopes in Dayton, Tennessee, in 1925 for allegedly teaching the theory of evolution, insisted the best defense lay in dogmatically asserting a narrow definition of Christian doctrine by, for example, lifting up the verbal inerrancy of Scripture. Other Evangelicals, however, continued to advocate more reasoned and moderate engagement with the wider culture. Such internal controversies diverted Evangelical energies, especially in the period between the First and Second World Wars.

Jonathan Lamb, formerly with the Langham Partnership, speaks at Keswick 2013. *Photo: Keswick Ministries*

Since the end of the Second World War, however, Evangelicals in the West, and especially in the United States, have regained some lost ground. Under the leadership of, among others, Billy Graham in America and John Stott in Great Britain, they articulated a theology that was robustly conservative but eschewed the negative anti-liberal polemics of the fundamentalists in favor of the positive proclamation of the gospel and its relevance to contemporary life.

Evangelicals Grow and Gain Political Influence

In Great Britain, in the face of pervasive secularization and church decline, Evangelicalism has proven to be more resilient than other forms of Christianity and hence has become increasingly prominent within existing denominations, not least the Church of England. It

Leaders like John Stott articulated a theology that was conservative and relevant to contemporary life.
Photograph by John W. Yates III © 1998. Used by permission of Langham Partnership.

has also stimulated significant growth in Independent and Pentecostal churches. The migration of Christians from Africa, the Caribbean, and South Asia has also swelled British Evangelical numbers.

A survey in the United States in 2007 indicated around a third of the population identified with Evangelicalism,[10] though probably less than half of these people were actively committed church members. Nevertheless, the American Evangelical subculture remains strong, providing financial and educational resources that have continued to exert significant influence on global Evangelicalism. American Evangelicalism makes full use of contemporary technology, promoting itself through broadcast media and online, as well as developing megachurches as a form of organization that is attractive to widely dispersed but mobile congregations.

Elsewhere, however, growth has been much more spectacular. In South America, for example, the estimated membership of Pentecostal churches increased from 1.16 million to 22.22 million between 1960 and 2000.[11] At

the turn of the millennium, following decades of exponential growth, there were 12.2 million Evangelicals in Korea, making up around a quarter of the total population. These two examples illustrate well the capacity of Evangelicals to grow their numbers in highly diverse cultural and religious contacts and against a background of historic Roman Catholicism in Latin America and of Buddhist and Confucian tradition in Korea. There has also been rapid growth across sub-Saharan Africa, grounded in the ability of Evangelicalism to adapt to a wide diversity of indigenous cultures. Here, as in the eighteenth-century North Atlantic world, the structural fluidity of Evangelicals alongside their articulation of spiritual certainties has been a winning combination in appealing to impoverished and vulnerable communities.

Charles Finney was an itinerant preacher involved with many revivals during the nineteenth century.
Image: North Wind Picture Archives

10. http://religions.pewforum.org/reports.

11. John Wolffe, ed., *Global Religious Movements in Regional Context* (Aldershot: Ashgate, 2002), 69, 88.

Evangelicals hold the religious allegiance of up to a tenth of the world's population.

The global upsurge of Evangelicals in the later twentieth century gave them renewed political influence. The most prominent, but not necessarily the most representative instance, was the Religious Right in the United States, a significant electoral force behind Republican presidents, notably Ronald Reagan in the 1980s and George W. Bush in the 2000s. Evangelical political associations have, however, been complex and diverse; while naturally tending to align with the political Right on moral issues, a recognition of the implications of the gospel for social justice can also inspire support for the political Left. Hence in Great Britain, Evangelicals have been found among the active supporters of the Liberal and Labour parties, and a similar diversity of allegiances can be discerned in African and Latin American politics.

Who, then, are Evangelicals? There can be no clear-cut answer to this question in the face of shifting and sometimes contentious definitions, and in the face of the fluidity and individualism of Evangelicals themselves. Nevertheless, a convincing argument can be made for the continuity and distinctiveness of Evangelicalism as a dynamic and committed form of Christianity. It claims a prehistory back to the early church but has its more immediate origins in the eighteenth century. By the early twenty-first century, depending on how one interprets the statistics, Evangelicals hold the religious allegiance of up to a tenth of the world's population. Evangelicals have included prominent aristocrats, scholars, social reformers, and political leaders. But Evangelicals are also countless otherwise obscure men and (especially) women on all six continents who have found a source of dignity and abiding purpose in a personal encounter with Jesus Christ, the assurance of sins forgiven, and a trust in the Bible as a guide for life.

Who, then, are Evangelicals? There can be no clear-cut answer to this question.

Bibliography

Much of this chapter summarizes material drawn from Mark Hutchinson and John Wolffe's book *A Short History of Global Evangelicalism* (New York: Cambridge University Press, 2012), which provides a starting point for readers seeking further details and bibliographic information.

Bebbington, D. W. *Evangelicalism in Modern Britain: A History from the 1730s to the 1980s*. London: Unwin Hyman, 1989.

de Tocqueville, Alexis. *Democracy in America*. 2 vols. London: Everyman's Library, 1994.

Edwards, Jonathan. *A Faithful Narrative of the Surprising Work of God in the Conversion of many Hundred Souls in Northampton, and the Neighbouring Towns and Villages of New-Hampshire and New-England. In a letter to the Rev. Dr. Benjamin Colman of Boston. By the Rev. Mr. Edwards, Minister of Northampton*. Elizabeth-Town, NJ: Shepard Kollock, 1790.

Hilton, Boyd. *The Age of Atonement: The Influence of Evangelicalism on Social and Economic Thought, 1785–1865*. Oxford: Clarendon Press, 1988.

Milner, Joseph, and Isaac Milner. *The History of the Church of Christ*. London: Thomas Nelson, 1849.

Wolffe, John, ed. *Global Religious Movements in Regional Context*. Aldershot: Ashgate, 2002.

Dr. John Wolffe is professor of Religious History at The Open University based in Milton Keynes, United Kingdom. He is the author of many works, including *The Protestant Crusade in Great Britain, 1829–1860*; *God and Greater Britain: Religion and National Life in Britain and Ireland, 1843–1945*; *Evangelical Faith and Public Zeal: Evangelicals and Society in Britain, 1780–1990*, edited with introduction and *The Expansion of Evangelicalism: The Age of Wilberforce, More, Chalmers and Finney*.

"Evangelicalism, along with Orthodoxy and Roman Catholicism, is one of the three most resilient and encompassing currents within the world Christian family. The great John Stott once defined Evangelicals as gospel people and Bible people. We are heralds of the Good News of Jesus Christ—meant for all peoples everywhere—and we find the basis for our witness in the life-giving words of Holy Scripture. As we stay true to these primary principles, I believe that God will continue to use Evangelicals as a transformative movement of grace and renewal in the world today."

—Dr. Timothy George, Dean of Beeson Divinity School of Samford University, Chairman of the Board, Colson Center for Christian Worldview, United States

DEMOGRAPHICS OF GLOBAL EVANGELICALISM

By Gina A. Zurlo

Evangelicalism is a social phenomenon that transcends traditional methods of definition. Evangelicals are found across many traditions, making it difficult to define who exactly an Evangelical is.[1] Are Evangelicals just those who are associated with particular denominations or communions? Or are they individuals who adhere to a particular set of theological criteria? Or maybe they are both? Recent scholarship suggests that what has traditionally been called Evangelicalism is changing. Numerous texts have been released about the concerns of young Evangelicals, the challenges facing the evangelical church, and the impact the increasingly global face of Evangelicalism will have on the movement and on Christianity as a whole.[2]

Contemporary use of the term *Evangelical* originated with eighteenth-century revivalism in Europe, whose emphases included born-again, or new-birth, experiences and intense spiritual piety. Although driven by particular beliefs and emphases, however, these revival movements were not themselves churches or denominations with specific theological creeds. Instead, the revival tradition united believers from varied backgrounds within a shared experience and spiritual focus. This shaped the movement that became known as Evangelicalism, which, more than 250 years after its inception, continues to encompass many kinds of Christians all around the world. The historical progression of Evangelicalism raises two important issues: (1) the problem of defining what, and who, an Evangelical is and (2) how one goes about counting Evangelicals.

Evangelicalism is clearly a global movement and has grown dramatically in Africa, which now has the highest percentage of Evangelicals of any continent.
Photo: The Langham Partnership

Defining Evangelicals

The historical origins of modern Evangelicalism lie in the search for "a 'true religion of the heart'" beginning in the first half of the eighteenth century in Europe.[3] English-speaking Protestantism was renewed by a series of religious revivals, flamed by prominent evangelists like George Whitefield and John Wesley but supported by

---

1. Corwin Smidt, "The Measurement of Evangelicals," *The Immanent Frame: Secularism, Religion, and the Public Sphere* (blog), August 29, 2008, http://blogs.ssrc.org/tif/2008/08/29/the-measurement-of-evangelicals/.

2. See David P. Gushee, ed., *A New Evangelical Manifesto: A Kingdom Vision for the Common Good* (St. Louis: Chalice Press, 2012); Soong-Chan Rah, *The Next Evangelicalism: Freeing the Church from Western Cultural Captivity* (Downers Grove, IL: InterVarsity Press, 2009); Marcia Pally, *The New Evangelicals: Expanding the Vision of the Common Good* (Grand Rapids: Eerdmans, 2011); John S. Dickerson, *The Great Evangelical Recession: 6 Factors That Will Crash the American Church—and How to Prepare* (Grand Rapids: Baker, 2013); Tom Krattenmaker, *The Evangelicals You Don't Know: Introducing the Next Generation of Christians* (Lanham, MD: Rowman & Littlefield, 2013). Brian Stanley's recent text, *The Global Diffusion of Evangelicalism: The Age of Billy Graham and John Stott* (Downers Grove, IL: InterVarsity Press, 2013), aims to put the story of English-speaking Evangelicalism in a wider global context.

3. Mark A. Noll, *American Evangelical Christianity: An Introduction* (Oxford: Blackwell, 2001), 10.

the lives of "ordinary men and women."[4] Initially, *Evangelical* was simply synonymous with *Protestant*, especially in Germany, where even today the German *Evangelische* is better translated as "Protestant" rather than "Evangelical."[5] Among English speakers many Lutherans in particular still use the term in this sense, as in the "Evangelical Lutheran Church." Over time the term *Evangelical* largely came to describe the network of Protestant Christian movements in the eighteenth century in Britain and its colonies, the individuals who were associated with those movements, and a larger pattern of theological convictions and religious attitudes.[6]

John Wesley led many revival meetings in the eighteenth century.
Photo: North Wind Picture Archives

Today, because Evangelicalism is a movement without a magisterium (a teaching authority like in the Roman Catholic Church), it is generally described in terms of adherents' denominational affiliations, self-identification on surveys and polls, or theological leanings; that is, defining the movement from the bottom-up rather than from a prescriptive set of criteria. Additionally, there is significant overlap between Evangelicalism and the Pentecostal/Charismatic movement. It is important to note that classical Pentecostals are normally considered Evangelicals, whereas Charismatics in mainline churches and Independent Charismatics are usually not. This is because mainline churches have Evangelical minorities that are often not the same as Charismatic minorities in terms of self-identification. Independent Charismatics often see Evangelicalism as part of the denomination from which they are breaking away.

Denominational Affiliation

The Protestant Reformation originating in sixteenth-century Germany was highly generative in the fragmentation of Christianity. Its emphasis on individual reading and interpretation of Scripture, combined with renewed religious freedom, resulted in the development of a multitude of new Christian groups, each an attempt to capture a more "pure" version of the faith. As the Reformation expanded in Germany, similar movements began to occur elsewhere in Europe, the beginning of what is known today as *denominationalism*. Reformed Christianity, based on the teachings of John Calvin and Ulrich Zwingli, developed in Switzerland. Presbyterianism, influenced by John Knox, grew out of Reformed Christianity in the Scottish context. In 1534 England's King Henry VIII split from Roman Catholicism and brought the Church of England into the Reformation. The Church of England would be the root of both the Episcopal Church in the United States and eventually Methodism, based on the teachings of John Wesley.

With these and other developments, denominational affiliation became the foundation of Protestant Christian group identity. This is particularly true in Europe and North America, but with the spread and continued growth of Christianity worldwide—notably through the vast denominationally oriented enterprises of Western missionaries—it also characterizes the global South. Global South is defined in geopolitical terms by sixteen United Nations regions: Eastern Africa, Middle Africa, Northern Africa, Southern Africa, Western Africa, the Caribbean, Central America, South America, Central Asia, Eastern Asia, Southern Asia, South-Eastern Asia, Western Asia, Melanesia, Micronesia, and Polynesia.

---

4. Ibid., 10.

5. American religion historian Martin E. Marty was one of those who equated the two terms for greater clarity. See Martin E. Marty, *Protestantism: Its Churches and Cultures, Rituals and Doctrines, Yesterday and Today* (New York: Holt, Rinehart & Winston, 1972), xi.

6. Ibid., 13.

Many missionaries to these parts of the world initially introduced Christianity in the form of a Western denomination, but processes of cross-cultural translation have led to indigenous expressions of Western denominations in addition to independent break-off congregations and movements in the global South.

Defining Evangelicals by denomination affiliation. Using denominational affiliation to define Evangelicals is a method generally popular among social and political scientists. Anglican missionary and church statistician David B. Barrett pioneered the field of reporting on Christian affiliation and activities worldwide, beginning his work in Kenya in the 1960s. The first edition of his *World Christian Encyclopedia* offered the following definition of *Evangelical*: "A sub-division of Protestants consisting of affiliated church members calling themselves evangelicals, or all persons belonging to Evangelical congregations, churches or denominations; characterized by commitment to personal religion (including new birth or personal conversion experience), reliance on Holy Scripture as the only basis for faith and Christian living, emphasis on preaching and evangelism, and usually on conservatism in theology."[7] This definition is grounded in denominational affiliation, but it also goes a step further to suggest what an evangelical denomination might actually look like.

Defining Evangelicals by denominational affiliation is helpful because it allows for analysis based on an already established structure. However, this method has three important weaknesses. First, not every congregation holds to its denomination's official statements of faith. For example, the Presbyterian Church (USA) (PC[USA]), is a mainline, mostly theologically liberal denomination. Since the early twentieth century, the PC(USA), including its precursor bodies, has seen the departure of numerous theologically conservative congregations to form new denominations, such as the Presbyterian Church in America (PCA). By virtue of its memberships in the National Association of Evangelicals and the World Evangelical Alliance, the PCA is listed as 100% Evangelical in the *World Christian Database*, the electronic successor to Barrett's *World Christian Encyclopedia*.[8] Despite the splits, however, a contingent of theologically conservative churches has remained within the PC(USA). The *World Christian Database* estimates the PC(USA) as 35% Evangelical, even though the denomination is not a member of an evangelical communion.

Second, and perhaps obviously, not all individuals affiliated with "100% Evangelical" congregations or denominations are actually evangelical. Historian Diana Butler Bass suggested a shift in Western Christian consciousness in which *belonging* to a community might trump what one actually *believes* about matters of faith.[9] Such a shift could result in more diversification of church institutions.

Third, identifying Evangelicals based solely on denominational affiliation does not take into consideration nonchurchgoers, such as the rising numbers of unaffiliated in the West,[10] and house church movements, such as those in China.

The declining importance of denominationalism should also be considered, since "members of nondenominational churches often identify themselves on surveys as unaffiliated or even as having 'no religion'" altogether.[11] In addition, denominational divides are sometimes not as clear-cut in those parts of the world where Evangelicalism is growing the fastest, such as in Africa among indigenous Christian movements.

---

7. David B. Barrett, ed., *World Christian Encyclopedia: A Comparative Study of Churches and Religions in the Modern World, AD 1900–2000* (Nairobi: Oxford University Press, 1982), 826.

8. Todd M. Johnson, ed., *World Christian Database* (Leiden: Brill, accessed March 2013), http://www.worldchristiandatabase.org/.

9. Diana Butler Bass, *Christianity After Religion: The End of Church and the Birth of a New Spiritual Awakening* (New York: HarperOne, 2012), 47–63. See pages 204–9 for an assessment of belonging, behaving, and believing as presented throughout the Bible.

10. See Grace Davie, *Religion in Britain Since 1945: Believing Without Belonging* (Oxford: Blackwell, 1994).

11. Byron Johnson, "The Good News About Evangelicalism," *First Things*, February 2011, http://www.firstthings.com/article/2011/01/the-good-news-about-evangelicalism.

Defining Evangelicals by self-identification. Another method of defining Evangelicals is by self-identification on surveys and polls. The philosophy behind this method, roughly stated, is that if one wants to know who or what someone is, then ask.[12] This method is beneficial in that it bypasses the complexities of denominationalism and puts the power of definition into the hands of the actual people being studied (similar to polling about political ideology). Gallup first asked the American public about having a "born-again experience" in 1976 (deemed "the Year of the Evangelical" by *Time*, *Newsweek*, and others) and polled about evangelical identity up until 2005; results have ranged between 34 percent and 47 percent.[13] The Pew Research Center Religion and Public Life Project also relies heavily on surveys and polls for identifying members of religious groups, including Evangelicals.[14] However, the seemingly simple question, "Are you a born-again or Evangelical Christian?" in a survey or poll introduces quite a number of problems. Many respondents simply do not know what the terms mean or whether they fall into either of those categories.

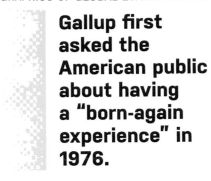

Gallup first asked the American public about having a "born-again experience" in 1976.

Defining Evangelicals by theology. David Bebbington's 1989 fourfold set of descriptors—conversionism, activism, Biblicism, and crucicentrism—dominates theological definitions of *Evangelical*.[15] According to Bebbington, these characteristics are the common features defining the movement over time, despite all of the changes Evangelicalism has undergone since its inception in the eighteenth century. While some of the particulars within each of these descriptors vary among denominations, the general scope and importance of each remains the same for the broader evangelical movement.

Conversionism is an individual's turn away from sin and toward repentance in Christ, an act of justification by faith resulting in confidence in one's personal salvation. *Activism* has roots in conversionism and reflects a desire to share the gospel message with others so that they, too, can claim a unique conversion experience. *Biblicism* is the belief that all spiritual truth is found in the Bible. Although theories of infallibility or inerrancy of the text have been common among Evangelicals, historically there has been fluidity concerning such theories, and a broader opinion of the Bible simply as truth has predominated.[16] The standard evangelical *crucicentric* view has been Christ's death as a substitute for sinful humankind. However, like biblical inerrancy, this opinion has not been uniform across the movement.

The Bebbington Quadrilateral has become ubiquitous but not without criticism. The definition gives the impression that Evangelicalism can be pinned down theologically when, in fact, the movement is quite diverse. It is unclear as to whether the four points define the center of the movement theologically or represent a set of boundaries. If they are boundaries, how are these boundaries defined without an evangelical headquarters or magisterium? It is difficult to argue that Evangelicalism, as a movement rather than as an organization or institution, can have clearly defined boundaries for "right" belief. In addition, Bebbington did not indicate in his evaluation whether an individual must subscribe to all of the four points in order to be considered an Evangelical.

---

12. Christian Smith, *American Evangelicalism: Embattled and Thriving* (Chicago: University of Chicago Press, 1998), 233.

13. Frank Newport and Joseph Carroll, "Another Look at Evangelicals in America Today," *Gallup*, December 2, 2005, http://www.gallup.com/poll/20242/another-look-evangelicals-america-today.aspx.

14. The Pew Forum also measures by denominational affiliation, largely as a result of its partnership with the Center for the Study of Global Christianity, which collects and analyzes a large amount of data on Christian denominations worldwide. See Pew Research Center Religion & Public Life Project, "Methodology for Estimating Christian Movements," Appendix B in "Global Christianity: A Report on the Size and Distribution of the World's Christian Population," *Pew Research Center Religion & Public Life Project*, December 19, 2011, http://www.pewforum.org/files/2011/12/ ChristianityAppendixB.pdf.

15. David Bebbington, *Evangelicalism in Modern Britain: A History from the 1730s to the 1980s* (London: Unwin Hyman, 1982).

16. Ibid., 13.

Perhaps the most serious weakness in utilizing the Bebbington Quadrilateral is contextual. Bebbington defined his four characteristics explicitly in reference to Evangelicalism in Britain from the 1730s to the 1980s. Others have taken them out of this context and at times applied them less than appropriately elsewhere. This has become most apparent with the growth of Christianity in Africa, Asia, and Latin America over the course of the twentieth century. Many of these new Christians often place high value on different characteristics—in particular, more Charismatic expressions of faith—and do not identify with the historical meanings these claims carry.[17]

Counting Evangelicals

Any effective and comprehensive method for counting Evangelicals must take into consideration denominational affiliation, self-identification, and theology. The Center for the Study of Global Christianity (CSGC) at Gordon–Conwell Theological Seminary in South Hamilton, Massachusetts, has been working on quantifying Christians around the world for nearly fifty years. The CSGC utilizes membership statistics from denominations in every country and has identified approximately forty-four thousand Christian denominations worldwide as of the middle of 2013.[18] The results of counting Evangelicals are directly related to denominational membership figures. Strictly speaking, denominational affiliation means official membership on a church roll.

Method 1: Individuals in Denominations That Are 100% Evangelical

According to the CSGC, the first category of Evangelicals includes individuals who are found in denominations that are coded 100% Evangelical. That is, membership in an evangelical council (either national, regional, or global) is assessed for every denomination, and those denominations that have evangelical affiliations are classed as 100% Evangelical. Consequently, 100 percent of the members of these denominations are considered Evangelicals. Utilizing this method alone, the *World Christian Database* estimates there are 150 million Evangelicals in the world. As of 2010, the nine largest 100% Evangelical denominations in the world are all Protestant, and the five largest 100% Evangelical denominations are found in Brazil, Ethiopia, Nigeria, and Indonesia, reflecting the global scope of the movement.

Method 2: Individuals Who Self-Identify as Evangelical in Non-100% Evangelical Denominations

For those denominations not identified as 100% Evangelical, an estimate is made of the percentage (0–99%) of members who self-identify as Evangelical. Self-identification percentages for Evangelicals in non-100% Evangelical denominations are verified by contacting key figures within each denomination, and each estimate is sourced in documentation housed at the CSGC. Adding together figures from both 100% and partially Evangelical denominations gives a total of 285 million Evangelicals worldwide. Looking at both 100% and non-100% Evangelical denominations reveals that the movement has a significant presence beyond Western Protestantism. Some of the denominations with the most Evangelicals are within Anglicanism in the global South, such as the Anglican Church of Nigeria and the Church of Uganda. Chinese house churches (classified as Independents) taken together constitute the denomination with the third most Evangelicals globally. The United Kingdom (the Church of England) and the United States (the Southern Baptist Convention), however, are still important locations of the movement.

---

17. Mark A. Noll, "Evangelical Identity, Power, and Culture in the 'Great' Nineteenth Century," 31–51 in *Christianity Reborn: The Global Expansion of Evangelicalism in the Twentieth Century*, ed. Donald M. Lewis, (Grand Rapids: Eerdmans, 2004), 40.

18. Todd M. Johnson and Peter F. Crossing, "Christianity 2013: Renewalists and Faith and Migration," *International Bulletin of Missionary Research* 37, no. 1 (January 2013): 33.

Method 3: Evangelicals Not Affiliated with Any Denomination (Unaffiliated Evangelicals)

To date, no studies have addressed directly how many Evangelicals are denominationally unaffiliated. However, two well-known realities (in Western Christianity, in particular) appear to provide indirect evidence for this undocumented trend. The first is reflected in recent research indicating the unaffiliated are not uniformly nonreligious.[19] The Pew Research Center Religion and Public Life Project reported that 68 percent of America's unaffiliated believe in God.[20] It is reasonable to assume that a notable proportion of Christians is among the ranks of the unaffiliated by virtue of Christianity being the largest religion in many of the countries studied. The second reality is the acknowledged fact that unaffiliated Christians often attend and are active in churches, including evangelical churches, without becoming official members. These unaffiliated Christians profess allegiance and commitment to Christ but do not maintain church affiliation.

Without specific survey or polling data on the activities or beliefs of unaffiliated Evangelicals, calculating their number worldwide requires a broad estimate.[21] One starting point is to consider the percentage of unaffiliated Christians in a particular country and evaluate it in light of the country's Evangelical presence. For example, South Africa was home to 35.8 million affiliated Christians in 2010 (71.4 percent of the country's population). Of these, 4.7 million were Evangelicals, found in both 100% Evangelical denominations and in non-100% Evangelical denominations (methods 1 + 2). The population also included 5.3 million unaffiliated Christians (10.6 percent of the population), for a total of 41.1 million Christians (82.0 percent of the country's population). Assuming that the same proportion of unaffiliated Christians as affiliated Christians are Evangelicals yields an additional 695,000 Evangelicals, raising the number of Evangelicals in South Africa to a total of 5.4 million (both affiliated and unaffiliated; methods 1 + 2 + 3).

Applying the calculation to the world's Christian population, country by country, results in an additional 14.3 million unaffiliated Evangelicals globally. (Over 70 percent of the world's unaffiliated Evangelicals live in the United States.) Adding together the results for unaffiliated and affiliated Evangelicals gives a total of 299.8 million Evangelicals worldwide (13 percent of the global population). This compares to 285.5 million affiliated Evangelicals, according to the structural definition of the *World Christian Database* (see figure 1).[22]

---

19. Pew Research Center, "Global Religious Landscape," *Pew Research Center Religion & Public Life Project*, December 18, 2012, http://www.pewforum.org/2012/12/18/global-religious-landscape-exec/. This report states that of the world's 1.1 billion unaffiliated, a significant portion maintains some kind of religious belief: "Various surveys have found that belief in God or a higher power is shared by 7% of unaffiliated Chinese adults, 30% of unaffiliated French adults and 68% of unaffiliated U.S. adults" (1). Many also participate in a variety of religious practices, such as prayer and attendance at religious services.

20. Pew Research Center, "'Nones' on the Rise," *Pew Research Center Religion & Public Life Report*, October 9, 2012, http://www.pewforum.org/2012/10/09/nones-on-the-rise/.

21. The ratio of unaffiliated Evangelicals to affiliated Evangelicals in any particular country is assumed to be the same as the ratio of unaffiliated Christians to affiliated Christians. This yields a simplified formula of unaffiliated Evangelicals = (unaffiliated Christians) x (affiliated Evangelicals) ÷ (affiliated Christians).

22. There are, of course, limitations to using such a blunt tool for measuring unaffiliated Evangelicals. The assumption that Evangelical and non-Evangelical Christians are equally likely to be unaffiliated might result in an inflation of the actual number of Evangelicals in a particular country. Little data are available on the probability that someone who self-identifies only as Christian, with no church affiliation or other descriptor specified, is an Evangelical. This is even more true for the totally unaffiliated, those who self-identify as nothing in particular. While some might consider the likelihood that either type of individual is Evangelical to be slim, however, it is not impossible, given the individualistic tendencies of the movement.

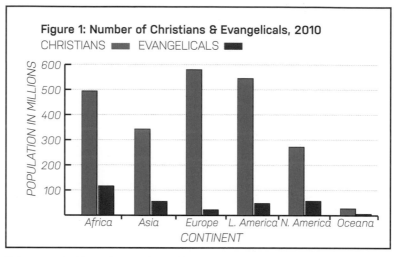

Data source: Todd M. Johnson, ed., *World Christian Database*
(Leiden: Brill, accessed March 2013).

Evangelicals are individuals in 100% Evangelical denominations (method 1), Evangelicals in non-100% Evangelical denominations (method 2), and unaffiliated Evangelicals (method 3).

Method 4: Individuals Who Align with a Specific Set of Theological Descriptors

In demographic analysis, one primary supporter of a theological definition of *Evangelicalism* is *Operation World*. Begun by Patrick Johnstone and continued first by Jason Mandryk and currently by Molly Wall, *Operation World* has appeared in seven editions since 1964, with the most recent edition released in 2010.[23] It is an easy-to-read, accessible resource intended primarily for equipping missionaries and mission-minded laypeople to pray for the nations and the church around the world. The 2010 edition defined Evangelicals as all those who adhere to all four theological articles that paint a picture very close to the Bebbington Quadrilateral.[24]

Although both *Operation World* and the *World Christian Database* are based on denominational data, *Operation World*'s theological definition of *Evangelicals* differs from the *World Christian Database*'s strictly structural approach. The *Operation World* team consists of individuals, who themselves adhere to the previously mentioned theological descriptors, trying to identify other people around the world who also hold those characteristics. The team's methodology does not rely on self-identification as Evangelical but rather on assessment and educated estimates. Theological criteria such as these tend to produce much larger Evangelical figures. Globally, *Operation World* reported 545.9 million Evangelicals in 2010, while the *World Christian Database* reported 299.2 million, nearly half as many.[25]

---

23. Jason Mandryk, *Operation World: The Definitive Prayer Guide to Every Nation,* 7th ed. (Colorado Springs: Biblica, 2010).

24. Ibid., 958–59. The definition of evangelical is as follows: "All who emphasize and adhere to all four of the following: The Lord Jesus Christ as the sole source of salvation through faith in Him, as validated by His crucifixion and resurrection. Personal faith and conversion with regeneration by the Holy Spirit. Recognition of the inspired Word of God as the ultimate basis and authority for faith and Christian living. Commitment to biblical witness, evangelism and mission that brings others to faith in Christ."

25. With the addition of the unaffiliated Evangelicals (methods 1 + 2 + 3).

The larger *Operation World* figure includes people who do not self-identify as Evangelical with respect to their denomination but who match a set of theological descriptors. It is telling that some of the largest discrepancies occur in countries in the global South (except for the United States, explained in the next paragraph), where Evangelicalism is relatively young and where denominational affiliation, of either the individual with a denomination or the denomination with regional Evangelical bodies, might not be as strong or apparent (i.e., where structural Evangelicalism is more difficult to enumerate).

One example of significant denominational discrepancy is the African American population in the United States. African Americans are often excluded from sociological and political discussions of Evangelicalism because of the perception that Evangelicalism is a white phenomenon. In reality, many African American Christians generally adhere to the theological characteristics of historical Evangelicalism, which is why *Operation World* includes them in its figures for Evangelicals in the United States. Of the eight largest denominational discrepancies between *Operation World* and *World Christian Database*, six are within predominantly African American traditions. Together, these six denominations add another 18.7 million individuals in the United States that *Operation World* considers Evangelical but the *World Christian Database* does not.

China is the most challenging country in terms of counting Evangelicals. *Operation World* reported 76.0 million Evangelicals in China as of 2010, while the *World Christian Database* reported only 15.2 million (a difference of 60.8 million). Despite the significant growth of the house church movement in China, no overtly Evangelical organization can be easily identified and tracked there. On the other hand, if all of the house churches in China suddenly joined the World Evangelical Alliance, a global Evangelical communion, then the *World Christian Database* would automatically consider all house church members Evangelical. *Operation World*, however, already considers most members of Chinese house churches Evangelical, based on *Operation World*'s assessment of their theological leanings. In many other churches in the global South it is difficult to apply the label *Evangelical* because of the historical and cultural context in which the movement was born.

Putting It All Together

The differences in methodologies described in the preceding sections result in differing figures. Table 1 presents global totals for all four methods together to provide a more comprehensive picture.

Table 1. Global totals for the four methods, 2010

	METHOD 1	METHOD 2	METHOD 3	METHOD 1+2+3	METHOD 4
	100% Evangelical Denominations	Non-100% Evangelical Denominations	Unaffiliated Evangelicals	*World Christian Database*	*Operation World*
Globe	150.6 million	134.9 million	14.3 million	299.2 million	545.9 million

Data source: Todd M. Johnson, ed., *World Christian Database* (Leiden/Boston: Brill, accessed March 2013); Jason Mandryk, *Operation World* (Colorado Springs: Biblica, 2010), 3.

Evangelicals Around the World

However it is defined, Evangelicalism is clearly a global movement. Figure 2 shows that Europe, the birthplace of Evangelicalism, is now the least Evangelical continent in the world, by percentage, at 3.8 percent. Evangelicalism has grown dramatically in Africa, which now is the highest percentage Evangelical of any continent (23.6 percent of African Christians, or 115 million Evangelicals in 2010). Both North America and Oceania are almost 21 percent Evangelical, though North America has a much larger number (56.9 million, compared to Oceania's 5.6 million).

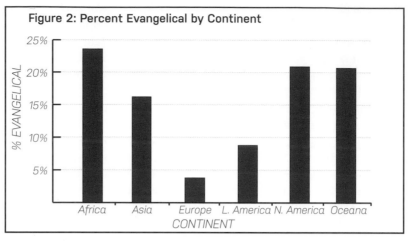

Figure 2: Percent Evangelical by Continent

Data source: Todd M. Johnson, ed., *World Christian Database* (Leiden: Brill, accessed March 2013).*Percentages are of all Christians in the region; Methods 1 + 2 + 3.*

Although the United States remained the country with the largest Evangelical population in 2010, it is clear the movement has achieved a significant level of global spread. Table 2 shows that in 1970, six of the ten countries with the largest Evangelical populations were in the global South. By 2010, eight were in the global South, each of which has had tremendous growth since 1970. Nigeria's Evangelical population swelled from 4.7 million to 32.6 million, while Brazil's grew more than fivefold over the forty-year period. The United Kingdom's Evangelical population is the only one among the top ten to have decreased over the forty-year period, dropping from almost 13 million in 1970 to just above 12 million in 2010.

Table 2. Countries with the largest number of Evangelicals (E), 1970 & 2010

RANK	COUNTRY	E 1970*	COUNTRY	E 2010**
1	United States	33,625,000	United States	54,805,000
2	United Kingdom	12,972,000	United Kingdom	32,630,000
3	Brazil	5,748,000	Brazil	29,100,000
4	Nigeria	4,771,000	China	15,250,000
5	India	2,781,000	South Korea	12,800,000
6	South Africa	2,541,000	United Kingdom	12,600,000
7	Canada	2,086,000	Ethiopia	12,170,000
8	Australia	2,081,000	Kenya	11,460,000
9	South Korea	2,076,000	India	9,330,000
10	Indonesia	1,767,000	Indonesia	7,800,000

Source: Todd M. Johnson, ed., *World Christian Database* (Leiden/Boston: Brill, accessed February 2013).
* Methods 1+2
** Methods 1+2+3

The ten countries with the highest percentage of Evangelicals (table 3) reflect two different sets of circumstances. They include countries with relatively small total populations and a significant Evangelical presence, resulting in high Evangelical percentages, such as Bahamas (1), Solomon Islands (6), and United States Virgin Islands (8) in 1970, and Vanuatu (1), Barbados (2), and Bahamas (3) in 2010. The countries with the highest percentage of Evangelicals also include countries that have had rapid growth of both Christianity in general and Evangelicalism specifically over the course of the twentieth century. In 2010 this included South Korea (6), Central African Republic (8), Papua New Guinea (9), and Nigeria (10). Note that in 1970 the United Kingdom (2),

New Zealand (3), Australia (9), and the United States (10) appeared on the list, but by 2010 all were replaced by countries in the global South.

Table 3. Countries with the highest percentage* of Evangelicals, 1970 & 2010

RANK	COUNTRY	% 1970*	COUNTRY	% 2010**
1	Bahamas	25.2	Vanuatu	37.9
2	United Kingdom	23.3	Barbados	32.1
3	New Zealand	23.2	Bahamas	30.7
4	Central African Republic	21.3	Kenya	27.6
5	Barbados	21.2	Solomon Islands	26.0
6	Solomon Islands	20.4	South Korea	25.9
7	Channel Islands	17.3	Saint Vincent	25.4
8	United States Virgin Is	16.6	Central African Republic	25.0
9	Australia	16.4	Papua New Guinea	22.1
10	United States	16.1	Nigeria	20.6

Source: Todd M. Johnson, ed., *World Christian Database* (Leiden/Boston: Brill, accessed February 2013).
* As a percentage of total country's population

The countries that experienced the largest evangelical growth between 1970 and 2010 are all in the global South (table 4). Three are in Asia (Mongolia, China, Nepal) and six in Africa (Reunion, Mauritius, Western Sahara, Mauritania, Togo, Cote d'Ivoire). While some of this growth was a result of Western Evangelical missionary efforts, most of these movements have taken on indigenous forms in their continued growth. In Nepal, for example, a significant portion of Christians is Charismatic or Pentecostal, who also tend to be Evangelical. This is the case for "hidden" converted Hindu believers as well, who choose to remain within their Hindu culture as witnesses to Christ.

Table 4. Countries with the highest growth rates of Evangelicals, 1970–2010

RANK	COUNTRY	1970–2010*
1	Armenia	16.99
2	Mongolia	16.95
3	China	15.23
4	Nepal	14.65
5	Reunion	9.58
6	Mauritius	9.10
7	Western Sahara	8.87
8	Mauritania	8.72
9	Togo	8.60
10	Cote d'Ivoire	8.50

Source: Todd M. Johnson, ed., *World Christian Database* (Leiden/Boston: Brill, accessed February 2013).
* Annual average growth rate, percent per year, between dates specified

Evangelicals in All Christian Traditions

Evangelicalism was birthed out of a largely Protestant context, but today the movement extends far beyond that tradition. Table 5 shows that significant contingencies of Evangelicals exist within each of the six major Christian traditions, though in varying percentages. Almost half of all Protestants worldwide are Evangelicals, but so are nearly 40 percent of Anglicans and 15 percent of Independents (the Independent percentage would more than double and reach 32 percent with the addition of 60 million Chinese house church members). Catholic Evangelicals are growing, particularly in Latin America, with many Roman Catholics becoming members of Evangelical Catholic and/or Charismatic Catholic churches.

Table 5. Evangelicals in all major traditions, 2010

TRADITION	EVANGELICALS	% OF TRADITION	% OF ALL EVANGELICALS
Protestant	198,373,000	47.6%	69.5%
Anglican	34,414,000	39.7%	12.1%
Independent	49,199,000	14.4%	17.2%
Catholic	2,577,000	0.2%	0.9%
Orthodox	808,000	0.3%	0.3%
Marginal	108,000	0.3%	0.0%
Total	285,481,000	100.0%	100.0%

Source: Todd M. Johnson, ed., *World Christian Database* (Leiden/Boston: Brill, accessed February 2013).

Various methods of defining Evangelicals—in terms of denomination, of self-identification, or of theology—have both strengths and weaknesses. In terms of a demographic assessment, though, it is important to consider as many angles as possible in order to arrive at the most accurate and representative evaluation. It is clear that, however described, Evangelicalism is now a global, diverse movement within Christianity that requires a nuanced approach to classification and counting that takes into consideration its historical progression and sociological complexities.

Bibliography

Barrett, David B., ed. *World Christian Encyclopedia: A Comparative Study of Churches and Religions in the Modern World, AD 1900–2000*. Nairobi: Oxford University Press, 1982.

Bass, Diana Butler. *Christianity After Religion: The End of Church and the Birth of a New Spiritual Awakening*. New York: HarperOne, 2012.

Bebbington, David. *Evangelicalism in Modern Britain: A History from the 1730s to the 1980s*. Grand Rapids: Baker, 1989.

Davie, Grace. *Religion in Britain Since 1945: Believing Without Belonging*. Oxford: Blackwell, 1994.

Dickerson, John S. *The Great Evangelical Recession: 6 Factors That Will Crash the American Church—and How to Prepare*. Grand Rapids: Baker, 2013.

Gushee, David P., ed. *A New Evangelical Manifesto: A Kingdom Vision for the Common Good*. St. Louis: Chalice Press, 2012.

Johnson, Byron. "The Good News About Evangelicalism." *First Things*. February 2011. http://www.firstthings.com/article/2011/01/the-good-news-about-evangelicalism/.

Johnson, Todd M., ed. *World Christian Database*. Leiden: Brill, accessed March 2013. http://www.worldchristiandatabase.org/.

Johnson, Todd M., and Peter F. Crossing. "Christianity 2013: Renewalists and Faith and Migration." *International Bulletin of Missionary Research* 37, no. 1 (January 2013): 32–33.

Krattenmaker, Tom. *The Evangelicals You Don't Know: Introducing the Next Generation of Christians*. Lanham, MD: Rowman & Littlefield, 2013.

Mandryk, Jason. *Operation World*. Colorado Springs: Biblica, 2010.

Marty, Martin E. *Protestantism: Its Churches and Cultures, Rituals and Doctrines, Yesterday and Today*. New York: Holt, Rinehart & Winston, 1972.

Newport, Frank, and Joseph Carroll. "Another Look at Evangelicals in America Today." *Gallup*. December 2, 2005. http://www.gallup.com/poll/20242/another-look-evangelicals-america-today.aspx.

Noll, Mark A. *American Evangelical Christianity: An Introduction*. Oxford: Blackwell, 2001.

———. "Evangelical Identity, Power, and Culture in the 'Great' Nineteenth Century." In *Christianity Reborn: The Global Expansion of Evangelicalism in the Twentieth Century*. Edited by Donald M. Lewis, 31–51. Grand Rapids: Eerdmans, 2004.

Pally, Marcia. *The New Evangelicals: Expanding the Vision of the Common Good*. Grand Rapids: Eerdmans, 2011.

Pew Research Center. "Global Religious Landscape." *Pew Research Center Religion & Public Life Project*. December 18, 2012. http://www.pewforum.org/2012/12/18/ global-religious-landscape-exec/.

———. "Methodology for Estimating Christian Movements." Appendix B in "Global Christianity: A Report on the Size and Distribution of the World's Christian Population." *Pew Research Center Religion & Public Life Project*. December 19, 2011. http://www.pewforum.org/files/2011/12/ChristianityAppendixB.pdf.

———. "'Nones' on the Rise." *Pew Research Center Religion & Public Life Project*. October 9, 2012. http://www. pewforum.org/2012/10/09/nones-on-the-rise/.

Rah, Soong-Chan. *The Next Evangelicalism: Freeing the Church from Western Cultural Captivity*. Downers Grove, IL: InterVarsity Press, 2009.

Smidt, Corwin. "The Measurement of Evangelicals." *The Immanent Frame: Secularism, Religion, and the Public Sphere* (blog). August 29, 2008. http://blogs.ssrc.org/tif/ 2008/08/29/the-measurement-of-evangelicals/.

Smith, Christian. *American Evangelicalism: Embattled and Thriving*. Chicago: University of Chicago Press, 1998.

Stanley, Brian. *The Global Diffusion of Evangelicalism: The Age of Billy Graham and John Stott*. Downers Grove, IL: InterVarsity Press, 2013.

Gina A. Zurlo *is assistant director of the Center for the Study of Global Christianity in South Hamilton, Massachusetts, as well as a PhD candidate at Boston University School of Theology in Boston, Massachusetts.*

Introduction to Diagrams on Evangelicalism

The diagrams on the next two pages chart important features of the global evangelical movement. The first diagram, "Evangelical Traditions by Proportion," shows how various Christian traditions are situated within Evangelicalism as a whole. The number is how many Evangelicals there are in that tradition, while the blue shading shows the intensity of Evangelical affiliation. One surprising fact is that nearly 30% of all Evangelicals are Pentecostals. The second diagram, "Evangelicalism by Tradition," illustrates how global Evangelicalism fits into global Christianity. The relative percentage of each of the major traditions (e.g., Evangelicals are 13% of all Christians, 40% of all Anglicans, etc.) is given at the top of the graphic. Further down are some minor traditions that are located in relation to the major traditions (e.g., Mennonites under Anabaptists) and the percentage of each that is Evangelical (e.g., 21% of all Methodists are Evangelicals). Note that some minor traditions are 100% Evangelical. Further information related to both diagrams is presented in Zurlo's article above.

EVANGELICAL TRADITIONS BY PROPORTION

Source: *World Christian Database*, 2010 data

OTHER 31 million	**LUTHERAN** 9 million / **BRETHREN** 3 million / **FUNDA-MENTALIST** 4 million / **LUTHERAN / REF. UNITED** 3 million
ANGLICAN 35 million	**HOLINESS** 12 million / **UNITED CHURCHES** 7 million / **METHODIST** 6 million
	REFORMED, PRESBYTERIAN 20 million / **UNAFFILIATED** 12 million
PENTECOSTAL 97 million	**BAPTIST** 43 million

Traditions have been subdivided, accounting for differences in totals compared to the diagram on the facing page.

Each rectangle's size is determined by the number of Evangelicals worldwide in 2010.

Each rectangle's color is determined by the percentage of Evangelicals worldwide in 2010.

The figure presented is the number of Evangelicals in that tradition in 2010.

EVANGELICALISM BY TRADITION

Source: *World Christian Database*, 2010 data

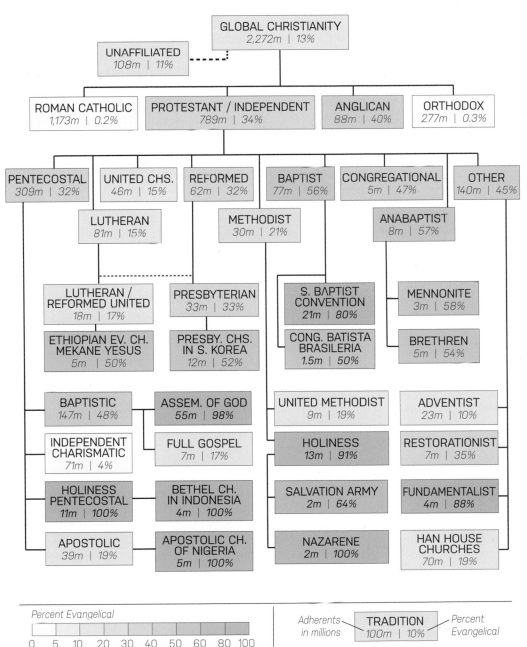

GLOBAL CHRISTIANITY
2,272m | 13%

UNAFFILIATED
108m | 11%

ROMAN CATHOLIC
1,173m | 0.2%

PROTESTANT / INDEPENDENT
789m | 34%

ANGLICAN
88m | 40%

ORTHODOX
277m | 0.3%

PENTECOSTAL
309m | 32%

UNITED CHS.
46m | 15%

REFORMED
62m | 32%

BAPTIST
77m | 56%

CONGREGATIONAL
5m | 47%

OTHER
140m | 45%

LUTHERAN
81m | 15%

METHODIST
30m | 21%

ANABAPTIST
8m | 57%

LUTHERAN / REFORMED UNITED
18m | 17%

PRESBYTERIAN
33m | 33%

S. BAPTIST CONVENTION
21m | 80%

MENNONITE
3m | 58%

ETHIOPIAN EV. CH. MEKANE YESUS
5m | 50%

PRESBY. CHS. IN S. KOREA
12m | 52%

CONG. BATISTA BRASILERIA
1.5m | 50%

BRETHREN
5m | 54%

BAPTISTIC
147m | 48%

ASSEM. OF GOD
55m | 98%

UNITED METHODIST
9m | 19%

ADVENTIST
23m | 10%

INDEPENDENT CHARISMATIC
71m | 4%

FULL GOSPEL
7m | 17%

HOLINESS
13m | 91%

RESTORATIONIST
7m | 35%

HOLINESS PENTECOSTAL
11m | 100%

BETHEL CH. IN INDONESIA
4m | 100%

SALVATION ARMY
2m | 64%

FUNDAMENTALIST
4m | 88%

APOSTOLIC
39m | 19%

APOSTOLIC CH. OF NIGERIA
5m | 100%

NAZARENE
2m | 100%

HAN HOUSE CHURCHES
70m | 19%

Percent Evangelical

0 5 10 20 30 40 50 60 80 100

Adherents in millions — **TRADITION** 100m | 10% — Percent Evangelical

WHAT EVANGELICALS BELIEVE

By C. Rosalee Velloso Ewell

Evangelical theology is perhaps best described as a kaleidoscope of convictions and practices that shape everyday life for countless Christians around the world. In the same way that it is practically impossible to answer the question, what is the image seen through a kaleidoscope? so it is with evangelical theology. It will always depend on who is looking through the glass and the way the light is hitting the colorful beads and mirrors inside. Even the slightest movement can change the image. So it is with what Evangelicals believe. Times, contexts, and life stories alter the image and emphasize different theologies at different times, making a simple definition not only impossible but also unhelpful insofar as it would not do justice to the various colors of our convictions. And yet, of course, there are certain trends and characteristics that shape and identify evangelical theology. Such convictions vary in importance and emphasis according to the circumstances of each Christian community.

Tokunboh Adeyemo, a theologian, biblical scholar, and former general secretary of the Association of Evangelicals of Africa, (at that time known as the Association of Evangelicals of Africa and Madagascar) identified an Evangelical as "one who believes in [the] good news, who has experienced . . . redemption, who is committed to its propagation; and who lives steadfastly in obedience to the authority of the Book—the Word of God—as his rule of faith and practice."[1] Adeyemo's statement offers us a place to begin unpacking the breadth of evangelical theology. Following his lead, this chapter will focus on four general areas: (1) the holy Scriptures, (2) salvation and the person of Jesus Christ, (3) the gathered community, and (4) mission. This chapter offers a brief analysis of each area, plus narratives and anecdotes that, it is hoped, provide a flavor for evangelical theology and a desire to study its multiplicity in greater depth. These four areas are not exhaustive or even comprehensive. They serve mainly to organize and guide descriptions and stories of what Evangelicals believe.

Holy Scriptures

Whether your travels take you to a megachurch in South Korea, an African American congregation in the Deep South of the United States, or a village hall in the Andean mountains, you will see the Bible being carried by the few or the many congregants who gather in those places of worship. At the heart of evangelical theology is the conviction that the holy Scriptures are something very, very special. The Bible, as the Word of God, is not something to be taken lightly, but is the tool and the means God has given God's people to shape and transform lives.

Throughout the twentieth century debates raged about definitions and what was meant by *Word of God* when such a term was applied to the Bible. In which ways is this collection of books genuinely God's word for humanity, or indeed for all of creation? What is the place of the human element in the writings of the texts? What is the role of the Holy Spirit in its composition? What does *inerrancy* really mean? Most of the debates were driven by scholars and prominent evangelical leaders in North America and Europe. They sought rational grounds and means by which to prove false the claims of those they called liberals. However, since the 1970s there have been major shifts in evangelical theology prompted mainly by the changing landscape of global Christianity. This shift is no less significant in the ways Scripture is read and interpreted around the world.

---

1. Tite Tiénou, "Evangelical Theology in African Contexts," in *The Cambridge Companion to Evangelical Theology*, ed. Timothy Larsen and Daniel J. Treier (Cambridge: Cambridge University Press, 2007), 214.

While world wars, the Cold War, and postcolonial wars tore communities and the planet apart, set up and brought down superpowers and economic powers, and saw the rise of natural disasters around the globe, Christians who called themselves Evangelicals turned to the Scriptures in varying ways to examine and learn what God had to say to God's people in such turbulent times. In some contexts, such collective Scripture reading led Evangelicals to start new movements for peace and justice. In South Africa a white pastor read the Bible and prayed with Nelson Mandela and other prisoners on Robben Island and later was himself imprisoned for his peaceful witness against apartheid. In London another Christian leader started a group of street pastors who walked through violent parts of town, armed only with their Bibles, to reach out to at-risk youth in the city's alleyways and dark corners.

In the history of Christian Protestantism (in general terms, Evangelicals are a subset within the Protestant movement) it is a mistake to see the evangelical emphasis on Bible reading as a stereotype of those who draw a sharp divide between Scripture reading and practices of social justice. Certainly mistakes have been made and an emphasis has been placed on the Bible that can lead to bad practices or the failure to live as disciples of Jesus. But such events do not take away from the importance the Scriptures have had and continue to have in shaping evangelical beliefs and in promoting practices of justice and peace. It was precisely the shift of the centers of Christianity from the North to the global South—which is made up of Central and Latin America, Africa, and most of Asia—that helped Evangelicals recover this very important aspect of their biblical theology. With questions being raised by voices from the political or economic margins, the authority of the Bible gained new light and new life in the evangelical world. Its careful study and use in Africa, Asia, and Latin America have brought new perceptions and new emphases to theological reflection and made the Bible just as powerful and transformative in those contexts as it was when Martin Luther diligently worked through Paul's letter to the Romans in the early years of the sixteenth century.

The challenge for Evangelicals (and for all Christians) around the globe is not to take the Bible for granted or to be satisfied with shallow meanings or interpretations that are used simply to justify positions of power or wealth. The evangelical conviction that the Bible is the Word of God remains the primary means by which communities learn what it is to live in the reign inaugurated by Jesus of Nazareth. Without the Bible, Evangelicals not only lose the narratives of the reign of God but the entire framework that shapes their beliefs and practices.

Salvation and the Person of Jesus Christ

Intimately related to the conviction that the holy Scripture is God's word to all of creation is the affirmation that salvation comes through transformation in Jesus Christ alone. There is no consensus about what this transformation looks like, or even its timing within God's plan for the creation. However, Evangelicals firmly believe Jesus is the means of salvation and this salvation is tied to a particular view of God's justice. At a funeral in the large city of São Paulo, Brazil, an evangelical pastor and theologian preached to his church, "We can't say for certain if [the deceased] knew Jesus or not, but we can say that she is in the best possible hands—in the hands of a just and loving God who sent his Son for the redemption of all. This is good news for all of us."

The gospel narrative, with its climax in the person of Jesus of Nazareth, is told and retold around the world in many different ways and also appropriated in a variety of contexts. Within such diversity, through the power of the story of Jesus, people are saved, one story at a time. This story of the Jewish carpenter is central to what Evangelicals believe. Yet the story of Jesus and salvation that characterizes evangelical theology does not do so in a purely academic manner. Rather, such evangelical beliefs are tied to issues of life. In this way we see the orthodox doctrines of christology (the person and work of Jesus Christ) and soteriology (having to do with salvation) lived out in the daily prayers and songs of Pentecostals in Asia or at a peace fellowship in Canada.

Just as the Bible is central to what Evangelicals believe, so is the connection between who Jesus is, what he has done for our salvation, and the ways in which this gets worked out in daily living. For many Christians around the world, affirming salvation through Jesus can be a very risky thing. Persecution and even martyrdom can be the result of their witness. In the history of Evangelicalism there have been times when Evangelicals have used the doctrine of salvation as a means to power, as a way to lord it over those who look or believe or behave differently. But a description of the evangelical conviction in salvation through Christ alone would be incomplete without the witnesses of countless disciples who have learned from Christ to love their enemies and to pray for those who persecute them. Learning from the story of Peter and Cornelius in chapter 10 in the book of Acts, we see that salvation in Jesus is a challenge to each and every person. It is in our encounters that we are challenged and transformed by the good news of the gospel, but the ways in which this happens are as different today as they were in the first century. To return to the metaphor of the kaleidoscope, the emphases and the types of transformation salvation brings will be different depending on whether you are in Japan or Jordan or Jamaica.

The Gathered Community

At the heart of the transformation Jesus makes possible is the community that gathers in his name and is led forward by the Spirit. The history of global Evangelicals shows just how many shapes, sizes, colors, and forms this community can assume. There is no mold or one-size-fits-all sort of church, yet the belief that getting together matters is central to evangelical convictions and practice.

Drawing on the narratives of the formation of Israel in the Old Testament, the calling and training of the disciples in the gospels, or Paul's letters to the many churches, Evangelicals believe God is at work in particular ways when we gather together for worship, prayer, confession, thanksgiving, or mourning. In places where the church suffers persecution there is an urgency to gathering that is often lost in many Western countries. The chants of freedom that recount Israel's exodus from Egypt serve as formative narratives for both Quechua and African American Evangelicals. These and so many other different contexts highlight the diversity of the people of God and the different challenges that come within each place.

Yet what does it mean to affirm that Evangelicals believe in the gathered church?

First, it is to say such particular gatherings are part of a particular history; that is, all theology is contextual and historical, grounded in people, movements, or ideas set in time and space. Evangelical theology of the church is no exception. Whether one's tradition follows the revivals set in motion by people like Jonathan Edwards, Alice and Annie Armstrong, Kwame Bediako, or Muriel Lester, the church that gathers is itself historical and multifaceted, shaped by the culture and time in which it grows.

Second, the diverse ways in which Evangelicals gather point both to the divisions and to the unity within the history of Evangelicalism. On the one hand, an emphasis on individual pietism and spirituality, especially in more conservative circles in Europe and North America, has led some Evangelicals to place less emphasis on the gathered church while still maintaining its general importance. On the other hand, political turmoil and economic oppression have led other Christians to see the church as *the* place where God's justice can be seen and experienced by everyone.

Finally, the belief in the gathered church stems directly from the importance of the Scriptures in evangelical theology. At its best, evangelical conviction that God is at work in the church is an affirmation of the work of the Holy Spirit in calling together people who would otherwise not be together at all. It is the formation of a community, much like the disciples or the little band that gathered at Philippi, where rich and poor, black and white, Jew and Gentile came together (Acts 16:11–40). As a not-so-evangelical writer put it, "They met Him again after they had seen him killed. And then, after they had been formed into a little society or community, they found God somehow inside them as well: directing them, making them able to do things they could not do before."[2] Evangelicals around the world

At the heart of evangelical theology is the conviction that the holy Scriptures are something very, very special.
Photo: www.designpics.com

2. C. S. Lewis, *Mere Christianity* (London: HarperCollins, 1952), 163.

getting together for church is a witness to God's power that another world is not only possible but has already been inaugurated by Jesus and the sending of the Holy Spirit at Pentecost.

Mission

If the priority of the Scriptures reveals both the importance of Christ for salvation and the testimony of the Spirit that calls Christians to gather as church, it is this same grand narrative that informs the firm conviction that God is a missionary God and therefore God's people are to be a missionary people. Evangelism—that is, witnessing to Jesus Christ in word, deed, and character—is not optional for the Christian life but is the joy and duty of every person. We are to give an account for the hope that is within us, "with gentleness and respect" (1 Peter 3:15–16 GNT).

From the beginnings of the evangelical movement in the sixteenth century through the postcolonial theologies of Latin America or India to the missional movements across the globe, mission itself has always played a key role in defining evangelical convictions, both negatively and positively. These convictions stem from the belief that the Spirit gathers Christians and enables them to embody a particular way of life that in itself witnesses to the power of the gospel. In its most positive expressions, this belief in being a missionary people shows itself in small communities that offer shelter, safety, and genuine Christian hospitality to people living in the slums of Bangkok as well as in the group of university students who visit a care facility for the elderly each Sunday after church, bringing music and life to a group of people waiting for death.

Evangelical belief in mission is also characterized by its expression in education and the formation of seminaries and Bible schools all around the world. For many of these schools in the late twentieth century it was the Lausanne Covenant of 1974 that shaped both the theology and the practice of evangelical higher education and its vision for mission. According to the covenant, God "has been calling out from the world a people for himself, and sending his people back into the world to be his servants and his witnesses, for the extension of his kingdom, the building up of Christ's body, and the glory of his name. We confess with shame that we have often denied our calling and failed in our mission, by becoming conformed to the world or by withdrawing from it."[3] Such a vision for mission became known as a holistic or an integral mission and emphasized the importance of holding both proclamation and social justice practices as key aspects of the mission of the church; both are necessary.

In the twenty-first century the reality of interreligious conflicts and wars has further shaped evangelical convictions about mission and its relation to everyday practices. The document "Christian Witness in a Multi-Religious World: Recommendations for Conduct"[4] addresses the particular issues Christians face when witnessing to Christ in situations of conflict or tension. The document begins and ends with the word *mission* and shows the importance of what loving one's neighbor means in today's world. Although the statement was written cooperatively with Christians from all around the globe, it reflects the evangelical belief that God has called all Christians to be witnesses to Jesus and such witness must always be exercised and practiced in Christ-likeness.

Evangelical convictions about mission are intimately tied to the ways in which we read the Bible: God's call to Israel to live in such a way that those around them might know who the one true God really is; Jesus' reminder to the disciples that they must go out and disciple and teach all Jerusalem, Judea, and the ends of the earth; Paul's admonitions to the Corinthians to live as sanctified people for the sake of their witness of Christ in their culture. This poses a challenge to the way we view mission today, because too often it is tied up with cultural identities, with issues of power and control, and with money. Yet despite these obstacles, Evangelicals continue to engage in practices of mission and to see these practices as inherent to their identity as Christians. What

---

3. "The Lausanne Covenant," The Lausanne Movement, accessed February 17, 2014, http://www.lausanne.org/en/documents/lausanne-covenant.html.

4. World Council of Churches, Pontifical Council for Interreligious Dialogue, and World Evangelical Alliance, "Christian Witness in a Multi-Religious World: Recommendations for Conduct," World Evangelical Alliance Resources, [2011], http://www.worldevangelicals.org/resources/source.htm?id=288/.

remains to be seen is the ways in which prophetic voices are enabled and raised up within the church: voices that offer Evangelicals critical self-assessments and lead revival movements within our various communities, and voices that remind us that despite all our efforts and beliefs, salvation belongs to the Lord.

The Evangelical Kaleidoscope of Convictions

The holy Scriptures, salvation and the person of Jesus, the gathered community, and mission are just four of the key themes that offer a way to describe some of the hallmarks of evangelical theology. They are not ideal types, nor are they described here in full detail or variety. The study of any set of convictions is indefinite and long lasting, and this is no less the case with Evangelicals. And just as the images inside a kaleidoscope look different to each viewer, so do evangelical theology, beliefs, and practices appear dissimilar because of what each viewer brings to the image being seen at that moment. If we look at the set of convictions that guide a congregation in Ghana, such beliefs will take on the particularities of that place—just as the image will be different if the church is gathered in Georgia. For Evangelicals, the massive explosion of numbers, primarily in the Global South, poses a particular challenge to our beliefs and faithful practices. Are we going to fall into the sin of Babel and try to make a name for ourselves, or will we follow the Spirit at Pentecost, affirming both the diversity among us yet the one Spirit that works through each and every person and community?

The challenges of belief and practice were different for Paul's churches because the people and their contexts were different. One wonders, why did Paul leave them on their own to work things out with nothing but a few occasional letters? Perhaps it was because he knew they were not alone but were guided by the same Spirit that guides the church today. As we look toward the next hundred years, it is urgent always to learn to trust anew, knowing God is faithful and has sent the Spirit to convict, to challenge, to guide the church wherever it is gathered, and to lead it to be the people God has called us to be.

Bibliography

The Lausanne Movement. "The Lausanne Covenant." Accessed February 17, 2014. http://www.lausanne.org/en/documents/lausanne-covenant.html.

Lewis, C. S. *Mere Christianity*. London: Geoffrey Bles, 1952.

Tiénou, Tite. "Evangelical Theology in African Contexts." In *The Cambridge Companion to Evangelical Theology*, edited by Timothy Larsen and Daniel J. Treier, 214–224. Cambridge: Cambridge University Press, 2007.

World Evangelical Alliance Resources. World Council of Churches, Pontifical Council for Interreligious Dialogue, and World Evangelical Alliance. "Christian Witness in a Multi-Religious World: Recommendations for Conduct." 2011. http://www.worldevangelicals.org/resources/source.htm?id=288/.

Dr. C. Rosalee Velloso Ewell is the executive director of the Theological Commission for the World Evangelical Alliance. She is a Brazilian Baptist theologian from São Paulo with a PhD in theological ethics from Duke University in Durham, North Carolina. She also serves as the New Testament editor for the forthcoming *Latin American Bible Commentary* (Certeza Unida and Kairos, 2015) and is the author and editor of various books and articles.

"The Evangelical community has grown significantly in the last twenty-five years in Latin America. We have seen the grace of God in many ways. However, we have not seen social changes and cultural impacts according to this numerical growth. We must experience other dimensions of growth. The challenge ahead is a radical discipleship that will produce new men and women for a new Latin America."

—Dr. Norberto Saracco, President, International Faculty of Theological Schools, Theological Institute FIET, Pastor, Good News Church, Buenos Aires, Argentina

EVANGELICALS IN MAINLINE DENOMINATIONS

By John Bowen

In many parts of the world the term *Evangelical Christian* would seem rather puzzling and the adjective *evangelical* redundant. For many of the world's growing churches, especially those in the global South (Central and Latin America, Africa, and most of Asia), the only kind of Christian is an Evangelical Christian, one whose faith is marked by the characteristics of Evangelicalism (see the following discussion on Bebbington's Quadrilateral). Yet even the global South has large denominations—Roman Catholic and Orthodox, in particular—that do not self-identify as Evangelical.

In the West, however, many Evangelical Christians belong, with varying degrees of comfort, to denominations that, broadly speaking, are not evangelical and are often referred to as mainline churches. In North America, for example, Anglican, Lutheran, Orthodox, Presbyterian, Roman Catholic, and United Methodist are considered mainline. Other large denominations, such as Baptist and Pentecostal, and also groups like the Salvation Army are labeled evangelical.

Like so many labels, however, the distinction between mainline and evangelical is not always accurate or helpful. In Britain, for instance, denominations like Baptist and Pentecostal are more often called nonconformist after those churches that refused to conform to the requirements of the Act of Uniformity in 1662, which tried to impose Anglicanism on the whole country. In the British context, therefore, the word *evangelical* is not tied to any particular denominational tradition or style of worship, but by characteristics that transcend such differences.

Historian David Bebbington has identified four such characteristics, sometimes referred to as the Bebbington Quadrilateral: *crucicentrism* (the cross is central to the gospel), *Biblicism* (the Bible is central to our knowledge of God and the gospel), *conversionism* (the gospel calls us to turn from sin and follow Christ), and *activism* (the gospel deserves the complete dedication of our lives).[1] In a sense, however, each of these four is only a logical outcome of a single conviction: that the gospel of Jesus Christ is truly good news and that this good news is to be found in the Bible. Sadly, sometimes churches that call themselves evangelical for historical reasons lack Bebbington's four characteristic marks. In Germany and North America, for example, the adjective *evangelical* in a denominational name, such as Evangelical Lutheran, means little more than "Protestant," rather than "Evangelical" in Bebbington's narrower sense.

Why Are Evangelicals in Mainline Churches?

The founders of mainline denominations, many of which date back to the Protestant Reformation of the sixteenth and seventeenth centuries, often held evangelical convictions and wrote those convictions into the founding documents of their denominations. A classic example is "The Thirty-nine Articles of Religion" of the (Anglican) Church of England, which affirms, among other things, the authority of the Bible (e.g., "Holy Scripture containeth all things necessary to salvation," article 6) and the centrality of the death of Christ for salvation ("The Offering of Christ once made is the perfect redemption, propitiation, and satisfaction, for all

---

1. D. W. Bebbington, *Evangelicalism in Modern Britain: A History from the 1730s to the 1980s* (London: Unwin Hyman, 1989), 1–19.

the sins of the whole world, both original and actual" article 31)—two of Bebbington's characteristic marks of Evangelicals.[2]

Many Evangelicals in mainline denominations would add that they appreciate three things in particular about their denomination's tradition. One is the kind of liturgical worship, normally following a form of service from a book, generally found in mainline churches. They value this kind of worship because it resonates with the worship of sister churches around the world and throughout several centuries, and thus it is a reminder of the oneness of the church.

Second, they like that the mainline tradition frequently holds a higher view of communion, and perhaps of baptism as well, than is found in many non-mainline evangelical churches. This emphasis on the sacrament of the Lord's Supper is often represented in the frequency with which Communion is celebrated, which may be weekly or even daily rather than monthly or quarterly, and the positioning of the Lord's Table in the worship space, often placing it higher than the pulpit. Finally, many mainline churches—such as Anglican, Lutheran, and United Methodist—are overseen by bishops. Such an arrangement, while not clearly mandated by Scripture, is seen by most Evangelicals as being compatible with Scripture and a healthy link to other churches, throughout history and across the globe.

Returning Mainline Denominations to Their Evangelical Roots

One of the reasons for the common distinction that is made between evangelical churches and mainline churches is that some mainline churches have, to one extent or another, moved away from their original evangelical characteristics over the centuries. Again, the Anglican world offers a straightforward example: while some Anglicans consider themselves evangelical, others prefer to describe themselves as liberal or progressive, while yet others prefer the designation *Anglo–Catholic*. These latter two groups, on the whole, do not embrace Bebbington's Quadrilateral, though there are, of course, degrees of overlap between the categories; some, for instance, might call themselves evangelical liberals or Anglo–Catholic Evangelicals.

A denomination like the Anglican Church sometimes takes pride in attempting to embrace such a breadth of Christian theology and spirituality, and, at its best, seeks to cultivate mutual respect, learning, and enrichment between the different strands. At the same time, Evangelicals in mainline denominations may feel they have more in common with fellow believers in non-mainline denominations than they do with those of different persuasions in their own churches.

It is not uncommon for Evangelicals within mainline denominations to view themselves as being in direct line of descent from the founders of the denominations and even to see themselves as being the "true" adherents of that particular church. They may, therefore, perceive part of their role as being to recall the denomination to its founding convictions and purpose, that is, to effect a return to a more evangelical faith. This concern often causes Evangelicals within mainline denominations to band together under such banners as, to give three Canadian examples I am familiar with, the Renewal Fellowship within the Presbyterian Church in Canada, the Anglican Communion Alliance (within the Anglican Church of Canada), and the Community of Concern within the United Church of Canada.

The last of these three, which was founded in 1988, is typical of such groups in that it seeks to be "a permanent force for orthodoxy . . . to work for the Church's founding principles set out in the Twenty Articles of Faith."[3] Formulated in 1925, those articles stated the United Church of Canada's faith in Scripture (e.g., "We receive the Holy Scriptures of the Old and New Testaments, given by inspiration of God, as containing the only infallible rule

---

2. "The Thirty-Nine Articles," ESVBible.org, accessed December 30, 2013,
http://www.esvbible.org/resources/creeds-and-catechisms/article-the-thirty-nine-articles/#1908/.

3. "History; Community of Concern: Its Beginning," Community of Concern within the United Church of Canada, accessed December 30, 2013, www.communityofconcern.org/?page_id=26/.

of faith and life, a faithful record of God's gracious revelations, and as the sure witness of Christ," 2.2 article II) and faith in the death of Christ (e.g., "For our redemption, He fulfilled all righteousness, offered Himself a perfect sacrifice on the Cross, satisfied Divine justice, and made propitiation for the sins of the whole world," 2.7 article VII) in language reminiscent of the Church of England's "The Thirty-nine Articles."[4]

How far such movements are successful in their goal of encouraging their denomination to return to its evangelical roots is somewhat questionable. Some have been in existence twenty years or more without noticeable effect on the overall direction of the denomination. But at least they provide a safe place of fellowship for Evangelicals who may otherwise feel isolated and even marginalized in their denomination. At present I am not aware of any examples of such groupings in the churches of the global South, because most denominations in those countries have not departed from their evangelical roots. Over time, of course, this may change.

Evangelical Division within Mainline Denominations

While mainline denominations often speak of the necessity for church unity and plead for the toleration of many theological positions, issues arise from time to time that test the patience of Evangelicals, occasionally to the breaking point. These issues may be doctrinal, such as attitudes toward Scripture; moral, such as, most recently, the blessing of same-sex couples; or having to do with church order, such as the ordination of women. Evangelicals in mainline denominations tend to disagree as to what issues, if any, are sufficiently significant to justify breaking fellowship. Tensions may then arise between those who leave and found a new denomination (and who may be branded as schismatics as a result) and those who stay (and who may in turn be accused of compromising the gospel).

Evangelicals within mainline denominations face many challenges.
Photo: www.designpics.com

One famous disagreement of this kind took place in 1966 at the second National Assembly of Evangelicals in the United Kingdom. Dr. D. Martyn Lloyd-Jones, pastor of Westminster Chapel, a Congregational church in the heart of London, made an appeal that was understood as an invitation to Evangelicals in mainline churches to leave those churches and help form a new Evangelical denomination. In his thanks to Dr. Lloyd-Jones for his remarks, the chairman of the session, Rev. John Stott, a prominent Evangelical Anglican, advised against immediate action, saying, "I hope no one will make a precipitate decision after this moving address. We are here to debate this subject and I believe that history is against Dr. Jones in that others have tried to do this very thing. I believe that Scripture is against him."[5] Stott's defense of staying within a mainline church is typical of how many would argue; he "referred to his own conscientious continuing membership of the Church of England on the ground that *its formularies were biblical and evangelical*, and that evangelicals were therefore the Anglican loyalists, and non-evangelicals the deviationists" (italics added).[6]

---

4. "Faith Statements; The Basis of Union: General and Basic Doctrine Sections," The United Church of Canada, updated May 2, 2013, http://www.united-church.ca/beliefs/statements/union/.

5. Timothy Dudley-Smith, *John Stott: A Biography*, vol. 2, *A Global Ministry: The Later Years* (Downers Grove, IL: InterVarsity Press, 2001), 68.

6. Ibid., 66.

This kind of division continues between, on the one hand, mainline Evangelicals who think they should stay and work for reform from within and, on the other hand, those who come to feel at some point that a non-negotiable line has been crossed and it is time for Evangelicals to leave and form a new, more purely Evangelical, denomination. Respected voices are to be heard for both arguments. Evangelicals on both sides of the divide tend to look to Evangelicals in mainline denominations in the global South as encouraging examples of how these traditional churches can be predominantly Evangelical.

Growth in the Global South and Blurred Distinctions in the West

Two more recent trends are worth noting. The first has already been alluded to. In the past fifty years or so, as denominations of all persuasions have been shrinking in North America and Europe, they have been growing in the global South. Many of these expanding churches are Evangelical, and often Pentecostal, in character. Many are also the long-term fruit of the work of Western missionaries during the nineteenth and twentieth centuries, though now completely owned by indigenous Christians.

Among these churches are large numbers that belong to mainline denominations. Whereas Evangelicals may be a minority in those same mainline denominations in the West, in the global South, Evangelicals are often the overwhelming majority. (Research suggests more Anglicans are in church in

A communion service at an evangelical Anglican church.
Photo: Sue Careless

Nigeria on a Sunday than in all of Europe and North America combined, and most of those Nigerian Anglicans are Evangelical.) The reason for this predominance of Evangelicals in the global South is simple: most of the missionaries, of whatever denomination, who evangelized these areas were themselves Evangelical, their zeal motivated by Scripture, the gospel, and the activism Bebbington identified. Among the world's Anglicans, this has led to renewed tensions between Evangelicals and non-Evangelicals, with the powerful evangelical churches of the global South sometimes threatening to withdraw from the international fellowship of Anglicans (the Anglican Communion) and form their own Evangelical Anglican denomination.

The second trend concerns what some have called the Canterbury Trail, after a book of that name by Robert Webber. Webber based the book on his own experience as an Evangelical who felt himself being drawn toward a more liturgical (what this chapter has been calling *mainline*) kind of church, and his discovery that others have made the same journey. He identified six things he felt he needed and found in a mainline church: a sense of mystery, Christ-centered worship, a sacramental reality, a historical identity, a feeling of being part of Christ's entire church, and a holistic spirituality.[7]

Perhaps this kind of move of Evangelicals to mainline denominations goes hand in hand with the decline of denominational loyalty, at least in the West. This decline has left many young Evangelicals dissatisfied and looking for a spiritual home that depends less on "the kind of church I happen to like" and more on the ideal of

---

7. Robert E. Webber, *Evangelicals on the Canterbury Trail: Why Evangelicals Are Attracted to the Liturgical Church* (Waco: Word Books, 1985).

the historic church. To them, there is a strong attraction in a tradition that stresses historical continuity rather than novelty, and community more than individual choice. As a result, it is at least possible that in the next fifty years the distinction between mainline and Evangelical will once again, in the West as in the global South, become less clear.

Bibliography

Bebbington, D. W. *Evangelicalism in Modern Britain: A History from the 1730s to the 1980s*. London: Unwin Hyman, 1989.

Community of Concern within the United Church of Canada. "History; Community of Concern: Its Beginning." Accessed December 30, 2013. http://wwwcommunityofconcern.org/?page_id=26.

Dudley-Smith, Timothy. *A Global Ministry: The Later Years*. Vol. 2 of *John Stott: A Biography*. Downers Grove, IL: InterVarsity Press, 2001.

ESVBible.org. "The Thirty-nine Articles." Accessed December 30, 2013. http://www.esvbible.org/resources/creeds-and-catechisms/article-the-thirty-nine-articles/#1908.

The United Church of Canada. "Faith Statements; The Basis of Union: General and Basic Doctrine Sections." Updated May 2, 2013. http://www.united-church.ca/beliefs/statements.union/.

Webber, David E. *Evangelicals on the Canterbury Trail: Why Evangelicals Are Attracted to the Liturgical Church*. Waco: Word Books, 1985. Rev. ed., with Lester Ruth (New York: Morehouse, 2013).

Dr. John Bowen is the director of the Institute of Evangelism at Wycliffe College in Toronto. He is the editor of *Green Shoots Out of Dry Ground: Growing a New Future for the Church in Canada* (Eugene, OR: Wipf & Stock, 2013) and the author of several books.

"Evangelicals can, in the coming years, have a crucial role in being the link between Christians in all confessions and Christian traditions who are firmly committed to the historic gospel message rooted in the Bible. By transcending denominational barriers the Evangelical Movement can mobilize the broadest spectrum of Christians worldwide to live out and proclaim the Evangel to a lost world."

—Ramez Atallah, General Secretary, The Bible Society, Cairo, Egypt

EVANGELICALS AND THE LAUSANNE MOVEMENT

By Rose Dowsett

The Lausanne Movement is a global network of individuals, agencies and churches sharing a vision for commitment to the evangelization of the whole world. There is no formal membership, and only a simple coordinating structure. The goal is to see the whole church taking the whole gospel to the whole world. As a long-term movement, it began almost accidentally, as we shall see.

The Lausanne Movement began in 1974 when Evangelicals gathered in the Swiss city of that name. This first Lausanne congress was convened at the instigation of the well-known evangelist Billy Graham at a time of social and political upheaval throughout the world. The Cold War had led many to believe the world could come to an end at any moment: China and Russia were locked down under communism, and many regional wars raged.

Against such a backdrop, it seemed world mission was never more urgent. At the same time, some Evangelicals, particularly some North Americans, believed it was more possible than ever before to reach the whole world with the gospel within a generation with strategic use of resources. Although the church in Europe was shrinking, the church in Latin America and sub-Saharan Africa was growing by leaps and bounds against a background of widespread social injustice, political upheaval, and much poverty. In Asia, despite conflict and the dominance of Buddhism, Islam, and Hinduism, there were growing Christian communities in several countries. The world church was tipping on its historic northern axis. It was heading South.

Back in 1966 Graham had invited Christian leaders to West Berlin for the World Congress on Evangelism. It was intended to be a one-time meeting, but by 1971 Graham, at the peak of his ministry as a mass-rally Evangelist, believed there needed to be another. It would be strictly evangelical and focused entirely on the evangelization of the world. Graham had the global standing to convene it, so in 1974 some 2,700 people from over 150 countries gathered in Lausanne, Switzerland. Among them were over a thousand participants from the non-Western world. This gathering became known as Lausanne I: The International Congress on World Evangelism.

Billy Graham presenting at conference.
Photo: Courtesy of Billy Graham Center Archives, Wheaton, Illinois

The Global South Perspective on the Role of Evangelism

The planning committee for the first Lausanne congress, chaired by Bishop Jack Dain of Australia, wisely included a number of Latin Americans, Africans, and Asians. Perhaps for the first time in the history of the church and mission, leaders from the global South were able to speak out on equal terms with those from the Northern and Western worlds. These speakers challenged some of the assumptions and practices relating to the nature of mission and evangelism, and they brought new insights from which the entire Evangelical community has benefited.

In North America, evangelism and evangelization had grown to be synonymous, partly as a reaction to the more liberal social gospel that defined many churches earlier in the twentieth century. Ralph Winter and Donald McGavran, two North Americans at the first Lausanne congress, powerfully highlighted the urgency of reaching the unreached peoples of the world with the gospel and of the importance of doing so in an intentional and systematic manner. The gospel in its simplest form must be proclaimed to every human being. With careful planning this should be achievable within a generation. The goal was for individuals to profess faith and for churches to be planted. But it would not be the task of the church to be concerned with social transformation. Social transformation could be done by others, of any faith or none. Evangelism, however, could be done only by the church.

The world's media paid attention to what was happening at Lausanne.
Photo: Courtesy of Billy Graham Center Archives, Wheaton, Illinois

Undoubtedly this clarion call woke many up to the reality that very large parts of the world's population still had not heard the gospel and that this was a scandal. The first Lausanne congress gave birth to many new initiatives to address this gap. But at this congress, Latin Americans and Africans in particular insisted that evangelization and mission must have wider dimensions than personal Evangelism. They argued that the historic pattern of Evangelicalism, and the historical understanding of evangelization, had actually been to address many areas of social injustice, to engage in compassion ministries that dealt with physical and mental needs, and to challenge the factors that give rise to poverty and exploitation and disease. An authentic demonstration of the kingdom of God demanded no less. Personal conversion and piety were essential, but genuine faith involved becoming bold disciples, with the lordship of Christ impacting every dimension of life. Evangelism could not be credible if it led only to "saved souls," concerned only for personal salvation and not to personal and societal transformation.

René Padilla, Samuel Escobar, and Orlando Costas, three Latin American Evangelicals, rattled the gathering in Lausanne by firmly declaring that evangelism without depth—that is, without concern for the whole person in the whole of society—was not enough; it was not truly gospel. John Gatu, a Kenyan representative, said the African Church needed freedom to develop as authentically African and should be sending missionaries, not still receiving them.

Evangelism through Social Transformation

Forty years after that first Lausanne gathering, these divergent views about the task of world mission have continued to find a home within the congress that became a movement. Gatu's vision has been greatly realized, with strong new mission movements originating from Latin America, Africa, and much of Asia. Winter and McGavran's passion for reaching the unreached people groups of the world—that is, distinct language or cultural groups where currently there is no known established Christian community—has catalyzed many initiatives and much greater awareness of who has been neglected, and attention and resources have been focused on them. There has also been significant investment in developing those Evangelicals around the world who have the gifts and vocation of an evangelist.

Escobar and Padilla's insistence on the holistic nature of biblical mission has recaptured advocacy and action in fighting social injustice and serving the poor with a full range of ministries for many evangelical churches and for much missionary endeavor. There is a renewed awareness that you cannot preach the gospel with credibility while ignoring the suffering of those to whom you preach. Evangelicals now more fully believe that the Enlightenment separation of sacred and secular is false. The biblical worldview integrates body and mind and soul, personal and communal, word and deed and character. The good news of the gospel must reflect this. The Lausanne Movement, stemming from the first Congress onwards, convinced many in the evangelical world that making disciples is about more than profession of faith.

The First Lausanne Congress Becomes the Lausanne Movement

When the first congress was convened in 1974, no one envisaged it would lead to an enduring organization. However, at the conclusion of the congress, the majority pressed for an ongoing structure to continue to address the concerns that had been raised. Some argued that the World Evangelical Fellowship (WEF), as the WEA was called at that time, already provided a global evangelical structure and it would be unhelpful to set up another. Furthermore, they pointed out, many of those attending the congress were already members of, or had links with, their national evangelical alliances. Perhaps the WEF did not appear at that time to have the resources or the energy to be the main global vehicle for world mission. On the other hand, some argued that an ongoing movement was needed that would focus specifically on world mission and resourcing evangelism, while the WEF was concerned with the whole life of the Church. Some felt that the contemporary church was, in any case, too focused on its own struggles of maintenance to engage energetically in world mission.

At the encouragement of the participants at the first congress, leaders established the Continuation Committee. After a short time this led to the more formalized structure, regionally and internationally, that we see today: the Lausanne Committee for World Evangelization. Over the years the Lausanne Movement has established its own commissions and working groups. Some of these have duplicated WEF/WEA commissions and working groups, while others have ventured into different areas. The movement's leadership structure has been light in touch, with a very small, dedicated team and most of the leadership provided by volunteers who are also engaged in other ministries. As with the WEA, this has led to times of great energy and advance, and to other times of little progress.

Today the Lausanne Movement has a number of ongoing working groups. The core four have been the Theology, Strategy, Intercession, and Communication Working Groups, while numerous others take up particular issues as needed. Over the years many consultations have been held. These have responded to issues that benefit from attention by international study, and their findings have frequently gone on to inform and benefit the global Church. Many of these consultations have resulted in publications that range from numerous Lausanne Occasional Papers, to booklets and pamphlets, to weighty books that serve church and agency leaders and seminaries, to popular paperbacks that include study guides for the Lausanne Covenant (from the 1974 congress), the Manila Manifesto (from the second congress, in 1989), and the Cape Town Commitment (from the third congress, in 2010). Some of these resources are extremely valuable, especially where they represent significant international consensus or where they address pressing missiological challenges, that is, challenges in the theology and practice of mission in numerous contexts across the world.

Since that first gathering in Lausanne in 1974, there have been only two more global congresses under the Lausanne Movement's aegis. These were held in Manila, Philippines, in 1989, and in Cape Town, South Africa, in 2010. However, there have been numerous smaller consultations and regional meetings, and gatherings of people and agencies involved in a particular type of ministry, for example, statistical research or employing business as a platform for ministry or working with refugees.

Evangelicals from around the world gathered for the first Lausanne congress. It would become a significant movement amongst Evangelicals.
Photo: Courtesy of Billy Graham Center Archives, Wheaton, Illinois

Documents of the Movement

Many of the concerns expressed by the leaders from the global South were captured in the highly influential Lausanne Covenant, created during the first Lausanne congress in 1974. Crafted under the wise and gifted leadership of the Reverend John Stott of London, this document has been widely seen as the most acceptable evangelical statement of faith of the twentieth century, uniting believers around the world. Many denominations have their own confessional statements, but the Lausanne Covenant transcends both denominational and national fault lines while being considerably more detailed than the World Evangelical Alliance (WEA) Basis of Faith.

The Manila Manifesto, a product of Lausanne II: International Congress on World Evangelization held in 1989, has perhaps done less to shape the global Evangelical community, though that second congress did give rise to many energetic new initiatives such as the AD2000 movement. It is probably too soon to evaluate the impact of the Cape Town Commitment from the third Lausanne congress, held in 2010, though it appears to have wide acceptance and has been vigorously promoted in many countries. These three documents do not supplant but complement one another. They each combine doctrinal statements with exhortations to consequent practical action. They are available in a number of languages and have been a precious gift to the global Church.[1]

The Movement and Other Missions Leaders

The Lausanne Movement has always had a strong link with other mission agencies and leaders and with individuals. Many of the key contributors from the global South at the first Lausanne congress were men and women John Stott had met during his world travels. They represented mature, theologically acute leadership beyond the North and the West. Initially through the influence of Stott, there has also been a long-term close relationship with the International Fellowship of Evangelical Students (IFES) staff.

Although this does vary from region to region, in most parts of the world the movement has had weaker links directly with churches and denominational structures, the more natural focus of much of the WEF/WEA ministry. This is not to imply that the movement's leaders have been less than committed to the church. Far from it. But it does illustrate a dilemma at the heart of Evangelicalism and especially in interdenominational networks: what is our ecclesiology when our unity in the essentials of the gospel, across church boundaries, is (understandably) more important than our loyalty to a particular congregation or denomination? There is no easy answer to this conundrum, and the Lausanne Movement just happens to be caught up in it. One way or another, the movement claims to have links with two hundred nations.

The WEA has supported the Lausanne Movement in its work, and was a formal partner in the Cape Town congress in 2010. Many of the individuals associated with Lausanne are also members of their national evangelical alliance or serve in one of the WEA's commissions, such as the Mission Commission or Theological Commission.

Cape Town 2010 and Beyond

Following Cape Town 2010: The Third Lausanne Congress on World Evangelism, the Lausanne Movement embarked on a ten-year plan for consultations. These are international and regional, occurring in alternating years. In addition, ongoing consultations are addressing some of the key issues raised at this third congress. Some 4,200 delegates from almost two hundred nations and ethnic groups contributed to the consultations

---

1. For the English translation, see "Lausanne Documents," The Lausanne Movement, accessed January 7, 2014, http://www.lausanne.org/en/documents/all.html/.

held during the congress, and many more who were not present were involved in prior discussions or through online participation.

The Cape Town Commitment, a document that synthesizes the discussions of the third congress, has six overarching themes underlying the structure of the text. These emerged from extensive consultation with global leaders in the initial planning stages for the congress:

- The importance of truth as revealed in Scripture and through the person of Jesus Christ
- Witness among those of other faiths
- Evangelism and integral mission
- A commitment to eradicate Bible poverty
- A call "back to humility, integrity, and simplicity"
- The development of partnerships to further the cause of the gospel.[2]

All of these are themes the WEA would wholeheartedly affirm, though perhaps wishing to make the role of the church—which is certainly implicit in the Lausanne Movement's thinking—more explicit.

Like other large international gatherings of Christian people, the Lausanne congresses offer wonderful opportunities for experiencing firsthand the inspiring global nature of the evangelical church today. For those able to be there, it is almost impossible to put into words adequately the privilege of being in such a multicultural manifestation of the body of Christ. Without a doubt there are things to be learned about and agreed to and acted upon at the congresses that would not happen otherwise. Such gatherings absorb huge amounts of time and energy and, above all, money, and it is hard to balance these two competing realities. But the Lausanne Movement is committed to ensuring that such investment truly serves the cause of the gospel worldwide, strengthening the church and bringing delight and glory to God.

Bibliography

The Lausanne Movement. "The Cape Town Commitment." Accessed January 7, 2014. http://www.lausanne.org/en/documents/ctcommitment.thml#p2/.

———. "Lausanne Documents." Accessed January 7, 2014. http://www.lausanne.org/en/documents/all.html/.

Rose Dowsett is a founding member of the Evangelical Alliance Scotland and served as missiological adviser to the Evangelical Alliance-UK, and as vice-chair of the World Evangelical Alliance's Mission Commission. She was a member of the Lausanne Theology Working Group and of the small international team that drew up the Cape Town Commitment.

> **"The Evangelical Movement, especially as born by the companion movements of the WEF and Lausanne, is in my view, the main and major hope for the forwarding of the gospel in our time. This will, however, require it to remain true to the Bible as the Word of God and not lose its nerve in terms of the vital necessity of evangelistic proclamation combined with a credible socio-political witness."**
>
> **—Michael Cassidy, Founder, African Enterprise, South Africa**

---

2. "The Cape Town Commitment," The Lausanne Movement, accessed January 7, 2014, http://www.lausanne.org/en/documents/ctcommitment.html#p2.

EVANGELICALS AND ECUMENISM

By Rolf Hille

The term *ecumenism* arouses ambivalent reactions within Evangelicals. Evangelicals are—not the least through the establishment of the Evangelical Alliance in the mid-nineteenth century—one of the first ecumenical movements in modern church history. On the other hand, Evangelicals historically have been reserved toward the Roman Catholic Church and the Orthodox Church, viewing them with theological skepticism. In some countries with a strong Roman Catholic majority, there are historical experiences of discrimination and sometimes even persecution against Evangelicals. The topic of ecumenism must be considered, therefore, in the context of this ambivalence between desiring and fearing ecumenism felt by many Evangelicals around the world.

Confessional Confrontation

The nineteenth-century evangelical movement was very strongly characterized by confessionalism, in Europe as well as North America. With this, the different understandings of truth of the denominations are exclusively pitted against each other. A confessional church requires that all the dogmatic teachings that are binding in their respective confessional tradition be affirmed without restriction by all the others. The question of some possible truth insights in other denominations is not seriously considered. Confessionalism can take on sectarian characteristics in extreme cases, namely when it leads to the exclusion of other denominations as part of the one church of Jesus Christ. The church movements that emerged from the Reformation of the sixteenth century denied, for example, that the others had a proper understanding of the Eucharist. So the Lord's Supper in the Lutheran sense means the real presence of Jesus Christ; yet, for the Reformed and Anabaptist churches, the body and blood of Christ are only to be understood symbolically. Another key example is the importance of ordination for the full-time leadership roles in the church congregation. Or the question of whether it is right to baptize infants.

This kind of sectarian confrontation not only went on between the Roman Catholic Church and the Protestants but also, and quite massively, between the Protestant churches that emerged from the Reformation of the sixteenth century. The three great movements of Lutheranism, the Reformed tradition (Jean Calvin, Huldrych Zwingli, and John Knox), and the Anabaptists (the so-called third, or radical, wing of the Reformation) had opposed one another in controversy since the late sixteenth century. Well into the nineteenth century the religious climate was distinguished by these churches polemicizing against and condemning one another.

Protestant Unity Granted by Common Spirituality

In the very act of its 1846 founding in London, the Evangelical Alliance managed a first ecumenical breakthrough. It brought together Christians of Lutheran, Reformed, and Anabaptist traditions into its ranks. This was possible because of a very low threshold ecclesiology, which focuses on the essential Christological and soteriological issues and allows other Christian denominations the freedom to take different positions on the question of the sacraments and of the ministry. Such a low threshold ecclesiology relativized confessional boundaries for Evangelicals. It was not questions of dogma, church order, or liturgy that were most important in the founding of the Evangelical Alliance but first and foremost the personal relationship to Christ of the individual people involved. The 920 participants who assembled in London to create something new came from the piety tradition of Anglo–Saxon Puritanism, Methodism, and the Baptists, as well as from the continental Pietism of the eighteenth century and the diverse revival movements in nineteenth-century Europe and North America.

For all these Christians of evangelical provenance, the experience of the personal relationship to Jesus Christ in the sense of conversion (repentance) and (spiritual) rebirth was fundamental. They did not ask first about church membership or church background but about a person's relationship to Christ. This individual approach was then deepened by the concept of personal sanctification. The group held in common the belief that conversion and being born again leads to a lifelong process of becoming holy.

The movement begun by the Evangelical Alliance, now known as the World Evangelical Alliance (WEA), bases its unity primary on personal piety and does not have the organizational unity of churches as its goal. This distinguishes the World Evangelical Alliance from the World Council of Churches, which arose in the mid-twentieth century.

Mission: A Strong Ecumenical Impetus

Instead of focusing on organizational unity among churches, the aim of the Evangelical Alliance was on the personal union of Christians for the purposes of joint prayer and witness. This was expressed both in the formation of a joint week of prayer and also in common evangelistic outreach. With regard to the aspect of mission, a basic motif of modern ecumenism was anticipated, namely, the impetus of the high priestly prayer of Jesus found in John 17:21 (NRSV): "[T]hat they may all be one. As you, Father, are in me and I am in you, may they also be in us, so that the world may believe that you have sent me."

The separation and disunity of Christians in denominationally oriented churches in conflict with one another appeared as a burdensome hindrance to missionary witness against the backdrop of the enlightened and increasingly secularized Western societies. With the great Protestant missionary movement of the nineteenth century, the impression of Western churches in conflict was reinforced on the mission fields of Africa and Asia. The denominational differences proved themselves to be highly counterproductive. Should the missionaries bring their respective denominational beliefs into the new churches and thus laden them with the conflicts of European or North American Christendom?

Under the leadership of American John Mott, the first World Missions Conference was held in 1910 in Edinburgh, Scotland. At that time, missionaries from all Christian nations had taken up the topic of unity, providing a first important impetus for the emerging ecumenical movement that later became the World Council of Churches.

Unity Anchored in Truth

The basis of ecumenical efforts among Evangelicals is very much focused on individual faith and spirituality, which could cause one to judge this kind of ecumenism as being less anchored doctrinally. This is not the case. With the founding of the Evangelical Alliance in 1846, and then, particularly, again at the 1951 founding of the World Evangelical Fellowship (renamed the World Evangelical Alliance in 2008), a common basis of faith in the dogmatic sense was immediately set in writing. In doing so, the *essentials* of the Christian faith, which all the Evangelical Alliance participants in London unanimously stood for, were consciously brought to the forefront. All denominational peculiarities were deliberately omitted. The Evangelical Alliance was, from the very beginning, not only a fellowship of believers but also a fellowship of faith. The diverse formulations of creeds in the history of the movement reveal a common consensus does exist.

The Evangelical Alliance was, from the very beginning, not only a fellowship of believers but also a fellowship of faith.

Rooted in the Historic Christian Faith

With its reference to the "historic Christian faith" (i.e., the trinitarian understanding of God) and the elementary early patristic (meaning from the early church fathers) statements regarding Christology (i.e., Jesus is truly God and truly human), the WEA emphasizes that it understands itself to be in complete agreement with the Christian churches since the apostolic age.

The Exclusive Articles of the Reformation

The WEA is evangelical in the sense that it connects itself to the common root, the Reformation of the sixteenth century. With all of the differences between Lutheranism, the Reformed churches, and the Anabaptists, it is the four so-called exclusive articles of the Reformation that have always come to the center of this alliance. The term "exclusive articles" means the Latin word *solus* or *sola* is used four times by the Reformation in the following sense: Christ alone (*solus Christus*); Scripture alone (*sola scriptura*); grace alone (*sola gratia*); faith alone (*sola fide*). It is the emphasis of the exclusive authority of the Holy Scripture as the only and authoritative record of revelation that determines as the canon all contents of the doctrine of faith and ethics. The World Evangelical Alliance takes on the *sola scriptura* (by Scripture alone) principle of the Reformers. The doctrine of salvation (soteriology), which is the theological reflection on all that is subjectively and objectively necessary for salvation, as well as the doctrine of justification, is essential to the faith. The objective basis of salvation is that Jesus Christ came into the world and has reconciled the world to God through the blood of his cross. The subjective side of the appropriation of salvation is then effected by personal faith in the salvation worked by Christ. The exclusivity of faith only in Christ and the fact that salvation is solely and only by faith and grace, so it cannot be brought about by good works, is the fundamental content of Reformation doctrine. We are saved by grace alone through Christ and by faith alone. This overall soteriological (theory of salvation) horizon is summed up in the statement *solus Christus* (Christ alone), the defining center of all ecumenical unity.

The Kingdom of God

With respect to the doctrine of the church (ecclesiology), Evangelicals stress the church as the fellowship of individual members of the body of Christ, which ultimately only Jesus himself knows in its entirety. He will gather her at his return in his kingdom. Until then, the church is hidden as a spiritual reality, although the disciples of Jesus Christ also join together for common prayer and action.

In summary, three points comprehensively describe the ecumenical profile of the WEA in all of its shades of color. The three points are: the historical Christian faith within the meaning of the early church confession with regard to the Trinity and Christ as human and divine; the doctrine of salvation of the Reformation, that man is saved by faith alone, and through the grace of Jesus Christ and that the Scriptures should be the sole and exclusive foundation of all Christian doctrine; and the basic understanding for Evangelicals of personal conversion and sanctification.

The Ecumenical Importance of the Lausanne Movement

Missions has always been the driving force of evangelical ecumenism. This becomes visible in outstanding clarity through the Lausanne Movement, called together in 1974 by Billy Graham as the first great International Congress for World Evangelization in Lausanne, Switzerland. The meeting, which about 2,700 evangelists from almost all countries of the world attended, was an important event in church history, not just with respect to Evangelicals but to world Christendom as a whole.[1] Until Lausanne I, as the first congress came to be known, the

---

1. Robert T. Coote, "Lausanne Committee for World Evangelization," in *Dictionary of the Ecumenical Movement,* 2nd ed., ed. Nicholas Lossky et al. (Geneva: WCC Publications, 2002), 673.

general public had assumed there were three kinds of churches: the Roman Catholic Church in the West; the Orthodox churches, especially those of Eastern Europe; and finally, all of Protestantism, which, in particular, was also represented by the World Council of Churches.

By this time the World Council of Churches had developed into a prominent liberal Protestant movement. To an increasing extent Evangelicals, who held firmly to their biblically conservative beliefs, began to feel excluded. Lausanne I made it evident there was a second very strong and vital movement in Protestantism that could not be ignored. It was clear Evangelicals represented not only individual independent churches worldwide or small minorities in the big mainline churches, but also a statistically significant movement worldwide in global Christianity.

The two initiatives, the World Evangelical Alliance and the Lausanne Movement, represented the concerns of Evangelicalism in different forms. Today, the WEA, through its national and regional members as well as its established commissions, has a well-functioning infrastructure. The Lausanne Movement, with its concentration on the issues of mission and evangelism, promotes the core concerns of Evangelicals: evangelism, church planting, apologetics, and the full range of mission theology. These concerns are described mainly by the three great international congresses for world evangelization held since that first one in Lausanne.

Ecumenical Dialogues with the Roman Catholic Church

An important event in the relationship between the WEA (then known as the World Evangelical Fellowship), and the Roman Catholic Church was the General Assembly that took place in Hoddesdon, England, in 1980. Two representatives of the Roman Catholic Church spoke a word of greeting at the gathering. This led to a heated debate among the Evangelical participants, especially between representatives of the Italian Evangelical Alliance, which withdrew its membership from the World Evangelical Fellowship, and the Spanish Evangelical Alliance, which suspended its membership. As a result of this incident, the World Evangelical Fellowship Theological Commission appointed a task force, consisting of a working group of evangelical theologians who had a special ecumenical interest and whose job was to consider the problem in more detail, which published a document titled: *Roman Catholicism: A Contemporary Evangelical Perspective* under the direction of Dr. Paul G. Schrotenboer.

At the annual meeting of the conference of Christian World Communions in 1988, it was agreed an official dialogue between theologians of the World Evangelical Fellowship and the Pontifical Council for Promoting Christian Unity should take place to promote greater mutual understanding and relationships between Evangelicals and Catholics. A series of five rounds of dialogue were completed in 2002 in Swanwick, England. This was the first time a joint comprehensive document under the heading of *koinonia* fellowship between Evangelicals and Catholics was written and then published as a paper for further theological studies. The series of dialogues was viewed positively in evangelical circles and the result can be a basis for the discussion between Evangelicals and Roman Catholic Christians to this day. It is noteworthy that the paper adopted in Swanwick was published in the fourth volume of the "Growing Consensus Documents."[2]

Since 2009 the ecumenical dialogues between the World Evangelical Alliance and the Pontifical Council for Promoting Christian Unity have continued. With the conviction that the exchange between the denominations should not take place only at the theological level but should reach those at the grassroots as well, in 2013 the PCPCU sent out a questionnaire to Catholic bishops' conferences and the WEA office sent it to national alliances. This is an attempt to discover at the ground level how Evangelicals and Catholics experience and judge their relationship with one another.

---

2. "Church, Evangelization and the Bonds of Koinonia: a Report of International Consultation between the Catholic Church and the World Evangelical Alliance, Swanwick, UK, 1993-2002," in Gros, J., T. F. Best, & L. F. Fuchs, eds.

Other Ecumenical Dialogues

From 2006 to 2007 the WEA held dialogues with the international church leadership of the Seventh-day Adventists. The WEA recorded in a final agreement that the Adventists may participate as an independent evangelical church in the national alliances, although doctrinal differences still definitely exist. These differences include the celebration of the Sabbath instead of Sunday, and the importance of the edifying and prophetic writings of Ellen G. White, not only for the Adventist Church, but for all Christians worldwide.

Ecumenical dialogues will continue with the Orthodox Church. In consultation with the senior representatives of the Orthodox churches, particularly the Patriarch of Constantinople, Evangelicals are planning to select a national church as a model for dialogue. So far, however, no ecumenical talks with one of the Orthodox churches have taken place. This can begin, for personnel and financial reasons, only after completion of the ongoing discussion with the Roman Catholic Church. Ongoing discussions with the World Council of Churches (WCC) are necessary to work through the still-existing tensions between the WCC and the WEA. The WCC has created the Global Christian Forum, an ecumenical network in which representatives of all the major Christian traditions meet together regularly as equal dialogue partners for regular exchanges.

The World Evangelical Alliance has become one of the most powerful engines of the ecumenical movement in the modern age. It promotes ecumenical dialogue beyond the Protestant realm and thus opens up new horizons of cooperation and mutual respect.

Bibliography

Coote, Robert T. "Lausanne Committee for World Evangelization." In *Dictionary of the Ecumenical Movement*, 2nd ed., edited by Nicholas Lossky. Geneva: WCC Publications, 2002.

Gros, J., T. F. Best, and L. F. Fuchs, eds. *Growth in Agreement III: international dialogue texts and agreed statements, 1998–2005*. Faith and Order Paper 204. Geneva/Grand Rapids: World Council of Churches/Eerdmans, 2007.

Schrotenboer, Paul G. *Roman Catholicism: A Contemporary Evangelical Perspective*. Grand Rapids: Baker, 1988.

Dr. Rolf Hille is director of ecumenical affairs of the World Evangelical Alliance, Germany, and former chair of the Theological Commission of the World Evangelical Alliance.

"Evangelical futures will be as varied as global Evangelicals themselves. In the USA they will be younger, increasingly Hispanic, less politically homogeneous, perhaps fewer overall, and hopefully spending less time fighting each other. In Europe they will grow in fresh and missional ways from a small present base. In Africa and Latin America they will continue to multiply, but unless the prosperity teaching is renounced, the growth may not be everywhere healthy and truly Evangelical. In Asia, China and India may come to be the world's major blocs of Evangelical Christianity."

—Rev. Dr. Christopher J. H. Wright, International Ministries Director, Langham Partnership International, author of *The Mission of God: Unlocking the Bible's Grand Narrative*, IVP Academic, 2006, UK

EVANGELICALS AND ROMAN CATHOLICS

By Timothy George

The three most resilient forces within twenty-first century world Christianity are Eastern Orthodoxy, Roman Catholicism, and Protestant Evangelicalism. Historically, the relationship between Catholics and Evangelicals has been one of antipathy and mutual hostility stemming from the divisions of the Protestant Reformation, a movement of renewal led by Martin Luther, John Calvin, and other Reformers that emphasized justification by faith alone and the priority of Holy Scripture over church tradition. The scars of religious wars, the centuries of hatred, bitterness, separation, and isolation have become deeply lodged in the collective memories of the two communities. However, in recent decades Evangelicals and Catholics have made substantial progress in overcoming suspicions and mistrust from the past.

While many evangelical groups worldwide participated in the International Missionary Council (founded in 1921 and integrated into the World Council of Churches in 1961), the International Congress on World Evangelization, held in Lausanne, Switzerland in July 1974, was an important marker in the emergence of a maturing, self-conscious world Evangelical Movement. Evangelicals are concerned not only with spreading the Gospel around the world but also with nurturing a more positive relationship with other Christians, including Roman Catholics. This rise of evangelical interest in Christian unity coincided with two developments: the decline of mainline Protestant ecumenism on the one hand (due to the collapse of its bureaucracy and the rise of theological relativism as well as divisions within its churches) and a new Catholic emphasis on Christian unity on the other. On the Catholic side, the reforms of Vatican II gave momentum to this movement toward unity, which reached a high point in the papal encyclical *Ut Unum Sint* (That All May Be One), released by Pope John Paul II in 1995.[1]

A Growing Dialogue

Among the various bilateral dialogues and other initiatives, such as the Alpha Course and Groupe des Dombes, that have taken place in recent decades, four major discussions between Catholics and Evangelicals are significant. The first is ERCDOM, the Evangelical-Roman Catholic Dialogue On Mission, carried out between 1977 and 1984. This dialogue, with evangelical leader John Stott as a principal participant, grew out of points raised at the Lausanne Congress, in particular the mutual recognition of a growing convergence in both the Evangelical and Roman Catholic understandings of mission and evangelization. This dialogue identified issues which required further discussion, thus providing a basis on which more progress toward Catholic and Evangelical cooperation could be made.[2]

The second exchange was carried out between Catholics and Pentecostals. The full five reports from the Pentecostal-Roman Catholic Dialogue (1976, 1982, 1989, 1997, 2006) are notable both for their durability and

---

1. Basil Meeking and John Stott, *The Evangelical-Roman Catholic Dialogue on Mission, 1977–1984: A Report* (Grand Rapids: Eerdmans, 1986).

2. "Evangelization, Proselytism and Common Witness: The Report from the Fourth Phase of the International Dialogue (1990–1997) between the Roman Catholic Church and Some Classical Pentecostal Churches and Leaders," *Pneuma* 21, no. 1 (Spring 1999): 11–51.

their substance.[3] In particular, the 1997 document "Evangelization, Proselytism, and Common Witness" was a breakthrough on the controverted themes of proselytism (the use of manipulative methods in seeking adherents from other confessions), evangelism (the sharing of the witness of the gospel), and religious liberty.[4] The 2006 document, "On Becoming a Christian: Insights from Scripture and the Patristic Writings," shows significant insights from a common exploration of the sacred Scriptures and early Christian writers, which both traditions hold dear as critical to their development.[5]

The third discussion is the movement known as Evangelicals and Catholics Together (ECT), a nonofficial theological project between Evangelical and Catholic theologians first convened by Richard John Neuhaus and Charles Colson. The ECT project began in 1992 with a conference occasioned by growing and sometimes violent conflicts between Catholics and Evangelical Protestants in Latin America. The initial ECT statement, "Evangelicals and Catholics Together: The Christian Mission in the Third Millennium," was released in March 1994.[6] The signers of the statement referred to one another as "brothers and sisters in Christ," and they pledged their mutual support both in world evangelization and in the need to address the most pressing moral and cultural threats of the time. Despite an initial flurry of controversy, largely from a sector within the Evangelical community, the ECT collaborators have produced eight additional joint statements in twenty years. These statements cover a range of topics, including salvation/justification, Scripture and tradition, the communion of saints, the sacredness of life, marriage as the lifelong union of one man and one woman, and the role of the Virgin Mary in the plan of salvation.[7]

The fourth dialogue project is the international consultation between the Catholic Church and the World Evangelical Alliance. This took place between 1993 and 2002, issuing in the 2003 report "Church, Evangelization, and the Bonds of Koinonia." The report provides a summary of recent Evangelical and Roman Catholic discussions. It acknowledges the many spiritual treasures these two Christian communities share in common, such as the Holy Scriptures, the Lord's Prayer, the classic creeds, a high Christology, the gospel call to conversion and discipleship, and the common hope of Christ's return. At the same time, this document frankly acknowledges differences as well as convergences and concludes with a stirring call to conversion—a turning away from the prejudices and stereotypes of the past, and a fresh turning toward one another in Christian charity (Vandervelde, 2005). The report declares: "On the basis of our real but imperfect communion, we ask God to give us the grace to recommit ourselves to having a living personal relationship with Jesus as Lord and Savior and deepening our relationship to one another."[8]

---

3. Cecil M. Robeck Jr., "On Becoming a Christian: Insights from Scripture and the Patristic Writings with Some Contemporary Reflections," *Cyberjournal for Pentecostal-Charismatic Research* 18 (January 2009): ATLA Religion Database with ATLASerials.

4. Charles W. Colson, "Evangelicals & Catholics Together: The Christian Mission in the Third Millennium," *First Things* 43 (May 1994): 15–22.

5. Evangelicals and Catholics Together, "The Gift of Salvation," *First Things* 79 (January 1998): 20–23; Evangelicals and Catholics Together, "Your Word is Truth," *First Things* 125 (August-September 2002): 38–42; Evangelicals and Catholics Together, "The Communion of Saints," *First Things* 131 (March 2003): 26–33; Evangelicals and Catholics Together, "The Call to Holiness," *First Things* 151 (March 2005): 23–26; Evangelicals and Catholics Together, "That They May Have Life," *First Things* 166 (October 2006): Evangelicals and Catholics Together, "Do Whatever He Tells You: The Blessed Virgin Mary in Christian Faith and Life," *First Things* 197 (November 2009): 49–60, 18-25; Evangelicals and Catholics Together, "In Defense of Religious Freedom," *First Things* 221 (March 2012): 29–36. The ECT statement on marriage is forthcoming in 2015.

6. George Vandervelde, "Church, Evangelization, and the Bonds of Koinonia," *Evangelical Review of Theology* 29, no. 2 (April 2005): 100–130.

7. Ibid., 123.

8. *The Mission of an Evangelist: Amsterdam 2000* (Minneapolis, MN: World Wide Publications, 2001), 455.

A Deepening Dialogue

Geoff Tunnicliffe, then Secretary General of the World Evangelical Alliance, meets Pope Francis.
Photo: World Evangelical Alliance

An Evangelical is a herald charged to deliver an urgent message, the greatest news ever spoken or heard. Evangelicals are people with passion to know the living God—the Father, the Son, and the Holy Spirit—and to make his grace and love known to every person on earth. The theological dialogues between Evangelicals and Catholics are best understood in this light. Jesus prayed to the heavenly Father that his disciples "may all be one . . . so that the world may believe" (John 17:2–21 NRSV). The coinherence (things that exist in connection with one another) of mission and Christian unity is essential to the nature and purpose of the Church. The gospel message we proclaim will not carry credibility apart from the oneness of its witnesses. Jesus prayed for His followers to be one as he and the heavenly Father are one—even as he sent them forth to proclaim his message of love and grace unto the ends of the earth until the end of time. The closer Evangelicals and Catholics draw together in Christ, the closer they will come to one another. As John Calvin put it: "that we acknowledge no unity except in Christ; no charity of which he is not the bond, and that, therefore, the chief point in preserving charity is to maintain faith sacred and entire."[9]

Billy Graham has been a key figure in seeking greater mutual understanding between Evangelicals and Catholics. He was a personal friend of Pope John Paul II, who invited Graham to preach in Poland on several occasions. In the year 2000, Graham invited some 12,000 evangelists and Christian leaders from 215 countries to Amsterdam to prepare themselves to be more effective witnesses for the gospel in the twenty-first century. The confessional fruit of Amsterdam 2000, known simply as the Amsterdam Declaration, depicts the church and Christian unity in this way:

We pledge ourselves to pray and work for unity in truth among all true believers in Jesus and to cooperate as fully as possible in evangelism with other brothers and sisters in Christ so that the whole church may take the whole gospel to the whole world. [. . .] In the widest sense, the church includes all the redeemed of all the ages, being the one body of Christ extended throughout time as well as space. Here in the world, the church becomes visible in all local congregations that meet to do together the things that according to Scripture the church does. Christ is the head of the church. Everyone who is personally united to Christ by faith belongs to his body and by the Spirit is united with every other true believer in Jesus.

Bibliography

Calvin, John. *Institutes of the Christian Religion*, 1536 ed. Translated by Ford Lewis Battles. Grand Rapids: Eerdmans, 1975.

Colson, Charles W. "Evangelicals & Catholics Together: The Christian Mission in the Third Millennium." *First Things* 43 (May 1994): 15–22.

Evangelicals and Catholics Together. "The Call to Holiness." *First Things* 151 (March 2005): 23–26.

---

9. Ibid., 458.

———. "The Communion of Saints." *First Things* 131 (March 2003): 26–33.

———. "Do Whatever He Tells You: The Blessed Virgin Mary in Christian Faith and Life." *First Things* 197 (November 2009): 49–60.

———. "The Gift of Salvation." *First Things* 79 (January 1998): 20–23.

———. In Defense of Religious Freedom." *First Things* 221 (March 2012): 29–36.

———. "That They May Have Life." *First Things* 166 (October 2006).

———. "Your Word is Truth." *First Things* 125 (August-September 2002): 38–42.

Pictured here with Pope John Paul II, Charles Colson founded Evangelicals and Catholics Together in 1994 to unite the two Christian communities around common convictions of faith and mission.
Photo: Prison Fellowship

"Evangelization, Proselytism and Common Witness: The Report from the Fourth Phase of the International Dialogue (1990–1997) Between the Roman Catholic Church and Some Classical Pentecostal Churches and Leaders." *Pneuma* 21, no. 1 (Spring 1999): 11–51.

"Final Report of the International Roman Catholic/Pentecostal Dialogue (1972–1976)." *Pneuma* 12, no. 2 (Fall 1990): 85–95.

"Final Report of the International Roman Catholic/Pentecostal Dialogue (1977–1982)." *Pneuma* 12, no. 2 (Fall 1990): 97–115.

Meeking, Basil, and John Stott. *The Evangelical-Roman Catholic Dialogue on Mission, 1977–1984: A Report*. Grand Rapids: Eerdmans, 1986.

"Perspectives on Koinonia." *Pneuma* 12, no. 2 (Fall 1990): 117–142.

Pope John Paul II. *Encyclical letter Ut unum sint of the Holy Father, John Paul II on Commitment to Ecumenism*. Washington, DC: United States Catholic Conference, 1995.

Robeck, Cecil M., Jr. "On Becoming a Christian: Insights from Scripture and the Patristic Writings with Some Contemporary Reflections." *Cyberjournal for Pentecostal-Charismatic Research* 18 (January 2009): ATLA Religion Database with ATLASerials.

Vandervelde, George. "Church, Evangelization, and the Bonds of Koinonia." *Evangelical Review of Theology* 29/2 (April 2005): 100–130.

Dr. Timothy George is dean of Beeson Divinity School of Samford University in Birmingham, Alabama, and general editor of the Reformation Commentary on Scripture.

"My hope for the future is that Evangelicals would be less concerned about their own self-interests and be more focused on God's love for the world. In Brazil specifically, the church has great potential for developing a major missionary-sending movement. However, although Brazil is one of the largest Christian nations in the world today (by percentage), per capita mission sending from Brazil is relatively low. I'd like to see the Brazilian church go to the least evangelized, least loved, least embraced, and least cared for around the world and make a difference among them."

—Ludmila Ghil, Brazilian missionary to Asia

EVANGELICALS AND OTHER RELIGIONS

By Miriam Adeney

All truth is God's truth, and all religions contain glimpses of this. Yet the good news that the Creator of the cosmos has come close to us in sacrificial love and transforming power in Jesus is something qualitatively distinct.

A Theological Paradox

Humans are created in God's image, yet are also sinners. Religions reflect this tension. People everywhere have thought and prayed and married and buried with an awareness of the supernatural. Bodies of wisdom, ritual, and everyday ethics have emerged to give order and a sense of meaning and identity to human life. These positive patterns are gifts of God, the results of God's gift of creativity to those formed in the Creator's image.

Even so, the people who shape cultures also are sinners. Religions themselves are warped by sin. Every human institution carries tendencies toward selfishness, exploitation, and idolatry. Cruelty and evil are part of religious history. Furthermore, when Christ is not the center of worship, demonic powers may insinuate themselves into religious systems, enslaving people and intensifying suffering.

How shall we deal with the tension between good and evil in religions? Different Evangelicals have weighed these factors differently. In this chapter we will glimpse several approaches. Against that backdrop, we will explore several religions.

Much Error, Little Value

Some Evangelicals have believed that truth is so mixed with error in other religions that those faiths are of little value. Religions follow a cycle of "sin, repression and suppression, substitution, and more sin," according to missiologist Samuel Schlorff, who went on to say,

> **Islam provides a perfect illustration . . . The *Quranic* view of God, especially in its doctrine of absolute transcendence, cuts the Muslim off from the knowledge of God that he or she has by means of general revelation, and from a saving knowledge of Christ. God appears to be so distant, essentially unknown and unknowable, and the Trinity in unity impossible, because Islam has repressed the truth about God and substituted for it untruth. Islam has also repressed and suppressed the truth about ourselves . . . which we have received through general revelation. It attributes our separation from God and our sinful human condition to God's transcendence and not our sin, and considers our present condition to be normal . . . The *Quran* teaches that we are basically good and able to do the good; we are just weak.[1]**

---

1. Samuel Schlorff, "The Translational Model for Mission in Resistant Muslim Societies: A Critique and an Alternative," *Missiology* 28, no. 3 (July 2000): 319.

Following in the tradition of Karl Barth and Hendrik Kraemer, Schlorff spoke of a chasm between human thoughts and God's thoughts: an absolute qualitative difference. The gospel "falls from above like a stone into the water,"[2] says Kramer, whereas, to change the metaphor, religions are, in the words of C. S. Lewis, "all *eros* steaming up, no *agape* darting down."

In this view, religions are skewed and incorrigibly misdirected. They represent resistance rather than response. As a result, Schlorff explained, "The *Quran* and Islamic culture cannot be considered as neutral vehicles that may be used as a contextual or theological starting point, or source of truth, and filled with Christian meanings. These are used only as a communicational starting point to help the receptors connect to the biblical message."[3] J. H. Bavinck, a veteran Dutch missionary to Indonesia, concurred. From a strictly theological point of view, Bavinck argued, there is no point within Islam that offers a truth that can be simply taken over and utilized as a basis for Christian witness.

The Gospel Fulfills

Job restored to health and wealth after keeping his faith. Woodcut.
Photo: North Wind Picture Archives

By contrast, other Evangelicals have viewed religions more positively, emphasizing their ethical truth, if not their saving truth. Japanese theologian Toyohiko Kagawa compared the partial glimpses of God provided by various religions to stages on the pilgrimage up Mount Fuji. Each rest stop yields a different vista. "Christian faith 'comprehends' and 'fulfills' all the partial truths found in the other religions, while at the same time purging them from their errors and supplementing them with truths and values that they do not themselves possess. In them we see 'broken lights,' in the gospel the full radiance of God's glory. This means that, much as Jesus came long ago 'not to abolish the law and the prophets . . . but to fulfill them' (Matthew 5:17), so his gospel comes today to the laws and prophets of other religions."[4]

In a broad sense, all theologians would affirm that God communicates to people across cultures through nature (Psalm 19), conscience (Romans 2), and dreams and visions (Acts 10). Every person receives light from Jesus (John 1:9). Justin Martyr and Clement of Alexandria spoke of Jesus as the divine reason in every human being. These gifts are bestowed indiscriminately on people of all faiths, or no faith at all.

Outside of the descendants of Abraham—people who had received special covenants from God—Scripture records God's guidance to people like Melchizedek, Job, Balaam, and Jethro. Jesus pointed out several non-Jewish people as models of faith in God. These include the widow of Zarephath, Naaman, the Roman centurion who asked for healing for his slave, a Canaanite woman, the good Samaritan, and a Samaritan leper, who was the only one among ten healed lepers to return and give thanks to God. The apostle Paul quoted pagan poets authoritatively to Athenians, to Cretans, and to Corinthians, and he told the pagan Lystrans that God had revealed himself to their forefathers.

---

2. Hendrik Kraemer, *The Christian Message in a Non-Christian World* (Grand Rapids: Kregel, 1956), 102.

3. Schlorff, "Translational Model," 321.

4. Toyohiko Kagawa, quoted in Gerald Anderson, *The Theology of the Christian Mission* (New York: McGraw-Hill, 1961), 208.

Given this general affirmation, some Christians who were born into families with other faiths have come to refer to their former religions' scriptures as the "Old Testament for our people," the law that can serve as a "schoolmaster" (in the apostle Paul's terminology, Gal. 3:24 KJV) to bring people to an awareness of their need for God. The Indian poet Narayan Tilak spoke of the Hindu Vedas in this sense. Chinese filmmaker Yuan Zhiming has commented similarly about the writings of Lao Tse, the sacred writings of Taoism.

However, American theologian Timothy Tennant and others have argued that it is wrong to equate these scriptures with the Old Testament. When God introduced himself to Abraham and David and Isaiah, this was a unique, cumulative series of self-disclosures. It is not paralleled in other religions.

Job lamenting that what God gave, God has taken away. Engraving. *Photo: North Wind Picture Archives*

Still, many would agree the general wisdom found in other faiths is a gift of God. Indeed, there may be indigenous ideas that display the gospel particularly well. Writing in a Hindu context, Indian theologian A. J. Appesamy argued that Christianity's sojourn in the West robbed it of some key meanings: "It is when the Bible is placed in its old environment (in Asia) that it can be fully understood."[5] More emphatically, Indian Christian leader Joseph D'Souza called Christians to learn from India's "vast and ancient philosophical ideas," asserting that "the Christian captivity to Greek philosophical systems must end."[6]

Those Who Seek, Find

For other Evangelicals, what matters is the process rather than the content. The focus here is a person's sincere search for God, rather than the ethical or theological teaching in that person's non-Christian faith. Canadian theologian Clark Pinnock has explored this avenue. If people seek after God, it is because God's grace draws them. Their sincerity will be demonstrated on Judgment Day when they recognize Christ and worship him. Religion's role in this seeking is ambivalent. People may search by means of their religion or through their concerns for health, art, peacemaking, ecology, relationships, and so on. In Jesus' day, Pinnock observed, religious orthodoxy did not guarantee responsiveness to him. Often the religiously ignorant received his teaching more readily than the Pharisees.[7]

For other Evangelicals, what matters is the process rather than the content.

5. Timothy T. Tennent, *Theology in the Context of World Christianity: How the Global Church is Influencing the Way We Think about and Discuss Theology* (Grand Rapids: Zondervan, 2009).

6. Joseph D'Souza. "The Indian Church and Missions Face the Saffronizaiton Challenge," in *Global Missiology for the 21st Century: The Iguassu Dialogue*, ed. William Taylor (Grand Rapids: Baker, 1999), 402.

7. Clark Pinnock, *A Wideness in God's Mercy: The Finality of Jesus Christ in a World of Religions* (Grand Rapids: Zondervan, 1992), 172.

Search matters, but the search alone is not enough for theologians like J. Robertson McQuilken. The search must lead to Jesus. Acts 4:12 is considered a key text: "Salvation is found in no one else, for there is no other name under heaven given to mankind by which we must be saved" (NIV). The word *name* indicates Jesus in his particularity, McQuilkin asserted. He believed those who respond to the light they have will receive more light. Eventually this will lead seekers to the gospel. This is a process with many steps, a dynamic interchange. "The repeated promise of additional light to those who obey the light they have is a basic and very important biblical truth concerning God's justice and judgment," McQuilkin affirmed.[8]

Muslim followers of Jesus often still feel connected to their ancestral religion.
Photo: Sue Careless

Religion Below the Neck

Religion is more than doctrine. Community is another significant dimension. Faiths are *lived*. A religion not only provides a cognitive map for relating to ultimate questions with coherence and commitment, it also manifests behaviors through sacred rituals, everyday ethics, and folk practices, all demonstrated in community.

It is true that deep social splits—sectarian, geographical, and generational—often fragment the brotherliness of a religion. Nevertheless, the communal dimensions of a faith may be as important for adherents as its creedal tenets. Evangelicals who witness across cultures dare not underestimate the power of community.

Insider movements constitute a controversial type of church growth that emphasizes community. Today, hundreds of thousands of Hindu, Buddhist, and Muslim followers of Jesus claim that, while their beliefs and spiritual experiences have changed radically, they remain part of their ancestral religions. Even though these believers have been born again through faith in Jesus and follow the Bible as authoritative, they still view themselves as Hindu, Buddhist, or Muslim. This identity is cultural more than religious, they assert.

Some followers of Jesus from Muslim backgrounds continue to worship at the mosque, pray the traditional Muslim prayers five times daily while facing Mecca, and use the Qur'an as authoritative when they witness to Jesus. Not surprisingly, Christian theologians differ strongly in their interpretations of this phenomenon. Concerns are raised about doctrinal understandings, Christian community, the sacraments, and the next generation. Yet historic churches (Presbyterian, Anglican, Baptist, and others) in such regions often are not contextualized to the majority-Muslim culture, whether in their terminology about Jesus, or political passions about Palestine, or even the wearing of beards. To Muslim-background followers of Jesus, such churches may not appear to offer a viable option for community that is relevant and honors God.

These large, dynamic movements of people who acknowledge Jesus as Lord constitute another evangelical approach to religions. They must be recognized, even though they may not identify with the word *Christian* any more than do Messianic Jews.

Now we turn briefly to the religions themselves.

Islam

For Muslims, God is all-powerful, the Creator of the cosmos, the sustainer of all systems, and the culminator of history. As the fount of righteousness, God communicates to humans through nature, prophets, and scriptures, especially the Qur'an. God is also merciful and compassionate, although his mercy does not extend to taking on human form, much less going to the cross.

---

8. J. Robertson McQuilkin, "Lost," in *Perspectives on the World Christian Movement: A Reader*, ed. Ralph Winter and Steven Hawthorne (Pasadena, CA: William Carey Publishers, 1999), 159.

A Shia Mosque.
Photo: Sue Careless

In Islam human beings are called to worship God through daily prayers, weekly worship services, and annual events, all celebrated communally whenever possible. Muslim mystical orders, known as Sufis, go further, cultivating intense spiritual experience of God. Humans are also called to live ethically in society in obedience to God, acting as God's capable but humble regents on earth. A particular subset of Muslims, political radicals, hunger for justice and righteousness in society and struggle vigorously to bring that to reality.

Adam, Noah, Abraham, Moses, and David are all considered Muslims, according to Muslims. God communicated to them, and they obeyed him and led his people in ways of righteousness. Similarly, Jesus is a Muslim, one of the greatest of all the prophets. When Jesus claimed to be "the way, and the truth, and the life," and said, "No one comes to the Father except through me" (John 14:6 NRSV), that was correct—for his day. Only when the prophet Muhammad arrived five hundred years later was this superseded. Jesus is mentioned in ninety-two verses in the Qur'an, and called the Messiah eleven times. He will play a key role in the final judgment. Yet he is not God. How could God become a baby, crying and colicky, diapered and nursed? How could the eternal become a point in time? How could he take on the features of a particular race? To say Jesus is God is blasphemy, making something like God.

Despite these significant differences, Evangelicals clearly have a great deal in common with Muslims. Today there is intense discussion about the best terms to use in witness and in Bible translation when referring to the person of Jesus, so as to communicate effectively to Muslims. Perhaps, though, the focus should be on God first of all. "God is great," Muslims affirm in their prayers. What could be greater than a God who loves so much that he enters into suffering and even death, absorbs it, but is not conquered by it, and comes through strong and glorious? Could anything be more mind-boggling? Nowhere is God's greatness demonstrated more powerfully than in the death and resurrection of God in Jesus.

With genuine empathy, Christians also must express sorrow for the Crusades, European colonization of Muslim-majority countries, Palestine's pain, and the loose, disrespectful immorality that spills into conservative countries through Western media. On the other hand, Evangelicals deplore Muslim laws on apostasy, which forbid conversions, and the severe persecution that is sometimes visited upon Muslims who choose Jesus.

Buddhism

With its first *noble truth*, that all life is suffering, Buddhism calls us beyond glib optimism and cheap cheerfulness to recognize the pain, paradox, and ambiguity in this world. Buddhism also shows a way forward. If we see that suffering is pervasive, if we recognize that it is exacerbated by our own desires, and if we can learn to quench those desires, then peace will come. This encapsulates the first three *noble truths*. Chaiyun Ukosakul, a Thai who became a Christian as an adult, has summarized the way to peace he was taught: "When I am angry, a tiger grows in my heart. But when I am enlightened, the tiger dies."[9]

A Buddhist Temple.
Photo: Sue Careless

9. Personal conversation with Chaiyun Ukosakul (April 20, 2000).

From a Christian perspective, Buddhism offers a degree of serenity in a hard world. If there were no God, or if God had not reached out to us, we might settle for this. But the amazing news is that there is a God, and he has cared so strongly for us that he chose to walk with dusty feet right to the painful, bloody cross. This is not tranquility. This is passionate involvement. This is love. And it is what makes our own love possible. Having opened ourselves to receive the love of God, we can pass it on.

This has implications for the value of individuals and for committed relationships. In Buddhism human beings are described in transient terms, such as candle flames, or drops of water, or temporary psycho-physical events. Committed relationships are seen as snares. By contrast, the Christian faith teaches that individuals are profoundly valuable and committed relationships are possible, significant, and good.

Evangelicals can value Buddhists' quest for transcendence and their sensitivity to suffering, balanced moderation, care for animals and plants, core ethical teachings, and beautiful artistic creations. Professor Prabo Mihindukulasuriya of Sri Lanka expressed his appreciation in the essay "Without Christ I Could Not Be a Buddhist: An Evangelical Response to Christian Self-Understanding in a Buddhist Context."[10] In a similar spirit an all-Asia evangelical network called SEANET (Southeast Asian Network) meets annually in Thailand to focus on some aspect of witness among Buddhists. Each conference results in a book. There are now ten volumes.

In various countries Buddhism may be mixed with Confucianism, Taoism, Shinto, or animism. Major variations include Theravada Buddhism in south Asia, Mahayana in East Asia, and Tibetan in central Asia. Intriguingly, Japanese Jodo Shinshu Buddhism teaches a strong doctrine of grace through faith. However, a careful study by Timothy Tennant reveals the object of this faith is not Jesus Christ but the words of Jodo Shinshu's founder, Shinran.

Hinduism

We are souls, Hindus affirm, not just animals, or machines, or producers, or consumers. We are born with a destiny to rise to union with the Ultimate Soul. A hunger for this union has pulsed powerfully through Hinduism. Rabindranath Tagore, who won the Nobel Prize for Literature for his book *Gitanjali* (*Song Offerings*), wrote, "I have been seeking and searching for God for as long as I can remember, for many, many lives."[11] The dynamic teacher Vivekenanda lamented, "In temple, church and mosque, in Vedas, Bible, and Koran I searched for You in vain. Like a child in the wildest forest lost, I cried and cried alone, 'Where are You gone, my God, my love?'"[12] Their quests reflect the ancient Upanishadic prayer:

Lead me from the unreal to the real,

Lead me from darkness to light,

Lead me from death to immortality.[13]

Hinduism is a complex amalgamation of beliefs and practices, squeezing many local religions into one system. Honored by all, the sacred Veda Scriptures are collections of hymns, poems, and liturgical aids. From these, India's great thinkers, such as Sankara and Ramanuja, developed systematic theologies. Key doctrines include *Brahman*, the Ultimate Soul; *atmans*, souls of living creatures; *maya*, the illusions and deceptions that surround us and veil our understandings; *samsara*, the wearying round of reincarnation; *karma*, the possibility of building

10. Prabo Mihindukulasuriya, "Without Christ I Could Not Be a Buddhist: An Evangelical Response to Christian Self-Understanding in a Buddhist Context," *Current Dialogue* (December 2011): 73–86.

11. Rabindranath Tagore, *Gitanjali,* quoted in Ivan Satyavrata, "India's Search for Jesus," in *Faith Seeking Understanding: Essays in Memory of Paul Brand and Ralph D. Winter,* ed. David Marshall (Pasadena, CA: William Carey Publishers, 2012), 78.

12. Letter from Vivekananda on September 4, 1893 to Prof. J. H. Wright of Boston who introduced the swami at the Parliament of Religions.

13. Brhadaranyaka Upanishad, Yajur Veda, 53:28.

up merit and improving our station in the next life; and *moksha*, breaking free from the round of samsara to merge with the Ultimate. In the end, our individuality dissolves into the great whole, and we cease to exist as distinct persons.

To progress spiritually, Ramanuja suggested three paths now considered classic: the way of *bhakti*, or worship; the way of *jnana*, or theological study; and the way of *karma*, or building merit through good deeds. To be good means fulfilling the duties of one's station, including those associated with caste, gender, and age. Within this framework, myriad methods have evolved, from asceticism to sacred prostitution.

Bhakti is a bridge Evangelicals may employ. Through songs, quietness, recitation, or other spiritual approaches, Hindus have sought to practice the presence of God. Some have learned how to go deep, to lose themselves in worship. Certain Vedic concepts also may be bridges. In the oldest scripture, the Rig Veda, for example, the Lord of creation, Prajapati, is said to offer himself as a divine sacrifice for the world. Christian theologian Khrishna Banerjea believed this pointed to Jesus: "It is the voice of your primitive ancestors calling upon you in the voice of their *Vedas* . . . not to waver in your duty to acknowledge and embrace the true *Prajapati*, the true *Parusha* begotten before the world, who died that you might live, who by death has vanquished death, and brought life and immortality to light through the Gospel . . . You will find in Him everything worthy of your lineage, worthy of your antiquity, worthy of your traditions."[14]

While Hinduism calls us to withdraw from the world as we grow in spirituality, Hindu-background Christians have heard Jesus' call to plunge more deeply into the world to serve it. Consider the Vedic scholar Narayan Tilak. When Tilak was introduced to the New Testament, he discovered the God for whom he had been searching. Tilak became known as a Jesus *bhakta*, a worshipper of Jesus. Eventually this prize-winning poet would write hundreds of Christian hymns. Tilak honored earlier Hindu writers and singers for the insight they had provided. Yet he recognized that the gospel differed from his tradition. Tilak emphasized not detachment (viraga) but attachment (anuraga). Instead of reciting sacred sayings passively, he created a darbar, a Christian study community whose members served the surrounding neighborhood.

Primal Religions

Stories, not doctrinal teachings, shape the worldviews of primal religionists. These myths are not mere tales. They metaphorically explore the ultimate questions: Where did we come from? Where are we going? What is a healthy society? How is justice restored? How can pain be endured? Taken all together, the mythological cycle rolls out a cosmic story. This is reenacted regularly in rituals.

The Bible is rich in stories of people who encountered God and responded, sometimes well and sometimes badly. Jesus himself told a lot of stories. Many of the issues in the Bible's stories are similar to those faced by primal religionists today, as American historian Philip Jenkins observed, "Robbers on the roads, streets full of crippled and sick, the struggle to pay gouging tax and debt collectors, demanding landlords . . . immanent national collapse . . . personality cults of dictators . . . judgments on the rich and haughty . . . sowing and reaping and shepherding . . . feasts of plenty, and wells that never go dry . . . deliverance from evil."[15] Such themes can constitute natural bridges for Evangelicals to communicate with primal religionists.

The oral wisdom in primal heritages contains much Evangelicals can appreciate. Native North Americans, for example, value a circular worldview. While Christians traditionally have emphasized a linear movement from Eden to the final kingdom, Native Americans emphasize the circles of the seasons and the generations, the spiral of the process of learning, and the rise and fall and renewal of many things. We can see the traits of our grandparents in our grandchildren. We can rejoice that Easter comes round again every year.

---

14. Khrishna Banerjea, *The Relation Between Christianity and Hinduism* (Calcutta: Oxford Mission Press, 1881).

15. Joel Carpenter, "Back to the Bible," review of *The New Faces of Christianity: Believing the Bible in the Global South* by Philip Jenkins, *Books and Culture* 13, no. 3 (2007): 23.

Although primal religions are diverse, the motifs of the Creator and creation, cosmic struggle, spirit power, and holistic integration of the physical and spiritual world often appear. The universe throbs with sacredness. It is a place, as written in Psalm 19, where the heavens can declare the glory of God, where the trees of the field can praise him, where the stones can cry out his glory, where everything that has breath will bow to the Creator.

Yet when Christ is not central, a vacuum is created. Then other powers tend to move in and take over. Primal religionists may propitiate impersonal powers by magic, and demonic powers by sacrifices and other rituals. Evangelicals believe Jesus Christ died to liberate people from just such domination.

However, primal religionists are not unique in this bondage. All religions can be skewed. All can invite idols. In the tragic history of colonialism, as well as in the ungodly preoccupations promoted through global media today, the idols of Christian-majority societies stand out starkly. German theologian Hendrik Berkof offered an illustration of such idols from his European context:

> **When Hitler took the helm in Germany in 1933, the powers of *Volk*, race, and state took a new grip on men. Thousands were grateful, after the confusion of the preceding years, to find their lives again protected from chaos, order and security restored. No one could withhold himself, without utmost effort form the grasp these Powers had . . . I myself experienced almost literally how such Powers may be "in the air" . . .**

> **The state, politics, class, social struggle, national interest, public opinion, accepted morality, the ideas of decency, humanity, democracy—these give unity and direction to thousands of lives. Yet precisely by giving unity and direction, they separate these many lives from the true God: they let us believe that we have found the meaning of existence, whereas they really estrange us from true meaning.[16]**

Idols are everywhere. When bringing God's good news to primal religionists, then, Evangelicals must also demonstrate how Christ liberates us from the idols of our own cultures. When *anything* exalts itself above the Lord Jesus Christ, Evangelicals condemn it. When faced with other people's idols, however, we should not be hasty. Eschewing syncretism but cultivating contextualization, Christians will differ as we face drums, feathers, smoke, or the ritual killing of animals. Humility is required, expressed in a teachable spirit and a passion to learn from and work under indigenous leaders, immersed in the Word and the Spirit together.

Although the systems or powers of this world are not evil in themselves, since they were created by Christ and are held together in him (Col. 1:16–17), Evangelicals believe systems can become evil when they usurp the central place in ordering our values. Since in recent centuries Christian-majority peoples have dominated others, Evangelicals believe we must begin with our own idols, the "beam" in our own eye (Matt. 7:5).

Religions Are Not the Final Focus

Writing an essay on the Trinity from his home in the Middle East, Arab Christian professor Martin Accad critiqued scholars of religion who try to pigeonhole each other as inclusivist, exclusivist, or pluralist. Religions are not the final focus, Accad argued. God in his sovereignty can use religions just as he uses nature. Even the Christian religion is not the ultimate concern. "The good news is Christ himself (rather than Christianity)." At the core, Evangelicals believe God in Jesus shatters all our categories.

---

16. Hendrik Berkhof, *Christ and the Powers* (Scottsdale, PA: Herald Press, 1962), 32.

Bibliography

Accad, Martin, and John Corrie. "Trinity." In *Dictionary of Mission Theology: Evangelical Foundations*. Nottingham, UK: InterVarsity Press, 2007.

Anderson, Gerald. *The Theology of the Christian Mission*. New York: McGraw-Hill, 1961.

Banerjea, Khrishna. *The Relation Between Christianity and Hinduism*. Calcutta: Oxford Mission Press, 1881.

Berkhof, Hendrik. *Christ and the Powers*. Scottsdale, PA: Herald Press, 1962

D'Souza, Joseph. "The Indian Church and Missions Face the Saffronization Challenge." In *Global Missiology for the 21st Century: The Iguassu Dialogue,* edited by William Taylor, 391–406. Grand Rapids: Baker, 1999.

Kraemer, Hendrik. *The Christian Message in a Non-Christian World*. Grand Rapids: Kregel, 1956.

McQuilkin, J. Robertson. "Lost." In *Perspectives on the World Christian Movement: A Reader*. Edited by Ralph Winter and Steven Hawthorne. Pasadena, CA: William Carey Publishers, 1999.

Mihindukulasuriya, Prabo. "Without Christ I Could Not Be a Buddhist: An Evangelical Response to Christian Self-Understanding in a Buddhist Context." *Current Dialogue* (December 2011).

Pinnock, Clark. *A Wideness in God's Mercy: The Finality of Jesus Christ in a World of Religions*. Grand Rapids: Zondervan, 1992.

Satyavrata, Ivan. "India's Search for Jesus." In *Faith Seeking Understanding: Essays in Memory of Paul Brand and Ralph D. Winter*, edited by David Marshall. Pasadena, CA: William Carey Publishers, 2012.

Schlorff, Samuel. "The Translational Model for Mission in Resistant Muslim Societies: A Critique and an Alternative." *Missiology* 28, no. 3 (July 2000): 305–328.

Tennent, Timothy, T. *Theology in the Context of World Christianity: How the Global Church is Influencing the Way We Think about and Discuss Theology*. Grand Rapids: Zondervan, 2009.

Dr. Miriam Adeney is an anthropologist and missiologist at Seattle Pacific University in Washington, United States and Regent College in Vancouver, Canada. She is the author of *Kingdom Without Borders: The Untold Story of Global Christianity, Daughters of Islam: Building Bridges with Muslim Women, God's Foreign Policy: Practical Ways to Help the World's Poor, How to Write: A Christian Writer's Guide*, and *A Time for Risking: Priorities for Women*. She has served as the president of the American Society of Missiology and is on the board for Christianity Today International, as well as task forces for the World Evangelical Alliance and the Lausanne Committee for World Evangelization. She has received the Lifetime Achievement Award from Christians for Biblical Equality.

"For more than two hundred years, Evangelical missionaries have been known for grassroots inventiveness and sometimes disruptive behavior. After all, they launched and extended the parachurch movement to translate Bibles and plant churches. Disruption is what typically happens when people try new things. For Evangelical missions, risk-taking comes with the territory. Creativity is a must. Are Evangelical Christians still up to the task?"

—Dr. Roy L. Peterson, President and CEO of The Seed Company, United States

EVANGELICALS AND MISSIONS

By Allen Yeh

The word *Evangelical* has the Gospel embedded within its name: the Greek word *euangellion* is composed of *eu* (good) and *angellion* (message), or *Gospel* (lit. "good news"). Evangelicals by definition are called to be good messengers (lit. "angels"), or evangelists. Just as the angel Gabriel in Luke 1:30–33 announced the good news to Mary, Evangelicals are called to model the angels by announcing the Gospel. They are Christians specifically committed to announcing the good news. Though the word *evangelism* is not synonymous with missions, the two words are indispensable to one another. To be an evangelical means to have mission at the heart of one's identity.

The definition of mission is comprised of five inextricably linked characteristics: 1) Holy Spirit-initiated, 2) church-driven, 3) diverse, 4) ecumenical, 5) holistic.

Holy Spirit-Initiated

Mission is the theme of the entire Bible,[1] or at least has been since the fall. From Genesis to the Gospels to Revelation, mission is the common thread that runs throughout Scripture. The Enemy attempts to corrupt and destroy what God has created, and God acts to redeem and restore the cosmos. "You will strike his heel" is a reference to Satan's temporary victory over Jesus on the cross, and "he will crush your head" is anticipating God's final triumph over Satan in Revelation 20.

The book of Acts is the climax and the most obvious starting point of post-Resurrection mission. It begins with Jesus and the Holy Spirit. There are four Great Commissions in the Bible.[2] Though the one in the book of Matthew ("Therefore go and make disciples of all nations . . .") is by far the most famous, the others are also considered Great Commissions because they are the final earthly words of Jesus to his disciples before his ascension. The Great Commissions focus on mission. God incarnate (Jesus) chose mission as the subject of his final earthly message. The very last thing that Jesus gives his followers is a commandment to mission, changing them from disciples (learners) to apostles (ones who are sent out).

All four Great Commissions, though spoken by Jesus and carried out by the Holy Spirit, are Trinitarian in formula, so they involve all three persons of the Godhead.[3] God the Father sends out the Son and breathes the

> **Evangelicals by definition are called to be good messengers.**

---

1. Christopher J. H. Wright, *The Mission of God: Unlocking the Bible's Grand Narrative* (Downers Grove: InterVarsity Press, 2006).

2. Matt. 28:18–20; Mark 16:15–18; Luke 24:36–49; John 20:19–23; Acts 1:4–8. The Markan Great Commission, however, has dubious attestation (In most Bibles there is a note such as: "The earliest manuscripts and some other ancient witnesses do not have Mark 16:9–20.") and thus will not be considered seriously in this discussion.

3. See Tim Tennent, *Invitation to World Missions: A Trinitarian Missiology for the Twenty-First Century* (Grand Rapids: Kregel, 2010).

Holy Spirit. The Father and Son together send out the Holy Spirit. Ultimately, the way we do mission is to imitate the Son being sent by the Father, and imitate the Spirit as sent out by the Father and the Son.

The persons of the Trinity have different functions with regard to the *missio Dei* (a Latin term that can be translated as mission of God). God the Father is the source, initiator, and goal of the *missio Dei*, God the Son is the embodiment of the *missio Dei*, and God the Holy Spirit is the empowering presence of the *missio Dei* as seen in the Acts version of the Great Commission.

During the twentieth century, two leading missiologists, David Bosch and Lesslie Newbigin, insisted on the shift of terminology from missions (plural) to mission (singular). Bosch defined missions as the work of humans and mission as the work of God (Bosch, 1991, p. 391). Even earlier than Bosch, the World Council of Churches discussed this distinction at their fifth World Missionary Conference in 1952.[4] Soon, missiological institutions and scholars followed suit. Today, the U.S. Center for World Mission, the Oxford Centre for Mission Studies and others have adopted the word mission, acknowledging God as the source of mission in the world.

Church-Driven

Though God is the originator of mission, the *missio Dei* works with the mission ecclesiae. It is no coincidence that Acts is the beginning of the Holy Spirit's actions, of the Church and of mission/missions. John Piper writes that worship is actually the ultimate goal of the church and worship fuels mission:

> **All of history[5] is moving toward one great goal, the white-hot worship of God and his Son among all the peoples of the earth. Missions is not that goal. It is the means. And for that reason it is the second greatest human activity in the world . . . Worship, therefore, is the fuel and goal in missions . . . The goal of missions is the gladness of the peoples in the greatness of God . . . Missions begins and ends in worship." Missions will not exist in heaven, suggesting that mission is God's action in history. Even while on earth, though, Evangelicals believe mission must be in service to something greater.**

Thomas Aquinas suggested that philosophy is the handmaiden to theology. So one might say that mission is the handmaiden to worship, as the second-most important activity of the church. Yet, while every church worships, unfortunately not every church engages in missions. The Greek word for church is *ekklesia*, which is a compound of the words *ek* (out from) and *kaleo* (to call). Therefore the church is the community of people who are called out, just as the apostles were sent out. If mission is not an integral part of a church's life, it is not acting out its very definition. A church is never meant to be insular.

If the church is the People of God, then it existed in nascent form in the Old Testament. Israel was God's missionary arm: "It is too small a thing for you to be my servant to restore the tribes of Jacob and bring back those of Israel I have kept. I will also make you a light for the Gentiles, that my salvation may reach to the ends of the earth" (Isa. 49:6, cf. Isa. 60:3). This was later echoed in Simeon's song in Luke 2:32, though in the latter case the reference is to Jesus fulfilling the task that Israel failed to do.

The missionary impulse came from God's Covenant, expressed in six parts in theology: Noahic (Gen. 9:8–17), Abrahamic (Gen. 12–17), Judaic (Gen. 49:10), Mosaic (Ex. 19-24), Davidic (2 Sam. 7), and New (Luke 22:20).

---

4. Lesslie Newbigin, "Mission to Six Continents," in *A History of the Ecumenical Movement*, ed. Harold E. Fey, vol. 2, 1948–1968 (Geneva: World Council of Churches, 1970), 178–179. There was a reaction against the perceived church-centric view of missions present in the assembly, with the result that the affirmation of mission being the *missio Dei* was an enduring contribution of Willingen. Their statement was, "There is no participation in Christ without participation in His mission to the world."

5. John Piper, Let the Nations Be Glad! The Supremacy of God in Missions (Grand Rapids: Baker, 1993), 11, 15.

Evangelicals understand these not as six separate covenants, but one that evolved over time. Through them, God intended that humans spread over the face of the earth in order to care for it; that was how mission was defined before God chose a people for himself. However, when humans proved to be no longer fit to be entrusted with the God-imaged lordship of the earth, but instead idolized themselves as expressed in the Tower of Babel story in Genesis 11, God found a new way, through one man named Abraham in Genesis 12 who he called out of Ur of the Chaldeans. The mission of the people of God truly begins when universal history becomes specific, namely from Abraham, known as the Father of Faith—and considered so by not only Jews and Christians but also Muslims—onward.

The church is a continuation of the Covenant that is inherently missional. The Jews of Israel were the people of God ethnically; the Gentiles in the church are the people of God by adoption. Therefore, Evangelicals must take up the promises and responsibilities of the Covenant.

Diversity

Church is meant to be diverse. Mission goes out to people and draws disparate elements back into the fold of God, expressed as reconciliation.

What diverse elements need to be reconciled? Galatians 3:28 explains, "There is neither Jew nor Gentile, neither slave nor free, nor is there male and female, for you are all one in Christ Jesus" (NIV). The apostle Paul, writer of Galatians, clearly spells out that reconciliation covers race, class, and gender. Paul further carries out his race/class/gender categories of reconciliation in two other Bible epistles. The books of Ephesians and Colossians repeat the need for racial reconciliation, gender reconciliation, and class reconciliation. Reconciliation can be reduced to the second-greatest commandment: love your neighbor. But horizontal reconciliation (love neighbor, as seen in Ephesians 2:11–22) is a reflection of vertical reconciliation (love God, as expressed in Ephesians 2:1–10), the greatest commandment of all.

Evangelicals believe that mission is essentially God reconciling the world to himself (2 Corinthians 5:17–20). God bridged the greatest divide: the holy Lord reached down to reconcile himself with us who were disobedient, and deserving of wrath. If God can bridge that greatest divide and reconcile himself with us, then surely we can bridge lesser divides and reconcile ourselves with other people.

In Acts we have Pentecost, the coming of the Holy Spirit, and the birth of the church. Diversity is seen clearly here, as there are Jews living in every nation. This allows for unity in diversity; the Jews can all understand each others' languages. Faith expands among Jews from Jerusalem, Judea, and Samaria. In Chapter 10 of Acts Peter has a vision of a sheet descending from Heaven carrying unclean animals to eat. The sheet symbolizes that Gentiles now have full access to the gospel and salvation, a thought that flabbergasts Peter. This is immediately followed by a description of Antioch, the first multiethnic church in history, where Gentiles and Jews worshipped together. It is also, not coincidentally, the first time the believers are called Christians.

It is in the nature of Christianity to be multiethnic. The name Christians was originally a nickname for followers of Jesus the Christ—invented in Antioch where the church included believing Jews and Gentiles. God's promises to Israel in the Old Testament were being fulfilled as people from many ethnic backgrounds became part of Israel as the people of God in Christ. They were all children of Abraham, as Paul assured the Galatians. What God had promised Abraham (that all nations on earth would be blessed through him and his people) is being fulfilled through the mandate Jesus gave—to the ends of the earth. In that sense, Christianity has taken up the missionary thrust of Old Testament prophecy in a way that is not so much the case within Judaism, where the mission of Jews in the world is not seen in the same geographical, missionary way.

Diversity is also seen in geography. Why did God choose Israel to be the promised land? Partly, because Israel is where Africa, Asia, and Europe all meet. It is the crossroads of three continents, and the gospel was meant to spread in three directions, which it did. Ethiopia, India, and Greece all received the good news in the first century. Christianity was never meant to be a Western religion (it started out as a Middle Eastern/Semitic religion) and, despite the stereotype, Christianity is not synonymous with Europe. Christianity actually starts in Asia, then went to Africa (Acts 8) before it reached Europe (Acts 16).

Diversity is also seen in the language of Scripture. Why was the New Testament written in koine (common) Greek? It was not the language of the Jews (Hebrew), nor the language that Jesus spoke (Aramaic). It was the *lingua franca* of the Eastern Mediterranean. From the start their language was translated into a foreign tongue allowing them to reach many. Christianity is the only religion in which the Scriptures were not written in the language of its founder.

Diversity is also spoken of with regard to the parts of the body in 1 Corinthians 12:12–31 (and echoed in the book of Romans) where each part of the body/church is indispensable because each brings various kinds of gifts. Gifts not only include ministry roles such as teaching and evangelism but also gifts of the Spirit such as prophesying and speaking in tongues, a language of worship and prayer commonly used by Pentecostal and Charismatic Christians.

Ecumenism

All Christians really ought to be both evangelical and ecumenical. Ecumenism is all those efforts and initiatives at Christian unity by diverse parts of the church. It is an attempt to find unity among diversity.

Cooperative efforts that happen among Evangelicals often are best expressed in missional organizations. Organizations such as OMF (Overseas Missionary Fellowship), LAM (Latin American Mission), AIM (Africa Inland Mission), and SIM (Serving in Mission), campus ministries including Cru (formerly known as Campus Crusade for Christ), InterVarsity Christian Fellowship, and The Navigators, and movements like Lausanne Committee for World Evangelization (LCWE) are cross-denominational, pan-denominational and multidenominational evangelical organizations. Evangelicals cannot be confined to a denomination. Evangelicalism is diverse, and within that diversity we see a truer picture of what it means to be God's Church.

Modern ecumenism began at the famous Edinburgh 1910 World Missionary Conference,[6] considered to be the birthplace of the Modern Ecumenical Movement. Contemporary evangelical ecumenism began in Lausanne. Here some 2,700 Evangelicals were called together by Billy Graham to the 1974 Congress on World Evangelization.[7] Out of this came not only a cooperative worldwide missionary effort among Evangelicals, but the Lausanne Covenant, whose chief architect was British theologian and church leader John Stott. The Lausanne Covenant's main theme is mission. Mission is what unites Evangelicals.

Lausanne has since gone on to host two more worldwide Congresses, one in Manila, Philippines, in 1989, and second in Cape Town, South Africa, in 2010. The last of these three was dubbed by the American publication *Christianity Today* magazine as the most diverse gathering of Christians ever in history.[8]

In John 17, Jesus, in what is known as his High Priestly Prayer, expounds on the topic of unity. Perhaps, then, it should be not so much that missions is the mother of ecumenism (as an old saying goes) but rather that ecumenism is the mother of missions. Jesus clearly states that when the world sees that Christians are united, it is a powerful witness. When it sees that we are not, the world disbelieves the message. In heaven our distinctions are not wiped away but rather there is "a great multitude that no one could count, from every nation, tribe, people and language, standing before the throne and before the Lamb" (Rev. 7:9) in worship of God. Jesus' High

---

6. For the definitive history behind this, see Brian Stanley, *The World Missionary Conference, Edinburgh 1910* (Grand Rapids: Eerdmans, 2009).

7. The collected papers from this Congress can be found in J. D. Douglas, ed., *Let the Earth Hear His Voice: A Comprehensive Reference Volume on World Evangelization* (Minneapolis: World Wide Publications, 1975).

8. John W. Kennedy, "The Most Diverse Gathering Ever," *Christianity Today*, September 29, 2010, http://www.christianitytoday.com/ct/2010/september/34.66.html/.

Priestly Prayer and the ending of the early statement of Christian faith, the Apostles' Creed ("I believe in the Holy Spirit, the holy catholic [universal] Church, the communion of saints, the forgiveness of sins, the resurrection of the body, and life everlasting") demonstrate that Evangelicalism and ecumenism work together. Evangelicalism is unity in diversity, not unity in uniformity.

Holistic Mission

Conversionism (the belief that humans need to be converted) and activism (working to bring about positive change in the world) are two hallmarks of evangelicals. Conversionism and activism point to what comprise mission: evangelism and social justice. Missions call us to be holistic and include both evangelism and social justice, as seen in the life of John Wesley, often dubbed the First Evangelical. Wesley, an eighteenth-century clergyman and theologian, not only preached and evangelized, he also helped the poor. William Wilberforce, the great slavery abolitionist, wrote in his journal that he held "two great objects: the suppression of the Slave Trade and the Reformation of Manners [morals]."[9] This is almost a virtual echo of James 1:27, "Religion that God our Father accepts as pure and faultless is this: to look after orphans and widows in their distress and to keep oneself from being polluted by the world" (NIV).

A group of consuls, explorers and missionaries in East Africa.
Photo: Anti-Slavery International/Panos

An important shift in the twentieth century came at the 1974 Lausanne gathering as Evangelicals sought to recover an emphasis on social justice as an essential element to mission. In John Stott's Lausanne paper "Evangelism and Social Justice: An Evangelical Commitment" he states that "social activity not only follows evangelism as its consequence and aim, and precedes it as its bridge, but also accompanies it as its partner. They are like the two blades of a pair of scissors or the two wings of a bird. This partnership is clearly seen in the public ministry of Jesus, who not only preached the gospel but fed the hungry and healed the sick."[10]

A group of Latin American Evangélicos known as the Fraternidad Teológica Latinoamericana (FTL), made up of leaders such as Emilio Nuñez, Samuel Escobar, and Orlando Costas, coined a phrase called *misión integral,* translated as "holistic mission." One of the FTL's leading spokesmen, René Padilla, made the case for *misión integral* at Lausanne '74 which was a major part of the impetus behind Stott drafting the Lausanne Covenant.

Latin American Evangelicos, however, sometimes still see Stott's definition as too bifurcated. Looking back at the model of Jesus himself, we see that he quotes Isaiah 61 in his famous Nazareth Manifesto in Luke 4; his mission statement to initiate his public ministry. Jesus never preached or evangelized without also healing and/or feeding people.

Holistic mission involves both evangelism and social justice, preaching and helping the poor, spiritual and material realities. The main thrust of mission is discipleship and the Kingdom of God. Matthew's text (specifically, Matt. 28:16–20) on the Great Commission has three verbs: go, teach, and baptize. Discipleship is to follow Jesus continuously. Evangelism and discipleship are like a wedding and a marriage. Evangelism/wedding is the initiating act; discipleship/marriage is the ongoing, day-to-day reality, lived out relationship with the other.

---

9. "The Abolition of Slavery and "The Better Hour" William Wilberforce and the Clapham Group," Wilberforce Central, accessed March 25, 2014, http://www.wilberforcecentral.org/wfc/Wilberforce/.

10. "Evangelism and Social Justice: An Evangelical Commitment," http://www.lausanne.org/en/connect/regions/europe.html?id=79.

Until William Carey, the "Father of Modern Missions," wrote his manifesto "An Enquiry into the Obligations of Christians to Use Means for the Conversion of the Heathens" in 1792, and launched the "Great Century of Missions,"[11] Protestants actually did not think the Great Commission was binding. They thought it was only for the original twelve disciples. From Luther to Carey, Protestants mostly did not care about missionary activity.[12] One of Carey's great contributions (and why he deserves his moniker) is that he rallied Protestants to take the Great Commission seriously as an evangelical responsibility. From Carey's influence, missions became core to the Protestant, and Evangelical, identity.

Carey's other great contribution is the injunction to start missionary societies. He realized Protestants had no vehicle for missionary activity as the Roman Catholics had, through monastic orders such as the Franciscans, Dominicans, and Jesuits. Protestants, in order to effectively do missions, needed the equivalent. Thus arose the Baptist Missionary Society, the London Missionary Society, the Church Missionary Society, and the American Board of Commissioners for Foreign Missions, among others.

Despite all that these societies accomplished, ironically, they have sometimes had the unintended consequence of separating global missional responsibility from local congregational life, causing a professionalization of missionary life rather than furthering the "priesthood of all believers." American missiologist Ralph Winter picked up on this idea of missionary societies and made a distinction between church and denominational missions versus parachurch and missionary societies, advocating for the latter.[13]

Twenty-First-Century Mission

Mission has changed much since Edinburgh 1910, and even since Lausanne 1974. In this century possibly the most significant change is the phenomenon now known as World Christianity.

Andrew Walls, who *Christianity Today* magazine calls "the most important person you don't know,"[14] is the father of the new branch of study of World Christianity broadly defined as the shift of the center of gravity of Christianity to the global South in the last half-century or so. This phenomenon is nothing less than a Copernican shift in Christianity, but has largely been lost on much of the secular media and among Christians.

If more Christians now live in Africa, Asia, and Latin America (the three most prominent Christian heartlands today are sub-Saharan Africa, China, and Brazil) than in North America and Europe, this should drastically change the way we do missions. Reverse mission is becoming an increasing reality. Non-Westerners are increasingly becoming missionaries to the West, the traditional origin point of missionaries going out.

World Christianity returns us to the roots of the Great Commission, which is discipleship. Even with the growing numbers of Christians in the global South, the Western world (the First World) has the majority of well-stocked and staffed seminaries, books, and influence. New and younger churches and schools in the global South are in need of training and education and resources. It is not that Western missionaries should stop going to the global South, but they are increasingly refocusing their efforts on discipleship over evangelism. The challenge is to do this in a spirit of partnership.

This focus away from evangelism does not apply, however, to the church's approach toward the other Westernized continents and nations such as Europe, Australia, and Canada, which are mostly post-Christian and

---

11. Carey's manifesto was dubbed thus by the great Yale church historian Kenneth Scott Latourette in *A History of the Expansion of Christianity* (New York: Harper & Brothers, 1937–45).

12. Count Nicolaus Ludwig von Zinzendorf and the Moravians were the exception.

13. Greg H. Parsons, Ralph D. Winter, *Early Life and Core Missiology* (Pasadena, CA: William Carey International University Press, 2012), 266.

14. Tim Stafford, "Historian Ahead of His Time," *Christianity Today*, February 8, 2007, http://www.christianitytoday.com/ct/2007/february/34.87.html.

highly secular and postmodern. Those places need evangelism but of a different kind than before; this is no longer frontier evangelism (the bringing of the gospel to areas where there is no indigenous church). This is now post-Christian evangelism, to people for whom the good news is no longer news.

The lone exception to the post-Christian/secular Western world is the United States. However, it must be qualified that the main reason the United States is still mostly Christian today is because of a domestic form of World Christianity. Philip Jenkins wrote the definitive book on World Christianity, *The Next Christendom*, in which he describes the shift of the center of gravity of Christianity to the non-Western world.[15] Soong-Chan Rah's *The Next Evangelicalism* applies Jenkins' thesis to the US and notes the shift of Christianity in the U.S. is to the ethnic minorities and immigrants.[16]

Frontier missions is, though, still a priority. If Ralph Winter is correct in redefining the *panta ta ethne* (the nations referred to in Matt. 28:19) as ethno-linguistic groups rather than political nations, evangelism then is still necessary to reach those who have not heard the gospel because of their isolation or adherence to other religions. There are many indigenous groups in Mexico and China, for example, who are not part of the mainstream language and culture, and thus would be sorely in need of missionary work among them, even though these nations are already considered reached or evangelized.

Radio and television made Billy Graham the most heard and watched evangelist in history.
Photo: Billy Graham Evangelistic Association

Andrew Walls in *Mission in the 21st Century*[17] spells out five marks of twenty-first century mission: (1) proclamation, (2) discipleship, (3) social justice on a personal level, (4) social justice on a structural level, and (5) creation care. These five marks are now widely accepted and used by mission agencies as well as denominations.

Challenges and Opportunities

Mission today is a recovery, not a discovery. There are other challenges we face, which may well prove to be opportunities:

1. **Technology changing the way we do missions.** Technology has often been an ally with Christianity. The Roman roads of Jesus' day were the information superhighway that carried the gospel all around the Mediterranean. The printing press allowed the Protestant Reformation to explode. Ships of the colonial era brought missionaries to the far corners of the earth. Radio and television made Billy Graham the most heard and watched evangelist in history. The Internet today connects countless millions. The airplane makes short-term missions possible, greatly multiplying the presence of long-term missionaries. The challenge is for Evangelicals to find ways to utilize growing technologies.

---

15. Philip Jenkins, *The Next Christendom: The Coming of Global Christianity* (Oxford: Oxford University Press, 2002).

16. Soong-Chan Rah, *The Next Evangelicalism: Freeing the Church from Western Cultural Captivity* (Downers Grove: InterVarsity Press, 2009).

17. Andrew Walls and Cathy Ross, eds., *Mission In The 21st Century: Exploring the Five Marks of Global Mission* (Maryknoll, NY: Orbis, 2008).

2. **Missionaries have other vocations.** The era of faith missions, popularized by Hudson Taylor and the China Inland Mission, is no longer the only or primary way missions is done. Tent-making—as practiced by the apostle Paul—is increasingly a pattern. Business-as-mission and microfinance are natural outflows of this type of mission.

3. **Urbanization is changing the world landscape.** In 2008, there were more people living in cities than outside. Eighteen of the world's twenty largest cities are outside North America and Europe. The world's population has risen to 7 billion with projection to 9.6 billion by 2050. Developed nations are rapidly aging while developing nations are becoming younger. The 10/40 Window[18] is not the only thing we must watch: the 4/14 Window (children between the ages of 4 to 14) is the time of life when most people become followers of Jesus Christ.[19]

4. **Ideology is replacing politics.** Islam is the fastest-growing religion in the world. Politics may no longer be the main dividing fence between people.

5. **The Three Self church.** Though this phrase is most often used in reference to registered churches in China, it really is a sign of younger churches coming into maturity, when they can be self-sustaining, self-governing, and self-propagating. A fourth self is now included with this, namely self-theologizing. Without this last point, global South churches could easily just end up parroting their counterparts in the West. When they contextualize Christianity to their own circumstances, that is a sign of maturity.

Christianity is unique among the religions of the world because of its diverse makeup. There is no ethnic majority, a shifting geographic center, and mission is from everyone to everywhere. Mission is at the heart and core of evangelical identity. Without it, Evangelicals would not be who we are.

Bibliography

Bosch, David. *Transforming Mission*. Maryknoll, NY: Orbis, 1991.

Douglas, J. D., ed. *Let the Earth Hear His Voice: A Comprehensive Reference Volume on World Evangelization*. Minneapolis, MN: World Wide Publications, 1975.

Jenkins, Philip. *The Next Christendom: The Coming of Global Christianity*. Oxford: Oxford University Press, 2002.

Latourette, Kenneth Scott. *A History of the Expansion of Christianity*. New York: Harper & Brothers, 1945.

Newbigin, Lesslie. "Mission to Six Continents." *In A History of the Ecumenical Movement*. Edited by Harold E. Fey. Vol. 2. Geneva: World Council of Churches, 1970.

Parsons, Greg H. Ralph D. Winter: *Early life and Core Missiology*. Pasadena: William Carey International University Press, 2012.

Piper, John. *Let the Nations Be Glad! The Supremacy of God in Missions*. Grand Rapids: Baker, 1993.

Rah, Soong-Chan. *The Next Evangelicalism: Freeing the Church from Western Cultural Captivity*. Downers Grove, IL: InterVarsity Press, 2009.

Stanley, Brian. The World Missionary Conference, Edinburgh 1910. Grand Rapids: Eerdmans, 2009.

Tennent, Tim. *Invitation to World Missions: A Trinitarian Missiology for the Twenty-First Century*. Grand Rapids: Kregel, 2010.

Walls, Andrew, and Cathy Ross, eds. *Mission In The 21st Century: Exploring the Five Marks of Global Mission*. Maryknoll, NY: Orbis, 2008.

---

18. A phrase coined by Luis Bush to indicate 10 degrees latitude north to 40 degrees latitude north, the least-evangelized regions on earth.

19. http://4to14window.com/.

Wright, Christopher J. H. *The Mission of God: Unlocking the Bible's Grand Narrative.*
  Downers Grove, IL: InterVarsity Press, 2006.

Dr. Allen Yeh is associate professor of Intercultural Studies and Missiology at Biola University in La Mirada, California. He is the coauthor of *Routes and Radishes and Other Things to Talk About at the Evangelical Crossroads*, and coeditor of *Expect Great Things, Attempt Great Things*: William Carey and Adoniram Judson, Missionary Pioneers.

"The future of global Evangelicalism depends on how Christian leaders today consider children and youth as vital to mission strategy. We should give them opportunity and a voice in mission. Twenty to thirty years from now, their generation will take over after the great mission leaders have come and gone."

—Carmen Menchit Wong, International Child Advocacy Director,
Compassion International, United States

Samuel Escobar
was part of a group
of theologians who
stressed the
importance
of holistic mission.
Photo: Dana L. Robert

PENTECOSTALS: THEIR RISE AND ROLE IN THE EVANGELICAL COMMUNITY

By Allan Heaton Anderson

Pentecostalism's growth during the twentieth century, from humble beginnings on the fringes of Evangelicalism to some half-billion adherents at the end of the century, is an astonishing fact even the most skeptical do not doubt. The experience of the Holy Spirit and belief in world evangelization are hallmarks of Pentecostalism, and Pentecostals believe they are called to be witnesses for Jesus Christ to the farthest reaches of the globe in obedience to Christ's commission. The message is centered exclusively on Christ, with a view of the Bible as the supreme source of authority and an emphasis on conversion as a complete break with the past through personal faith in Christ.

In these ways Pentecostals are thoroughly, even radically, Evangelical. Their contribution to the southward shift of Christianity's geographical center of gravity is a powerful argument against the inevitability of secularization, a European idea based on an age-old experience of and reaction to monopoly by state churches. Outside Europe, religious ideas continue to be strong, and Pentecostalism's growth is convincing evidence of that.

During the second half of the twentieth century the most significant changes in the global demography of Christianity have occurred through the growth of Pentecostalism. It is arguably the fastest growing religious movement in the contemporary world. "Charismatic Christianity . . . is largely responsible for the dramatic shift in the religion's center of gravity," wrote Gambian-born theologian Lamin Sanneh.[1] Religious historian Philip Jenkins has offered a comprehensive account of the shifting locus of world Christianity in the twentieth century, an epochal shift in demography that has been discussed by scholars at least since the 1970s. Jenkins has speculated that Pentecostal and independent churches will soon "represent a far larger segment of global Christianity, and just conceivably a majority," resulting in Pentecostalism being "perhaps the most successful social movement of the past century."[2] Considering this movement—with its origins in a series of revival movements within evangelical groups and missionary networks at the beginning of the twentieth century—began with a tiny number of adherents, this is remarkable.

Historical Connections

Making sense of the bewildering varieties of Pentecostalism is not easy. There are thousands of different Pentecostal denominations, and many of those in the global South are independent of the forms founded in North America and Europe. Complex historical and theological developments led to the emergence of the various global movements that make up contemporary Pentecostal and Charismatic Christianity.

From Pietism to Pentecostalism

In what follows, a genealogy of influence and consecutive historical links in the history of Evangelical Christianity resulting in Pentecostalism is outlined. Seventeenth-century Pietism with its emphasis on personal conversion and piety gave rise to the first Protestant missions and, in particular, to the Moravian movement. Mora-

---

1. Lamin Sanneh, *Disciples of All Nations: Pillars of World Christianity* (New York: Oxford University Press, 2008), 275.

2. Philip Jenkins, *The Next Christendom: The Coming of Global Christianity* (New York: Oxford University Press, 2007), 8–9.

vian missionaries had a profound influence on John Wesley and eighteenth-century Methodism, from which emerged the nineteenth-century Holiness Movement. This in turn influenced the Keswick Conventions and Reformed revivalism, and all this had a decisive role in the emergence of twentieth-century Pentecostalism, as we shall see below. Early Pentecostalism arose within the radical Evangelical and Holiness movements worldwide and was an integral part of those movements. It took several years, however, before Pentecostal denominations were to be created as distinct from the rest of Evangelicalism.

The Holiness Movement and Baptism with the Spirit

In eighteenth century Britain, Anglican cleric and theologian John Wesley founded the Methodist movement. John Wesley's doctrine of entire sanctification and the possibility of spiritual experiences subsequent to conversion was the key factor that produced the nineteenth-century Holiness Movement and its twentieth-century offspring, Pentecostalism. The historical and theological origins of Pentecostalism are to be found in Methodism, probably its most important precursor.

Evangelical Protestantism, especially of the Methodist variety, was the dominant American subculture by the middle of the nineteenth century. It stressed personal liberty and allowed the emotional element of popular religion. It also extended its offer of religious power and autonomy to the dispossessed, African Americans recently freed from slavery, subjugated women, and the poor. Important Methodist figures like American missionary bishop William Taylor were instrumental in spreading revivalist ideas across the globe.

Several early Pentecostal missionaries were once part of Taylor's Methodist Episcopal Church at the beginning of twentieth century, including T. B. Barratt in Europe, Minnie Abrams and Albert Norton in India, Willis and May Louise Hoover in Chile, Samuel and Ardel Mead in Angola and J. M. L. Harrow and John Perkins in Liberia. These and other missionaries had not only been associated with Taylor but were deeply influenced by his focus on the autonomy of indigenous churches. This was to have profound repercussions for the shape of Pentecostalism later.[3]

The Holiness Movement stressed an instantaneous experience of sanctification (holiness) as a second distinctive work of grace. Developments within the Holiness Movement itself, and the influence of other revival movements, resulted in Pentecostalism becoming less Methodist in orientation in the late nineteenth century and the term *Pentecostal* becoming more prominent. The experience of the Holy Spirit was linked with a search for the power of Pentecost, a new development that was to gain momentum and overtake the earlier emphasis on perfection.

Minnie Abrams, an early Pentecostal missionary.
Photo: The Flower Pentecostal Heritage Center

In particular, this change of emphasis was taught by revivalist R. A. Torrey, who wrote "the Baptism with the Holy Spirit" was a definite experience "distinct from and additional to His regenerating work" and "always connected with and primarily for the purpose of testimony and service." Torrey explained that Spirit baptism was "not primarily for the purpose of making us individually holy," and the power received during Spirit baptism varied according to "a wide variety of manifestations of that one Baptism with that one and same Spirit." Although Torrey endorsed the belief that Spirit baptism would be accompanied by manifestations or gifts of the Spirit, he (like many in evangelical revivalist circles), reacted to the new Pentecostal movement and declared "the teaching that speaking with tongues was the inevitable and invariable result of being baptised with the Holy Spirit" was "utterly unscriptural and anti-scriptural."[4]

3. Donald W. Dayton, *Theological Roots of Pentecostalism* (Metuchen, NJ: Scarecrow Press, 1987); Allan H. Anderson, *Spreading Fires: The Missionary Nature of Early Pentecostalism* (Maryknoll, NY: Orbis, 2007), 20–21.

4. R. A. Torrey, *The Holy Spirit: Who He Is and What He Does* (Old Tappan, NJ: Fleming H. Revell, 1927), 112, 117–23.

The tension caused by the differing beliefs concerning the baptism of the Spirit became the major reason for the splits between Evangelical and Pentecostal groups in the early twentieth century. But Torrey's influence on the doctrine of Spirit baptism as being distinct from and subsequent to conversion, which is the central and distinctive theme of Pentecostal doctrine, was considerable. His writings were quoted widely, though selectively, by Pentecostals. By the end of the nineteenth century the idea had grown that there would be a great outpouring of the Spirit throughout the world before the second coming of Christ (and, it was hoped, this would happen at the beginning of the twentieth century), and those upon whom the Spirit had fallen were to prepare for this by offering themselves for missionary service. Mission became the preoccupation of early Pentecostals.[5]

Keswick and the Power for Service to Others

A.J. Gordon was an American Reformed teacher who had an impact on the Keswick Convention.
Photo: Flower Pentecostal Heritage Center

The Keswick Convention's annual gatherings in England from 1875 onward recognized two distinct experiences of the new birth and the fullness of the Spirit, and the gatherings represented another major Evangelical influence on Pentecostalism. Although the fullness of the Spirit was seen at Keswick in terms of holiness or the higher Christian life, Keswick was more affected by Anglican Evangelicals and American Reformed teachers like A. T. Pierson, A. J. Gordon, and A. B. Simpson, and the South African revivalist Andrew Murray Jr.

Murray taught sanctification was a possible but progressive experience. Being filled with the fullness of God, he wrote, was "the highest aim of the Pentecostal blessing" and attainable by the believer who would prepare for it by humility and faith. Although Murray continued to link the fullness of the Spirit with purity and overcoming sin, he added the new Keswick emphasis on power for service to others, what he called "the full blessing of Pentecost."[6] This form of holiness teaching became more acceptable to Reformed people with Calvinist leanings and was an important supporter of the faith missions, especially the China Inland Mission. Increasingly in the Holiness and revivalist movements, the phrase *baptism with the Spirit* was used to indicate the "second blessing."

By the end of the nineteenth century, Spirit baptism in Keswick and elsewhere was no longer understood primarily in terms of holiness but as empowering for mission service. Keswick meetings became international events and featured prominent missionary speakers, emphasizing the need for the higher Christian life in missionary service. Murray, Pierson, and other leaders wrote regular reports to the Christian press on the work of missions. Pierson, as editor of *The Missionary Review of the World*, was one of the most influential mission motivators in the Western world, regarding missions as "the indispensable proof and fruit of all spiritual life."[7]

The Growth of Pentecostalism

Independent Pentecostal churches have proliferated worldwide. Those formed in the first half of the twentieth century and birthed in local revival movements were the thin end of the wedge. They expanded rapidly and formed their own traditions, remaining isolated from mainstream Christianity for decades. Increasingly, complex and diverse networks of new independent churches have mushroomed in recent years, making them possibly the largest grouping within Pentecostalism as a whole. The recent history of Pentecostalism is littered with revival movements causing schisms that have become Pentecostalism's defining feature.

---

5. Dayton, *Theological Roots*, 95–100; D. William Faupel, *The Everlasting Gospel: The Significance of Eschatology in the Development of Pentecostal Thought* (Sheffield, England: Sheffield Academic Press, 1996), 84–87.

6. Andrew Murray, *The Full Blessing of Pentecost: The One Thing Needful* (Fort Washington, PA: Christian Literature Crusade, 1954), 22–27, 95–96.

7. A. T. Pierson, quoted in "A Revival Promised," *Word and Work* 23, no. 8 (August 1901), 237.

Growth in the Global South

Although Pentecostalism had relatively slow beginnings, the global South has seen its remarkable expansion in the last quarter of the twentieth century, an expansion that has altered global religious demographics considerably. In Latin America, Africa, and Asia, many large, urban megachurches have arisen, and much of the rapid growth in Chinese Christianity has come among those who have a Pentecostal orientation. The opening up of what was formerly a closed world after the fall of the iron curtain and the post-1980 reforms in China, rapidly accelerated the expansion of this transnational movement.

Latin America, with more than a century of independence, has its own momentum, and there Pentecostalism has taken a different turn. Large denominations have emerged in Latin America, from the mid-1950s onward, following the first denominations founded by foreigners. African Christianity may be the most Pentecostalized of all the continents, with massive new African denominations and enormous Charismatic movements in older mission churches. China developed its own forms of Christianity without recourse to the outside world. Although we may describe much of this as having been affected by the western Pentecostal missionaries in China in the early twentieth century, applying that nomenclature indiscriminately to Chinese independent churches founded at the same time is inappropriate. India, with its closer ties to the West, has more claim on the title *Pentecostal* for many of its independent churches than China does. But this too must be qualified. The Philippines, with its centuries of majority Catholicism, have presented a somewhat similar situation to that of Latin America, and Filipino leaders have emerged to form new movements that are making a considerable impact on the religious scene.

How Many Pentecostals Are There in the World?

Facts and figures on the growth of any global religious movement are notoriously difficult to come by. The most well-known statisticians of global Christianity, the successors to Christian demographer David Barrett, stated there were 612 million "Pentecostals, Charismatics, Neocharismatics" in the world in 2012, a figure projected to rise to 828 million by 2025.[8] Here, three distinct forms are included. Although not expressly defined, *Pentecostal* in this context probably means "classical Pentecostals"; *Charismatic* means those who practice spiritual gifts in the older Catholic and Protestant denominations, with Catholics forming the great majority; and *Neocharismatic* includes all others, especially the vast number of independent churches—perhaps two-thirds of the total.

Social scientists and others group all these movements under the generic title *Pentecostalism*, based on perceived evidence but with little regard to theological and historical differences. This figure was placed at only 67 million in 1970,[9] and the tenfold increase since then has curiously coincided with Europe's secularization zenith. Pentecostalism in North America made steady progress over the course of the twentieth century, but classical Pentecostalism, while influential, is not as numerically significant as is sometimes claimed. A survey conducted by the Pew Forum on Religion and Public Life in 2007 on religious affiliation in the United States found that Pentecostals were 4 percent of the total population. This constituted part of the 26 percent classified as "Evangelical Protestant Churches," compared to the 18 percent called "Mainline Protestant Churches," and 24 percent "Catholic." Of course, this 4 percent refers only to classical Pentecostal denominations.[10]

---

8. Todd M. Johnson, David B. Barrett, and Peter F. Crossing, "Christianity 2012: The 200th Anniversary of American Foreign Missions," *International Bulletin of Missionary Research* 36, no. 1 (January 2012): 28.

9. Ibid.

10. "Affiliations," Pew Research Religion & Public Life Project, accessed June 7, 2013, http://religions.pewforum.org/affiliations.

Europe is very different, retaining significant remnants of state churches: Catholic, Orthodox, Protestant, and Anglican. Although Pentecostals have made modest increases, they remain a very small minority, less than 2 percent of the overall population in all European countries except Portugal, where Pentecostalism has been influenced by the vibrant Brazilian variety. Pentecostals are more significant as a proportion of the European church-going population. British sociologist David Martin, who has taken issue with the common secularization theories in explaining the exceptionalism of Europe, has suggested Pentecostalism is less likely to succeed in the developed world because it "represents the mobilization of a minority of people at the varied margins of that world, whereas in the developing world it represents the mobilization of large masses."[11]

Reasons for the Growth of Pentecostalism in the Majority World

When considering the role of Pentecostalism within Evangelicalism today, it is important to keep in mind that over three-quarters of Pentecostalism's adherents live in the Majority World (continents of the south and east). There are indeed many reasons for the emergence and growth of Pentecostalism in the Majority World. Pentecostalism is an ends-of-the-earth form of Christian mission, with a transnational orientation based on personal enterprise, the ubiquitous voluntarism of its membership, and the constant multiplication of multicentered, variegated organizations whose primary purpose is to evangelize and spread their influence worldwide.

These constant efforts to expand and proselytize are underpinned by a firm belief in the Bible as an independent source of authority—one that resonates with local customs and relates better to a spiritual and holistic worldview—and by theological convictions based on a common experience of the Spirit that empowers believers' mission to the world. The personal conversion of individuals is the goal of these efforts. To their credit, the Pentecostal missionaries, themselves largely untrained and uneducated, practiced indigenous church principles. They quickly found and trained thousands of local leaders, and the swift transfer to local leadership was unprecedented in the history of Christianity. Pentecostal churches became indigenous and three-self (i.e., self-governing, self-supporting, and self-propagating) before the established missions from older churches and mission agencies had even begun the process.

Why Pentecostalism Appeals, Then and Now

Contemporary Pentecostalism is the product of a long process of development, with precedents going back to a much earlier time. Its mission was to liberate very ordinary people from colonial and ecclesiastical hegemony and to free women from male patriarchy. It encouraged free enterprise in a global religious market. The revival movements worldwide challenged Western hegemony and created a multitude of new indigenous churches, a type of Christianity in the local idiom that included emphases on power to overcome an evil spirit world and manifestations of the miraculous.

Pentecostalism addressed allegations of both the foreignness and the irrelevance of Christianity in pluralistic societies. With its emphasis on the priesthood of all true believers, Pentecostalism broke down barriers of race, gender, and class, and it challenged the exclusive preserves of ordained male, foreign clergy. Of course, this development included multiple schisms that, while increasing division and creating a new form of religious charlatan, also proliferated local leadership and encouraged multiplication.

Pentecostalism has a remarkable ability to adapt itself to different cultures and societies and to give contextualized expressions to Christianity. These are expressed in its energetic and energizing worship and liturgies, in its music and dance, in its prayer with the free use of the emotions, and in its communities of concerned and committed believers. Pentecostals are also becoming more socially aware and active in efforts to relieve the poverty and disease around them. Pentecostalism can transpose itself into local cultures and religions so

11. David Martin, *Pentecostalism: The World Their Parish* (Oxford: Blackwell, 2002), 67–70.

effortlessly because of its primary emphases on the experience of the Spirit and the spiritual calling of leaders who do not have to be formally educated in church belief and practice. In particular, the ministry of healing and the claims of the miraculous have assisted Pentecostalism in its appeal to a world where such supernatural events are taken for granted.

The ability of Pentecostalism to adapt to and fulfill people's religious aspirations continues to be its strength. A belief in a divine encounter and the involvement or breaking through of the sacred into the mundane—including healing from sickness, deliverance from hostile evil forces, and perhaps, above all, a heady and spontaneous spirituality that refuses to separate *spiritual* from *physical* or *sacred* from *secular*—are all important factors in Pentecostalism's growth.

Pentecostalism has been able to tap into ancient religious traditions with one eye on the changing world of modernity. The widespread use of mass media, the setting up of new networks that often incorporate the word *international* into their titles, the frequent conferences with international speakers that reinforce transnationalism, and the growth of churches that provide total environments for members are all features of a new multidimensional Pentecostalism.

This combination of the old with the new has enabled Pentecostalism to attract people who relate to both worlds. With its offer of the power of the Spirit to all—regardless of education, language, race, class, or gender—Pentecostalism has been a movement on a mission to subvert convention. It has not been so dependent on Western specialists and trained clergy or on the transmission of Western forms of Christian liturgy and leadership. In fact, Pentecostalism in its earliest forms broke down the dichotomy between clergy and laity that was the legacy of older churches.

Present Prospects

It is no accident the southward shift in Christianity's geographic center of gravity over the course of the twentieth century has coincided with the emergence and expansion of Pentecostalism. Worldwide, the number of Christians has doubled in forty years, from 1.1 billion in 1970 to 2.2 billion in 2010. It was estimated that in Africa in 1985 Christians exceeded Muslims for the first time, and Christians are now almost the majority. This is a phenomenon so epoch-making that Lamin Sanneh described it as "a continental shift of historic proportions."[12]

There are now over four times as many Christians in Africa as there were in 1970 and almost the same is true in Asia, while the Christian population of Latin America over this period has almost doubled. Of course, some of this has to do with differentials in population growth, but it remains true that much of the global growth of Christianity has occurred through conversion in the global South, where the influence of Pentecostalism is strongest. In contrast, the Christian population of Europe during the same period has increased by only about a quarter, and that of North America by about a third. The decrease in the percentage of world Christianity in the global North is likely to continue.[13]

The rise of the Charismatic Movement in the Western world certainly made Pentecostal ideas and practices more acceptable to traditional forms of Christianity. But this might also be seen as one result of the privatization of religion beginning in the 1960s, when the established churches no longer held monopoly and authority over all things sacred. It could be argued that Charismatic Christianity provided a panacea for the spiritual deficit in organized religion and in Western society as a whole. Or, as American theologian Harvey Cox put it, not only were people disillusioned with traditional religions in the 1960s, but they were also disappointed by "the bright promises of science and progress." Cox opined that the "kernel of truth" in the "overblown claims" of the "death

12. Sanneh, *Disciples of All Nations*, 274–75.

13. Douglas Jacobsen, *The World's Christians: Who they are, Where they are, and How they got there* (Hoboken, NJ: Wiley-Blackwell, 2011), 373; Jenkins, *New Faces of Christianity*, 188.

of God" theologians was that "the abstract deity of western theologies and philosophical systems had come to the end of its run."[14] For Cox, the dramatic growth of Pentecostalism seemed to confirm rather than contradict what he had written about the "death of God" in *The Secular City* three decades earlier, but it had provided an unanticipated and unwanted solution.

After the 1980s, the Pentecostalization of older churches outside the Western world, especially in Africa and Asia, accelerated as those churches adjusted to the rapid growth of new Pentecostal churches in their midst. They began to adopt their methods, which appealed to the young and urbanized in particular. Simultaneously, the new form of Pentecostalism exhibited a fierce independence that eschewed denominations and preferred associations in loose fellowships. This gave rise to the megachurches that operate in cities like Lagos, Rio de Janeiro, Seoul, and Singapore, and also in unexpected European places like Kyiv (a Ukrainian church with a Nigerian leader), Budapest, London, and Uppsala. Each of these European examples is the largest congregation in its respective country. The megachurches form networks of similar churches across the world, and these transnational associations are not only North–South but also South–South and East–South. In most cases, the transnational churches in the North have been unable to break free from their ethnic minority character.

Contemporary Pentecostalism is very much the result of the process of globalization, and health and wealth advocates are as much at home in Lagos and Rio as they are in Tulsa or Fort Worth. In many cases, the only ones who get rich in poverty-ravaged countries are the preachers.

The mass media, beginning with the use of periodicals and newsletters, followed by a ready acceptance of new technologies—first radio, then television, and now the Internet—tourism and pilgrimages to megachurches, and an international economy, have combined to create conditions conducive to the spread of a globally friendly religion like Pentecostalism. Some of the networks of churches have begun to take on the appearance of new denominations. Some have passed to a second generation of leadership whose organizational ideas are quite different from those of their founders. Some of the new churches leave much to be desired, especially those with wealthy leaders whose questionable and exploitative practices continue to be debated in public forums.

The adaptability of Pentecostalism to a culture is more easily achieved in those parts of the world where a spiritual universe exists, and healing and the supernatural are regarded as normal experiences. Pentecostalism also grows where a pluralistic religious environment is the norm. The Christian world has become more interconnected than ever before, and increasingly Pentecostals are conversing with other Christians, who are bringing them out of their largely self-imposed isolation. Whether this will result in more unity or more division and diversity is anyone's guess. It is certain that the continuous change and transformation in world Christianity will continue. But Pentecostalism in the Majority World, as Philip Jenkins has observed about Christianity in the global South, does not represent a global religion with roots in the North but a new type of Christianity altogether.[15]

The emphasis on a personal, heartfelt experience of God through the Spirit is offered to all people without preconditions, enabling them to be powerful and assertive in societies where they have been marginalized. They are offered solutions to all varieties of their felt needs. This will continue to draw people in the Majority World to Pentecostal churches. When yours is an all-encompassing, omnipotent, and personal God who enters into a personal relationship with individual believers, everything becomes a matter for potential prayer. The born-again experience focusing on a radical break with the past attracts young people disenchanted with the traditional ways of their parents.

Pentecostalism's constant evangelism, offering healing and deliverance, draws large crowds. Its organized system of following up on contacts means that more unchurched people are reached with this message and joined to Pentecostal communities. Pentecostalism's cultural flexibility in its experiential and participatory liturgy, offering a place to feel

---

14. Harvey Cox, *Fire from Heaven: The Rise of Pentecostal Spirituality and the Reshaping of Religion in the Twenty-First Century* (Cambridge, MA: Da Capo Press, 2001), xvi, 83, 104.

15. Jenkins, *The Next Christendom*, 254.

at home, a measure of religious continuity with the past spirit world, and (at least to some observers) the appearance of an egalitarian community that is meeting the felt needs of ordinary people—all combine to provide an overarching explanation for the universal appeal of Pentecostalism and the transformation of Christianity in the Majority World.[16]

Bibliography

Anderson, Allan H. *Spreading Fires: The Missionary Nature of Early Pentecostalism*. Maryknoll, NY: Orbis, 2007.

———. *To the Ends of the Earth: Pentecostalism and the Transformation of World Christianity*. Oxford: Oxford University Press, 2013.

Cox, Harvey. *Fire from Heaven: The Rise of Pentecostal Spirituality and the Reshaping of Religion in the Twenty-First Century*. Cambridge, MA: Da Capo Press, 2001.

Dayton, Donald W. *Theological Roots of Pentecostalism*. Metuchen, NJ: Scarecrow Press, 1987.

Faupel, D. William. *The Everlasting Gospel*. Sheffield, UK: Sheffield Academic Press, 1996.

Jacobsen, Douglas, *The World's Christians: Who they are, Where they are, and How they got there*. Hoboken, NJ: Wiley-Blackwell, 2011.

Jenkins, Philip. *The Next Christendom: The Coming of Global Christianity*. New York: Oxford University Press, 2007.

Johnson, Todd M., David B. Barrett, and Peter F. Crossing. "Christianity 2012: The 200th Anniversary of American Foreign Missions." *International Bulletin of Missionary Research* 36, no. 1 (January 2012): 28.

Martin, David. *Pentecostalism: The World Their Parish*. Oxford: Blackwell, 2002.

Miller, Donald E., and Tetsunao Yamamori. *Global Pentecostalism: The New Face of Christian Social Engagement*. Oakland, CA: University of California press, 2007.

Murray, Andrew. *The Full Blessing of Pentecost*. Fort Washington, PA: Christian Literature Crusade, 1954.

Pew Research Religion & Public Life Project. "Affiliations." Accessed June 7, 2013, http://religions.pewforum.org/affiliations.

Pierson, A. T. "A Revival Promised." *Word and Work* 23, no. 8 (August 1901).

Sanneh, Lamin. *Disciples of All Nations: Pillars of World Christianity*. New York: Oxford University Press, 2008.

Torrey, R. A. *The Holy Spirit: Who He Is and What He Does*. Old Tappan, NJ: Revell, 1927.

Dr. Allan Heaton Anderson is a professor of Mission and Pentecostal studies in the Department of Theology and Religion at the University of Birmingham, United Kingdom.

"Evangelicals bring to the world the message of the 'good news' that God was 'in Christ reconciling the world to himself.' In the life, death, and resurrection of Jesus Christ, God is at work healing the brokenness, hurts and sinfulness of the world. Evangelicals, called to be ambassadors of Christ, tell of this good news, seeking by God's grace to live as exemplars of this faith, as communities of believers who love God, and who imperfectly but genuinely reflect God's love and grace to others. We are inspired by the hope that God's gracious rule, already begun, will be fulfilled when Christ returns to create a new heaven and a new earth."

—Leighton Ford, Leighton Ford Ministries, Lifetime Honorary Chair of Lausanne Movement, United States

---

16. Donald E. Miller and Tetsunao Yamamori, *Global Pentecostalism: The New Face of Christian Social Engagement* (Oakland, CA: University of California Press, 2007), 221; Allan H. Anderson, *To the Ends of the Earth: Pentecostalism and the Transformation of World Christianity* (Oxford: Oxford University Press, 2013), 247–257.

EVANGELICALS AND EVANGELISM

By Frances S. Adeney

Evangelism, the process of bearing the good news of new life in Jesus Christ to others, has been described and evaluated since Philip was first named an evangelist in Acts 21:8. For contemporary Evangelicals, the Lausanne Covenant of 1974 defines *evangelism* this way: "Evangelism itself is the proclamation of the historical, biblical Christ as Savior and Lord, with a view to persuading people to come to him personally and so be reconciled to God."[1] This definition, in combination with the rest of the Lausanne Covenant, stresses the offer of forgiveness of sins through Jesus Christ and the promise of the gift of the Holy Spirit. It also includes the forthright telling of the cost of discipleship and the results of evangelism, including obedience to Christ, incorporation into his church, and responsible service in the world.

The Early Church Onward

Since the time of the early church, Christians have practiced evangelism in numerous ways. Jesus reached out to the outcasts, graciously listening to and healing those who came to him. Paul explained and propagated that gospel of grace, preaching and training leaders of the new church to do likewise. The early church fathers institutionalized the good news of the gospel, and monastic communities demonstrated God's love through their community and spirituality. Although much was lost over the ages, many Christian values became part of European mores in the ensuing centuries. In the sixteenth century Protestant Reformers rediscovered the gospel of redemption through faith alone, *sola fides*. Individuals could approach God in faith and find salvation, reviving outreach as a vital part of evangelism.

Messengers of the gospel brought Christianity to many countries during the seventeenth and eighteenth centuries as European colonial expansion grew. Christians sometimes cooperated with economic interests, giving evangelism some troubling associations that later became part of postcolonial critiques. But communities felt God's power moving through them, and many turned to Christ.

The nineteenth-century missionary movement saw Protestant Christians from all sectors of the church sending missionaries from the United States and England to all parts of the world. Whether Presbyterian, Methodist, Lutheran, Anglican, Baptist, Nazarene, or another denomination, Christians agreed that the word of salvation through Jesus Christ must reach the world. Evangelism was at the core of this missionary movement, and churches soon grew in many parts of the world.

A Movement Divided

Evangelism became a divisive issue in the early twentieth century. The fundamentalist/modernist debate created a dividing line between the Christians who separated those who saw proclamation at the heart of evangelism and the Christians who put social service and justice at the center of missionary activity. The fundamentals stressed the centrality of Jesus Christ, the importance of individual salvation, the primacy of the Bible, and the eschatological view, which held that Christ would soon return. These central tenets of the Christian faith called for a vigorous evangelism that combined preaching with a call to commitment.

---

1. "The Lausanne Covenant," The Lausanne Movement, accessed January 11, 2014, http://www.lausanne.org/en/documents/lausanne-covenant.html/.

Although the fundamentals remained strong among Evangelistic efforts of churches in many parts of the world, that separation of approaches to evangelism took root in the United States. The Lausanne Covenant of 1974, an international declaration by church leaders from around the world, challenged the division, putting social justice alongside of proclamation. Latin American theologians René Padilla, Orlando Escobar, and Samuel Escobar stressed the importance of economic justice as a part of Christian outreach. Protestant leaders Billy Graham and Tony Campolo tied evangelism to social issues, even as they focused on individual commitment to Christ. Material and spiritual blessings both became important parts of Evangelistic preaching in the prosperity gospel among African Americans. The Lausanne Movement followed up with conferences on evangelism, stressing the holistic nature of Christ's call to follow him.

In the latter half of the twentieth century, changes in the global church also brought proclamation and justice emphases in evangelism closer together. Growth of Pentecostal and Charismatic churches in South America brought an emphasis on the importance of faith for everyday life. Independent African churches saw phenomenal growth as poor people across that continent encountered Christianity. Churches in South Korea began to send missionaries to other parts of Asia. The shift of the church to the global South brought attention to the needs for social goods (such as education and social services) and social justice (such as human rights and just political systems) as part of the good news of the gospel.

The Unique Role of Women

During the nineteenth and much of the twentieth centuries, more than half of the missionary force was made up of women. Across the world women worked together for the good of women, whether rich or poor. Catherine Booth taught wealthy women in London to care for the wretched poor as part of their missionary efforts. Lottie Moon trained Bible Women in China[2] to carry the gospel to towns and villages. Women's missionary societies in Baptist and Methodist denominations in the West sent funds and missionaries to work with the poor in Africa, Asia, and Latin America. Christian women in Indonesia formed a national theologians conference. A movement of Women's Work for Women[3] brought issues of housing and health care for women to the attention of churches in the United States. Women practiced theologies that broke down the dividing wall between proclamation and social service.

Women such as Catherine Booth played an essential role in the Salvation Army.
Photo used with permission The Salvation Army Archives, Canada and Bermuda Territory

Diversity among Evangelicals

Today the diversity among Evangelicals is greater than ever all around the world. Responses to postcolonial critiques of Christian mission and evangelism vary as Christians evaluate good and ill effects of the global missionary activities of the previous two centuries. Self-identified Evangelicals attend churches across the theological spectrum. Methodist, Episcopalian, Lutheran, and Presbyterian denominations all include evangelical congregations. Baptist, Nazarene, African Methodist Episcopal, and Mennonite congregations may also consider themselves evangelical. Many Charismatic churches, Friends meetings, and African American congregations, as well as independent congregations, in the United States include themselves under the evangelical umbrella.

2. Regina D. Sullivan, *Lottie Moon: A Southern Baptist Missionary to China in History and Legend* (Baton Rouge, LA: Louisiana University Press, 2011), 51.

3. Dana Robert, *American Women in Mission: A Social History of Their Thought and Practice* (Macon, GA: Mercer University Press, 1997), 130.

Theologies of evangelism among Evangelicals range from fundamentalist understandings of proclamation geared to conversion as the only way to God, to ministries that include stating the gospel along with caring for a person's physical well-being and working toward structural change in society. Spirituality as a major component of a theology of evangelism takes a central place in renewing practices of evangelism for some. For others, a welcoming community marks the center of evangelism.

Defining *evangelism* as "an initiation into the kingdom of God" makes room for diverse methods under a single, broad theology of evangelism. A needs-based approach to evangelism, an emphasis on preaching, or a focus on multiplying the church can each fit under that rubric. Creative ministries and emerging churches spread the gospel through art fairs, Internet sites, sports events, and coffee hours. The McDonald's Church in Manila, Philippines, meets at McDonald's restaurants, providing breakfast for all comers. The Sweaty Sheep ministry in Louisville, Kentucky, holds worship services after triathalons and foot races. The Arbor ministry in Oregon sponsors website meetings along with community worship. The Riverside Church in New York City offers jackets and ties to homeless men who want to participate in Sunday services. New College Berkeley in Berkeley, California, offers low-cost courses for people who want to develop their understanding of Christianity. Jonah House in Baltimore, Maryland, focuses on political critique. Food pantries and shelters across run by churches in multiple countries provide services to the poor along with the good news of salvation.

What Evangelicals Hold in Common about Evangelism

Although the ministries just described each have a particular nuance to their theology of evangelism, many commonalities on evangelism exist among Evangelicals. Contemporary Evangelical theologies of evangelism often stress a trinitarian foundation. God is the source and reason for evangelism. Evangelism is God's work, which humans carry out. The Christological emphasis in evangelical views of evangelism is very strong. Jesus, the God-man, incarnated, crucified for the sins of the world, and resurrected is the core evangelistic focus among Evangelicals. The work of the Holy Spirit is another emphasis that predominates. It is the Holy Spirit that convicts persons of their sinfulness and draws them to the mercy and grace of God expressed in the gospel.

Most Evangelicals agree that the church exists by mission both as God's people and as a manifestation of God's work in the world, a sign of the kingdom. The universality of the gospel is another feature of evangelical theologies of evangelism. The gospel is for all people; everyone is invited into the family of God through Christ. The imminent return of Christ is also stressed, giving urgency to the task of spreading the gospel.

Finally, a conversion model prevails. People can choose to answer Christ's call on their lives or they can turn away from God's grace offered through Jesus Christ. Respecting that freedom to choose means that methods of evangelizing must honor people not manipulate them.

Current theologies and strategies can be evaluated from the commonalities among evangelical theologies of Evangelism. Evangelistic preaching in the congregation and deepening spiritual practices can become central methods of evangelism. Cross-cultural sensitivity can increase as congregations recognize that God goes before them, doing the work of evangelism and strengthening people for the task of expressing God's mercy in the gospel. The church then becomes a faithful witness to God's reign in its setting.

Different Contexts, Different Evangelical Approaches

Despite these general common features, there are a number of differences among evangelical theologies and ministries of evangelism. While many methods of evangelism are biblical, they are suited to different contexts and theological emphases. Evangelicals believe it is the context that determines the most appropriate approach to use for evangelism in a given setting.

The contexts for evangelism in our global and connected world vary widely. Many places in Africa receive the gospel with joy. In Asia, by contrast, it is often difficult to establish a Christian presence. In North America and Europe, Christian scholars note that Evangelicals live in a post-Christian society; in this context, churches need to become communities that evangelize, reaching out to those all around them who do not know Christ.

Popular rock band, the Newsboys, perform at a Festival of Hope outreach event in 2014.
Photo: Billy Graham Evangelistic Association of Canada

Some churches and ministries of evangelism focus on the verbal message. Calling people to repentance and salvation through preaching, vacation Bible school, literature distribution, and revival meetings predominates in these ministries. The theology behind this approach lies in the Great Commission of Matthew 28:18–20: "And Jesus came and said to them, 'All authority in heaven and on earth has been given to me. Go therefore and make disciples of all nations, baptizing them in the name of the Father and of the Son and of the Holy Spirit, and teaching them to obey everything that I have commanded you. And remember, I am with you always, to the end of the age'" (NRSV). This approach focuses on discipleship and eternal salvation as the most important features of the gospel.

Church planting, another evangelism strategy used by Evangelicals, has similar goals. Multiplying the church by establishing congregations of worshippers and spreading the gospel among unreached peoples strives toward the goal of all people having the opportunity to accept the gospel. A love for the world and an eschatological theology, which asserts that Christ will unexpectedly return, lends urgency to this approach. To the Thessalonians Paul wrote, "For the Lord himself will come down from heaven, with a loud command, with the voice of the archangel and with the trumpet call of God, and the dead in Christ will rise first. After that, we who are still alive and are left will be caught up together with them in the clouds to meet the Lord in the air. And so we will be with the Lord forever" (1 Thess. 4:16–17 NIV). Anticipating their question as to when this would happen, he added, "Now, brothers and sisters, about times and dates we do not need to write to you, for you know very well that the day of the Lord will come like a thief in the night" (1 Thess. 5:1–2 NIV).

The witness of the Holy Spirit provides another focus for evangelism among some Evangelicals. The Holy Spirit draws one to Christ. Preaching about the Holy Spirit and waiting for the action of the Holy Spirit becomes central to evangelism. Coming forward to publicly declare one's intent to follow Jesus—the call to conversion and commitment—changes the direction of one's life. Accounts of receiving the Holy Spirit in the Acts of the Apostles are numerous, providing a powerful biblical base for the importance of the Holy Spirit in the work of evangelism. Peter assured the Pentecost crowds that when they were baptized in the name of Jesus, they would receive forgiveness of their sins and "the gift of the Holy Spirit," a "promise" for all who were called by God (Acts 2:38–39).

A needs-based approach offers much to Evangelicals working in poverty-stricken areas of the world. People who are hungry or sick need care before they can appropriate a verbal message into their view of life. A theology of service and compassion to others underlies this method. Jesus as a model for living demonstrates needs-based evangelism. When Jesus encountered people seeking healing, he healed them. When people sought spiritual knowledge, he taught them. As he sent out the seventy-two ahead of him, he instructed them to heal the sick and to tell them the kingdom of God was near (Luke 10:9).

Daily Christian living provides another model of evangelism that brings hope to others. Paul's letter to the Philippians reminded Christians that "it is God who is at work in you, enabling you both to will and to work for his good pleasure" (Phil. 2:13 NRSV). The result? They would "shine like stars in the world," despite being "in the midst of a . . . perverse generation" (Phil. 2:15 NRSV).

Approaching others in friendship and care also leads to opportunities to share the story of the good news of salvation in Christ. "Always be ready to make your defense to anyone who demands from you an accounting for the hope that is in you; yet do it with gentleness and reverence" (1 Peter 3:15–16 NRSV). Through sharing the gift of the gospel in this way, gifts are also received by Christians. The hospitality of friendship enriches all.

Relieving oppression can be another form of evangelism. By showing Christian concern for the freedom and well-being of others, Christians demonstrate God's concern for justice. At the beginning of his public ministry, Jesus announced,

> **The Spirit of the Lord is upon me,**
> **because he has anointed me to bring good news to the poor.**
> **He has sent me to proclaim release to the captives**
> **and recovery of sight to the blind, to let the oppressed go free,**
> **to proclaim the year of the Lord's favor (Luke 4:18–19 NRSV).**

Lastly, an evangelism based on community practices highlights the church as a welcoming society that exhibits love and worship for Christ. The church itself witnesses to God's love and redemptive power. Jesus sent his disciples into the world with the prayer, "As you have sent me into the world, so I have sent them into the world. . . . that the world may believe that you have sent me" (John 17:18–21 NRSV). The countercultural message of the cross leads to an embodied witness to God's reign as others see the sacrificial service of Christian communities. Some congregations look to the example of Saint Patrick and the Celtic way of evangelism that places community at the heart of witness. Mennonites, for example, stress the witness of the community as an Evangelistic outreach. Many churches combine that community emphasis with an accent on liberation themes as part of evangelism.

The biblical models of the Great Commission, the work of the Holy Spirit, the meeting of needs, the relieving of oppression, the focus on daily Christian living, and the witness of the church are practiced in different ways by Evangelicals around the world. The setting itself and the emphasis on a biblical model of evangelism combine to provide a vast array of evangelical theologies and approaches to evangelism in the many different contexts that exist in this world.

Contemporary Holistic Approach

A holistic approach is more and more the norm in Evangelistic efforts around the world. During the Consultation on the Church in Response to Human Need meeting held in Wheaton, Illinois, in 1983, the World Evangelical Fellowship (WEF) affirmed that evangelism cannot be separated from serving the needs of people.[4] Cross-cultural understanding is foundational to this approach. Listening to others, cooperating with existing programs, and voicing the concerns of local people become strong components in holistic evangelism.

Receiving from others finds a place alongside bringing the good news to them. Preaching the good news of salvation works hand in hand with demonstrations of Christ's compassion and respect for the integrity of all people. Rather than focus on the distinctions between proclamation and social concerns, such approaches often emphasize the kingdom of God, continuing Jesus' mission to announce the good news of the release of captives, the restoration of sight to the blind, and the proclamation of the year of the Lord (Luke 4:18–19). A holistic approach can also include a focus on structural reform and liberation.

Evangelicals entering the political realm and working for the social good have increased around the world since the 1970s, providing another form of Christian witness. Some universities in Indonesia, for example, offer graduate programs that train Christian leaders to engage in political leadership. Emerging churches utilize the

---

4. "Transformation: The Church in Responses to Human Need," The Lausanne Movement, accessed January 11, 2014, http://www.lausanne.org/en/documents/allconsultation-statements/423-transformation-the-church-in-response-to-human-need.html/.

common interests of people who come together for worship, meeting people where they are by using the Internet and cafés and other places for their gatherings. Finally, a holistic approach includes a focus on spirituality, bringing individual and communal prayer to bear on community and personal witness.

Evangelism lies at the heart of Evangelical identity around the world. Current changes in context and approach may require more study and expansion of descriptions of evangelism by Evangelicals. Structural, liberation, and spirituality components may need to be considered in new ways. It will be fascinating to see how Evangelicals address these issues in global contexts, revising definitions without compromising the evangelical call to biblical faithfulness.

Suggested Reading

Adeney, Frances S. *Graceful Evangelism: Christian Witness in a Complex World*. Grand Rapids: Baker, 2010.

Guder, Darrell L., ed. *Missional Church: A Vision for the Sending of the Church in North America*. Grand Rapids: Eerdmans, 1988.

Haney, Marsha Snulligan. *Evangelism among African American Presbyterians: Making Plain the Sacred Journey*. Lanham, MD: University Press of America, 2007.

Heath, Elaine A. *The Mystic Way of Evangelism: A Contemplative Vision for Christian Outreach*. Grand Rapids: Baker, 2008.

Hunter, George G., III. *The Celtic Way of Evangelism: How Christianity Can Reach the West—Again*. Rev. exp. ed. Nashville: Abingdon, 2010.

"The Lausanne Covenant." The Lausanne Movement. Accessed January 11, 2014. http://www.lausanne.org/en/documents/lausanne-covenant.html/.

"Transformation: The Church in Responses to Human Need." The Lausanne Movement. Accessed January 11, 2014. http://www.lausanne.org/en/documents/allconsultation-statements/423-transformation-the-church-in-response-to human-need.html/.

Muck, Terry, and Frances Adeney. *Christianity Encountering World Religions: The Practice of Mission in the Twenty-first Century*. Grand Rapids: Baker, 2009.

Robert, Dana L. *American Women in Mission: A Social History of Their Thought and Practice*. Mercer, GA: Mercer University Press, 1997.

Stone, Bryan P. *Evangelism after Christendom: The Theology and Practice of Christian Witness*. Grand Rapids: Brazos, 2007.

Sullivan, Regina D. *Lottie Moon: A Southern Baptist Missionary to China in History and Legend,* Louisiana University Press, 2011.

Dr. Frances S. Adeney is the William A. Benfield Jr. Professor of Evangelism and Global Mission at Louisville Presbyterian Theological Seminary in Kentucky. She is currently working on a book about women and Christian mission.

"God has placed within the global Church all that is required to finish the task of world Evangelization. To make this happen, denominational leaders and local church pastors are crucial. However, the challenges include insufficient visionary leaders who are committed to the task and are willing to make sacrifice."

—Amos Aderonmu, Immediate Past International Director, Calvary Ministries (CAPRO), Nigeria

EVANGELICALS AND PRAYER

By Molly Wall

What image comes to your mind at the mention of prayer? A small child kneeling, hands folded, uttering a bedtime prayer to God? The early morning call of the local muezzin beckoning the devoted, "Come to prayer"? Or clusters of orthodox Jewish men, cloaked in white prayer shawls, offering prayers before Jerusalem's Western Wall? One thing is clear: we are all familiar with this idea of prayer, regardless of our background or religious tradition. Followers from most all the world's religious groups, and even the nominally religious or agnostic, engage in some form of prayer.

What about prayer for evangelical Christians? What are the forms, practices, and expressions of prayer within this body of adherents currently dwelling within thousands of cultures and in every country of the world? Why do Evangelicals pray? How are twenty-first-century realities affecting Evangelicals in their practice of prayer worldwide? Recent decades have brought a flourish of evangelical prayer activity—prayer movements, ministries, gatherings, resources—each uniting and spurring Evangelicals on toward focused, impassioned prayer in unprecedented numbers.

Creativity of Expression

Evangelicals pray as individuals, retreating or secluding themselves for prayer; but they also participate in times of corporate prayer, whether with one or two others, a local congregation, or mass gatherings. Some pray in total silence, even while in groups, such as at the Taizé Community in France. Others cry out to God, either in continuous songs of praise, such as at the International House of Prayer in Kansas City, Missouri, or with weeping and intense pleading, such as on the prayer mountains of Korea.

Photo: www.designpics.com

Prayers can be scripted, either reciting from Scriptures like the Lord's Prayer or the Psalms, or they can come from other texts across the centuries like the Anglican *Book of Common Prayer*. But prayers need not be patterned or prepared, and Evangelicals are free to pray directly to God—without the mediation of a priest or leader and regardless of their training or background—and to speak directly to God from whatever state, from gratitude to grief, they find themselves.

One person may lead a prayer, speaking aloud with others agreeing along, a common practice of European traditional churches. Alternately, and most famously in Korea, each individual may cry out loudly in prayer, simultaneously within a group. Different times of day can be devoted to prayer, such as in the early mornings or as part of bedtime routines, before each meal, or as a set rhythm of five or more formal times throughout the day. Some evangelical groups or communities meet once daily for prayer or hold weekly prayer meetings at set times. Some follow a liturgical calendar, with seasons set aside for fasting and prayer, such as the Lenten season preceding Easter. The Bible instructs us to "pray without ceasing," or pray at all times (1 Thess. 5:17 NRSV; Eph. 6:18).

Prayer meetings may be held in homes, schools, churches, or other public places, where allowed (or held in secret where not). Sometimes prayer meetings are held outdoors, in parks or common areas, in sporting arenas, and, more recently, through the Internet and mobile technology. But prayer need not even be held in one gathering place. Prayer walking is a way for Evangelicals to engage practically with their own neighbourhoods and cities. They may even travel to neighbourhoods and communities where there are not yet any local believers and engage in prayer walks there. There is no one version, method, or even form that can be assigned to evangelical prayer. It is as varied and diverse as Evangelicalism itself.

What Evangelical Prayer Holds in Common

Evangelical prayer reflects a set of assumptions about God and humans. Patrick Johnstone, the British founder of prayer ministry Operation World, once asked, "How can we weak, frail, puny creatures speak to our omnipotent Creator to make a difference to our world? It is a breath-taking mystery."[1]

Prayer assumes God is present, hears the prayers offered him, and has the ability, if not desire, to respond. Evangelicals believe a relationship exists between humans and God, that God can receive thanks, be petitioned for the needs of humankind, and then be received from in return. This assumes God can be perceived—whether audibly, through thoughts or visions, through the Scriptures, or in some other form—all through the Holy Spirit, God's gift to believers.

Prayer is at its very core *relational*, and it restores something of the fellowship experienced between God and humankind as expressed in the creation story, where in the garden of Eden God and humans walked and talked together freely. It reflects a future time when that communion will be fully restored. For respected twentieth-century British Evangelical leader John Stott, "Prayer . . . is the very way God Himself has chosen for us to express our conscious need of Him and our humble dependence on Him."[2]

The Lord's Prayer as a Guide

Jesus himself taught his band of first-century Jewish followers how to pray, telling them,

Pray then like this:

> "Our Father in heaven,
> hallowed be your name.
> Your kingdom come,
> your will be done,
>   on earth as it is in heaven.
> Give us this day our daily bread,
> and forgive us our debts,
>   as we also have forgiven our debtors.
> And lead us not into temptation,
>   but deliver us from evil."

These words of Jesus, recorded in Matthew 6:9–13 (ESV), are commonly known as the Lord's Prayer.

For Evangelicals, prayer is not a kind of magic, reflecting belief in a deity who can be manipulated or controlled by human offering or ritual. God is understood as a God that can potentially be persuaded or part-

---

1. Patrick Johnstone and Jason Mandryk, *Operation World, 21st Century Edition.* (Carlisle, England: Paternoster Lifestyle, 2001).
2. John Stott, *Christian Counter-Culture: The Message of the Sermon on the Mount* (Leicester, England: Inter-Varsity Press, 1978).

nered with in his work in the world. As Walter Wink, an American Bible scholar and activist, put it, "Prayer is not magic; it does not always work; it is not something we do, but a response to what God is already doing within us and the world. Our prayers are the necessary opening that allows God to act without violating our freedom. Prayer is the ultimate act of partnership with God."[3]

Evangelicals most commonly pray in Jesus' name not as a magical incantation to evoke desired results but in keeping with Jesus' own instruction about asking of the Father (God) in Jesus' name (John 14:13–14). Praying in Jesus' name reflects the evangelical understanding that it is in Jesus (the Christ) that humans are reconciled to God and that restored fellowship with God exists through and in Christ. Praying "in Jesus' name" is a prayer of faith, prayed with confidence and

Photo: The Langham Partnership

based on who Evangelicals understand God to be and also on how they understand God to have acted before, as recorded throughout Scripture and Christian history.

A hallmark of evangelical prayer is its accessibility to all. Evangelicals believe that in Christ, anyone can pray directly to God at any time and from any place. This is equally true whether the one praying is a child or a senior, a woman or a man, from any cultural or religious background, praying in any language. No human can ever take from another this ability to pray to God. It is an equalizing force: the earnest prayers of a fearful, forgotten child are received just the same by her Creator God as are the honest prayers of a revered global church leader.

Prayer is a call, a command and a gift. Prayer is the indispensable foundation and resource for all elements of our mission.[4]

Prayer is well understood as being a gift from God, an immediate, secure place to turn with a need, a problem, a perplexing or tragic situation. Evangelicals rally to pray in response to such events as a young Iranian pastor receiving a death sentence for sharing his faith with compatriots, or for such needs as those of the Japanese people in 2011 in the wake of a devastating natural disaster, a tsunami. Over one million attended the three-day prayer and fasting event in Haiti following the disastrous earthquake in 2010.

But for Evangelicals, prayer is also proactive, entered into specifically to pray for the kingdom of God to come on earth, now. David Wells, a professor at Gordon-Conwell Theological Seminary in South Hamilton, Massachusetts, described prayer as an act of "rebelling against the status quo" whereby Evangelicals refuse to resign themselves to the corruptions of this world and so rebel against it by engaging in prayer in order to see it changed.[5] Prayer is thereby work and even warfare, a work all are called to regardless of what may also be happening in the life of each individual believer or local church. It is a command and, in some cases, an act undertaken at great personal cost, a means of engaging in battle with the present evils of this world.

In the introduction to his book listing vital prayer needs for every country of the world, Jason Mandryk wrote, "We do not merely pray about the many points featured herein, we pray toward something, and that something is magnificent—the fulfilment of the Father's purposes and His Kingdom come. . . . May we become intercessors with a world vision that prays Satan-defeating, Kingdom-taking, people reaching, captive-releasing revival-giving, Christ-glorifying prayers."[6]

3. Walter Wink. *Engaging the Powers: Discernment and Resistance in a World of Domination* (Minneapolis, MN: Fortress Press, 1992).

4. "The Cape Town Commitment," The Lausanne Movement, accessed January 24, 2014, http://www.lausanne.org/en/documents/ctcommitment.html/. The Cape Town Commitment is an Evangelical confession of faith and call to action.

5. David F. Wells, "Prayer: Rebelling Against the Status Quo," *Christianity Today,* November 2, 1979.

6. Jason Mandryk, *Operation World*, 7th ed. (Downers Grove, IL: InterVarsity Press, 2010).

Persistence in Prayer

Evangelicals do not believe God must answer every prayer request just as it is prayed. However, they do believe God will answer and will do so beyond what humans can themselves imagine, ask, or think (Eph. 3:20). Evangelicals are persistent in their prayers. If God does not answer right away, they believe it best to pray repeatedly until God chooses to answer or shows them a different way. Some Evangelicals pray for the healing or salvation of a loved one for decades before the answer comes. Sometimes no answer comes in their lifetime. Still, believers pray in faith, trusting God to answer according to his ways and timings. This persistence allows the evangelical church to pray for things like an end to corruption, poverty, human trafficking, infanticide, and violence against women. Sri Lankan Bible teacher and church leader Ajith Fernando reminds us, "Often great prayer movements start with one or more individuals with a burden to pray, who share this burden with others, and then keep on praying with them until the blessing comes."[7]

For places like Nepal, Mongolia, or Albania, groups of believers from around the world prayed persistently over the years, asking God to work in these lands. Now each has a growing, thriving church where ten, twenty, or fifty years ago there were no churches at all. Prayer circles, from which activists rose to abolish slavery and work toward the betterment of British society, provide another example of Evangelicals persistent in prayer. Others would point to the now thousands-strong Korean mission movement, which is seeing a great surge of workers on the heels of the 1984 International Prayer Gathering hosted by the South Korean Church. (The subsequent 2012 World Prayer Assembly hosted by Indonesia has many watching for a similar surge to go forth from that great nation as well.)

American John Robb, the chairman for the International Prayer Council, feels both prayer and social action are essential: "I am not saying that prayer is all that is necessary to change the world. Many evangelical Christians have used prayer for too long as a substitute for action—dumping back on God the responsibility for doing what He has already commanded us to do throughout the Bible. Yet neither is social action a substitute for prayer. There is still a profound air of mystery surrounding prayer and how God uses our praying to transform the world."[8] Historically, kingdom-focused prayer among Evangelicals has led directly to engaged social action and believers being sent forth to the world to demonstrate and proclaim the love of Christ through acts of mercy, justice, and care for the poor and vulnerable, always teaching the words and ways of Jesus.

Gathering Together for Worldwide Prayer

We can speak confidently of the emergence, the veritable explosion, both in fervency and numbers, of prayer ministries, networks, and movements now cultivating focused, informed prayer for the nations, peoples, issues, and needs of the world. Early British Protestant missionary William Carey wrote in his *Enquiry*: "One of the first, and most important of those duties which are incumbent upon us, is *fervent and united prayer*."[9]

Indeed, this duty is now shouldered enthusiastically by millions of Evangelicals, particularly from the churches of the global South—Central and Latin America, Africa, and most of Asia. Some of the largest prayer meetings in history have been in Nigeria, and gripping visions for establishing prayer groups in every village of a state or nation come from prayer networks in places like Indonesia and parts of India. The National Jubilee Prayers in Uganda (2012) included prayer leadership from the country's president. Prayer networks, especially among women, are the backbone and strength of a vibrant Brazilian Church.

---

7. Ajith Fernando, *The NIV Application Commentary: Acts* (Grand Rapids: Zondervan), 1998.

8. John Robb with Larry Wilson, "In God's Kingdom … Prayer Is Social Action," *World Vision*, Feb/March 1997.

9. William Carey, *An Enquiry into the Obligations of Christians, to Use Means for the Conversion of the Heathens* (Leicester, England: Ann Ireland, 1792). Available online at www.gutenberg.org/files/11449/11449-h/11449-h.htm.

Evangelicals have gathered together to pray, both virtually and in person, more than ever before in recent years, and they do so with greater unity of focus, as technology allows people to connect and share information more widely in ways undreamt of even ten years ago.

Gatherings take place at the local level as always, though now often connected by relationship (or even virtually) to similar gatherings around the world. The influence of the 24/7 Prayer movement, which sets up prayer chains or rooms dedicated to round-the-clock prayer, has spread to many major world cities. Prayer houses on university campuses or in churches often have a dedicated focus on prayer for the needs of the local community and the wider world. People continue the centuries-old tradition of gathering for all-night prayer vigils or concerts of prayer, now often in large numbers, to focus prayer on geographical areas or special issues.

These gatherings often bring together Evangelicals from diverse denominations within a city or nation. Where strident discord previously existed, Evangelicals in many countries often find God building unity and trust among them as they gather and pray together for the suffering believers of the persecuted church around the world, for a nation in a time of need, or for God to send his people out to the world to show Christ's love and care for people.

Movements of children and youth in prayer are growing rapidly, with resources and prayer information available at their reading levels. With humility, vulnerability, and dependence on God as the starting place for prayer, adults have much to learn from children and young people in their prayers.

The Unifying and Reconciling Work of Prayer Gatherings

It is impossible to pray for someone without loving him, and impossible to go on praying for him without discovering that our love for him grows and matures.[10]

Evangelicals believe that when they are honest and humble in prayer—about themselves, their situations, and their actions—there is strength of relational intimacy among them in which God can work in powerful ways. Wrongs and sins can be confessed, forgiveness extended, and broken and damaged relationships reconciled, whether between spouses in a marriage, parents and children, or churches or mission teams experiencing conflict and division. Earnest prayer requires trust, and as God forgives and humans forgive, trust once broken begins to be rebuilt.

This is no less true among groups long divided—between hardened oppressors and those they formerly abused, between warring tribes or ethnic groups, between nations who pillaged and destroyed neighboring nations. Perhaps some of the most powerful prayer events of recent decades have seen Evangelicals from enemy nations or tribes go by delegation one to the other to confess the sins of their ancestors and people toward each other, to cry together, to seek forgiveness, to extend it, and then to join together in united prayer for one another and for God's kingdom to come on earth as in heaven.

How Prayer Requests Are Shared

The intertwined realities of a globalizing, interconnected world have both fueled and benefited evangelical prayer efforts. In the early church the apostle Paul and his small team shared the needs of the churches as they traveled from place to place. Believers could rejoice and thank God together for answers to prayer and also share the burdens and challenges faced by their brothers and sisters in Christ. The global body of Evangelicals today continues to both rejoice and share burdens in prayer for one another. As in the early church, this prayer leads to action and practical help.

---

10. John Stott, *Christian Counter-Culture*.

Global resources like the *Operation World* handbook provide information and prayer requests from every country of the world. Numerous websites supply information specifically for a region, for a country, for a particular people group, and even for special needs such as those of the world's most vulnerable children, those caught in human trafficking, or those places where the church faces persecution and violent oppression.

Most evangelical ministries produce prayer guides and materials concentrating on the focus of their own work or their own specific needs for prayer as an organization. Each evangelical missionary often has a team or a sending church committed to praying for them with which they share personal prayer needs. Evangelical churches typically produce weekly bulletins highlighting needs for prayer within that local group, often including the needs of ministries or missionaries with whom they have a relationship and information about national or issue-specific days for prayer, inviting congregants to participate on their own or together with others in the church.

The needs of the persecuted and suffering church around the world rightly draw the focus of Evangelicals to prayer. Believers devote themselves to prayer for those who, for the sake of following Christ, are beaten, tortured, held captive, and physically and emotionally harmed. Ministries like Open Doors, Voice of the Martyrs, and Release International provide current information on specific situations needing prayer, as well as longer-term reflection on ways to pray for peoples or churches living in a prolonged state of oppression and injustices.

Information is no longer simply written or shared orally but now also distributed through videos, charts and maps, and other visual cues and reminders to pray for a person or event. Individuals often make use of social media to solicit prayer during times of need. Only in our day has it been possible to immediately rally hundreds or thousands from all around the world to pray simultaneously for a specific need.

Comfort, Conviction, and Contradiction

Comfort can drive out prayer. If prayer is recognition of human limitation and inadequacy in the face of world needs, then the more a people feel able to address comfortably their own needs, whether physical or emotional, the further this perspective slips from their reality. When a need suddenly appears in the face of human tragedy or impossibility, it presents a stark contrast to what has otherwise become a more self-sufficient daily existence.

It seems the church of the global South better understands this reality and gives time—at the expense of sleep, food, leisure time, and more—to engaging, with fervency and urgency, in this work for personal sustenance and for God's glory. In contrast, prayer meetings in the West may be filled with only a handful of people and left aside by those who consider themselves too busy to afford time for focused, communal prayer. Wide swathes of the evangelical church (particularly the European and North American churches) are disengaged from the work and privilege of world-changing prayer, this foundation of our call and command. Present and long-term effects of this widespread trend in some cultures can be surmised but remain fully to be seen.

What Lies Ahead

Were there ever a time for Evangelicals to connect with one another, and with the work of world evangelization, the time is now. This season of fervent and united global prayer may erode long-standing barriers of culture, gender, ethnicity, or denomination. It may usher

The needs of the persecuted and suffering church around the world rightly draw the focus of Evangelicals to prayer.

in revival and a host of missionaries sent forth for the remaining work of world evangelization and the glory of God among all peoples.

Opportunity beckons Evangelicals to spur one another to *informed* prayer—prayer of substance, depth, and breadth based on information afforded them for which no other generation has had such privilege or responsibility. It is prayer beyond individual blessings and personal needs and toward the extreme needs of their fellow humans.

Prayer remains a mysterious communion between humans and the divine, yet perhaps in no other century has the church borne such opportunity to watch and wait with excitement to see firsthand what God might do in this generation in answer to a globe-covering wave of fervent and united prayer.

Global Events and Evangelical Prayer

Global events now play a major role in evangelical prayer.

- The South African-initiated **Global Day of Prayer** engages participants from almost every country, who come together on Pentecost Sunday every year to pray for the world.
- The **World Prayer Assembly of 2012** in Indonesia gathered leaders of the world's evangelical prayer movements for several days of focused prayer and worship, bringing together many streams of evangelical prayer and the global church: men, women, children, and the elderly, from Brazilian Pentecostals to Chinese church leaders, from British Anglicans to independent African groups, and from many places in between.
- The **International Prayer Council** provides a connection point for prayer movements and networks to communicate and coordinate with one another, to share ideas and resources, and to invite the global body to join together in prayer for various issues, on various days, and for specific reasons. 24/7 Prayer, Children in Prayer, Prayer 24–365, Jericho Walls, Global Day of Prayer, Operation World, and others are among the best known.

Bibliography

"The Cape Town Commitment." The Lausanne Movement. Accessed January 24, 2014. http://www.lausanne.org/en/documents/ctcommitment.html/.

Carey, William. *An Enquiry into the Obligations of Christians, to Use Means for the Conversion of the Heathens.* Leicester, England: Ann Ireland, 1792.

Fernando, Ajith. *The NIV Application Commentary: Acts.* Grand Rapids: Zondervan, 1998.

Johnstone, Patrick, and Jason Mandryk. *Operation World, 21st Century Edition.* Carlisle, England: Paternoster Lifestyle, 2001.

Mandryk, Jason. *Operation World,* 7th ed. Downers Grove, IL: InterVarsity Press, 2010.

Robb, John, with Larry Wilson. "In God's Kingdom ... Prayer is Social Action." *World Vision* (Feb/March 1997).

Stott, John. *Christian Counter-Culture: The Message of the Sermon on the Mount.* Leicester, England: Inter-Varsity Press, 1978.

Wells, David F. "Prayer: Rebelling Against the Status Quo." *Christianity Today,* November 2, 1979.

Wink, Walter. *Engaging the Powers: Discernment and Resistance in a World of Domination.* Minneapolis, MN: Fortress Press, 1992.

Molly Wall is a researcher, editor, and program manager with Operation World in the United Kingdom. She has served as a researcher and curriculum developer with the U.S. Center for World Mission in Pasadena, California.

A group of Christians meet for prayer in India.
Photo: The Langham Partnership

"God reveals his original intent before the Fall that males and females share in relationship and dominion on the earth. Evangelicals who live redeemed relationships between males and females (on earth as in heaven) and work together to complete his mission, reveal a powerful prophetic statement across all religious blocs that Jesus can redeem a fragmented world."

—Dr. Leslie Neal Segraves, Cofounder and Executive Director of 10/40 Connections, Inc. and Lausanne Senior Associate of Male/Female Partnership, United States

EVANGELICALS AND GENDER

By Aída Besançon Spencer

The heart of *evangelical* is "the proclamation of good news." Women have been active in promoting the good news about God from the very beginning, when Eve acknowledged that God had given Cain, their first child, to her and Adam (Gen. 4:1). However, Evangelicals have differed on their understanding of the appropriate roles for women in leadership in the church and home. The Bible has much support for female leadership but also places that appear to restrict women.

A Biblical Survey

In the Old Testament, women served as leaders in the household and the society. God appointed Miriam, along with Moses and Aaron, as a leader over Israel when they left Egypt for their promised land (Mic. 6:4; Ex. 15:20–21). Deborah, a judge, prophet, and ruler commended by God, gave Israel rest from its enemies for forty years (Judg. 4:4–10; 5:7, 31). Even though male prophets were available (e.g., Jeremiah, Nahum, Zephaniah, and Obadiah), only the prophetess Huldah was sought by the devout King Josiah and his cabinet to interpret authoritatively God's written word, the rediscovered book of Deuteronomy (2 Kings 22:8–20).

Mary Magdalene and other women were commissioned by Jesus and by the angelic messenger: "Then go quickly and tell [Jesus'] disciples: 'He has risen from the dead and is going ahead of you into Galilee'" (Matt. 28:7 [NIV].
Image: North Wind Picture Archives

Symbolically, wisdom was portrayed as a wise woman standing at the gates of the city with the elders (Prov. 8:1–36). Consequently, wise women assumed leadership over cities and communicated God's message to kings (2 Sam. 14:1–20; 20:15–22). The prophet Joel proclaimed God would pour out God's Spirit on both women and men, young and old, poor and rich, so they would prophesy (Joel 2:28–29; Acts 2:17–18).

In the New Testament, the presence of women in leadership continued. Anna, together with Simeon, recognized in the infant Jesus the Savior about whom Anna preached throughout Jerusalem (Luke 2:36–38). Women prophets were preaching and praying in Corinth (1 Cor. 11:5). The woman in Samaria was the first person in the Gospels to be told by Jesus that he was the Messiah. After her life-changing conversation with Jesus, she returned to her village of Sychar as an evangelist, inviting everyone to meet this Messiah (John 4:4–42).

Women served as apostles, being commissioned eyewitnesses of Jesus' life and resurrection. Mary Magdalene, Joanna, Mary the mother of James and Joseph, Salome the mother of James and John, and other women were commissioned by Jesus and by the angelic messenger: "Then go quickly and tell [Jesus'] disciples: 'He has risen from the dead and is going ahead of you into Galilee'" (Matt. 28:7 [NIV]; Mark 115:40; 6:1–8; Luke 24:1–10, 22–24; John 20:1–18).

Junia, along with Andronicus, were considered "prominent among the apostles" (Rom. 16:7 ISV). Priscilla, also called Prisca, and her husband, Aquila, accurately taught the rhetorician Apollos the way of God (Acts 18:26) and led the way in establishing numerous house churches (Rom. 16:3–5; 1 Cor. 16:19). As nineteenth-century

Presbyterian pastor A. T. Pierson expressed it so beautifully, "Apollos, the scholar and orator of Alexandria, puts himself under the instruction of two poor tent-makers of Corinth, one of them a woman, to be taught the way of God more perfectly. The first theological seminary was a humble lodging, with a single student and two professors, a man and his wife the head of the faculty."[1]

Other women opened up their homes for churches to meet in and led them as church overseers. These included the elect lady and the elect sister (2 John), Lydia (Acts 16:14–15, 40), and Stephana(s) (1 Cor. 16:15–18). Phoebe served as a minister in Cenchreae, being deemed worthy to be welcomed by the Christians in Rome. She had been a leader over many and even over Paul (Rom. 16:1–2). The apostle Paul affirmed women and men as his coworkers in ministry, including Prisca, Euodia, and Syntyche (Rom. 16:3; Phil. 4:2–3).[2]

How Jesus Interacted with Women

Most Evangelicals recognize Jesus both affirmed and elevated the status of women. His teachings and actions were favorable to women, and women were an important part of his ministry. He conversed with them in public despite discouragement by some Jews (e.g., John 4:27). Jesus' teachings were favorable to women as was evidenced by his affirmation of a monogamous marriage commitment for both men and women (Matt. 5:27–32). Women were such an important part of Jesus' ministry they were reflected in his genealogy (Matt. 1:3–16) and cited as positive examples of the faith (e.g., Mary [Luke 1:27–56; 2:19, 51]). Jesus also at times employed women's perspectives in his teachings. He used female images for himself (Luke 13:34; 15:8–10) and illustrations drawn from household activities common to women (e.g., sewing and cooking [Luke 5:36; 6:38; 13:20–21]).[3]

Different Conclusions

Evangelicals, however, differ over the implications of the actions of Jesus and Paul toward women for church leadership roles. Some Evangelicals conclude that women, no matter how devout or prepared, may not authoritatively lead or teach the gospel to men in the public assembly of the church or in colleges and seminaries. In other words, they may not serve as governing or teaching elders. Some Evangelicals exclude women from serving as deacons as well, and even from reading Scripture and praying in public. Others exclude women from having any authority over their husbands in the home. The key functions debated are women's authority and their teaching of Christian doctrine to adults, especially males.[4]

While all Evangelicals agree Jesus and Paul affirmed women, some Evangelicals believe some Bible passages limit women. If Jesus chose women to be included among witnesses to his resurrection, why then did he not include women among the twelve apostles? If newly baptized heirs of the promise, clothed "with Christ," are no longer Jew or Greek, slave or free, male and female (Gal. 3:27–29), how then can women "learn in silence" but not be permitted to teach or have authority over a man (1 Tim. 2:11–12 KJV)? How can the Scriptures affirm the Samaritan woman who preached to her village and assume women could prophesy in Corinth, yet Paul write that women should be silent in the churches and be subordinate (1 Cor. 14:34)? How can the church be exhorted to be submitted to one another, yet wives be submitted to their husbands (Eph. 5:21–24)? What does it mean for a man to be the "head" of a woman (1 Cor. 11:3)?

1. A. T. Pierson, *The Dream as Interpreting the Man* in *How Christ Came to Church* (Grand Rapids: Kregel, 2010), 120.

2. See Aída Besançon Spencer, *Beyond the Curse: Women Called to Ministry* (Grand Rapids: Baker, 1985); "'El Hogar' as Ministry Team: Stephana(s) Household," in *Hispanic Christian Thought at the Dawn of the 21st Century: Apuntes in Honor of Justo L. González*, ed. Alvin Padilla, Roberto Goizueta, and Eldin Villafañe (Nashville: Abingdon, 2005), 71.

3. See Aída Besançon Spencer, "Jesus' Treatment of Women in the Gospels," in *Discovering Biblical Equality: Complementarity without Hierarchy*, 2nd ed., ed. Ronald W. Pierce and Rebecca Merrill Groothuis (Downers Grove: InterVarsity Press, 2005).

4. E.g., www.moodyministries.net/crp_MainPage.aspx?id=338, accessed May 15, 2013.

For some Evangelicals, passages such as these limit women's roles in the church, religious institutions, and the home. For others, these passages indicate inconsistencies in the biblical writings. Other Evangelicals believe that when passages are studied in their literary, historical, and cultural contexts, God and God-incarnate (Jesus) and Jesus' apostles support the leadership of gifted women and men in the church and the home, as well as in society.

God's truth is sometimes not fully developed immediately in all cultures and times. Thus, the twelve apostles symbolically reflected the twelve Jewish patriarchs, while the female and male witnesses reflect the New Covenant where the Holy Spirit equips every believer to be a priest and proclaimer. To learn in silence is a positive means of education employed for all rabbinic students, not just women. Disorder in worship may be acceptable to pagan worship, but not in worship of the unique, living God (1 Cor. 14:36–40). A positive authority is always affirmed for orthodox women, but never a destructive domination. A "head" of someone may be that person's source (such as the source of a river or the source of life), not necessarily her boss (1 Cor. 11:8, 12). This view posits that submission and humility toward wholesome church leadership are positive actions for all, men and women, as Jesus exhorted, "Whoever may wish to become great among you will be your servant and whoever may wish to be first among you will be slave of all. For also the Son of Humanity came not to be served but to serve, and to give his life a ransom for many" (Mark 10:43–45 author's translation). And Paul is very clear that a wife has authority over her husband's body, as he does over hers (1 Cor. 7:2–4).

Different Interpretations, Different Impact

Varying interpretations of the Bible have affected the extension of Christianity from its earliest years until now. In some cultures the native leadership of women is curtailed, while in other locations it is affirmed, as in Macedonia and Crete, where Lydia's aggressive hospitality is welcomed and where female elders are encouraged to teach (Acts 16:15, 40; Titus 2:3). Inscriptions honoring female elders in the church may still be found dating from the second to the fifth centuries.[5] The great ecumenical councils, Nicea and Chalcedon, did not restrict women in church leadership.

Slowly, after the fourth century, women began to be restricted at the same time as leadership by laymen and the use of the gifts of the Holy Spirit.[6] For example, the Synod of Laodicea in Phrygia (Asia) in AD 343–81 concluded that "women may not approach near the altar."[7] The Synod of Carthage in 398 stated, "A layman may not teach in the presence of the clergy, except at their command. A woman, however learned and holy, may not take upon herself to teach in an assembly of men. A woman may not baptize."[8] The institutionalization of the church, which occurred when Emperor Constantine nationalized Christianity, and the transference of Old Testament temple theology to the church were both factors that affected the role of women in the church.

> The great ecumenical councils, Nicea and Chalcedon, did not restrict women in church leadership.

5. Kevin Madigan and Carolyn Osiek, eds., *Ordained Women in the Early Church: A Documentary History* (Baltimore, MD: Johns Hopkins University Press, 2005).

6. Ronald Kydd, *Charismatic Gifts in the Early Church* (Peabody, MA: Hendrickson Publishers, 1984); William David Spencer, "Chaining of the Church," *Christian History* 17, no. 1 (1988): 25.

7. Spencer, *Beyond the Curse,* Canon 44, 63.

8. Ibid., Canons 98–100.

Always a Remnant

Throughout history a remnant of the evangelical church, having noted the Bible's more permissive examples and teachings about women, would support women in leadership roles. In her 1667 pamphlet, Margaret Fell, known as the mother of Quakerism, declared "women's speaking" was "justified, proved and allowed by the Scriptures" because "women were the first that preached the tidings of the resurrection of Jesus, and were sent by Christ's own command before He ascended to the Father, John 20.17."[9] Abolitionist Lydia Maria Child in 1837 credited "the sects called evangelical" to be "the first agitators of the woman question."[10] In 1859 Catherine Booth, who with her husband, William, founded The Salvation Army, promoted the "woman's right to preach the gospel" in a pamphlet titled "Female Ministry."[11] In 1952 Helen Barrett Montgomery, the first woman selected as president of a major American denomination in 1921, translated the New Testament from the original Greek. Her translation, *The New Testament in Modern English,* is still in print today. What these women began in the 1800s was revived and continued in the 1970s, 1980s, and later.

Abolitionist Lydia Maria Child credited Evangelicals as "the first agitators of the woman question."
Image: North Wind Picture Archives

Freedom and Restrictions

Often when Christianity is first welcomed into a culture women are freed from many of that culture's restrictions. Later, however, those Christian women may encounter limitations to their leadership possibilities. In India, for example, Christians brought education to girls and decreased female infanticide, abortion, and prostitution.

When English missionary William Carey witnessed a newly widowed Indian woman voluntarily being burned on her husband's funeral pyre in 1799, Carey and others, such as Raja Ram Mohan Roy, campaigned against this practice in India for thirty years until it became illegal.[12] This legal change has kept thousands of women alive.

Christian thinking prompted the condemnation of infanticide in 1802, saving millions of girls. Christians also worked against child marriage. Indian social reformer Pandita Ramabai saved the lives of thousands of orphans and widows. Irish missionary Amy Carmichael rescued

Catherine Booth founded The Salvation Army, along with her husband William.
Photo used with permission The Salvation Army Archives, Canada and Bermuda Territory

9. Ruth A. Tucker and Walter L. Liefeld, *Daughters of the Church: Women and Ministry from New Testament Times to the Present* (Grand Rapids: Zondervan, 1987).

10. Aída Besançon Spencer, Donna F. G. Hailson, Catherine Clark Kroeger, and William David Spencer, *The Goddess Revival: A Biblical Response to God(dess) Spirituality* (Eugene, OR: Wipf and Stock, 1995).

11. Catherine Booth, "Female Ministry; or, Woman's Right to Preach the Gospel," *Indiana University Victorian Women Writers Project,* accessed January 27, 2014, http://webapp1.dlib.indiana.edu/vwwp/view?docId=VAB7105.

12. Aída Besançon Spencer, William David Spencer, and Mimi Haddad, eds., *Global Voices on Biblical Equality: Women and Men Serving Together in the Church* (Eugene, OR: Wipf and Stock, 2008).

hundreds of children from temple prostitution. Christian missionaries, as well as the Indian men and women they trained, have made an effort to educate girls as well as boys, women, and men. A Christian worldview promoted literacy and just legislation for women. Nevertheless, even now a Christian fiancé in India may demand an excessive dowry from a prospective father-in-law, or a Christian daughter may be forced to marry an undesirable man. Abortion in India is almost always female abortion. Patriarchy may still restrict women from traveling outside their homes.[13]

Sometimes women are encouraged during times of revival and outreach but then restricted when positions become institutionalized. In the early decades of the twentieth century, women outnumbered men on the mission field by a ratio of two to one. But when the women's missionary agencies were forced to merge with the male-dominated denominational boards, many fewer women were appointed as missionaries, and women had less freedom in the running of the restructured mission.[14]

The percentage of women ordained in a particular denomination does not necessarily increase over time. For example, the Assemblies of God has historically championed the cause of women's ministry; however, the proportion of credentialed ministers has declined. In 1987 almost one-half of all Assemblies of God women ministers were sixty-five years of age or older. The Evangelical Free Church used to ordain women, but after 1988 women no longer could be ordained or be pastor-teachers. The Southern Baptist Convention also ordained women up to 1987, after which it stopped doing so. This action then limited women as missionaries and became a precedent for Baptists around the world. In the 1930s, 34 percent of all Church of God ministers were women, but since World War II women ministers in this denomination have declined to about 10 percent.

A.B. Simpson, the founder of the Christian and Missionary Alliance, called the Holy Spirit "our Mother God" and included women on the executive board committee, employing them as Bible professors and supporting female evangelists and branch officers (the early Christian and Missionary Alliance equivalent to a local minister). But by 2013 women were no longer allowed to have "elder authority."[15] Dwight L. Moody worked together with a number of women preachers. At the turn of the twentieth century, female graduates of Moody Bible Institute openly served as pastors, evangelists, pulpit supply preachers, and Bible teachers, and were even in the ordained ministry.[16]

Descriptive or Prescriptive?

Evangelicals believe part of the fall of humanity was that the male would rule over the female (Gen. 3:16). But, is that passage descriptive or prescriptive? If it is descriptive, it is a type of destructive authority (Mark 10:42) that should be avoided. If it is prescriptive, it would serve as a positive model for men and women that would affect their roles in society, the church, and the home.

Both Paul and Peter appeal to Christians to accommodate to society in order to evangelize it (Titus 2:5, 8; 1 Peter 2:13–15; 3:1), but this appeal may be misinterpreted to result in Christians never being prophetic and countercultural. Evangelicals may not know how to handle the clash between traditional and Christian values. To what extent have Evangelicals accommodated to culture for the sake of outreach at the cost of allowing the culture and ethnic traditions to dilute and reshape the gospel? To what extent should the priesthood of all be-

---

13. Ibid.

14. Dana L. Robert, *American Women in Mission: A Social History of Their Thought and Practice* (Macon, GA: Mercer University Press, 1996); Ruth A. Tucker, *Guardians of the Great Commission: The Story of Women in Modern Missions* (Grand Rapids: Zondervan, 1988).

15. www.cmalliance.org/about/beliefs/perspectives/women-in-ministry, accessed May 15, 2013.

16. Janette Hassey, *No Time for Silence: Evangelical Women in Public Ministry Around the Turn of the Century* (Grand Rapids: Academie Books, 1986); Aída Besançon Spencer, "God's Order Is Love," *Brethren in Christ History and Life* 13, no. 1 (April 1990): 39–50.

lievers (e.g., 1 Peter 2:9) be a real-life model for the ministry of the church? Those are the questions with which many Evangelicals still grapple.

Spiritual equality has not always been reflected in functional equality. Some Evangelicals think spiritual equality should not affect social equality in leadership, especially in the church. In many countries the majority of believers are women, though the majority of visible leaders are male.

Evangelical denominations differ over their view on the ordination of women in ministry. Here are some examples from United States denominations, which have a global impact. Denominations outside the United States also differ over support for female clergy. These statistics reveal the difference is not simply between "liberal" versus "conservative" denominations.

Female Christian Clergy Percent by Denomination and Year of First Ordaining Women[17]

DENOMINATION	YEAR:			Year Women First Ordained
	1994	(2011)	(2012)	
Assemblies of God	8%			1914
Church of God, Anderson, IN	10%			1974
Church of the Nazarene	11%			1912
Cumberland Presbyterian Church		(13%)		1889
Evangelical Covenant Church		(19%)	(26%)	1976
Evangelical Free Church	0%			
Free Methodist Church	1%			
Southern Baptist Convention	4%			
Wesleyan Church	11%			1853
Presbyterian Church (USA)	19%	(26%)		1956
United Church of Christ	25%			1810

Different Rationales

Here are the rationales from three different evangelical denominations with three different conclusions about women in church leadership: to allow flexibility, to restrict, and to support. The Conservative Congregational Christian Conference states that the "ministerial standing of women" is a negotiable decision, not a non-negotiable doctrine: "Christians, equally committed to the authority of Holy Scripture, may disagree on whether or not the Scriptures allow for the ordination of women." Thus, each congregation may ordain "whom it freely chooses, thus preserving its own autonomy."[18] The Southern Baptist Convention states that "women participate equally with men in the priesthood of all believers . . . While . . . pastoral leadership is assigned to men, [Scripture] also teaches that women are equal in value to men."[19] In contrast, "the Evangelical Covenant Church affirms women in all ministry and leadership positions within the church, both lay and clergy."[20]

---

17. hirr.hartsem.edu/research/fast-facts.html#womenpast, accessed May 15, 2013; Kris Valerius, Office of General Assembly Records Coordinator, Presbyterian Church USA, e-mail message to Aída B. Spencer, May 16, 2013; "Women in Leadership Positions," ECC, received from Tyler Uhl, May 20, 2013; Pam Phillips-Burk, Women's Ministries, Cumberland Presbyterian Church, e-mail message to Aída B. Spencer, June 4, 2013.

18. www.ccccusa.com/wp-content/uploads/2011/07/PPLH-Ministerial-Standing-of-Women.pdf, accessed May 16, 2013.

19. www.sbc.net/aboutus/pswomen.asp, accessed May 16, 2013.

20. www.covchurch.org/resolutions/2006-women-in-ministry, accessed May 16, 2013.

Where Evangelicals Agree

All Evangelicals agree, no matter their position on gender and faith, that authentic Christianity includes promoting the respect and dignity of women and men and the spiritual equality of women and men, modeling the love of Christ in every facet of life. In many evangelical denominations, the role of women in the church and the home has been decided, at least officially. Other evangelical denominations and groups are still wrestling with clarifying the Bible's teachings of the role of women and men in the church and the home. The Bible, considered God's authoritative revelation, and the church's particular interpretations of it are the foundational bases for this quest.

Evangelical Views of Women in Ministry

By Debra Fieguth

When it comes to the role of women in the church, there is little consensus among Evangelicals. Rather, there is a spectrum of views that falls into approximately four camps, though even the number of camps and the views they contain are hotly contested. There is no clear demarcation between the camps, as there are differences within each and some overlap with others.

On one end of the spectrum is the *traditional*, or hierarchical view, which holds that women should keep silent and teach only children and other women. They should not be allowed to speak in church or lead worship. Nor can they be elders or deacons or serve communion. Among the texts this group refers to are 1 Corinthians 11:3, which states Christ is the head of the man, and the man is the head of the woman; 1 Corinthians 14:34, which commands women to be silent in church; and 1 Timothy 2:12, which does not allow a woman to teach or exercise authority over a man.

The *complementarian* position is that the woman's role is different from that of the man, and the two roles complement each other, although the man is considered the head of the woman. Women are seen as subordinate but not inferior. Some observers say complementarians are actually the same as traditionalists. But complementarianism differs from one theologian to another. For example, some believe women can teach men in a seminary, as long as they have permission from the male leadership. Others do not allow women to teach or preach at all when there are men are present.

The third position, *egalitarianism*, or biblical feminism, believes since "there is neither male nor female in Christ" (Gal. 3:28 NASB), women can be partners in every aspect of ministry and should be permitted to do whatever men can do. This view states that roles should be assigned according to gifts rather than to gender. Egalitarians believe inequality is a result of the fall, and therefore Christians should strive to end that inequality, or undo the effects of the fall and the subsequent curse.

Finally there is the concept of *plural leadership*, which overlaps with egalitarianism but goes further. This view posits there is no biblical basis for ordination, but rather ordination was an invention of the church as it developed over the first three centuries. The position suggests neither men nor women should be ordained; instead, each person should be designated to positions of service according to spiritual gifting. The celebration of communion, therefore, is open to all believers, or "priests," in God's kingdom, including women.

Strategically, the World Evangelical Alliance has a Women's Commission that "exists to serve the Church by uniting women leaders and organizations, encouraging, equipping and mobilizing them to help women globally to be all that God created and called them to be. WEA provides a global identity, platform and voice, enabling the Commissions to address issues and concerns of women around the world.[21]

---

21. "The Unique Role of the WEA's Women's Commission," World Evangelical Alliance, accessed June 10, 2014, http://www.worldevangelicals.org/commissions/wc/.

Bibliography

Booth, Catherine. "Female Ministry; or, Woman's Right to Preach the Gospel." *Indiana University Victorian Women Writers Project*, accessed January 27, 2014, http://webapp1.dlib.indiana.edu/vwwp/view?docId=VAB7105/.

Hassey, Janette. *No Time for Silence: Evangelical Women in Public Ministry Around the Turn of the Century.* Grand Rapids: Academie Books, 1986.

Kydd, Ronald. *Charismatic Gifts in the Early Church.* Peabody, MA: Hendrickson Publishers, 1984.

Madigan, Kevin, and Carolyn Osiek, eds. *Ordained Women in the Early Church: A Documentary History.* Baltimore, MD: Johns Hopkins University Press, 2005.

Pierson, A. T. *The Dream as Interpreting the Man* in *How Christ Came to Church.* Grand Rapids: Kregel, 2010.

Robert, Dana L. *American Women in Mission: A Social History of Their Thought and Practice.* Macon, GA: Mercer University Press, 1996.

Spencer, Aída Besançon. *Beyond the Curse: Women Called to Ministry.* Grand Rapids: Baker, 1985.

———. "'El Hogar' as Ministry Team: Stephana(s) Household." In *Hispanic Christian Thought at the Dawn of the 21st Century: Apuntes in Honor of Justo L. González,* ed. Alvin Padilla, Roberto Goizueta, and Eldin Villafañe. Nashville: Abingdon, 2005.

———. "God's Order Is Love." *Brethren in Christ History and Life* 13, no. 1 (April 1990): 39–50.

———. "Jesus' Treatment of Women in the Gospels." In *Discovering Biblical Equality: Complementarity without Hierarchy,* 2nd ed., ed. Ronald W. Pierce and Rebecca Merrill Groothuis. Downers Grove: InterVarsity Press, 2005.

Spencer, Aída Besançon, Donna F. G. Hailson, Catherine Clark Kroeger, and William David Spencer. *The Goddess Revival: A Biblical Response to God(dess) Spirituality.* Eugene, OR: Wipf and Stock, 1995.

Spencer, Aída Besançon, William David Spencer, and Mimi Haddad, eds. *Global Voices on Biblical Equality: Women and Men Serving Together in the Church.* Eugene, OR: Wipf and Stock, 2008.

Spencer, William David. "Chaining of the Church." *Christian History* 17, no. 1 (1988): 25.

Tucker, Ruth A. *Guardians of the Great Commission: The Story of Women in Modern Missions.* Grand Rapids: Zondervan, 1988.

Tucker, Ruth A., and Walter L. Liefeld. *Daughters of the Church: Women and Ministry from New Testament Times to the Present.* Grand Rapids: Zondervan, 1987.

World Evangelical Alliance, "The Unique Role of the WEA's Women's Commission," accessed June 10, 2014, http://www.worldevangelicals.org/commissions/wc/.

Dr. Aída Besançon Spencer is professor of New Testament at Gordon-Conwell Theological Seminary in South Hamilton, Massachusetts, and an ordained minister in the Presbyterian Church (USA).

"It is my hope that we as Evangelicals will continue to serve God and love the world just like Jesus loves this world. Times might become more difficult for Christians, but with God's help we will overcome and continue to proclaim the Gospel amidst growing adversity and greater economic challenges. Men and women side by side, both reconciled through forgiveness of their sin and equipped by the power of the Holy Spirit."

—Elke Werner, Senior Associate for Women in Evangelism, Lausanne Movement, member of the board of Lausanne Int., Germany

EVANGELICALS AND RELIGIOUS LIBERTY

By Godfrey Yogarajah and Roshini Wickremesinhe

The Ottoman Empire (present-day Turkey) of the mid-nineteenth century, where conversion was punishable by death, was not a pleasant place for a Christian convert. In addition, the declining empire was caught in the power struggle between Imperial Russia and European powers. By the fall of 1853 these powers and the Ottoman Empire were engaged in the Crimean War, which resulted in bloody massacres and the deaths of thousands on all sides.

It was at such a time as this that the British Evangelical Alliance (BEA) received a plea from some Turkish Christians, following the execution of a convert in 1853, to advocate for the freedom of Christians under the Ottoman Empire. The BEA, together with its Turkish counterparts, worked its contacts in several European governments. Immediately after the end of the Crimean War in 1856, Sultan Abdülmecid I, ruler of the Ottoman Empire, in a delicate political maneuver influenced by the support extended by British and other European powers during the Crimean War, issued the Imperial Reform Edict. Among other reforms, it granted freedom of worship to followers of all faiths and abolished the death penalty for religious conversion.[1]

Christians have historically been in the forefront of advocating religious liberty for all. Early church fathers recognized the significance of religious freedom. Second-century Christian apologist Justin Martyr wrote, "Nothing more contrary to religion than constraint."[2] A century later the author Tertullian, against a decree issued by Emperor Septimus Severus banning conversions to Christianity, wrote, "It is a matter of both human and natural law that every man can worship as he pleases . . . it is not in the nature of religion to impose itself by force, but should be adopted freely."[3]

One of the earliest accounts of Evangelicals promoting religious liberty is found in the account of the BEA advocating for and securing the return to Berlin of the exiled Baptist leader Johann Gerhard Oncken in 1852.[4] Starting in 1855 concerted efforts by the BEA to promote religious freedom in Germany through dialogue with several German emperors, kings, and chancellors culminated in a meeting with Austrian Emperor Franz Joseph I at the Hofburg Palace. This led to greater freedom for Protestants and their legal recognition in 1880.[5]

More than two centuries later Evangelicals worldwide continue to be in the forefront of advocating for religious liberty. The oppressors of the Ottoman Empire are no more, but there are more persecution victims living on almost every continent in the world today than ever before. These are faithful men, women, and children who refuse to deny Christ. Some pay the ultimate price. Others languish in prison. Some suffer unspeakable torture, are left destitute, and endure beatings, while others face ridicule and discrimination for bearing Christ's name.

---

1. Thomas Schirrmacher, "The Early History of the Evangelical Alliance and of its Advocacy of Religious Freedom," ProMundis (blog), May 8, 2012, http://www.thomasschirrmacher.net/blog/the-early-history-of-the-evangelical-alliance-and-of-its-advocacy-of-religious-freedom/.

2. In M. Searle Bates, *Religious Liberty: An Inquiry* (New York: International Missionary Council, 1945), 137.

3. Tertullian, *Apologeticum* [Apology], http://www.tertullian.org/works/apologeticum.htm, accessed March 21, 2014.

4. Schirrmacher, "Early History of the Evangelical Alliance" (blog).

5. Thomas Schirrmacher, "The Early History of the Evangelical Alliance and of its Advocacy of Religious Freedom," *International Journal of Religious Freedom* 5, no. 1 (2012): 164.

Why Advocate for Religious Liberty?

Evangelicals believe religious liberty is a God-ordained, fundamental, and inalienable human right to be enjoyed by every human being. The only creature God created in his own image is the human being (Gen. 1:26–31). Hence, every human being must be treated with dignity, irrespective of race, religion, gender, and any other difference. Scripture demonstrates God's impartiality in dispensing both justice and grace when dealing with every human being (Gal. 3:26–29). This concept of equality also spills over to God's gift of free will bestowed on human beings to make choices, tempered with reason and conscience. In sending out the twelve disciples, Jesus Christ himself endorsed every person's right to choose his or her own religion or belief (Matt. 10:1–14).

To those who choose to follow him, Christ warned that persecution is to be expected: "No servant is greater than his master. If they persecuted me, they will persecute you also" (John 15:19, 20 NIV). Scripture also commands us to speak up on behalf of those who are oppressed and to defend their rights (Prov. 31:8, 9). We are also to identify with and care for those who are imprisoned and ill-treated (Heb. 13:3). This is the basis of the evangelical response to persecution: advocating on behalf of the persecuted and ministering to those who are persecuted, providing for their needs.

Go . . . and Do Likewise

Andrew van der Bijl lay on a hospital bed nursing a severely wounded ankle. He had been injured in Indonesia, fighting for the Royal Dutch East Indies Army (KNIL) in Indonesia's post–World War II independence struggle. The joyful, selfless service and love of the Franciscan nuns who cared for him and the hundreds of other wounded men prompted the cynical young man to read the Bible for the first time. That was the beginning of God's call to a lifetime of adventure as a servant of the persecuted church in lands far away.

Following a visit to Poland in 1955, Brother Andrew, as he is now known, pioneered a ministry to Christians in the Communist-ruled Soviet Union and Eastern Europe, smuggling Bibles behind the iron curtain in his Volkswagen Beetle. Every time he approached the border, Brother Andrew risked arrest and imprisonment for smuggling banned religious literature. Seeing how meticulously the border guards searched each vehicle, sometimes removing the seats, hubcaps, and even the engine, Brother Andrew chose to rely on God. "I know that no amount of cleverness on my part can get me through this border search. Dare I ask for a miracle? Let me take some of the Bibles out and leave them in the open where they will be seen. Then, Lord, I cannot possibly be depending on my own stratagems, can I? I will be depending utterly upon You." Miraculously, he sailed through the Romanian border with the Romanian-language Bibles stacked on the seat beside him.[6] A firm believer that life is more than self and there is no higher calling than to live and be poured out for Jesus Christ, Brother Andrew epitomizes the biblical call to serve the suffering. Wryly nicknamed "God's Smuggler," he founded Open Doors, an agency specializing in providing for the needs of the persecuted church worldwide.[7]

During the Cold War, when Christian persecution intensified in countries ruled by Communist regimes (particularly in Eastern Europe), a new breed of Evangelicals grew. They ministered to the persecuted and their families by providing for their needs and speaking up for religious freedom. These included pioneers like Brother Andrew, as well as leaders like Richard Wurmbrand. Wurmbrand was himself a victim of persecution, imprisoned many times for preaching the gospel in the underground churches he established to escape Communist control. He was also persecuted for his outspoken denouncement of Communist persecution of Christians in his native Romania.

---

6. Brother Andrew, with Elizabeth Sherrill and John Sherrill, *God's Smuggler* (New York: New American Library, 1967), 174, 198.

7. Brother Andrew, John Sherrill, and Elizabeth Sherrill, *The Narrow Road: Stories of Those Who Walk this Road Together* (Grand Rapids: Revell, 2011).

In 1945, while about four thousand religious leaders in Romania were gathered to pledge loyalty to the new Communist regime, Wurmbrand made the bold statement that a Christian's duty is to glorify God alone.[8] Three years later the secret police arrested him. Wurmbrand spent a total of fourteen years in prisons, three of which were in solitary confinement. He was severely tortured, both physically and psychologically.[9] His wife, Sabina, was also imprisoned for three years for refusing to denounce Christ, leaving their young son, Mihai, to fend for himself. In 1964 Richard Wurmbrand was granted an amnesty.

Fearing Wurmbrand would be imprisoned again, underground church leaders urged him to leave Romania. Two concerned Christian organizations negotiated with Communist authorities for his release from Romania in exchange for a large sum of money.[10] In 1966 Wurmbrand testified before the United States Senate Internal Security Subcommittee. He showed his scars of torture and focused media attention on the persecution of Christians by Communist regimes. Known as the "father of the underground church," Wumbrand devoted the rest of his life to advocating for and ministering to the persecuted church. He and Sabina founded Voice of the Martyrs, which carries out their vision throughout the world.

Written Witness

Writing that documents persecution and various aspects of religious liberty—covering theological, spiritual, and practical dimensions—is one of the greatest legacies evangelical champions of religious freedom have given the world. Wurmbrand and Brother Andrew each wrote many books documenting their experiences. In more recent years Paul Marshall, Glenn Penner, Ronald Boyd-MacMillan, and many others—as well as organizations like Voice of the Martyrs, Open Doors, Release International, and Christian Solidarity Worldwide—have published extensively on the subject. *Sorrow and Blood: Christian Mission in Contexts of Suffering, Persecution, and Martyrdom*,[11] a compendium of writings by authors from around globe and produced by the World Evangelical Alliance Missions Commission and Religious Liberty Commission, is an excellent resource on global persecution. Publications like this one stand as a testimony of the horrific and increasing violations of religious freedom and human rights worldwide and provide a testimony of the living history of the church, the faithfulness of the persecuted church, and, of course, God's glory.

Advocates for Religious Freedom

Many organizations with an evangelical heritage—such as Advocates International, Christian Solidarity Worldwide, Jubilee Campaign, and Release International—are professional advocates for religious freedom worldwide. The tireless, unseen, and often forgotten work of these organizations and many more has contributed immensely to the cause of promoting religious liberty and human rights for all.

Equipping and strengthening the persecuted church to not lose faith as it goes through times of trial and persecution is another critical component in serving the persecuted church. Hence, "an indispensable tool in combating

Richard Wurmbrand said that a Christian's duty is to glorify God alone.
Photo: Voice of the Martyrs

8. "The History of VOMC," Voice of the Martyrs, http://www.persecution.net/history.htm/.

9. Richard Wurmbrand, *Tortured for Christ* (Bartlesville, OK: Living Sacrifice Book Company, 1967).

10. Richard Wurmbrand, *With God in Solitary Confinement* (Bartlesville, OK: Living Sacrifice Book Company, 2001), 127–28.

11. William D. Taylor, Antonia van der Meer, and Reg Reimer, eds. *Sorrow and Blood: Christian Mission in Contexts of Suffering, Persecution, and Martyrdom* (New York: World Evangelical Alliance, 2012).

persecution is mature disciples."[12] Unfortunately, churches often neglect this aspect of preparation. There are amazing stories of church growth stemming from persecution from the time of the early church, recorded in the book of Acts, to the present day. However, history is also littered with examples like those of the once thriving Christian communities in Japan, Turkey, and North Africa that were annihilated by savage persecution.

Organizations concerned with protecting religious liberty help train Evangelicals in the biblical theology of persecution and the practical aspects of facing and enduring persecution, as well as on advocacy and basic human rights, depending on the need. This training enables Christians in restricted nations to understand the true nature of persecution as a spiritual battle, to stand firm in their faith, to practice forgiveness, and to speak up and seek justice wherever possible. As history demonstrates, churches rooted in Scripture and prepared for persecution thrive in spite of it, but churches based on shallow teaching and unprepared to face persecution will not survive.

Religious Liberty as a Human Right

The importance of human rights has spread across the globe as a standard of good governance and justice. The Universal Declaration of Human Rights, the International Covenant on Civil and Political Rights, and other international instruments enshrine the freedom of religion or belief among the other fundamental human rights. Article 18 of the Universal Declaration of Human Rights, which is the universal measurement of human rights standards, has declared, "Everyone has the right to freedom of thought, conscience and religion; this right includes freedom to change his religion or belief, and freedom, either alone or in community with others and in public or private, to manifest his religion or belief in teaching, practice, worship and observance."[13] The International Covenant on Civil and Political Rights echoes the same standard of religious freedom.

Religious freedom advocates and organizations increasingly use these standards, as well as national and international legal mechanisms, when seeking justice for victims of religious liberty violations. Activists also engage in quiet diplomacy with governments of nations where there is repression, as well as with nations that can be positive influencers, in order to promote religious liberty. The World Evangelical Alliance (WEA), for example, has had fruitful dialogue with China, Bhutan, Sudan, and many other countries.

Religious freedom advocates also approach international bodies like the United Nations Human Rights Council, making recommendations and filing stakeholder reports during the process of the United Nations Human Rights Council Universal Periodic Review of countries.[14] Advocates engage the United Nations Special Rapporteur on Freedom of Religion or Belief and the United States Commission for International Religious Freedom, and they appear before the International Criminal Court.

The Jubilee Campaign, which promotes human rights and religious liberty and holds special consultative status with the United Nations Economic and Social Council, has been in the forefront of a campaign against violence in Nigeria. Christian Solidarity Worldwide and others have worked tirelessly for decades, campaigning for international human rights bodies to address violations, imprisonments, and illegal detentions in many nations around the world, including North Korea, Eritrea, Myanmar, China, Iran, Libya, Egypt, and others.

Advocates International, a global network of Christian lawyers begun in 1991, trains, mentors, and encourages Christian law professionals to do justice with compassion. Advocates International and its regional affiliates have been active in promoting religious freedom through advocacy, litigation, and legislation. In 1992

---

12. Reg Reimer, "Persecution, Advocacy and Mission," in *Suffering, Persecution and Martyrdom: Theological Reflections*, ed. Christof Sauer and Richard Howell (Edleen, South Africa: AcadSA, 2010), 340.

13. Adopted by the United Nations General Assembly in 1948, following the experiences of World War Two. http://www.un.org/en/documents/udhr/, accessed March 21, 2014.

14. In the UPR process, all member nations are called to report on their human rights record once every four years. http://www.ohchr.org/en/hrbodies/upr/pages/uprmain.aspx, accessed March 21, 2014.

two board members of Advocates International intervened on behalf of the First Evangelical Congregation Church in Sofia, Bulgaria, to recover properties confiscated by Communist authorities years earlier.[15] Since then, Advocates International has inspired hundreds of Christian legal professionals from the world over to advocate for religious liberty and other human rights.

In an effort to promote religious freedom as a human right of all people in a part of the world where there are high incidents of violations, a network of religious liberty activists was formed in South Asia. This network happened as the result of discussions led by Christian Solidarity Worldwide, the WEA Religious Liberty Commission, and the Asia Evangelical Alliance Religious Liberty Commission. An inaugural consultation on the Freedom of Religion or Belief held in 2013 in Sri Lanka brought together religious freedom advocates and experts in South Asia, including the United Nations Special Rapporteur on Freedom of Religion or Belief and religious freedom advocates from different faiths—Christians, Muslims, Hindus, and Buddhists—who were experiencing persecution in their respective countries.

Since its inception as the Evangelical Alliance in 1846, the WEA, which represents around six hundred million Evangelical Christians worldwide, has been involved in the religious liberty movement worldwide. In 1992 WEA formed the Religious Liberty Commission with the specific purpose of promoting freedom of religion worldwide, as defined by Article 18 of the United Nations Declaration on Human Rights[16] and in accordance with God's Word.[17] The WEA's commitment to religious liberty is ongoing. This was reiterated in the "Resolution on Religious Freedom and Solidarity with the Persecuted Church," adopted at the 2008 WEA General Assembly.[18]

In 1997 the organization received consultative status with the United Nations Economic and Social Council. This propelled the WEA's work on human rights and religious liberty, enabling and fostering an official Evangelical response to religious freedom issues worldwide. The WEA has submitted reservations and recommendations to the United Nations Human Rights Council on countries where religious persecution persists.

The WEA and the National Alliances

The WEA also promotes and equips national evangelical alliances to engage the issue of religious liberty in their respective nations. Some national alliances have excelled as pioneers of religious liberty in their own right through their own national and regional religious liberty commissions. The BEA was the first national alliance to engage in advocacy for religious liberty as far back as the 1850s, petitioning and advocating for the freedom of worship with governments around the world and with a high degree of success in campaigns in Turkey, Russia, Italy, and Spain.[19] Today a large number of the national evangelical alliances have an active religious liberty commission.

The Evangelical Alliance in the United Kingdom, The Evangelical Fellowship of Canada, the Evangelical Fellowship of India, the National Christian Evangelical Alliance of Sri Lanka, and the Religious Liberty Commissions in Germany, Switzerland, and Austria are notable for their work toward promoting and protecting religious liberty. Their work includes targeting the very roots of oppression through effective advocacy and instigating legal action to repeal repressive laws and regulations, as well as ministering to and providing for the needs of individual victims in the midst of oppression and persecution.

---

15. http://www.advocatesinternational.org/content/chronology-advocacy-mentoring-1991-2010, accessed March 21, 2014.

16. Universal Declaration of Human Rights (1945), Article 18, "Everyone has the right to freedom of thought, conscience and religion; this right includes freedom to change his religion or belief, and freedom, either alone or in community with others and in public or private, to manifest his religion or belief in teaching, practice, worship and observance."

17. 2 Timothy 3:12; Hebrews 13:3; 1 Peter 2:13–17; Hebrews 10:32–29.

18. http://worldevangelicals.org/pdf/Christof%20Sauer%20Pattaya%2009.pdf, accessed March 21, 2014.

19. http://www.eauk.org/connect/about-us/upload/The-Evangelical-Alliance_-A-brief-history.pdf, accessed March 21, 2014.

In 2012 the Evangelical Fellowship of India challenged a religion act in the state of Himachal that operated as an anti-conversion law. The state's high court quashed some draconian sections of the oppressive law, a small but significant victory in a country where anti-conversion laws still operate in five states.[20] The Asia Evangelical Alliance Religious Liberty Commission, the Socio-Political arm of the European Evangelical Alliance, and the Ethics, Peace and Justice Commission of the Association of Evangelicals in Africa promote and facilitate the defense of religious liberty in their respective regions.

Active national alliances also quickly respond when there is a significant development affecting religious freedom in their country, be it the murder of a pastor, a violent attack on a church, the passing of an oppressive law, or an act of state-enforced repression. Local knowledge and presence on the ground give alliances a vital advantage for deciding the best response or action, an advantage larger international organizations often lack. They are also uniquely placed to touch individual victims and minister to each one.

A pastor ministering to a small congregation in a rural Sri Lankan village was facing numerous challenges that continued over a period of time. This pastor received death threats, the home where his wife and three small children lived was attacked, the well from which the family drew its drinking water was poisoned, mobs held public demonstrations against him, and he was denounced as a criminal and a beggar. The pastor decided not to complain to the police about his tormentors. When asked why, he replied, "I want them to see Jesus. If I retaliate and go against them to the authorities, they will not see Jesus."[21] Today he continues to minister in the same village. His attackers saw his decision as a willingness to suffer without complaint for what he believed in.

In the aftermath of the horrific attacks in 2008 on Christians in Orissa and Kandamal in India, which left many Christians dead and over fifty thousand homeless, some widows living in temporary tents with their children were asked what they needed. "We want our children to grow up in the faith for which their fathers sacrificed their lives" was the answer of these women who were surviving with little food and no proper sanitation or running water.[22]

Christianity was introduced to North Africa around the first or early second century AD and spread to other parts of Africa. These were among some of the earliest Christian communities in the world. King Ezana, who ruled Aksum (the region covering modern-day Ethiopia) during the fourth century, embraced Christianity and declared it the official religion of his kingdom. Subsequently, while Christianity declined in many parts of Africa due to the advancement of Islam, it remained strong in Ethiopia.

Many centuries later, in 1974, the Communist regime that came to power banned all evangelical activities. Recognizing the evangelical church in Ethiopia would not survive repression if the churches did not unite, the evangelical leaders there banded together to form an umbrella association encompassing not only main churches but also most local churches spread all over the country. This was the birth of the Evangelical Churches Fellowship of Ethiopia. After the formation of the fellowship in 1976, its leaders were arrested. They were imprisoned and tortured by the Communist state. Even in the face of such hostility and suffering, the fellowship conducted frequent meetings, extending spiritual and physical support and guidance to member church leaders.[23] Today the Ethiopian Fellowship continues to function as a vibrant body in a country where Evangelicals are the minority.[24]

20. "Some Relief for Freedom of Religion," Press Release issued by the Evangelical Fellowship of India (August 31, 2012). Refers to Section 4 of the Himachal Pradesh Freedom of Religion Act 2006 and Rule 3 of the Himachal Pradesh Freedom of Religion Rules 2007.

21. Roshini Wickremesinhe of the National Christian Evangelical Alliance of Sri Lanka, in conversation with the victim in a location in Sri Lanka. Name of Sri Lankan pastor cannot be used due to security.

22. Godfrey Yogarajah of the WEA, in conversation with victims during a visit to Orissa and Kandamal with the Evangelical Fellowship of India. Names of widows cannot be used due to security.

23. http://www.ecfethiopia.org/history.htm, accessed March 21, 2014.

24. 3% of the population where 43% are Christians; see http://www.csi-int.org/world_map_africa_religion.php.

There are nations where national alliances and religious liberty commissions function under oppressive circumstances. The local alliance of an Asian nation, which for decades has suffered under the yoke of military oppression, formed a religious liberty commission. Within two months the group had initiated dialogue between Christian leaders, which brought together Evangelicals and the traditional church, and the leaders of the majority religious group in the country. Scattered across the globe are also groups and individuals who advocate religious liberty and serve the persecuted and oppressed while braving persecution themselves for their convictions.

Speaking as One Voice

Leaders from the WEA, Voice of the Martyrs Canada, and Open Doors International discussed and initiated the Religious Liberty Partnership in 2008, bringing together twenty-five like-minded agencies working against religious persecution around the world. The Religious Liberty Partnership facilitates, encourages, and nurtures partnerships, collaboration, and transparency between the different organizations for the purpose of accurate information gathering and dissemination, effective advocacy, and timely assistance for victims. The Religious Liberty Partnership has engaged in collective advocacy and work in cooperation on issues of common interest, such as apostasy laws in the Middle East and an early warning system for religious liberty violations.

A further organized dimension to evangelical engagement for religious liberty has been added by the founding of the International Institute for Religious Freedom (IIRF) of the World Evangelical Alliance in 2006. It is harnessing scholarly research and academia for the cause of religious freedom. Scholars from various disciplines contribute to its consultations and to the *International Journal for Religious Freedom,* as well as various book series and periodicals. Doctoral students researching religious liberty and persecution find competent promoters and a network of peers. The IIRF also established the first professorship at a theological faculty that is focusing on religious freedom and persecution in 2014. Consultancy, such as on the methodology of the World Watch List of Open Doors International, is helping to make the publications of advocacy agencies more reliable. Courts, parliaments, and politicians call for witness and documentation by the institute. Long-term theological reflection on martyrdom and persecution helps the worldwide church in theological education and in appropriate responses to discrimination and persecution.

Pray Without Ceasing

"Our prayers can go where we cannot . . . there are no borders, no prison walls, no doors that are closed to us when we pray," said Brother Andrew.[25] Persecuted Christians from every continent consistently ask the global church for prayer. The International Day of Prayer for the Persecuted Church, a global event held in November, takes the message of the persecuted church to millions around the world, answering that call.

Prayer is the greatest and most important response a Christian can offer to the persecuted. The majority of countries classified as the worst offenders of religious persecution are situated in the global South, which is comprised of Central and Latin America, Africa, and most of Asia. Due to the intensity and magnitude of violations, there is a perception that religious liberty is under threat only in those regions. However, religious liberty is also under threat in the global North. The threats are subtle and often veiled in the language of secularism, individual freedom, inclusiveness, or choice. As much as the church in the global South needs prayer, the church in Europe and North America needs prayer, too.

---

25. Susan Devore Williams, *And God Changed His Mind* (Grand Rapids: Revell, 1991), 165.

In the Palm of His Hand

Throughout history Evangelicals have displayed a keen commitment to religious liberty, and they continue to champion freedom of religion around the world. Awareness of religious liberty violations has increased significantly. Many who hear the reports allow their hearts to be broken by the stories of the persecuted. They embrace them with love and minister to them in humility. They bind their wounds, wipe their tears, feed and clothe them, share their stories with the world, speak up for them where they have no voice, seek justice for them, and stand in the gap for them and intercede. Those who are persecuted and those who work on their behalf are the true heroes of our faith.

Bibliography

Bates, M. Searle. *Religious Liberty: An Inquiry*. New York: International Missionary Council, 1945.

Brother Andrew, with Elizabeth Sherrill and John Sherrill. *God's Smuggler*. Grand Rapids: Baker, 2001.

Devore Williams, Susan. *And God Changed His Mind*. Grand Rapids: Revell, 1991.

Miller, Alexei, and Alfred J. Rieber, eds. *Imperial Rule*. Budapest, Hungary: Central European University Press, 2004.

Reimer, Reg. "Persecution, Advocacy and Mission." In *Suffering, Persecution and Martyrdom: Theological Reflections*, edited by Christof Sauer and Richard Howell. Edleen, South Africa: AcadSA, 2010.

Schirrmacher, Thomas. "The Early History of the Evangelical Alliance and of its Advocacy of Religious Freedom." ProMundis (blog), May 8, 2012, http://www.thomasschirrmacher.net/ blog/the-early-history-of-the-evangelical-alliance-and-of-its-advocacy-of-religious-freedom/.

———. "The Early History of the Evangelical Alliance and of its Advocacy of Religious Freedom." *International Journal of Religious Freedom* 5, no. 1 (2012): 164.

Taylor, William D., Antonia van der Meer, and Reg Reimer, eds. *Sorrow and Blood: Christian Mission in Contexts of Suffering, Persecution, and Martyrdom*. New York: World Evangelical Alliance, 2012.

Wurmbrand, Richard. *Tortured for Christ*. Bartlesville, OK: Living Sacrifice Book Company, 1967.

Wurmbrand, Richard. *With God in Solitary Confinement*. Bartlesville, OK: Living Sacrifice Book Company, 2001.

Roshini Wickremesinhe is the director of the Colombo office of the International Institute for Religious Freedom.

Godfrey Yogarajah is the executive director of the Religious Liberty Commission of the World Evangelical Alliance.

"I rejoice in the growth of Evangelicalism around the world and I hope it will be able to express and teach Evangelical truth with joy and without defensiveness, to practice mission with an enthusiasm fostered by a deep spirituality, to remain creative in the invention of new forms of service to the human needs of the poor, to denounce evil in persons and structures, and to announce the good news of God's Kingdom."

—Dr. Samuel Escobar, Professor Facultad Protestante de Teología UEBE, Madrid, Spain

EVANGELICALS AND SOCIAL JUSTICE

By Ron Sider

Social justice exists when justice prevails in society. But what is justice? For millennia, many thinkers have agreed with Aristotle that justice exists when people receive their due. But people are not isolated individuals. They live in groups and institutions. Justice, therefore, requires that people, groups, and institutions all receive their due. But what is due to them?

To answer that question it is helpful to distinguish three aspects of justice: commutative, procedural, and distributive. *Commutative* justice requires fairness in agreements and exchanges (e.g., honest weights and measures) between private persons and groups. *Procedural* justice requires fair procedures and processes (e.g., unbiased courts and a transparent legal framework). *Distributive* justice refers to the ways in which all the goods of society (e.g., money, land, education, etc.) are divided.

Photo: www.designpics.com

Because everyone's understanding of what justice requires flows significantly from each person's deepest religious/philosophical views, our world is full of competing definitions of justice that are grounded in a variety of different religious and secular philosophies. Since Evangelicals seek to allow biblical revelation to shape their thinking decisively, we must ask: What does the Bible tell us about the nature of justice?

God is the ultimate foundation of justice. "Endow the king with *your* justice, O God" (Ps. 72:1 NIV; italics added). God loves justice (Isa. 61:8) and calls God's people to do justice (Deut. 10:18–19).

While the Bible is not an academic or philosophical treatise on justice, throughout the Scriptures we receive teaching about the nature of justice. God clearly demands *commutative* justice. Weights and measures should be fair because "honest scales and balances belong to the LORD" (Prov. 16:11 NIV). That God demands *procedural* justice is clear from the several texts about the way God demands unbiased courts and hates bribes that corrupt the judicial process (Ex. 23:6, 8; Deut. 1:16–17; 16:18–20).

Does God demand *distributive* justice as well? Some Evangelicals in recent decades have said no. All that is needed for justice to prevail is for the societal procedures to be fair (e.g., laws should apply to everyone and the courts should be transparent and unbiased), no matter how society's goods are divided, no matter how poor or rich some people may be. Other Evangelicals believe the Bible demands not only procedural but also distributive justice. The Bible contains important material relevant to this debate.

The Scriptures and Distributive Justice

Throughout the Scriptures we are taught the Creator made people designed to flourish precisely as material *and* spiritual beings. If we were only "souls," then very unequal distribution of material things like food, money, necessary clothing, housing, and health care would be irrelevant to human flourishing. But since we are material as well as spiritual beings, we can flourish only if there is a just distribution of material things.

The Hebrew words for "justice" (*mishpat*) and "righteousness" (*tsedaqah*) underline the importance of distributive justice. These words refer to both fair courts (procedural justice) and fair economic systems (distributive justice). The prophets denounced the way powerful people seized, often through legal trickery, the land of weaker people and thus forced them into poverty (Isa.5:7–9; Mic. 2:2). In fact, God became so angry with the economic injustice among God's chosen people that God sent them into foreign captivity. But the prophets also promised a future Messianic time when injustice would be abolished. In that day, each person would have his own land again without fear of oppression (Mic. 4:4). The Hebrew words for *justice* and *righteousness* clearly refer to distributive justice in this context.

The hundreds and hundreds of biblical verses about God's special concern for the poor underline the importance of distributive justice. God acts in history to lift up the poor and the oppressed (Ex. 3:7–8; Ps. 140:12). God tears down those who get rich by oppression (Jer. 5:26–29). Self-proclaimed believers who do not share God's concern for the poor are really not Christians at all (Matt. 25:41–43; Jer. 22:13–19). God's special concern for the poor does not mean God is biased. God loves everyone equally. But precisely for that reason God is not neutral in situations of poverty and oppression. When some people oppress others, God actively sides with the oppressed—in order to liberate both the oppressed and the oppressor. God measures people and societies by what they do to the people on the bottom. God demands fair distribution of society's resources.

But does the Bible offer any concrete definition of distributive justice? Old Testament material concerning the land provides an important clue. Since Israel was an agricultural society, land was the most important resource (capital) for producing wealth. When Israel moved into the land of Canaan, God commanded that every family receive its own land. God also stipulated that every fifty years, the family land would be returned, no matter how or why the land had been lost (Lev. 25). As we have seen, the prophets denounced the way powerful people seized the land of their poorer neighbors. Indeed, the prophets said God punished this economic injustice with national exile. But when the Messiah came, each person would have his land again.

God wants every person and family to have access to the available productive resources so that, if they work responsibly, they can earn a sufficiency of material resources and be dignified members of their community. In a world where billions live in poverty—lacking adequate food, clean water, affordable health care, and good education—while others live in enormous wealth, the biblical principles of distributive justice demand sweeping change if social justice is to prevail.

Searching for Social Justice

There is another biblical teaching that is important for an evangelical understanding of social justice. Sin is both personal and social, and social structures (i.e., legal and economic systems) can be unjust. While Evangelicals are quite clear that God condemns personal sin (i.e., lying, stealing, or committing adultery), they often overlook the fact that God also abhors unjust socioeconomic systems (i.e., legalized slavery, apartheid, and economic systems designed to benefit some unfairly and deprive others entirely).

The prophets condemned both sexual sin *and* economic injustice (Amos 2:6–7), drunkenness *and* systemic exploitation of the poor (Isa. 5:8–9, 11). They denounced unfair legal and economic systems (Ps. 94:20–23; Isa. 10:1–4). When we choose to create or benefit from unfair socioeconomic systems, we sin against God and neighbor. When we ask why poverty and oppression exist and seek their structural, systemic causes and corrections, we are engaged in the search for social justice.

Abolitionists and the Social Sin of Slavery

In the eighteenth and nineteenth centuries Evangelicals often played a major role in promoting and, alas, sometimes also undermining social justice. William Wilberforce was a prominent member of the British parliament in the late eighteenth and early nineteenth centuries. A committed Evangelical, he was deeply engaged in evangelism in England and abroad. But Wilberforce's great calling was to battle the terrible evils of the slave trade and slavery itself. He used his political skills to persuade the British parliament first to end the slave trade and then, as he lay dying, to abolish slavery itself, thus transforming the British Empire.

At the same time, tragically, some American Evangelicals were defending and perpetuating slavery. But others disagreed. Charles Finney was the Billy Graham of mid-nineteenth-century America. He held evangelistic crusades around the country. But he also preached against the social sin of slavery, demanding that converts at his evangelistic meetings abandon their connections to slavery. Oberlin College, the evangelical college in Ohio where Finney taught theology for part of every year, became an important center of the abolitionist movement. (Thoroughly evangelical, Oberlin College was the first American college to grant degrees to both African Americans and women.[1]) Finney was an important leader in one of the major abolitionist societies. And the Oberlin students he encouraged to go out to evangelize Native Americans also tried to force the federal government to keep the many treaties they made (and then regularly violated) with the Native Americans.

The Missionary Influence

Nineteenth-century missionaries who went to Africa and Asia also contributed to social justice. They taught a new understanding of the dignity and value of women that elevated the status of women in important ways. As they built hospitals and schools, these Evangelicals contributed significantly to social justice. In Africa, many of the African leaders who led the twentieth-century movements for freedom and independence from Western colonialism were educated in mission schools.

Unfortunately, toward the end of the nineteenth and into the early twentieth centuries, the Great Reversal occurred. Partly because of the emergence of dispensational theology (which was pessimistic about any improvements in society before Christ's return), Evangelicals despaired of Wilberforce and Finney's hope that society could be improved. As theologically liberal Christians in the early twentieth century emphasized more and more a social gospel focused largely or exclusively on socioeconomic change via politics, Evangelicals (especially Americans) turned inward, focusing almost entirely on evangelism and ignoring social justice in the larger society. And, because of the large number and influence of missionaries from the United States, this one-sided emphasis on evangelism and neglect of social justice influenced many younger churches in Africa and Asia.

Embracing Social Justice in the Twentieth Century

Slowly, by the middle of the twentieth century, things began to change. People like Carl Henry and Billy Graham spearheaded movements and organizations (e.g., the magazine *Christianity Today*) that slowly promoted greater concern for social justice. By the early 1970s, younger Evangelicals, dismayed that their elders had ignored or even opposed Dr. Martin Luther King Jr.'s great civil rights movement against American racism and segregation, issued the "Chicago Declaration of Evangelical Social Concern" in 1973.[2]

The next year saw a very important step toward the embrace of social justice by Evangelicals around the world. Evangelicals from all continents gathered in Lausanne, Switzerland for Lausanne I: The International Congress on World Evangelization. Powerful plenary addresses by younger Latin American Evangelicals René Padilla and Samuel Escobar helped move thousands of Evangelicals at Lausanne to make a historic declaration on social justice: "We . . . should share [God's] concern for justice and reconciliation throughout human society and for the liberation of men and women from every kind of oppression. . . . [W]e express penitence both for our neglect and for having sometimes regarded evangelism and social concern as mutually exclusive. . . . [E]vangelism and socio-political involvement are both part of our Christian duty. . . . [W]e should not be afraid to denounce evil and injustice wherever they exist."[3]

---

1. Public Broadcasting Service (PBS), "People and Ideas: Charles Finney," *God in America*, October 11, 2010, http://www.pbs.org/godinamerica/people/charles-finney.html/.

2. "Chicago Declaration of Evangelical Social Concern," *Evangelicals for Social Action*, accessed January 16, 2014.

3. "The Lausanne Covenant," The Lausanne Movement, accessed January 19, 2014, http://www.lausanne.org/en/documents/lausanne-covenant.html/.

Social Justice in the Global South

This historic global document, the Lausanne Covenant of 1974, affirmed and encouraged a growing engagement with social justice by younger Evangelicals all around the world, especially in Latin America, Africa, and Asia. Interaction with their own local context as they sought to apply the Scriptures faithfully had already prompted many younger Evangelicals from the developing world to challenge racial and economic oppression and work for social justice. The Lausanne Covenant's affirmation of social responsibility provided affirmation that nurtured a steadily expanding engagement on all kinds of social justice issues.

In Latin America, Evangelicals like René Padilla, Samuel Escobar, and Orlando Costas led the Latin American Theological Fraternity in a vigorous and simultaneously sympathetic and critical dialogue with liberation theologians and their vigorous critique of global economic injustice. In Kenya, David Gitari, trained by the International Fellowship of Evangelical Students (IFES), modeled a superb combination of evangelism and social action in his Anglican diocese and boldly challenged national political injustice as bishop and then as archbishop for all of Kenya. In South Africa, younger black Evangelicals like Moss Nthla condemned white evangelical acceptance of apartheid and developed an evangelical movement in the black church that contributed to the eventual overthrow of apartheid.

In India, Evangelicals Vinay and Colleen Samuel developed a large holistic ministry in a huge slum of Bangalore and then pioneered what became a vast program of microloans that empowered thousands of poor people to start tiny businesses to improve their economic lives. In the Philippines, Evangelical university graduates formerly active in the IFES formed the Institute for Studies in Asian Church and Culture (ISACC) led by Melba Maggay. They developed programs promoting holistic ministry and took an active role in the famous People Power Revolution, which nonviolently overthrew the vicious dictatorship of President Ferdinand Marcos in 1986.

In the 1980s and 1990s the International Fellowship of Evangelical Mission Theologians (INFEMIT) led by Vinay Samuel nurtured a rapidly growing concern for holistic ministry, especially among younger evangelical leaders in the global South. Three global conferences on economics sponsored by INFEMIT deepened evangelical thinking about economic justice and produced the "Oxford Declaration on Christian Faith and Economics" (1990), which combined biblical principles on justice with careful economic thinking. The INFEMIT network also led to the establishment of the Oxford Centre for Mission Studies, which has enabled scores of global South evangelical leaders to write doctoral dissertations on a wide variety of topics based on social justice and holistic mission.

Turn-of-the-Century Evangelicals and Social Justice

In the last decade of the twentieth century and the first decade of the twenty-first, evangelical engagement with issues of social justice has greatly expanded and deepened. A massive increase in evangelical participation in campaigns on issues like religious freedom, sex trafficking, and human rights around the world prompted one prominent secular journalist (Nicholas Kristof) to speak in 2002 of Evangelicals as the "newest internationalists" in *The New York Times*. Global Pentecostalism, the fastest growing part of both Evangelicalism and Christianity as a whole, has increasingly embraced social justice. More and more Pentecostals in countries all around the world are actively engaged in holistic ministries and programs that lift people out of poverty and promote social justice.

The World Evangelical Alliance (WEA) has greatly strengthened its work on a wide range of social justice issues, including reducing global poverty and promoting religious freedom and peacemaking. Increasingly, more Evangelicals have abandoned a one-sided pro-Israeli position in favor of a strong affirmation of the right of both Israelis and Palestinians to live in freedom, safety, and economic well-being in a state of their own.

Micah Challenge, a global evangelical campaign to end extreme poverty, is a striking illustration of the change that is happening in evangelical circles. In the year 2000 the world's top political leaders adopted the

United Nations Millennium Declaration, now known as the Millennium Development Goals, to cut global poverty in half by 2015. The WEA and Micah Network, a global structure that had emerged from decades of rapidly growing evangelical work in relief and economic development, responded by creating Micah Challenge.

The Micah Challenge mobilizes Evangelicals for political advocacy
Image: Public Domain

Now active in fifty countries, Micah Challenge hosted a Global Leaders Forum in 2007 at which the secretary-general of the United Nations spoke. In 2010 Micah Challenge organized a day of prayer that engaged over seventy million people. Micah Challenge goes beyond relief and development, mobilizing Evangelicals for political advocacy to urge public policies that reduce poverty and promote economic justice.

Evangelical Engagement in Politics

Particularly striking has been the massive growth of Evangelical reflection on and participation in politics. Whereas forty years ago relatively few Evangelicals were involved in politics, more recently Evangelicals have flooded into the political arena. Evangelicals have filled the top political posts in a number of countries, and large numbers have joined the legislative process either by winning elections or by joining organizations explicitly formed to influence politics.

In one study of this political engagement, political scientist Paul Freston pointed out that the new Evangelical political engagement was too often unwise because frequently it was not grounded in careful systematic reflection on how biblical Christians should do politics.[4] That failure happened in part because for decades there had been very little systematic Evangelical thought and writing about politics. But in the last ten years especially that has changed dramatically. Scores of recent Evangelical books have reflected carefully on how to engage in politics in a genuinely Christian way.[5]

Concerns Remain

In spite of the massive growth of global Evangelical engagement on issues of social justice, there are still reasons for concern. One weakness is the ongoing failure of many Evangelicals to understand the reality of social sin and structural injustice (Micah Challenge is an exception). As a consequence, many Evangelicals still think that the only or primary way to solve social problems is "one person at a time." Evangelicals now understand the importance of both immediate relief (e.g., when a famine, flood, or earthquake occurs) and long-term community development (e.g., to enable poor people to create wealth). But they still often overlook the clear biblical teaching about social sin and neglect the importance of correcting or abolishing economic and social structures that perpetuate injustice.

Some Evangelicals today have become so focused on social justice that there is a danger they will lose the historic Evangelical passion for evangelism. It would be a tragedy if contemporary Evangelicals repeated the mistake of Social Gospel Christians who, a century ago, embraced social justice in a way that neglected or abandoned evangelism. The Evangelical community needs a biblical balance that vigorously and wholeheartedly embraces both.

---

4. Paul Freston, *Evangelicals and Politics in Asia, Africa and Latin America* (New York: Cambridge University Press, 2001).

5. Ronald J. Sider, *Just Politics: A Guide for Christian Engagement* (Grand Rapids: Baker, 2012), xiii–xvi.

Further Reading

Cannon, Mae Elise. *Social Justice Handbook: Small Steps for a Better World*. Downers Grove, IL: InterVarsity Press, 2009.

Dayton, Donald W. *Discovering an Evangelical Heritage*. New York: Harper & Row, 1976.

Evangelicals for Social Action. "Chicago Declaration of Evangelical Social Concern." Accessed January 16, 2014. http://www.evangelicalsforsocialaction.org/chicago-declaration-of-evangelical-social-concern/.

Freston, Paul. *Evangelicals and Politics in Asia, Africa and Latin American*. Cambridge: Cambridge University Press, 2001.

Gitari, David. *In Season and Out of Season: Sermons to a Nation*. Carlisle, UK: Regnum, 1996.

Hertzke, Allen D. *Freeing God's Children: The Unlikely Alliance for Global Human Rights*. New York: Rowman & Littlefield, 2004.

The Lausanne Movement. "The Lausanne Covenant." Accessed January 19, 2014. http://www.lausanne.org/en/documents/lausanne-covenant.html.

Lee, Matthew T., Margaret M. Poloma, and Stephen G. Post. *The Heart of Religion: Spiritual Empowerment, Benevolence, and the Experience of God's Love*. New York: Oxford University Press, 2013.

Maggay, Melba Padilla. *Transforming Society*. Quezon City, Philippines: Institute for Studies in Asian Church and Culture, 1996.

McNeil, Brenda Salter and Tony Campolo. *A Credible Witness: Reflections on Power, Evangelism and Race*. Downers Grove, IL: InterVarsity Press, 2008.

Miller, Donald E., and Tetsunao Yamamori. *Global Pentecostalism: The New Face of Christian Social Engagement*. Berkeley, CA: University of California Press, 2007.

Public Broadcasting Service (PBS). "People and Ideas: Charles Finney." *God in America*, October 11, 2010. http://www.pbs.org/godinamerica/people/charles-finney.html.

Samuel, Vinay, and Chris Sugden, eds. *Mission as Transformation: A Theology of the Whole Gospel*. Oxford: Regnum, 1999.

Sider, Ronald J. *Good News and Good Works: A Theology for the Whole Gospel*. Grand Rapids: Baker, 1996.

———. *Just Politics: A Guide for Christian Engagement*. 2nd ed. Grand Rapids: Brazos, 2012.

Tizon, Al. *Transformation after Lausanne: Radical Evangelical Mission in Global-Local Perspective*. Carlisle, UK: Regnum, 2008.

Wolterstorff, Nicholas. *Until Justice and Peace Embrace: The Kuyper Lectures for 1981 Delivered at the Free University of Amsterdam*. Grand Rapids: Eerdmans, 1983.

Dr. Ron Sider is the Senior Distinguished Professor of Theology, Holistic Ministry, and Public Policy at Eastern University's Palmer Theological Seminary in King of Prussia, Pennsylvania. He has published more than thirty books, including *Rich Christians in an Age of Hunger*, lauded by *Christianity Today* as being among the top one hundred most influential books in religion in the twentieth century.

A Fresh Statement on Social Action from the World's Evangelicals

More than four thousand Evangelicals from 198 countries gathered in Cape Town for six days in October 2010. It was The Third Lausanne Congress on World Evangelization.

This congress, standing in line with the other two Lausanne gatherings, had a lofty goal: "To bring a fresh challenge to the global Church to bear witness to Jesus Christ and all his teaching—in every nation, in every sphere of society, and in the realm of ideas."[6]

The Cape Town Commitment (CTC) is the document—and hopefully the global action—that resulted. The CTC, building on the original Lausanne Covenant and The Manila Manifesto, is a document setting out biblical convictions with a call to action for the Evangelical community.

"The CTC reflects the Lausanne call for the whole Church to take the whole gospel to the whole world; it is framed in the language of love—love for the whole gospel, the whole Church, and the whole world."[7]

The call to action portion of the CTC includes the following sections:

• Bearing witness to the truth of Christ in a pluralistic, globalized world
• Building the peace of Christ in our divided and broken world
• Living the love of Christ among people of other faiths
• Discerning the will of Christ for world evangelization
• Calling the Church of Christ back to humility, integrity and simplicity
• Partnering in the body of Christ for unity in mission. —eds.

A Force for Good: The Salvation Army

Brass bands, Christmas kettles, uniformed churchgoers, ministry to the down-and-out, responding to disasters—these are some of the images that arise when we think of The Salvation Army. Yet William Booth and his wife, Catherine, likely had no idea the East London ministry they started in the mid-nineteenth century would have such a far reach, eventually working in 126 countries.

In 1865 William, a London minister, decided to leave the pulpit of his comfortable Victorian church and take the gospel message to the streets to reach the poor, homeless, and hungry. Many people responded to his message, but when he tried to send them to existing churches, they didn't feel comfortable.

Nor were they always welcomed. Churchgoers were well dressed, and they frowned upon the shabbily clothed, unwashed new Christians entering their churches. So the Booths formed a church just for them called East London Christian Mission. It was a place where all were welcome, no matter how poor.

In 1878 William asked his son Bramwell to read the mission's annual report. When Bramwell saw the phrase "The Christian Mission is a volunteer army," he objected vigorously. He did not see himself as a volunteer but as someone who was compelled to do God's work. William changed the word *volunteer* to *Salvation Army*, and The Salvation Army was born. William became the general of the new organization, and Catherine became known as "the mother of The Salvation Army."

Catherine, who as a young girl was concerned about the social problems caused by alcohol, was an integral part of the ministry from the beginning. An early feminist, she published her first pamphlet in 1859,

---

6. "The Cape Town Commitment," The Lausanne Movement, accessed July 7, 2014, http://www.lausanne.org/en/documents/ctcommitment.html.

7. Ibid.

Female Ministry: Or, Women's Right to Preach the Gospel. Although timid and at first restricting her own teaching to children, she eventually overcame her shyness and became a much sought-after preacher. While William preached mostly to the poor, Catherine's audience was usually the wealthy, from whom she received financial support for their growing ministry.

In the early years many workers from London's textile industry, as well as domestic servants, became soldiers and officers of The Salvation Army. The organization quickly grew, spreading overseas in the 1880s. By the early twentieth century it was established in many countries, including Korea in 1908. Now hospitals, colleges, and other institutions all over the world are named after the Booths.

From the beginning it was a two-pronged ministry: both a church and a social services agency. Perhaps this has to do with how its workers have viewed poverty. Poverty is not just a lack of food or money but a breakdown of relationships: with people, financial systems, the environment, and, ultimately, with God. The Salvation Army workers believe in an integrated mission that helps people rebuild those broken relationships.

The Salvation Army is well equipped to respond quickly during emergencies—floods in Indonesia and Australia, uprisings in the Democratic Republic of Congo, earthquakes in New Zealand and Japan, drought in India, extreme cold in Ukraine, tornadoes in the United States, a volcano in Chile. One of its biggest relief efforts came in 2005 when Hurricane Katrina raged through the southern United States. More recently The Salvation Army has been working with Lutheran World Relief to provide assistance for Syrian refugees in Jordan.

The organization also tackles the root causes of some the most difficult social issues. For example, it has done much work to address the causes and results of human trafficking, a growing and insidious phenomenon. Over the past ten years the number of women and children sexually trafficked is on par with the estimated number of Africans enslaved in the sixteenth and seventeenth centuries.

In 2013 The Salvation Army's General André Cox called for the worldwide Salvation Army to join in echoing Pope Francis's call to end world hunger. —Debra Fieguth.

"Evangelism is at its best when Jesus is seen as truly and properly God and truly and properly human. The Good News gospel then becomes a headline which reads with a divine intuitiveness to questions of our humanity. Holding in tension both the message and the audience sits the gospel in the midst of prophetic connections."

—Commissioner Christine MacMillan, Senior Advisor for Social Justice (WEA), Founding Director of The Salvation Army, International Social Justice Commission; Former Territorial Commander Canada and Bermuda, The Salvation Army

EVANGELICALS AND POLITICS

By Tim Costello

Politics is about handling the complexities of how individuals and groups live together. It involves a deliberation and negotiation around power, capital, and labor: how to share the benefits of growth and, in tough times, the burden of sacrifice. It does so within governing frameworks of easing the possibilities for exchange in the market and therefore power balances needed to ensure a free and fair market. In relatively peaceful times politics is the choice, through negotiation or edict, that gives directions to subjects/citizens that will be obeyed because of the coercive power of rule.

Even in a democracy, the notion of a majority in parliament hides the implicit ancient threat of a greater force. That coercive power of the state is the means to impose its edicts, whether in taxing, imprisoning, or even executing its adversaries. In revolutionary times of instability and times of external threat from other powers, it is a flexing of explicit might, usually in a military campaign, to advance perceived interests. In both peaceful and violent periods, politics is the means to decide who gets what they want and who loses and misses out.

Polis is the root word of politics and literally means "Greek city–state," where cosmopolitan groups with different gods, ethnicities, and preferences had to compromise in order to live together despite their differences. Aristotle believed the very purpose of politics was to form character and shape citizens who would learn virtue through political participation. Politics in ancient Greece was inescapable and worth embracing enthusiastically. Deliberation, debate, and active citizenship were inherently good in themselves. Politics, therefore, was an essential requirement.

This Aristotelian approach to politics as character formation has never been the explicit understanding of Christians, particularly Evangelicals, who see repentance and obedience to God who has shown his face in his son Jesus as shaping character and a way to know the good. With politics, the struggle for Evangelicals has centered on two questions: Should Evangelicals be involved in the quicksand of politics? And how should they be engaged in politics given the myriad of issues and disparate concerns?

Evangelicals are people of evangelism, conversion, and missionary endeavor, but ultimately they are people of the Book. All Christian traditions source the Bible, but the signature for final evangelical authority for doctrine is, what does the Bible say? When it comes to politics, it is the same question, what does the Bible teach? Before attempting to answer that question, I want to peruse what the evangelical experience of political engagement has been.

Evangelical Political Engagement

Political engagement for Evangelicals has varied from a full-blooded commitment like that in the Westminster Houses of Parliament of Victorian times, when the Evangelical Party was at its zenith (as seen in the factory and child labor reforms of that era); to periods of withdrawal and isolation; to an

Aristotle believed the very purpose of politics was to form character and shape citizens who would learn virtue through political participation.
Image: North Wind Picture Archives

apolitical stance after the modernist and social gospel reactions. And everything in between. Today there is a resurgence of political activity of both the Evangelical left and the right around the world. There is indeed a left and a right side to the political bias and positioning of people who consider themselves as being Evangelical, and this is true the world over.

The current Evangelical consensus is that nonengagement and political neutrality are impossible and lack faithfulness to God. Beyond this consensus, however, the varied responses and support of Evangelical Christians for mainstream or Christian parties reflect a varied understanding of which particular Scriptures are given the most weight.

Wilberforce, Finney, and Postmillennialism

Some Evangelicals today are fond of citing William Wilberforce and Charles Finney (the Billy Graham of his time) as political exemplars for their leadership against eighteenth- and nineteenth-century slavery. Wilberforce was a politician who chose to stay in the British Parliament rather than leave and take up a spiritual calling, namely to train to be an Anglican minister and preach the gospel. As an Evangelical, Wilberforce was torn. Preaching and saving souls was regarded as a higher calling than the temporal realm of politics. However, he came to see clearly that his calling as a Christian was to be in the political fray.

Finney was an effective evangelist in the 1830s in northern New York. He employed controversial new methods of public appeals for conversion and the use of the "anxious seat," a place at the front of a meeting for those people in need of prayer or considering conversion. Both Wilberforce and Finney lived before the advent of religious modernism and biblical criticism that undermined faith in the Bible as the infallible, inerrant word of God, and before the social gospel that precipitated an Evangelical withdrawal from political engagement.

The renewed interest in these two men as Evangelical heroes has emboldened Evangelical commitment to political struggle as a fruit of the gospel. Wilberforce's story is better known but perhaps not the details of opposition he faced in his time from Bible believers and the church. The Evangelical group that published *The Record* used this magazine to attack him for straying away from the gospel. They reminded him Jesus had said nothing about slavery and the apostle Paul had sent the runaway slave Onesimus back to his master (Philem. vv. 10–19). So why, they asked of Wilberforce, would focus on some inconsequentials and not the good news of salvation of souls? Wilberforce had to go deeper into the text and beneath the literal words to consolidate his view that all people, including slaves, are made in the image of God and that the good news should set them free.

Finney as an evangelist from the northern part of the United States was strongly pro-abolition, but it was his methods that raised eyebrows. Finney wanted people saved so he could enlist them in the abolitionist cause. He refused the sacraments to slave owners and slavery supporters, and he was president of a theological college that trained blacks for the ministry. No one could question Finney's power as an evangelist in seeing conversions, but they did criticize his politics.

Both Wilberforce and Finney shared a view of strong postmillennialism common to Evangelicals at that time. Postmillennialism can mean many things, but it always refers to the biblical vision of a final golden age within history. It was a positive view of politics and engagement as building the reign of God on earth and holding the belief that Jesus would return to complete this advance.

Up until 1830, postmillennial thinking motivated missionary movements. Millennialism is based on chapter 20 in the book of Revelation and refers to a thousand-year rule of Christ. Every prayer for revival and Evangelistic endeavor assumed an immediate missionary dimension. God was viewed as wanting to bring the message of redemption to glorious fulfilment. Christ's reign was not just a wish, a dream, a plan, and an ideal. Instead, his reign was on the verge of being inaugurated through the church and its far-flung missionary efforts.[1] But this

---

1. H. Richard Niebuhr, *The Kingdom of God in America* (New York: Harper & Brothers, 1959), 26, 46.

postmillennial hope of a golden age of prosperity and universal peace followed by the return of Christ (after the millennium) would soon fragment Evangelicals.

Many began to sense individual salvation was becoming secondary to political humanization and social development. They worried that postmillennialism meant the accent was falling on the gradual improvement of society through political and social struggle in moving toward the dawn of the millennium. For a majority of Evangelicals, service of the soul, not the body, became primary, a distinction unfamiliar to Wilberforce and Finney.

Moody and Premillennialism

Around 1840, when the terms *pre-* and *postmillennial* were coined, the premillennial view emerged as the dominant one for most Evangelicals. Christians would be raptured from earth to heaven, and Christ would return (pre-, before, the millennium). This belief was a radical reversal of the accepted attitude to politics, because it saw there would be the gradual deterioration (not improvement) of the world until Christ returned to usher in the millennium. It was a shift from a focus on the here-and-now of earthly concerns to heaven, and this shift became a distinctive Evangelical position. This emphasis on the return of Christ and of seeing the individual's choices as decisive, imbued deep misgivings with the world of transient politics.

Dwight Moody typified this shift for Evangelicals in the second half of the nineteenth century as he pictured the sinner standing alone before God. The response to Moody's preaching of the message of salvation was essentially a decision each individual person was able to make. The vision had shifted from engagement in all areas of God's world as an expression of a spiritual life that includes politics, justice, and society as a sign of the reign of God (and, therefore, concern with structural sins) to a concentration on personal sins. It was a shift away from social involvement and toward exclusively verbal evangelism. Indeed, soon all progressive social concern, whether political or private, became suspect for Evangelicals.

Yet Moody and others saw that evangelism still had definite social consequences, largely in the private areas of indulging in alcohol, adultery, and gambling. The social consequences came through individual conversions that took precedence and effectively squeezed out any priority on Christian political and social work. Conversions were depicted as the root that would eventually produce fruit that might include social reform.

Nonetheless, the premillennialist position saw little hope for society before Christ returned to establish his kingdom. Moody's most quoted statement summarized this disengagement and the pointlessness of politics: "I look upon this world as a wrecked vessel. God has given me a lifeboat and said to me, 'Moody, save all you can.'"[2] Salvation meant being saved from this world. This was a significant departure from what had been the dominant tradition of American and British Evangelicalism (Moody's revivals in Britain were huge). Until then, Evangelicals had had a positive view of the reformability of society consistent with the gospel spreading and precipitating a golden age as in postmillennialist thinking.[3] Politics was a tool for reforming society.

Dwight L. Moody preached a message of personal salvation
Image: North Wind Picture Archives

---

2. Quoted in Mark A. Noll, *The Old Religion in a New World: The History of North American Christianity* (Grand Rapids: Eerdmans, 2002), 131.

3. George M. Marsden, *Fundamentalism and American Culture. The Shaping of Twentieth-Century Evangelicalism: 1870–1925* (New York: Oxford University Press, 1980), 322–27.

Henry's Call for an Evangelical Social Ethic

Carl Henry called for an Evangelical social ethic.
Photo: Public Domain

The challenge to address this retreat began in earnest in the 1940s with Carl Henry, a Wheaton College graduate, lecturer at Fuller Theological Seminary, and editor of the evangelical magazine *Christianity Today*. At Fuller, professors were quietly dropping premillennial views. They were moving away from the kingdom-later idea that Christians would be raptured or removed from this world before the millennium and therefore needed to have no interest in this world or the reign of the kingdom of God of earth and social change now.

In his 1947 book *The Uneasy Conscience of Modern Fundamentalism* Henry indicted the "evaporation of fundamentalist humanitarianism"[4] and asked why, in its opposition to religious modernism and the social gospel, it had retreated and given up on humanitarian efforts. Instead of acknowledging the world-changing potential of the gospel, it had narrowed the gospel to world-resisting doctrinal concerns, such as alcohol, dancing, and movies. Should it not, Henry argued, be addressing war, totalitarianism, inadequate international dealings, and the evils of racial hatred and intolerance and the exploitation of labor-management relations? "There is no room . . . for a gospel that is indifferent to the needs of the total man nor of the global man," he concluded.[5] Henry questioned why Evangelicalism, in revolting against the social gospel, seemed to also revolt against the Christian social imperative. He criticized religious modernists who cultivated a social gospel in efforts to build a "higher civilizations" but did so to the exclusion of personal salvation.[6]

Although this book proved to be a bombshell for Evangelicals, Henry's conception of social engagement consisted largely of placing redeemed individuals into positions of social importance so as not to sacrifice "world statesmanship to men of godless convictions."[7] Henry was clear about there being no one direct line from the Bible to the ballot box.

Readers at the time might have discerned a mildly conservative bent in the pages of *Christianity Today* because political activity was still only a marginally legitimate activity for Evangelicals. Lewis Smedes, a former Evangelical colleague of Henry's at Fuller, wished Henry "would land on some specific points and call his shots. . . . Is he against the War on Poverty? Is he against social security and Medicare? Is he for the government legislation on civil rights?"[8] Smedes concluded that the net impression of Henry's essay was Evangelicals did not yet have a social ethic.

But Henry's signal against retreat and his call to Evangelicals to engage reflected the fluidity of post–World War II Evangelical politics. Although the basis for social change remained, personal conversion Evangelicals were now more likely to bring their spiritual values into the political realm. They were considering political activism, rather than their dominant spiritual and otherworldly isolation from politics. As Swartz noted, Henry's journey to reengage the gospel in social change led Evangelicals in many directions. It was a call to go public, including the political sphere, with their convictions grounded in their faith and interpretation of Scripture.[9]

---

4. Quoted in David R. Swartz, *Moral Minority The Evangelical Left in an Age of Conservatism* (Philadelphia: University of Pennsylvania Press, 2012), 20.

5. Ibid., 21.

6. Ibid., 20.

7. Ibid., 21.

8. Lewis Smedes, "The Evangelicals and the Social Question," *Reformed Journal* 16 (February 1966): 9–13.

9. Swartz, *Moral Minority*, 24–25.

Saving Bodies and Social Structures as Well as Souls

This reengagement received further fine-tuning at Lausanne I: The International Congress on World Evangelization held in 1974 and instigated by Billy Graham. Lausanne I attracted 2,700 leaders from 150 nations, at least half from the global south for debate over the task of evangelism. British Evangelical Anglican John Stott admitted he had changed his mind on the Great Commission, no longer interpreting it exclusively in terms of evangelism. He wrote, "I now see more clearly that not only the consequences of the commission but the actual commission itself must be understood to include social as well as evangelistic responsibility, unless we are to be guilty of distorting the words of Jesus."[10]

This elevation of social responsibility (and political intent) to a status alongside evangelism was seen by some as a return to the holism of the nineteenth-century Evangelicals. For others, like Samuel Escobar and other Latin American delegates, it was to redress a North American type of evangelism that focused on results and techniques that sought to save souls so efficiently it served only to baptize the conservative status quo. Escobar declared, "Christians, evangelicals in particular, oppose the violence of revolution but not the violence of war; they condemn the totalitarianism of the left but not that of the right; they speak openly in favor of Israel, but very seldom speak or do anything about the Palestinian refugees; they condemn all the sins that well behaved middle class people condemn but say nothing about exploitation, intrigue, and dirty political maneuvering done by great multinational corporations around the world."[11]

Escobar charged that North American Evangelicals failed to understand the multidimensional aspects of the gospel beyond saving souls. He said the gospel was also about saving bodies and social structures. He urged the Lausanne delegates to understand "discipleship in the daily social, economic and political aspects of life as a sign of the kingdom and an anticipation of the new creation."[12] Here was an Evangelical who had participated in the key international congresses on world evangelism in Berlin (1966), Bogota (1969), Ottawa (1970), and Madrid (1974) and taken part in the drafting of the 1974 Lausanne Covenant, raising fundamental questions. Escobar was criticizing a reduced gospel that was technique driven and grounded in efficiency.

Scholar and activist René Padilla, who was also involved in Lausanne I, declared that evangelization based on a "systemization of methods and resources to obtain pre-established results found no precedent in Scripture but in fierce pragmatism."[13] He charged that Western Christians were trying to think through the Great Commission in a politically uncritical context while Southern Evangelicals were living out discipleship in the heat of life-and-death political battles. Not surprisingly, those from the global South (Central and Latin America, Africa, and most of Asia) regarded the Western evangelical effort of saving souls as quickly as possible as preserving the conservative status quo and hegemony of oppressive military, dictatorial, and powerful business domination of political rule.

Their cry restored a bridge between the Western Evangelical left and Evangelicals in the global South, asserting a multidimensional gospel that included social justice and engagement with politics. The legacy of this protest from the global South is with us today. It is now impossible to do mission and evangelism without a prophetic engagement with the powers that cripple human bodies and not just their souls.

Mission Outreach as a Political Act

For many Evangelicals the very essence of politics, namely compromise, is difficult. To even mention the word raises the innate difficulty of engaging truth with the flux and ambiguities of politics. Evangelicals believe

10. David J. Bosch, *Transforming Mission: Paradigm Shifts in Theology of Mission* (Maryknoll, NY: Orbis, 1991), 415.

11. Quoted in Swartz, *Moral Minority*, 123.

12. Ibid., 123.

13. Ibid., 123.

God's truth and word is absolute and to compromise is disobedient and even idolatrous. How do you compromise the Word of God? How then, without absolute clarity, can you be involved in politics which is of essence about compromise and lesser choices?

Not that this barrier has impeded evangelical action. Evangelicals have an extraordinary history of mission and outreach, and almost always integral in its wake has been the practical care for the poor that inevitably displaces and disturbs power: a political act. Whether it has been expressed through caring for the lower castes in India, through establishing health and education outposts in the toughest places, or through empowering women who are marginalized, this missional activity has invited hostility from Brahmin rulers, from men, and from the powerful.

While the motivation is spiritual and not political, an upsetting of the given order is always an outcome. Defeating poverty is impossible without addressing power entrenched in injustice and inequality. It is also impossible without changed hearts that demand of rulers they practice transparency and accountability for all children of God, whatever gender or caste or tribe. Such a call is inherently political. It requires political checks and balances and structural changes to accommodate an evangelical vision of justice.

Many evangelical bodies have risen up and engaged in the work of transforming lives. The Evangelical Alliance TEAR, a movement of Christians to address poverty around the world, is one such example. A creation of the Evangelical community, it has been a quintessential vehicle for combining faith, evangelism, politics, and development. World Vision was also born of this evangelical vision and is now the largest development agency in the world with forty-five thousand staff in more than one hundred countries. In Australia, which is regarded as a secular country, twenty of the twenty-five largest charities are Christian faith based, and many of those are evangelical.

Globally, the number of projects and dollar commitment to the global poor through evangelical organizations is breathtaking. Without the service of these Evangelical agencies, the world would be in even more dire straits. Likewise, the costly service of evangelical churches throughout Africa and Asia and Latin America and their courageous, prophetic voice have transformed communities and given hope to millions of impoverished lives. But the journey to such worldly engagement that does not shy away from power and politics has not always been smooth.

The Bible and a Blueprint for Politics

This chapter opened by asking the central Evangelical question, what does the Bible teach about politics? In truth, the ambivalence experienced by Evangelicals in their journey is a direct result of the difficulty in answering this question unambiguously. Evangelicals are not alone in searching for a biblical answer to the meaning of politics. The Bible with its parables, commandments, kings, judges, prophets, priests, and Messiah revealed in Jesus has served as a reference point for Western politics for centuries. Just about every political movement has extracted its own message and legitimated its own cause from the text. For the left, it has inspired calls for social justice, democracy, and wealth redistribution. The Exodus story has even inspired revolution and the overthrow of the status quo. For the right, the Hebrew Bible has been preached to validate monarchy, traditional social arrangements, patriarchy and family structure (despite polygamy), and opposition to gay marriage. Both sides can select preferred texts and come to radically opposite political policies.

The truth in Scripture is that the stories, messages, and political contexts are simply too diverse to fit neatly into any unified view of politics and theory of government. The Bible is full of political incidents but not political theory or appreciation for politics as a way of life. Much has been said about domestic policy and special regard for the poor, but no foreign policy has been addressed other than not to trust in chariots but to trust God and his judgments through other nations. The Hebrew Bible has largely religious and moral teachings but not political ones.

So how do Evangelicals read the New Testament in relation to politics? The language of the New Testament is highly political. It speaks of an alternative kingdom and the rule of God (not Herod) that is good news for the poor and the prisoner. But beyond that, there is again the same absence of any campaign blueprint or real politick.

Jesus has refused Israel's expectation and demand for a political messiah to liberate them from national humiliation under the Romans. His distinctive announcement is that the kingdom of new power relationships has begun in his ministry. His kingdom is highly political in one sense, as "the last shall be first" and the least shall be the greatest (Matt. 20:16 KJV; Luke 9:48). But it is an entirely new definition of who gets what they want and who misses out. This is because enemies and Samaritans and lepers are all included. This kingdom is plausible only in the light of the resurrection that says this radical way of inclusion does not end with Jesus' crucifixion. In fact, it has now taken root. It will ultimately triumph, and it invites us in faith to live this way here on earth whatever the cost.

So a blueprint for Evangelicals when it comes to politics is not possible. We Evangelicals find our way in the real world as we faithfully seek to serve the God of our Lord Jesus Christ in the place he has put us, constantly allowing Scripture to challenge our preconceptions and penetrate our souls. Many of us live in democracies where we can elect to vote. We are citizens with the responsibility to participate—to live out the alternative way of Jesus and see the poor as he did—as being of utmost importance. For some of us there will be opportunities to participate or to address the powers and principalities of our times as William Wilberforce did. For others our calling will be to live with integrity and to discern our times prayerfully, to stand up for justice, mercy, and truth telling.

Successes and Failures of Evangelicals in Politics

By Debra Fieguth

The story of Evangelicals involved in politics is, not surprisingly, mixed. Some have had remarkably godly successes, and others have been marked by abject failures. What follows are some examples from countries around the world that illustrate both.

In Africa . . .

Olusegan ("The Lord Is Victorious") Obasanjo, a former president of Nigeria, fought the corruption for which the country was notorious and championed debt relief and democratic institutions. During his 1999–2007 term, Nigeria's economic growth doubled, partly due to rising oil prices. In the years since, Obasanjo has worked through his United Kingdom-based foundation to advance human security in Africa, increase agricultural capacity, promote youth employment and empowerment, support the education of girls, and combat disease.

Further south, now-deceased Frederick Chiluba, a former trade unionist who was elected president of Zambia in 1991, gave Evangelicals much hope at the beginning. He declared Zambia a Christian nation, even beginning meetings with prayer. He denounced corruption and witchcraft. But after ten years in power he was accused of personal corruption. Although he was eventually acquitted of all charges, a cloud remained. It is an example of how the best of intentions can be corrupted by power.

South Africa officially declared itself a Christian country during the apartheid years of 1961 to 1994, yet it was known for its oppression of blacks by a small group of white Christians. Throughout the country's history there have been varying levels of involvement by Evangelicals. Frank Chikane, a black pastor and human rights advocate, later an advisor to President Thabo Mbeki, had earlier been arrested by the South African police and tortured by a white deacon from his own apostolic denomination. Chikane is currently president of Apostolic Faith Mission and a consultant to President Jacob Zuma.

In Latin America . . .

Latin America has experienced an enormous growth of Evangelicals over the past few decades. Pentecostals especially have supplanted Catholics in many parts of the region. Some countries are known to be majority Evangelical. The politics of some, however, are troubling. In Guatemala, for example, General Efrain Rios Montt, an Evangelical convert from the Roman Catholic Church, ruled as a dictator from 1982 to 1983. Human rights abuses, particularly toward indigenous Mayas, were widely documented during his regime. In 2012 he was indicted for genocide and crimes against humanity, and convicted. Although his convictions were later overturned, and supporters say he did not know of the abuses, it seems improbable for a military general not to have known about them.

In contrast, Marina Silva, a poor woman from the Amazon region, became involved in liberation theology, a movement often associated with Roman Catholic theologians. A member of the Workers' Party, she was elected senator and converted to Pentecostalism. Rather than changing her politics or leaving it altogether, Silva remained with the party. In 2003 she was made minister of the environment, a post she held for several years. Eventually she resigned from the government because she felt environmental issues were not getting the traction they needed. She eventually switched parties to join the Green Party and then ran for president, winning 20 percent of the vote. She has since left the Green Party to start her own party and plans another run for the presidency.

Evangelicals in politics, especially in Latin America, generally follow two models, observed Professor Paul Freston, who divides his time between universities in Canada and Brazil. One is the lone ranger, a model used by many who run for political office only to fall prey to the temptations of power. The second is the corporatist model. Candidates are nominated by a church leadership, and members are instructed to vote for them. That approach, Freston noted, is also flawed. Christians who fall into that camp "have been disproportionately involved in corruption." Freston has advised solid preparation, broad knowledge, and apprenticeship for any Evangelicals contemplating the challenges of politics.

In Asia . . .

South Korea is a country with a significant number of Evangelicals, Protestants making up 40 percent of the members of the National Assembly. The country has had three Christian presidents in recent years: Syngman Rhee (1948–60), Kim Young-sam (1993–98), and Lee Myung-bak (2008–13). During his presidency Kim presided over a massive anticorruption campaign, granting amnesty to thousands of political prisoners. After his presidency he traveled the world promoting democracy. Under Lee's leadership Korea's global visibility and influence increased, and Korea hosted the G20 Summit in 2010. Among his other accomplishments, he set a goal to fight global warming.

Until recently, Evangelicals in Korean politics have worked within existing parties. In recent years a few parties using *Christian* in their name have been formed. Some note this is because Evangelicals believe politics has become corrupted and hope to make a change with a more explicit emphasis on Christian principles.

In North America . . .

In the United States a string of presidents have declared themselves to be born-again Christians. The best known was Jimmy Carter, now known globally for his humanitarian work and post-presidency peacemaking efforts. While in office (1977–81) Carter was seen as being less than successful, particularly because he seemed unable to solve the Iranian hostage crisis in 1979. Yet he signed the Panama Canal Treaty in 1977 and the Camp David agreements in 1979. During a 1978 visit to Brazil, he refused to meet leaders of a Baptist denomination because he saw them as being too cozy with the military regime. After his presidency, he and his wife, Rosalynn, founded the Carter Center to advance human rights. The center conducts peace negotiations, observes elections, and has worked in Sudan, South Sudan, Nigeria, Cote d'Ivoire, Liberia, Tunisia, Egypt, Democratic Republic of Congo, Nepal, and other countries. The center has ongoing work for democracy in China.

Tommy Douglas, a Canadian Baptist pastor who served as the premier of Saskatchewan (1944–1961), was concerned about social needs. He enacted the first universal medical plan on the continent, becoming the forerunner to Canada adopting universal health care in 1966.

In Europe . . .

Political work by Evangelicals is not always on the frontlines. Christians in Eastern Europe were tireless in their opposition to communism. One of the most striking examples took place in East Germany in 1989. After years of weekly *Friedensgebete* (translated as "prayers for peace") at a church in Leipzig, the anti-Communist movement reached a peak. A groundswell of protestors grew week by week until October 1989, when seventy thousand people met in and outside the church, followed by candlelight processions with the Christian message of no violence.

In her book *Candles Behind the Wall*, Barbara von der Heydt documented the peaceful protests that took place, with millions of East Germans eventually gathering in cities throughout the country. The *Stasi* (state police) were out in force, creating fear the regime might copy the "Chinese solution." (It was just months after the brutal crackdown on prodemocracy protestors on Beijing's Tiananmen Square.) Soldiers in East Germany had been ordered to shoot at the least provocation. Yet they held back, many believing it was the Spirit of God at work, helping to bring to an end the persecution of the regime. While the protestors came from many faith and nonfaith sectors, their common commitment to nonviolence kept the revolution peaceful. And though the prayer movement was but one factor in the fall of the Berlin Wall in early November of 1989, von der Heydt believed it "significantly influenced" the tone of the revolution.

Bibliography

Bosch, David J. *Transforming Mission: Paradigm Shifts in Theology of Mission*. New York: Orbis, 1991.

Marsden, George M. *Fundamentalism and American Culture. The Shaping of Twentieth-Century Evangelicalism: 1870-1925*. New York: Oxford University Press, 1980.

Niebuhr, H. Richard. *The Kingdom of God in America*. New York: Harper & Brothers, 1959.

Noll, Mark A. *The Old Religion in a New World: The History of North American Christianity,* Grand Rapids: Eerdmans, 2002.

Smedes, Louis. "The Evangelicals and the Social Question." *Reformed Journal* 16 (1966).

Swartz, David. *Moral Minority: The Evangelical Left in an Age of Conservatism*. Philadelphia: University of Pennsylvania Press, 2012.

von der Heydt, Barbara. *Candles Behind the Wall: Heroes of the Peaceful Revolution That Shattered Communism*. Grand Rapids: Eerdmans, 1994.

Tim Costello is the chief executive officer, of World Vision Australia, a Baptist minister, and a global leader on social justice issues.

"The future of the Evangelical Church is important for us all. Here I discovered a deep and passionate commitment to the whole Gospel: a deep conviction of the salvation and redemption of people and systems that enslave and oppress. It is critical that we maintain a deep and active prayer life, loving Christ through scriptural holiness. I believe God will graciously use us to achieve His loving will in the world."

—Graham Power, Chairman of the Power Group of Companies. Founder: Global Day of Prayer;Unashamedly Ethical, South Africa

Photo: www.designpics.com

EVANGELICALS IN THE CITY

Challenges Emerge for Christian Faith and Mission in a New Urban World

By Ash Barker

When I first met Mali,[1] she greeted us with, "I am a Christian! Are you?" It was 1999, and I was entering Klong Toey slum in Bangkok for the first time, about to begin a sabbatical with my family. All we really knew about Klong Toey was its notorious reputation as Bangkok's largest slum. We knew there was only one small church for its eighty thousand mostly Buddhist residents in two square kilometers. Mali's welcome in English came as a wonderful surprise for us. She quickly found us a home to live in and helped orientate us into the community. When we moved to live in Klong Toey permanently in 2002, Mali became part of our family and vice versa. When our son Aiden was born in 2003, Mali was right there with us in the birthing unit.

Mali loves Friday night worship at a house church we belong to in Klong Toey, and she prays fervently there for those in need. She knows firsthand what it is like to be in desperate need and for God to answer prayers. Born as one of sixteen brothers and sisters, Mali was just a little girl when her family's fishing village in southern Thailand could no longer sustain them. In search of work and the promise of a better life, they traveled by train to Bangkok with what little they had. The dream quickly became a nightmare, with only slum housing and hard, low-paying work in sweatshops. Mali's family could hardly afford even small daily rations of rice. When HIV/AIDS claimed one of Mali's brothers, the family debts started to mount up.

Mali, still a teenager at the time, was "married off" to raise money. This kind of prostitution of a vulnerable girl is common, and it saved Mali's family from starvation and dangerous moneylenders, but it scarred Mali. She told me the low point was after a fire burnt down part of her slum neighborhood. Her family was blamed and expected to pay compensation. The offer for Mali to go to Hong Kong and Singapore to pay these debts quickly was accepted.

When she arrived, she discovered she had been tricked into a trafficking ring. As a trafficked prisoner in a basement in Hong Kong, Mali tried to commit suicide numerous times between servicing customers. She cried out to God for help, and God answered. Amazingly, Mali was led to the Lord by one of her customers who had met Jesus and was new in the faith. He helped her escape and get back to Klong Toey.

The way in which Mali came to Christian faith is not in any evangelistic strategy manual. Yet her faith is real. She continues to grow in Jesus. It was only a month after Mali's return to Bangkok that she welcomed us to Klong Toey.

Just because you know Jesus, though, does not mean crippling debts suddenly disappear. Within a few years of her return, Mali began to get sick and needed to do far worse things for far less money. Eventually, my wife, Anji, and Mali worked together to find alternative employment for her by making and selling handicrafts. Mali was skilled at finding good materials and making bracelets, and this initiative soon took off. Rather than hoard success for herself, however, Mali invited neighbors in similar circumstances to join her in her enterprise, and together they founded a business called Klong Toey Handicrafts. Last year more than eighty women were involved, and they made over $200,000 in sales all around the world. The fact that Mali survived and got back to Klong Toey is a miracle, but that she shared her opportunities with others is a sign of God's grace and hope.

---

1. Mali's name was changed to protect her identity.

Growing Urban Slums: The New Norm

Mali's coming to faith may be unusual, but her circumstances are increasingly the new global norm. Complex movements from rural to urban centers, increased population growth, and free-flowing globalized markets are creating the rapid growth of urban areas the planet has not seen before. When the famous evangelical revivals began in 1800s, less than 3 percent of the population lived in urban areas. The vast majority of these urban people identified themselves as Christian. Today this has drastically changed. Evangelicals now find themselves, as of 2009, part of the first generation of the humans species who are majority urban,[2] and only about 39 percent of them identify as Christian.[3] What is especially challenging is the rise of urban slums like Klong Toey, where today one in six people live. Slums are growing by about one million people a week.[4]

Chart 1: Rural and urban population of the world, 1950-2050[5]

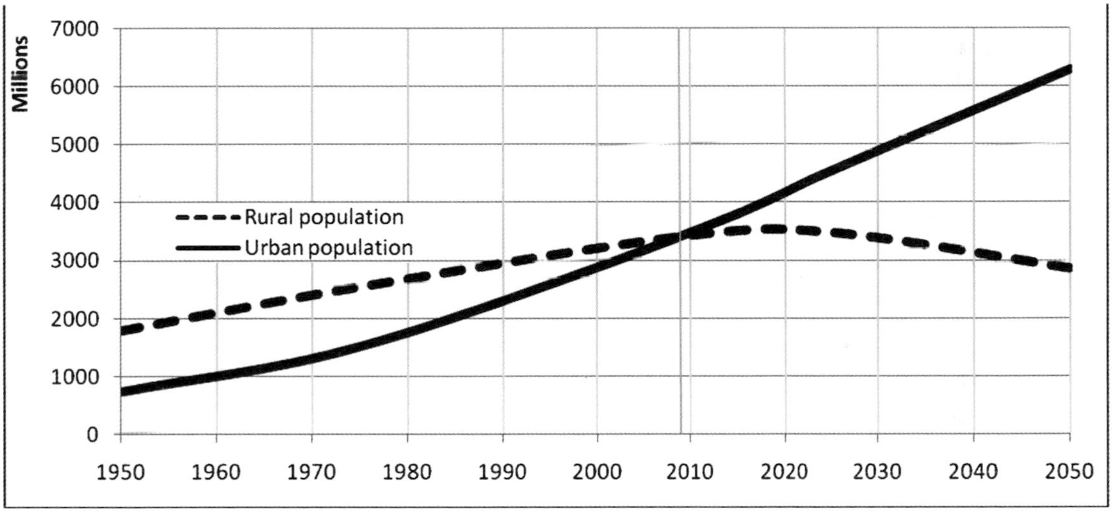

Source: United Nations, *World Urbanization Prospects*

The lives of today's urban slum residents like Mali are hard for most of us to imagine. To put this sudden growth into context, consider that when Christians were first called to go out "into all the world" (Mark 16:15 NRSV), that world contained fewer than two hundred million people. It took humanity until 1804 to reach one billion.[6] That one-billionth slum resident created this ratio: one in every six humans live in slums.[7] While it is difficult to predict with any certainty, today's urban slum residents could double within twenty years, leading to one in

---

2. United Nations, *World Urbanization Prospects—The 2009 Revision* (New York: United Nations, 2010), 2.

3. David B. Barrett, Todd M. Johnson, and Peter F. Crossing, "Christian World Communions: Five Overviews of Global Christianity, AD 1800–2025," *International Bulletin of Missionary Research* 33, no.1 (January 2009): 25–32.

4. UN-Habitat, *The Challenge of Slums: Global Report on Human Settlements 2003* (London: Earthscan, 2003), iv.

5. United Nations, *World Urbanization Prospects*, 2.

6. Matt Rosenberg, "Current World Population: Current World Population and World Population Growth Since the Year One," About.com Geography, accessed February 2, 2010, http://geography.about.com/od/obtainpopulationdata/a/world-population.htm/.

7. UN-Habitat, *Challenge of Slums*, iv.

five people (two billion) living in urban slums by 2030,[8] the entire world population of 1930.[9] The United Nations Human Settlements Programme (UN-HABITAT) has warned the number of slum residents could well reach three billion people by 2050 "if left unchecked."[10]

As chart 2 shows, Mali is not alone. Her experiences are quickly becoming the most normal human experience.

Chart 2: The rapid rise of slum and squatter neighborhoods, 1800-2025

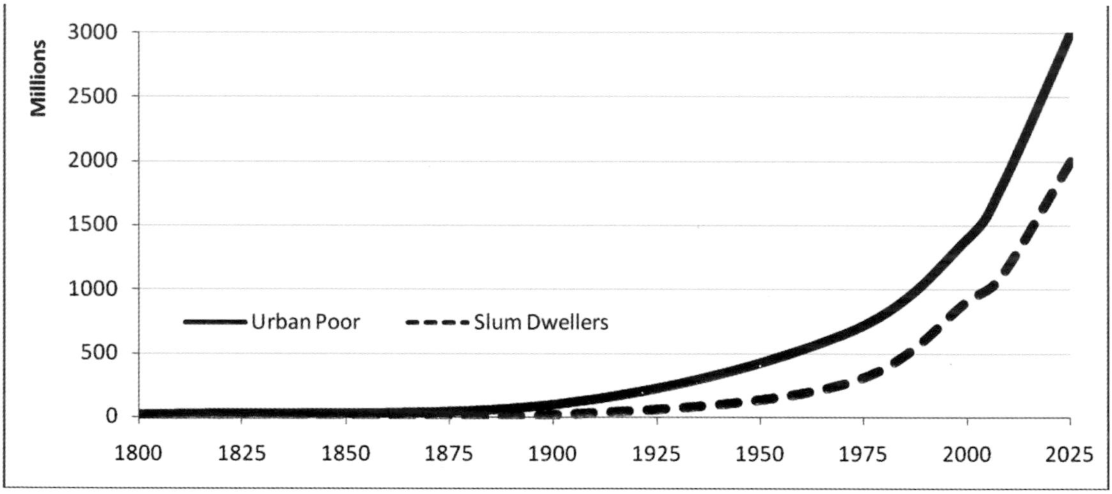

Source: UN-Habitat 2003 and David Barrett[11]

The Urban Influence of Christianity

Although Christian faith began with Jesus in the rural villages of Galilee, it grew to be an influential movement throughout Roman cities and urban centers. From its early beginnings in Jerusalem to its growth in Roman colonial cities like Ephesus and then to its eventual status as the official religion of the Roman Empire, Christianity has a history of adapting to urban conditions and finding resonance among urban populations.

Christian faith even sees its eternal life in the city of New Jerusalem (Rev. 3:12). However, this attention to the urban has not been consistently strong. At its best, for example, during the plagues in Roman cities when pagan priests and most who were able to flee did so, the courage of early Christians to stay with the afflicted is credited as an important dimension in the rise of Christianity.[12] The credibility of the Christian faith rose, too.[13]

---

8. Ibid., xxiv.

9. Rosenberg, "Current World Population."

10. http://www.un.org/youthenvoy/un-agencies/un-habitat-united-nations-human-settlements-programme/ (accessed June 26, 2014).

11. UN-Habitat, *The Challenge of Slums*, xxiv. David Barrett, 'Status of Global Mission, 2009, in the Context of 20th and 21st Centuries' http://www.movements.net/wp-content/uploads/2012/12/2012-01-028-johnson.pdf (accessed June 26, 2014).

12. Rodney Stark, *The Rise of Christianity: How the Obscure, Marginal Jesus Movement Became the Dominant Religious Force in the Western World in a Few Centuries* (San Francisco: HarperCollins, 1996), 73–94.

13. Ibid., 91–93.

Christianity can be seen at its worst when entwined with the dark spectre of European colonization. Certainly this became the case when Christianity became the official religion of the Roman Empire. Later the British, Dutch, Spanish, and Portuguese Empires—which intertwined the tasks of civilizing and Christianizing—were an especially oppressive force upon indigenous populations around the world. Cities became important bases for this colonization agenda.

Almost certainly, Christianity's urban influence began to wane prior to 1900. According to Barrett and Johnson's *Status of Global Mission*, cities seem to have been tough places for Christianity to find resonance since then. The authors note that in 1900 urban Christians made up over 68 percent of the global urban population; but by 2004 the figure was down to 39.67 percent, with projections at just 36.90 percent for 2025.[14] The decline can be seen in chart 3.

Chart 3: Proportion of Christians in global urban populations

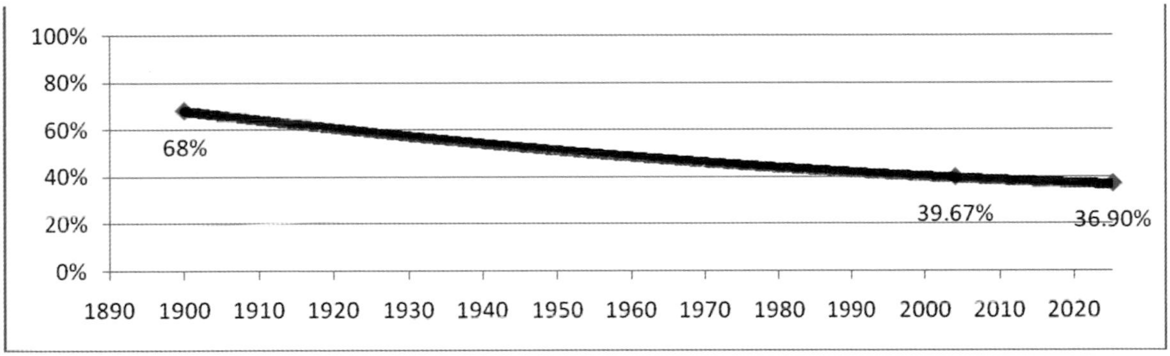

Source: Status of Global Mission, 2004[15]

Large Slums, Small Christian Populations

Some Evangelicals are adapting to this new urban world. Some Christian populations are finding resonance and growth, especially in many cities in Latin America, sub-Saharan Africa, and a few Asian countries. These, however, are now the exceptions. Urban Christianity in the West is either declining or starting to bottom out. The new, rapidly growing 10/40 Window cities (cities located approximately between 10 degrees north and 40 degrees north, covering the area of North Africa, the Middle East, and Asia) are dominated by Islam, Hinduism, or, in Bangkok's case, Buddhism. This is especially so in slum and squatter neighborhoods, where two out of three urban slum residents live in cities. In Bangkok, for example, the percentage of Evangelicals in the city could be as low as 0.3 percent,[16] with over one and a half million slum residents who have fewer than than twelve Christian churches among them.

These 10/40 Window cities are the new norm. They are where the future relevance and faithfulness of Christian faith will be found or found out. For instance, the majority of the largest fifty cities in Asia have both large numbers of slum residents and small Christian populations (see chart 4).

---

14. David B. Barrett and Todd M. Johnson, "Status of Global Mission, 2004, in Context of 20th and 21st Centuries," *International Bulletin of Missionary Research* 28, no. 1 (January 2004): 25.

15. Ibid.

16. Peter Wagner, Stephen Peters, and Mark Wilson, *Praying Through the 100 Gateway Cities of the 10/40 Window* (Seattle: YWAM, 1995), 134.

Chart 4: 50 largest urban areas in Asia by total population, 2010

	Urban area	Country	Population	Largest	%	Religions Adherents by percentage
1	TOKYO	Japan	35,467,000	Buddhists	56.0	
2	Mumbai	India	20,036,000	Hindus	69.0	
3	Delhi	India	16,983,000	Hindus	78.0	
4	Shanghai	China	15,790,000	Chinese folk	30.0	
5	Kolkata	India	15,548,000	Hindus	69.0	
6	JAKARTA	Indonesia	15,206,000	Muslims	65.0	
7	DHAKA	Bangladesh	14,625,000	Muslims	90.0	
8	Karachi	Pakistan	13,252,000	Muslims	93.0	
9	MANILA	Philippines	11,799,000	Christians	93.8	
10	BEIJING	China	11,741,000	Agnostics	36.0	
11	Osaka-Kobe	Japan	11,305,000	Buddhists	55.0	
12	Istanbul	Turkey	10,546,000	Muslims	95.0	
13	SEOUL	South Korea	9,554,000	Christians	45.7	
14	Guangzhou	China	9,447,000	Agnostics	36.0	
15	Shenzhen	China	8,114,000	Agnostics	35.0	
16	TEHRAN	Iran	7,807,000	Muslims	95.0	
17	Chennai	India	7,545,000	Hindus	83.0	
18	Wuhan	China	7,542,000	Agnostics	36.0	
19	Tianjin	China	7,468,000	Agnostics	38.0	
20	Hong Kong	China	7,416,000	Agnostics	37.0	
21	Bangaluru	India	7,216,000	Hindus	76.0	
22	Lahore	Pakistan	7,201,000	Muslims	97.0	
23	BANGKOK	Thailand	6,963,000	Buddhists	78.0	
24	Hyderabad	India	6,749,000	Hindus	83.0	
25	Chongqing	China	6,690,000	Agnostics	38.0	
26	BAGHDAD	Iraq	6,593,000	Muslims	93.0	
27	Ahmadabad	India	5,716,000	Hindus	86.0	
28	Ho Chi Minh City	Viet Nam	5,698,000	Buddhists	43.0	
29	Pune	India	5,000,000	Hindus	75.0	
30	Shenyang	China	4,952,000	Agnostics	40.0	
31	Chittagong	Bangladesh	4,914,000	Muslims	88.0	
32	RIYADH	Saudi Arabia	4,863,000	Muslims	85.0	
33	Dongguan	China	4,850,000	Agnostics	36.0	

0%   50%   100%

	Urban area	Country	Population	Largest	%	Religions Adherents by percentage
34	Bandung	Indonesia	4,786,000	Muslims	84.0	
35	HANOI	Viet Nam	4,703,000	Buddhists	43.0	
36	YANGON	Myanmar	4,635,000	Buddhists	74.0	
37	SINGAPORE	Singapore	4,590,000	Chinese folk	40.0	
38	Chengdu	China	4,266,000	Agnostics	39.0	
39	Xi'an	China	4,178,000	Agnostics	32.0	
40	Surat	India	4,166,000	Hindus	87.0	
41	Harbin	China	4,003,000	Agnostics	34.0	
42	Guiyang	China	3,980,000	Agnostics	38.0	
43	ANKARA	Turkey	3,914,000	Muslims	100.0	
44	Nanjing	China	3,813,000	Chinese folk	32.0	
45	KABUL	Afghanistan	3,753,000	Muslims	98.0	
46	Pusan	South Korea	3,529,000	Christians	52.0	
47	Surabaya	Indonesia	3,473,000	Muslims	83.0	
48	PYONGYANG	North Korea	3,439,000	Agnostics	56.0	
49	Changchun	China	3,400,000	Agnostics	35.0	
50	Kanpur	India	3,363,000	Hindus	76.0	

0%   50%   100%

*Rate = average annual growth rate, per cent per year, between dates

Source: Atlas of Global Christianity, 2000[17]

Some postcolonial cities do have high numbers of slum residents and high rates of Christian identification. This is especially the case in Latin America, sub-Saharan Africa, and Manila. But colonial-instigated Christianity is difficult to measure when nominalism and syncretism can easily be undermining active faith. If Christian community participation is one indicator of genuine Christianity, then we see mixed results in urban slums. In Manila, which has a Christian identification rate of 93.8 percent,[18] and where there are 3.3 million slum residents, urban missiologist Viv Grigg found there were 677 churches in 1998 and more than 1,000 by 2004, but only 8 percent of those churches were in slums.[19] Grigg did find higher rates of churches in slums in other postcolonial cities, such as Lima, Peru. Lima has 2.7 million slum residents and 594 churches, 90 percent of them located in the slums.[20]

In the slums of postcolonial cities with high rates of Christian identification there are reports of both high and low levels of church participation. It is difficult to make a generalized statement about the state of Christianity in the slums of these cities. What the International Society for Urban Mission can say is that, to our

17. Todd M. Johnson and Kenneth R. Ross, *Atlas of Global Christianity* (Edinburgh: Edinburgh University Press, 2009), 246.

18. Ibid., 246.

19. Viv Grigg, "Where Are the Churches of the Poor?" Urban Leaders, accessed January 11, 2011, http://www.urbanleaders. org/weburbpoor/04Context(CX)/Global%20Movements/where%20are%20the%20churches%20of%20the%20poor/churches%20of%20the%20poor.htm/.

20. Ibid.

knowledge, there are no reports of high rates of church participation in the slums of postcolonial cities where there are *few* Christians overall.

Urban slums are especially prevalent in large numbers in cities where one of three other major religions (Buddhism, Islam, and Hinduism) are a majority. We can see, for example, that Bangkok slums have over 1.5 million residents who are mostly Buddhist, and the slums have fewer than twelve Christian churches. Large Muslim cities like Dakar in Senegal have more than a million slum residents,[21] but few are Christian since 89 percent of the residents are Muslim.[22] Hindu cities like Delhi have 1.5 million slum residents,[23] 78 percent of them Hindu.[24] Majority Hindu, Muslim, and Buddhist cities all have very few Christians, but many have large numbers of slum residents.

Where urban poverty is most concentrated, and that includes where the most slum residents live, Christianity struggles the most. The so-called 10/40 Window has been highlighted as a geographical area where poverty is highest and Christianity is weakest. This region also accounts for over 630 million slum residents. That is, approximately 63 percent of all slum residents, or almost two out of every three.[25] Yet Christians make up only 8.5 percent of the population in that region, a total of 352 million.[26] Given that over 140 million of these Christians live in Eastern Asia, which includes South Korea and China,[27] the numbers become far starker for the other parts of Asia and North Africa that have higher numbers of slum residents. Indian cities like Mumbai, for instance, have 3.2 million slum residents, Delhi has 1.8 million, and Kolkata (also known as Calcutta) has 1.5 million;[28] those three cities have tiny percentages of Christians. Similar stories can be found throughout Asia, the Middle East, and Northern Africa, where all three urban conditions—rapid urbanization, postcolonialism, and the existence of another world religion in the majority—help to ensure a large number of slums with few Christians living in them.

The Evangelical Response

It is no exaggeration to say Evangelicals could well be found wanting in this new urban world. In an interconnected world, rapidly growing urban slums are a challenge to everyone's global security, equality, and stability. But Christians have a special mandate from God to seek God's "will be done, on earth as it is in heaven" (Matt. 6:10 NRSV).

Evangelical faith and mission, then, is especially challenged in how to respond to this new, urbanizing earth. It is estimated, for example, that only one in five hundred international missionaries and less than ten thousand national Christian workers focus on slums. Many of our Christian aid and development agencies are now very effective in rural areas, but most struggle in urban slums, with even

Where urban poverty is most concentrated, and that includes where the most slum residents live, Christianity struggles the most.

21. "Dakar, Senegal," Earth Observatory, accessed January 10, 2011. http://earthobservatory.nasa.gov/IOTD/view.php?id=8886/.

22. Johnson and Ross, *Atlas of Global Christianity*, 244.

23. Jeremy Page, "Indian Slum Population Doubles in Two Decades," *The Sunday Times*, December 21, 2010, http://www.timesonline.co.uk/tol/news/world/asia/article1805596.ece/.

24. Johnson and Ross, *Atlas of Global Christianity*, 246.

25. UN-Habitat, *State of the World's Cities 2006/7*, 72.

26. Johnson and Ross, *Atlas of Global Christianity*, 136.

27. Ibid., 140.

28. Jeremy Page, "Indian Slum Population."

our largest like World Vision spending only 1.3 percent of their 2004 global budget on slum projects.[29] We also know personal relationships are a key part of sharing faith, yet as Todd Johnson of the Center for Global Christianity reports, among Muslims, Hindus, and Buddhists—the three largest religions other than Christianity and the dominating religions of the growing 10/40 Window cities—less than 14 percent (or one in seven) have had personal contact with a Christian. It would not be an understatement to say Evangelical engagement is mostly missing the action in some of the most important, growing cities demographically today.

Mali's life shows what God can do in an urban slum like Klong Toey. Despite the darkest of circumstances, it is not impossible for real transformation through Jesus to shine through. Will a new generation of Christian workers rise up to submerge themselves deeply, relationally, and strategically to be part of seeing more of this happen?

Many urban Christian activists on the front line today resonate with Jeremiah 29:7: "But seek the shalom of the city where I have sent you into exile, and pray to the Lord on its behalf, for in its shalom you will find your shalom" (NRSV with "shalom" substituted for "peace"). This promise of shalom—the well-being found in the harmony between God, people, and place—is remarkable because the city in these verses, where God's people have been asked to live, pray, and seek shalom, is none other than Babylon, a city possessing the most villainous qualities in the biblical narrative.

Perhaps God is calling God's people to seek the shalom of the world's cities again, even in the most challenging of places? If for no other reason, we will have the privilege of seeing God at work in the lives of people like Mali, and in this we have the chance of finding our own shalom.

Bibliography

Barker, Ash. *Slum Life Rising: How to Enflesh Hope in a New Urban World*. Melbourne: Urban Neighbours of Hope, 2012.

Barrett, David B. and Todd M. Johnson, "Status of Global Mission, 2004, in Context of 20th and 21st Centuries," *International Bulletin of Missionary Research* 28, no. 1 (January 2004).

Barrett, David B., Todd M. Johnson, and Peter F. Crossing. "Christian World Communions: Five Overviews of Global Christianity, AD 1800–2025." *International Bulletin of Missionary Research* 33, no.1 (January 2009)

Earth Observatory. "Dakar, Senegal." Accessed January 10, 2011, http://earthobservatory.nasa.gov/IOTD/view.php?id=8886/.

Grigg, Viv. "Where Are the Churches of the Poor?" Urban Leaders, accessed January 11, 2011, http://www.urban-leaders.org/weburbpoor/04Context(CX)/Global%20Movements/where%20are%20the%20churches%20of%20the%20poor/Churches%20of%20the%20poor.htm/.

Johnson, Todd M., and Kenneth R. Ross. *Atlas of Global Christianity*. Edinburgh: Edinburgh University Press, 2009.

Page, Jeremy. "Indian Slum Population Doubles in Two Decades." *The Sunday Times*, December 21, 2010, http://www.timesonline.co.uk/tol/news/world/asia/article1805596.ece/.

Rosenberg, Matt. "Current World Population: Current World Population and World Population Growth Since the Year One." About.com Geography, accessed February 2, 2010, http://geography.about.com/od/obtain-populationdata/a/worldpopulation.htm/.

---

29. The Urban Working Group, World Vision, "The Keys to the City: Finding New Doorways to Urban Transformation— A Report and Recommendations," accessed January 8, 2010, http://www.transformational-development.org/Ministry/TransDev2.nsf/A6748A23BB21C3F08825725700707E73/$file/Urban%20R&D%20Report%20-%20Summary%20(Draft)%20%20Jan%209,%202007.pdf/.

Stark, Rodney. *The Rise of Christianity: How the Obscure, Marginal Jesus Movement Became the Dominant Religious Force in the Western World in a Few Centuries*. San Francisco: HarperCollins, 1996.

UN-Habitat. *The Challenge of Slums: Global Report on Human Settlements 2003*. London: Earthscan, 2003.

United Nations. *World Urbanization Prospects—The 2009 Revision*. New York: United Nations, 2010.

United Nations Human Settlements Programme. *The Challenge of Slums: Global Report on Human Settlements, 2003*. London: Earthscan, 2003.

The streets of Hong Kong, one of the world's largest urban centres.
Photo: The Langham Partnership

The Urban Working Group, World Vision. "The Keys to the City: Finding New Doorways to Urban Transformation—A Report and Recommendations." Accessed January 8, 2010, http://www.transformational-development.org/Ministry/TransDev2.nsf/ A6748A23BB21C3F08825725700707E73/$file/Urban%20R&D%20Report%20-%20Summary%20(Draft)%20-%20Jan%209,%202007.pdf/.

Wagner, Peter, Stephen Peters, and Mark Wilson. *Praying Through the 100 Gateway Cities of the 10/40 Window*. Seattle: YWAM, 1995.

Dr. Ash Barker founded Urban Neighbours of Hope (www.unoh.org) in Melbourne, Australia, in 1993. The organization has grown into numerous neighborhood-based teams in Thailand, Australia, and New Zealand. In 2002 Barker moved with his family to the largest slum in Bangkok, Thailand, where they have lived since then. Barker is now the convener for the newly formed International Society for Urban Mission (www.newurbanword.org).

"The innovative movements of the Holy Spirit, discerned all over Asia and Africa, surprise us with joy, precisely because the Triune God is inexhaustible, living and creative in His being. The emphasis now is on local churches which are culturally rooted in their particular contexts. It is indeed a new kairos moment for the church."

—Dr. Richard Howell, General Secretary: Evangelical Fellowship of India and Asia Evangelical Alliance

EVANGELICAL ENGAGEMENT WITH ETHNODOXOLOGY

Toward a Vision of Worship from Every People and Tongue

By Robin P. Harris

In one church in Africa, worship is announced through drums, "speaking" to those who have not yet arrived: "Hurry, the service is about to begin!" As the drumming continues, rattles and bells enter in, and singing starts. Often in a call-and-response style, the singing includes vibrato and improvised harmony. The congregation rises and moves energetically in celebration of their new life in Christ.

One newly arrived missionary joined in the celebration of song and dance. Others sat motionless, uncomfortable with the non-Western form of worship and unaware of the statement they were making through their refusal to participate.

The service ended and the believers surrounded the dancing visitor with expressions of welcome and thanks for worshipping with them. Then they asked, "Why don't the others worship with us? Do they have sin in their lives?"

Apparently among these Africans only those who have sin in their lives find it difficult to enter into worship and dance.[1]

From Whence We Have Come

During the nineteenth and twentieth centuries, as Euro-American Evangelical Christians traversed the globe, they often took with them the prevalent philosophies of their home cultures. In particular, they unknowingly succumbed to the idea of cultural evolutionism, in which one's own culture is considered to be the most highly developed, or further along on the evolutionary scale, than other more "tribal" societies and cultures. These ideas often resulted in the musical and artistic expressions of the newly encountered cultures being labeled *primitive* and *heathen*. Some Western Christians even tried to "help" local music makers by encouraging the translation of Western Christian songs into indigenous languages and teaching new converts to do things like sing in four-part harmony.

Because of the widely accepted but erroneous view of music as a universal language, it never occurred to most early mission workers that just as they needed to learn new, complex, and strange-sounding languages in order to communicate with local people, so also did they need to study and understand local music and other artistic systems. These artistic systems included dance and drama, as well as visual and verbal arts like proverbs, poetry, and storytelling. Instead, many workers simply brought their Bible in one hand and their translated hymnbooks in the other. The unfortunate result was that people in new church plants were worshipping in truth (i.e., worshipping the True God) but not in spirit; it was difficult for their hearts to engage with God using styles of music and arts unfamiliar to them.

---

1. Roberta R. King, "Do They Have Sin?" in *Worship and Mission for the Global Church: An Ethnodoxology Handbook*, ed. James R. Krabill et al. (Pasadena, CA: William Carey Library, 2013), 184.

Concerned by the charges of music colonialism, a number of evangelical missionaries from around the world have begun to resist this trend by incorporating into their thinking and practice the principles of ethnodoxology. The ethnodoxology movement—engaging locally grounded arts in worship, witness, discipleship, and meeting the needs of hurting communities—is a movement that is slowly but surely changing the face of the twenty-first century evangelical church.

One of the leaders in this movement, Dr. Brian Schrag, reminisced on the impact of the first use of a *kundi,* an indigenous harp, in a rural church in the Democratic Republic of the Congo:

> When I began to study the *kundi,* other Christians joined me and we formed a *kundi* choir called Chorale Ayo (the Love Choir). Our teacher, Punayima, composed a song for us about God creating man and woman from the earth. When we played and sang the song in a church service, the normally boisterous congregation was still and silent. I feared that we had somehow made a mistake, making people think of old gods. So after the service I asked a friend why everyone was so quiet. His reply: *'What could we do? The song cut our hearts.'*[2] (italics added).

From a Trickle to a Stream

More than a half century ago American author A. W. Tozer summed up the state of worship in the evangelical church in his book *Worship: The Missing Jewel of the Evangelical Church.*[3] And although the historical streams feeding the rise of ethnodoxology stretch back decades, if not centuries, a few notable forerunners of the movement appeared in the 1960s, around the same time as Tozer's book. For example, Dr. Vida Chenoweth was an early pioneer in connecting culturally appropriate music to cross-cultural ministry. She began applying linguistic and ethnomusicological research methods to Papua New Guinean music styles in her work with Wycliffe Bible Translators. This resulted in locally composed Scripture songs that reflected the "heart music" of their creators. Chenoweth taught this approach at Wheaton College, an evangelical campus in Illinois, in the 1980s and 1990s to many now-influential arts in mission practitioners.

Dr. Tom Avery of Wycliffe Bible Translators gathered many of these practitioners into a large team of ethnomusicologists in mission while continuing to train others. By the beginning of the twenty-first century, Wycliffe and other mission organizations around the world were expanding this approach to include not just music but all artistic forms of communication, another hallmark of what was going to be called the ethnodoxology approach.

In the late 1990s worship leader and missionary Dave Hall coined the term *ethnodoxology* by combining three Greek terms—*ethne* (peoples), *doxa* (glory), and *logos* (word). The English word *doxology* combines "words" and "glory" into a concept signifying "words to glorify" or "worship" God. Hall defined ethnodoxology as "the study of the worship of God among diverse cultures." Hall stressed a broad understanding of worship beyond the Sunday morning corporate gathering, emphasizing worship "first and foremost as a life to be lived and secondarily as an event in which to participate."[4]

The term *ethnodoxology* has gained increasingly wide usage. At the beginning of the twenty-first century a journal called *EthnoDoxology* began offering articles devoted to the multifaceted music, arts, and worship o

---

2. Brian Schrag, *Creating Local Arts Together: A Manual to Help Communities Reach Their Kingdom Goals,* James R. Krabill, gen. ed., (Pasadena, CA: William Carey Library, 2013), xxviii.

3. A. W. Tozer, *Worship: The Missing Jewel of the Evangelical Church* (Camp Hill, PA: Christian Publications, 1961).

4. "Ethnodoxology," ICE: International Council of Ethnodoxologists, accessed January 31, 2014, http://worldofworship.org/Ethnodoxology.php.

every tribe, tongue, and nation. Contributors to the journal included a growing number of evangelical ethno-musicologists and mission workers from around the world who were applying their training to a wide diversity of ministry contexts.

The ICE Network

By 2003 a group of evangelical missionaries launched a network for this global tribe of worship- and mission-focused musicians and artists. The charter members expressed their desire to use the newly emerging term *ethnodoxology* as a part of the group's identity. The International Council of Ethnodoxologists—or ICE, as it is more commonly referred to—was born. Growing steadily by its tenth anniversary to a group of more than three hundred associates in more than seventy countries and six continents, ICE launched an e-journal, *Global Forum on Arts and Christian Faith*.[5] In addition ICE has published a large, two-volume set of ethnodoxology resources.[6] These volumes clearly demonstrate the global nature of the ethnodoxology movement, with more than one hundred contributors from twenty-five countries. The largest group of countries represents the global South (Central and Latin America, Africa, and most of Asia), with the remainder coming from European and North American contexts.

In addition to providing resources and networking for the new movement, ICE has spawned regional networks of ethnodoxologists, such as ALDEA (Asociación Latinoamericana De Etno Artes), PECOP (Philippine Ethnoarts Community of Practice), and the Korean Ethnodoxology Initiative. These networks are producing their own materials and training seminars in languages that best serve their constituents.

Teaching and Learning

Although in the past, seminary courses on worship have been rare, several colleges, seminaries, and graduate schools in England, the United States, the Philippines, Thailand, Indonesia, India, and various countries in Africa (to name a few) have begun collaborating with ICE to host intensive courses on topics related to ethnodoxology. A few evangelical educational institutions now offer both undergraduate and graduate degrees in ethnodoxology-related fields, such as world arts, ethnomusicology, ethnoarts, and global worship studies. At mission conferences various seminars, tracks, and task forces on ethnodoxology, using the term in either their title or their approach, have been launched. One-week intensive ethnodoxology training events called "Arts for a Better Future," cosponsored by ICE and its partner organizations, are conducted on a regular basis. All of these new streams of teaching, learning, thinking, writing, and ministry are being energized by the emerging ethnodoxology movement.

The ethnodoxology-influenced streams of training, although gathering speed with each year, are, in fact, still relatively small compared to other approaches to worship and the arts in the cross-cultural engagement of the evangelical church. An overview of arts and mission paradigms shows three basic approaches:[7]

. "Global Forum on Arts and Christian Faith," Global Forum on Arts and Christian Faith, accessed January 31, 2014, http://www.artsandchristianfaith.org/.

. James R. Krabill, gen. ed.; Frank Fortunato, Robin P. Harris and Brian Schrag, eds., *Worship and Mission for the Global Church: An Ethnodoxology Handbook* (Pasadena, CA: William Carey Library, 2013).

. Adapted with permission from Brian Schrag, "Ethnoartistic Cocreation in the Kingdom of God," in *Worship and Mission for the Global Church*, eds. James Krabill et al., (Pasadena, CA: William Carey Library, 2013), 51–52 (see note 1). These three models are discussed in an expanded form in Schrag's chapter, "Determining Your Role as an Arts Advocate and Facilitator," in *Worship and Mission for the Global Church*, eds. James Krabill et al., (Pasadena, CA: William Carey Library, 2013), 364–366.

1. **Bring It—Teach It.** Some cross-cultural workers approach the arts in the "Bring It—Teach It" framework teaching their own arts to people in another community. This can lead to unity among diverse Christian communities, but it excludes the distinctive creations of local arts and artists.

2. **Build New Bridges.** In another framework, "Build New Bridges," artists from one community find ways to connect artistically with members of another. This approach results in collaborative artistic efforts, often in response to traumatic events or specific community needs. It is frequently used in short-term mission engagement and can have positive impact, especially if local culture is taken into consideration.

3. **Find It—Encourage It.** In a third approach, arts advocates take the "Find It—Encourage It" stance, learning to know local artists and their arts in ways that spur those artists to create in the forms they know best. The advocate enters the local creative processes, helping give birth to new creations that flow organically from the community. This approach usually requires longer-term relationships with people and, above all, a commitment to learn.

It is the "Find It—Encourage It" stance that is growing. This is ethnodoxology in action.

Practitioners of these three approaches in arts and mission are increasingly in dialog with one another working toward greater collaboration and effectiveness. In May 2013 the Mission Commission of the World Evangelical Alliance (WEA) and Lausanne Arts, in partnership with ICE, held a three-day roundtable for North American arts and mission leaders, hosted by the World Arts program of the Graduate Institute of Applied Linguistics in Dallas, Texas. This historic gathering of key leaders identified the current challenges and opportunities for arts and mission engagement worldwide. Similar future gatherings are being planned for North America and beyond, and collaborative projects between the attendees multiplied in the months following the event. The periodic Global Consultation on Music and Missions (GCoMM), which has twice gathered ethnodoxologists from around the world to venues in North America, has in recent years expanded to include locations like Singapore and Chiang Mai.

From *Monochrome* to *Mosaic*: The Growth of Multicultural Music and Arts in Gathered Worship

The principles of ethnodoxology apply not only to cross-cultural and rural contexts of ministry but also to churches located in urban centers. In communities with ethnic and cultural diversity, which are increasingly the case in urban centers around the world, ethnodoxologists are addressing the worship wars by emphasizing the importance of accepting diverse corporate worship styles, especially those of marginalized groups, as a way of showing love to our fellow worshippers and illustrating vital theological truths regarding the body of Christ. They aim to change the current reality that 11:00 Sunday morning is the most segregated hour of the week. These proponents of multicultural worship hold conferences and have formed large networks and created Facebook groups to help and support one another.

Ethnodoxologists around the world are united in four concepts:

1. Music and other art forms are *not* universal languages. Our responses to the arts are learned, not intrinsic.

> They aim to change the current reality that 11:00 Sunday morning is the most segregated hour of the week.

2. Just as in spoken language, music and other arts must be understood in their historical and cultural contexts to be interpreted correctly.

3. All people should have the opportunity to worship God in the forms that best express their hearts—their own languages, music, and other art forms.

4. Evangelical churches that value and encourage heart music and arts in worship, reflecting the various and multiple cultures in their communities, demonstrate the love of Christ to a watching world.

What difference does it make? What kinds of outcomes are we seeing from the ethnodoxology approach to arts in mission? Here is one picture, from Jim and Carla Bowman's ministry, Scriptures in Use:

The listeners in Togo are electrified as the biblical story of creation begins: "In the beginning God created the heavens and the earth." The poetic, melodious pattern of the story flows from Antoine's lips. When he reaches the repeating phrase "and God saw that it was good," he sings a song composed by a local musician, Timothée, in call-and-response style. The song is designed to reinforce the story; the words of the song are: "In the beginning God created heaven and earth. It was empty, and darkness was over the surface of the deep." The call and response is choreographed by the composer in a traditional style that glorifies God the Creator. As the villagers quickly memorize the song response and join Antoine, their voices become a chorus of blissful harmony.

Then dancing intercepts the story. The headman dances as well, thus placing his approval on the story and the event. The drum language continues. Amidst the steaming equatorial heat sitting stiffly in the air, the pulsating rhythm of the drum reaches to the stars and sounds deep into the tropical night. The storytelling and singing continue in this way. As the fire dims, the story ends. *There is not one villager who wishes to leave that place. The story in this setting has connected them to the Word and to their history. It has involved and inspired them as they interact with the story through song and dance.*[8]

Stories like this abound and multiply every day as the creativity of evangelicals from many tribes and tongues around the world is released in artistic and heartfelt response to the Lord. They are worshipping in spirit and in truth.

[This article has been adapted with permission from *Worship and Mission for the Global Church: An Ethnodoxology Handbook* (James R. Krabill, gen. ed., with Frank Fortunato, Robin P. Harris, and Brian Schrag, eds. [Pasadena: William Carey Library, 2013]) with elements from chapter 10 (Brian Schrag; 41–52), chapter 16 (Robin P. Harris; 84–88), chapter 37 (Roberta R. King; 184), and chapter 58 (Jim and Carla Bowman; 229–230). It also includes a story from page xxviii of the companion volume, *Creating Local Arts Together: A Manual to Help Communities Reach Their Kingdom Goals* by Brian Schrag, James R. Krabill, gen. ed. [Pasadena: William Carey Library, 2013]).]

Photo: The Langham Partnership

Jim and Carla Bowman, "Story and Song in Kpele-Dafo: An Innovative Church Planting Model among an Oral Culture of Togo," in James R. Krabill, managing ed. with Frank Fortunato, Robin P. Harris, and Brian Schrag, eds., *Worship and Mission for the Global Church: An Ethnodoxology Handbook* (Pasadena, CA: William Carey Library, 2013), 229–231.

Bibliography

Bowman, Jim, and Carla Bowman. "Story and Song in Kpele-Dafo: An Innovative Church Planting Model Among an Oral Culture of Togo." In *Worship and Mission for the Global Church: An Ethnodoxology Handbook*, ed. James R. Krabill et al., 229–231. Pasadena, CA: William Carey Library, 2013.

Global Forum on Arts and Christian Faith. "Global Forum on Arts and Christian Faith." Accessed January 31, 2014. http://www.artsandchristianfaith.org/.

Harris, Robin P. "The Great Misconception: Why Music is Not a Universal Language." In *Worship and Mission for the Global Church: An Ethnodoxology Handbook*, ed. James R. Krabill et al., 82–89. Pasadena, CA: William Carey Library, 2013.

ICE: International Council of Ethnodoxologists. "Ethnodoxology." Accessed January 31, 2014. http://worldofworship.org/Ethnodoxology.php/.

King, Roberta R. "Do They Have Sin?" In *Worship and Mission for the Global Church: An Ethnodoxology Handbook*, ed. James R. Krabill et al., 184. Pasadena, CA: William Carey Library, 2013.

Krabill, James R., ed. *Worship and Mission for the Global Church: An Ethnodoxology Handbook*. Pasadena, CA: William Carey Library, 2013.

Schrag, Brian. "Ethnoartistic Cocreation in the Kingdom of God." In *Worship and Mission for the Global Church: An Ethnodoxology Handbook*, ed. James R. Krabill et al., 49–56. Pasadena, CA: William Carey Library, 2013.

Schrag, Brian, and James R. Krabill, eds. *Creating Local Arts Together: A Manual to Help Communities Reach Their Kingdom Goals*. Pasadena, CA: William Carey Library, 2013.

Tozer, A.W. *Worship: The Missing Jewel of the Evangelical Church*. Camp Hill, PA: Christian Publications, 1961.

Resources and Further Reading

"Arts in Mission." *Connections: The Journal of the WEA Mission Commission* 9, nos. 2 and 3 (September 2010): 1–98.

Global Consultations on Music and Missions. http://www.gcommhome.org/.

Global Forum on Arts and Christian Faith. http://www.artsandchristianfaith.org/.

ICE: International Council of Ethnodoxologists. http://www.worldofworship.org/.

The Lausanne Movement. "Truth and the Arts in Mission." Part 2A, section 5. The Cape Town Commitment. http://www.lausanne.org/en/documents/ctcommitment.html#p2-1/.

Multicultural Worship Leaders Network Facebook page. https://www.facebook.com/groups/ 115159921876519

"Videos from the Consultation on Arts in Mission." The Lausanne Movement. http://www.lausanne.org/en /multimedia/videos/arts-in-mission-videos.html. The videos are of speakers from the May 2013 Lausanne Arts–WEA MC–ICE Consultation on Arts and Mission.

Links of interest regarding ethnoarts in the global South:

"Aldea: Asociación Latinoamericana De Etno Artes."

http://etnoartes.com/.

"Korean Ethnodoxology Initiative." Glocal Worship. http://glocalworship.net/2011/12/05/korean-ethnodoxology-initiative/.

Philippine Ethnoarts Community of Practice. http://pecop.org.

Dr. Robin P. Harris is president of the International Council of Ethnodoxologists (ICE). She is an assistant professor and Director of the Center for Excellence in World Arts at GIAL in Dallas, Texas. She has served for decades in cross-cultural contexts, including ten years in Russia, and helped launch the Arts in Mission task force of the WEA Mission Commission.

"The wonderful growth of the Evangelical Church in the Global South needs to be accompanied by conscientious Bible teaching, especially on Christian character and ethics. Earlier, liberalism brought nominalism to the church by denying God's power to act miraculously and to give us an infallible Scripture. Now a new nominalism could emerge with a generation of Christians who believe in God's power but neglect Christian character and ethics."

—Ajith Fernando, Author and Teaching Director, Youth for Christ, Sri Lanka

A church worships in Kenya.
Photo: The Langham Partnership

EVANGELICALS AND THE ARTS

By John Franklin

It is not that long ago that a chapter on the arts in a book on Evangelicals would not have been considered. The last twenty-five years have witnessed profound changes within the Evangelical community that include a new sensitivity to the arts. A growing interest, appreciation, and engagement of the arts have become a characteristic of contemporary Evangelicalism.

A Brief Pre-Twentieth-Century History

The connection between Christian faith and art has a long and distinguished history. This is particularly true with respect to visual art and music. Catholicism has typically been more arts friendly than Protestantism given a sacramental bent that discerns God in the ordinary things of life. Protestantism and its founding Reformers carried a certain suspicion about the arts, not least the visual arts, and turned attention instead to word rather than image. At the heart of this new focus on word was a shift in understanding how faith apprehends what is true. It was a shift from a more objective, communal account to one where the inner experience of the subject became paramount.

In the nineteenth century it was believed that through the aesthetic sense one could come to knowledge of the divine. Along with the elevation of the artist as a special figure able to live outside the religious and moral norms of society came warnings against the moral bankruptcy of the artist and the loss of spiritual reality in an increasingly secularized society. The evangelical voice was very much a part of the discussion (as seen in the writing of John Ruskin, a leading art critic in the Victorian era). The romantic view of the arts prevalent in the nineteenth century was characterized by its attention to feeling and dissatisfaction with a merely rational account of the world. Romanticism was a voice that allowed room for the arts as a valued component of human experience in the journey of faith. Artists of this era included William Blake and J. M. W. Turner (Britain), Caspar David Friedrich (Germany), and Eugene Delacroix (France).

As artistic expression moved further from religious sensibilities in favor of the rugged individualism of the artist, Christians in the twentieth century began to remove themselves from the world of the arts. In the early part of the twentieth century artists such as Kandinsky, Picasso, and Paul Klee turned more to abstraction. Then as culture became more secularized, so did art. The prevalence of Christian understanding diminished in the culture, so religious sensibility in the arts was also in decline. With absence came the loss of influence.

Affirmation of the arts was exchanged for a pervasive suspicion of the arts among Evangelicals. The social and spiritual revolution of the 1960s, however, contained within itself the seeds of a new openness to creativity. Authors like Hans Rookmaaker and Francis Schaeffer, who both believed in the lordship of Christ over every area of life, began to disciple a new generation of believers to understand the place of the arts within a biblical worldview. Rookmaaker's strong assertion that "art needs no justification"[1] was a breath of fresh air to many in the Evangelical community. Others remained unconvinced, believing that art has a subversive side and Christians need to be vigilant and avoid coming under its influence. The majority of evangelical faith communities, though, simply neglected the arts, receiving no teaching about the place of the arts in the life of faith.

---

1. Hans Rookmaaker, *Art Needs No Justification* (Downers Grove, IL: InterVarsity Press, 1978).

With the advent of postmodernism, the emphasis on abstract reason has been overtaken by an emphasis on concrete embodiment. The visual has eroded the primacy of the word, and in a pluralistic world of competing stories and relative truths, no one has claim to final truth. In leaving the rigor of Western reason behind, postmodernism readily embraces the arts, whether music, dance, film, visual, or theater. Symbol, narrative, and the poetic have become common and accepted ways to communicate. This new trend brings some balance to the lopsided approach—which allowed reason to dominate all of life—Evangelicals inherited from the Enlightenment of eighteenth century Europe.

Ad Deum in Angels. Choreography by Steve Rooks.
Photo: Ad Deum Dance Company

The power of the arts to move both heart and mind is unquestionable, and their presence is everywhere. We are in a transitional moment in art history. Religious believers long marginalized by the art world in the West are finding a voice through the production of high quality art work that gains the attention of believer and unbeliever alike. We are witnessing important changes as the evangelical faith community seeks to give shape to its global mission.

A Grounding in Bible and Theology

Evangelical sensibility to Scripture and theology has sometimes fueled a negative perspective of the arts. Much has been written, both past and present, that cautions of the dangers—the risk of moral compromise, the possibility of lapsing into idolatry, or simply over-indulging our passions—of the dramatic arts, of images, and of human imagination. Yet Scripture itself engages artistic expression in poetry, narrative, metaphor, parable, and image. After all, those first said to be filled with "divine spirit of God" were artists (Ex. 35:30–36:1). The created order itself offers us a glimpse into who God is and tells us of his power and glory (Ps. 19:1; Rom. 1:20).

The creation story introduces us to what has been called the cultural mandate: to be fruitful, to multiply, and to care for and steward the earth. This has profound implications for how we respond to what is given to us in our various cultural settings. Evangelicals believe those who stand in covenant relationship with God are called to approach nature and culture in a way that complies with what God requires of us. Humanity is called to draw on its own resourcefulness in maintaining order that is God honoring and allows for human flourishing. This call to order the world is an implicit affirmation of the goodness of creation. It is a call not out of the world but into the world. Making art is a key component of the exercise of stewardship.

Evangelicalism has been inclined to measure the value of its activity in terms of its contribution to evangelism. The doctrine of redemption has overshadowed the doctrine of creation and left the arts, for some, valuable only as instruments for spreading the gospel. A more holistic evangelical theological understanding considers creation as well as incarnation. These theological themes are fertile ground for Evangelical reflection on the arts.

The Sacrifice Scene in THE BIG PICTURE by Dennis Hassell.
Photo: Tara Whittaker from The Arts Engine production at "The Big Picture" by Dennis Hassell.

Art Meets Church and Culture

In the last few decades there has been a growing momentum among Evangelicals globally to give more attention to the arts. There has been significant growth in Christian artist networks, conferences, arts organizations, annual gatherings, and events, all of which focus on the intersection of art and faith. Add to this the development of art galleries, theater companies, film productions, dance troupes, writers' collectives, music making, and an ever-increasing number of books on art and faith by Evangelical authors, and it is clear that Evangelicalism is experiencing a renaissance in artistic expression. There are two main streams in which these activities flow. One is church centered, the other culture centered.

Art in the Church

Much of what is found in popular culture runs contrary to Christian values and moral practices. To resist this influence, Evangelicals often create a subculture that offers an alternative to the mainstream options. The idea that Christians should make "Christian art" can be viewed as a result of Evangelical discomfort with art. The discomfort is commonly linked to a wish to separate from mainstream culture. Art is deemed acceptable if it has religious content or is employed in the service of evangelism or worship. A more robust doctrine of creation would eliminate the too common Evangelical need for legitimizing art through religious practice. The early chapters of Genesis make clear that we are called to be those who make culture, who engage our God-given gift of imagination to innovate and create in ways that only humans can. Art is deeply personal and so inevitably will be influenced by the faith of the artist.

The history of Western music and visual art is intimately tied to the church and its faith communities, a relationship that has been conflicted in recent years, not least among Evangelicals. However, the celebration of the arts taking place in evangelical churches around the globe makes it clear we are at the dawn of a new day. Churches all over the world are finding space for visual art displays and hosting concerts and literary readings. Pastors who have a specialty in arts and worship are being hired to oversee worship life and to foster involvement of artists in the community.

In the Western part of the globe, the road to bringing the arts into the church has had its obstacles. The bleak simplicity encouraged by many within the Evangelical tent has resisted the enriched, colorful, and emotionally charged presence of art in places of worship, preferring stark auditoriums over sanctuaries that generate aesthetic pleasure. The involvement in the arts of a younger generation in the Western Hemisphere is eroding this trend and allowing the arts to be a place of hope and beauty for evangelical faith communities.

Churches in the Global South have an easier path, as they are more familiar with artistic expression. The arts are woven into the fabric of life in many of these cultures, and the presence of the arts in the church is more readily accepted. The arts are being accepted as a context in which one can meet God and be touched by the divine presence in both heart and mind. Unlike the West they are not bound by an emphasis on an intellectual account of the faith but are open to a more personal expressive practice of faith, and have less discomfort with the body as an instrument for praise and worship.

Daniel Cossette and Shizu Yasuda in Unconfined Choreography. *Photo: Ad Deum Dance Company*

Art in Culture

Evangelicals have not always felt comfortable engaging the world around them. They have sometimes failed to learn the language of the culture and hence been poorly equipped to communicate. Certainly this is true with respect to the arts. Although Evangelicals still find themselves stammering in discussions about the place of art and its value, here too there are encouraging signs of change.

"The Healing," sandstone, cast glass set on granite base with printed fractal, 10" x 20" x 18".
Credit: By Heidi Brannan

The clear call of Scripture to human salvation through Christ and the attendant responsibility to exercise a moral influence in a fallen world have the potential to lead some within Evangelicalism to adopt the goal of changing the world. Two recent cautions on this matter of transforming the world are found in books by Andy Crouch and James Davison Hunter. In his book *Culture Making: Recovering Our Creative Calling*, Crouch warned we should not be driven by an agenda to change the world.[2] ("Making culture" refers to anything from cobbling together institutions, making roads and buildings to creating music or visual art.) Instead, Evangelicals should recognize that by culture making, including art, we open up the possibility of making a difference, if only in our own circumscribed context.

Hunter, in his book *To Change the World: The Irony, Tragedy, and Possibility of Christianity in the Late Modern World*,[3] encouraged Evangelicals to resist the drive to shape the world in Christian terms; rather, they are to be a faithful presence and expect surprising outcomes from that faithfulness. One expression of faithful presence is surely to be found in the arts. Evangelical credibility in the arts will increase as less attention is given to advocating for art that preaches and more for art that is aesthetically excellent.

The work of art making is increasingly being viewed around the globe as a legitimate Christian calling. The artists need the blessing of their communities to take up their gift and engage it with integrity and authenticity so that they might be a kingdom presence in the marketplaces of the world. What follows is a list of examples of some of the ways in which Christians all over the world are bringing the gift of art to others.

- **In South Africa**. In 1993, when South Africa was in crisis over apartheid, a group of Christians from many quarters gathered over a four-year period and shaped the "Manifesto: Christians and the Arts."[4] At the heart of this document was the belief that art could speak redemptively into the social upheaval caused by apartheid. It was a call to the church to be more intentional about the oft-neglected resource of creativity.
- **In New York**. In 2005 the American Bible Society in New York City opened the now independent Museum of Biblical Art. Located on Broadway, just a few blocks from the Lincoln Center for the Performing Arts, the museum offers ongoing exhibitions of work that demonstrates the influence of the Bible on

The work of art making is increasingly being viewed around the globe as a legitimate Christian calling.

. Andy Crouch, *Culture Making: Recovering Our Creative Calling* (Downers Grove, IL: InterVarsity Press, 2008).

. James Jefferson Hunter, *To Change the World: The Irony, Tragedy, and Possibility of Christianity in the Late Modern World* (Oxford University Press, 2010).

. http://www.artsreformation.com/a001/arts-manifesto.html.

art through the ages. Although it seeks to be religiously neutral, its resonance with evangelical faith is evident.

- **In Manila**. One of the most energetic and vibrant organizations engaging culture through the arts is Kaloob Philippine Music and Dance Ministry in Manila. Ed Lapiz, the founder and the artistic and dance director, is also a pastor and conference speaker who travels internationally. At the heart of this venture is the desire to preserve the artistry of the Philippine culture that is integral to Philippine identity. There is no hesitation to bring that artistry into the context of evangelical faith.

Drama plays a big part in the Christian arts scene. "The Missionary
Photo © Dennis Hasse

- **In Europe**. Christian Artists Seminars in Europe has brought together artists in all of the disciplines to celebrate their work and consistently includes workshops and plenary sessions on political and social issues relevant to the European context. A growing number of faith-based arts initiatives have been born out of the evangelical church in Europe.

- **In Texas**. Ad Deum Dance Company in Houston has provided a fusion of faith and artistry speaking into contemporary culture since 2000.

- **In Canada**. Imago is a Canadian arts initiative founded by InterVarsity Christian Fellowship leader Wilber Sutherland in 1972. Forty years later it continues to flourish in advocating for Christian artists as it seeks to exercise a biblically based influence on Canadian culture.

- **Everywhere**. The image-based character of our culture has taken much of its shape from the long-standing influence of film. Evangelicals have written a host of books that discuss film and its significance as a location for exploring moral and spiritual values. Many evangelical publications now carry film reviews. Films—as well as novels, poetry, visual art, theater, and music—have become locations for discussion and exploration of things we hold in common as humans and settings to open conversations on important themes of religious faith. Art becomes a bridge for dialogue between Evangelicals and others.

Arts and Mission

In missions scholar Andrew Walls's important essay "The Western Discovery of Non-Western Christian Art," he noted that both Catholic and Protestant observers held that Western art in the early part of the twentieth century was "breaking down with fatigue."[5] Western art was becoming clearly secular with the declining influence of Christianity. There was some faint hope that non-Western art might breathe new life into the arts and provide for a recovery of Christian presence in the world of the arts. Non-Western art done by Christians readily took up Christian subject matter, which some thought would be an antidote for the art of the secularized West.

The arts received some attention at the 1938 International Missionary Council meetings in Tambaram, India. Later, conversations expanded to include concern that missionary work "evangelize not colonize,"[6] referring to the tendency to export Western culture to "the regions beyond." J. F. Butler's 1958 article in *The Hibbert Journal* actually raised the question "Can Missions Rescue Modern Art?"[7] Important conversations were happening. Leaders like Butler inspired the founding in 1978 of the Asian Christian Art Association, an organization intended to engage in advocacy and encouragement for Christian artists in Asia.

---

5. Andrew F. Walls, *The Missionary Movement: Studies in the Transmission of Faith* (Maryknoll, NY: Orbis, 2006), 175.

6. Ibid., 176.

7. Ibid., 178.

The discussions about art and mission that were present in the 1950s and 1960s faded into silence soon after. Then, in 2004 the Lausanne Committee for World Evangelization hosted a Consultation, the 2004 Forum for World Evangelization, in Pattaya, Thailand. About 1,500 people gathered for this event, and over thirty groups formed to discuss diverse themes related to missions and to produce a corresponding document. Forty members took up the theme "Redeeming the Arts."[8]

This discussion and the subsequent document focused on three topics believed to be essential for furthering the conversation on arts and mission: arts and a renewed theological vision, arts and discipleship in the church, and arts and the transformation of culture. Plans for Cape Town 2010: The Third Lausanne Congress on World Evangelization sought to follow up on the call articulated in that document. The program committee for this Cape Town meeting included those who brought an arts presence to that historic gathering. Drama played an important role at the Congress in the plenary gatherings, as did visual art, with a display in the Cape Town Convention Centre as well as images in the plenary sessions.

In 2008 the World Evangelical Alliance (WEA) held meetings in Pattaya, Thailand, followed by a special meeting of the Mission Commission of the WEA. At that gathering, the Mission and Art Task Force was inaugurated. So far two important projects, guided by members of the task force, have resulted. The first occurred in the fall of 2010 when the Mission Commission took the imaginative risk of publishing a double issue of its magazine *Connections* on the theme "Arts in Mission." The magazine was filled with articles detailing ways in which the arts were being engaged around the world to carry out the missional task.[9] The second project guided by the task force was a conference held in the fall of 2011 at All Nations Christian College in Hertfordshire, United Kingdom, for training in cross-cultural mission and exploration of issues related to art and mission. A third project is currently underway to convene a Global Consultation on Arts in Mission by 2016.

There have been other important steps forward for Evangelicals, arts, and mission as well.

- **Youth with a Mission (YWAM)** has for more than fifty years exercised a global reach employing innovative strategies for communicating the gospel that has given a major role to the arts.
- Operation Mobilization (OM) has developed **OM Arts International** to tap the extraordinary resources found in creative artistic imagining and to harness them for the missional task.
- **StoneWorks** provides leadership in nurturing young artists, instructing mission leaders, and bringing together networks of artists across Europe.
- The American-based **Artists in Christian Testimony Intl (ACT Intl)** commissions artists to missionary work that takes seriously the value of the arts in Evangelism and discipleship.

A number of organizations are committed to promoting and preserving indigenous artistic expression in new faith communities around the world:

- **International Council of Ethnodoxologists (ICE)** is devoted to encouraging worship arts that fit with their cultural locations.

> **There have been other important steps forward for Evangelicals, arts, and mission as well.**

. "Lausanne Occasional Papers, LOP46: Redeeming the Arts: The Restoration of the Arts to God's Creational Intention," he Lausanne Movement, accessed January 21, 2014, http://www.lausanne.org/en/documents/lops/861-lop-46.html/.

. *Connections: The Journal of the WEA Mission Commission* 9, nos. 2 and 3 (September 2010).

- Wycliffe Bible Translators has broadened its **Summer Institute of Linguistics (SIL)** to include training in the arts.
- Operation Mobilization has developed an initiative to focus specifically on the arts. OM Arts International seeks to empower artists to engage their gifts in both missional and worship settings.

An important expression of arts and mission is found in community art projects, where those marginalized by mainstream culture or those whose lives have taken a bad turn can find healing and hope. There are scores of projects around the globe set in inner-city contexts that draw the poor and disenfranchised into a safe context where they can give expression to the pain and hurt in their lives through art making. It may be drama or dance, visual art or music, poetry or photography—all of which serve to lift some of the burden their artists bear and contribute to the healing process.

Promise for the Future

The signs are positive for a continued engagement of Evangelicals with the arts. Scores of Evangelicals have published books on the arts, and many websites host conversations and promote artists of faith. One important site is ArtWay (http://www.artway.eu), which has links to activities and networks around the world. Education is another area that will influence the future for the arts among Evangelicals. The Institute for Theology, Imagination and the Arts at the University of St. Andrews in Fife, Scotland, provides a rich set of programs for those interested in graduate study in theology and the arts, and it hosts Transpositions, a blog site to encourage conversations about theology and the arts (http://www.transpositions.co.uk). The shaping of a similar center at Duke University in Durham, North Carolina, under the direction of Jeremy Begbie, is another sign of promise for the future. There is also the excellent work of the Brehm Center at Fuller Theological Seminary in Pasadena, California, which carries the vision to revitalize the church through the arts and the culture through attention to beauty.

Evangelicals are increasingly engaged with popular culture and social media, both of which have a profound shaping influence in our lives. In these and other places are signs of promise that the Evangelical embrace of the arts is on the threshold of a new era. Old habits die hard, but a bright and energetic younger generation is taking the torch and illuminating a way forward to include the arts on the Evangelical agenda.

Art sometimes becomes a substitute for religion. Museums, theaters, and concert halls become sanctuaries, stand-ins for the church, for those seeking "spiritual" experiences not readily available in our secular culture. The answer to this reality is not to run from the arts or ignore them but rather to set the arts in the broader context of God's good creation and to receive them as blessing and gift.

Art can be idol or icon. It can become a substitute for God or a window through which we come to discover more deeply who God is and to what God has called us. Art can also be a way to speak the language of hope in a world that lives with uncertainty. Evangelicalism is recovering a lost heritage and becoming attuned to the Holy Spirit's movement through the arts.

Evangelicals are increasingly engaged with popular culture and social media, both of which have a profound shaping influence in our lives.

Bibliography

Connections: The Journal of the WEA Mission Commission 9, nos. 2 and 3 (September 2010).

Crouch, Andy. *Culture Making: Recovering Our Creative Calling.* Downers Grove, IL: InterVarsity Press, 2008.

Hunter, James Davison. *To Change the World: The Irony, Tragedy, and Possibility of Christianity in the Late Modern World.* New York: Oxford University Press, 2010.

The Lausanne Movement. "Lausanne Occasional Papers, LOP46: Redeeming the Arts: The Restoration of the Arts to God's Creational Intention." Accessed January 21, 2014. http://www.lausanne.org/en/documents/lops/861-lop-46.html/.

Rookmaaker, Hans. *Art Needs No Justification,* Downers Grove, IL: InterVarsity Press, 1978.

Schaeffer, Francis. *Art and the Bible,* Downers Grove, IVP, 1973.

Seerveld, Calvin. *Bearing Fresh Olive Leaves: Alternate Steps in Understanding Art.* Toronto, ON: Tuppence Press, 2000.

Taylor, W. David, ed. *For the Beauty of the Church.* Grand Rapids: Baker, 2010.

Walls, Andrew F. *The Missionary Movement: Studies in the Transmission of Faith.* Maryknoll, NY: Orbis, 2006.

"The Portal," earthenware and cast glass, 12" x 12" x 15".
By Heidi Brannan

John Franklin is executive director of Imago (www.imago-arts.org), a Toronto-based initiative designed to support Christians in the arts in Canada. He is chair of the Arts in Mission Task Force for the WEA Mission Commission, was a member (with an arts focus) of the program team for Cape Town 2010: The Third Lausanne Congress on World Evangelization, and serves as chair of Lausanne Canada.

The Other Side of the River,
A Musical Parable.
Photo © Dennis Hassell

EVANGELICALS AND THEOLOGICAL EDUCATION

By Riad Kassis

"If you pursue theological training for three years you will save at least twelve years attempting to figure out the foundations of Christian ministry."[1] This was the advice given to a young man by an experienced pastor and gifted preacher at one of the largest evangelical churches in Damascus, Syria, a pastor who himself had not had the opportunity to receive formal theological training. Their quest to understand and share the Word of God is a major motivation for Evangelicals to devote time, effort, and resources toward obtaining theological training. This chapter focuses on global theological education and provides sketches of the major players in formal evangelical theological education globally.

International Council for Evangelical Theological Education

The International Council for Evangelical Theological Education (ICETE) emerged in 1980 in response to an urgent need for regional theological associations to collaborate in their accreditation endeavors, as well as to foster cooperation and genuine partnership among them. ICETE was formed as a global partner of the World Evangelical Alliance (WEA) out of its Theological Commission. It is a global community that links nine regional theological networks comprising more than one thousand theological schools in 113 countries.

ICETE exists to promote the enhancement of evangelical theological education worldwide and to serve as a forum for contact and collaboration among those around the world who are involved in evangelical theological education. It provides mutual assistance, stimulation, enrichment, networking, and support services for regional associations of evangelical theological schools worldwide. ICETE facilitates among these bodies the enhancement of their services to evangelical theological education within their regions.

Langham Partnership

In 1969 the late John Stott founded Langham Trust, which has been known as Langham Partnership since 2001, naming it simply after the street in London where his church stood, All Souls Church, Langham Place. Stott had observed on his travels that many evangelical institutions of theological education on the continents of the south and east (called the "Majority World") lacked faculty members with adequate academic training. Through Langham Partnership he established the Langham Scholars program to provide funding for able men and women to study for doctorates in biblical and theological disciplines, scholars who would then return to teach in seminaries in their home countries.

Initially these students enrolled in departments of theology in the United Kingdom but then also in institutions in the United States, Australia, Canada, New Zealand, and Hong Kong. The landscape of theological education has shifted considerably in the thirty years since the Langham Scholars program was established. Majority World seminaries have begun doctoral programs, providing viable opportunities for training within the context of the Majority World. Leaders continue to gain voice as theologians, addressing contextual issues and engaging in global theological discourse.

---

1. Rev. Farid Khoury, private conversation with author, Damascus, Syria, April 1983.

Today, with the growth of quality programs of doctoral-level theological education on other continents (which is partly the fruit of Langham Scholars's investment in faculty development), close to 40 percent of the students currently supported by Langham Scholars are being funded for doctorates outside the West in schools like Africa International University (Nairobi), Jos ECWA Theological Seminary (Nigeria), and South Asia Institute of Advanced Christian Studies (Bangalore). In 2013 the number of Langham Scholars around the world passed three hundred, with approximately seventy currently being supported by the program. They come from, and serve in, many countries: Africa, Latin America, the Middle East, Central and Eastern Europe, the Caribbean, the Pacific, and all parts of Asia.

The global network of the Fellowship of Langham Scholars, which supports the alumni who received their theological education through the support of Langham Scholars, allows news and information about colleagues' publications to be shared and arranges some regional consultations. The Fellowship has also created post-doctoral opportunities, such as the International Research and Training Seminar program, for the professional development of Langham Scholars alumni.

When we think of theological education we often think in terms of formal training with a focus on academics. However, Stott's vision was not limited to academic excellence, though he was certainly committed to that. Stott saw theological education as a servant of the church, contributing to the effectiveness of the church in fulfilling its mission in the world. In its vision and mission statement, Langham Partnership declares its intent "to see churches in the majority world equipped for mission and growing to maturity in Christ through the ministry of pastors and leaders who believe, teach and live by the word of God."[2]

Stott's aim was to raise the standards of biblical preaching not only by raising the standards of theological education to result in better-trained pastors but also by providing resources and training for preachers. So the Langham Scholars program integrates with two others: Langham Literature provides books for pastors, students, and seminary libraries, and Langham Preaching establishes national indigenous movements for practical training in biblical preaching.

Many Langham Scholars alumni have gone on to be writers and publish widely, including contributing to multiauthor, one-volume commentaries like the *Africa Bible Commentary* (Zondervan, 2010). The majority of them serve the cause of theological education by teaching in seminaries (in some cases providing leadership as deans and principals), while some move into other positions of leadership in church and society. Several Langham Scholars alumni hold international posts within global networks like the Lausanne Movement or serve on international scholarly bodies like the Committee on Bible Translation. The vision of John Stott for enhancing theological education is alive and vibrant in the heartbeat of such ministries.

ScholarLeaders International

ScholarLeaders International exists to encourage and enable Christian theological leaders from the Majority World for the sake of the global church. It has supported more than 230 Christian leaders from fifty-two countries in Africa, Asia, Latin America, the Middle East, and Eastern Europe.

Inspired by Stott's conviction that Christians in the Majority World must have the opportunity to equip themselves and assume church leadership in their homelands, two former study assistants for Stott, Mark Labberton and Tom Cooper, joined with another colleague, Steve Hayner, in 1984 to form Christian International Scholarship Foundation (CISF), as ScholarLeaders was initially called. Rather than send missionaries and teachers from the West, CISF funded proven indigenous leaders to obtain advanced theological education, mostly at seminaries in the United States, so they could return home as highly respected and uniquely effective Christian leaders.

---

2. "Langham Vision and Mission," Langham Partnership, accessed February 16, 2014, http://us.langham.org/who-we-are/vision-mission/.

As time passed, CISF focused increasingly on regions of greatest opportunity and need: Africa, China, Brazil, and the Middle East. Beginning in 2001, it backed strategic institutions in the Majority World as those institutions initiated their own doctoral programs, often led by faculty who had received CISF scholarships for their advanced education. By 2010 less than half of those supported by the organization were pursuing their degrees as full-time residential students in the West. The organization has supported students at more than two dozen schools in fifteen countries around the world.

Lami Bakari is a Langham scholar from Nigeria.
Photo: The Langham Partnership

In 2010 CISF was rechristened ScholarLeaders International to reflect its expanded programs, which encourage lifelong professional growth, support new ministry initiatives, and enable a more prominent global voice for Majority World Christian leaders. These new programs continue the investments in theological leadership made through scholarship support for advanced education by serving leaders in support of their professional development. This support is particularly strong with regard both to writing and publication efforts and to the gathering of senior leaders to create opportunities for them to offer and receive counsel and support from one another. Through programs like ScholarLeader of the Year, ScholarLeaders has sought to encourage "South to South" dialogue by highlighting the work being done by exemplary leaders from the global South and providing opportunities for those leaders to share from that work with interested parties in another region of the world. These events are held in global South countries to encourage interaction among global South leaders through seminars, lectures and workshops.

ScholarLeaders increasingly works collaboratively with Majority World institutions with regard to strategic faculty development and across institutions to address theological issues that are especially pertinent to the Majority World church. Working collaboratively with Majority World institutions and several like-minded organizations, ScholarLeaders believes the next decades will see even greater change and provide new opportunities for the encouragement and enabling of theological leaders for the global church.

Overseas Council

Since its founding in 1974, Overseas Council (OC) has focused its ministry on strengthening seminaries and other programs of theological education where Christian leaders are being formed. Currently OC partners with 130 strategic seminaries that serve fifty-eight thousand students each year in seventy countries across the Majority World. From its inception, OC has opened the door to formal theological education training at the first-degree and post-graduate levels for hundreds of gifted women and men through scholarship support. OC also supports seminaries in their staff and faculty development programs. While historically OC has assisted numerous seminaries with major capital development projects, current projects now also include building library collections and IT infrastructure.

In addition to the strategic use of resources, OC focuses on building organizational capacity through its Institute for Excellence in Christian Leadership Development, which schedules regular gatherings of the leaders of seminaries in the different regions in which OC has partners. The institute develops administrative and faculty leadership and strengthens the capacity of its partner schools to respond to the needs of the local church. In 2013 OC conducted twelve such institutes involving approximately four hundred seminary leaders from eighty seminaries.

Beyond partnering with individual seminaries, OC has either initiated or is involved in projects of a regional scope. A few current examples are described here.

- In collaboration with SAT-7, a Christian television station that broadcasts in the Middle East, and the Middle East Association for Theological Education (MEATE), OC is developing TEACH (Theological Education for Arab Christians at Home), a broad array of contextually relevant, online, distance-learning opportunities accessible to the Arab-speaking church.

- In partnership with the China Christian Council (CCC), OC is providing a core library of up to two thousand evangelical Chinese-language books for a network of twenty-two CCC seminaries in the People's Republic of China.
- In 2014 OC inaugurates FLITE (Foundations for Leadership in Theological Education), which provides newly appointed seminary leaders with a yearlong, mentored, training course in effective seminary leadership.

Based in Indianapolis, Indiana, OC maintains indigenous consultants in each region in which it works. These regional directors assist OC in developing strategy and strengthening relationships with regional partners. Current regional directors function in Latin American, the Caribbean, Africa, Europe, Eurasia, the Middle East, non-Chinese Asia, and China.

OC also collaborates with a larger network consisting of affiliates in Canada (ReSource Leadership International), Europe (OC Europe), Australia (OC Australia), and New Zealand (Leadership Development International). Although they function as independent entities with a national or regional base, these affiliates share a similar history and ministry focus.

Libraries and Evangelical Theological Education

Celebrating the power of books to transform lives is an excellent description of one of the many roles of libraries in the work of advancing evangelical theological education. There is a tremendous hunger in a majority of the world for access to sound theological scholarship. At the same time, challenges to providing access to quality resources exist. Some of the challenges are simply logistical, while others are both more extreme and even seemingly insurmountable.

One of the main challenges is, of course, language. English has eclipsed both German and French as the primary language of theological resources, while the great need for non-English theological resources in places like the Middle East, Vietnam, China, India, and other parts of Asia continues to explode with the expanding core of schools offering theological education.

Groups like Theological Book Network (TBN) work diligently to raise awareness among scholars and libraries about the value of sharing their surplus with students and faculty-scholars in countries with fewer resources. Shipments of books from TBN are sent to schools where both students/faculty, and churches benefit greatly from them. At the same time, there is a growing sense of urgency for the need for contextually relevant materials. Faculty and librarians are looking not only for materials that are language relevant but are also contextually relevant, appropriate, and accessible.

Evangelical theological education is growing rapidly in Latin America and the Caribbean, making the need for resources in Spanish increasingly urgent. Efforts are underway to create an interinstitutional Christian repository of materials so that institutional libraries can readily share materials that have already been created but are not currently easily accessible. Rather than sharing tattered copies of chapters of books (a growing practice born out of need in many places), repository access will make relevant materials available.

Librarians embrace the power of collaboration and are sharing resources and knowledge at unprecedented levels. At the same time, one of the many challenges facing evangelical schools worldwide is the lack of trained library staff. There is an expanding recognition of the need to provide training to nationals, who will help make the libraries more usable.

Increasingly, the understanding that theological education occurs on many levels and in many places is becoming widespread. Students need to be able to think critically and read reflectively in order to become informed and effective practitioners. They also need to be able to evaluate the validity of the source of the research materials they use. Thus, teaching information literacy, including how to engage in ethical research practices, has become another important role for theological librarians; in this way, particularly, libraries are playing a larger and larger part in effective evangelical theological education.

This chapter has dealt mainly with formal evangelical theological education. However, it is worth noting the growing trend of nonformal theological education Evangelicals are keen to develop and use. The trend is in alignment with the Reformation concept of the priesthood of all believers, since such training is mainly geared toward equipping God's people for the ministry. This sort of training is taking various formats and modes of delivery. Theological Education by Extension (TEE), distance learning that is accessible and cost effective for training pastors and laity, is one of the early developments. Church-based training is another growing trend. Training in theology and ministry skills are provided at local churches, adding another level of accessibility to education. Evangelicals are progressing in the use of distance education, using the media and the Internet to provide accessible and affordable theological education.

Evangelicals have seen the importance of having qualified pastors, preachers, professors, librarians, leaders, and change agents who are engaged in understanding the Christian faith and are able to reflect intelligibly on their social, religious, and political contexts. The organizations that support theological education around the world and embrace nontraditional methods of providing such education show just how much Evangelicals value learned and formally trained leaders.

Bibliography

Langham Partnership. "Langham Vision and Mission." Accessed February 16, 2014. http://us.langham.org/who-we-are/vision-mission/.

Dr. Riad Kassis is the program director for Langham Scholars (Langham Partnership), the international director for International Council for Evangelical Theological Education, and a theological educator and writer based in Lebanon. The writer would like to acknowledge the input of Chris Wright, Evan Hunter, Scott Cunningham, and Melody Mazuk.

> **"The future of Evangelicals has never been brighter. We are in relationships with the leaders of more national governments than ever. We are serving the poor and vulnerable on a scale unimaginable until now. We are partnering to solve global problems from poverty to pollution, human trafficking to hunger. Most importantly, we are helping others trust Christ for salvation all along the way."**
>
> **—Rev. Dr. Joel C. Hunter, Senior Pastor, Northland, Longwood, Florida**

EVANGELICALS AND THE MARKETPLACE

By R. Paul Stevens

I was interviewed on a Canadian evangelical television program about faith in the marketplace. The big question was, "How do you go about witnessing in the workplace?" Various callers indicated that in their workplaces it was politically incorrect to speak about their faith. That is the situation in the post-Christian West. Yet, when my wife and I drove into a parking lot in Cape Town, South Africa, the parking attendant said, "I am sorry to tell you that it is closed today because this is Good Friday. This is the day my Jesus died for us. And today we are honoring him. And he died for you too."

With all the complications of a post–Christendom society, it is wonderfully true that—globally, in the twenty-first century—the marketplace is the most strategic mission field. Why is this? Because most Evangelicals spend forty to eighty hours a week in the marketplace. That is where life's problems are shared between workers. People watch how others work and wonder what makes them tick. And, most significant of all, believers have access to workplaces where no pastor or professional missionary can even enter. Inevitably, questions of faith will arise. When I worked as a carpenter it took just a few weeks before a colleague asked me, "Paul, what happens when we die?" No pastor would have received that question because that man would never have gone to church.

So whether in a politically correct, religiously plural environment or in a substantially Christian culture, Evangelicals have opportunities, especially when one has earned the right to speak. But there is more to Evangelicals in the marketplace than witnessing, as important as that is.

Empowering Church People for Full-Time Service in the Marketplace

Some churches, like Redeemer Presbyterian Church in New York City, believe members doing good work in the world, whether that be fixing toilets or administering huge investment plans, are actually doing kingdom work. Kingdom work is not religious work, but neither is it secular work. Evangelicals believe it is work that engages in the mission of God to bring well-being to people, create new wealth, improve human life, and bring shalom.

Kingdom work also includes bringing people under the life-transforming rule of Jesus. It is work in which pastors and missionaries spend most of their time, and it is the proper work of all Christians. But if people in the marketplace are doing kingdom work, if in the dispersed life of the church the members are in "full-time service" and "doing the Lord's work," then they should be empowered and equipped for this task. Increasingly, around the world Evangelicals are being converted to this New Testament perspective where even the slaves in Colossae were serving the Lord Jesus as full-time ministers (Col. 3:22–25). Evangelicals are also doing very strategic work for the unemployed, the underemployed, and especially the poor.

Job and Wealth Creation

Virginia Juan heads up APPEND, a large organization in Manila that is teaching and equipping people who would otherwise be enduring a barely subsistence-level life. Juan and her team teach basic business start-up skills, lend money for seed capital, develop support networks, and help people save and give to others. They are working to curb or eradicate poverty by changing the buying, sell-ing, and consumption patterns, and by reeducating youth to analyze and evaluate the economy through the lens of a supply or value chain, replacing greed and the economic force with Christ's love.[1]

Photo: www.designpics.com

It may be an overstatement to say business is the best hope of the world, as the premier Roman Catholic marketplace theologian Michael Novak in the United States has said,[2] but it is certainly a major hope. Evangelicals are taking major leadership in wealth creation, hands up instead of handouts, not only in Asia and Africa but also in Central Eu-rope and the formerly Communist countries, where Integra Foundation is a leading evangelical movement. Integra was started by two Evan-gelicals, Milan Cicel, a Slovakian, and Allan Bussard, a Canadian. They invest in sustainable business ventures in Africa.[3] In the final judgment there will be a lot of people hearing Jesus say, "I was barely alive, but you gave me the means of thriving." Behind this is a theology and worldview.

Integrating Work in the World into Theological Studies

Regent College in Vancouver, Canada, began in the early 1970s with the vision of giving the same theolog-ical integration to people undertaking societal careers as is normally given to people preparing for a Christian service career. At that time it was countercultural, that is, counter church and counter seminary culture. Thank-fully, the vision is catching on in other theological institutions and universities around the world, such as the Biblical Graduate School of Theology in Singapore and Bakke Graduate University in Seattle, to name just two. The Frateridad Teologica Latinoamericana, with leaders like René Padilla in Argentina and Ricardo Barbosa de Sousa in Brazil, is doing critical work in teaching, publishing, and empowering the whole people of God for the ministry of everyday life.[4]

These efforts are not merely lightening up theology so the laity can get it. They are taking the service of people in societal occupations as being as seriously in need of biblical and theological integration as that of pas-tors and missionaries. Theological education is too good to be reserved for the clergy. Undergirding this move-ment toward theological education for all are wonderful New Testament truths: the priesthood of all believers, the demolishing of the sacred-secular divide by Jesus, the abolition of the laity (considered as second-class, untrained people in the church), and the raising of the whole people of God as prophets and priests, and princes and princesses. Also implicit is the holistic nature of the mission of God, which includes evangelism but does so in all the ways in which God's life-giving kingdom breaks into this world and this life.

Transforming Cities and Nation-Building

A Kenyan graduate of Bakke Graduate University recently spent a whole day teaching the theology of work to the parliamentarians and bishops of the Republic of South Sudan. He spent another whole day with all the deputy ministers, and a third day with the pastors of the country. All three groups asked for more. The impact of this input on a new nation could be immeasurable in spite of the convulsions that new country has experienced.

Along the same lines of developing national infrastructures and healthy national cultures, Integra, men-tioned earlier, has undertaken anticorruption projects in the former Soviet Union countries, where deals are rife

1. APPEND, Inc., www.append.com.ph.

2. Michael Novak, *Business as a Calling: Work and the Examined Life* (New York: The Free Press, 1996), 84.

3. Integra Foundation, www.integra.sk/en.

4. Frateridad Teologica Latinoamericana, www.ftl-al.org.

with under-the-table payments. Dr. Dwight Mutonono, another Bakke Graduate University alumnus and the director of Africa Leadership and Management Academy (ALMA), has invested himself in tackling leadership, a fundamental issue in nation-building, in Zimbabwe. His leadership and management institute, associated with the University of Zimbabwe, is preparing a new generation of servant leaders for African countries.[5] Alvin Ung, a Malaysian author and business consultant, has crafted an important book on what he calls "barefoot leadership," which highlights and promotes people in Malaysia who are making a difference and thus contributing to nation-building at all levels. Many are Christians.[6]

A Spanish-speaking Seattle lawyer, Chi-Dooh Li, had the idea of breaking the cycle of poverty in Guatemala by using donated money to buy land from private owners on behalf of the poor, who otherwise would not have the means to purchase it. With their harvests they repay the cost of the land and receive titles to the property. Ten villages have completed the process, and twenty-four thousand people have directly benefited from the program.[7] Behind this idea is the example of a biblical character, Erastus, the director of the city's public works (Rom 16:23; Acts 19:22). New Testament scholar Bruce W. Winter observed, "If the evidence of Acts 19:22 is accepted, Erastus was a Christian of substantial financial means, active in two spheres [church and city]. . . . If this is correct, then there was no dichotomy in the thinking of the early church between the gospel/church ministry and the seeking the welfare of the city of Corinth as benefactors. . . . the secular and spiritual welfare of the city were two sides of a single coin and not separate spheres."[8] Some Evangelicals are directly crafting companies that reflect the kingdom of God in all aspects.

Creating Kingdom Companies

Dennis Bakke cofounded Applied Energy Sources (AES), a company chronicled in his book *Joy at Work*. Bakke was the CEO of the largest energy company in the world, and his governing concept, derived from his reading of Genesis, is based on the dignity and decision-making capability of human beings, who are made in the image of God. (Adam, we remember, was given the charge of naming the animals and filling the earth, that is, making a difference.) Bakke's biblically based concept led him to craft a company that pushed decision-making down in the organization and gave people dignity and joy in work, even though most of the employees were not Christians.[9]

Flow Automotive is another example of a kingdom company. Don Flow took over his father's car business in North Carolina and created a company that would bring glory to God and also provide extraordinary service to customers. His transformative approach to business includes personnel policies, pricing of new cars, caring for the community, and helping employees develop potential.[10] All the workers from the car washers to the managers are treated with equal dignity. New cars have a single "fair" price thus not disadvantaging people without advanced negotiating skills. He invests in the community through major sports and recreational services and securing new employment possibilities when industries have folded. All employees are part of ongoing learning and education.

---

5. Africa Leadership and Management Academy, www.africaleader.net.

6. Alvin Ung, *Barefoot Leadership: The Art and Heart of Going That Extra Mile* (Kuala Lampur, Malaysia: Alvin Ung, 2012), www.barefootleadership.my.

7. Chi-Dooh Li, *Buy This Land* (n.p.: Chi-Dooh Li, 2012), http://www.buythislandbook.com.

8. Bruce W. Winter, *Seek the Welfare of the City: Christians as Benefactors and Citizens*, First Century Christians in the Graeco–Roman World (Grand Rapids: Eerdmans, 1994), 1996–97.

9. Dennis W. Bakke, *Joy at Work: A Revolutionary Approach to Fun on the Job* (Seattle: PVG, 2005), http://www.dennisbakke.com.

10. Flow Automotive, www.flowauto.com.

Kingdom companies are not simply platforms for announcing the gospel, as has tragically been the case with some companies started in restricted-access countries. Rather, kingdom companies see their product or service as contributing to the kingdom of God. They intentionally develop their relationship with employees, suppliers, government, nation, and customers in a way that leads to an "Aha!" with people wondering what makes this company tick. Behind this approach to business is a critical view of Christian mission.

Implementing Integral Mission

Evangelicals have been in the forefront of refining a theology of mission. Mission has been reframed from something the church does to bring the gospel to the world in response to the Great Commission, to something *God is doing* to bring God's kingdom and God's shalom into the world—"As the Father has sent me, I am sending you" (John 20:21 NIV).

This missional action of God created the church, and God invites the people of God to join God in this cooperative work of building both the human and the faith communities. This call is holistic for the individual person. It calls for conversion of heart and mind. It is holistic for society. It brings justice and righteousness to the thought-forms and culture that shape the way people think and act. And it is holistic for creation through sustainable development and renewal. The mission of God is also prophetic in that it names sin and calls for justice in the world. Missional theologians like Regent faculty members Charles Ringma and Ross Hastings have led the way in this new way of thinking, publishing books on the missional God and teaching mission in an integral and holistic way.[11]

There are enormous implications for the marketplace, which is now seen as not merely a place to evangelize but as an arena, if not the most strategic one, for the full-orbed mission of God. Evangelicals view the church as a rhythm of gathering and dispersion; as Quaker theologian Elton Trueblood once said, "'Church-goer' is a vulgar ignorant term and should never be used. You cannot go to church; you are the church wherever you go."[12] Dr. Sunki Banf, a marketplace theologian from South Korea, said "business itself *is* mission."[13] And there is a special part of the marketplace where Evangelicals have had an especially transformative influence.

Developing Entrepreneurial Leadership and Innovation

Dr. Richard Goossen, a professor of entrepreneurship and a business entrepreneur, has researched more than 250 Evangelical business entrepreneurs and published his findings in several books, one of which was coauthored with me, *Entrepreneurial Leadership: Finding Your Calling, Making a Difference*.[14] In addition, Goossen has developed a major resource of Christian entrepreneurs through an annual conference and web-based resources under the umbrella of the Entrepreneurial Leaders Organization.[15]

It is not surprising Evangelicals have provided innovative leadership in the marketplace. Why? Because our creative God invested humankind, who was made in God's image, with a creative capacity. We are creating creatures. Furthermore, the triune God inspires risk taking, a trait so amply developed in the well-known parable of the talents (Matt. 25:14–30). The will of God itself is not inexorable; it is not something to make one fearfully

---

11. Ross Hastings, *Missional God, Missional Church: Hope for Re-evangelizing the West* (Downers Grove, IL: InterVarsity Press, 2012).

12. Unpublished public lecture at McMaster Divinity College, Hamilton, Ontario, 1959.

13. Sunki Bang, "Tensions in Witness," *Vocatio*, 1, no. 2 (July 1998): 17–18, quoted in R. Paul Stevens, *Doing God's Business: Meaning and Motivation for the Marketplace* (Grand Rapids: Eerdmans, 2006), 80.

14. Richard J. Goossen and R. Paul Stevens, *Entrepreneurial Leadership: Finding Your Calling, Making a Difference* (Downers Grove, IL: InterVarsity Press, 2013).

15. ELO: Entrepreneurial Leaders Organization, www.eleaders.org.

compliant and subservient like the person in the parable with just one talent. God's will is an empowering vision that inspires innovation and entrepreneurial activity as it did for Joseph in the book of Genesis. But not all these enterprises, so inspired and implemented, are for profit. Not that profit making is wrong. Indeed, profit is like the blood of the body. You must have it to live, but you should not live for it.

Establishing Christian Social Enterprises

Many Evangelicals have created social enterprises that meet a social need by giving people work skills and needed employment. The Banqueting Table in Vancouver, Canada, is a catering business that provides dignity, work skills, and needed income to dozens of single mothers.[16] Grandview Calvary Baptist Church, also in Vancouver, has started a pottery studio, landscaping firm, and home renovation company, all under the umbrella of Just Work.[17] While not always completely self-supporting, these businesses go a long way toward bringing the kingdom into a very needy part of their city. Behind such enterprises is another arena in which Evangelicals have made a major contribution, vocational discernment.

Vocational Discernment

Philip Wu, in Hong Kong, has crafted Vocation Creation, a resource that helps people find out what to do with their lives, or discern their vocation. He consults with businesses, leads seminars, and teaches. But Wu does so in a way that is accessible to people who do not share a full Christian faith.[18] His assumption, verified by research, is that people who have identified and then practice their calling find satisfaction in their work. They thrive. Gray Poehnell, a Canadian, has worked for decades in the same area. He specializes in helping Aboriginal people in Canada and Australia learn how to discern the way they have been made by God and the way they are summoned by God to serve their neighbors through work.[19] While Poehnell does not always use Christian language, his evangelical theology undergirds all he does. Through books and manuals and by speaking at international vocational conferences, he provides a theological worldview and life view for career development, even for people who have not yet embraced the Christian faith. But there is one final dimension of faith–work integration that is critical for Evangelicals: spiritual formation.

> **God's will is an empowering vision that inspires innovation and entrepreneurial activity as it did for Joseph in the book of Genesis.**

Spiritual Formation in the Marketplace

As one of the leading professors and authors in the area of spiritual formation, Eugene Peterson, translator of *The Message*, has affirmed the marketplace is the most significant arena of spiritual formation. "I'm prepared to contend that the primary location for spiritual formation is the workplace"[20] Really? Is not the marketplace

---

16. The Banqueting Table, www.thebanquetingtable.ca.

17. Just Work Economic Initiative, www.justwork.ca.

18. Vocation Creation, http://www.vocatiocreation.com.hk.

19. Vocational.ca, www.vocational.ca; Ergon Communications, www.ergoncommunications.com.

20. Eugene H. Peterson, *Christ Plays in Ten Thousand Places: A Conversation in Spiritual Theology* (Grand Rapids: Eerdmans, 2005), 127.

where all the seven deadly sins—pride, greed, envy, gluttony, lust, wrath, and sloth—find expression?[21] Yes, they do. It is in the workplace that we are found out for who we are. Our inner life is revealed by our outer work, and areas of need become a cry for what the Bible calls the fruit of the Spirit: love, joy, peace, patience, kindness, goodness, faithfulness, gentleness and self-control (Gal. 5:22–23). It is certainly a surprising thing in the twenty-first century that many business schools now offer courses in spirituality, even though the curriculum is pluralistic and sometimes even New Age. People now understand they take their whole selves to work. Famously Henry Ford said, "Why is it that I always get the whole person, when all I want is just a pair of hands?"[22] We take our souls to work. "When work is soulless, life stifles and dies," said the existentialist philosopher Albert Camus.[23] The primary location for spiritual growth is not church services, retreats, or even quiet times, as important as these are, but the warp and woof of everyday work in our places of employment, where we live for most of the week. So alongside the initial affirmation that the marketplace is both a mission field and the mission of God, is the affirmation that the marketplace is a school for the Christian life and spiritual formation.

Consider an alternative. Suppose you were independently wealthy and had no need to work. Would that be a good thing spiritually? Absolutely not. So, Evangelicals say to people in the marketplace, go to work because God is still working, and God invites you to join in God's work on earth creating, sustaining, fixing, and consummating. Go to work because it is the primary way in which you can love your neighbor, whether near or far, seen or unseen. Go to work to love God through your work, as God will love you in it. And go to work to become more like Christ, who came to earth and worked in the marketplace and used marketplace images and terms almost exclusively to describe the best thing that has ever happened on earth, the good news that he preached, the in-breaking of the kingdom of God.

Bibliography

Bakke, Dennis W. *Joy at Work: A Revolutionary Approach to Fun on the Job*. Seattle: PVG, 2005. http://www.dennisbakke.com.

Ray Bakke, Lowell Bakke, and William Hendricks. *Joy at Work Bible Study Companion*. PV: http://www.dennisbakke.com.

Goossen, Richard J., and R. Paul Stevens. *Entrepreneurial Leadership: Finding Your Calling, Making a Difference*. Downers Grove, IL: InterVarsity Press, 2013.

Hastings, Ross. *Missional God, Missional Church: Hope for Re-evangelizing the West*. Downers Grove, IL: InterVarsity Press, 2012.

Winter, Bruce W. *Seek the Welfare of the City: Christians as Benefactors and Citizens*. First Century Christians in the Graeco–Roman World. Grand Rapids: Eerdmans, 1994.

Witherington, Ben, III. *Work: A Kingdom Perspective on Labor*. Grand Rapids: Eerdmans, 2011.

Wong, Kenman L., and Scott B. Rae, *Business for the Common Good: A Christian Vision for the Marketplace*. Downers Grove: InterVarsity Press, 2011.

---

21. The seven deadly sins have developed over a long history in the church starting in the third century. They are roughly equivalent to what the apostle Paul calls "the works of the flesh" (Gal 5:19–21).

22. Quoted in Kenman L. Wong and Scott B. Rae, *Business for the Common Good: A Christian Vision for the Marketplace* (Downers Grove: InterVarsity Press, 2011), 207.

23. Quoted in Eric Steven Dale, *Bringing Heaven Down to Earth: A Practical Spirituality of Work* (New York: Peter Lang, 1991), 8.

Dr. R. Paul Stevens is professor emeritus of Marketplace Theology at Regent College in Vancouver, Canada. He is a marketplace ministry mentor and author and coauthor of numerous books, including *Work Matters: Lessons from Scripture*, *Taking Your Soul to Work*, and *Entrepreneurial Leadership*.

Photo: www.designpics.com

"I see the future of Evangelicals as one of opportunity and challenge. Evangelicals will be presented with challenges that result from church growth. For only growth that is matched with strong discipleship will enable churches to gain greater strength, depth and maturity; to uphold the highest moral and ethical standards that are biblically shaped and guided; and to be seen to be credible entities. The result of all this is that Evangelicals will be presented with opportunities to impact society through words and deeds that are informed by a transforming vision of God's purpose in and for the world."

—Dr. Desta Heliso, Vice President, Ethiopian Kale Heywet Church, Ethiopia

EVANGELICALS AND SCIENCE

By Harry Lee Poe

Science and evangelical faith came into conflict at several points during the twentieth century, but the conflict rarely arose because of science or religion. It usually began because of philosophical assumptions. These assumptions generally involved problems of empiricism, what we can know and how we can know it. In addition to the problem of philosophical assumptions was the problem, in both science and religion, of hermeneutics, the method of interpretation. Science posed a particular problem for Evangelicals in the twentieth century because science, as it has been understood in the modern world, did not exist when the Bible was written. This caused tension, since faithfulness to the Bible as revelation from God has been a cornerstone of evangelical faith throughout its history.

Clashing Movements

Western Christianity gave birth to modern science during the same period as the Protestant Reformation, and science represents an aspect of the same broad movement that sought a more reliable basis for authority than tradition. Protestant theologians turned to God's revelation in the Bible as their source for theological knowledge. Scientists turned to God's revelation in creation as their source for scientific knowledge. In fact, when Sir Francis Bacon first described the scientific method in *The New Organum* (1624), he preceded it with his *Advancement of Learning* (1605) in which he declared "let no man upon a weak conceit of sobriety or an ill-applied moderation think or maintain, that a man can search too far, or be too well studied in the book of God's word, or in the book of God's works."[1] The old Greek deductive method began with universal principles and applied them to the world, but Bacon's scientific inductive method began by making a large number of observations of particular situations and determining the universal conclusions from analysis of the observations.

The Protestant Reformation and the scientific method both addressed what seemed to be an obstacle to truth. In both arenas, a vast human tradition had formed over the previous thousand years that held both theology and science in its grip. Traditions not found in the Bible, such as Purgatory and the Immaculate Conception, disturbed the Protestant Reformers, so they sought to reform the theology of the church based on what they discovered in the Bible. In the area of science, no new discoveries had occurred since the time of the ancient Greeks because science was based largely on the philosophical explanations of Aristotle and the Greek philosophical tradition. The earth was the center of the universe because the Greeks said so. The heavenly bodies were perfectly smooth spheres because the Greeks said so. Objects fell to the earth because, the Greeks explained, the objects were returning to their place of origin. If "the heavens declare the glory of God" (Ps. 19:1 NIV), then the heavens and all of creation should be a more reliable source of knowledge than the pagan Greeks. In this manner, experimental science of the inductive method replaced philosophical science of the deductive method.

By the beginning of the twentieth century, the various sciences had shown remarkable success in describing the laws of nature. For Evangelicals, the two greatest areas of conflict concerned the age of the earth and Charles Darwin's theory of natural selection. Both of these issues relate to the interpretation of the first chapter of Genesis.

---

1. Francis Bacon, *The New Organum*, ed. Lisa Jardine and Michael Silverthorne (Cambridge: Cambridge University Press, 2000), and Francis Bacon, *The Advancement of Learning*, Great Books of the Western World, vol. 30 (Chicago: Encyclopedia Britannica, 1952), 4.

The Problems of the Age of the Earth and How the Humans on It Came to Be

At the beginning of the scientific revolution of the seventeenth century, Archbishop James Ussher of Armagh, Ireland, a contemporary of Sir Francis Bacon and Galileo, sought to develop a scientific method for interpreting the Bible. A pioneer in higher critical method, Ussher also proposed that God created the world in 4004 BC, in keeping with the traditional understanding that the period from creation to the last judgment would be seven thousand years. By the twentieth century, Ussher's dating of the age of the earth had become part of the evangelical tradition. In contrast to the biblical teaching of a beginning to the universe, Aristotle had taught that the universe has always existed.

Galileo Galilei, astronomer and physicist.
Hand-colored engraving.
Image: North Wind Picture Archives

During the eighteenth century, Scottish philosopher David Hume proposed that in an eternal universe, life could have emerged by chance as one of an infinite number of possibilities. This view provided the philosophical foundation for Darwin's theory of natural selection. The idea of the evolution of humans from lower forms of life had been around for decades before Darwin, but in his book *On the Origin of Species* (1859), Darwin proposed that the evolution had occurred as a result of purely natural causes. Asa Gray, an Evangelical American botanist, agreed that humans may have evolved from lower forms but disputed Darwin's attempt to link the scientific idea of evolution with the philosophical/theological idea of naturalism which argues that everything in the world can be explained by natural causes. B. B. Warfield, an Evangelical American theologian, also accepted the possibility of evolution as a compatible interpretation of God's creation of humans, but he joined Gray in disputing the confusion of science and philosophy.

David Hume.
Digitally colored steel engraving.
Image: North Wind Picture Archives

The question of the age of the earth grew into an issue in the nineteenth century due to the development of the science of geology. As geologists mapped the earth's layers and types of rocks and minerals, they proposed that the earth was significantly more ancient than six thousand years old. Several theories emerged to reconcile the new dating of the age of the earth with Ussher's earlier dating. The day-age theory proposed that each day of creation in the first chapter of Genesis represented an entire age. Another theory proposed a cosmic upheaval of an indeterminate period of time between Genesis 1:2 and Genesis 1:3. The most outrageous proposal came from Edgar Allan Poe in his book *Eureka* (1848), a little-known treatise on the universe and God. Poe concluded that God had created the universe by creating a "primordial particle," which God then caused to expand into the universe we now see. For this idea, which conflicted irreconcilably with Aristotle's view of an eternal universe, Poe was regarded as mentally disturbed.[2]

---

2. Literary people continued to refer to Poe's huge errors in science, such as the relativity of time and space, the continuity of electro-magnetism and light, and the existence of a finite expanding universe as evidence of insanity. In his 1926 biography of Poe, Hervey Allen argued that *Eureka* "passed the last admitted borders of sanity." See Hervey Allen, *Israfel* (New York: Farrar & Rhinehart, 1934), 473. Allen went on to talk of *Eureka* as the product of "insane dreams" (586) and excuses the book as the work of a man who was mentally ill when he wrote it (592).

New Discoveries and New Challenges

With the dawn of the twentieth century, the scientific world was shaken to its foundation with new discoveries. German-born physicist Albert Einstein proposed his theories of relativity in 1905 and argued that time is another dimension of the physical world with length, width, and depth. Danish physicist Nihls Bohr's work in 1913 opened the quantum world of subatomic particles in which electrons were found to exhibit the mutually exclusive attributes of waves and particles. Between 1929 and 1931, Georges Lemaître, a Belgian priest, and Edwin Hubble, an American astronomer, provided experimental and theoretical support for Poe's proposal for a beginning to the universe. This big bang theory would be strongly resisted by scientists like Einstein, who relied upon Aristotle's explanation of the universe. By the last quarter of the twentieth century, however, the scientific world had rejected Aristotle's eternal universe for a universe that had a beginning.

With all of this upheaval in science, Evangelicals could be expected to come into conflict with scientific ideas at some point. Probably the best-known confrontation came in 1925 over the issue of evolution with a staged trial designed to attract publicity for the small town of Dayton, Tennessee. Unfortunately, this episode established a pattern for dealing with scientific issues in mass media arenas that did not allow for in-depth examination of the issues. William Jennings Bryan, a former Democratic presidential candidate and secretary of state under President Woodrow Wilson, was the most prominent Evangelical in public life at the time. Local officials asked Bryan to prosecute John Scopes, a local schoolteacher accused of teaching evolution in the public school. What came to be known as the Scopes Monkey Trial was misrepresented in the national press and assumed a carnival atmosphere as Clarence Darrow, the most famous criminal trial lawyer of his era, defended Scopes. The subtleties of the distinction between the science of evolution and the philosophy of naturalism were lost in the media confusion.

Evangelicals Become Organized

In 1941 a group of five Evangelical scientists formed the American Scientific Affiliation (ASA) as a forum where Christians in the sciences could freely discuss the issues surrounding science and the Christian faith. By the end of the twentieth century the ASA would grow to a membership of over two thousand members. Between 1955 and 1968 the ASA held six joint conferences with the Evangelical Theological Society. The ASA began publishing a journal in 1949, now known as *Perspectives on Science and Religion*. Because the ASA has as its mission being a place where Christians can discuss without judgment or retribution the interpretation of science and the interpretation of the Bible, the organization does not take a position on controversial issues among Christians. Members advocate positions in the papers they present at the annual meeting and in the articles they submit to *Perspectives*, but the ASA does not advocate specific interpretations of the Bible or science.

Charles Darwin
Image: North Wind Picture Archives

In contrast to the approach of the ASA, a variety of science and religion organizations that do take a stand on issues concerning science and religion arose within the broad family of Evangelicals during the twentieth century. Many Evangelicals were attracted to the activities of the Seventh-day Adventist scientists who organized the Society for Deluge Geology and Related Sciences, followed by the Society for the Study of Natural Science and the Bible. These groups took the position that the geological formations of the earth's crust were created by Noah's flood, based on Ussher's dating of the age of the earth. The Geo-Science Research Institute was founded in 1957 at Andrews University in Berrien Springs, Michigan, and later moved to California's Loma Linda University, a Seventh-day Adventist school.

Controversy Keeps Arising

The age of the earth and evolution became key components of the controversy among Evangelicals known as the Battle for the Bible from the mid-1960s to the mid-1980s. Questions of science and faith almost disappeared from discussion at the Evangelical Theological Society meetings. Concerned over theological liberalism, many Evangelicals rallied around the term "inerrancy" to describe their view of the Bible as revelation from God. Expounded in the Chicago Statement which many prominent evangelical leaders signed, inerrancy came to mean that the Bible is inerrant in the original autographs. Many conservative Christians, however, failed to grasp the difference between their views about the Bible and what the Bible actually said. To defend the Bible meant to defend a particular interpretation of the Bible. For some theologians, discussions of the relationship between the Bible and modern science seemed dangerous to their employment at evangelical schools. To others, it seemed pointless. For whatever reason, evangelical theologians avoided the subject.

Young Earth, Old Earth

In 1961 John Whitcomb and Henry Morris published *The Genesis Flood*. This book formed the catalyst for the formation of the Creation Research Society (CRS) in 1963, which advocated a young earth view of creation it sought to defend with scientific data. Eight of the ten founding members of the CRS belonged to the ASA and continued to hold their membership in that broader organization for many years.

During this same period a major controversy arose in the Southern Baptist Convention (SBC) over *The Message of Genesis* written in 1961 by Ralph Elliott, a professor at Midwestern Baptist Theological Seminary in Kansas City, Missouri. His book, which regarded Genesis 1–11 as mythological, was condemned by the annual SBC in 1962. Elliott lost his job at the seminary, and Broadman Press, the publishing arm of the Baptist Sunday School Board, withdrew the book. In 1969 the SBC condemned Elliott's treatment of Genesis in its new *Broadman Bible Commentary*, written by G. Hinton Davies, and withdrew *The Message of Genesis* from its bookstores.

For many conservative Evangelicals, a young earth position became a major test of orthodoxy. Few evangelical seminaries offered courses on science and religion during this period. The same could also be said for non-evangelical Protestant seminaries, where Karl Barth's aversion to natural theology led to a general disapproval of thinking about how faith relates to modern science. Unlike philosophical naturalism, natural theology attempts to develop an understanding of God by observing nature. An exception to the disapproval of natural theology could be found in the small Process Theology movement among more liberal theologians, which attempted to develop a theology based on evolution in which God is also in the process of "becoming."

Throughout the twentieth century, both young earth and old earth advocates ignored what might be considered the most important information in interpreting the text of Genesis and arriving at a theological position on the age of the earth. The English language tradition of the Bible has translated Genesis 1 as a sequence of seven consecutive days, beginning with the first day and ending with the seventh day. But the Hebrew text actually begins with "one day" instead of on "the first day," and the next act of creation takes place on "a second day" rather than on "the second day." Thus, in the Hebrew text the first five acts of creation occur on indeterminate days in sequence. At every other place in the Pentateuch (the first five books of the Old Testament) in which consecutive days are described, however, the Hebrew text uses the definite article to indicate the events took place on "*the* first day, "*the* second day, "*the* third day," or the like. Biblical scholars have said little about this discrepancy.

For the most part, however, twentieth-century liberal and conservative theology proceeded on the basis of Newtonian physics of the seventeenth century. Newton's assumption of Aristotle's view of absolute time had an influence on the debate over what God knows. The concept of absolute time asserts that time is constant throughout the universe as opposed to Einstein's view that time is relative. Under Newtonian physics, God cannot know the future, but under Einstein's physics God can know the future.

Darwin Revisited

A new interest in science and faith developed in the 1990s among both evangelical and mainline Christians. A new challenge to Darwinian assumptions about naturalism came in 1991 with the publication of *Darwin on Trial* by Philip Johnson, who founded the Discovery Institute as a think tank to engage naturalism. *Darwin's Black Box* written by Michael Behe in 1996, and the intelligent design movement led by American philosopher and theologian William Dembski proposed "irreducible complexity" as a mathematical indicator that an effect resulted from design rather than by chance. One of the most important aspects of this movement was its re direction of the discussion to the problem of naturalistic philosophical assumptions. At the end of the century however, intelligent design became confused with creation science when a creation science textbook was re vised and the term *intelligent design* was incorporated into it. A school district in Pennsylvania, which used the textbook, was sued for violating the constitutional ban against the establishment of religion, and an American federal court ordered the school district to stop using the textbook.

By the early twenty-first century a number of Evangelical scientists believed that God could have created humans by evolution as well as by fiat. Francis Collins, an Evangelical American biologist who led the Human Genome Project's effort to map the human genome, became a leader of this group and also took the lead in found ing BioLogos, an organization dedicated to advancing the idea that God created humans through evolution.

Looking Ahead

The discussion between Evangelical scientists and theologians has been minimal over the last fifty years but issues like these will form a major aspect of the cultural climate in which evangelism takes place in the twenty first century. Scientific discovery and technological application of science now impacts humans directly. Our culture now assumes that "science" is true, without distinguishing between science and philosophies of science.

Biblical faith stands in stark contrast to a growing cultural materialism that no longer assumes the values of Scripture. Evangelism that does not take this dynamic into consideration will not be able to present the gospel in a meaningful way to people who are ignorant of the content of the Bible. Evangelicals need to know how to talk to this scientific culture.

Bibliography

Allen, Hervey. *Israfel*. New York: Farrar & Rhinehart, 1934.

Bacon, Francis. *The Advancement of Learning*. Great Books of the Western World, vol. 30. Chicago: Encyclopedia Britannica, 1952.

Bacon, Francis. *The New Organum*, ed. Lisa Jardine and Michael Silverthorne. Cambridge: Cambridge University Press, 2000.

Behe, Michael. *Darwin's Black Box*. New York: Free Press, 1996.

Darwin, Charles. *On the Origin of Species*. London: John Murray, 1859.

Davies, G. Hinton. *Broadman Bible Commentary*. Nashville: Broadman, 1969.

Elliott, Ralph H. *The Message of Genesis*. Nashville: Broadman, 1961.

Johnson, Philip. *Darwin on Trial*. Downers Grove, IL: InterVarsity Press, 1991.

Poe, Edgar Allan. *Eureka*. New York: George P. Putnam, 1845.

Whitcomb, John, and Henry Morris. *The Genesis Flood*. Grand Rapids: Baker, 1961.

Dr. Harry Lee Poe is a theologian, author, and the Charles Colson Chair of Faith and Culture at Union University in Jackson, Tennessee.

Francis Bacon. Hand-colored engraving of painting by Honbraken, 1738.
Image: North Wind Picture Archives

"In the early twenty-first century, Evangelical Christianity is both thriving and imploding. It thrives in places where Spirit-filled, Bible-guided, and Christ-centered faith inspires worship, works of comfort, evangelization, reconciliation, and peace-building. It implodes—sometimes in the same places—wherever poverty, political partisanship, materialism, or superstition draws believers away from the transforming power of Jesus Christ. What comes in the future will depend on how central Christ remains."

—Mark Noll, Francis A. McAnaney Professor of History, University of Notre Dame; author *The Rise of Evangelicalism: The Age of Edwards, Whitefield, and the Wesleys* (InterVarsity Press), United States

EVANGELICALS AND ENVIRONMENTAL STEWARDSHIP

By Ken Gnanakan

Evangelicals have gradually grown into engagement with various environmental initiatives over the last several decades. Evangelicals are beginning to recognize that ours is a Creator as well as a redeemer God. Today we find efforts ranging from tree planting and food production in the developing world, to ecosensitive attitudes to consumption and waste in the developed nations. These have been encouraging trends.

A History of Concern

A brief scan of various attitudes of Christians toward the environment over the centuries reveals contrasting views. In an impressive survey in the 1980s, ecological theologian Paul Santmire noted Christian theology's history of ecological concern, particularly in Western Christian thought. He described it as "the ambiguous ecological promise of Christian theology," with two opposing theological motifs: the spiritual and the ecological.[1] According to Santmire, the spiritual motif expresses a religious worldview that, if not outright hostile to the natural world, is at the very least unconcerned.[2] Characteristic of the spiritual motif is the belief that God is a being separate from the world, choosing to intervene in its affairs only at certain times. The ecological motif, in contrast, stresses God as the power of life itself, a presence in nature, humanity, and the rest of the cosmos.

While both of these motifs have prevailed, church history is decorated with prominent figures with remarkable attitudes to God's creation. Often referred to as "the Patron Saint of Ecology," Francis of Assisi recognized creation as a powerful manifestation of the beauty of God. He wrote the "Canticle of the Sun" praising God for creations such as "Brother Sun" and "Sister Moon."[3] Stories that surround his life deal with his love for the natural world, animals in particular. Saint Francis believed the world was created good and beautiful by God but is in need of redemption because of human sinfulness. Francis's message was to enjoy nature, as we too are creatures.

Saint Francis of Assisi addressing a group of birds. Hand-colored woodcut
Image © North Wind Picture Archive

---

1. H. Paul Santmire, *The Travail of Nature: The Ambiguous Ecological Promise of Christian Theology* (Minneapolis: Fortress, 1985), 9.

2. Ibid., 9.

3. "The Canticle of the Sun," or the "Laudes Creaturarum" ("Praise of the Creatures"), was composed by Saint Francis of Assisi in the Umbrian dialect of Italian. It has been translated into many languages and is easily accessible on various websites.

The Doctrine of Creation Attacked

Over the latter part of the last century there has been increasing alarm about the rapidly degrading environment. Proper attitudes toward environmental conservation have been called for, with reminders we live in a world where not all is right. Strangely, the Christian doctrine of creation has been blamed. Almost fifty years ago medieval historian Lynn White Jr. in a lecture called "The Historical Roots of Our Ecological Crisis" argued that the biblical doctrine of creation has largely contributed to our present predicament: "Especially in its Western form, Christianity is the most anthropocentric [human-centered] religion the world has seen. Christianity, in absolute contrast to ancient paganism and Asia's religions (except, perhaps, Zoroastrianism), not only established a dualism of man and nature, but also insisted that it is God's will that man exploit nature for his proper end."[4] The Genesis passages commanding Adam and Eve to "rule" and have "dominion" (Gen. 1:28 NIV; Gen. 1:28 NRSV), White contended, have led to this arrogant exploitation of nature.[5]

Criticisms like this have provoked Christians to dig deeper into the Bible and rediscover the God-given mandate to care for creation. White's short but seminal lecture, which was later published as an article, raised a huge controversy and has been quoted more often than any other environmental challenge. Many biblical scholars, particularly Evangelicals with their commitment to the Word of God, responded strongly, some accepting the criticism and others defending themselves. Concerned Christians with biblically backed action-oriented programs set out to make a difference as a result, as we see being demonstrated all over the world.

The Contemporary Context

During the 1950s, 1960s, and 1970s public awareness of the dreadful damage to the environment caused by human exploitation increased. Rachel Carson's "Silent Spring" articles in 1962 powerfully depicted the environmental devastation caused through pesticide poisoning.[6] Various factors led to the Earth Day demonstrations of April 22, 1970, the date often cited as the start of the modern environmental movement. At the same time, many Evangelicals retreated from getting involved in creation care during the so-called environmental movement in the United States. But why were we unconcerned for so long? Those were also the days of the emergence of New Age beliefs.[7] Perhaps Evangelicals feared identifying with environmental concerns would be perceived as aligning themselves with New Agers.

In Europe, Norwegian philosopher Arne Naess was advocating deep ecology as early as 1973. Naess argued that human destruction of the natural world posed a threat not only to humans but to the entire natural world. Deep ecology's core belief defined the living environment as an interdependent whole and stated it should be respected and regarded as having equal rights to survive. This movement was "deep" because it looked more deeply into the actual reality of humanity's relationship to the natural world. The movement criticized anthropocentric environmentalism and adopted a more holistic, biocentric view.[8]

---

4. Lynn White Jr., "The Historical Roots of the Ecological Crisis," University of Vermont, accessed January 31, 2014, http://www.uvm.edu/~gflomenh/ENV-NGO-PA395/articles/Lynn-White.pdf. The lecture was delivered in 1966 at the University of California, Los Angeles, and published as an article in *Science* magazine in 1967. Since then it has appeared in many publications all over the world and is widely quoted.

5. Ibid.

6. *Silent Spring* was initially serialized in three parts in 1962 in the *New Yorker* magazine (June 16, 23, and 30). It was first published as a book by Houghton Mifflin, Mariner Books in 1962.

7. Various New Age practices and beliefs prevail as alternative spirituality and religion. Associated holistic and alternative medicinal practices speak of the integration of mind, body, and spirit and are becoming increasingly popular.

8. Arne Naess and George Sessions, "Basic Principles of Deep Ecology," The Anarchist Library, accessed October 10, 2013, http://theanarchistlibrary.org/library/arne-naess-and-george-sessions-basic-principles-of-deep-ecology/.

In north India, the Chipko movement started in the early 1970s, creating worldwide awareness amid the increasing threats of deforestation. Advocates practiced Gandhian nonviolent resistance, hugging trees to protect them from being felled for commercial reasons. By the 1980s the movement had spread throughout India and was being practiced in other parts of the world.[9] The Chipko movement was one of the first environmental movements in the developing world. It raised an awareness of the rights of tribal people who are sustained by forests.

Meanwhile in Africa, there were similar small movements. One of the most well-known was spearheaded by Wangari Maathai.[10] In 1976 she introduced the idea of planting trees to fight deforestation and of working with communities concerned for the sustainable use of natural resources. Maathai wanted to improve people's livelihoods. She established The Green Belt Movement in 1977, mobilizing women in rural Kenya to combat deforestation, restore their main source of fuel for cooking, generate income, and stop soil erosion. Maathai was awarded a Nobel Peace Prize in 2004 for her laudable efforts.

All of these movements not only exposed the fragile condition of the environment but also blamed increasingly insensitive Western (and sometimes Christian) activities for causing the irreversible damage in the first place. Recognition of the interdependence between humans and nature was the fundamental solution offered. Creation depends on humans, and humans depend on creation. The Dalai Lama of Tibet, expressing his Buddhist sentiments, put it very clearly: "Because of the interdependent nature of everything we cannot hope to solve the multifarious problems with a one-sided or self-centered attitude. . . . What we need now is a holistic approach towards problems combined with a genuine sense of universal responsibility based on love and compassion."[11]

The Evangelical Response

Provoked by all these reminders, Evangelicals have been urged to do much more. It has often been said that we Evangelicals are more concerned about evangelism and church planting than about practical expressions of Christlike concern. Such a charge indicates to us a need to return to Scripture to discover the firm biblical grounds on which we can build our stand. We believe in a Creator God. Our environmental action needs to demonstrate this belief. As God's created beings we have a responsibility to the wider created order.

Ecological and environmental concerns are central to the Bible. The Word of God starts with the glorious account of God's creation. God created the intricate natural world within which he placed his people. Although sin entered in, the prophets looked forward to a renewed creation. Jesus, our redeemer, displayed a very positive attitude toward everything around him. Paul spoke about creation groaning for redemption, just as much as human beings (Rom. 8:22–23). The Bible claims it is through creation that even God is known (Ps. 97:6; Rom. 1:20).

Evangelicals must respond to the criticisms leveled against the creation accounts. The first is that being created in the image of God seems to make Christians feel they are superior to everything else in creation. The doctrine of creation has been viewed as meaning we are created as being *like* God; hence, everything was made for us. The second criticism is that Christians perceive themselves as being the rulers of all creation. This belief is based on God having been said to have given "dominion" to humans (Gen. 1:28 NRSV). These two aspects of the doctrine of creation have been blamed for the ecological disaster in which we now find ourselves.

To correct these accusations we must rediscover what the Bible actually says. In response to the criticism to be made in the image of God implies humans have been created in order to represent God responsibly in

9. Ken Gnanakan, *Responsible Stewardship of God's Creation* (Bangalore, India: World Evangelical Alliance Theological Commission, 2004), 97.

10. See the official website, The Green Belt Movement, http://www.greenbeltmovement.org/.

11. "Caring for the Earth," His Holiness the 14th Dalai Lama of Tibet, accessed October 2, 2013, http://www.dalailama.com/messages/environment/caring-for-the-earth/.

:reation. God and humans have a link that is different than the link betweeen God and the rest of creation. Humans are entrusted with a special task, a privilege and a responsibility. We are to protect God's creation as stewards, or caretakers, and not as reckless exploiters. Possessing God's image, instead of being seen as authoritative or in hierarchical terms, reveals itself in godly attitudes and gracious actions toward nature.

Adam and Eve.
Image: North Wind Picture Archives

The second criticism deals with the word *dominion*. The Genesis mandate to Adam and Eve over earth was to "subdue it; and have dominion" (Gen. 1:28 NRSV). The Hebrew words in this verse literally mean "to tread down," "to bring into bondage," or even "to rape," "to trample" or "to press" and therefore "to rule or dominate." Hebrew words, like many of the words in most of our Asian languages, have a rich array of meanings. Evangelicals must therefore consider the wider context of the word *dominion*. Ezekiel 34 depicts the prophet reminding the kings of Israel that God is shepherd. In contrast, the kings "ruled them harshly and brutally" (Ezek. 34:4 NIV). Here, *radah*, "to rule," is placed alongside the concept of a caring shepherd, not harshness and domination. When we examine the commands given to Adam and Eve at creation, it is necessary to also consider the nuances of later commands. Man and woman are instructed to "till" and "keep" the garden (Gen. 2:15 NRSV). These are words that beautifully tone down the harshness of the others on which we have been focusing. They speak of serving. An increasing number of Evangelicals believe humans must serve creation, and in doing so they serve the Lord God.

Human sinfulness is another biblical fact to keep in mind as we consider how we have cared (and not cared) for the environment. God created a wonderful world. But sin and the fall reverted it back to chaos. Environmental complications and ecological disasters are to be expected. When the reality of the image of God and dominion are placed in the context of the human fall and sin, sinfulness exploits the privileges humans have been given. Far too many discussions on the environmental crisis make no reference to sin and the fall of humanity. The crisis then becomes inexplicable, and the attack on the doctrine of creation becomes justifiable. Creation's perfection is marred by human imperfection.

A New Day of Evangelical Action

We Evangelicals are gradually waking up to our responsibilities. As we briefly survey the varied actions of the community today, it is heartening to see changing attitudes being converted into ecofriendly actions. Eco-action has become an integral part of the Christian life and mission. An NGO (nongovernmental organization) in Kenya is encouraging the use of ecotoilets that use minimal amounts of water, convert sewage to organic fertilizer, and keep the surrounding areas clean to minimize spread of disease. In Nigeria, churches are actively engaged in AIDS awareness programs and assisting families that have been devastated by the dreaded social pandemic and its associated environmental issues, such as lower agricultural production due to impacts on human capacity and a depleted work force and the overuse of some natural resources, particularly those managed by women such as water, firewood, and medicinal plants. As AIDS-affected rural households lose salary earners and agricultural labor, many are turning to natural resources as a safety net.[12]

---

12. An excellent article quoting UNAIDS (a joint United Nations program on HIV/AIDS) surveys is Judy Oglethorpe and Nancy Gelman, "HIV/AIDS and the Environment: Impacts of AIDS and Ways to Reduce Them: Fact Sheet for the Conservation Community," World Wildlife Fund, Inc., http://awsassets.wwf.org.au/downloads/mc_fs_hiv_aids_and_the_environment_07.pdf.

A Bible school in Bangalore, India, has taken a holistic perspective and minimized its waste. Water, garbage, food waste, and even sewage are all recycled through natural means. Cooking gas is made available for the community kitchen using environmentally friendly natural technologies, a few hours of lighting is provided converting this gas through mechanical means, and wastewater (containing small amounts of urine) goes into the garden, making it a complete ecofriendly campus. Nearby villagers have been taught to grow their own vegetables, purify their water naturally, and follow healthy habits for a wholesome lifestyle.

In Singapore, a mission group is targeting young people to build up appropriate environmental attitudes for the future. Groups of students are taken to Mongolia to plant trees, converting deserts into green forests. They return as changed individuals. This experience, the director feels, will help Christian youth become more powerful in their witness, rather than only preaching the gospel.

Many Christian families in Europe and North America are adopting an ecofriendly lifestyle, believing it is what God desires. They are decreasing their meat consumption, convinced that larger acreages of land are required for producing meat than to grow vegetable products. They carry reusable shopping bags, and old plastic grocery bags are used for disposing trash. The use of compost bins for fruit and vegetable scraps is being introduced. This will cut down on the amount of garbage disposed of as well as produce organic compost for their gardens.

Called to Be Stewards

Undoubtedly, there is a growing commitment to be good stewards. In his book *The Steward* Canadian theologian Douglas J. Hall stresses the "stewardship" metaphor "because it encapsulates the two sides of human relatedness, the relation to God on the one hand and to nonhuman creatures of God on the other."[13] The steward metaphor provides the corrective for the flawed relationships that have caused devastation. "The human being is, as God's steward, accountable to God and responsible for his fellow creatures."[14]

In both the Old and the New Testaments various words are used to describe a delegated responsibility that has been given to us. These words appear in the powerful parables of "the laborers" and "the dishonest manager" (Matt. 20:1–16 NRSV; Luke 16:1–13). We are called to be responsible stewards. Responsible stewardship demonstrated through God's love will result in practical actions for exemplary living today. As Evangelicals who are called to care for creation, we recognize the need for harmony, unity, purity, and integrity in creation. A respect for creation will elicit our love to protect, conserve, and bring healing to our wounded world.

Ultimately, we are responsible to God to honor him for the way in which he has honored us with responsibility over all of creation. All that we believe will turn into a powerful witness when we see God as the one who invests such responsibility to us. This relationship to God will reveal itself in a more responsible relationship to the world.

Bibliography

Carson, Rachel. "*Silent Spring.*" Boston: Houghton Mifflin, 1962.

Gnanakan, Ken. *Responsible Stewardship of God's Creation*. Bangalore: India: World Evangelical Alliance, 2004.

Hall, Douglas J. *The Steward: A Biblical Symbol Come of Age*. Eugene, OR: Wipf & Stock, 2004.

His Holiness the 14th Dalai Lama of Tibet. "Caring for the Earth." Accessed October 2, 2013. http://www.dalailama.com/messages/environment/caring-for-the-earth/.

---

13. Douglas J. Hall, *The Steward: A Biblical Symbol Come of Age* (Eugene, OR: Wipf & Stock, 2004), 46.

14. Ibid., 47.

Children now have clean water for laundry, drinking and wash in certain communities and schools in Latin America, Burundi and Vietnam, thanks to World Vision.
Photo: José Luis R © 2014 World Vision

Photo: Achel Bayisenge © 2014 World Vision

Naess, Arne, and George Sessions. "Basic Principles of Deep Ecology." The Anarchist Library. Accessed October 10, 2013. http://theanarchistlibrary.org/library/arne-naess-and-george-sessions-basic-principles-of-deep-ecology/.

Santmire, H. Paul. *The Travail of Nature: The Ambiguous Ecological Promise of Christian Theology*. Minneapolis: Fortress, 1985.

White, Lynn, Jr. "The Historical Roots of the Ecological Crisis." University of Vermont. Accessed January 31, 2014. http://www.uvm.edu/~gflomenh/ENV-NGO-PA395/articles/Lynn-White.pdf.

Dr. Ken Gnanakan is an educator, environmentalist, and theologian based in Bangalore, India. He is the founder and chancellor of the ACTS Group, chair of the International Council for Higher Education, and chair of Theological Book Trust.

Photo: Le Thiem Xuan © 2014 World Vision

EVANGELICALS IN THE MIDDLE EAST

A Community Commitment to Witness and Ministry

By Wafik Wahba

The Middle East is the birthplace of the Christian faith. The early disciples went out through the whole region to preach the message of the gospel. By the third century Middle Eastern Christians were instrumental in preaching the good news of God's salvation to the ancient world of the Mediterranean and beyond. Significant historical records illustrate the role of Christian leaders, as well as that of ordinary Christians like merchants and travelers, in spreading the Christian faith to Asia, Africa, and Europe.

The Mesopotamian Syriac church in what is modern-day Iraq and Iran sent missionaries to India and across Asia to China. By the ninth century records appear of churches along the Silk Road in countries like modern-day Afghanistan, Azerbaijan, and Tajikistan. The Egyptian church sent missionaries to Europe as well as to Ethiopia. These missionary-minded churches were very active in mission ministries during the early centuries of Christianity. However, the advent of Islam restricted their ability to reach out beyond their Middle Eastern territories after the seventh century.

More than twenty million Christians now live in the land where Christianity began. The story of the endurance of Middle Eastern Christians despite centuries of suffering and persecution is a living testimony of God's faithfulness. Although their numbers have dwindled through the centuries, Evangelicals continue to be salt and light through their sacrificial life of service and witness. Their committed prayer and worship is a living witness of God's glory shining in the darkness of this world.

Current Christian Population in the Middle East

The majority of the Middle East population is Muslim, with Christians composing less than 5 percent of the total population, and the majority of those Christians are Eastern Orthodox. Between the eleventh century and the fourteenth century several Catholic churches were established in the region, including the Maronite in Lebanon, the Coptic Catholic in Egypt, the Chaldean Church of Iraq, and others. By the mid-nineteenth century various evangelical communities were present across the Middle East.

Egypt is home to the largest Christian community, an estimated twelve million. The evangelical churches of Egypt also represent the largest Evangelical community in the region, with over one million Evangelicals. Evangelical communities in Syria and Lebanon present a smaller (less than half a million in total) but vibrant and influential community. There are also several evangelical churches in Iraq, Jordan, and Israel/Palestine, with a total estimated half a million Evangelicals. Several evangelical churches and ministries are also present in the Persian Gulf States of Dubai, Abu Dhabi, Bahrain, Kuwait, Qatar, and Oman.

Although the majority of those who attend churches in the Persian Gulf region are originally from other Middle Eastern countries, a handful of indigenous believers have begun to associate themselves with these churches. One of the current pastors in the Evangelical Churches of Kuwait comes from a native evangelical family that traces its history of Evangelicalism to 1961, when the country itself gained its independence.

As large numbers of Middle Eastern Christians have immigrated to other countries over the last sixty years or so, several Middle Eastern countries have been drained of their native Christian population. Countries like

Jordan, Syria, and Palestine boasted a large number of Christians, reaching to over 30 percent of the population, at the beginning of the twentieth century. But today the number of Christians in those countries is less than 5 percent of the total population. Lebanon was a majority Christian nation until its civil war (1970–90); now its population is less than 30 percent Christian. An estimated three million Egyptian Christians have left Egypt since the 1960s, due to persecution and harassment starting from the 1950s, the 1952 revolution, and for economic reasons. The impact of Christians leaving the Middle East has had dire consequences on the life and ministry of the church. However, in the last twenty years, thousands of non-Christians searching for God became believers. God is using them to make a significant difference in the region through their committed life of sacrificial witness.

Evangelical Influence

Middle Eastern Evangelicals are influencing today's society at large through worship, prayer, and service. The presence of evangelical churches influences the theology and worship of the larger Christian community in the region. One of the early steps taken by Evangelicals, in the mid-nineteenth century, was to translate the Bible into the modern Arabic language, the dominant language used by contemporary Middle Easterners today. The translation of the Scriptures into the daily language of the people gave the larger Christian community the ability to read and study God's Word and ground their faith on the truth of the Scripture. Soon after the Arabic translation became available, Bible study meetings spread across all denominations. This opened the door for people to ask the hard questions about Christian beliefs and styles of worship. It also enabled Christians to examine their own Christian traditions in the light of God's Word.

One of the remarkable stories about the influence of God's Word in shaping contemporary Middle Eastern Christian communities is demonstrated in the calling of Pope Shenouda III (1923–2012) to ministry. As a young man he regularly passed the Bible Society bookstore in downtown Cairo. One day he stopped to read a passage from the page of an open Bible on display: "So Jesus said to them, 'The light is among you for a little while longer. Walk while you have the light, lest darkness overtake you'" (John 12:35 ESV). The young man decided to dedicate his life to serving the Lord.[1] In 1971 he became the pope of the Coptic Orthodox Church of Egypt and spiritual leader to more than twelve million Middle Eastern Christians, who form more than half of all Arabic-speaking Christians in the Middle East. Pope Shenouda III initiated one of the largest Bible study meetings in the region, attended by thousands of people every week.

The Impact of Bible Translation

Today, Bible societies across the Middle Eastern countries are instrumental in making God's Word available for Christians as well as the millions of non-Christians who are searching for the truth and are hungry to know the true God. The influence of the Bible in shaping the theology and worship of the Middle Eastern church today is remarkable. Preaching is focused on an accurate interpretation of God's Word that speaks to the needs of contemporary people. Worship is also focused on a strong biblical foundation, which is reflected in the many contemporary praise and worship songs that can be heard in the churches. More than ten thousand contemporary Middle Eastern worship lyrics and songs today are used for worship across the region today.

During the first two centuries of Christianity, the Scripture was translated to the Middle Eastern languages of Coptic and Syriac, long before it was translated into Latin and other European languages. (Europe did not begin translating Scripture into English, German, and other languages until the fourteenth century.) This availability of Scripture in the Middle East helped keep the Christian faith alive through centuries of persecution and hardship.

---

1. Bible Society of Egypt, Monthly Newsletter, May 2013.

Evangelicals and Education

Theological education has become one of the key features of the evangelical movement in the Middle East. From the 1860s to the present, several theological seminaries were established by indigenous churches to prepare Christian leaders for various forms of ministry across the region. In 2013 the Evangelical Theological Seminary in Cairo, the oldest evangelical seminary in the region, celebrated 150 years of ministry. Four seminaries are instrumental in preparing leaders for the region: Jordan Evangelical Theological Seminary in Amman, Jordan; Arab Baptist Theological Seminary and the Near East School of Theology, both in Beirut, Lebanon; and Bethlehem Bible College in Bethlehem, West Bank. Thousands of pastors and church leaders who have graduated from Middle Eastern seminaries serve the Lord in more than thirty countries across the globe.

Elie Haddad is president of the Arab Baptist Theological Seminary in Lebanon
Photo: The Langham Partnership

Education, however, has not been confined to theological education. The evangelical communities across the Middle East have been instrumental in establishing hundreds of primary and secondary schools, along with institutions of higher education for educating Christians and non-Christians alike. Their vision is to transform society through quality education that enables younger generations to influence change and build a modern and democratic society. The American Universities in Cairo (1919) and Beirut (1866) were established by Evangelicals to provide quality higher education and influence change in the larger society. During the last 150 years, thousands of influential leaders have graduated from such institutions as these.

Evangelicals are also credited for encouraging women's education as early as the start of the twentieth century. Beginning in the 1940s, women gained the rights to vote and assume high political offices in countries like Egypt, Lebanon, Syria, and Iraq. The evangelical movement played a key role in these advancements, by preparing qualified women leaders through education and empowering them to assume leadership positions in the church and in society at large. The evangelical movement also advocates for gender equality, which contributed to significant social transformation in Middle Eastern societies.

Mission in the Middle East

Building on such a remarkable history of Christian mission, contemporary Middle Eastern Christians are keen to spread the message of the gospel to their own people and to other nations around the world. From the mid-twentieth century onward, hundreds of Middle Eastern missionaries have been sent to the Persian Gulf states, Africa, Europe, Asia, and the Americas.

Middle Eastern Christian mission organizations today embrace an all-inclusive kingdom approach in their ministries. They serve the social and spiritual needs of the community and reach out to millions of people in their constituencies. Many evangelical social organizations minister to the larger community in their countries. For example, the Lebanese Society for Educational and Social Development (LSESD) serves thousands of people through education and social services. The Coptic Evangelical Organization for Social Services (CEOSS) reaches two million people through education, small businesses, and health care programs, empowering them to break out of a cycle of poverty and oppression.

The Media Movement

Mass media presents an unprecedented opportunity for Middle Eastern Christians to communicate the message of the gospel to the millions around them. Satellite television is key in reaching out to people, with programs also being viewed through the Internet. At least twelve Middle Eastern Christian satellite television channels are broadcasting around the clock the message of salvation to the millions in the region. It is estimated that more than five million non-Christians across the Middle East and North Africa have come to believe in Jesus Christ through mass media in the last twenty years alone. The last decade has seen a new wave of communications through Facebook, Twitter, and other forms of social media that contribute to the acceleration of preaching the gospel across the region.

Satellite TV was instrumental in reaching out to Iranians starting from the 1980s when traditional means of evangelism were prohibited. After the Iranian Revolution of 1979, when several churches were destroyed and pastors murdered, the number of Christians in Iran was less than 2% of the total population. Today there are reports of a strong church in Iran that attracts the younger generations frustrated with the political and religious turmoil in their country. It is estimated the number of Christian believers in Iran is ten times that of 1979.

Middle Eastern Christianity is associated with the monastic tradition, one of the most remarkable spiritual movements in Christian history. It was in the desert of Egypt that monasticism was born, and by the fourth century it had become a global movement that influenced Africa, Asia, and Europe. The spread of Christianity into many parts of Europe is credited to the monks and nuns who preached the gospel, teaching people the Christian faith and attending to their social needs.[2]

The spirituality that stems from this Middle Eastern spiritual movement is instrumental today in shaping the life and ministries of Middle Eastern Christian communities. A renewed desire for prayers, fasting, and worship is spreading across the region. In the midst of the current events of turmoil and persecution, several Middle Eastern churches are dedicating long hours for worship services and prayer. Even before the Egyptian revolution in 2011, Kasr El-Dobara (KED) Evangelical Church in downtown Cairo dedicated days of prayers and fasting for the country. The church continues to pray constantly for God's intervention to transform the Egyptian and Middle Eastern countries, to expose the corruption, oppression, and injustices. This is exactly what has been happening since the revolution.

Although one cannot say Middle Eastern countries today are more democratic or less corrupt than before the revolutions and uprisings of the early twenty-first century, a remarkable change is taking place in exposing the sources of corruption, injustices, and confusion that have dominated the region for many centuries. An example of this change is the prayer movement spreading across Egypt and the Middle East. Many churches have weekly prayer meetings that sometimes last over twelve hours.

One of the most remarkable prayer meetings took place on November 11, 2011, when more than fifty thousand people gathered for overnight prayer at the Cave Church in Cairo. That night of prayer, fasting, and repentance was unprecedented in the recent history of the Middle Eastern church. The prayer was led by church leaders from all denominations and attended by Christians and non-Christians, who were drawn to the praise and worship. God's glory was manifested, and the prayer movement spread to many churches and communities.

One of the very significant outcomes of this prayer movement has been a renewed desire for unity among churches and Christians in the region. In early 2013 several churches in Egypt came together to form a unified church body committed to prayer and service in a new spirit. Evangelicals believe prayer leads to unity, and a united body of Christ glorifies the Father and empowers the testimony of the church in the whole world.

. Historically the monastic movement that started in Egypt was introduced to Europe during the fourth and fifth centuries. Many European church leaders actually came to Egypt to be educated in the monastic life and spirituality. They were instrumental in starting the European monastic spirituality.

About half a million Evangelicals live in the Middle East, including Israel/Palestine. *Photo: www.designpics.com*

Today's Middle Eastern Christians face renewed cycles of persecution. The conflict that began in Syria a few years ago has resulted in uprooting and scattering thousands of Syrians, many of whom are Christians. Across the region, Christian homes are destroyed and properties are confiscated. Churches are bombed in Syria, Iraq, and Egypt. Christians are killed and kidnapped. Their ancestors faced the same realities throughout the centuries.

Middle Eastern Evangelicals put their trust in the Lord, who is given all authority in heaven and on earth. They trust in the promise "surely I am with you always, to the very end of the age" (Matt. 28:20 NIV). Evangelicals in the Middle East would describe themselves as "hard pressed on every side, but not crushed; perplexed, but not in despair; persecuted, but not abandoned; struck down, but not destroyed" (2 Cor. 4:8–9 NIV).

Dr. Wafik Wahba is professor of Global Christianity at Tyndale University College and Seminary in Toronto, Canada. He has taught theology and intercultural studies in the United States, the Middle East, Africa, Asia, and South America. He co-led the unit on theological education for mission at the Lausanne 2004 Forum for World Evangelization in Pattaya, Thailand, and is one of the authors of "Effective Theological Education for World Evangelization," Lausanne Occasional Paper No. 57 (May 2005). Dr. Wahba serves on the board of directors for several international Christian organizations.

EVANGELICALS AND BIBLE TRANSLATION

By Roy Peterson and Gilles Gravelle

"The purpose of Bible translation is to enact the way, the truth, and the life in new settings, to make Christ live within new contexts."

—Kevin Vanhoozer

"When I read the Bible in the national language, it was like reading in moonlight. Now that I have a translation in my own language, it's like reading it in bright sunlight. It's all so clear!"

—A Kupang Malay speaker

Little Wolf, the First Bible Translator to the "Ethne"

As the resurrected Christ was about to ascend to heaven, he made one more thing perfectly clear to his followers: they must go and tell the good news to everyone, everywhere. The gospel was evangelical from the start. And that would require translation.

In 267 AD, The Goths raided Cappadocia, modern-day southern Turkey and carried off a number of Greek-speaking Christians; Bible translation had begun. A little boy named Ulfilas, "Little Wolf," was among the captives.[1] By the time he was thirty-two, Ulfilas would develop a Gothic alphabet and translate most of the Bible. It was innovation par excellence. No manuals existed on developing an alphabet or translating from Greek and Hebrew into another language. Ulfilas's work may have been the first time the Bible was translated by a linguistic and cultural outsider.[2] The translated gospel came through cross-cultural contact, even if it was forced contact.

The Silk Road Translator

Bible translation did not become any easier for missionaries, especially when it came to languages that are nothing like the biblical languages. In AD 638 a foreign traveler along the Silk Road—the commerce highway system of the time—attempted the seemingly impossible: translating the Bible into Chinese. It was "the sort of Chinese that would be likely if you've got a meeting with people who don't know the language and other people who know the language but don't know the subject."[3]

In seventh-century China, the Silk Road translator struggled to describe Christ in terms the Chinese would understand. Even with mistakes, this new translation began to describe the One who made all things. It included the account of the fall, the law, and the Christian teaching of redemption. It was messy. But it was progress.

. Other translations, such as Syriac, were done as early as AD 150–200 by an indigenous community of believers.

. Andrew F. Walls, "Bible Translation and Scripture Use in Christian History" (unpublished manuscript, 2009)

. Andrew F. Walls, "Missionary Societies and the Fortunate Subversion of the Church," *The Evangelical Quarterly* 88, no. 2 (1988): 141–155.

The Risk Takers: Wycliffe, Tyndale, and Luther

John Wycliffe translating the Bible into English, 1300s. Hand-colored woodcut.
Image: North Wind Picture Archives

Pre-Reformation Europe had only one acceptable language for the Bible: Latin. In England, church officials did not think common folk needed their own English translation. However, there were three men who acted on an uncommon belief. John Wycliffe's translation from Latin into common English in 1384 was not officially commissioned, nor was William Tyndale's English translation from Greek in 1526. Wycliffe was persecuted for his work the rest of his life. Tyndale was executed for his efforts. Yet, the work continued.

Germany was a somewhat safer place to be a Bible translator, and Johannes Gutenberg's printing press innovations made mass production of these Bibles possible. This technological improvement was just in time, because religious revolution was in the air, led by a theologizing monk named Martin Luther. Luther thought ordinary people should be able to read and interpret the Bible. His views would embolden others. Bible translation would play a major role in giving millions access to the Scriptures for the first time.

Rebellious William

Against the wishes of the official Church, a defiant, young, evangelical-minded Baptist named William Carey launched a grassroots mission society in 1793. One of his goals was to translate the Bible into major Indian languages. The society was called the Particular Baptist Society for the Propagation of the Gospel Among the Heathen. It was likely the first parachurch organization.

Like Luther and his predecessors, Carey continued to set the pace for the future of Bible translation, even if it meant agitating the status quo. His work created a surge in Bible translation and church planting work, carried out by like-minded volunteers over the following two hundred years.

Peaking in the late 1990s, all of the major languages in the world had Bible translations. Several thousand more had Bible portions. Over one thousand translations were in progress. Certainly, people from across the spectrum of church denominations have done Bible translation work. But the translation surge from Carey until the present can be largely credited to the work of evangelical grassroots believers, organizations, and churches.

Bible Translation in the Twenty-First Century

Because of Evangelicals' obedience to the great commission, over four billion people have access to some Scripture in their language. In every era, translators used the technology of the time to accelerate the work and improve the results. The translators included mother-tongue speakers, cross-cultural workers, and national workers in their work.

Today, Bible translation is a global church movement.

After hundreds of years of cross-cultural Bible translation work, the winds of change are blowing. It is possible that the last generation of new translators, an indigenous movement translating the Bible into their own languages, is at work. Rapid gains in technology enable new and better ways of working. For the first time in church history, the global church is collaborating like never before to finish the translation task.

In every era, translators used the technology of the time to accelerate the work and improve the results.

Finishing the Task—In This Life?

For more than two hundred years, evangelical missionaries have been known for grassroots inventiveness and sometimes disruptive behavior. After all, they launched and extended the parachurch movement to translate Bibles and plant churches.

For evangelical missions, risk taking comes with the territory. Creativity is a must. "It is the contributors of the funds who are the real association [. . .] the individuals, churches, congregations, who freely act together, through such agencies for an object of common interest. The Protestant form of free, open, responsible, embracing all classes, both sexes, all ages, the masses of the people, is peculiar to modern times, almost to our age."[4] This comment was made in the year 1837. It is still true today.

How will this creative DNA further Bible translation work in the coming decades? If the surge illustrated in the two charts are indicators, then expect faster, better, deeper and wider results—and quite possibly completion before this century ends.

Translation Is More than Spreading Christianity

In his book *Liberating Word: The Power of the Bible in the Global South*, Philip Jenkins shows that Bible translation is no longer viewed primarily as a tool for spreading Christianity, as it was under the modern Western mission period. Translation is increasingly viewed by local pastors in in certain regions of the world as a need-driven, urgent task. These pastors often live and serve in contexts where people have suffered from civil and religious wars, the negative impact of colonialism, disintegration of social structures, disease, and severe famines.

Evangelicals believe that any language community needs Scripture to provide lasting solutions to social problems, fueling the translation movement even more. As Nigerian Bishop Emmanuel Egbunu said: "The indigenizing principle ensures that each community recognizes in Scripture that God is speaking to its own situation."[5]

Spiritual, social and physical problems also present theological challenges in knowing God. Explaining the importance of Scripture in local language and cultural context, Cambodian-born Hwa Yung says, "It is not a fad or a catch-word, but a theological necessity demanded by the incarnational nature of the Word."[6]

Peruvian missiologist Samuel Escobar agrees. "The text of Scripture can be understood adequately only within its own context, and the understanding and application of its eternal message demands awareness of our own cultural context"[7] (Escobar, 2003, p. 21).

Martin Luther. Hand-colored engraving from the original picture by Holbein. *Image: North Wind Picture Archives*

. Walls, Andrew F. "Bible Translation and Scripture Use in Christian History." Unpublished manuscript, 2009.

. Emmanuel Egbunu, "Teach, Baptise, and Nurture New Believers," in *Mission in the 21st Century: Exploring the Five Marks of Global Mission*, ed. Andrew Walls and Cathy Ross (Maryknoll, NY: Orbis, 2008), 25–46.

. Hwa Yung, *Mangoes or Bananas? The Quest for an Authentic Asian Christian Theology* (Oxford: Regnum International, 1997), 7.

. Samuel Escobar, *The New Global Mission: The Gospel From Everywhere to Everyone* (Downers Grove, IL: InterVarsity Press, 2003), 21.

Finally, Ghanaian theologian Kwame Bediako understood that partial Bible knowledge only results in partial heart understanding. This is what happens when people can only read Scripture in a foreign language. Bediako questioned, "How can we minister the Gospel effectively if we cannot reflect theologically in the language in which we dream and pray?"[7]

Evangelism is still a significant reason for Bible translation. But Christians living in war-torn zones, experiencing social and economic upheaval, and losing loved ones to hunger and disease seek the comfort, solace, and solutions found in Scripture as never before. Bible translation is an urgent and practical task for these times, perhaps more so than at any other time in history.

Today Bible translation is changing significantly. Translation workers are asking the end users what they want most from a translation. Ministry leaders from around the world have indicated they require Scripture translations sooner than ever. People are profoundly experiencing the complete story of God's love and redemption through multiple channels. Video, audio, and printed Scriptures are the triad of Bible translation.

William Tyndale, English trans lator of the New Testament Hand-colored woodcut
Image: North Wind Picture Archive

Bible translation today is much more social than in the past—thanks in part to social media. What began as an initiative born of autonomy has now become an initiative born of community, seen in the way teams use social media to give and receive real-time feedback on their drafts.

It is remarkable how fast and wide a new translation spreads digitally through a community. Through progressive publishing, readers receive new Scripture portions hot off the digital press. It is Gutenberg's printing press in warp speed.

Web-based crowdsourcing made it possible for a people in Bihar, India to help voluntarily with the translation in one recent translation project. More than thirteen hundred people from the local community helped. They offered feedback on the quality of the text, suggested improvements, corrected spelling, and asked questions. The eager community of online workers spread the Word through numerous social networks. Together they viewed the translation as their own. It originated with them—and they spread it to others. Within only a few short months, awareness of the translation work spread throughout this language group of 1.5 million speakers.

This is translation, distribution, and impact in real time. All of this occurred because of a Web-based, crowd sourced rough draft of the Gospel of Luke. It was a pilot project, and the results were astonishing.

Translation Changes Everything

We have come far since Little Wolf's fateful beginning. Billions of people speaking thousands of language now have some, if not all, of God's Word in their languages. Yet, hundreds of millions of people in more than 1,900 language groups still do not have even one verse of Scripture. And more than one billion people do not have a full Bible. How are Evangelicals helping to finish the translation task?

- Making Bible translation a central rather than peripheral activity in missions, especially among unreached people.
- Directing funds to areas of most potential impact.
- By having specialists train local leadership and build greater capability.

---

7. Bediako, Kwame. "The Challenge of Mother Tongue for African Christian Thought." *Journal of African Christian Thought* no. 1 (June 2002): 1–60.

Evangelicals have always taken calculated risks to translate the Bible. Evangelicals have been creative and innovative. Although roles and ways of working may be different, the ultimate reason remains the same. Evangelicals believe that God's Word changes everything.

Major Bible Translation Agencies

The Seed Company: www.theseedcompany.org
Wycliffe Global Alliance: www.wycliffe.net
SIL International: www.sil.org
The United Bible Societies: www.unitedbiblesocieties.org
The Bible League International: www.bibleleague.org
Pioneer Bible Translators: www.pioneerbible.org
Lutheran Bible Translators: www.lbt.org

Bibliography

Bediako, Kwame. "The Challenge of Mother Tongue for African Christian Thought." *Journal of African Christian Thought* 5, no. 1 (June 2002): 1–60.

Egbunu, Emmanuel. "Teach, Baptise, and Nurture New Believers." In *Mission in the 21st Century: Exploring the Five Marks of Global Mission*, edited by Andrew Walls and Cathy Ross, 25–46. Maryknoll, NY: Orbis, 2008.

Escobar, Samuel. *The New Global Mission: The Gospel from Everywhere to Everyone.* Downers Grove, IL: InterVarsity Press, 2003.

Finishing the Task. "The Task." Accessed May 26, 2014. http://finishingthetask.com/.

Jenkins, Philip. *The New Faces of Christianity: Believing the Bible in the Global South.* Oxford: Oxford University Press, 2006.

Walls, Andrew F. "Bible Translation and Scripture Use in Christian History." Unpublished manuscript, 2009.

———. "Missionary Societies and the Fortunate Subversion of the Church." *The Evangelical Quarterly* 88, no. 2 (1988): 141–155.

Yung, Hwa. Mangoes or Bananas? *The Quest for an Authentic Asian Christian Theology.* Oxford: Regnum International, 1997.

Dr. Gilles Gravelle is the director of research and innovation at The Seed Company. His forthcoming book, *The Age of Global Giving* (William Carey Library, Pasadena) discusses the critical changes taking place in mission finance.

Dr. Roy L. Peterson is president of the American Bible Society and former president and CEO of The Seed Company, a Wycliffe Bible Translators affiliate. Earlier in his career, he served in Ecuador and Guatemala, also for Wycliffe organizations.

"Providing God's Word to those who have not yet heard it in their heart language is a compelling urgency of our time. When people hear Jesus speaking their own heart language, his message means so much more. When Jesus' message becomes incarnated within a Bibleless culture, the results are awesome!"

—Dr. Alex Phillip, Executive Director, New India Evangelistic Association, India

THE CHALLENGE OF EVANGELICAL DIVERSITY

By Rose Dowsett

Careful study indicates the early church was never as monochrome as some people assume. While the Roman Empire and the Greek language imposed some uniformity, these did not succeed in stamping out significant variety. The Council at Jerusalem (Acts 15, probably AD 48) wisely recognized the leading of the Holy Spirit to accept the limits of conformity and allowed Gentile believers to live differently from Jewish believers in many ways. The Epistles reveal very different cultural and religious contexts, with varying issues and challenges at play in the lives of believers. Even essential teaching about the person and work of Christ is expressed differently for different audiences and by different New Testament writers.

While the pre-Reformation churches sought to impose uniformity through liturgy and directives from its bishops, it is doubtful that in reality they ever achieved it. Not only did the Eastern (mostly Orthodox) and Western (mostly Roman Catholic) churches operate under different structures that were often very hostile to one another from the early centuries onward, but even within those two major blocs there was also considerable fragmentation.

The Protestant Reformation of the sixteenth century made it clear that it was not possible to keep the church looking, believing, and behaving in one form. Protestantism, including Evangelicalism, is especially vulnerable to fragmentation. Placing authority in God's Word rather than in church structures did not lead to agreement about how to understand and apply it. Different scholars and church leaders interpreted some points differently.

As the Bible became more widely available, lay believers also sometimes reached different conclusions about its meaning and how to obey it. Sometimes the differences in interpretation were very minor and sometimes more significant, and both led to the creation of new denominations. As the church has been established in more and more countries and ethnic groups, the need to contextualize expressions of church and gospel has led to even greater variety.

As well as differences over interpreting Scripture, some divisions have been sparked by culture and context, some by conscientious conviction, and some by dominant personalities. Sometimes there has been a desire to recover some neglected truth or to protest against what is perceived to be unfaithfulness to God's Word. Sadly, sometimes differences have been reinforced by painful history, even civil war or imperialism. We cannot escape the impact of history.

Cultures and Countries

Other problems have revolved around the relationship between church and state. In America the separation of church and state is very important to most Christians, while in many European countries church and state have a much closer and happier relationship. In some countries today there is a tolerant acceptance of plural forms of the church, with freedom for many different denominations. In other countries, such as China or Greece, that freedom is severely restricted.

In some cultures, plurality is a matter of individual freedom, including freedom of conscience, and that freedom is sacrosanct. It is taken for granted there should be plenty of choice and that such choice is a human right. In other cultures, especially those with a strongly hierarchical or tribal tradition, loyalty is often to a specific leader—a matter of communal identity rather than doctrinal distinctive—and individual choice is not part of the landscape. For some the overriding issue is absolute doctrinal orthodoxy as the leader or group defines it. For others, doctrinal particularities are of far less importance than the immediacy of experience of hope or healing or well-being. All of these positions are found within the World Evangelical Alliance (WEA) family.

The WEA and Denominational Plurality

The birth of the Evangelical Alliance in 1846 (in which the WEA finds its roots), was a response to the problem of denominational pluralism—and often even hostility between one denomination and another—in the light of the Lord Jesus Christ's impassioned prayer just before his crucifixion that his disciples should be united. Clearly this was not to be something vague and abstract, but organic as the relationship between Father and Son and Spirit is organic (as well as a mystery). From the time of the church fathers onward there have been those who have argued that such unity is only spiritual (a position taken to this day by many Evangelicals) and any kind of visible or structural unity is not what Christ was referring to. So, *alliance* rather than organizational unity enabled believers from across denominational divides to ally with one another around a core of commonly held beliefs while allowing secondary issues to be as diverse as you please. Alliance enabled believers regardless of denomination to join together in common cause in agreed actions.

Three core beliefs—the authority of Scripture, the centrality of Jesus Christ and his atoning death on the cross, and the need for people to come to personal faith in him—remain a unifying basis of shared identity for Evangelicals. The WEA Statement of Faith (see the sidebar) is carefully expressed, designed in its simplicity to accommodate the widest possible number of those who self-define as Evangelicals. It avoids the expanded details that would divide.

Nonetheless, there is disagreement over what exactly falls into the category of secondary issues, where we can agree to disagree. How inclusive, and how exclusive, should the evangelical family be? What are valid differences in focus, in ways of expressing theology, and in interpreting Scripture? Is it possible to keep the peace between those who call themselves "conservative Evangelicals," those who call themselves "open Evangelicals," those who call themselves "Charismatic," those who call themselves "Reformed," and those who find most or all of those terms utterly irrelevant and prefer no label at all other than "Christian" or perhaps "Bible-believing Christians"? And what about those for whom "Evangelical" simply means "Protestant" (as in some of continental Europe), or others for whom "Charismatic," "Pentecostal," and "Evangelical" are all interchangeable (as in some parts of Latin America and Africa)? Against such a confusing backdrop, we turn to look at a few specific areas of tension today, as an illustration of our difficulties.

Scripture and Its Interpretation

How inclusive, and how exclusive, should the evangelical family be?

Evangelicals hold a high view of Scripture. They would agree it carries final authority for belief and conduct, and it should shape the life of both church and individuals. But there is a spectrum of views about how to interpret Scripture, from exact literalism to uncovering the cultural context, from the shaping of its original form and content to the seeking of some inner kernel of abiding truth, and many points in between. How do you make the bridge between the ancient worlds of the eastern Mediterranean and the far different (and diverse) worlds of the twenty-first century? Different ways of interpreting the Bible and different convictions about how to transpose these ancient texts into contemporary contexts can lead to painful confrontations.

The Death of Christ

The person and work of Christ lie at the very heart of our Christian faith. The Lord's death and resurrection are the grounds upon which we are reconciled with our heavenly Father. For some today, this can only be expressed through "penal substitutionary atonement" and the use of those specific words. For others, while accepting the importance of this absolute reality, other models of the death of Christ are also used in the New Testament. Reconciliation and victory over the powers of darkness are two examples of great significance and may be more readily understood as entry points to the gospel. This discussion is taking place on every continent.

Doing Theology

Until the mid-twentieth century, Protestant theology was formulated in the Western world. First it was shaped by its inheritance from the Greco-Roman classical world and that world's ways of organizing material, then by the medieval world, and then by the Enlightenment, with its stress on logic and human reasoning. For some, their systems of theology—for instance, Reformed theology or dispensationalism—became more controlling than the Scriptures from which they were supposed to be derived. Hebrew thinking can happily accommodate concepts that to many Western minds may appear contradictory, such as the apparent incompatibility of human free will and predestination. This is not a problem at all in the biblical world, where they are simply both true. In the same way, much Western theology has little room for mystery (or humility) and wants to tie up every loose end neatly.

Today, as believers all over the world reflect on Scripture, there are many new insights into God's truth and many fresh ways of expressing and organizing theology. This is often less philosophical and more concrete, sometimes expressed through narrative, parable, music, or drama rather than in logical discourse. Furthermore, some of the issues that have occupied Western theologians are of lesser concern to those in the global South (Central and Latin America, Africa, and most of Asia). Conversely, theologians are bringing to our attention new areas the global North/West did not notice or regarded as of lesser importance, for example, the reality of the spirit world. In some parts of the world the task of formulating and developing theology has passed from being the preserve of professional academic theologians (which it should never have been in the almost-exclusive way adopted by the West) into a communal activity practiced naturally by a group of believers moving backward and forward between Scripture and daily life.

Word and Deed

For some Evangelicals, the sole business of the church has been proclamation of the gospel. For others, words alone lack credibility, and mission must include attention to the whole person in the whole of that person's life, in the whole of society. So it is of the essence of mission, not a dangerous diversion, to address issues of poverty and injustice and environmental degradation, alongside speaking of the Lord and explaining the gospel. For some, their eschatology (i.e., their understanding of what will happen at the end of the world) means that this world will be utterly destroyed and is not worth worrying about; only people's souls have eternal significance. For others with a different interpretation and who believe the world will be renewed rather than utterly destroyed, it is important to care for the world because God who created the world still declares his love for it and sustains it. And because God cares passionately about justice and about the poor and sick, as evidenced throughout Scripture, we should do so too. In practice, Evangelicals are often at the forefront of compassion ministries, alongside verbal proclamation.

> **The person and work of Christ lie at the very heart of our Christian faith.**

The Holy Spirit

A group of Evangelicals called Cessasionists believe that the gifts of the Spirit were given only for the first era of the church. However, from the Evangelical Revivals of the eighteenth century onward, there has been a widespread experience of the gifts of the Spirit. This was reinforced through the beginnings of Pentecostalism at the start of the twentieth century, movements of the Spirit in the mid-twentieth century, and the influence of many parts of the global South churches since then. Most Evangelicals want to keep Word and Spirit firmly together, but disagreements remain about healing, prophecy, miracles, prosperity, and speaking in tongues. The majority of Evangelicals in the global South are Charismatic or Pentecostal in the expression of their faith, and this is changing the face of the world church. The church is called to be fully trinitarian.

What Is the Church?

From its beginnings in mid-nineteenth century, the WEA has accommodated both adult/immersion baptism and infant baptism, varieties of leadership models, and differing relationships to the state, along with various kinds of denominations or independent congregations. Today, especially in such post-Christian societies as most of Europe, there are many experiments in different forms of being and doing church, some of which do not look very much like church in its traditional forms. In addition, there are experiments in establishing disciple groups in particularly hostile environments, such as the insider movements in the Islamic world, the Hindu world, and the Buddhist world. (Insider movements refer to apparent movements of the Holy Spirit, where people of another faith hostile to the Christian faith come to personal trust in Jesus Christ, but try to remain as closely within the socio-religious culture of origin as possible, retaining many practices of the former faith.) Is it possible to establish an absolute irreducible core of what has to be believed and practiced for a group to be authentically church? What is the relationship between a local church and the wider community of believers across a country and then across the whole world? If the church is the body of Christ as Scripture tells us it is, then how do we live that out in our fractured world, expressing unity as well as diversity?

Practice, Ethics, and Discipleship

In Matthew 7:3 Jesus says it is easier for us to see the splinter in someone else's eye than the large piece of wood in our own. We can easily be blind to our own failure to meet God's standards while being judgmental about practices somewhere else in the world. Depending upon where they are in the world, and also on their interpretation of Scripture, Evangelicals disagree about the role of women in church and society, about what is acceptable in relation to human sexuality and what constitutes truthfulness, about whether divorce or polygamy is permissible, whether it is right for there to be financial and economic inequality across the world, whether materialism is simply a Western problem, and a host of

Baptism of Virginia Dare, first English child born in the New World, Roanoke Colony, 1587. Hand-colored woodcut.
The World Evangelical Alliance embraces a variety of traditions ranging from, for example, infant baptism to baptism by full-immersion.
Image: North Wind Picture Archives

207

other matters. Our reading of Scripture is often filtered through the assumptions of our culture and worldview, our minds and hearts are often selective about what we hear and respond to in God's Word, and so our grasp of what it means to be a disciple is often different from that of others. These are just some of the areas in which our diversity can stretch our unity to a breaking point. There are, sadly, many more.

Should Evangelicals be dismayed and defeated by these disagreements? No! Is there anything we need to do? Yes! The God who delighted to create myriads of different butterflies and birds and trees and flowers does not expect his children all to be the same. But, we *are* all called to be increasingly transformed into the image of our Lord Jesus Christ. We are all called to live out the unity that is ours in him: one body, one family, one people, with a shared calling, a shared gospel, one faith, and one baptism. Siblings in a family may be very different from one another, but we recognize that something is badly wrong when they are at war with one another.

We Evangelicals are often passionate about our faith (as we should be). But alongside that we need to be deeply humble in recognizing none of us is infallible, and we need to show love and grace toward those from whom we differ. However much we may be blessed and at home in our own traditions, we need the breadth of heart to rejoice with those who live out their love for the Lord in worship, life, and service, differently from ourselves.

The great diversity of God's people today could be deeply enriching for us all. It is a gift of God to our generation. Let us celebrate.

Rose Dowsett is a founding member of the Evangelical Alliance Scotland and served as missiological adviser to the Evangelical Alliance-UK, and as vice-chair of the World Evangelical Alliance's Mission Commission. She was a member of the Lausanne Theology Working Group, and of the small international team that drew up the Cape Town Commitment.

The WEA Statement of Faith

We believe

. . . in the **Holy Scriptures** as originally given by God, divinely inspired, infallible, entirely trustworthy; and the supreme authority in all matters of faith and conduct . . .

One God, eternally existent in three persons, Father, Son, and Holy Spirit . . .

Our **Lord Jesus Christ**, God manifest in the flesh, His virgin birth, His sinless human life, His divine miracles, His vicarious and atoning death, His bodily resurrection, His ascension, His mediatorial work, and His Personal return in power and glory . . .

The **Salvation** of lost and sinful man through the shed blood of the Lord Jesus Christ by faith apart from works, and regeneration by the Holy Spirit . . .

The **Holy Spirit**, by whose indwelling the believer is enabled to live a holy life, to witness and work for the Lord Jesus Christ . . .

The **Unity** of the Spirit of all true believers, the Church, the Body of Christ . . .

The **Resurrection** of both the saved and the lost; they that are saved unto the resurrection of life, they that are lost unto the resurrection of damnation.[1]

---

1. "Who We Are: Statement of Faith," World Evangelical Alliance, accessed March 3, 2014, http://www.worldea.org/whoweare/statementoffaith/.

Evangelicals Join Together in a Global Forum

The Global Christian Forum is designed to facilitate all Christian communities to have a common gathering place. This forum provides opportunity for Christians from all parts of the world—and from each and every Christian communion—a place in which they each can discover mutual interest, wrestle with issues and to forward plans and initiatives for the nurturing of Christian unity.

Conceived in 1988 by Konrad Raiser, general secretary of the World Council of Churches, the Forum began with a consultation at Fuller Theological Seminary in 2000 and has continued regular international and regional meetings under the banner, "Our journeys with Jesus Christ."

The guiding purpose statement of the Global Christian Forum is: to create an open space wherein representatives from a broad range of Christian churches and inter-church organizations, which confess the triune God and Jesus Christ as perfect in His divinity and humanity, can gather to foster mutual respect, to explore and address together common challenges (www.globalchristianforum.org).

In the spirit of John 17:21 the Forum seeks to:

- Deepen our commitment to God's Word and mission in the world;
- Enhance our understanding of contemporary expressions of Christian mission;
- Pursue principles and practices that enable us to deal freely, responsibly and peaceably with our Christian differences and distinctive qualities;
- Engage in theological reflection in areas of mutual concern;
- Strengthen the wholeness of the church by encouraging communication and cooperation;
- And foster relationships that may lead to common witness.

"The global rise in strength and influence of Evangelicals has made it imperative to find ways within the wider Christian community to foster understanding and common action. We believe that the Global Christian Forum made up of the World Evangelical Alliance, The World Council of Churches, and the Roman Catholic Church, enables us to forge new means of cooperation for the good of humanity and the witness of Jesus Christ."

—Rev. Dr. Larry Miller, Secretary, Global Christian Forum, France

THE STORY OF THE WORLD EVANGELICAL ALLIANCE

By Ian Randall

In 129 nations around the world, evangelical churches have formed alliances for mutual support, identity, and influence, and for the sake of the gospel. The World Evangelical Alliance (WEA) gathers those alliances together, along with one hundred other international organizations, to give a worldwide identity, voice, and platform to more than six hundred million Evangelicals in the world today. The WEA, as it exists today, was years in the making. This is its story.

A Desire to Join Together

The World Evangelical Fellowship (WEF) began in 1951. (The WEF changed its name to WEA fifty years later.) An ongoing impetus toward Evangelical unity, stemming back to the creation of the Evangelical Alliance in London in 1846, contributed to the creation of the WEF. The aim then was a world body that would counter Evangelical fragmentation. This hope foundered over deep disagreements about whether or not slaveholders in the southern states of America could be members. The opposition to membership by slaveholders was led especially by British Evangelicals.[1]

When an international body could not be formed, national Evangelical alliances began to emerge around the world. There was still a strong desire to foster transnational Evangelical cooperation, however, and moves in the 1940s to promote Evangelical unity in North America contributed to a renewed vision for a global body. During this period the American branch of the Evangelical Alliance officially ceased to function, and the National Association of Evangelicals (NAE) was formed.

The 1948 formation of the World Council of Churches (WCC), which significant Protestant denominations joined, galvanized the movement for a global Evangelical body. The range of theological opinion embraced in the WCC would become a contentious issue for Evangelicals. But the British Evangelical Alliance, which was present in Amsterdam when the WCC was formed, advised an Evangelical presence, arguing in its quarterly periodical, *Evangelical Christendom*, "If Evangelicals oppose the WCC or abstain from co-operating with it, the Council may well be captured by the Modernists or the Ritualists, but if we play our part we may be an instrument in the hand of God for reviving the churches."[2]

> **When an international body could not be formed, national Evangelical alliances began to emerge around the world.**

---

1. Ian Randall and David Hilborn, "An Evangelical and Catholic Union," in *One Body in Christ: The History and Significance of the Evangelical Alliance*, ed. Ian M. Randall and David Hilborn (Carlisle, UK: Paternoster Press, 2001), 18–44; Ian Randall and David Hilborn, "Across the Partition Wall," in *One Body in Christ: The History and Significance of the Evangelical Alliance* (Carlisle, UK: Paternoster Press, 2001), 45–70.

2. *Evangelical Christendom* (January–March 1949): 1.

Early Talks

The NAE was shaped by developments within the New England Fellowship, founded by J. Elwin Wright, which in the 1940s was calling for a national Evangelical fellowship.[3] The NAE explored a more progressive "new Evangelicalism."[4] The energetic Wright, as the NAE's first executive secretary, visited Europe and suggested convening an exploratory meeting about international fellowship. This was held in Switzerland in 1948. In early March 1950 an International Delegate Conference was held in Kent at Hildenborough Hall, a center set up by the British evangelist Tom Rees, where NAE delegates met with representatives from twelve European countries. Sir Arthur Smith, chairman of the British Evangelical Alliance, was elected chairman of the new International Committee, and it was agreed that a "basis of belief would be the foundation stone" for the NAE, while each affiliated group would have freedom in "the application of this basis to their national situation."[5]

World Tour

Further concrete moves toward a world Evangelical fellowship were taken at a conference at Gordon Divinity School in Boston in early September 1950. The conference recommended the establishment of an International Association of Evangelicals to witness to evangelical and historic Christianity, to encourage and promote fellowship among Evangelicals, to stimulate evangelism, and to promote united evangelical action in all spheres. The NAE's involvement was a notable feature during this period of organizational development. The NAE formed a Commission on International Relations to encourage worldwide Evangelical cooperation. Together with NAE leader Clyde W. Taylor, Wright traveled to Tokyo, Manila, Hong Kong, Bangkok, Calcutta, Bombay, New Delhi, Beirut, Damascus, Amman, Jerusalem, Athens, Rome, Zurich, Geneva, Marseilles, Barcelona, Paris, Amsterdam, and London from October 1950 to January 1951 to further the NAE's goal.[6]

John Langlois was well-known for his significant legal and political work, increasingly took on responsibilities for the World Evangelical Fellowship, which would later become the WEA.

The trip bore fruit. The International Committee formed at Hildenborough Hall met in January 1951 at Woudschoten, a student conference center near Utrecht. The committee recommended that a body with the name World Evangelical Fellowship be formed and invited Evangelicals from around the world to an international convention at Woudschoten in August 1951. Forty-six delegates from evangelical associations in eighteen nations met at that summer's convention; others came to observe, doubling the numbers present. John R. W. Stott, the rector of All Souls Church in London, was among the speakers.

The delegates approved the name World Evangelical Fellowship, stating, "The Fellowship is not a council of churches nor is it in opposition to any other international or inter-denominational organization. It seeks to work and to witness in a constructive manner ever 'maintaining the truth in love.'"[7] The proposed basis of faith included statements on the inspiration of Scripture, the Trinity, the person and work of Christ, salvation, the

---

3. Bruce L. Shelley, *Evangelicalism in America* (Grand Rapids: Eerdmans, 1967), 72–73.

4. For this, see George Marsden, *Reforming Fundamentalism: Fuller Seminary and the New Evangelicalism* (Grand Rapids: Eerdmans, 1987).

5. *World Evangelical Fellowship Bulletin*, no. 2 (1964): 1–2.

6. Gilbert Kirby to Everett Cattell, 6 May 1965, in David M. Howard, *The Dream That Would Not Die: The Birth and Growth of the World Evangelical Fellowship, 1846–1986* (Exeter, UK: Paternoster Press), 29.

7. Norman Goodall, *The Ecumenical Movement: What It Is and What It Does* (London: Oxford University Press, 1961), 154.

Holy Spirit, and the spiritual unity of all believers. Stott and A. J. Dain, also from England and both Anglicans, summarized the WEF's threefold purpose:

1. The furtherance of the gospel (Phil. 1:12)
2. The defense and confirmation of the gospel (Phil. 1:7)
3. Fellowship in the gospel (Phil. 1:5)[8]

A constitution consisting of five points was drawn up:

1. Belief without mental reservations in the basic doctrines of our faith as expressed in the statement of faith
2. Acceptance into active cooperation with all who hold these doctrines and give evidence of loyalty to them, though there may be differences in conviction on other points of doctrine or of ecclesiastical policy
3. Obedience to the commands of Scripture by renunciation of all cooperation with unbelief in or apostasy from these doctrines
4. Recognition of the complete autonomy of every constituent national or area-wide body within the WEA
5. Dedication to a program of mutual helpfulness in the propagation of the gospel, the defense of Christian liberties, and the attainment of objectives that are of common concern

Not All Agreed

Evangelicals from eleven countries were in favor of the proposal to establish the WEF. There was hesitation among the representatives of the British Evangelical Alliance, but they ultimately decided to join.[9] Spain, however, was the only continental European country that joined. Evangelicals from Germany abstained from voting on the motion, while France, Denmark, Norway, and Sweden opposed it.

Some of the opposing delegates wanted the Evangelical Alliance work to continue as before. Some were concerned the word *infallible*, which delegates from the United States insisted on, implied too mechanical an understanding of biblical inspiration. There were also worries that cooperation with those who might not hold to the basis of faith in its entirety was being prohibited. Minutes from a meeting of the European Baptist Federation in 1952 reflected these misgivings: "Dr Petersen [from Denmark] spoke of a plan to form a World Evangelical Fellowship which would embrace Continental branches of the World's Evangelical Alliance and certain Evangelicals in America. He feared this might tend to introduce American controversies into Europe."[10] In the same year representatives from several European countries met in Germany and established their own, separate, European Evangelical Alliance. The breach with the WEF would not be healed until 1968. Until then, the WEF was able to make little headway in Europe.

B. E. Fernando, from Sri Lanka, became chairman of the new Asia fellowship
Photo: World Evangelical Alliance

---

8. Harold Fuller, *People of the Mandate: The Story of the World Evangelical Fellowship* (Grand Rapids: Baker, 1996), 31–32.

9. Minutes of the British Evangelical Alliance Executive Council, 24 July 1952.

10. Minutes of the European Baptist Federation Council, Copenhagen, 29–31 July 1952, Box 801, European Baptist Federation Archives, International Baptist Theological Seminary, Prague, 81; see Keith G. Jones, *The European Baptist Federation: A Case Study in European Baptist Interdependency, 1950–2006* (Milton Keynes, UK: Paternoster Press, 2009), 92–93.

A Growing Fellowship

In order to implement the fifth point of its constitution more fully, WEF commissions were set up to stimulate evangelism, coordinate activities where appropriate between evangelical mission agencies, coordinate the work of evangelical literature producers, and speak up for religious liberty on behalf of persecuted minorities. WEF membership was made up of national evangelical fellowships, such as early member Evangelical Fellowship of India (EFI). Early secretaries and other officers of the WEF were unpaid volunteers.

Visiting the member national WEF associations became the role of cosecretary J. Elwin Wright. In December 1951 Wright, together with Paul Rees, the president of NAE, embarked on a thirty-one thousand mile journey to twenty-one countries. Wright commented that he believed the WEF was "destined to exercise a great influence on the spiritual life of India."[11] He suggested that Western fellowships needed to take a servant role to the growing churches in the rest of the world.[12] Wright repeated his global travels in subsequent years and attracted more national fellowships of Evangelicals into the WEF.

Spiritual Unity in Action

In 1959 Wright handed over his leadership role to Fred Ferris, the executive director of the NAE Commission for WEF. Ferris was concerned that the WEF should not appear to be an arm of evangelical work in the United States. At his instigation the first General Committee of the WEF was held in Asia—in Hong King—in 1962. An Asia fellowship was also created, with B. E. Fernando from Sri Lanka as chairman and J. B. Kawet from Indonesia, K. Thirumalai from India, D. V. Mieng from Vietnam, and Ernet Tak from Pakistan serving in other roles. A pattern of General Committees, later called General Assemblies, of being held every six years was established. In Hong Kong in 1962 some delegates from the United States suggested that the second article in the WEF constitution, which concerned Evangelical cooperation, should be tightened to forbid any member from being in any association which might compromise its loyalty to the WEF's statement of faith. Many delegates from other countries, however, felt this would bring the WEF into open conflict with the WCC. Eventually the proposal was dropped.[13]

Gilbert Kirby, general secretary of the British Evangelical Alliance, followed Ferris as the WEF's international secretary. Kirby sought to counter polarized attitudes, and he commended the slogan for the WEF: Spiritual unity in action. For Kirby, the WEF was to serve: "We are essentially a service organization and will gain the respect of our Evangelical brethren across the world as we are able to offer a practical service."[14] This was increasingly done through publications, scholarships for theological students, and meetings of Evangelical leaders. During Kirby's tenure the WEF began to focus more on Africa as well.[15]

A New Watershed

When Kirby became principal of London Bible College, Dennis Clark, who had been working for the Toronto-based Bible and Medical Missionary Fellowship, was appointed WEF international secretary in his place.

---

11. Travel Reports, box 1, folder 30, Records of the World Evangelical Fellowship, Billy Graham Center Archives, Wheaton, IL; see also http://www2.wheaton.edu/bgc/archives/GUIDES/338.htm/.

12. Arthur H. Matthews, *Standing Up, Standing Together: The Emergence of the National Association of Evangelicals* (Carol Stream, IL: National Association of Evangelicals, 1992), 109–10.

13. J. B. A. Kessler, *A Study of the Evangelical Alliance in Great Britain* (Goes, Netherlands: Oosterbaan & Le Cointre, 1968), 99–100.

14. Gilbert Kirby, "A Britisher Writes a Letter to Americans," *United Evangelical Action* (September 1962): 12–13.

15. Howard, *Dream*, 62–67.

Clark, who served from 1966 to 1970, was seen by some critics as being anti-American, although others viewed his approach as properly internationalist. He also spoke out in favor of social action, which was controversial in much of American Evangelicalism at the time. In his report to the General Council in 1968, which met in Lausanne that year, Clark wrote, "WEF stands at a new watershed. The challenge is to move forward with a positive programme that is truly international in scope and operation. Anything less than this is unthinkable, and if the challenge is not tenable the Council should consider dissolution."[16] Of the sixty-five WEF delegates from thirty-six countries who had gathered in Lausanne, only three were Americans, although other Americans were also present.

John Langlois from Britain, who was to be known for his significant legal and political work, increasingly took on WEF responsibilities. Bruce Nicholls from New Zealand, a BMMF missionary in India, was appointed theological coordinator of the WEF. This was a crucial step. A WEF budget was set, and it seems that contributions to the international office came largely from the United States and Europe. However, internationalization was proceeding. Ben Wati from India was elected president of the WEF, the first president from the global South.[17]

Gordon Landreth, the British Evangelical Alliance general secretary, served as the WEF's interim international secretary from 1970 to 1971. Clyde Taylor then held the international secretary's post until 1975. Taylor, who led the NAE and the Evangelical Foreign Mission Association, had been involved in the WEF for a number of years and traveled to many places where evangelical fellowships were operating. He stressed the importance of national leadership, of non-Western missionary societies, and of theological education.

In 1972 Taylor and Langlois visited evangelical fellowships across Africa, which from 1966 had had the Association of Evangelicals of Africa and Madagascar. During this period the Asia Theological Association was developing its work and became the world's largest evangelical theological association.[18] Taylor was also active in the planning for the International Congress on World Evangelization, which was held in Lausanne in July 1974 and sponsored by the Billy Graham Evangelistic Association. The goals for the conference were to impart vision for world evangelism, inform churches of strategies, encourage unity in evangelization, and identify unreached people. Of the 2,700 delegates, 1,200 were from the Third World, and 150 nations were represented. This congress, with its record-breaking Third World attendance, was an indicator of the church growth occurring in the global South, an area comprised of Central and Latin America, Africa, and most of Asia. Many participants had WEF connections. The 1974 WEF General Assembly was held in Switzerland, and Billy Graham, who was supportive of the WEF, attended.

Gaining Traction

In 1974 an important decision was made: the post of international secretary should become a full-time position. All agreed. Waldron Scott of the evangelical group the Navigators was appointed on this basis, succeeding Taylor. Scott devoted more time to policies, such as raising the profile of evangelical leaders around the world. WEF commissions—the Theological Commission, the Missions Commission, the Communications Commission, and the newer International Forum of Evangelical Women (later called Women's Concerns)—were all active. Church renewal, religious liberty, youth, and international relief and development were also areas that developed during Scott's tenure.

In 1980 the WEF General Assembly was held near London. Afterward Scott Waldron resigned. He was followed by Wade Coggins, executive secretary of the EFMA, on an interim basis, and then by David Howard, who

---

16. International Secretary's Report to the General Council [1968], Records of the World Evangelical Fellowship, Billy Graham Center Archives, Wheaton, IL.

17. Howard, *Dream*, 85–86, 89–90.

18. I am indebted to John Langlois for information he provided me about this and other aspects of the WEF's global development

served from 1982 to 1992. Howard was an InterVarsity Christian Fellowship leader and had been involved in Lausanne and in the huge Urbana conferences for students.[19] He brought to the WEF a vision for teamwork and mission that was relevant to varied cultural settings around the world.

A Moment of Crisis and a Move to Singapore

Howard saw his lowest point with the WEF in 1985. Finances had become a recurring problem, and he worried that responsible stewards would not support a work that they did not know enough about or understand. Howard reported to the International Council and, in an effort to save the situation, eliminated staff and cut his own salary by half. But by the end of 1985 he felt there was no alternative but to resign. When the council met in January 1986, its chairman, Tokunboh Adeyemo from Africa, told the group they needed to seek God's face and His will for the future. For the next thirty-five hours the council did just that, engaging in heart searching, prayer, and Bible study, followed by a serious evaluation of the WEF.

An unexpected phone call from Brian Stiller, executive director of the Evangelical Fellowship of Canada, while the council was still meeting helped to confirm to the council that the WEF had significant support. John Langlois, as the WEF's treasurer, was one of those present when Stiller called, and he experienced the mood of the meeting change completely from despair to hope.[20] Howard remained on and, in a significant development, oversaw with Langlois and others a move of the WEF's headquarters from the United States to Singapore. Other important events included influential publications for the evangelical world, perhaps most notably *In Word and Deed: Evangelism and Social Responsibility*, edited by Bruce Nicholls.[21]

The First Majority World Leader

Agustin "Jun" Vencer of the Philippines became the international director of WEF in 1992. A lawyer by profession, Vencer was executive director of the Philippine Council of Evangelical Churches, a member of the International Council of the WEF, and a member of the International Relief and Development Alliance, a consortium encouraged by the WEF. He was also chairman of the Evangelical Fellowship of Asia.[22] Regional groupings were playing an important role in Africa, the Caribbean, Latin America, the South Pacific, the United States, Canada, and Europe.[23]

For the first time the WEF had a Majority World leader. Vencer, like his predecessors, was committed to the growth and strengthening of the national alliances and to integrating the gospel with social action. During his nine years as international director he traveled tirelessly, creating strong relationships. In the early 1990s a new evangelical impetus took place across Eastern Europe as those national evangelical alliances outlawed under communism were re-formed. In Bulgaria, Vencer helped Evangelicals achieve recognition, after explaining to government officials that the Bulgarian Evangelical Alliance, through the WEF, was part of a worldwide community of 110 fellowships. Vencer's productive period concluded at the WEF General Assembly in Kuala Lumpur in 2001, during which a new name was adopted—the World Evangelical Alliance.

---

19. Keith Hunt and Gladys Hunt, *For Christ and the University: The Story of InterVarsity Christian Fellowship of the USA, 1940–1990* (Downers Grove, IL: InterVarsity Press, 1991), 306.

20. Fuller, *People of the Mandate*, 34–36.

21. Bruce J. Nicholls, ed., *In Word and Deed: Evangelism and Social Responsibility* (Exeter, UK: Paternoster Press, 1985).

22. Fuller, *People of the Mandate*, 7.

23. Ibid., 48–49.

A New Day

David Detert, an American based in France who had chaired the WEF International Council, led an interim WEF international team. Funding issues had reemerged, and in 2001 the WEA asked Interdev, an international organization committed to strategic partnerships at a global level, for a comprehensive evaluation of the movement. The associate international director of Interdev, Gary Edmonds, who was involved in establishing cross-sector partnerships in impoverished nations, presented the evaluation.

At a 2002 WEA gathering in England, the International Council invited Edmonds to be the WEA's director. Edmonds accepted. Although he worked to reduce debts, in part by selling the Singapore property, he did not see Interdev's recommendations being implemented. After he resigned in 2004, Geoff Tunnicliffe, a Canadian, became the next international director. The Evangelical Fellowship of Canada, based in Toronto, offered the WEA administrative and financial support. Tunnicliffe oversaw the opening of WEA centers near Vancouver, San Francisco, Washington, D.C. and in Geneva.

Since 1951 the WEA has grown. It has survived crises and challenges to reach a point of significant influence around the world. In recent years its commissions have been given fresh impetus to be active agents of change and influence in the global Church. The Mission Commission and its practitioners have been especially pioneering. The Religious Liberty Commission and the WEA's presence in the United Nations are significant. Major evangelical leaders from the global South have been playing a crucial role in the WEA. The alliance is truly a world Christian body.

Bibliography

European Baptist Federation Archives, International Baptist Theological Seminary, Prague.

Fuller, Harold. *People of the Mandate: The Story of the World Evangelical Fellowship*. London: Oxford University Press, 1961.

Goodall, Norman. *The Ecumenical Movement: What It Is and What It Does*. London: Oxford University Press, 1961.

Howard, David M. *The Dream That Would Not Die: The Birth and Growth of the World Evangelical Fellowship, 1846–1986*. Exeter, UK: Paternoster Press, 1986.

Hunt, Keith, and Gladys Hunt. *For Christ and the University: The Story of InterVarsity Christian Fellowship of the USA, 1940–1990*. Downers Grove, IL: InterVarsity Press, 1991.

Jones, Keith G. *The European Baptist Federation: A Case Study in European Baptist Interdependency, 1950–2006*. Milton Keynes, UK: Paternoster Press, 2009.

Kessler, J. B. A. *A Study of the Evangelical Alliance in Great Britain*. Goes, Netherlands: Oosterbaan & Le Cointre, 1968.

Marsden, George. *Reforming Fundamentalism: Fuller Seminary and the New Evangelicalism*. Grand Rapids: Eerdmans, 1987.

Matthews, Arthur H. *Standing Up, Standing Together: The Emergence of the National Association of Evangelicals*. Carol Stream, IL: National Association of Evangelicals, 1992.

Nicholls, Bruce J., ed. *In Word and Deed: Evangelism and Social Responsibility*. Exeter, UK: Paternoster Press, 1985.

Randall, Ian, and David Hilborn. "Across the Partition Wall." In *One Body in Christ: The History and Significance of the Evangelical Alliance*. Edited by Ian Randall and David Hilborn. Carlisle, UK: Paternoster Press, 2001.

———. "An Evangelical and Catholic Union." In *One Body in Christ: The History and Significance of the Evangelical Alliance*. Edited by Ian Randall and David Hilborn. Carlisle, UK: Paternoster Press, 2001.

Records of the World Evangelical Fellowship, Billy Graham Center Archives, Wheaton, IL.

Shelley, Bruce L. *Evangelicalism in America*. Grand Rapids: Eerdmans, 1967.

Dr. Ian Randall is a senior research fellow at the International Baptist Theological Seminary in Prague and Spurgeon's College in London. He is the author of a number of books on evangelical history.

"The Evangelical Movement holds firmly the vital tradition of the historical Christian church; we uphold the divine character of the Holy Scriptures, Old and New Testaments, we confess with all churches through the ages and on all continents, the creeds of the early Church, and we stick firmly to the principles of the Reformation of the sixteenth century, Christ alone, Scripture alone, salvation alone by grace, through faith alone. As far as the Evangelical movement continues in the twenty-first century with a strong evangelistic outreach, and keeps these foundations faithfully, she has the promise of our Lord Jesus Christ that 'the gates of Hades will not prevail against her' (Matthew 16:18)."

—**Dr. Rolf Hille, Director for Ecumenical Affairs of the WEA, Germany**

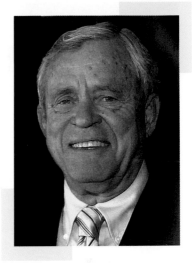

David Howard led the WEF from 1982 to 1992. The WEF later became the WEA.

THE FUTURE OF THE EVANGELICAL MOVEMENT

By Paul Joshua Bhakiaraj

I am neither a prophet nor the son of a prophet, and so I begin this chapter with not a little fear and trepidation. If history is littered with examples of failed predictions it seems foolhardy for me to predict the future of the Evangelical Movement. This chapter, therefore, does not pretend to be a definitive guide to the future. Instead, what I offer are reflections on the current state of some aspects of the Evangelical Movement and turn my gaze to some trends that call for our attention. My use of the word *Evangelical* employs the traditional understanding of the term[1] and I do not exclude Pentecostal and Charismatic groups from this category.

History as Teacher

Historians are correct to trace an insistence on the evangel, the good news, the gospel, as that which represents what is unique to the Evangelical Movement and also ties it together. Many trace this back to the sixteenth century Reformation where the centrality of the gospel of grace was a central point of contention. But what the reformers did was to in fact reclaim the early church's faith itself. They saw their efforts as a going back to the basics that were expressed in the life and ministry of the early church. The Evangelical Movement, which draws its inspiration from those emphases, therefore claims to be a gospel centered movement. It insists that the evangel of Jesus Christ is, or ought to be, at the heart of the church, supplying what is so unique to it, its very life and identity.

History teaches us that the Evangelical Movement is constituted by gospel people, whose identity is derived from that scriptural witness to the activity of the triune God in the world. This is then believed to be just as real to them in the here and now. For as Paul says in Romans 8:11, it is the same Spirit that raised Christ from the dead that lives in the disciples of Christ. In as much as the reformers laid claim to this heritage of the early church, we observe that theirs was a movement of protest as well as a reformation. A protest because it decried the dilution of the Christian faith that crept into the institution of the church and saw that regression as, in fact, another gospel, not the one delineated in the Scriptures. It was a reformation because it was a call back to the foundations that the apostles and the earliest church laid and built on.

So, as we retell this fascinating history, beginning from the early church right up to the present age, spread as it is around the world, we affirm the centrality of the gospel of Christ, as both forming the legacy we have inherited and the identity we possess. It teaches us to be people who steadfastly build on the foundation of the gospel of Jesus Christ as expressed in the Scriptures. And such a loyalty enables us to constantly reform ourselves when we inadvertently, or perhaps more consciously, build on another gospel. Recognizing the centrality of the evangel for the Christian faith is therefore essential for our contemporary identity and even future action, if we are to remain as gospel people, marked by our allegiance to Jesus Christ even as we are empowered by the Holy Spirit to be and do so.

Crisis or Kairos?

Remaining as gospel people today is crucial for many sections of the Evangelical Movement face severe challenges of various kinds. Approximately two decades ago some sections of the Evangelical Movement were

---

1. For a popular and well received definition see David Bebbington, *Evangelicals in Modern Britain: A History from the 1730s to the 1980s* (London: Unwin, 1989).

aid to be in a state of crisis.[2] The very word *Evangelical* was thought to lack a precise meaning and questions about its propriety were raised.[3] Twenty years later we find ourselves at a similar place.[4] One commentator even goes so far as to quip: "It is my considered opinion that the evangelical movement no longer exists. As a cohesive movement, it has dissolved . . . What was once a relatively united movement has become little more than a memory."[5] While he clarifies that an "evangelical ethos" may endure, he is less sure that the movement as such remains. Another commentator, with equally sharp insights, calls this malaise that Evangelicalism suffers under is no less than a captivity to the Western worldview of the twentieth century. His indictment is sharp:

> **What we are witnessing in the twenty-first century is the captivity of the church to the dominant western culture and white leadership, which is in stark contrast to the demographic reality of Christianity in the twenty-first century. Even if we could justify the western captivity of the church in the early part of the twentieth century, there is no justification for it now . . . For most of its history (but particularly in the last fifty years) American evangelicalism has more accurately reflected the values, culture and ethos of western, white American culture than the values of Scripture. At times, the western evangelical church has been indistinguishable from Western, white American culture. In the emerging culture and the next evangelicalism of the twentieth-first century, we must consider how evangelicalism has been held captive to western, white culture and explore ways that the Christian community can reflect biblical more than cultural norms.[6]**

It appears that the time is ripe for a protest and a reformation. The crisis that attends this section of Christianity requires serious and sustained attention. It seems an appropriate time to return to and renew our insistence on the evangel, the gospel of Jesus Christ, a clear focus on which we seem to have lost. While it is true that crisis, captivity, and syncretism, to mention only three, have all been words used to describe the current state of Evangelicalism, it may also be wise to recognize that times of crises can also be *kairos* moments. This seems to be a *kairos* moment that affords us opportunities to protest against that which we have allowed to stagnate the faith. And a moment to scripturally and substantially reform ourselves by returning to and rebuilding on the centrality of the gospel of Jesus Christ. The time is ripe to review the integrity of our claim to gospel centeredness, indeed even our evangelical credentials.

Protest against What? Reformation for Whom?

It may be prudent to recognize that the malaise alluded to revolves primarily around Western Evangelicalism. The cultural realities, theological emphases, and institutional trends these commentators have focused on center almost exclusively around expressions of Western Evangelicalism. There is a marked absence of such

---

. Stanley J. Grenz, *Revisioning Evangelical Theology: A Fresh Agenda for the 21st Century* (Downers Grove, Il: InterVarsity Press, 1993), 14.

. Donald Dayton, "Some Doubts About the Usefulness of the Category 'Evangelical,'" in *The Variety of American* Evangelicalism, ed. Donald Dayton and Robert Johnston (Downers Grove, Il: InterVarsity Press, 1991), 251, quoted in Stanley Grenz, *Revisioning Evangelical Theology*, 14.

. See for example, David E. Fitch, *The End of Evangelicalism? Discerning a New Faithfulness for Mission* (Eugene: OR, Cascade Books, 2011), xiv.

. Roger Olson, "The Future of Evangelicalism," Patheos (blog), accessed June 5, 2013, http://www.patheos.com/blogs/rogereolson/2013/03/my-talk-about-the-future-of-evangelicalism-at-george-fox-evangelical-seminary/.

. Soong-Chan Rah, *The Next Evangelicalism: Freeing the Church from Western Captivity* (Downers Grove, Il: InterVarsity Press, 2009).

a diagnosis on the Evangelical Movement around the world. To be sure there are significant threats the world Evangelical Movement faces, and we would be less than wise to ignore them. They surely need urgent attention. But the crisis that these commentators refer to pertain to forms of Western Evangelicalism.

It is important to make this distinction, because when we speak of the future of the Evangelical Movement I believe that a Eurocentric framework is all too often applied to the worldwide movement. For example, in *Evangelical Futures: A Conversation on Theological Method*,[7] too little is discussed about the Evangelical Movement around the world. Similarly in another, *The Futures of Evangelicalism: Issues and Prospects*, the global nature of the movement is largely ignored. There is a particularly helpful chapter in which the author focuses on the role of the Majority World Church:

> **And as we seek a more biblical understanding of what it means to live and relate in truly human ways as an expression of the gospel itself, we in the West will have a lot to learn from the less impoverished traditions of humanity in community found among Christians in the non-Western world. In this as in so much else, the strength of evangelicalism in the Two-Thirds World will be a major asset to the world church in mission.[8]**

It sometimes seems that it is a rare Western scholar who recognizes the vitality of the Evangelical Movement in the Majority World, and rarer still to identify it as being an asset to the world church.[9] But thankfully, this is changing. The unfortunate neglect of the colorful and vibrant character of the Evangelical Movement around the world needs to be reversed. To the extent that the Evangelical Movement is thought to be primarily a Western phenomenon, we are the poorer for it and less able to appreciate the value of Majority World Christians as legitimate co-partners and indeed as a valuable resource.

Surely Western Evangelicalism and that of the Majority World need each other to sharpen each other as iron sharpens iron. Both have numerous gifts to offer to each other and the wider church. And more importantly, as the Scottish historian Andrew Walls has reminded us, it will take no less than the whole church to grow into the full stature of Christ.

> **The Ephesian metaphors of the temple and of the body show each of the culture-specific segments as necessary to the body but as incomplete in itself. Only in Christ does completion, fullness, dwell. And Christ's completion as we have seen, comes from all humanity, from the translation of the life of Jesus into the lifeways of all the world's cultures and subcultures through history. None of us can reach Christ's completeness on our own. We need each other's vision to correct, enlarge, and focus our own; only together are we complete in Christ.[10]**

---

7. John Stackhouse Jr., ed., *Evangelical Futures: A Conversation on Theological Method* (Grand Rapids: Baker, 2000). One author includes a subsection: "Challenges from Africa and Asia," 35.

8. Craig Bartholomew, Robin Parry, and Andrew West, eds. *The Futures of Evangelicalism: Issues and Prospects* (Leicester: IVP, 2003).

9. Three books that affirm the role majority world Christians play are: Mark Hutchinson and Ogbu Kalu, eds., *A Global Faith: Essays on Evangelicalism and Globalization* (Sydney: CSAC, 1998); Donald Lewis, *Christianity Reborn: The Global Expansion of Evangelicalism in the Twentieth Century* (Grand Rapids: Eerdmans, 2004); Ogbu Kalu, ed., *Interpreting Contemporary Christianity: Global Processes and Local Identities* (Grand Rapids: Eerdmans, 2008).

10. Andrew Walls, *The Cross-Cultural Process in Christian History* (Maryknoll, NY: Orbis, 2002), 79.

Part of this process of learning together will include a critique of the dominance of forms of western Evangelicalism, its theology and practice of ecclesiology and mission. It will call to question the propensity of western Evangelicalism to speak for and represent the movement around the world. It will interrogate the status of Western Evangelicalism, particularly in the light of the crisis it faces, to serve as the sole gatekeeper of the rich and lengthy evangelical legacy we, around the world, possess.

More positively the Evangelical Movement around the world will continue its life and witness in its own respective contexts, and from that missional engagement yield productive patterns and sharp insights into the calling of the church in the world. The resulting fuller and more complete vision of Christ will represent a boon for the larger church worldwide. Consequently from the neglect it has suffered, it will increasingly come to be seen that the Evangelical Movement worldwide is a legitimately co-equal even prophetic and reformational voice for western Evangelicalism. But the question is: Is Western Evangelicalism willing to learn from the strengths of the movement in the Majority World? Some existing literature and current practice seems to suggest a reticence.[11] In other quarters some seem to be waking up to the possibility.

The Evangelical Movement in the Majority World

Christianity is increasingly present in the majority world, with Latin Americans, Africans, and Asians adding color to a faith that was once thought of as a white, Western religion. At the start of the twentieth century, only about 10% of the world's Christians lived in the Majority World whereas 90% lived in the Western world of Europe, North America, with Australia and New Zealand also being counted in. But in the early years of the twenty-first century more than 60% of Christians live in the Majority World.[12] Within the Evangelical Movement, more particularly Asia, Africa, and Latin America each have more Evangelicals than North America and Europe combined.[13] This suggests that in the twenty-first century the Evangelical Movement, not to say anything of Christianity as a whole, will be lived out and shaped by Christians from those Southern and Eastern continents. The numerically strong and growing Eastern and Southern centers of Christianity will become more significant for the life of the faith, more particularly for evangelical expressions of the Christian faith. What will that imply for the future of the Evangelical Movement?

The Evangelical Movement of the Future

The Evangelical Movement of the future will be a recognizably global movement, spread predominantly throughout the southern and eastern continents. Not necessarily characterized by its western features and represented by its western celebrity leaders alone, it will clearly be a world Christianity, a movement that is recognized as a truly global phenomenon. It will become increasingly more globally representative and expressive of the realities of Southern and Eastern continents. A representative Evangelical will probably be a Chinese woman engaged in the marketplace, rather than a white Western theologically educated male. The Evangelical Movement may not be centered any longer in Colorado Springs or in London, but will move, if it already has not, equally to Beijing, Lagos, and Sao Paulo.

This is not to say that the visibility of Western Evangelicalism nor its power will dissipate overnight. The economic and institutional power that lies in the West will continue to fuel Western dominance in the representation, interpretation, and the organization of the Evangelical Movement. Nevertheless, that will also begin to

---

1. An essay that throws some light on this issue particularly for theological education is Tite Tienou's "Renewing Evangelical Identity from the Margins," in *Renewing the Evangelical Mission*, ed. Richard Lints (Grand Rapids: Eerdmans, 2013), 31–50.

2. Todd M. Johnson and Kenneth R. Ross, *Atlas of Global Christianity* (Edinburgh: Edinburgh University Press, 2009), 8.

3. David B. Barrett, George T. Kurian, and Todd M. Johnson, eds. *World Christian Encyclopedia*, 2nd ed., vol. 1, *The World by Countries* (New York: Oxford University Press, 2001), 13–14.

lose its shine over the next decades as new economic powers in the Majority World assume greater prominence though much of those resources will likely remain outside the church. Demographically speaking the future of the movement lies in the Majority World, a shift that is already clearly visible.

If the Evangelical Movement of the future will be characterized by such a shift, this will signify a concurrent shift in the cultural patterns of the movement around the world. The cultural frameworks within which the movement will exist will be another of its characteristic features of the future. The movement will inhabit the diverse cultural realities characteristic of the Majority World rather than the unified framework that Christendom constructed in the West. The political and ecclesiastical structures and idioms that were employed by Western Christianity derived their currency from that particular historical situation. The Evangelical Movement of the future can assume no such common and unified cultural framework within which to understand and situate itself. We will find instead a layered set of diverse realities made up of multiple histories, cultures, religions and political realities, which will all merge together to form the complex and plural contexts within which the Evangelical Movement will have to grow and establish its identity. The late African theologian Kwame Bediako called this process "a reconfiguration of the cultural manifestation of the Christian faith in the world" because "Christianity now lives through other cultures, in other historical, social, economic and political realities than those that appear to prevail in the West."[14] And therefore it is crucial to recognize that, as René Padilla, another stalwart from Latin America, suggests, "The end of Constantinian era, marked by the 'death of Christendom' is the essential starting point for understanding the role of the [majority world and western] churches at the outset of the third millennium."[15]

A New Context for a New Future

The south and eastward shift of the Christian Church implies a fundamental cultural shift, not least among which will be the economic and political dimensions. For the Evangelical Movement it will be these realities that will provide the context within which the future will take shape. It will be in the intensities of these environments that fresh and new ways of being church will be forged. The Evangelical Movement will be a church largely of the poor; a minority church faced with conditions that are shaped and even dictated by non-Christian majorities, many of whom could even be antagonistic to the gospel. It will be a demographically young church with younger and lay (non-ordained) leadership; yet a vibrant and active church defying odds, and in many ways representing the yeast of the kingdom of God that leavens the whole loaf.

The reader will have noticed a difference in word choice to distinguish between Western Evangelicalism and the Evangelical Movement in the Majority World. The Evangelical Movement as it developed in the West has taken on, for the most part, the shape of an Evangelicalism, which among other things has become a recognizable sub culture complete with its political sympathies and social mores, though there has been some measure of diversity. In the Majority World, however, while there is a common theological core by virtue of its insistence on the evangel of Jesus Christ, there is a cultural plurality such that one will be hard pressed to describe the Evangelical Movement there as an 'ism.' We will find there is an evangelical character and spirit and perhaps even an evangelical social grouping, animated by church and missional links both global and regional, rather than a clear and identifiable sub culture that imitates and parallels Western Evangelicalism. On the ground we find a plurality of cultures and a diversity of histories, national and ecclesiastical. Latin America, for example, possesses its own histories, cultures, and economic realities that contribute to the production of a distinctive Latin American expression of the faith, not least among which are the particular political compulsions that the

---

14. Kwame Bediako, "The Emergence of World Christianity and the Remaking of Theology," in *Understanding World Christianity: The Vision and Work of Andrew* Walls, ed. William Burrows et al. (Maryknoll, NY: Orbis, 2011), 243–256.

15. René Padilla, "The Future of Christianity in Latin America: Missiological Perspectives and Challenges," *International Bulletin of Missionary Research* 23, no. 3 (July 1999): 105–112.

face and trends we see.[16] The manner in which Latin Americans have shaped their faith and life in dialogue with their complex contexts is particularly unique to them. While one may learn from them it is not necessarily a template for the world. The same can be argued for Africa and Asia. Animated by these multiple engagements with their manifold contexts, the future will see the development of a marked cultural plurality within the worldwide movement. We are just beginning to comprehend the nature, extent and gravity of this shift.

If the Evangelical Movement of the future will be characterized by a fundamental demographic and cultural shift, to be sure a theological shift will also follow and/or accompany it. Some may grow nervous, fearing the impending loss of evangelical theological orthodoxy and a decline into theological anarchy. I would like to submit that rather than such a reaction we could choose to view this as an expansion of the horizons of theology, rather than a surrender of our deep evangelical convictions.

This theological expansion of horizons is not unlike the experience of the early Church. When it outgrew its Jewish cradle and faced the host of conundrums in the Greco-Roman world, including meat sacrificed to idols, sexual ethics, and community care, the early church was widening its missiological engagement and therefore its theological horizons. All through the Epistles we observe how the apostles guided the early church as she wrestled with these fresh and new missiological challenges. This was unexplored territory, hitherto unknown contexts in which one was called to be a disciple of Christ. The early church was faced with new sociological contexts, new cultural frameworks, new economic realities, new philosophies, and new religious movements, all of which needed to be responsibly engaged and brought under the Lordship of Christ. New and challenging questions called for fresh and suitable answers. Accordingly, "In as much as the . . . historical shifts of the heartlands of the Christian faith . . . have been cultural crossings" suggests Kwame Bediako, "they are privileged moments for understanding the meanings inherent in the faith, that is, for the development of theology." He then asserts that "since the significant cultural crossings of the Christian gospel are taking place in the churches of the South and East], it is to these theatres of Christian interaction that we must turn for the reorientation that is needed for embracing the task of theology afresh in our time."[17]

This is what we seem to be witnessing, as Christianity crosses geographical and cultural boundaries. A development of theology is being necessitated and undertaken as old horizons fade and new ones appear. As the heartlands of the Evangelical Movement shift toward the Eastern and Southern continents, we see its missiological engagement calling for and yielding fresh theology. The emphases may be different compared to the classical themes of Western theology; the issues it has to engage with diverse and dissimilar to what some are normally accustomed to; the resources required to answer these questions may not always recall and be tightly moulded by revered milestones of Western theology. The customs of theological production and modes of articulation may not necessarily adopt established patterns in the West. Yet they are as legitimate, valid and indeed necessary for the life of the church as she is engaged in mission in these multidimensional Majority World contexts.

The issues that these theological developments work with may evolve around globalization and technology, poverty and prosperity, spiritual warfare and deliverance, persecution and suffering, to cite just a few more obvious features. They will require a fresh and faithful examination of the Scriptures, of history and a fresh analysis of contexts. As it represents an expansion of our theological horizons it presages fresh opportunities for constructive theological

This theological expansion of horizons is not unlike the experience of the early Church.

5. For example, see the brief discussion in Padilla, "The Future of Christianity," 106–8.

7. Bediako, "Emergence of World Christianity," 249, 252.

development. Surely such missional opportunities are not to be missed for fear of transgressing what some may consider sacrosanct boundaries? For as surely as that process continues responsibly, our estimation and appreciation of Christ and of the Holy Spirit will grow ever wider and deeper as Christians from the Majority World take captive every thought of theirs to Christ. It will be as though Christ himself actually grows and becomes as thoroughly at home in these diverse contexts and realities.[18] The Evangelical Movement of the future will increasingly see the creative development of theology in these multiple centers of resourceful missional activity. A theology that accompanies mission and not theology for theology sake. And so it should be, if we are to be worthy inheritors and faithful custodians of the legacy of the Evangelical Movement which has and continues to maintain mission as one of its defining features.

Futures of the Evangelical Movement

The demographic changes that we see call for a deep appreciation for and a wide recognition of the global nature of the movement. The Evangelical Movement of the future will need to become an intentionally and consciously globally aware and globally engaged movement, in the true spirit of gospel partnership. This will need to be reflected in our awareness, our engagement, our studies, our leadership and our self-representation both internally and externally. It will call for resolve on the part of those who are blessed with greater resources and those in leadership positions to seek ways by which such a reality is actually reflected in our life and ministry. We will need to help the world see that being Evangelical does not mean primarily holding fast to one particular political position, or adhering strictly to one particular social-cultural expression, but rather represents a way of living in and living out that gospel of Jesus Christ around the world. The compelling vision of Revelation 7:9 ought to be that which draws us forward.

The cultural changes that we will increasingly see call for an Evangelical Movement that is gracious in its life and ministry. For centuries the western mould seemed to be a defining feature of the Evangelical Movement and this became the exacting standard for the rest of the world. As this practice fades and multiple patterns of cultural existence and identity will be freely expressed, it will call for a graciousness on the part of all to allow for and even appreciate cultural diversity within the movement. Our own and preferred way of life and cultural patterns, including ecclesiastical and intuitional, may need to be seen as one of the many God-given varieties that are just as legitimate as any other and/or perhaps just as open for judgment as any other. A gracious Evangelicalism will shy away from waging cultural wars that do more disservice to the faith than protect it. While biblically responsible and faithful patterns of life are developed and adhered to, we will be characterized by a graciousness that was so true of Jesus Christ our Lord.

The theological changes that we are witnessing call for an underlining of the true nature of the Evangelical Movement: as a gospel centered people in multiple and complex contexts. While our contexts will differ and our responses vary we must never lose sight of the centrality of the gospel itself. We will be vigilant to watch for any tendency to substitute the gospel of Christ for another gospel, whatever shape and form. Occasions to define, perhaps even demarcate,

Apostles Paul and Barnabas preaching Christianity at Antioch. Hand-colored woodcut
Image © North Wind Picture Archive

---

18. Walls, *The Missionary Movement*, xvii.

certain aspects of our worldview will present themselves, yet in all of that, we must retain our allegiance to the Triune God of the Bible rather than let these boundary markers replace the central object and dynamic of our faith. The Evangelical Movement will have to be known essentially for its insistence on the evangel, the gospel of Jesus Christ, as the true touchstone for the Christian faith. This gospel critique of the movement, even as we participate in and animate the movement itself, will be a sure guide for our life and ministry in the future.

May we move forward in the twenty-first century with a bold humility to live in and live out the gospel of Jesus Christ through the power of the Holy Spirit, to the praise and glory of God the Father.

Bibliography

Barrett, David B., George T. Kurian, and Todd M. Johnson. *World Christian Encyclopedia* (2nd ed.). New York: Oxford University Press, 2001.

Bartholomew, Craig, Robin Parry, and Andrew West, eds. *The Futures of Evangelicalism: Issues and Prospects.* Leicester: IVP, 2003.

Bediako, Kwame. "The Emergence of World Christianity and the Remaking of Theology." In *Understanding World Christianity: The Vision and Work of Andrew Walls.* Edited by William Burrows et al. Maryknoll, NY: Orbis, 2011.

Bebbington, David. *Evangelicals in Modern Britain: A History from the 1730s to the 1980s.* London: Unwin, 1989.

Dayton, Donald. "Some Doubts About the Usefulness of the Category 'Evangelical'." In *The Variety of America Evangelicalism.* Edited by Donald Dayton and Robert Johnston. Downers Grove, Il: IVP, 1991.

Fitch, David E. *The End of Evangelicalism? Discerning a New Faithfulness for Mission.* Eugene, OR: Cascade Books, 2011.

Grenz, Stanley J. *Revisioning Evangelical Theology: A Fresh Agenda for the 21st Century.* Downers Grove, Il: InterVarsity Press, 1993.

Hutchinson, Mark, and Ogbu Kalu, eds. *A Global Faith: Essays on Evangelicalism and Globalization.* Sydney: CSAC, 1998.

Lewis, Donald. *Christianity Reborn: The Global Expansion of Evangelicalism in the Twentieth Century.* Grand Rapids: Eerdmans, 2004.

Johnson, Todd M., and Kenneth R. Ross. *Atlas of Global Christianity.* Edinburgh: Edinburgh University Press, 2009.

Kalu, Ogbu, ed. *Interpreting Contemporary Christianity: Global Processes and Local Identities.* Grand Rapids: Eerdmans, 2008.

Olson, Roger. "The Future of Evangelicalism." Patheos (blog). Accessed June 5, 2013, http://www.patheos.com/blogs/rogereolson/2013/03/my-talk-about-the-future-of-evangelicalism-at-george-fox-evangelical-seminary/.

Padilla, Rene. "The Future of Christianity in Latin America: Missiological Perspectives and Challenges." *International Bulletin of Missionary Research,* 23, no. 3 (July 1999): 105.

Rah, Soong-Chan. *The Next Evangelicalism: Freeing the Church from Western Captivity.* Downers Grove, Il: InterVarsity Press, 2009.

Stackhouse, John Jr., ed. *Evangelical Futures: A Conversation on Theological Method.* Grand Rapids: Baker, 2000.

Tienou, Tite. "Renewing Evangelical Identity from the Margins." In *Renewing the Evangelical Mission.* Edited by Richard Lints. Grand Rapids: Eerdmans, 2013.

Walls, Andrew. *The Cross-Cultural Process in Christian History.* Maryknoll, NY: Orbis, 2002.

———. *The Missionary Movement in Christian History: Studies in the Transmission of Faith*. Maryknoll, NY: Orbis, 1996.

Dr. Paul Joshua Bhakiaraj is a professor at the South Asia Institute of Advanced Christian Studies (SAIACS), Bangalore, India. Among other affiliations he is an associate of the Missions Commission of the World Evangelical Alliance (WEAMC); a member of the Lausanne Theology Working Group; and a member of the International Networking Team of International Fellowship of Mission as Transformation (INFEMIT).

"The Evangelical community will be a global force to be reckoned with in the twenty-first century. With her continuing amazing growth, especially in the global south, comes clarity, confidence and courage in engagement with all the domains of society. Such robust witness must be tempered with grace and humility. But there must be an unapologetic witness to the power of the gospel to transform society."

—Dr. Daniel Ho, Senior Pastor, Damansara Utama Methodist Church, Malaysia

Dr. Daniel Ho
*Photo: Damansara Utama
Methodist Church (DUMC)*

EVANGELICALS YOU WOULD WANT TO KNOW

By Albert W. Hickman

The history of Evangelicals is fascinating and diverse. The personalities and leaders of Evangelicalism through the years and around the world reflect the complex and intriguing history of the movement. This list is a compilation of names from around the world. This list is not complete. It does, though, offer a peek into the amazing history of Evangelicalism and the individual leaders who contributed so much in so many powerful ways.

Africa

Mojola Abegbi [born David Brown Vincent] (1860–1917)—Nigerian African Independent Church movement leader. Agbebi, a Yoruba, helped establish the first indigenous church in West Africa, the Native Baptist Church in Lagos, as well as the African Baptist Union of West Africa. He was an ardent advocate for African leadership in churches.

Kwame Bediako [Manasseh Kwame Dakwu Bediako] (1945–2008)—Ghanaian Presbyterian theologian. Bediako did much to persuade mainstream Western theologians and institutions of African theology's importance to global Christianity. To produce scholars and scholarship grounded in the African Christian context, he founded the Akrofi-Christaller Institute of Theology, Mission, and Culture.

Nicholas Bheki Nkosi Hepworth Bhengu (1909–1985)—South African Pentecostal evangelist. At Bhengu's Back to God Crusades, converts surrendered weapons and stolen goods; congregations he started formed the Assemblies of God Movement. TIME called him "the black Billy Graham," and many consider him among Africa's most significant evangelists.

Samuel Adjai Crowther (c. 1809–1891)—Nigerian churchman and linguist. Fulani slave traders captured Crowther, a Yoruba. In Sierra Leone he was freed and converted. A priest and missionary, he became the first African ordained an Anglican bishop. His Yoruba Bible strongly influenced subsequent African translations.

William Wadé Harris (c. 1860–1929)—Liberian prophet/evangelist. While imprisoned for political activism, Harris received a calling to be a missionary in a dream. He walked throughout Cote D'Ivoire calling people to repent and burn their charms, baptizing around 120 thousand during an 18 month period.

Festo Kivengere (1919–1984)—Called "the Billy Graham of Africa" Kivengere was a leader in the East African Revival and founded African Evangelistic Enterprise. He wrote *I Love Idi Amin*, on forgiveness, after fleeing Uganda and the dictator's wrath, eventually returning to continue his ministry.

Gottfried Osei-Mensah (b. 1934)—Ghanaian evangelical leader. Osei-Mensah was trained as an engineer but left that profession to become Traveling Secretary of the Pan-African Fellowship of Evangelical Students. Following the Lausanne Congress on World Evangelization he was elected the first General Secretary of the Lausanne Committee for World Evangelization.

Matilda Smith [Machtilt Schmidt (Dutch)/Magtildt Schmidt (Afrikaans)] (1749–1821)—South African mission activist. Smith, from a Dutch family in Cape Colony, preached to and taught slaves and advocated on their behalf when there was no local church or mission activity among them. She later co-founded the South Africa Missionary Society.

Asia

Vedanayagam Samuel Azariah (1874–1945)—Indian advocate for indigenous evangelization. The first Indian Anglican bishop, Azariah promoted church unity and helped found missionary societies. His memorable address at the 1910 World Missionary Conference called for Western missionaries to treat non-Western Christians as brothers and equals.

Benjamin Chew (1907–1994)—Singaporean parachurch leader. A Methodist physician, Chew played a significant leadership role in numerous parachurch groups, including the Graduates' Christian Fellowship, Singapore Youth for Christ, the Evangelical Fellowship of Singapore, and OMF. His medical work enabled the control of tuberculosis.

David [formerly Paul] Yonggi Cho (b. 1936)—South Korean Pentecostal pastor. Cho is founder and pastor emeritus of the Yoido Full Gospel Church, considered the world's largest congregation (more than 750 thousand registered members). Though noted for such innovations as cell groups, Cho has been the subject of controversy over financial dealings in recent years.

Watchman Nee [born Ni Shu-tsu] (1903–1972)—Chinese church leader and author. Nee, heavily influenced by doctrines of the Plymouth Brethren, founded what became the Local Church (or Little Flock) movement. Arrested by an unfriendly government in 1952 for his work, he died in prison. His writings include *The Normal Christian Life*.

Petrus Octavianus (1928–2014)—Octavianus was a leading figure in Indonesian Evangelicalism. He founded the Indonesia Missionary Fellowship (YPIII) in 1960 and headed the Indonesian Gospel Institute (I-3), the Fellowship of Indonesia Evangelical Churches and Institutions (PII), and the Indonesian Evangelical Mission Church (GMII).

Pandita Ramabai [born Ramabai Shastri] (1858–1922)—Indian scholar and social reformer. Ramabai advocated for women's education and ending child marriage. After her conversion she founded girls' schools and homes for the destitute, widows, and women in need. Author of several books, she translated the Bible into Marathi.

John Sung [Song Shan] (1901–1944)—Considered the greatest Chinese evangelist of the twentieth century. Sung earned a doctorate in chemistry but abandoned it for preaching. His sermons focused on repentance and revival, and he formed converts into evangelistic bands to continue his work.

Oceania

Peter Ambuofa (d. 1937)—Solomon Islands missionary. Converted while a laborer in Australia, Ambuofa faced opposition upon his return home until success as a farmer attracted formerly hostile neighbors to the gospel. He subsequently became a leader in the South Sea Evangelical Mission.

Arthur John "Jack" Dain (1912–2003)—Anglican churchman. England-born Dain led the Church Missionary Society of Australia and Tasmania before becoming Assistant Bishop of Sydney in 1965. Active in the World Evangelical Fellowship, he chaired both the 1974 International Congress on World Evangelization and the Lausanne Continuation Committee.

Leon Lamb Morris (1914–2006)—Australian New Testament scholar. Author of more than fifty books, Morris also contributed to the New International Version and the English Standard Version translations of the Bible. A president of the Australian Evangelical Alliance he led in the creation of the TEAR Fund for emergency relief.

Eastern Europe

Aladár Szabó (1862–1944)—Hungarian missions advocate. Szabó established several home mission societies but also felt that foreign missions was important to the revival of home missions. His advocacy for interdenominational cooperation and foreign missions challenged the insularism of the Hungarian Reformed churches of his day.

Georgi Vins (1928–1998)—Russian Baptist pastor. Vins, a leader in the underground Baptist church, gained international attention in 1975 when imprisoned by the Soviets and again in 1979 when released to the United States, where he continued to preach and advocate for persecuted Baptists.

Richard Wurmbrand (1909–2001)—Romanian pastor and advocate for persecuted Christians. Twice imprisoned for his faith, Wurmbrand wrote of his experiences in *Tortured for Christ*. With his wife, Sabina, he founded Voice of the Martyrs in 1967 to minister to and advocate on behalf of persecuted Christians.

Western Europe

Reinhard Will Gottfried Bonnke (b. 1940)—German Charismatic evangelist. Bonnke went to Lesotho as a missionary in 1969 and founded the evangelistic organization Christ for all Nations in 1974. He has preached extensively in Africa (where a reported seventy-four million have responded to his message) as well as Asia.

Hans Nielsen Hauge (1771–1824)—Norwegian revivalist. After a religious conversion at age twenty-five, Hauge led a pietistic revival that swept Norway. A layman, he was opposed by religious authorities and imprisoned several times, but he greatly influenced Lutheranism at home and among immigrants to North America.

Carl Olof Rosenius (1816–1868)—Swedish Lutheran revivalist. A lay preacher, author, and songwriter, Rosenius was the leader of the New Evangelical revival in Sweden that brought together strains of traditional and pietistic Lutheranism. He edited the influential magazine *Pietisten* from 1842 until his death.

Corrie ten Boom (1892–1983)—Dutch author and speaker. During World War II, ten Boom's family hid Jewish people and resistance fighters. Imprisoned by the Nazis, only Corrie survived. Her subsequent books (notably *The Hiding Place*) and speeches conveyed the depth of God's love amid suffering.

Count Nicholas Ludwig von Zinzendorf (1700–60)—Founder of the Moravian Church. Refugees from Moravia flocked to the estate that Zinzendorf, a German nobleman, opened for oppressed religious minorities. The congregation he established there, based on the Unity of the Brethren, became a strong global missionary-sending force.

Latin America and Caribbean

Pedro Arana Quíroz (b. 1938)—Peruvian evangelical leader. An elder statesman among Peruvian Evangelicals, Arana Quíroz was regional secretary for Latin America with the International Fellowship of Evangelical Students and president of the Peruvian Bible Society. He also served in the national Constituent Assembly.

Gonzalo Báez-Camargo (1899–1983)—Mexican Methodist writer and journalist. The positive attention Báez-Camargo received as an author, poet, and columnist was unusual for a Mexican Evangelical at the time. He also served as an editor and Bible translator and was well known as an evangelical ecumenist.

Orlando Costas (1942–1987)—Puerto Rican missiologist and theologian. Costas was a prolific author and a founder of the International Fellowship of Evangelical Missiologists from the Two-Thirds World. He pastored several churches before becoming a theology professor in Costa Rica and later in the United States.

Samuel Escobar (b. 1934)—Peruvian theologian. A seminary professor and leader in the International Fellowship of Evangelical Students, Escobar is a founder and former president of the Latin American Theological Fraternity. Within the Lausanne Movement he has been a prominent voice on social justice issues.

Luigi Francescon (1866–1964)—Pentecostal missionary. Raised Roman Catholic in Italy, Francescon underwent an evangelical conversion in the United States and later became a Pentecostal. He was instrumental in founding denominations on three continents, including the Iglesia Pentecostal de Argentina and Congregação Cristã no Brasil.

Rolando Edgardo Gutiérrez-Cortés (1934–1997)—Nicaraguan pastor-theologian. Gutiérrez-Cortés moved from Nicaragua to Mexico after his infant daughter died while visiting there. He became an influential pastor and theologian, serving as president of the Latin American Theological Fraternity and the National Baptist Convention of Mexico.

Humberto Lay Sun (b. 1934)—Peruvian pastor and politician. Lay Sun, an influential pastor from 1979–2005, founded the National Restoration Party in 2005. Respected for his work on the National Reconciliation Commission, he was elected to Congress in 2011 and chairs the Ethics Commission.

Francisco Olazabal (1886–1937)—Mexican Pentecostal revivalist. Converted in California, Olazabal became first a Methodist and then a Pentecostal pastor. His American revival crusades birthed numerous Hispanic Pentecostal churches, and in 1923 he was a co founder of the Latin American Council of Christian Churches.

C. René Padilla (b. 1932)—Latin American theologian. Padilla, currently president of the Micah Network, is a leading advocate for integral mission, emphasizing proclamation and demonstration of the gospel as equally important. He is author of *Transformation: The Church in Response to Human Need*.

Luis Palau (b. 1934)—Argentinian Baptist evangelist. Palau has preached to an estimated thirty million people in seventy-five countries. Now based in the United States, he is the author of almost fifty books in English and Spanish and hosts two daily international radio programs.

United Kingdom

William (1829–1912) & Catherine [née Mumford] Booth (1829–1890)—Salvation Army founders. William and Catherine, both gifted lay preachers, established the Christian Mission in 1865 to meet the spiritual and physical needs of London's poor and marginalized. Known today as the Salvation Army, it continues their vision in 126 countries.

William Carey (1761–1834)—Known as the Father of Modern Missions. Reacting against Protestant disinterest in missions, Carey wrote and spoke of all Christians' obligation to carry out Christ's Great Commission (Matthew 28:19–20). His faith and perseverance as a missionary to India inspired the nineteenth-century missionary movement.

Selina [née Shirley] Hastings, Countess of Huntingdon (1707–1791)—Supporter of Methodist evangelism. Hastings directed her fortune and social position toward the evangelization of Britain's upper class. Expelled from the Anglican Church by authorities displeased with the Countess of Huntingdon's Connexion of sixty chapels, she continued her efforts until her death.

Hannah Moore (1745–1833)—Writer and social reformer. A former teacher, Moore became acquainted with the Clapham Sect of wealthy Evangelicals, including William Wilberforce. Her subsequent writings advocated for abolition of the slave trade and other evangelical causes, while much of her income was devoted to philanthropy.

John Newton (1725–1807)—Hymnist and preacher. Newton, a slave-ship captain who was converted to Christ, is best known for his hymn "Amazing Grace." Less known is his subsequent ministry as an Anglican preacher and his work as an abolitionist, including his influence on abolitionist William Wilberforce.

Charles Haddon Spurgeon (1834–1892)—Known as The Prince of Preachers. Spurgeon, a Particular Baptist, pastored the famous Metropolitan Tabernacle in London. He was perhaps the best-known preacher in Britain in his day. A prolific author, his writings and sermons are still widely read and studied.

John R. W. Stott (1921–2011)—Anglican preacher and teacher. One of the twentieth century's best-known Evangelicals, Stott was on staff at All Souls Church in London for most of his life. He was a principal drafter of the Lausanne Covenant, and his many books include *Basic Christianity*.

John Wesley (1703–1791) & Charles Wesley (1707–1788)—Founders and leaders of Methodism. The Wesley brothers, converted three days apart, became leaders of Methodism, originally a revival movement within Anglicanism. John is remembered for his preaching and writings; Charles, for the more than six thousand hymns he penned.

George Whitefield (1714–1770)—Known as the Apostle of the British Empire. Anglican preacher and evangelist Whitefield possessed a booming voice; his open-air preaching drew large crowds and could be heard from a great distance. He preached eighteen thousand sermons during his lifetime and made thirteen trips to North America, where he died.

William Wilberforce (1759–1833)—English statesman and philanthropist. Wilberforce became a leading abolitionist after his conversion. His work produced the Slave Trade Act of 1807 and contributed to the Slavery Abolition Act of 1833. He was also a founder of the Church Missionary Society.

North America

Henry Alline (1748–1784)—Known as The Apostle to Nova Scotia. Alline was an itinerant preacher and Canada's most prolific eighteenth-century author. He contributed to the region's neutrality during the American Revolution and established the Maritime Provinces as the center of Baptist faith in Canada.

Richard Allen (1760–1831)—African-American preacher. After black parishioners at St. George's Methodist Episcopal Church faced discrimination from white congregants and leaders, Allen, a former slave, organized the Bethel AME Church in Philadelphia. In 1816 he founded the African Methodist Episcopal Church, the first autonomous African-American denomination.

Isaac Backus (1724–1806)—American preacher and defender of religious liberty. Converted during the Great Awakening, Backus subsequently embraced Baptist doctrine and became a leading advocate of church-state separation. He was a delegate to the Massachusetts convention that ratified the US Constitution.

Fanny J. Crosby [Frances Jane Crosby van Alstyne] (1820–1915)—American hymnist. Blind from infancy, she penned more than eight thousand hymns, many still sung today. Among the best known are "Blessed Assurance," "Pass Me Not O Gentle Savior," "Jesus Keep Me Near the Cross," and "To God Be the Glory."

Jonathan Edwards (1703–1758)—American preacher and theologian. The writings and sermons of Edwards, one of America's greatest intellectuals, engendered New Light Calvinism and are considered classics of Reformed theology. The First Great Awakening began with revival under his preaching in Northampton, Massachusetts.

Charles Grandison Finney (1792–1875)—American known as Father of Modern Revivalism. Rejecting his rigid Calvinism, Finney promoted such innovations as the altar call (public declaration of repentance) and the anxious seat (where those convicted of sin could receive prayer). Later in life he was a social reformer.

William Franklin "Billy" Graham, Jr. (b. 1918)—American evangelist. Perhaps the world's best-known modern Evangelical, Graham has preached to 80 million in person and billions via radio and television. His Billy Graham Evangelistic Association has sponsored numerous international evangelism conferences, and among his legacies are the Lausanne Movement and *Christianity Today* magazine.

Adoniram (1788–1850) and Ann [née Hasseltine] Judson (1789–1826)—Known as the first American denominational missionaries. The Judsons, appointed as Congregationalists, became Baptists during their voyage to India. Denied residency there, they sailed to Burma. Adoniram's Burmese Bible translation is still used today; Ann contributed to it and also wrote catechisms.

George Liele [Lisle] (1750–1820)—Known as the First American Missionary. Born a slave in Virginia, Liele was converted in Georgia, encouraged to preach to other slaves, and later freed. To remain free after the American Revolution, he evacuated to Jamaica, where he ministered among the African population.

Dwight Lyman Moody (1837–1899)—American evangelist. His 1873–1875 British crusade made Moody, the pioneer of many features of modern evangelistic meetings, internationally famous. Legacies of his ministry include

Moody Bible Institute, Moody Memorial Church, Northfield Mount Hermon School, and the Student Volunteer Movement.

Harold John Ockenga (1905–1985)—Known as the American Father of Neo-Evangelicalism. Ockenga, long-time pastor of Boston's Park Street Church, was a founder of and first president of the National Association of Evangelicals, Fuller Theological Seminary, and Gordon-Conwell Theological Seminary. He also chaired the board of *Christianity Today* magazine.

Phoebe Worrall Palmer (1807–1874)—American holiness revivalist. Better-known than her co-revivalist husband Walter, Palmer also led the "Tuesday Meetings for the Promotion of Holiness" and wrote extensively. She played a significant role in spreading the doctrines of the Holiness Movement throughout North America and Britain.

INTRODUCTION TO REGIONAL ESSAYS

By Mark Hutchinson

In this section you will read fascinating profiles of Evangelicals around the world. Where they live; how they live; their histories and current situations. You will also read about ministries impacting communities across the globe.

There is something both absurd but also historically advantageous about attempting to put together an overview of global Evangelicalism. On the one hand, it is incredibly absurd—Evangelical Christianity as a global movement is now far too complex a category for any one person, or even a team of people, to adequately address. (Indeed, there are some who would suggest global Evangelicalism is now so dynamic that it strains the singularizing concept of a movement.)

The team of people who addressed the task for this volume were drawn from among those who live close to the subject, and yet were neither tempted to overemphasize its values, nor impose an external critical framework which, as is the case in too much scholarly literature, obscures its shared origins, pathways and objectives. Each contributor would say—even after the globe was partitioned along lines provided for by standard United Nations categories—that the available space for their particular regional focus was far too small to do their region justice. Naturally, there will be oversights, miscalculations, and gross generalizations. These are the ordinary outcomes of hypercompression. We are not the first to face such problems, and, indeed, the problem of the evangelist is now the problem of any scholar who seeks to encompass subjects on a global scale. For them, "the world itself could not contain the books that would be written" (John 21:25).

On the other hand, there is also something sublimely historically advantageous to the task. What we have attempted together—surrounded by books, empowered by the Internet, erected from the midst of historically unusual wealth and leisure—is what a former shoemaker attempted alone as the full-time pastor of a Leicester Baptist church in 1792. This volume treads, therefore, within a great tradition. William Carey's *Enquiry* of course, went on to become a work of profound influence. The authors of these regional pieces do not have such a large aim. It is simply suggested here that, by laying readable regional stories, trends, and literatures alongside one another, common themes and new insights may occur to the reader. If this is what is achieved, then we will consider ourselves well pleased.

> There is something both absurd but also historically advantageous about attempting to put together an overview of global Evangelicalism.

INTRODUCTION TO MINISTRY PROFILES

By Debra Fieguth

Just as the area essays in this section of *Evangelicals Around the World* tell the history, the composition and the present situation of Evangelicals in different regions of the world, the ministry profiles show the difference this community is making wherever they live out their faith.

The profiles have as part of their title "Evangelical Impact": and that is really what these stories are about. Although every attempt was made to balance geographical regions, type of ministry (evangelistic, justice-oriented social services, education, for example) and size, certainly there are countless stories we have not told.

Wherever possible the profiles focus on ministries developed in the specific country by nationals. Some were started by outsiders but are staffed almost entirely by national workers. The rest are indigenous.

The breadth and depth of evangelical impact around the world is both astonishing and inspiring. They bring heart and story to the statistics and surveys of this diverse community around the world

INTRODUCTION TO REGIONAL GRAPHICS

By Gina A. Zurlo

Each continent section (Africa, Latin America, North America, Asia, Europe, and Oceania) begins with a full page profile situating that continent in its global religious context. The profiles include three sections: global comparison data, Christianity, and missions. Global comparisons are made with three populations—total, Christian, and non-Christian—plus that continent's share of missionaries received. Narrowing in on Christianity, the graphic shows the continent's populations of all Christians and Evangelicals (the latter including both World Christian Database and Operation World estimates; see the "Demographics of Global Evangelicalism" article in this volume for an explanation of methodological differences) and the growth rates of each compared to their respective global populations. Finally, missions is highlighted by differentiating the number of missionaries sent from and received by the continent and how much personal contact Christians there have with non-Christians.

Following each full-page profile is a table listing every country on that continent, in alphabetical order. These tables include the following data:

Population, 2010: Total country population.

Christians, 2010: Total Christian population of that country (all traditions).

% Christian, 2010: Christians' share of total population.

WCD Evangelicals, 2010: The number of Evangelicals in that country according to the World Christian Database.

WCD % Evangelical, 2010: Evangelicals' share of total population according to the World Christian Database.

OW Evangelicals, 2010: The number of Evangelicals in that country according to Operation World.

OW % Evangelical, 2010: Evangelicals' share of total population according to Operation World.

AFRICA

POPULATION 1,031,084,000
MAJORITY RELIGION: ISLAM (41.7%)

AFRICA REPRESENTS

14.9% OF THE TOTAL
GLOBAL POPULATION

21.9% OF THE GLOBAL
CHRISTIAN POPULATION

11.5% OF THE GLOBAL
NON-CHRISTIAN POPULATION

21.5% OF THE GLOBAL
MISSIONARY FORCE RECEIVED

CHRISTIANITY IN AFRICA

POPULATION ■■■ CHRISTIAN ■■■ EVANGELICAL ■■■

CHRISTIAN & EVANGELICAL POPULATION

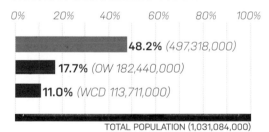

0%　　20%　　40%　　60%　　80%　　100%

48.2% *(497,318,000)*

17.7% *(OW 182,440,000)*

11.0% *(WCD 113,711,000)*

TOTAL POPULATION (1,031,084,000)

GROWTH RATE* 1970 2010

5.0%
4.5%
4.0%
3.5%
3.0%　　　　　　　　　GLOBAL EVANG.
2.5%　　　　　　　　　　(2.79%)
2.0%　　　　　　　　　GLOBAL CHRISTIANS
1.5%　　　　　　　　　　(1.55%)
1.0%
0.5%

*Rate = average annual growth rate, percent per year,
between dates specified.

MISSIONS IN AFRICA
FROM ALL CHRISTIAN TRADITIONS

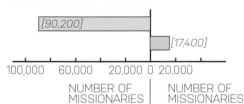

[90,200]

[17,400]

100,000　60,000　20,000　0　20,000

NUMBER OF　　　NUMBER OF
MISSIONARIES　　MISSIONARIES
RECEIVED　　　　SENT

1 MISSIONARY SENT
FOR EVERY **28,600** CHRISTIANS
IN AFRICA

1 MISSIONARY RECEIVED
FOR EVERY **11,400** PEOPLE
IN AFRICA

26 OF EVERY 100 NON-CHRISTIANS
PERSONALLY KNOW A CHRISTIAN
IN AFRICA

Source: *World Christian Database*, 2010 data

Christians and Evangelicals by country in Africa, 2010

	POPULATION, 2010	CHRISTIANS, 2010	% CHRISTIAN, 2010	WCD EVANGELICALS, 2010	WCD % EVANGELICAL, 2010	OW EVANGELICALS, 2010	OW % EVANGELICAL, 2010
Algeria	37,063,000	64,600	0.2%	2,600	0.0%	84,100	0.2%
Angola	19,549,000	18,235,000	93.3%	3,743,000	19.1%	4,277,000	21.9%
Benin	9,510,000	4,162,000	43.8%	741,000	7.8%	768,000	8.1%
Botswana	1,969,000	1,352,000	68.7%	92,000	4.7%	160,000	8.1%
Burkina Faso	15,540,000	3,483,000	22.4%	1,469,000	9.5%	1,442,000	9.3%
Burundi	9,233,000	8,509,000	92.2%	1,464,000	15.9%	2,303,000	24.9%
Cameroon	20,624,000	11,943,000	57.9%	1,216,000	5.9%	1,804,000	8.7%
Cape Verde	488,000	463,000	95.0%	9,900	2.0%	33,800	6.9%
Central African Republic	4,350,000	3,103,000	71.3%	1,277,000	29.4%	1,453,000	33.4%
Chad	11,721,000	4,077,000	34.8%	1,468,000	12.5%	1,161,000	9.9%
Comoros	683,000	3,300	0.5%	360	0.1%	1,300	0.2%
Congo	4,112,000	3,691,000	89.8%	212,000	5.2%	598,000	14.5%
Congo DR	62,191,000	59,086,000	95.0%	4,624,000	7.4%	12,689,000	20.4%
Cote d'Ivoire	18,977,000	6,511,000	34.3%	1,601,000	8.4%	2,256,000	11.9%
Djibouti	834,000	14,500	1.7%	300	0.0%	1,200	0.1%
Egypt	78,076,000	7,876,000	10.1%	417,000	0.5%	3,283,000	4.2%
Equatorial Guinea	696,000	617,000	88.7%	16,400	2.4%	30,400	4.4%
Eritrea	5,741,000	2,667,000	46.5%	35,000	0.6%	111,000	1.9%
Ethiopia	87,095,000	52,153,000	59.9%	12,155,000	14.0%	16,657,000	19.1%
Gabon	1,556,000	1,315,000	84.5%	45,200	2.9%	191,000	12.2%
Gambia	1,681,000	75,300	4.5%	4,700	0.3%	13,400	0.8%
Ghana	24,263,000	15,518,000	64.0%	4,686,000	19.3%	5,879,000	24.2%
Guinea	10,876,000	397,000	3.7%	92,800	0.9%	74,500	0.7%
Guinea-Bissau	1,587,000	194,000	12.2%	22,700	1.4%	27,100	1.7%
Kenya	40,909,000	33,245,000	81.3%	11,402,000	27.9%	19,992,000	48.9%
Lesotho	2,009,000	1,843,000	91.7%	146,000	7.2%	253,000	12.6%
Liberia	3,958,000	1,604,000	40.5%	321,000	8.1%	601,000	15.2%

Country							
Madagascar	21,080,000	11,997,000	56.9%	1,651,000	7.8%	2,311,000	11.0%
Malawi	15,014,000	11,975,000	79.8%	2,637,000	17.6%	3,069,000	20.4%
Mali	13,986,000	442,000	3.2%	102,000	0.7%	93,600	0.7%
Mauritania	3,609,000	9,500	0.3%	1,100	0.0%	2,100	0.1%
Mauritius	1,231,000	408,000	33.2%	98,900	8.0%	131,000	10.6%
Mayotte	204,000	1,400	0.7%	160	0.1%	240	0.1%
Morocco	31,642,000	31,300	0.1%	3,700	0.0%	4,700	0.0%
Mozambique	23,967,000	12,572,000	52.5%	2,476,000	10.3%	2,607,000	10.9%
Namibia	2,179,000	1,987,000	91.2%	288,000	13.3%	270,000	12.4%
Niger	15,894,000	56,100	0.4%	13,900	0.1%	21,500	0.1%
Nigeria	159,708,000	73,632,000	46.1%	32,594,000	20.4%	48,806,000	30.6%
Reunion	845,000	740,000	87.6%	45,000	5.3%	49,100	5.8%
Rwanda	10,837,000	9,916,000	91.5%	2,089,000	19.3%	2,761,000	25.5%
Saint Helena	4,200	4,100	95.8%	740	3.3%	390	9.1%
Sao Tome & Principe	178,000	171,000	96.1%	3,500	2.0%	7,000	3.9%
Senegal	12,951,000	697,000	5.4%	8,800	0.1%	25,800	0.2%
Seychelles	91,200	86,400	94.8%	3,700	4.1%	5,000	5.4%
Sierra Leone	5,752,000	763,000	13.3%	154,000	2.7%	229,000	4.0%
Somalia	9,636,000	4,500	0.0%	550	0.0%	4,300	0.0%
South Africa	51,452,000	42,199,000	82.0%	5,170,000	10.0%	10,650,000	20.7%
South Sudan	9,941,000	6,010,000	60.5%	1,319,000	13.3%	4,804,000	48.3%
Sudan	35,652,000	1,916,000	5.4%	394,000	1.1%	1,532,000	4.3%
Swaziland	1,193,000	1,046,000	87.6%	146,000	12.2%	302,000	25.3%
Tanzania	44,973,000	24,627,000	54.8%	6,919,000	15.4%	8,043,000	17.9%
Togo	6,306,000	2,962,000	47.0%	399,000	6.3%	723,000	11.5%
Tunisia	10,632,000	23,800	0.2%	610	0.0%	1,200	0.0%
Uganda	33,987,000	28,698,000	84.4%	6,326,000	18.6%	12,507,000	36.8%
Western Sahara	515,000	790	0.2%	30	0.0%	120	0.0%
Zambia	13,217,000	11,297,000	85.5%	2,565,000	19.4%	3,406,000	25.8%
Zimbabwe	13,077,000	10,678,000	81.7%	1,036,000	7.9%	3,911,000	29.9%

EVANGELICALS IN EASTERN AFRICA

By Girma Bekele

There are few more geographically diverse regions on earth than Eastern Africa, home to Africa's highes[t] peaks, earliest humans, and possibly even to ancient civilisations such as Punt, the land of the Biblical Quee[n] of Sheba. In the twentieth century, Eastern Africa was also home to a revival which was significant on a globa[l] scale, a movement which continues to shape world Christianity to this day.

Burundi and Rwanda

Burundi sits south of the equator, in East-Central Africa, bordering the Democratic Republic of Cong[o,] Rwanda, and Tanzania. With a population of 9.85 million (2012), it shares its major ethnic groups with Rwand[a] (85% Hutu, 14% Tutsi and 1% Twa). Some 91.5% of the country identify as Christians, with Catholics being th[e] largest group at 71.4% and Evangelicals at 27% (Johnson 2007).

Historically, Burundi was an independent Kingdom, mainly made up of three ethnic groups: The Twa Hut[u] (agricultural people) and Tutsi peoples (pastoralists). The Twa, also known as the Batwa pygmies, are a minorit[y] (1%). They are often marginalized and still experience ethnic prejudice, discrimination, and violence with almos[t] no bargaining power in the socio-political arena. During nineteenth-century European colonial expansion, th[e] two independent Kingdoms of Burundi and Rwanda fused into a new colonial entity known as Ruanda-Urund[i,] part of German East Africa, which included Burundi, Rwanda, and Tanganyika (part of present day Tanzania[).] Following the defeat of Germany in the First World War, Belgium was granted a League of Nations mandate i[n] 1923, and eventually Burundi, with Rwanda, became a Belgian protectorate.

The Catholic White Fathers (also known as the Society of Missionaries of Africa) established their first mis[-] sion station in 1900, during the German colonial period. Protestants from the German Bethel Mission launche[d] their mission in 1907, a precursor for the Evangelical Presbyterian Church in Rwanda. German Lutherans wer[e] expelled from Rwanda following World War I when Rwanda became a protectorate under Belgium. Seventh Da[y] Adventists from Belgium and Anglicans were also among the first to arrive. Their first success was among poo[r] Hutu, the first five being ordained in 1919.

Evangelicals, both in Burundi and Rwanda, have their roots in the 1930s East African Revival which com[-] menced at the Church Missionary Society mission station (an outpost of the Anglican Diocese of Uganda). Thi[s] significantly influenced Evangelicalism in East Africa as a whole, including Uganda, Tanzania, and Kenya. Evan[-] gelical missions such as the Ruanda Mission of the Church Missionary Society, especially under Drs. Joe an[d] Decie Church, had direct connection with the Keswick Convention in the U.K. and Canon Warner Theologic[al] College, which was established in Burundi by Lawrence Barham. All have contributed to the shaping of Evan[-] gelicalism in Burundi.

Post-Genocide Growth

During the twelve years from 1993 to 2005, ethnic conflicts in Burundi were severe. More than 300,00[0] from the nation's 8 million people were killed. The resurgence of Evangelicalism in both Burundi and Rwand[a] was primarily a post-genocide event, featuring a significant contribution by Pentecostalism. In Burundi, Evan[-] gelicals are affiliated with the National Council of Churches of Burundi, of which the Anglican Church of Burun[di] has the largest share of membership. Healing, restoration, peace building, and church planting are major missiological frontiers.

As in Burundi, modern Christianity began in Rwanda through the work of various mission organizations that followed the footsteps of colonial powers: Germany, Belgium, and Britain. Burundi and Rwanda were separated and became independent nations on July 1, 1962, but they continue to share many similarities, including ethnic groups (85% Hutu, 14% Tutsi and 1% Twa) (Johnson 2007). Racial division was intense during the colonial pe-

The 1994 ethnic conflict in Rwanda resulted in the death of as many as 800,000—mainly Tutsi.

riod, culminating in the 1959–1962 Hutu revolution in Rwanda. The Tutsi monarchy was abolished, and many Tutsi were killed or went into exile, and Rwanda became a Republic under Hutu government (Ischi 345–46). Similar atrocities happened in Burundi, primarily due to fear. The minority Tutsi who were in power in 1973 killed 100,000–150,000 Hutus, followed by years of restriction from schooling (including Catholic schools, which were nationalized by the ruling powers). Many missionaries were expelled during this period.

The 1994 ethnic conflict in Rwanda resulted in the death of as many as 800,000—mainly Tutsi. According to the United Nations Office for the Coordination of Humanitarian Affairs, there was a genocide of up to 30% of the Rwandan Batwa during the same 1994 ethnic conflict, but that tragedy received much less international attention. A significant turning point came in the post-genocide period when many Rwandans were seeking national healing. The established churches—Catholic and mainline Protestant—were tainted with the blood of innocents during the genocide. Evangelical spirituality became a genuine alternative to Catholic and mainline Protestant nominalism; renewal fomented by Pentecostal congregations, particularly those who were planted by some refugees who returned to their homeland after decades of living in neighboring countries to escape persecution. A notable example is the Zion Temple Pentecostal Church, which, within four years of its founding (2000), had grown to some 7,000 members.

Evangelicals Step Up

After the civil war, the international attention focused on Rwanda made it a real concern for evangelical ministries coming to help in the recovery. The Rwanda Evangelical Alliance is affiliated with the World Evangelical Alliance (WEA), and was instrumental in the establishment of The Rwandan Institute of Evangelical Theology (FATER), a key leadership training institution. Of its members, the 250,000—strong Association of Baptist Churches in Rwanda was commenced in 1967 by missionaries from the DRC. By way of contrast, the Presbyterian Church in Rwanda (300,000 members) emerged from German and Belgian roots and was founded as early as 1904; additionally the Province of the Episcopal Church in Rwanda (over one million members) was established in 1925. Of the 93.4% of the population who are Christian, Catholics are slightly in the majority (53%) and Protestants at 46.5% (Pew Research, 2012); about one-quarter of Protestants may be considered Evangelicals (Operation World, 2010). As in Burundi, Evangelicals in Rwanda now have an unprecedented open door for evangelism, church planting, and social action.

The Comoro Islands and Mayotte

Comoro consists of three volcanic islands (Grande Comore, Mohéli, and Anjouan), all of which are located in the Indian Ocean off the south-east coast of Africa, east of Mozambique and northwest of Madagascar. Its population of 717,500 (World Bank, 2012) is ranked 178/187 on the 2013 HDI. Political life is often very volatile due to struggles among leaders of the islands for control of the federal power. In this small country, there have been 19 coups since independence. The islands were occupied by France in 1886 and became independent in 1975. The major religion is Islam (98.5%, with a Christian population of only 1%) with some fundamentalist sentiment while other sectors are deeply involved in occult practices and spirit possession. Christian witness is still forbidden, except in the French territory of Mayotte. Various Christian relief and aid organizations have access to the other Comoro Islands, where evangelism is primarily carried out in the form of presence, radiating the love of God in practical actions. The well-known *Jesus* film is available in Shimaore and Shingazidja.

After having voted twice (1975 and 2009) to remain attached to France, Mayotte became the furthest region of the European Union in 2014. With a population of 212,600 (2012 national census), 97.4% are Muslims (relatively moderate) and 1.8% are Christians, the majority being nominal Catholics. Evangelicals form less than 0.1% (Operation World, 2010). A prominent evangelical church is the International Evangelical Church of Mayotte. With 73% totally unreached, the Evangelical community seeks encouragement and partnership with East African evangelical bodies to expand the missionary frontier.

Djibouti

Djibouti is a barren strip of desert between Ethiopia, Eritrea, and Somalia in the horn of Africa, home to two major demographic groups: the Somali (near the border with Somalia) and the Afar (bordering with Eritrea and Ethiopia). It is a strategic place for shipping, which is its main source of income. France retains a sizeable military base because until September 20, 1977, Djibouti was a French Colony. Arabic and French constitute the country's two official languages. Again, its main religion is Islam (97%) with Evangelicals maintaining a tiny minority (0.1%). Nevertheless, the Ethiopian Evangelical Church is very active in evangelizing among refugees and immigrants (Haustein and Fantini, 2013). The constitution of Djibouti allows relative religious freedom, though Afar and Somali converts are severely persecuted by their own people. Christian denominations—the Église Protestante de Djibouti, the Greek Orthodox Church, and the Red Sea Mission Team—work with considerable freedom. Established in 1960, primarily for French troops, the Église Protestante de Djibouti, has opened its doors to house various small evangelical ethnic churches, among them Reformed, Pentecostal, Mennonite, Lutheran, and Baptist.

Ethiopia

With a population of 91.73 million (World Bank, 2012), Ethiopia is one of the oldest Christian nations in the world. Around AD 330, Christianity became the state religion. The throne-altar and crown-clergy partnership in Ethiopia lasted until 1974 when the monarchy was overthrown by a military coup d'état. The beginning of Ethiopian Evangelicalism dates from the arrival of two Protestant missionaries, both sponsored by the Church Missionary Society (CMS): Samuel Gobat of Switzerland (1799–1879, later Anglican Bishop of Jerusalem) and Christian Kügler of Germany (1801–1830). Emperor Haile Selassie, the last Monarch of Ethiopia, gave royal permission for evangelical mission work in areas of the nation that were not traditionally dominated by the Ethiopian Orthodox Church. As a result the two largest evangelical churches are the Ethiopian Evangelical Church Mekane Yesus (EECMY), rooted in the mission work of the Lutheran and Presbyterian Missions in Ethiopia, and the Kale Heywot (Word of Life) Church (EKHC). Established as a national church in 1959, by the end of 2009 the EECMY had 5.3 million members in 6,644 established congregations and 2,818 preaching places in 21 Synods, predominantly in the region of Oromia.

The arrival of Thomas Lambie (1885–1954) in 1918, a medical doctor and a missionary of the United Presbyterian Board of Foreign Missions of North America, marks the beginning of EKHC. With the merger of the Abyssinian Frontiers Mission (AMF) and the Sudan Interior Mission (SIM—now named Serving in Mission), an evangelistic mission was launched in Hossaina, Kemabata, south of Addis Ababa. Predominantly located in Southern Ethiopia, the EKHC is the largest evangelical church in Ethiopia with 7.1 million members and 7,774 local churches across the nation.

The country was under a severe Marxist regime from 1974–1991. During that period, Ethiopian Evangelicalism was confined to being an underground movement but nevertheless experienced explosive growth. Now at 20% of the population, it is one of the fastest growing movements in the world. The Ethiopian Orthodox Tewahedo Church is 43.5% of the population, with Islam 33.9% and Roman Catholic .07% (Census, 2007). Although in its initiation Ethiopian Evangelicalism mirrored the traditions of founding western missionary agents, during the eighteen years of "survival" mode under Communist rule, it effectively re-emerged as Pentecostal.

Ethiopian Evangelicalism is challenged by excessive ethnic self-consciousness. One's theological or socio-political views, as well as one's actions or inactions, are seen through the prism of ethnicity, regardless of one's intention. Churches split easily and there is a professionalization (or even a personalization) of ministry, often characterized by feelings of insecurity. Lack of theological training is apparent. There is much need for mature leadership, Christian unity and visionary evangelical social action in the fight against acute poverty.

Eritrea

Located in North-East Africa along the Red Sea, Eritrea was part of Ethiopia until it became independent in 1994 following a referendum. It borders on Djibouti, Ethiopia, and Sudan, and is one of the poorest countries in Sub-Saharan Africa. Most of its land is dry, hot desert along the coastline, with a population of 6.13 million (World Bank, 2012). It was an Italian colony from 1890 to 1941. Eritrea united with Ethiopia as a federation in 1951. Ten years later Ethiopia annexed it, leading to a thirty-year war for independence.

Evangelicalism in Eritrea has its roots in the 1860s in a religious movement within the EOTC that was reminiscent of the Reformation in Europe. Due to growing tension on doctrinal issues, the renewal movement was considered heretical and was forced out of the EOTC. This resulted in the formation of a new Church, adopted by the Swedish Lutherans, Mekane Yesus (Eritrean Evangelical Lutheran Church). Operation World estimates the Christian population at 47.31%, with Evangelicals 2.1% (just under 100,000), and Islam 50.3% (Operation World). The Full Gospel Evangelical Church, Pentecostal, has significantly shaped Evangelicalism in Eritrea, including bringing elements of renewal within Orthodox and Catholic groups, known as Tehadiso (reformed). As of 2002, a government ruling banned all religious groups with the exception of the established Eritrean Orthodox, Roman Catholic, and Evangelical Lutheran churches. Of course, Sunni Muslims are free. Evangelicals are subjected to harsh persecution and Evangelicals in East Africa need to stand in solidarity with them.

Kenya

With its capital at Nairobi, Kenya's population of 43.18 million (World Bank, 2012) is 83% Christian: Evangelicals constitute 48.9 (Operation World). There is rampant nominalism, even among Evangelicals. The national average of church attendance is only 7%, less than one-tenth of all Christians. The Nairobi Evangelical Graduate School of Theology, the Pan African Christian University, St Paul's United Theological University in Limuru, and Daystar University serve all of anglophone Africa and are among the most prominent theological schools on the continent. Evangelicals are spread among major denominations such as the Africa Inland Church (1895), the Africa Gospel Church (an Evangelical Friends Church), and the African Church of the Holy Spirit

A group of pastors meet in Rwanda.

(700,000 members), which was born due to a split from Friends African Mission in 1927. Among the largest of the churches is the Anglican Church of Kenya (5 million), with its roots in the 1844 mission work of CMS and the Presbyterian Church of East Africa (4 million), a plant of the Church of Scotland in 1891. The African Israel Nineveh Church (500,000), planted by David Zakayo Kivuli, commenced out of a connection with the Pentecostal Assemblies of Canada in 1942.

Fastest growing are various indigenous/independent churches (such as the Baptist Convention in Kenya and the Mombasa Pentecostal Church). The Evangelical Alliance of Kenya (EAK), established in 1975, has 10 million members in 38,000 churches scattered in fifty-two denominations, making up 32% of Kenya's population (Johnson 2007). The Evangelicals are renewing their strength to fight against nominalism, government corruption, nepotism, and various fronts in the area of social concern, including a fight against HIV. Mission and evangelism have been identified as urgently needed, for despite the fact that the population of Kenya is considered to be over 80% Christian, nominalism remains a huge challenge. This privileged majority has yet to turn its energy towards transforming with Christian values the country's political and socioeconomic process.

Madagascar

Madagascar is a large island in the Indian Ocean off the east coast of Africa, with a population of 23 million (World Bank, 2012). In the two decades following independence in 1960 from France, the country was under harsh Marxist governments. The people of Madagascar, the Malagasy, have ethnic origins in Southeast Asia. The Church of Jesus Christ in Madagascar is the largest Protestant/Evangelical church. It was established in 1968 as a result of the union of three churches which have their roots in the work of the London Missionary Society (arrived in 1818), the Paris Missionary Society and the Friends Foreign Mission Association. It has 3.5 million members in 5,795 churches. Established in 1950 as a national church, the Malagasy Lutheran Church was established by Norwegian (1866) and American missionaries (1888). It has about 3 million members scattered in 5,000 churches (Johnson 2007).

In 1973, Evangelical Anglicans established the Province of the Indian Ocean as a structure to unify and support many small congregations that have roots in the 1864 work of the Society for the Propagation of the Gospel on several islands in the region. There are about 500,000 members in the islands of Madagascar, Mauritius, Seychelles, and La Réunion. The Baptist Evangelical Association of Madagascar (established in 1997) and other independent Evangelical/Pentecostal churches (such as the United Pentecostal Church of Madagascar) are flourishing. Nonetheless, the combination of religious syncretism and the practice of traditional African religions, such as Spiritism and Voodooism, are prominent in the country. Christians make up 53.53% of the population, of which the Evangelicals make up 11.5% (Johnson 2007), with evangelism and church planting at the heart of the missiological vision.

Mauritius

Mauritius consists of the outer island of Rodrigues, the islands of Agalega and the archipelago Saint Brandon. Located east of Madagascar in the western Indian Ocean, the country was colonized by Portugal, France, and finally Britain (1810–1968), and since 1992 it is a republic within the Commonwealth. It is a multiethnic nation with African, European, Indian, and Chinese descent. While Hindus account for the majority (48.60%), Christians represent 32.71%, the majority being Catholic, of which 10.1% are Evangelicals (Operation World 2010), including Anglicans, Baptists and Presbyterians. The Federation of the Mauritian Evangelical Churches (six churches), other Charismatic/Pentecostal and Independent churches are growing very fast. The Fellowship of Christian Churches in Mauritius (FCCM), established 1995, is a significant step in Mauritius Evangelicalism, fostering Christian unity, raising trained church leaders, and encouraging nationwide evangelism and church planting, particularly among the Hindus and Muslims.

Réunion

Located just east of Madagascar off the African coast, Réunion has been French territory from as early as the 1720s when settlers from the French East Indian Company arrived. Its population is about 880,000 with its citizens claiming ancestral roots in French, other European, African, Malagasy, Southern Indian, and Chinese homelands. 84% of the population is identified as Christian, including Roman Catholics (92%) and Protestants (7.8%) of which 5.2% are Evangelical (Joshua Project, Pew Research). Evangelical Churches of Reunion, planted by African Evangelical Fellowship (AEF/SIM missionaries), the Assemblies of God (France) and Protestant Church of Reunion Island, are some of the notable churches in the evangelical tradition in Réunion. Church planting is a high missional priority; it faces specific resistance from native religious spirituality (i.e., a mixture of Hinduism and African witchcraft, superstition, and Catholic nominalism).

Seychelles

The Seychelles is a country of 88,000 people spread across 115 islands stretched out in the Indian Ocean, northeast of the island of Madagascar. Nearly 95% of the population are Creoles, a people of mixed African, European, Indian, and Chinese origin. Great Britain gained control of the islands from France in 1814, ending a fifty-eight-year period of French rule. Seychelles remained a British colony from 1814 until independence in 1976. Catholics form a majority of the population (88.3%), of which 10.7% are Protestants and 6% are Evangelicals (Pew, 2012), but with evident nominalism that reveals itself in superstition and religious syncretism. Established in 1993, the Evangelical Alliance of Seychelles consists of small independent evangelical churches, notably the Pentecostal Assembly of Seychelles, Christ Holiness Church, Grace and Peace Baptist Church, Assemblies of God Church, Redeemed Christian Church of God, and Deeper Life Bible Church.

There are two main missionary challenges for Evangelicals in Seychelles. First is the need to capitalize on the religious freedom and the religiously fertile ground to evangelize and plant churches. Second is a need for Evangelicals to be proactive in social engagement. Ironically, the country has the highest human development index ranking in the sub-Saharan region and yet has the highest income inequality in the world.

South Sudan

With a population of 10.84 million (World Bank, 2012), South Sudan borders the Republic of Sudan to the north, Ethiopia to the east, Kenya to the southeast, Uganda to the south, the Democratic Republic of the Congo to the southwest, and the Central African Republic to the west. It became an independent state on July 9, 2011, following a referendum and a lengthy war of independence. South Sudan, with its capital in Juba, has its roots in the geopolitical and socioeconomic interests of the Colonial administration that effectively divided the country into North and South in 1930. The policy had two severe consequences: first, polarization (pitting black versus Arab; Christian/African traditional versus Muslim) and secondly, the intensification of the isolation and underdevelopment of the south through northern domination.

Dinka, Nuer, and Shilluk peoples dominate South Sudan. It is a region naturally very difficult to live in, with recurrent flood, drought, and famine. Civil war is also at the heart of the human suffering in this region. Although modern Evangelicalism has its roots during the British rule, Christianity in Sudan dates back to the early centuries of the Christian era because of influences from neighbouring Ethiopia. Following the defeat of the Sudanese Muslim Mahdi, by Anglo-Egyptian forces, Sudan became a British territory until 1956. This political change opened doors for missionaries to launch mission work, leading to the establishment of works by the CMS, American Presbyterians, Verona Fathers (a Catholic community), and Sudan United Mission.

The main challenge for South Sudan Evangelicalism is reconciliation, peace, and unity as this new country struggles to rebuild itself after decades of civil war. Christian communities work to develop a proper balance between tribal particularity and the new national identity. Historically, religion has always been at the heart of the Sudanese politics. Just as Islam unites and defines national identity in the north, so Christianity is intertwined with one's identity, rights, and aspirations in the south. Growing tribalism has affected both the prosperity of the country and the life of the churches. The largest church is the Episcopal Church of Sudan (4.5 million) followed by the Evangelical Presbyterian Church in South Sudan (1 million), the Sudan Interior Church (a Baptist church with 25,000 members and 120 parishes) and The African Inland Church Sudan (123,000) (Johnson 2007). Among the indigenous churches, the Evangelical Church of South Sudan (about 3,500 members) was founded by Sudanese refugees in Kenya who decided to return to war-ravaged South Sudan.

According to the Pew Research Center (2012), about 60% of South Sudanese identify themselves as Christians, and nearly half are Evangelicals scattered in the above churches and small newly planted independent Pentecostal churches, such as the Pentecostal Church of God. The already weak health and education infrastructure was further degraded by war and is a particular focus for churches. Evangelicals are challenged to rise above ethnic walls and to become involved in advocacy, justice, and social concern in mediating God's all-encompassing love in rebuilding a country stricken by extreme poverty due to civil wars, recurrent drought and famine.

Somalia

Located in the horn of Africa, Somalia is bordered in the west by Ethiopia, with Djibouti to the northwest, the Gulf of Aden to the north, and Kenya to the southwest. Its coastline on the Indian Ocean has been the source of much of its trade and strategic interest, while its proximity to Yemen in the north means that it participates in issues of key interest to the Muslim world. Its population of 10.2 million is predominantly Muslim (99%). Historically Somalia was divided between British rule (in the north, since 1884) and Italian control (in the south, since 1889), before it became independent in 1960 (World Bank, 2012). Years of war have devastated the people: war with Ethiopia in late 1970s and civil war since 1991. Recurring drought and famine have also kept the people in dire poverty. Most are completely dependent on foreign food aid to survive, but warlords control the flow of food to the people. Very few Somalis are Christians (less than .01%), and these live in constant fear of discovery and execution. Christian mission organizations, most of them Catholic, ran some schools, medical centers, orphanages and development work, but they were expelled during the Marxist rule in the 1970s. No known evangelical church exists in Somalia. Conditions for evangelism are perhaps most hopeful among the more than 3 million Somali refugees who live outside of their country where they can hear the gospel without fear of persecution. A few native evangelists help with a Bible translation in the Somali language and Christian radio broadcasts.

Tanzania

Christianity entered Tanzania in the mid-nineteenth century, following two consecutive colonial occupations (first German, then British). The Evangelical Lutheran Church in Tanzania (ELCT), with 3 million members, has its roots in the Berlin Mission III (also known as the Evangelical Missionary Society for East Africa) when the first mission station was opened in Dar es Salaam in 1887. In the Southern Highlands, at Ipagika, Berlin I Missionary Society opened a mission station in 1891, and two years later the Leipzig Missionary Society opened a missionary station in the Northern Highlands at Kidia.

The Anglican Church of Tanzania (2 million members) is an offshoot of the United Society for the Propagation of the Gospel and the Church Missionary Society. The Moravian Church in Tanzania (500,000 members) was also established during the same period, the first being at Rungwe in Southern Tanzania in 1891. Christians consist 54% of the population, with the Catholic Church as the largest church, representing about half of all the Christians. Baptist, Africa Inland, and various Pentecostal groups (nearly 20% of the Protestants and Independents) and Evangelicals scattered in the three large denominations make up 18% of the population (Johnson 2007). Tanzania Evangelical Fellowship (TEF) was created in 1993, and has fifty-three organizations. Christian nominalism and a lack of theologically-trained clergy are problems for the Christian majority. The need for improved health care, education, and sustainable rural development are primary concerns that await a strong Christian response.

Uganda

The Anglican Church Missionary Society (CMS) began working in Buganda Kingdom in 1877. By 1914, Christianity had reached much of Uganda, laying a basis for rapid growth in the 1930s through the East African Revival. As a result, the Anglican Evangelical community in Uganda is now one of the largest communities worldwide within the Pan-Anglican communion. Currently the Church of Uganda is an independent Province of the Anglican Community with 8,100,000 followers. Christians account for 84.74% of the population, with Evangelicals making up some 37% (Johnson 2007).

Political instability has led to several civil wars, the longest being the twenty-year struggle against the Lord's Resistance Army (LRA), during which more than 120,000 were killed. Independent indigenous churches, notably the Pentecostal Assemblies of God, have flourished since the country became independent in 1962, despite persecution under Idi Amin. There are two reasons for this diversification. First, Anglicanism became a kind of state church to the extent that nominalism crippled its evangelistic vision and associated the church with even some corrupt political leaders. Corruption, personal rivalries, and ethnic conflicts have all vitiated the effectiveness of the Church. Secondly, Pentecostalism has provided an alternative authentic Christian spirituality—resonant with the intense spirituality of the East African Revival—for which many otherwise dissatisfied members have sought. As in Kenya, Evangelicalism has yet to make a significant impact on peace building or on care of the poor and the sick, especially HIV-AIDS victims. The socioeconomic, political, and moral life of the nation does not reveal the presence of a transforming Christian social vision.

General Conclusion

Despite the rapid and consistent growth in East African Evangelicalism, four major missiological challenges still confront the churches. The most acute is systemic poverty. The combined effects of drought, famine, civil war, failed state-enforced sociopolitical and economic policies, and corruption and poor governance all have exacerbated human suffering in East Africa. Evangelicals can make a significant contribution to the fight against poverty and can influence the development of a fuller vision of responsible governance. One can only imagine the possibilities if the Christian majority in most East African countries were united around a common goal, searching for the most effective ways to expand common ground for mutual enrichment, reformation, and betterment of the life of the poor. The region's problems cannot be addressed with emergency foreign aid alone. Evangelicals might make a huge contribution to translating the all-encompassing love of God into action if they nurtured each other's strengths through common prayer, study, planning, and works. The united exploration of sound Christian social thought/public policy thought that addresses contemporary missiological issues in the region—poverty, leadership, public policy analysis (health, education, development, gender, globalization, and so forth)—is an essential challenge.

Secondly, the community-building capacity of Evangelical Christians is implicit in the realization of their own theologies of the divine gift of unity in Christ, which relativizes human-made differences. A sense of God-given ethnic innocence would be a real contribution to the area. Evangelicals need to be alert to the damage being caused to the unity and distinctiveness of the church as the unique body of Christ by excessive ethnic self-consciousness. Even in countries where they are in a minority, Evangelicals can make a meaningful contribution in the dialogue for a balance between ethno-linguistic particularity and national unity. The question of ethnic self-determination has been intertwined with much of East Africa's sociopolitical turmoil. The credibility of any federal-regional political system hinges upon the maintenance of a constitutionally inclusive, transparent, and sustainable distribution of power between the center and the regional states through a democratic process that allows for a meaningful dialogue for the mutual and common benefit of all. National unity is undermined by fear of each other and can be poisoned by vengefulness and paternalism. Unless these walls of fear and suspicion are transcended with genuine reconciliation and honestly negotiated sharing of power, they will make national unity very superficial and diminish the ground for mutual flourishing. In the healing process and in the genuine effort to resist resentment, exclusivism or neo-paternalism, East African Evangelicals (particularly in Ethiopia, Kenya, Rwanda, Burundi, South Sudan) are called to show an alternative way. The church lives neither for the north nor for the south. In living for Christ, she becomes the sign of the alternative community—the community of God, redeemed out of all tribes and languages and from all walks of life.

Thirdly, there is a great need for mature theological leadership. With the exception of Somalia and Eritrea, East African Evangelicals now enjoy unprecedented freedom. The pressing question is whether there is mature leadership to guide its current freedom towards healing, reconciliation, and reformation. There is a need to develop a local theology, authentically East-African, deeply rooted in evangelistic biblical theology to sustain the current evangelical growth. Theology has to be local (with global hermeneutical considerations), contextual and missional but must be rooted in the invariable truth of the Scriptures. Theological reflection occurs as a natural outcome when the church faithfully and thoughtfully lives out its missionary mandate.

Finally, there is the unfinished task: mission to the unreached peoples, particularly Muslims in Djibouti, the Comoro Islands and Mayotte as well as to Hindus in Mauritius. The barriers to this in some countries are political, but in others merely a matter of resources and focus.

Bibliography and Further Reading

Figures are taken from The World Christian Database (WCD)

Freston, Paul, *Evangelicals and Politics in Asia, Africa, and Latin America*, New York: Cambridge University Press, 2001.

Harris Ostwald, Connie, "A Deeper Look at Poverty: Challenges for Evangelical Development Workers," *Transformation: An International Journal of Holistic Mission Studies*, 26: 2 (April), 130–145, 2009.

Haustein, Jörg and Emanuele Fantini, "Introduction: The Ethiopian Pentecostal Movement—History, Identity and Current Socio-Political Dynamics," *PentecoStudies* 12:2, 150–161, 2013.

Johnson, Todd, ed. World Christian Database, Leiden: Brill, 2007 (et. seq.).

Kubai, Anne, "Post-Genocide Rwanda: The Changing Religious Landscape," *Exchange* (April) 36:2, 198–214, 2007.

Ranger, T. O., *Evangelical Christianity and Democracy in Africa*, Oxford: Oxford University Press, 2008.

Stoneman, Timothy H.B., "An "African" Gospel: American Evangelical Radio in West Africa, 1954–1970," *New Global Studies*, 1:1 (October), 3–26, 2007

World Bank; International Finance Corporation, "Doing Business in Hargeisa 2012." Washington, DC., 2012 https://openknowledge.worldbank.org/handle/10986/13417 License: CC BY-NC-ND 3.0 IGO, accessed 26 June 2014.

Dr. Girma Bekele is adjunct professor of Missions and Development Studies at Wycliffe College in the University of Toronto, Canada, and visiting professor of Global Mission, Covenant Theological Seminary, St. Louis, Missouri. He has worked in relief and development both as practitioner and consultant, and currently resides in Toronto, where he worships and ministers at the Ethiopian Evangelical Church in Toronto.

Evangelical Impact in Kenya: Heart and Mind Combine in Higher Education

A university in the suburb of Karen near the Kenyan capital of Nairobi is offering its students more than just an academic education. "We seek to be a learning community that practices loving God and neighbor with heart and mind," says Dankit Nassiuma, professor and vice-chancellor at Africa International University (AIU).

The university's professors strive to integrate their evangelical faith with their disciplines in seven departments: theology, business administration, finances and accounting, development studies, psychology and counseling, entrepreneurship, and education.

AIU's roots go back to the 1970s when a Nigerian church leader, Byang Kato, had a vision for a higher level of training for African pastors. He had already made arrangements to start a francophone graduate school in Bangui, Central African Republic, before he died in a swimming accident in 1975.

From there the vision expanded to an English-language counterpart for anglophone Africans. Nairobi Evangelical Graduate School of Theology (NEGST) began in 1983 with four students. The student body and the programs offered grew, and in 2011 the school was awarded a university charter. To reflect the diversity of its programs and students the school changed its name to Africa International University.

The student body continues to grow, and AIU now attracts students from many African countries. In addition to undergraduate programs, the school offers doctoral degrees in Biblical studies, intercultural studies, and theological studies, as well as a doctorate of ministry. Another francophone AIU campus began offering courses in 2011 in Niamey, Niger.

AIU is not the first Christian university in Kenya. Daystar University, with a current student population of 4,400, traces its roots to Zimbabwe when South African Motsoko Pheko and American missionaries Donald and Faye Smith cofounded Daystar Publications in 1964. With conflict brewing in Zimbabwe, the operation moved to Zambia and then relocated its headquarters to Kenya in 1974.

The ministry, then known as Daystar Communications, began offering courses in communications in downtown Nairobi. The course offerings steadily grew until Daystar became a Christian liberal arts university that now attracts students from all over Africa, plus Asia and North America. They study in fifteen undergraduate programs, at the master's level, and in doctoral disciplines.

Daystar was founded on the "principle of nurturing servant leaders for the transformation of the church and society," says James Kombo, deputy vice-chancellor of academics. A promotional video boasts that many of Africa's leading figures in media, the corporate world, sports, and service received their educational grounding at Daystar.

—Debra Fieguth

The Church in Africa is growing in leaps and bounds. Christians make up 54% of the population of Tanzania.
Photo: The Langham Partnership

EVANGELICALS IN NORTHERN AFRICA AND EGYPT

By Duane Alexander Miller

Indigenous populations in the countries of North Africa are often called Arabs. It is an ascription which is neither accurate nor, in many cases, welcome, so it is necessary to differentiate between arabophone peoples and Arabs. While almost all the indigenous peoples of North Africa are arabophone, there are substantial groups of Copts and Berbers who are not ethnic Arabs. As individuals convert to Islam for various reasons, the connection to their original ethnic community is sometimes lost and they have become Arabized in their language and customs. While labeling themselves as Arabs, they may have little or no actual genetic connection to the original bearers of Arab/Islamic imperialism in the seventh or eighth centuries. Nevertheless, the terms Arab and Berber may for statistical purposes be indistinguishable, but this is not to say that there are not important historical and cultural distinctions.

History and Composition

North Africa was the center of the Christian world from the second to the fifth centuries, a region which produced such influential church fathers as Augustine of Thagaste, Cyprian of Carthage, and Tertullian. The tale of the martyrdom of Saint Perpetua and her companions in the third century spread far and wide and encouraged Christians throughout the Mediterranean region to stand firm in their faith in the midst of persecution. With the decay of the Western Roman Empire, and the invasions of the Vandals and then the Arabs, however, the Church of North Africa virtually vanished.

How such a vibrant community could entirely die out is one of the more difficult questions of church history. Some of the factors suggested in the scholarly historical literature include a lack of monastic foundations which are important in the churches in Egypt and Ethiopia, the concentration of Christians in cities rather than villages, the Donatist schism, and the predominant use of Latin in the church as opposed to the indigenous languages (Shenk 1993; Daniel 2010). It is important to note that—culturally and in the resolution of theological and ecclesiastic disputes—the churches in Roman North Africa looked to the bishop of Rome for leadership, and not to the bishop of Alexandria.

Whatever the precise reasons may have been for the decline, by the time of the modern missionary movement there was effectively no North African indigenous church. The major strategies used by Evangelical and Protestant missionaries in other parts of what is today considered the Arab world could therefore not be used. That strategy, which was termed by Vander Werff (1977) the "via the Eastern Churches strategy" and by Blinco (1998) "the Great Experiment," recognized that direct evangelization of Muslims under Ottoman rule was both dangerous and quite often illegal. Missionaries therefore sought to revive and reform in an evangelical mould the ancient churches of the East with the expectation that the indigenous Christians would then evangelize Muslims. In North Africa, where the ancient churches had become extinct, this was not a possibility, except in Egypt, where converts from the Coptic Orthodox Church formed a first generation of Evangelicals.

In North Africa, therefore, a number of pioneer missionaries attempted to revive the extinct faith amid the relics of churches and Christian tombs in ancient towns. Charles Marsh of the Plymouth Brethren left a record of his lonely missionary career in *The Challenge of Islam*. One of his daughters, Daisy Marsh, grew up and ministered in Algeria until 1970. Being fluent in Amazygh, the dialect of the ancient indigenous Berbers of the Kabyl egion, Daisy used Christian radio to broadcast in that language from France rom 1973 through 1990 (Abu Banaat 2006).

Other pioneers in North Africa were Lilias Trotter (1853–1928, in 1888 he founder of the Algiers Mission Band), and agents of the new evangelical mission agencies (such as the North Africa Mission, Southern Morocco Mission, London Jews Society, and Radio School of the Bible). The Algerian War of Independence (1954–1962) saw the departure of that country's expatriate Christians. The Protestant Church of Algeria, known by its acronym EPA (Eglise Protestante d'Algérie), was established in 1972. This denomination, which races its origins back to early missionary work of French and then later American Methodists, was de-registered by the Algerian government in 1990. Despite attempts at reestablishment, many of its churches were forced to close until 2011, when the denomination regained official recognition.

The Coptic Evangelical Organization for Social Services (CEOSS) is helping women in Egypt to receive an education.
Photo: CEOSS

Egypt

Egypt has its own cherished tradition of ancient Christianity, tracing the oming of the gospel back to Saint Mark. The indigenous ancient church is alled the Coptic Orthodox Church. The word Copt is derived from the ancient Greek name of the country (Aigyptios). Copt then, is an ethnic, cultural, and linguistic term, and the Copts are an African people, not a Semitic people like later migrants such as the Arabs or Hebrews, direct descendants of the builders of the pyramids and the Sphinx. With the arrival of Islam in the seventh century and the imposition of dhimmitude and the jizya, a tax demanded of non-Muslims living under Islamic rule, the church gradually declined. Many Copts were Arabized and converted to Islam. Nonetheless, the Coptic Orthodox Church survived and—though under intense pressure—is today the largest indigenous Christian Church in the Middle East.

In the nineteenth century, the reforms of Muhammad Ali of Egypt meant that the Copts were no longer orced to pay the jizya and Protestant missions started to minister in Egypt. The Presbyterian mission of the American Board resulted in the founding of an actual evangelical denomination in the country called the Evangelical Church of Egypt (Synod of the Nile), which became officially independent in 1958. Presently, it has some eight presbyteries and about 250 congregations worldwide, though these figures may well decline domestically as Christian emigration from Egypt increases. One of the iconic ministries of the Presbyterians was the rental of a riverboat used to travel up and down the Nile, enabling the missionaries to distribute tracts and portions of scripture to enquirers.

The Anglican Church Mission Society (CMS) attempted establishment in 1818 but abandoned the field in 1862, only to return in the 1880s. Important events in the history of CMS ministry include the founding of the Harpur Memorial Hospital in Cairo and the career of the brilliant evangelical Anglican missionary and scholar, W. H. Temple Gairdner (1873–1928). With his colleague, Douglas Thornton, Gairdner rented a house near the city center from which they engaged in apologetics and lively intellectual discussions with the local educated Muslims. Gairdner also wrote plays in Arabic on biblical-Qur'anic figures such as King David and the Patriarch Joseph.

The Anglican mission, originally under the supervision of the Jerusalem bishopric, eventually became an independent Diocese of Egypt, North Africa, and the Horn of Africa, which continues to identify itself with the evangelical Low Church tradition of the CMS missionaries who helped found it. Individuals connected to the Presbyterian mission went on to found one of the most well-respected universities in the arabophone world—the American University in Cairo (Sharkey 2008). The late nineteenth and early twentieth centuries also saw the arrival and growth of other, smaller missions, such as that of the Assemblies of God, Baptists, Brethren, and Seventh-Day Adventists. All these efforts among the Coptic ethno-linguistic group make it appropriate to refer, therefore, to Evangelical Copts or the Coptic Evangelical Church.

Counting Christians

Because almost all of the indigenous Evangelicals in North Africa are (however nominal) converts from Islam, firm numbers are difficult to define. The number of Algerian Evangelicals present in Algeria around the year 1990 was very low. The combination of a number of factors, however, has made conversion to Christianity (mostly to Evangelicalism, but some to Catholicism) in Algeria one of the more significant movements from Islam to Christianity in the world today. Estimates of Christians in Algeria range between twenty thousand and eighty thousand, with somewhere around forty thousand being a reasonable compromise. The factors of conversion include Bible translation, the central role of indigenous leadership and vision, use of media, and personal contact with potential converts.

As may also be seen among Iranian converts, a key factor is that Islam is an Arabizing religion, while Christianity honors the local pre-Islamic culture and language (in this case, Berber) and does not force converts to choose Arabic names or pray in Arabic. That some of their ancestors in the days of the early Church may well have been Christians appears to be of importance to some of these new Christians. One early Berber convert explained "Islam is for the Arabs and not for Kabyles. I believe in God Almighty and in Jesus Christ. Our religion today is, as it always has been—The Cross" (Marsh 1980:157). By comparison, with about three hundred members apiece, Libya and Tunisia have only small numbers of indigenous Evangelicals. Moroccan Evangelicalism (with approximately two thousand members) experienced some growth through the 1990s but has lately stagnated. Western Sahara, which is occupied by Morocco, has a very small number of indigenous Evangelical Christians, if any.

The number of Christians in Egypt is a contested and politically sensitive topic. The population of Egypt has skyrocketed since 1900 when it was in the single-digits of millions. Estimates of the population today place it at above eighty million in a country that does not produce enough food or petroleum to meet domestic demand. Estimates of the Christian population of Egypt range between 6 and 20%, most of whom are Coptic Orthodox. The Evangelical-Protestant population is likely less than 1% of the entire population (WCE). The World Christian Encyclopedia estimates 42,000 "hidden Muslim believers in Christ" as of 1995, a number which to local observers seems high. Patrick Johnstone estimates some 10,000 Muslim-background believers (MBBs) in-country (Operation World).

Concerns and Issues

In North Africa and Egypt, conversion from Islam to Christianity, even where not technically illegal, remains dangerous and can lead to persecution from family members, the religious community, and the state. Even where the state does not actively persecute a convert, the authorities likewise may not protect the convert from harm.

The so-called Arab Spring has not been kind to the new Christians, as some of them call themselves, of North Africa. Rather than ushering in a period of greater human rights and freedom of religion, the opposite has taken place as traditionalist Islamic political parties (some with their own militias) have gained in influence.

The monarchy of Morocco has managed to stay in power, but the toppling of the regime of Muammar Gadhafi in Libya led to great instability in a country that is close to having the status of a failed state. In 2013 a church in Benghazi was burned down and, as in Egypt, severe economic problems have produced a pronounced increase in crime, including crimes targeted specifically at Christians. Meanwhile, tourism, one of the key sources of income for Egyptians, has deteriorated. The lack of political stability in the region and the increasing sway of Islamist politicians who endorse intolerant formulations of the shari'a are of grave concern to Christians in the region.

As may be seen in the Eglise Protestante d'Algérie's lengthy and difficult struggle for recertification, religious freedom remains one of the greatest concerns for the Evangelicals of North Africa. In 2010 Morocco ex elled some eighty foreign Christians from the country, alleging that some of them had engaged in proselytism German 2010). Morocco and Algeria technically guarantee freedom of religion, but in practice make speaking bout one's faith with a Muslim very risky. In 2006 Algeria passed an anti-proselytism law, leading to the appearnce of some Christians in court: there is little doubt that here, as in many Islamic countries, national obligations nder the United Nations Charter are honored in the breach.

Christians in North Africa thus live in a frustrating paradox, being told they have freedom of religion while ot being able to speak about it. The ability to ask questions and receive answers over the anonymity of the nternet, therefore, has become an important means of evangelism in North Africa, and indeed the entire Arab vorld. This leads to a different challenge. Christianity has always been a communal religion and important ritals such as baptism and the Lord's Supper cannot take place without the actual presence of living, breathing ellow Christians, gathered together. How does one integrate anonymous inquirers into such a tradition?

As the Christian Church in North Africa matures, there are inevitable difficulties, which are also seen in nigrant churches abroad, related to having a second generation in the church—children whose parents are onverts but who themselves have been raised in Christian households. According to the president of the glise Protestante d'Algérie (EPA), specific difficulties rotate around the right to choose a biblical (and non-Islamic ame) for a child, and not being forced to use family law that is based on shari'a.

Emigration is a final concern, common to all Christians in the Arab world. A veteran missionary with experince in Morocco reported that the churches there lose leaders and potential leaders when the people emigrate ɔ the West (personal correspondence). The further loss of security for Christians in the region after the Arab pring has seen increased emigration from Egypt, something that may well also be the case in other countries ι the region.

Mission

These concerns and difficulties faced by the local churches influence and help determine how they go bout discerning and carrying out their mission in the world. In North Africa, the mission of the churches grows irectly out of their context: many of the problems of converts from Islam living in Islamic countries relate to amily and work (Meral 2008). Choosing names for children is one of the simpler issues compared to the potenally crippling difficulties related to being forced out of employment or to suffering the application of shari'a ι the resolution of matters of family status (inheritance, child custody, marriage laws, etc). Therefore, in some ιstances churches and ministries help train MBBs to start their own businesses.

Identity-advocacy is another facet of the mission and life of some of the churches in North Africa. Converon from Islam to Christianity is taboo and considered a form of social pollution. The traditional punishment for postasy under the shari'a is execution. A *sahiih*—or authentic—hadith of the prophet of Islam states, "Whoever hanges his religion, slay him," which is an instruction taken literally in some communities.

In converting from Islam to Christianity, believers are trying to form a new identity—one which their larger ociety has not previously recognized as being possible. In Islam, political and religious identity are often very osely intertwined, such that betraying Islam is synonymous with betraying Algeria, Morocco, or Tunisia. Some f these Christians, however, are engaging in public discourse, including television, explaining that they are hristians, ex-Muslims, but that they are not traitors to their countries or their people.

Identity advocacy takes two forms. One is evangelism, wherein others are invited to also engage in the aboo act of conversion. Another aspect of identity-advocacy is sharing one's story and experience and explainɪg how it is that these new believers perceive themselves to be loyal to country, community, and family while 'so having departed from Islam for the Christian faith. The rise of Salafi Islam and the higher profile of shari'a dvocates in the governments of these countries after the so-called Arab Spring has made this sort of mission 1 the more difficult and dangerous.

To better represent and safeguard the rights of indigenous Christian communities, five of the main churches in Egypt—the Coptic Orthodox Church, the Catholic Church, the Evangelical (Presbyterian) Church, the Greek Orthodox Church, and the Anglican Church—joined together in 2013 to form the Egypt Council of Churches. The Anglican bishop of the diocese, himself an Evangelical, explained the endeavour in these words: "It is so important that this Council is born at this time while Egypt is going through a very challenging circumstance politically, socially and economically. It means a lot for the churches to face these challenges together with one heart and soul" (Zulu 2013).

The Future

It is noteworthy how many similarities there are between the contemporary evangelical Christians of the region and the local early Christians. Indeed, determining to what extent the church (or "the City of God") and the state ("the earthly city") can or should cooperate, occasioned the writing of that great North African classic Augustine's *City of God*. It is a question that remains relevant today. Early Christians were accused of being disloyal to the empire because they would not undertake what they considered to be an act of idolatry in offering incense to the genius of Caesar. Rather than accept the status quo, North African fathers such as Tertullian countered (in his *Apologeticus*) with a vigorous defense of how Christians were not only good, but the best, citizens of the empire.

Similarly, contemporary conversion in North Africa carries the stigma of not being merely a personal act but a form of social and political treachery. Even the ambiguous and constantly shifting realities regarding property are analogous—the early church experienced years of relative tranquility and was surprised by a sudden outbreak of persecution and expropriation of property. Finally, the close ties between Rome and North Africa in the early church are to some extent relived today in the attachment of the francophone churches of North Africa to France due to migration and greater freedom of religion there. The Coptic Churches in Egypt, by way of comparison, have fewer natural links abroad, and can be overlooked in the West's struggles to deal with the rise of political Islam. There are now more than a million Coptic Orthodox adherents in diaspora around the world.

The future of Christians (evangelical or otherwise) in Egypt and North Africa is very uncertain. There is growth in some regions in terms of people leaving Islam for Christianity (Algeria, Egypt), but there are immense political and economic pressures that make a continuing commitment to the new Christian identity difficult and dangerous. Many converts under pressure revert to Islam or become altogether nonreligious. As with the entirety of the arabophone world, these pressures can also lead to emigration or flight, flows which have decimated the church in countries like Iraq and are currently having a heavy impact on Syria.

The experience of evangelical churches in Iran suggests that the rise of Salafist Islam in North Africa will have two effects. First, it will result in increased persecution and marginalization of indigenous Christians, leading to emigration. Secondly, as Muslims have the chance to live under an ostensibly pure shari'a-based polity they will be able to test empirically the slogan that "Islam is the solution."

In Iran this has led to at least hundreds of thousands of people leaving Islam—some for atheism or agnosticism, and others for Christianity. Contemporary reformationist Islam in North Africa and Egypt does not allow for the separation of the political and the spiritual claims. This is both its strength and its weakness. It is a strength in that it can muster the coercive elements of society to stop the spread of the Christian message. But it is also a weakness because once people doubt the political viability of Islam to deliver a secure and prosperous state, the spiritual and theological claims of Islam may also be called into question.

Dr. Duane Alexander Miller serves on the faculty of both Nazareth Evangelical Theological Seminary in Nazareth, Israel and Saint Mary's University in San Antonio, Texas. His PhD dissertation was "Living among the Breakage: Theology-making and ex-Muslim Christians" (Edinburgh 2013–2014). His main areas of interest are religious conversion from Islam to Christianity and the history of Protestant missions in the Middle East.

Sources and Further Reading

Abu Banaat. "Daisy Marsh: Missionary to the Kabyles." *St Francis Magazine* 2, no. 3 (December 2006), 1–5.

Blincoe, Robert. *Ethnic realities and the church: lessons from Kurdistan: a history of mission work, 1668–1990.* Pasadena, Calif: Presbyterian Center for Mission Studies, 1998.

Carrel, Serge and Mustafa Krim. "'Les relations des protestants algériens avec l'Etat sont en voie de normalization!' confie optimiste Mustapha Krim" at Federation Romanded 'EglisesEvangeliques, 2011 and accessed March 25, 3013. www.lafree.ch/details.php/fr/actualite.html?idelement=1432

Church of the Nazarene (Holy Land). "Situation Assessment." Unpublished report. Jerusalem, 1995.

Daniel, Robin. *This Holy Seed: Faith, Hope and Love in the Early Churches of North Africa.* Silver Spring, MD: Tamarisk Books, 2010.

German, Erik. "Christian aid worker purge? Morocco orders dozens in five cities to be deported." *Christian Science Monitor,* March 11, 2010 and accessed March 26, 2013. *www.csmonitor.com/World/Middle-East/2010/0311/Christian-aid-worker-purge-Morocco-orders-dozens-in-five-cities-to-be-deported*

Guera, George. "The Church Planting Movement among the Kabyle Berbers of Algeria." Guest Lecture, Nazareth Evangelical Theological Seminary, Nazareth, Israel. Dec. 8. 2009.

Johnstone, Patrick; Mandryk, Jason, "Egypt," Operation World, http://www.operationworld.org/egyp, accessed 27 June 2014.

Madany, Bassam. "The New Christians of North Africa and the Insider Movement." *St Francis' Magazine* 5 no. 5 (October 2002): 49–57.

Madany, Shirley W. *Muslims Meeting Christ.* Upper Darby: Middle East Resources, 2005.

Mandryk, Jason, ed. *Operation World,* 7th edition. Biblica/WEC, 2007.

Marsh, Charles R. *The Challenge of Islam.* London: Ark, 1980.

Meroff, Deborah. "God's Time for Algeria: The power of the gospel is stirring souls in a once-impenetrable Muslim nation." *Christianity Today* 45, no. 1 (Jan/Feb 2007): 57.

Miller, Duane Alexander. "The Episcopal Church in Jordan: Identity, Liturgy, and Mission." *Journal of Anglican Studies* 9, no. 2 (November 2011): 134–153.

———. "Renegotiating the Boundaries of Evangelicalism in Jerusalem's Christian Quarter: Christian and Missionary Alliance Church, Jerusalem, 12 February 2010." *Anglican and Episcopal History* 79, no. 2 (June 2010): 185–188.

Rhodes, Matthew. *Anglican Mission: Egypt, a Case Study.* Cambridge: Henry Martyn Center, 2003.

Rowden, Rebecca. *Baptists in Israel: The Letters of Paul and Marjorie Rowden 1952–1957.* Nashville: Fields, 2010.

Sharkey, Heather J. *American Evangelicals in Egypt: Missionary Encounters in an Age of Empire.* Princeton: Princeton University Press, 2008.

Shenk, Calvin E.. "The Demise of the Church in North Africa and Nubia and Its Survival in Egypt and Ethiopia: A Question of Contextualization?" *Mission: International Review* 21, no. 2 (April 1993): 131–154.

Swim, Roy E. *A History of Missions of the Church of the Nazarene.* Kansas City: Nazarene Publishing House, 1936.

Thomas, Jacob. "A New Minority in North Africa." 2007. *www.stfrancismagazine.info/ja/A%20New%20Minority%20in%20North%20Africa%20(18th%20May%202007).pdf*

United Christian Council in Israel. *Celebrating 50 Years of History: 1956–2006.* Jerusalem: UCCI, 2006.

Vander Werff, Lyle L. *Christian mission to Muslims: the Record: Anglican and Reformed approaches in India and the Near East, 1800–1938.* South Pasadena, Calif: William Carey Library, 1977.

World Christian Encyclopedia 1 (WCE). The world by countries: religionists, churches, ministries. Oxford: Oxford Univ. Press, 2001.

Evangelical Impact in Egypt: Reaching the Marginalized

CEOSS helps at-risk children through psychological and emotional support and by providing assistance to families so that children don't have to work.
Photo: CEOSS

The Coptic Evangelical Organization for Social Services (CEOSS) has been reaching out to Egypt's marginalized people since 1950 and now helps about two million people annually. Some 750 staff and 5,000 volunteers make this work possible all over Egypt.

CEOSS seeks to contribute to the transformation of Egyptian society "by nurturing moral and spiritual awareness, enhancing a sense of belonging, promoting respect for diversity, addressing conflict, and advancing social justice for individuals and communities," according to its website.

The organization helps anyone in need regardless of religious faith, but because the country is approximately 90 percent Muslim, most recipients are Muslim. Children at risk (including street children and those working illegally), impoverished women, the disabled, and youth are among the groups for which CEOSS has developed special programs.

Since the revolution of January 2011, work among Egypt's youth has taken on increased significance. Young people, both Muslim and Christian, have come together to discuss the current economic and political situation, forwarding recommendations to the government for a better transition. Before the revolution, intercultural dialogue was difficult, says CEOSS media supervisor Maria Dous. "But now it's becoming easier because they're all working toward the benefit of Egypt."

CEOSS helps at-risk children through psychological and emotional support and by providing assistance to families so that children don't have to work. Nagah, a fifty-two-year-old widow and mother of six, put her young daughter to work selling vegetables because she could not afford to send her to school. When Nagah learned about a project that would pay the school fees, plus provide uniforms and supplies, "I agreed that my daughter could go back to school." Nagah was also trained to improve her business, so "my income has increased, my daughter continues her education, and I can afford the family expenses."

A young family, housing its four children in a mud brick home roofed with tree branches and sticks, lamented the dirt, insects, and rain that kept falling on them. Then the mother, Shadia, discovered she could obtain a CEOSS loan to construct a steel-and-concrete roof. "This year, we are not suffering from the winter cold as we used to in past years. The house also became clean."

CEOSS provides small loans to people in both rural and urban communities so they can start up clothing or hairdressing shops, raise animals to sell their products, and launch many other kinds of businesses. The loans are accompanied by training, so they receive the skills they need to run a business.

Health care, both curative and preventative, is another CEOSS priority. The work in this area includes nutrition for children and mothers, an eye hospital, and a mobile unit that assists the disabled by providing and repairing equipment.

The revolution of January 2011 resulted in significant physical damage as well as emotional needs. Following that chaotic time CEOSS repaired many houses, created hundreds of temporary jobs, trained workers, provided literacy education for almost two thousand women and girls, and built new houses for the very poor.

—Debra Fieguth

EVANGELICALS IN SOUTHERN AFRICA

By John Charles Kerr

Evangelicalism in southern Africa is a mustard seed story. Today's luxuriant growth stems from the tiniest of seeds, cast upon seemingly unpromising ground in the nineteenth century. It is a work, as Ezra would explain, done by our God. This was the brilliant, high-beamed diffusion of faith across the region to which David Livingstone looked when he penned his hopeful, defiant words as he lay castaway at Bambarrê in 1871: "I too have shed light?" (Livingstone 1874, 174).

Livingstone's words, spoken by a man who was at the mercy of slave traders, ring out like almost like prophecy. He was, to his biographers, a failed visionary in almost every venture that he attempted: "In everything he had failed: he had failed as a husband; he had failed as a father; he had failed as a missionary; he had failed as a geographer; he had failed most of all as a liberator" (Seaver 1957, 629). And yet today, southern Africa, where the great missionary-explorer poured out his life, is spoken of as the new center of global Christianity.

Author Philip Jenkins suggests that the twentieth century witnessed "the largest shift in religious affiliation that has ever occurred anywhere." He projects a continuing worldwide boom in faith in the twenty-first century, where "the vast majority of believers won't be white" (Jenkins 2006).

The 2013 report from Gordon Conwell's Center for Global Christianity likewise posits a twenty-year Christian growth trajectory in Africa from 38.7% of the population in 1970 to 49.3% in 2020 (van Klinken 2013). The bulk of this growth will occur in Southern Africa, particularly among renewalist Evangelical Christians, who, though only 18.8 million in 1970, will grow to 226.2 million by 2020. Compare those figures with Livingstone's Africa, and Melvin Hodges's words become prophetic: "There is no place on earth where, if the gospel seed be properly planted, it will not produce an indigenous church" (Hodges 1953, 14).

As president of the Association of Evangelicals for Southern Africa (AEA) and head of Lusaka's Bread of Life Church, Zambian Bishop Joe Imakando attempts to account for this vibrant growth: "We share a message which appeals to people . . . It is spiritual, but also looks after the whole person. . . . We preach the message of Jesus Christ, but we also motivate people and tell them they can excel." A similar note is sounded across the border in probably the largest non-Catholic denomination in Zimbabwe, the Zimbabwe Assemblies of God Africa of Ezekiel Guti (ZAOGA), where "dominant prosperity teachings have arisen from predominantly southern African sources and are shaped by Zimbabwean concerns . . . self-reliance, indigenous business and black empowerment'" (as cited in Imakando 2011).

Indigenizing Ingenuity

Western academics have tended to interpret prosperity teachings as the imposition of foreign fundamentalists, in part because of the disbelief that indigenous developments could be other than "a symptom of backwardness and of incomplete development" (Bompani 2010). "Real" Africans are animists living in grass huts—a judgment which ignores the rapid globalization of the African world, its teeming cities, the urgent pressures of modernization.

The work of Andrew Walls, Bengt Sundkler, and others, however, has demonstrated the indigenizing ingenuity of African religious communities. The prosperity gospel, which receives such broad appeal in today's southern Africa, reads like a replaying of Livingstone's theme of "Commerce and Christianity" for a new age. The University of South Africa's Tinyiko Sam Maluleke speaks of "the wave of creativity" among African Christians, "showing a remarkable knack for contextualization, dynamism and innovation" in a "dynamic, growing, multi faceted and dialectic movement."

Contrary to widespread expectations, Liberation Theology has not mushroomed in the region, though Christian belief and practice continue to grow out of social and economic realities among the poor. In southern Africa, liberation is holistic: it has political and economic implications, but is primarily concerned with deliver ance from supernatural evil. It is a combination that Africans do not seem to find as problematic as their Western associates.

In Mozambique, James Pfeiffer ties such grass-roots ministry to African Independent Churches (now more commonly known as African Initiated Churches, or AICs), and says that the economic crises of the 1990s cre ated a "perilous social environment," which found expression in "heightened fears of witchcraft, sorcery, and avenging spirits [which are] often blamed in Shona ideology for reproductive health problems." Thus people have turned for help to AICs, "which invoke the Holy Spirit to exorcise malevolent agents and then provide community of mutual aid and ongoing protection against spirit threats" (Pfeiffer 2002).

For African leaders such as Imakando, Evangelicalism's growth relates to its implicit ability to bring to gether the economic, the spiritual, the intellectual and the political, and so make life better across the boar for the people of southern Africa. Its mission includes engaging and influencing the prevailing political proces His Association of Evangelicals for Africa, the umbrella body for evangelical churches, has one hundred millio members, making it one of the continent's largest civic organizations. Its mission statement is "to mobilize and empower evangelical churches and agencies for total transformation of Africa through evangelization and e fective discipleship" (Imakando 2011).

In Imakando's words, "We have a lot of clout . . . We can speak for Christians, for the poor, for the unde privileged . . . We have a big following and we make politicians aware. They need votes and they know we hav votes. . . . We educate our people on the qualities of a good leader." Imakando speaks of the growing politic impact of Evangelicalism on his "Christian nation" and predicts that "it will influence the politics of the future In South Africa, Clint Le Bruyns observes a similar weight of influence: "Evangelicals are already participants i public life and can potentially contribute to the healing of a divided and scarred South Africa through their re spective ecclesial and theological capital" (Le Bruyns 2006).

Whether this influence amounts to anything like a prophetic role in speaking into government abuse an corruption—something seldom seen as strength in fractured, individualist Evangelicalism—remains to be see Effective opposition to governments which persecute and intimidate opposition voices requires a sort of unite protest from the Evangelical community that is rare. This can also be perilous terrain in nations where regime are still known to come down on dissent with full, often brutal, force. Dealing with church leaders who a "bought" by oppressive governments is one problem for evangelical partnerships (local or international), as organizing strong support for the victims of oppression and brutality. This sort of truly prophetic role vis-à-v governments of all stripes remains one of Evangelicalism's ongoing challenges and is a source of external c tique of the movement (Filipovic and McCormick 2013). Steps in this direction have been made by NGOs su as African Enterprise.

Political influence aside, deliverance is probably the keynote for the vast majority of churches in Southe Africa: churches which expound messages that "appear simplistically charismatic, visionary, and apocalypt In this thought world, prophecy is an everyday reality, while faith healing, exorcism and dream visions are fu damental" (Jenkins, 2002). There are widespread concerns about the loss of evangelical orthodoxy in Afric Zambia's Victor Chanda (2013), for instance, bemoans the fact that the "Word of Faith . . . has found a home Africa." Chanda notes the similarities between its concept of blessings and curses, built around the role of t prophet and preacher, and traditional African Religion. For Chanda, "the Faith Movement is not based on sour theological and philosophical ground. It is based on unique reading of the Bible which is more esoteric th theological, more Gnostic than Christian." Determining the balance between indigenization and syncretism appears, remains a problem in creating unity of action and belief.

Two Great Tenets

The two great defining tenets of Evangelicalism which are held by virtually all African Independent Church- es and most Protestants are a conversion experience and a high view of Scripture. According to Jenkins (2002):

"The Bible has found a congenial home among communities who identify with the social and eco- nomic realities it portrays and read it not just as historical fact but also as relevant instruction for daily conduct. . . . When observers complain that . . . revival crusades make little explicit reference to evangelical theology, that is partly because pastors can . . . assume their hearers will already know so many of these doctrines."

Even religious philosopher John Mbiti, normally sympathetic to traditional religions, says that a "biblical basis is all that matters for African theology. . . . Nothing can substitute for the Bible." Mbiti is suspicious of im- ported, nonbiblical theological debates, "propagated without full or clear grounding" (in Malukele 1997).

Sources of Growth

What are the origins of such a booming, variegated evangelical church, scattered across a diverse region in a rainbow of expressions which speak for the people themselves? Livingstone's death in a Zambian hut in May 1873 ironically evoked a greater missionary response than his life. Only two years after his death, the Free Church of Scotland reentered the Malawi's highlands and founded the Livingstonia Mission Centre. From that center a wave of evangelism spread across the southern half of the continent. Key figures include: Dr. Rob- ert Laws, head of Livingstonia for four decades, a great missionary strategist; W. A. Elmslie, missionary to the Ngoni people of the Zambezi region (Elmslie 1970); and the dynamic Donald Fraser, missionary to the Tonga and Ngoni tribes. The tribal context seemed often to play into the missionaries' cause: it was fear of the war-like Ngoni, for example, that drove many a tribe into the arms of the missionaries and the gospel. Migrating out of south Africa, these fierce warriors had raided the Tonga along with the Chewa, Henga, and Tumbuka. In fact, Zambia's great Tonga tribe was probably spared assimilation, if not extermination, at hands of the Ngoni by the arrival of Livingstonia missionaries.

Education proved to be the entry ticket for these Zambian tribes. By 1894, Livingstonia had built eighteen mission schools with more than one thousand pupils. By 1906, they had 107 schools with more than three thou- sand pupils (Elmslie 1970). Livingstonia's strong English curriculum, through its Overtoun Institute, began to produce prominent African intellectuals just as it had already begun to produce indigenous evangelists.

Livingstonia sent some of its best representatives to the Bemba people, including John Afwenge Banda, the Chewa evangelist and father of Dr. Hastings Kamuzu Banda, later first president of independent Malawi. Tonga evangelist David Kaunda, followed a year later, building up the Chinsali station and guiding rapid expansion.

The seeds sown at Livingstonia's Overtoun Institution scattered all over East and Central Africa. One of the great breakthroughs was when Livingstonia sent William Koyi, the Xhosa evangelist from Lovedale, South Africa, to preach to the Ngoni in their own language. To everyone's relief, the "wild Ngonis" followed the Tonga lead and put Koyi in charge of the school. Before long, the newly-evangelized Ngoni had produced fifty new hymns with their own flavor.

One of the most inspiring accounts of revival in these early days came under Keswick missionary Donald Fraser. From 1898, Fraser led annual gatherings in Ngoni country for baptism and Holy Communion, with up to ten thousand attending. He witnessed a corporate exodus from old tribal ways into the church in an "African Pentecost," a Christian version of their own traditional First Fruit ceremonies, typified by an urge for purification with individual and group confession.

A decade later, in 1910, the revivalist campaign of Charles Inwood gathered thousands of people.

Mr. Inwood was speaking on the Holy Spirit. At the close of his sermon all was very quiet. He asked for a time of silent prayer, and then called on those willing to receive fullness of Spirit to rise. An elder began to pray and make confession, then another, until two or three were praying together in a quiet voice. (Sundkler and Steed 2000)

Mrs. Fraser recounts, "And then suddenly there came the sound of a rushing mighty wind. It was the thrilling sound of two thousand five hundred people praying audibly, no man conscious of the prayer . . . a mighty volume of tumbling waters" (quoted in Sundkler and Steed, 2000, 824). Among others, the Tumbuka-Henga community, which had been driven to near extinction by the Ngonis, was now truly "saved," in the fullest sense of the word.

Meanwhile, the gospel was moving northward into Zambia's Barotseland from the south. By 1875, French missionary Francois Coillard, of the Paris mission to Lesotho, known by its English name as the Paris Evangelical Missionary Society, or PEMS, was building a mission station among the Lozi. Schooling began for the children of Chief Lewanika. In 1894 Coillard opened a Bible school with four pupils, while the Methodists under John Smith did similar work among the Ila. Baptist congregations in South Africa sent missionaries to the Bible school such as D. D. Doke, a well-known expert in Bantu languages. Frederick Stanley Arnot (1858–1914), a true successor to David Livingstone, arrived in Barotseland with the Plymouth Brethren, walking through Central Zambia, Angola and Katanga, while advancing the gospel and planting mission stations everywhere he went. South African missionary Jules Joseph Adolphe Jalla (1864–1946) reported breakthroughs at Sesheke, Zambia in 1901. Methodist ethnologist and Bible translator, E. W. Smith, arrived in the region in 1902, building up mission stations at Nazal and Kasenga, centers that produced alumni such as David Mibiana, the most powerful first generation preacher of the Zambezi valley.

Lesotho was the starting point for other missionary expeditions. Stephen Hofmeyr, the Boer missionary with Africkaans farmer, Conrad de Buys and his sons, led seven mission expeditions north, from 1872 to 1887. Berlin missionaries Schwellnus and Knothe were joined by trained African evangelists going north from their Mphome Evangelists' school in Venda country. Johannes Madima was one of their students, who later had very effective ministry among the chiefs, the key players in reaching a region with the gospel. David Funzane, educated by the English Methodists in Natal, was a well-known church leader in Venda country.

Such initiatives from the South were curtailed when, in 1890, Cecil Rhodes hoisted the British flag at Fort Salisbury and a full British protectorate was established over the entire region. The chiefs were pushed to the sidelines. Migrants were left with the task of advancing the gospel. An organized trek of some five hundred Mfengu families from Capetown streamed into Zimbabwe, mostly laborers and farmers, settling in Bulawayo. They brought with them a strong, literate Christian community that would produce great evangelical leaders: Gqweni Hlazo; Moses Mfazi, the Mfengu Methodist; John Boyana Radasi, a Mfengu Presbyterian trained in Scotland; Chikala, the son of a Zambian chief; and Jonas Chirembe Chihota. In short, the gospel by 1914 was well entrenched in African communities and was beginning to develop an indigenous voice. Energetic forms of the faith which had considerable impact on South Africa came out of the AICs and the Zionist Churches which gathered at this time around the preaching of missionaries from Zion City, Chicago and (later) the Azusa Street Revival, Los Angeles.

Lesotho was the starting point for other missionary expeditions.

Post-War Development

After World War I, Zambia's Copperbelt became a hub for development. Baptist A. J. Cross came to the mining center of Ndola in 1929 and found that a self-supporting, self-governing native church already flourished among the migrant labor force. Missionary Mabel Shaw and the congregationalists expanded in the north of Zambia. The Open Brethren established the Kalene Hills Mission among the Lunda with Dr. Walter Fisher. Fisher was closely involved with Frederick Stanley Arnot, and the Open Brethren brought spirituality, a healing community, agriculture skills, and adult baptism. The Primitive Methodists and E. W. Smith established strong mission centers among the Ila. A Grass-roots Church Movement sprung up around Alice Lenshina, the illiterate prophetess, who captivated Zambia for a time. The African Methodist Episcopal Church was formed in 1950, a fully Africanized church which would become a major denomination. A church union debate developed among Zambian Congregationalists, Methodists, and Lozi Reformed, resulting in 1965 in the formation of The United Church of Zambia.

In Zimbabwe, the Land Apportionment Act of 1930–1931 was forced through by the small white minority, against some missionary opposition. Mission schools were integrated into the government program. At the same time, partially in response to political disempowerment, Wesleyan Methodists grew nationwide, with the double mandate of caring for both black and white; the Salvation Army grew in the Mazoe Valley, and by 1961 claimed some sixty thousand members; Pentecostalism began to grow. Zimbabwe's Independent Churches produced strong Charismatic leaders like Samuel Mutendi, Johane Masowe, and Johane Maranke.

Namibia, a former German possession, was reached with the gospel by Finnish Lutherans and Martti Rautanene in 1927. Thereafter, the evangelical cause was advanced by a refugee movement. Ombandju refugees, fleeing the Portuguese oppression of Angola, received the gospel under Zacheaus Iihuhwa and became prolific agents for its advancement.

In South Africa, where the multiplication of denominations resulted directly from racial politics and divisive Protestantism, the "Christian Council" was tasked with bringing together the nation's factions under Dutch Reformed leadership. With the defiance campaigns of the 1950s, political protests were widespread. The strong leadership of Dr. J. S. Moroka and Chief Albert Luthuli was needed to rally the Church. Methodist Rev. Seth Mokitimi led the call for peace and goodwill. A timely statement was proclaimed by the evangelical voices in the SACC in 1960: "No one who believes in Jesus Christ may be excluded from any Church on the grounds of his color or race. The spiritual unity among all men who are in Christ must find visible expression in acts of common worship and witness" (quoted in WCC 1961, 48).

Political tensions notwithstanding, there was significant revival among South Africa's black population between 1955 and 1960. In 1900, the number of converts among Africans was about one in four; by the mid-1950s the number of converts had increased to one in two. Dutch Reformed missions grew from eight stations in 1955 to twenty-five in 1960.

A Pentecostal breakaway from the Dutch Reformed Church (DRC) resulted in the Apostolic Faith Mission in 1910, a movement which would enjoy rapid growth across southern Africa. Other growing evangelical churches included the Congregational Mission under Ray Phillips; the Salvation Army; and Methodists, Lutherans, and Pentecostals. The last found the tough Afrikaner community very open to its message, especially when one of the movement's significant international voices, "Mr. Pentecost" David Du Plessis, was so visibly from an old Afrikaner family. The Apostolic Faith Community grew to two hundred thousand under Rev. P. L. LeRoux and his Pentecostal message and experience. A greater surprise was the development of Pentecostalism among the Natal Asian community, usually thought of as homogenously Hindu and Muslim. J. F. Rowlands, a British Pentecostal, founded "Bethdesda" in Durban in 1931. Bethesda grew rapidly, with strong evangelical witness among Asians throughout Natal and Zululand, for a time demonstrating the strongest growth track in the entire region.

South Africa had the most rapid increase in African Initiated Churches (AIC). In 1918 they numbered 26; by 1932, 320; in 1980, 3000. Nicolas Bhengu (1909–1985), the great Zulu preacher and son of a Lutheran pastor, founded the Back to God Crusade in 1950. Related to the Assemblies of God in a loose association of Pentecostal groups, Benghu avoided political wrangling and "with his powerful command of the masses, emphasized the social and moral aspects of his teaching: 'We will only be taken to freedom when we have complete faith in God alone'" (Sundkler and Steed 2000, 837). The white population also had its Charismatic movements, including those associated with Swiss preacher, Johannes Buchler, Scots-Australian John A. Dowie, and prominent revivalists P. S. LeRoux and Edgar Mahon. The take-off period of such AICs was between 1940 and 1960; by 1970, they were reaching more than 4.5 million members across South Africa and nearly 17 million by 1995.

Churches and the Struggle for Independence

It was only a matter of time until the oppressive governmental systems generated by the European empire-builders gave way to independence movements. All church bodies during the 1950s and 1960s found it a most challenging task to speak the gospel of grace into an increasingly astringent climate. Zambia's first president was Dr. Kenneth Kaunda, born in 1925 as the son of Rev. David Kaunda, who had built the solid Presbyterian church of north-west Zambia. The personality of President Kaunda dominated relations among the churches. He came from a healthy Christian tradition and was a friend of the ecumenical movement.

Meanwhile, Zimbabwe struggled under the unsuccessful Central African Federation. When Zambia and Malawi became independent, Ian Smith's illegal declaration of independence by his own government instigated civil war. Wesleyan Pastor Canaan Banana became state president from 1980–1988, seeking to marry African socialism with Christian theology in Zimbabwe. Church leaders struck a forum that proclaimed such reconciliation was possible. Indeed, during these volatile times, the church made a major contribution toward retaining a semblance of national unity.

Meanwhile, in Mozambique, with its long-entrenched Portuguese colonial state, secret police, the International and State Defence Police (PIDE-DGS), and the Catholic Church, the Colonial army was beefed up to suppress the FRELIMO liberation movement. Ironically, many of the leaders of FRELIMO, with Charismatic Eduardo Mondlane, emerged from church school systems, including that established by the Swiss Presbyterians. After 1964, terror was the prevailing mode; whole villages and communities were torched, tortured, and destroyed. There was a great exodus of church and community leaders during this time.

In South Africa, the Sharpeville massacre of 1960, where sixty-nine Africans were killed by the police, brought the churches together in a call for unity and equality. Their forward-thinking proposals were rejected by the government. It was left to Dr. Beyers Naude to start the Christian Institute, a protest and reform movement against racialism and political and economic inequality.

The Christian Institute supported a strong evangelical response to racist legislation for more than a decade. There was, however, the need for extended confession and discussion before Evangelicals could overcome their differences. Balcomb, for example, identifies no fewer than four evangelical approaches to the liberation struggle: radical open struggle; conservative quietism more interested in fighting theological "liberalism" than in upsetting the status quo; "Third Way" reconciliationists such as Michael Cassidy; and "alternative communitarians," such as revivalist Nicholas Bhengu (Hutchinson and Wolffe 2012).

In the South African Council of Churches, Methodist John Rees was followed by Desmond Tutu as chair in 1976, two strong leaders with prophetic social concern. Tutu later led the church through the liberation struggle, with some inspired eloquence as part of the mix: "Many in the black community ask why I still waste my time talking to whites and I tell them that our mandate is biblical. Moses went to Pharaoh several times even if he knew that it was futile" (Sundkler and Steed 2000, 987).

The Kairos Document of September 1985 called upon "all who bear the name Christian to reject state theology, and church theology in favor for prophetic theology"—a theology which had a biblical understanding of structural inequality and discriminatory laws (Sundkler and Steed 2000, 987). Evangelicals produced their own statement in 1986, dissociating themselves from the State-approved Rhema Church and its word-faith theology.

Finally, in February 1990, Nelson Mandela was freed after twenty-seven years in jail. A national initiative for reconciliation attended by the representatives of eighty-five churches was undertaken resulting in the Rustenburg Declaration. Fundamentally, the initiative was based on a confession of:

> **our sin . . . our part in the heretical policy of apartheid which has led to such extreme suffering for so many in our land. We denounce apartheid, in its intention, its implementation and its consequences, as an evil policy, an act of disobedience to God, a denial of the Gospel of Jesus Christ and a sin against our unity in the Holy Spirit. (Rustenberg Declaration, November 1990)**

David Bosch (1929–1992) represented the evangelical tradition in the DRC, before his tragic death in a car accident. As Dean of Theology at UNISA, general secretary of South African Missiological Society and editor of *Missionalia*, Bosch was an internationally acclaimed missiologist with a heart for social reform. Through the inspired leadership of such men as Bosch and Willie Jonkers, bloodshed was averted as majority rule came to South Africa, and the basis laid for a church-led reconciliation process.

In Namibia, by 1969, the Liberation struggle had taken hold led by Sam Nujoma's SWAPO. Lutherans numbered 320,000, Catholics 120,000, Dutch Reformed 50,000, and Anglicans 20,000. The churches joined the liberation struggle. Leonard Auala became a very influential leader who faced Prime Minister Vorster of South Africa in a memorable showdown in 1970. It was a decisive moment for the public expression of Christian values regarding human rights and the equality of all people. It would be twenty years, however, before the fruit of the exchange was fully seen and Namibia achieved its independence.

Post Independence Southern Africa

Two developments stand out in assuring the ongoing growth of Evangelicalism in post-independence Africa. First in 1960, Vatican II gave the Bible new status with its "Dogmatic Constitution on Divine Revelation." Now was the time for "translations in every language . . . in cooperation with separated brethren." It was a new day for Bible translation, with a new understanding of "meaning by meaning translation" (*Dei Verbum* 1965). Even among the extensive Catholic populations of Southern Africa, therefore, key evangelical doctrines are increasingly common. Secondly, the Association of Evangelicals in Africa (AEA) was founded in 1966, with inerrancy as the fundamental, *Afroscope* its journal and Tokunboh Adeyemo as general secretary.

A structure could now develop which would see increasing numbers of evangelical leaders trained to graduate level in Africa, rather than in Europe or North America. The Theological Commission's Accrediting Council for Theological Education in Africa helped set standards for education, and both francophone and anglophone graduate schools emerged. The Association now supports both the Africa International University (Kenya) and a range of seminaries in southern Africa. These include: Bible Institute of South Africa and George Whitefield College (both in Cape Town, South Africa); Nazarene Theological College (Honeydew, South Africa); South African Theological Seminary (Johannesburg, South Africa); the Central Africa Baptist College and Seminary; and the Theological College of Central Africa (both in Zambia). These, and a vast array of church and denominational colleges and institutes, train pastors for one of the world's now definitional concentrations of Christian churches and communities. While "[t]here is no single southern Christianity, any more than there is such a thing as European or North American Christianity," Jenkins notes:

These newer churches preach deep personal faith and communal orthodoxy, mysticism, and puritanism, all founded on clear scriptural authority. . . . For better or worse, the dominant churches of the future could have much in common with those of medieval or early modern European times. (Jenkins 2006)

This concentration of biblical Christianity now has observable effects not only on the rest of Africa, but, through the global networks of related denominations and migration flows, into the rest of the world. The input of African dioceses into international divisions within the Anglican Church is a notable case.

Conclusion

David Livingstone's journals were prophetic. He had no way of knowing how overwhelming a harvest would follow his sowing:

I was permitted to sow the good seed among them, and I believe that seed is not dead. It is the living word of the living God. There are few souls which can withstand its force, and no hatred, howsoever deep, can quench its power. (quoted in Schapera, 1963, 303)

As the twenty-first century unfolds, his call to ongoing evangelical missions continues to resound. This is the way forward for the Evangelical Movement which he birthed:

The spirit of mission is the spirit of our master, the very genius of His religion. A diffusive philanthropy is Christianity itself. It requires perpetual propagation to attest its genuineness. (quoted in Schapera, 1963, 612)

Dr. John Charles Kerr has served at Trans-Africa Theological College in Kitwe, Zambia for eighteen years. He and his wife, Ruth, combine teaching and administration with ministry to all corners of Zambia. He is involved in sponsoring orphan care and community schools, conservation agriculture, and skills training. His book *Hidden Riches Among the Poor* chronicles highlights of his Africa experience.

Bibliography and Further Reading

Bompani, Barbara. "Religion and Development from Below: Independent Christianity in South Africa," *Journal of Religion in Africa* 40 (2010): 307–330.

Chanda, Victor. "The Word and the Spirit: Epistemological Issues in the Faith, Health and Wealth Movement in Zambia." Doctoral Dissertation in Theology, UNISA, 2013.

Elmslie, W. A. *Among the Wild Ngonis*. London: Cass & Co., 1970 3rd ed., LMS, 2004.

Filipovic, Jill, and Ty McCormick. "Angels and Demons." Foreign Policy, December 20, 2013. http://www.foreignpolicy.com/articles/2013/12/19/the_power_struggle_is_only_beginning_south_sudan#sthash.OX9Zea68.I1k5vX2e.dpuf

Hodges, Melvin. *The Indigenous Church*, Springfield, MO: Gospel Publishing House, 1953.

Hutchinson, Mark and John Wolffe. *The Cambridge Short History of Global Evangelicalism*. Cambridge: CUP, 2012.

Imakando, Joe. 2011. In the *Daily Maverick* and accessed November 29. www. dailymaverick.co.za.

Jenkins, Philip. *The Next Christendom: The Rise of Global Christianity*. New York: Oxford University Press, 2002.

———. "Believing in the Global South." *First Things*. Institute of Religion and Public Life, (December 2006). *www.firstthings.com*

Le Bruyns, Clint. "Can Any Good Come from Evangelicals?" *Religion and Theology* 13, no. 3 (2006), 341–358.

Livingstone, David, and H. Waller, ed. *The Last Journals of David Livingstone in Central Africa*, New York: Harper & Bros., 1874.

Maluleke, Tinyiko Sam. "Half a Century of African Christian Theologies." *Journal of Theology for Southern Africa* 99 (1997): 3–4.

Maxwell, David. "Witches, Prophets and Avenging spirits: The Second Christian Movement in North-East Zimbabwe." *Journal of Religion in Africa* 25, no. 3 (1995), 309–339.

Paul VI, Dei Verbum: Dogmatic Constitution on Divine Revelation, November 18, 1965, http://www.vatican.va/archive/hist_councils/ii_vatican_council/documents/vat-ii_const_19651118_dei-verbum_en.html, accessed 27 June 2014.

Pfeiffer, James. "African Independent Churches in Mozambique: Healing the Afflictions of Inequality." *Medical Anthropology Quarterly*, 16, no. 2 (June 2002): 176–199.

Schapera, I., ed. *Livingstone's African Journals*. London: Chatto & Windus, 1963.

Seaver, George. *David Livingstone: His Life and Letters*. New York: Harper & Brothers, 1957.

Sundkler, Bengt and Christopher Steed. *A History of the Church in Africa*. London: Cambridge University Press, 2000.

van Klinken, Adrian. "On the Growth of Christianity in Africa." June 12, 2013.

World Council of Churches (WCC) (1961), The "New Delhi Report," The Third Assembly of the World Council of Churches 1961, Geneva: WCC.

Evangelical Impact in South Africa: Word, Deed, and Impact Bring Change

An organization that started with a call to evangelize the cities of Africa also played a key role in bringing democracy to apartheid South Africa.

In 1961 a young Michael Cassidy felt a burden not only for his home country but for all of Africa. He set about visiting thirty-one African cities. The following year he formed African Enterprise (AE), whose mission statement is "to evangelize the cities of Africa through word and deed in partnership with the church." AE formed teams in South Africa and other African countries, and in 1971 Festo Kivengere, a well-known Ugandan evangelist, became joint leader of the ministry with Cassidy. AE now works in ten African countries.

Although the emphasis remained on evangelism, a focus on reconciliation and deed developed. In 1985 Cassidy launched the National Initiative for Reconciliation (NIR), which called together church leaders from a range of denominations and races. The outcome? A concerted drive for justice, peace, and reconciliation in apartheid South Africa.

Racial conflict was rife during those years of apartheid. In a country that had an official policy of racial segregation and where the majority of the population was relegated to a lower-class citizenship and violence was rampant, Cassidy and his team encouraged and worked toward racial reconciliation.

In 1996, two years after the first democratic elections, AE launched the Kolobe Lodge Dialogue weekends, which gathered together political leaders from virtually all political parties. The object was to create an opportunity for them to talk to each other—and listen to each other—some for the very first time in their lives. In workshop forums they shared grievances and life stories and were often able to come to a point of repentance forgiveness, and healing.

In the weeks leading up to the 1994 elections, when black South Africans were permitted to vote for the first time ever, AE played a critical role in convincing Zulu Chief Mangosuthu Buthelezi and his Inkatha Freedom Party (IFP) to participate in the elections after he had refused to do so unless special power would be given to the Zulu nation.

The specter of civil war hung over the country at that time. An international mediation team failed to bring the sides together. Then Cassidy invited Washington Okumu, a Kenyan economist, political scientist, and former diplomat who played a vital role in keeping the negotiations alive, to meet with Buthelezi.

Simultaneously, on April 17 some twenty-five thousand people met at King's Park Stadium in Durban. Observers described The Jesus Peace Rally, as it was known, as one of the most extraordinary prayer meetings South Africa has ever seen.

Okumu presented Buthelezi with a proposal that turned the intransigent chief around. Many who were either at the prayer rally or had heard of it saw Buthelezi's about-face as a miracle and a direct result of prayer.

On April 27 peaceful elections took place, with Nelson Mandela elected as the first black president of South Africa. Journalists reporting on the election described a "holy hush" in newsrooms as they wrote about the results. Headlines in South African newspapers declared it a miracle the election had taken place peacefully.

Twenty years later, AE focuses on evangelism and working with children and youth, as well as on continued healing and reconciliation. Although Cassidy remains involved, Stephen Mbogo of Kenya now heads AE.

In the summer of 2013 a Great Mission, organized by AE Kenya, in partnership with churches in Kitale and beyond, brought together more than five hundred church workers and evangelists from all over Kenya, South Africa, Malawi, the United Kingdom, the United States, and Canada.

AE used its method of stratified evangelism, which is a way of bringing the gospel to all levels of society, to reach the people of Kitale during the Great Mission. This included holding about one thousand meetings in the form of door-to-door visits, open air meetings, public rallies, and forums tailored to specific communities including schools and universities.

Many testimonies were recorded during the week of the Great Mission,[1] which reached at least 116,300 people with the gospel, and feedback indicated at least 7,390 people made decisions for Christ.

—Debra Fieguth

---

1. http://www.africanenterprise.com/index.php/en/australia/news-media/news/.

EVANGELICALS IN WESTERN AFRICA

By Mark Hutchinson

Western Africa has a long history of contact with Europe; indeed, it has been a place of significance for Evangelicals from their earliest years. A location for conflict with the French, Portuguese, Dutch, and Spanish empires, British exploration opened trading ports along the coast from the 1600s, resulting in the gradual connection of the region into the transatlantic trade routes then opening up in North and South America. As the shortest distance between one side of the Atlantic and the other (Senegal is less than half the distance from Brazil than London is to New York), favorable trade winds drove a triangular trade among African kings with a taste for European goods, Brazilian plantation owners dependent on African slaves, and Europeans hungry for cheaply-grown American-grown cash crops and Canadian cod.

Trade and Trouble

The availability of good harbors and rivers that were navigable into the hinterland thus determined European engagement with Africans on this "Windward Shore," hence the sites of Banjul (in Gambia), Bissau, and Freetown. In the latter, the British gradually supplanted the Portuguese, building trade forts or factories to exploit the riches of the turbulent inland politics of African kingdoms. "European willingness to sell such strategic items as muskets, gunpowder, and iron created clear military and economic advantages for those societies willing to engage in trade" (Lovejoy 1983, 16), while the expansion of inland kingdoms made it a necessity for survival on the coast. The invasion of plundering Mani, for example, and then the conquering Islamic Fula, had already disrupted Sierra Leone and Nigeria long before the British arrived. The trade, however, grew rapidly as a means for expansionary African kingdoms to consolidate and support their military and political control, with Dahomey (later Benin), the Sokoto and Bornu Caliphates and the Toucouleur empire (or "Tijaniyya Jihad") states also using it as a means of subjugation or "as a means of converting non-Muslims . . . as a form of religious apprenticeship for pagans" (Lovejoy 1983, 16). European trade, therefore, sparked a cycle of increasing African violence (Baum 1999, 111). The barriers of jungle and desert, the human boundaries of slavery, and Islam and traditional religions, would be determinative for the spread of Christianity in West Africa.

Enlightenment and Evangelicalism went hand in hand. As with missions to Aboriginal people in Australia, the Moravians—with their reputation for effectiveness in situations where other churches failed—were often the groundbreakers for European missions. Born in Ghana and educated in Copenhagen, Christian Jacob Protten, for example, was the grandson of the Ga Chief Ashangmo. Having met Zinzendorff in Copenhagen, he was sent back to found a school at Elmina on the Gold Coast as early as 1737. Though this failed, his efforts initiated change.

Later, when Henry Smeathman helped open up Sierra Leone both as colony and as collecting point for Joseph Banks's empire of science, he also effectively connected the region to the international Quaker network and made the location a matter of "romantic colonialism" on behalf of the Clapham Sect. It was statistician, University of London founder, and Claphamite Zachary Macaulay, who was appointed governor of Freetown in 1794, cooperating with evangelical friends such as John Clarkson to provide a solution to "the [largely Loyalist] black poor" who had been displaced by the American Revolution.

Evangelical Engagement

Sierra Leone was Britain's second colony in Africa, an often-struggling symbol of evangelical engagement with the continent. It was not a promising start—the colony was nearly wiped out several times by disease, internal dissension, the difficulties of the equatorial West Coast, and hostile action during European wars. The Amherst-educated Edward Jones, the first naturalized citizen of Sierra Leone, married three times, buried all three of his wives, and buried five of his six children during his pioneering life in education and colonization. Attempts to educate Africans in Europe as the basis for an indigenous clergy faced similar problems: just as yellow fever ruled in Africa, tuberculosis did so in Europe (Jones 1980, 334). As Beetham notes, in the fifteen years following 1835 the Methodists "made seventy-eight new appointments . . . in Gambia, Sierra Leone and the Gold Coast; thirty of these died within a year of arrival" (Beetham 1967, 11).

Sierra Leone survived, however, in part because it continued British colonialism and trade, acted as a support base for British political and naval action against slaving, and received the energies of new re-migration organizations such as the "Society for Missions to Africa and the East" (later the "Church Missionary Society") which fed support through the establishment and provisioning of churches, schools, and other institutions. One such society—The Society for the Colonization of Free People of Color of America (ACS)—was inspired by American merchant Paul Cuffee to set up an American-African colony just south of Sierra Leone. Though founded, it is now suggested, out of fear of the growing numbers of free Afro-Americans in the United States, it soon attracted and was overtaken by an alliance of Evangelicals, Quakers, and abolitionists (Tyler-McGraw 2007, 1).

In 1820, in part motivated by a transference of the frontier dream of an American empire to the shores of Africa, the new country of Liberia was established. Like Sierra Leone, it was tied to a Transatlantic vision of the redeeming influences of commerce and Christianity.

The actual path of these countries of Euro-American influence was rather less straightforward, their institutions producing generations of leaders who had their own ideas as to what constituted progress for Africans. While at first run by white ACS "colonial agents," such as Jehudi Ashmun, by 1852 Liberia had its first black leader and by 1857 had declared itself to be an independent republic.

Methodist leader Thomas Birch Freeman who, though a poor administrator proved a highly effective ecclesial diplomat with West African paramount leaders, would later build on such apparent false starts, planting schools and churches in the Gold Coast and training an expanding cloud of preachers and teachers. One of the greatest engines for influence in Sierra Leone was Fourah Bay College (FBC), many of the early faculty for which were drawn "from the United Brethren Mission of Moravia, Germany and the Basel Mission" (Paracka 2003, 7).

Leaders Emerge

For the first generation of African leaders, education seemed to be the key to the future. It was from this "Athens of West Africa" that indigenous leadership spread inland, beyond the more slowly advancing European missionary boundaries. Here the churches they established were only nominally under European control, spurring rapid indigenization far more quickly than had previously been done. Among those associated with FBC were Samuel Ajai Crowther, enslaved as a youth by Fulani raiders, and James Africanus Horton, who had family connections to the Igbo and Yoruba peoples in Nigeria. They became the founders of new missions and translated the Scriptures into African languages, particularly Yoruba, the lingua franca of the former Oyo Empire, the collapse of which projected so many Yoruba into captivity. When T. F. Buxton's Niger Expedition failed spectacularly (of the 145 Europeans, 130 contracted fever, and forty died), the indigenization theories of people such as Henry Venn gained ground.

The Church in Africa would be "self-supporting, self-governing, self-propagating." (It needed to be; European lives tended to be short and fruitless in regions afflicted by mosquitoes and the tsetse fly). Between 1841 and 1880, Krio and indigenous leaders were given the freedom "beyond the Niger"—as was recognized by the ordination of Crowther as the world's first African Anglican bishop in 1864—to create an indigenous church. It was a double-edged sword; the appointment beyond the River, some later reflected, was both a release and banishment from coastal settlements which were considered, even by Henry Venn, as "too English" for African leadership.

It was a spirituality that engaged with the traditional cosmos of regional religions and which (for Yoruba and Fante peoples in what would become respectively Nigeria and Ghana) was a direct response to the military threat of Islamic powers to the North and the kingdom of Dahomey to the West. The spontaneous preaching of former Sierra Leoneans in the threatened Yoruba enclave of Abeokuta, followed by representations by Birch and later Crowther to Egba chief Sodeke, demonstrates (as Andrew Walls has shown) the active appropriation of Christianity by Africans to solve African problems.

The self-interest of both British Church and Empire—which undermined regional powers by, for instance, restricting trade, and though technically allies or tenants of various regional powers, acted unilaterally by imposing European bishops or exchanging forts with the Dutch to create defined spheres of influence—engaged these African Christian leaders with the problem of how to conceptualize a specifically African Christianity.

> **It was a spirituality that engaged with the traditional cosmos of regional religions.**

It was from among FBC's Krio alumni and from Freeman's institutions that leadership arose to reconceptualize the African future. People such as James "Holy" Johnson came to believe that Christianity was practically the only benefit Europe could offer to Africa. Biblical passages referring to Ethiopia as "a sort of Black Zion" (Scott 2004) acted as the basis, in both political thought and popular spirituality, for African nationalism and the rise of independent African churches.

The result was the development of a "muscular" and "rather pan-African culture of the wider coastal world with its 'civilized' and Christian emphases" (Kalu 2008). By 1870, all the leaders of the Fante Confederation, which formed in 1868 to seek self-rule, were "Ethiopianist" Methodists: "people successfully merging African political aspirations of a modern sort with a measure of traditional culture as well as of Christian commitment" (Hanciles 2002, 25). Similar ethnic nationalist movements to oppose colonialist takeovers of African Christianity, for instance, among the Yoruba in Southern Nigeria, or in the "deep inner rejection of colonialism with its brutal 'pacification' . . . and . . . forced labor" under William Wadé Harris, led to the emergence of African Churches such as the Native Baptist Church, and, in the run-up to and aftermath of World War I and the global influenza pandemic, the Aladura churches, which some have seen as a form of indigenous Pentecostalism.

The "Windward Shore": Senegal, Gambia, Guinea, Guinea Bissau

In the countries of first African/European contact (i.e., the old "Windward Shore"), the pressure from the Muslim Sahel, and French Catholic dominance, led to a late and partial evangelical presence.

Indeed, it is only in those areas established or formerly ruled by Britain, the United States, or in isolated settings such as Cabo Verde, in which West African Evangelicalism manages to climb above the "2% visibility horizon." This effectively means that apart from Nigeria and Ghana, with the two smaller countries Togo and Benin squeezed between them, Liberia and Sierra Leone, the only francophone country in West Africa with a visible Evangelical population is Burkina Faso.

Senegal is thus in the mainstream, with only 0.2% of the population identifiably Evangelical. The early Portuguese attempt to impose Catholicism by force effectively closed large parts of the hinterland to missions, rendering, in the aftermath of the slave trade, Catholicism to entrench itself largely as identity religion among the white colonial and mixed-race populations in the trading ports. As Jones notes, at the same time as evangelical missions were gearing up, French Catholic missions were under extreme pressure from Enlightenment rationalism and Revolutionary dispossession: "The same generation which had experienced in Britain the Methodist and Evangelical revival had also seen the enthronement of the Goddess of Reason in the cathedral church of Our Lady of Paris" (Jones 1980, 326).

It was not until the Caribbean experience demonstrated to Louis Philippe's restored French constitutional monarchy that religio-cultural change was essential to avoid social and economic disaster that new Catholic orders directed at West Africa, such as the Congregation of the Holy Heart of Mary and the "Ploermel Brothers," began to receive the sort of official support that British Evangelicals had been able to leverage on a voluntary basis. By then, town (rather than city) based Sufism had captured much of the energy which was available through counter-European indigenous identity formation. This demonstrates in the Catholic context what Andrew Porter has demonstrated for the Protestant: that growing conflict with indigenization movements (particularly after 1870) can be overly credited to issues of race, when in fact Metropolitan and colonial administrative decisions were often at the root of ebbs and flows in missionary success (Porter 1977, 23).

Both Senegal and Gambia thus remain more than 90% Muslim, with overlap in traditional religions, particularly among the Floup Diolas in southern Senegal and the Jola people in Gambia.

Senegal's Evangelical minority has relied on either influence from nearby churches, (particularly Sierra Leone and Burkina Faso) or from European missions. A protestant presence in the country commenced when Eugène Casalis of the Société des Missions Evangéliques de Paris (SMEP) received an invitation from the interim governor, Jean–Bernard Jauréguiberry, to send a student to study the local languages. In 1863, Casalis sent Louis Jacques, from Vevey, Switzerland, resulting in a base in Casamance, at Sédhiou.

The next decade saw (in 1873) the baptism of the first Senegalese (Mademba Casalis Gueye) and the translation of the Gospel of Matthew into Wolof, the evangelization of Sor district and surrounding villages and the construction of a school for fifty students.

The SMEP received valuable help from Fourah Bay—one alumnus, Walter Taylor, was another well-educated Abeokutan who, on the death or withdrawal of European missionaries, singlehandedly carried on the mission finally making ground among Bambara people and ex-slaves fleeing the Fulani. Success among a refugee slave population was not a guarantee for success among the caste-oriented Wolof-speaking broader society.

It was not until the 1980s that Samuel Vauvert Dansokho, the Evangelical Protestant Church's first Senegalese pastor, was ordained. The 1990s and 2000s was really a period of restarts, assisted by evangelical pastors from other francophone countries in West Africa, particularly Togo and Cote d'Ivoire. Most of the small number of EPS pastors have had to leave the country to train at places such as the Protestant University of Central Africa (UPAC), or in Cameroon. Later-established churches have been able to depend more readily upon such intra-regional networks. With this sort of help, local churches (Glory Baptist Church's Reach Education Centre School project or the KJMI's Gambia Pastoral Institute) are now active in building a local institutional presence.

Proliferation thus came from external plantings. In 1936 the US-based Worldwide Evangelization Crusade (WEC) entered the field, followed by various Pentecostal and mainstream churches (such as the AOG, which arrived in 1956).

There are now a smattering of foreign-originated churches in the country, including the Baptist Church, Foursquare Gospel Mis-

Senegal's Evangelical minority has relied on either influence from nearby churches or from European missions.

sion, the Church of Christ, the Church of God, and a number of Methodist denominations. The national member of the Evangelical Alliance (the Fédération des Églises et Missions Évangéliques du Sénégal) now claims sixty missions, churches, and NGOs across the country, and a following of some seventy thousand missions. Such figures are naturally of some sensitivity and are used carefully, given a past record of mob violence against churches and known Christian figures. FEMES-related churches avoid activities that can lead to accusations of proselytism, a problematic position which points to the fundamental intolerance of the broader society, given the tendency of agitators to confuse Evangelicals with Jehovah's Witnesses.

President of the Fédération, Eloi Sobel Dogue of the Eglise Evangélique Keur Jamm, Grand Yoff, has been prominent in expressing Evangelical opinion, including bringing the problems of living as a minority religion even in a relatively successfully modernizing country such as Senegal. Gambian and Senegalese Evangelicals also struggle with their representation abroad. When, for example, Muslim Gambian President Yahya Jammeh made declarations before the United Nations about what he called the threat of homosexuality, US-based activists were less than nuanced in their repetition of anti-Evangelical statements, while broader literature repeats the assumption that West African Christianity is missionary religion.

Despite constitutional guarantees of religious liberty, overt Christian activism can result in charges of sedition or even treason being brought against missionaries, as was the case of Prison Fellowship and the arrest of David Fulton in 2008.

Sierra Leone and Liberia

As may be seen in many of their surrounding countries, Sierra Leone and Liberia became something of a bridgehead into West Africa in the colonial period, producing large numbers of leaders and indigenous missionaries for the rest of the region.

As the best known and perhaps most easily reached areas of Africa, the Livingstone "aura" transmitted by the travels and exploits of Methodist Episcopal evangelist and Bishop William Taylor drew religious innovators, including early Pentecostals from the mid-1890s.

When that movement formalized in such revivals as that at Azusa Street, Africa was uppermost on many minds; it will be remembered that Lucy Farrow and Julia W. Hutchins, key figures in Azusa Street, were both directing their steps towards Liberia when Azusa Street broke out.

Liberia and Sierra Leone acted as the entry point for many Pentecostals, both black and white, some of whom then went on to work in Ghana, Nigeria, even Angola. This was a role they continued to play after World War II with the rapid growth of Western missionaries; at one stage "Liberia had one of the highest populations of American missionaries per capita in the world." It was to a Liberian Lepers colony, for example, that Loren Cunningham sent the first two YWAM missionaries in 1961.

This overseas interest led to innovations based on the availability of capital and technical knowhow, including the establishment in 1954 of Station ELWA, the first evangelical radio station in Africa. Its programs reached a thousand miles into the hinterland and along the coast. As Tim Stoneman points out, however, the cultural issues (relating to translation and indigenization) took much longer to conquer than the technical challenges (Stoneman 2007). The broader importance of such developments may be seen in the fact that, as late as 2004, parts of West Africa, such as Ghana's Volta region, were effectively unconnected to national processes due to lack of radio coverage—a lack which churches were in the forefront of attempting to amend (BBC 2004).

Both Sierra Leone and Liberia have, since the 1960s, been the subject of long-running political instability and civil war, which has killed hundreds of thousands, and displaced millions. Many of these ended up over the border as refugees, subjected to continued peril. The war has been described as causing "untold suffering to its citizens with women and girls being singled out for widespread and systematic abuse" (Sierra Leone National Action Plan 2009, 3).

Institution maintenance was in some periods impossible, resulting in the collapse of social services, the flight of key leaders and educators to the West, and (in churches) widespread conflict between between formal and popular religious practices. In the last, there is a significant intermingling of Islamic, Christian, and traditional iconographies and spiritualities. Misfortune or impairment is directly linked in the local cosmology with spiritual causes; beliefs reinforced by the widespread involvement of Mende and Temne peoples in various secret societies.

The brutal culture-war activities of all parties to the various conflicts has led to large scale amputations, war disabilities, and orphaned children. The area has among the highest rates of child and maternal mortality in the world, is plagued by drug and human trafficking cartels, is subject to unfavorable international investment regimes, and has high rates of unemployment. These are the circumstances in which all churches operate, and the human problems, which shape their social ministries.

Inevitably, much of the work proper to governments (healthcare, welfare, education, micro-economic development), therefore, falls to international NGOs, leading to what Berghs (2012) calls the "NGOisation" of the region. Some of these are international evangelical bodies, and others operated by local churches.

Most NGOs work on the community level. In 2006, for example, WEC International's Rainbows of Hope Sierra Leone, Evangelical Fellowship of Sierra Leone and World Relief developed a Parental Training Manual a handbook for churches and communities to work with parents (van den Brink 2006). The limited counseling services that do exist directly support women and children, such as faith-based organizations such as Echoes of Mercy, Graceland Counseling Services, Center for Victims of Torture, and Community Advocates and Psychosocial Services) (Smith and Smith 2012).

Micro-finance, of the sort of life loans offered by evangelical churches in Liberia, has made such churches essential to life. The result, as Bill Massaquoi of the Association of Evangelicals in Liberia noted to a seminar on the aftermath of mass terrorism, is that churches have been "springing [up] all over the place." "In our case, the church just quickly gathered itself," Massaquoi says, "strengthened itself to minister to the people" (Moore 2001)

Burkina Faso

Landlocked Burkina Faso was originally dominated by the Mossi kingdoms, which managed to resist local jihadi states and maintain traditional religious beliefs. It began its absorption into the French sphere in 1894 was formally annexed in 1919, and gained self-governing status in 1960. This led to a series of unstable civil, military governments, some of a socialist stamp.

Colonization was not beneficial, an under-resourced but secularizing French colonial apparatus leaving Burkina Faso "among the poorest countries with the lowest school enrollment in sub-Saharan Africa" (Ouedraogo 2010).

The Assemblies of God entered Burkina Faso in 1921, commencing its work at Gounghin (Ouagadougou) followed by the Christian and Missionary Alliance (1923, in Bobo-Dioulasso), the Sudan Interior Mission (1930 Fada-N'Gourma) and WEC (World Wide Evangelical Crusade, in 1931 at Gaoua). The AOG emphasized the building of schools, opening its first in 1948, originally from a conviction as to the importance of an indigenous leadership. For this reason, in a relatively small public sector, AOG churches remain a significant presence—approximately 50% of about four thousand local churches (Ouedraogo 2010).

From the 1980s, Canadian Mennonite missionaries working in Koutoura began to see some success. The lack of local training institutions, however, has until recently been a problem in establishing an indigenous leadership. The social issues include food and water security, as a result of desertification, diseases such as AIDS and Ebola, human trafficking, and the like. Members of FEME have responded by developing extensive schooling and social welfare involvements, and with overseas assistance installing potable water plants and sustainable agriculture and small business startups.

As involvement in public issues increases, however, there is inevitably conflict over political positions. As one journalist wrote to the head of FEME, in evangelical churches "people with extreme right-wing ideas mingle . . . with people in far-left ideas" united largely by their common theology of salvation. Recent debates over the public expenditure required for establishment of a federal upper house have illustrated the problem of rising churches in incapable states throughout the region (Kourouma 2013).

The Sahel (Mali, Niger, Chad)

Countries in the Sahel are majority Muslim countries, mostly within the culturally divergent francophone zone. The emergence of faith missions and the British government's cantoning of Muslim sections of northern Nigeria and the Sudan off from missionary involvement actually meant that some parts of French West Africa were easier to reach by missionaries for those concerned about the Hausa and the Fulani (Cooper 2006, 10). The result, as Cooper notes, is that in Niger's Maradi and Tsibiri regions, where nineteenth century jihadism had been rejected, the basic patterns of life show markers of cultural adaptation largely mediated by missions such as The Sudan Interior Mission (SIM, founded 1893).

Local radio culture, trade goods, exotic goods such as bicycles and peanut butter: "Even the ambivalent radio repair man, who is a Christian in town and a Muslim in the village where his first wife resides, occupies a particular social space. All are evidence of a lively but largely Christian subculture that has contributed substantially to the quality and texture of life" (Cooper 2006, 3). This was particularly the case after the association of the Catholic Church with Vichy fascism in World War II. During and after the war, most Catholics were migrants, while the indigenous Christian movement in these countries became increasingly Protestant.

Today in the town of Maradi alone, there are more than 500 members of evangelical congregations from among local ethnic groups and evangelical churches dot the landscape of the entire region beyond the city of Maradi proper. This does not include the churches in what is known as Arewa, or the burgeoning Fulani Christian community, or the Christian churches that have burst onto the scene in the capital of Niamey as mobile Christians establish new communities there. The indigenous Christian church in Niger is Protestant, not Catholic. (Cooper 2006, 15)

The resistant Muslim culture, it is true, has meant that Christian communities have remained small, particularly with the spread across the Nigerian border of anti-Sufi, anti-Christian identity politics based on conflicts further south and east. In Chad, where Christian growth was largely concentrated in the south, Evangelicals form perhaps 11% of the population. A relatively moderate national range of versions of Islam, carefully overseen by the government, has meant that conflict here has been localized, and often between armed Chadian Mbarara and Houda herdsmen and Christian farming communities. Christian organizations, however, do not find it difficult to point to a systematic governmental pro-Muslim preference, and to the ambiguity of Chadian involvement in the United Nations stabilization mission in the neighboring Central African Republic.

As the Mali case demonstrated in 2012–2013, political instability in the region often sees the rapid expansion of Islamic militancy. Recently, parts of Mali were subjected to a particularly brutal and iconoclastic interpretation of shari'a. (International intervention assisted in stablilization of Mali, though at the time of writing, "stability" was still a relative term).

This is not only the case in Muslim majority nations. In the Central African Republic, the co-option of religion by tribal and militarised militias and the influx of Chadian-Sudanese mercenaries has drawn from the evangelical churches a rejection of the religious labels being used by the anti-Balaka defensive militias, responding to the genocidal tactics of Muslim Seleka insurgents into this majority Christian "phantom state" (Smith 2013; WEA's Bangui Declaration II of 4 February 2014).

Some of these conflicts relate to the broader environment, to population pressures, and to the creeping of the Sahara as signalled by increasingly long droughts, such as the Great Sahel Drought of the 1970s. Conflict over resources in the region places real pressure on the original Word-centered mission Christianity, preferencing forms of Christianity, which can combine preaching with social works. Though from a low base, there is some evidence of vigorous evangelical growth in these Muslim majority countries. In failed states, such as the CAR, churches, including evangelical ones, necessarily provide much of the institutional basis (Smith 2013).

Nigeria, Togo, Benin, and Ghana

Nigeria and Ghana stand out as not only the Christian metropoli of West Africa, but of the continent, and increasingly, through extensive worldwide diasporic communities, in many other parts of the world. Their numbers and mobility continue to play an important part in both missionizing Africa and "re-enchanting" the secularizing global space occupied by many Westerners (Stolz 2011; Jenkins 2007).

Divided by colonial borders and separated by Togo and Benin, both of which have sought alternative approaches to nation building, Nigeria and Ghana are intractably plural societies; the Ewe, for example, were largely incorporated "by the former German colony of Togoland until after World War I when it was divided and transferred to France and Britain. This artificial division resulted in two sections of Eweland, one in the Gold Coast (now Ghana) and the other in Togo" (Dotse 2011, 2).

Historically, they had been pressed by tribal conflicts to migrate west, competing for space with Yoruba, Aja, Fon, Ga, Ada, and the Ashanti. Such divisions structure inequality, with people groups such as the Konkomba living across borders and being considered landless, and so powerless, or, like many young Togolese women, committed to extended periods as guest workers in Nigeria (Talton 2010).

For many of these peoples, Christianity has become a powerful tool for negotiating modernity and change. Nigeria and Ghana, therefore, are a most dramatic confluence of dynamic indigenous traditions, geopolitics and the seeds blown from Sierra Leone and Liberia. Crowther and Freeman's spirituality encountered Ewe, Igbo, Hausa, and Yoruba traditions and exploded into a frenzy of religious creativity, from Africanized versions of high Anglicanism to African Initiated Churches, which have since spread all over the world. Kalu notes the indigeneity of these Christianities, in cases such as "the five young men who spoke in tongues in 1934 without a missionary and contrary to their church's belief. They were kicked out from the Faith Tabernacle, formed the Church of Jesus Christ, and in 1939 invited the Assemblies of God (AOG) to take them over" (Kalu 2008). Walls notes similar cases of self-conversion and indigenizing spiritualities stretching back to and beyond the Ethiopianist traditions noted above. Both countries remain centers for remarkable religious entrepreneurialism.

Ghana has at least sixteen million people who call themselves Christians (62% of the population), some five million (or 19% of the population) of which are identifiably Evangelical. Of the five people/ language groups with a population over one million, four are majority Christian (Ashanti/Twi Akan, Fante, Ewe, Dangme), with several dominant Protestant in form (Addai 2013).

These traditions date back to the work of the Freeman's Methodists and the Basel Mission, which established itself near Accra in 1828. In 1847, the North German Missionary Society (Bremen Mission), which was squeezed out of Gabon by the Spanish and French, settled in the Volta Region, establishing the first formal school at Peki along with the Evangelical Presbyterian Church, Ghana and, after the transfer of Togolese churches to the Société des Missions Evangéliques, the Eglise Evangelique Presbyterienne du Togo.

The Ewe are a significant people in both Ghana and Togo, but in the latter, first German and then French political dominance is still reflected in a majority of Ewe self-identifying as Catholic. Over the border, the Ewe are much more strongly Protestant and Independent. Further west in Cote d'Ivoire, Christianization was also largely Catholic, though the religious largest bloc in the country is still Islam, and there is a significant minority of Evangelicals (7.5%). It is also in the Ivory Coast that the Harrist Church, the outcome of the truly remarkable work of Liberian Glebo prophet William Wadé Harris, is strongest.

By way of contrast, Christianity in Ghana is very much a public religion. Paul Gifford suggests, "about fifty percent of vehicles have Christian slogans painted on them" with statements such as "God is King" or more cryptic messages such as "Don't Blame Judas." Numerous businesses field such inspiring names as "Jesus Way Upholstery, King of Kings Electrical, Jehovah Jireh Motorbody Repairs, the Lord is my Light Car Wash," and the "Wonderful Jesus Hardware" (Gifford 1998, 61).

The bodily impacts of belief and ritual leading to a strong emphasis on faith healing, prophecy, and spiritual deliverance are shared by both grassroots African Independent and Pentecostal groups, even some mainline Evangelicals. The connections are historical as well as ritual; the Musama Disco Christo Church, for instance, emerged from Methodist prayer meetings in the 1920s. Such churches operate in the same social spaces as evangelical churches. For Mennonite Bible teachers, Edwin and Irene Weaver, and David Shank, this widespread indigenized form of Christianity provided opportunities for introducing evangelical biblical understandings (Shank 2003).

Conversely, Pentecostal-like spirituality is common in many Presbyterian and Anglican churches, sometimes leading to friction and the emergence of new churches (see Zink 2013, 232).

On the other hand, cultural location can create conflict over polygamy ("an intractable predicament in some African denominations"), or what is seen as "human trafficking" in Togo (criticized by some Western academics as "neo-abolitionism" oriented more towards supporting the NGO business than correcting an actual problem). Recognising that these are Western problems more than problems with the base society as such, and that the culture itself has resources for reconciliation and empowerment, has been a step towards bringing about resolution in fraught problems.

Nigeria

While sharing with Ghana about the same percentage of Evangelicals, it is the massive population and regional influence of Nigeria, which makes it stand out. When scholars note that 65% of West Africans are Christians, a large part of that is made up of Nigeria's thirty-three million Evangelicals (Ranger 2006).

It is an influence with problems as well as advantages. On the one hand, the Nigerian state has led and funded regional efforts such as ECOWAS and military security interventions in Sierra Leone, Liberia, and, more recently, Mali. On the other hand, resource scarcity and unconstrained population growth place severe strains on land, water, petroleum, and the like, leading to local lawlessness and intercommunal tensions.

The problems of the state are reflected in its churches. Religious movements in Nigeria operate on a vast scale. In Ranger's words: "The country comprises many different kinds of evangelicals, as theology and lifestyle interact with ethnicity to create a bewildering variety of churches and sects" (Ranger 2006).

As early as 1915, the "prophet" and former CMS catechist Garrick Sokari Marian Braide attracted as many as a million followers, out of which arose one of the earliest Aladura churches, the Christ Army Church. With their emphasis on prophecy and healing, churches such as the C&S (Cherubim and Seraphim) and the Aladura, acted as the basis, first, for the relatively easy growth of Western Pentecostalism (with visits by evangelists such as T. L. Osborne in the 1950s and 1960s) and then the spread of Charismatic revival through Scripture Union and other interdenominational evangelical networks in the 1970s. This latter threw up multiple new mission agencies and churches, which impacted well beyond Nigeria's borders.

In Ghana, Nicholas Duncan Williams was among the first of many ministry founders who developed a Charismatic theology to material and political matters, tinged with prosperity preaching as a rejection of the missionaries' gospel of poverty and humility.

The "whole counsel" of God was for Africans to enjoy the whole blessing of God, no longer mediated by white men. From the mid-1980s, as Meyer notes, the Pentecostal megachurch Winners Chapel, typified for many by the building of the largest Protestant church building in the world, became a prominent form on the

Nigerian and Ghanaian landscape. So significant have their numbers grown that four out of five of Africa's largest churches are in Lagos, and church camps are of such a scale as to register in the national tourism returns.

Such bodies are capable of filling some of the gaps left by an impoverished state, founding universities, hospitals, and schools. Standards vary, and the profit motive has been a matter of criticism, particularly when associated with prosperity doctrine preachers. Mirroring ECOWAS and African Union involvements, such large Nigerian church networks can bring to bear moral suasion on the region's less tolerant regimes (All Africa 2014). There is also evidence that Protestant conversion plays a significant role in constructing a sense of well-being (Pokimica, Addai and Takyi 2012) and the essential, contractual trust which underlies developing economies, so uniting the public and the private through the economic (Addai, Opoku-Agyeman and Ghartey 2013).

The mainline evangelical churches, moreover, remain significant. Samuel Ajai Crowther's church did not gain Provincial status until 1951 when the five West African Dioceses (Sierra Leone, Accra, Lagos, On the Niger, and Gambia) came under a single Archbishop.

Between 1951 and 1977, the two Nigerian Dioceses produced fourteen new ones, as the church struggled with both population growth and extension across the complex Nigerian landscape. Nigeria became a separate Province in 1979, and in 1997 was split into three Provinces. With around twenty million members, the Nigerian Anglican Church is the second largest Province in the worldwide Anglican Communion, its influence in the Global Anglican Futures Conference and at Lambeth, becoming the cause of considerable debate. The Nigerian sense of leadership in the Global south can be heard in the statements of leaders such as Friday Imaekhai, Archbishop of Bendel and Bishop of Esan when reflecting on divisions in the global community: "The troubles of the Anglican Communion today," he noted, "flows from the Western rejection of the uniqueness and sufficiency of the Lord Jesus Christ as the one who is heir and therefore owner of all things" (in Taiwo 2013).

The Evangelical Church of West Africa, now the Evangelical Church Winning All, or ECWA, emerged from SIM networks in 1954. It is one of the largest church denominations in Nigeria with about five million people spread across six thousand churches. Two theological seminaries in Igbaja and Jos, eight Bible colleges, and fifteen theological training institutes produce leaders and ministers. The Church's Medical Department coordinates a wide network, which includes four hospitals, a community health program with more than 110 health clinics, a central pharmacy, and the School of Nursing and Midwifery. It has followed the path of reverse mission back along diasporic pathways, establishing congregations in Europe and North America, as well as supporting the largest missionary agency, the Evangelical Missionary Society, of any African country.

Regional Issues

The moral compass. Having been founded on a rationale of bringing "civilization and Christianity," energized by the internalized disciplines of education and Protestant spirituality, and structured by contrastive relationships with folk Islam and traditional religions, and more recently with Islamic caliphatism and identity politics, the "moral compass" of Western Africa remains the largest challenge to African Evangelicals. Most countries in the area are ranked well down the Transparency International Perceived Corruption Index, and in those countries, which have functionally nondemocratic regimes, there are real restraints on what many evangelical traditions have seen as their prophetic role. Internationally, this is sometimes mistaken for compliance or even collusion; locally, it is seen as survival and/or adaptation. The evangelical moral compass has also had to deal with ineluctable external factors: AIDS, poverty, desertification, and so forth, which challenge received views of the benevolence of God, Christian morality, and the effectiveness of gospel-based ministries.

Research-led interventions by organizations such as the Dutch Woord en Daad development organization, the anti-corruption campaigns by African Enterprise, and the advocacy of the Exposed network, among others, are attempting to find practical ways of dealing with structural issues from Christian perspectives (van den Toren-Lekkerkerke 2014).

The usual passengers on current flights from the West thus include not just the Peace Corps workers, politicians, and engineers of the 1960s, but also the "new Evangelicals" engaged in battling poverty, water scarcity, health issues, political corruption, environmental issues, and the like.

Conflict with Islam. The rise of Muslim identity politics in those areas with either a jihadist past, contemporary associations with Saudi-exported Wahhabism, or with tribalized associations with Islamic heritage, has meant that the Sahel and the northern areas of countries south of the Sahel have seen ongoing violence against a variety of Christian communities.

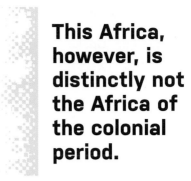

This Africa, however, is distinctly not the Africa of the colonial period.

Organizations such as the largely Hausa Congregation of the People of Tradition for Proselytism and Jihad ("Boko Haram") find churches a relatively easy, though not a unique, target in their campaign for shari'a and Islamicization of the state. As Ranger notes, the reverse impact on Evangelicals has been a like politicization, and "the effect of making debates about democracy focus on politics and law rather than on morality and personal conduct" (Ranger 2006). The power of Evangelical Christianity, which lies in its moral reformism and personal liberation under Word and Spirit, can be threatened by absorption into such debates, much as it was domesticated into Victorianism in nineteenth-century England.

Reactions to Islam, through application of evangelical theologies to legal or policy structures, can also produce reflexive global responses that affect Evangelicalism elsewhere. How Western secularists "hear" a Nigerian Archbishop's call for the death penalty for perjurers in court cases "just as it was for Ananias and Sapphira, or congratulations proffered to the Nigerian President on his passage of 'anti-gay laws,'" is detached from the social crises in which the original statements are made. A solution for Evangelicals in West Africa can become a stick used to ensure the marginalization of their brothers and sisters elsewhere.

Economic globalization and colonialism. Where there are failing states, such as in Guinea-Bissau, or as there has been at times in Sierra Leone or Togo, the collapse of order and social welfare provision has made West African states origination or transhipment points for criminal or neocolonial aberrations.

In 2008, for example, the *Washington Post* noted the growth of cocaine trafficking from Colombian cartels through Guinea Bissau (Sullivan 2008). Similar observations have been made with regard to the trafficking of blood diamonds (Sierra Leone), poached ivory (Togo), and the human trafficking of economic migrants (up to one-third of all irregular migrants to Europe, predominantly from Ghana and Nigeria, and most through Mali and Niger) and what some NGOs refer to as the "new slave trade" (UNODC 2010).

With the latter, we return to where this story began, with the impact of European and transatlantic economies and imperialism on already pressured and mobile West African societies. Now, however, the candidates for leaky boats heading for low-paid work in Europe propel themselves, falling into the hands of North African traffickers out of the desire for a better life. One could read such situations as a reprise on the problems of the nineteenth century, that, in the words of James Russell Lowell:

> Slavery, the earth-born Cyclops, fellest of the giant brood . . .
> Gropes in yet unblasted regions for his miserable prey;—
> Shall we guide his gory fingers where our helpless children play? (Lowell)

This Africa, however, is distinctly not the Africa of the colonial period. If anything, it is a realization not of colonial dreams, but of the vision of the Ethiopianist leaders of first wave nationalism.

Its Evangelicalism, its leaders and its churches, are African, constituting and leading communities, which are some of the most rapidly growing in the world. In the emerging markets and economies of the world, with massively mobile and increasingly educated populations, that is a recipe for global impact.

Sources and Further Reading

Addai, Isaac, Chris Opoku-Agyeman and Helen Tekyiwa Ghartey. "An Exploratory Study of Religion and Trust in Ghana." Social Indicators Research 110, no. 3 (February 2013): 993–1012.

AllAfrica. "Nigerian Church Leader Meets Veep." AllAfrica.com. Washington. Febryar 12, 2014.

Baum, Robert M. *Shrines of the Slave Trade: Diola Religion and Society in Precolonial Senegambia*. New York: Oxford University Press., 1999.

BBC. "Ghana: Volta region lagging behind in terms of radio stations." BBC Monitoring Media. March 16, 2004.

Beetham, T. A. *Christianity and the New Africa*. New York: Frederick A. Praeger, Publishers, 1967.

Berghs, Maria. *War and Embodied Memory: Becoming Disabled in Sierra Leone*. Farnham, UK: Ashgate, 2012.

Brown, Jonathan. "Judgment day in Gambia for the armed robber who found God." *The Independent,* London, UK, (December 30, 2008): 18.

Buchbinder, Liza Stuart. "After Trafficking: Naming Violence against Child Laborers in West Africa." University of California, San Francisco with the University of California, Berkeley. ProQuest, UMI Dissertations Publishing, 2012.

Cath.ch. "Attaques répétées au Sénégal contre les églises évangéliques." Cath.ch, 3 July 2011 and accessed April 1, 2013.

Cooper, Barbara MacGowan. *Evangelical Christians in the Muslim Sahel*, Indianapolis: Indiana University Press, 2006.

Currie Grant, M. J. E. "The development of Krio Christianity in Sierra Leone 1792–1861." Thesis, The University of Edinburgh, 1993.

Dotse, A. Kobla, "The Origins and Brief History of the Ewe People", np: XXXX Publications, http://ewechicago. org/Flyers/The%20ewes/, accessed 27 June 2014.

Fayose, Cyril Gershon. "Healing wounds: A Ghanaian Christian perspective on intractable conflict. The case of the Evangelical Presbyterian Church Ghana (EPCG)." Luther Seminary thesis, Proquest-UMI.

Gifford, Paul. *African Christianity: Its Public Role*. Bloomington, IN: Indiana University Press, 1998.

Hanciles, Jehu. *Euthanasia of a Mission: African Church Autonomy in a Colonial Context*. Westport: Praeger, 2002.

Jenkins, Philip. *God's Continent: Christianity, Islam, and Europe's Religious Crisis*. Oxford: Oxford University Press, 2007.

Jones, D. H. "The Catholic Mission and Some Aspects of Assimilation in Senegal, 1817–1852." *The Journal of African History* 21, no. 3 (1980): 323–340.

Kalu, Ogbu. *African Pentecostalism: An Introduction*, New York: Oxford University Press, 2008.

Kourouma, Issaka Luc. "Sénat: Au pasteur Samuel Yaméogo, président de la Fédération des églises et missions évangéliques." L'Observateur Paalga. August 12, 2013 and accessed 1 April 2014. *http://news.aouaga. com/h/11758.html*

Lovejoy, Paul. *Transformations in Slavery—A History of Slavery in Africa*, Cambridge: Cambridge University Press, 1983.

McGee, Gary B. "Shortcut to language preparation? Radical evangelicals, missions, and the gift of tongues." *International Bulletin of Missionary Research*. 25, no. 3 (July 2001): 118–123.

Meyer, Birgit. *Translating the Devil: Religion and Modernity Among the Ewe in Ghana*. Edinburgh University Press, 1999.

Moore, Art. "The hard-won lessons of terror and persecution." *Christianity Today* 45, no. 13 (Oct 22): 20–21.

Ouedraogo, Philippe. "The legacy of Christianity in West Africa, with special reference to Burkina Faso." *Comparative Education*. 46, no. 3 (August 2010): 391–405.

Paracka Jr., Daniel J. *The Athens of West Africa: A History of International Education at Fourah Bay College, Freetown, Sierra Leone*. New York: Routledge, 2003.

Pokimica, Jelena, Isaac Addai, Baffour K. Takyi. "Religion and Subjective Well-Being in Ghana." *Social Indicators Research* 106, no. 1 (March 2012): 61–79.

Porter, Andrew. "Evangelical enthusiasm, missionary motivation and West Africa in the late nineteenth century: The career of G. W. Brooke." *The Journal of Imperial and Commonwealth History*, 6, no. 1 (1977): 23–46.

Ranger, Terence O. *Evangelical Christianity and Democracy in Africa*. Oxford: Oxford University Press, 2006.

Scott, William. "The Ethiopian Ethos in African American Thought." *International Journal of Ethiopian Studies* 1, no. 2 (Winter/Spring 2004): 40–57.

Shank, David. "William Wadé Harris." *International Bulletin of Missionary Research*. 10, no. 4 (October 1986): 170–176.

Shank, Davis. "A Decade with God's Mission among African Initiated Churches in West Africa." *Mission FOCUS, Annual Review* 11 (2003): 85–104.

Smith, A. M. Akinsulure- and Hawthorne E. Smith. "Evolution of Family Policies in Post-Conflict Sierra Leone." *J Child Fam Stud* 21 (2012): 4–13.

Smith, David. "Unspeakable horrors in a country on the verge of genocide." *The Guardian*, November 23, 2013.

Steensland, Brian and Philip Goff. *The New Evangelical Social Engagement*, New York: Oxford, 2013.

Stolz, Jorg. "All Things Are Possible: Towards a Sociological Explanation of Pentecostal Miracles and Healings." *Sociology of Religion* 72, no. 4 (2011): 456–482.

Stoneman, Timothy H.B. "An "African" Gospel: American Evangelical Radio in West Africa, 1954–1970." *New Global Studies*, 1, no. 1, 2007.

Sullivan, Kevin. "Route of Evil: How a Tiny West African Nation Became a Key Smuggling Hub For Colombian Cocaine, and the Price It Is Paying." *Washington Post*. May 25, 2008: A.1.

Taiwo, Foluso. "Compromise and Conformity with the World, the Bane of the Church: Archbishop Imaekhai." Church of Nigeria Anglican Communion. February 20, 2014 and accessed APril 14, 2013. http://www.anglican-nig.org/formal%20opening.php

Talton, Benjamin. *The Politics of Social Change in Ghana*, London: Palgrave Macmillan, 2010.

Tyler-McGraw, Marie. *An African Republic: Black & White Virginians in the Making of Liberia*. Chapel Hill, NC: University of North Carolina Press, 2007.

UNODC. Smuggling of migrants into, through and from North Africa A thematic review and annotated bibliography of recent publications. New York: United Nations Office on Drugs and Crime, 2010.

van den Toren-Lekkerkerke, Berdine. "Beyond Fate and Hopelessness: The Need for a Contextual Approach to HIV/AIDS Prevention Programmes in the Evangelical Christian Community of French-Speaking Africa." *Transformation* 31, no. 1 (2014): 11–20.

Williams, Martin. "Scots missionary 'criticised Gambia." *The Herald*. Glasgow, December 6, 2008): 3.

Zink, Jesse. "'Anglocostalism' in Nigeria: Neo-Pentecostalism and Obstacles to Anglican Unity." *Journal of Anglican Studies*, 10, no. 2 (November 2013), 231–250.

Evangelical Impact in Nigeria: Wealthy Church Spreads

A church with a seating capacity of fifty thousand is the centerpiece of Canaanland, a community in Ota near Lagos, Nigeria.

David Oyedepo founded the ministry in 1981, when he claimed to have received an eighteen-hour vision from God that said, in part, "The hour has come to liberate the world from all oppression of the devil through preaching of the word of faith, and I am sending you to undertake this task." In response Oyedepo planted his first Living Faith Church in Kaduna in northern Nigeria in 1983. Three years later he built a Bible training center, which now has branches throughout Nigeria and in sixty countries, according to the David Oyedepo Ministries International (DOMI) website.[1]

In the early years, church planting was concentrated in Muslim-dominated northern Nigeria. But in 1989 Bishop Oyedepo, as he was by then known, started a church in the sprawling southern city of Lagos. Since then, Living Faith Chapel, called Winners' Chapel in some cities,[2] has grown exponentially. Winners' Chapels are found throughout Nigeria and other African nations. DOMI now claims five thousand assemblies in Nigeria and boasts a network of churches in thirty-four countries spread over five continents.

The centerpiece five-thousand-acre Canaanland campus, which opened in 1999, accommodates a university, nursery, primary and secondary schools, and several business ventures, including a publishing house, bottled-water processing plant, bakery, restaurants, shops, banks, and residences. In the works is Canaan City, a town of fifteen thousand housing units.

Part of Bishop Oyedepo's appeal to Africans, many of whom live in poverty, is that Oyedepo himself is the wealthiest pastor in Nigeria and preaches what is called a health and wealth, or prosperity, gospel. Oyedepo has a net worth estimated at $150 million USD. He has written some seventy books, many of them telling people how to rise from poverty.

—Debra Fieguth

Evangelical Impact in West Africa: Growth through Diversity

Nigeria, the most populous country in Africa, also has the highest population of Christians. Despite persecution and religious, political, and ethnic conflicts, the evangelical church continues to grow, with numerous African-initiated churches (AICs) springing up in the last several decades.

One of the largest denominations is Evangelical Church Winning All (ECWA). Originally called Evangelical Church of West Africa, the group started as an offshoot of Sudan Interior Mission (SIM) in 1954. It has since grown to some five thousand churches throughout the country with about six million people attending these churches.

ECWA also operates two seminaries, eight Bible colleges, and fifteen theological training institutes. In addition to providing theological education, ECWA cares for the physical health of Nigerians with four hospitals, more than one hundred medical clinics, a school of nursing and midwifery, and an HIV/AIDS ministry team.

In an address at the denomination's 2013 conference, ECWA president Rev. Dr. Jeremiah Gado noted that scores of churches have been destroyed and hundreds of worshippers killed, especially in the northeast, by Boko Haram, the anti-Western Muslim group. Yet the church continues to grow in the Muslim-dominated north and ECWA intends to plant more churches there as well as in other parts of Nigeria, Africa, and the world.

---

1. David Oyedepo Ministries International, Inc., http://www1.davidoyedepoministries.org.

2. http://www1.davidoyedepoministries.org/aboutus.

Ghana has about five million Evangelicals (or 19% of the population).
Photo: The Langham Partnership

ECWA's missionary agency, the Evangelical Missionary Society (EMS), is helping to carry out that vision. Some one thousand six hundred EMS missionaries are active in Nigeria, Burkina Faso, Chad, Cameroon, Niger, and The Gambia, as well as in the United States, Great Britain, and Israel.

Another offshoot of SIM, which now stands for Serving in Mission, is ELWA Ministries, which began as a radio station. Its call letters stand for Eternal Love Winning Africa. Started in 1954 in Liberia, ELWA was Africa's first Christian radio station.

ELWA has gone through difficult times. Liberia's civil war shut down the radio station from 1990 to 1992, and again in 1996. SIM helped resurrect it both times, but after the 1996 shutdown did so only "on the condition that the vision, initiative, and management remain in the hands of the nationals" instead of expatriates.

The radio station now features nineteen hours of English broadcasting a day and an hour and a half in Liberian languages. It is supported almost entirely by local funds. Since 2003 another radio ministry, HCJB (which stands for Heralding Christ Jesus' Blessings), has provided the resources needed for shortwave broadcasts that reach surrounding countries.

Like ECWA, ELWA Ministries has broadened its reach to include operating schools and hospitals. One committed Liberian pastor, who is also the principal of a school, oversaw the manufacture of several thousand bricks to build the school structure.

The effects of the civil conflicts of the 1990s are still apparent. For example, women raped who contracted HIV/AIDS are now being cared for by the ELWA Ministries AIDS ministry team.

—Debra Fieguth

LATIN AMERICA

POPULATION 596,191,000
MAJORITY RELIGION: CHRISTIANITY (92.4%)

LATIN AMERICA REPRESENTS

8.6% OF THE TOTAL
GLOBAL POPULATION

24.2% OF THE GLOBAL
CHRISTIAN POPULATION

1.0% OF THE GLOBAL
NON-CHRISTIAN POPULATION

25.7% OF THE GLOBAL
MISSIONARY FORCE RECEIVED

CHRISTIANITY IN LATIN AMERICA

POPULATION ▬ CHRISTIAN ▬ EVANGELICAL ▬

CHRISTIAN & EVANGELICAL POPULATION

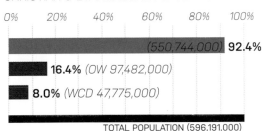

0%   20%   40%   60%   80%   100%

(550,744,000) **92.4%**

16.4% *(OW 97,482,000)*

8.0% *(WCD 47,775,000)*

TOTAL POPULATION (596,191,000)

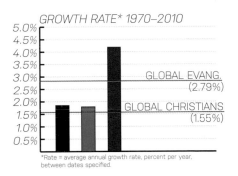

GROWTH RATE* 1970–2010

5.0%
4.5%
4.0%
3.5%
3.0%
2.5%
2.0%
1.5%
1.0%
0.5%

GLOBAL EVANG.
(2.79%)

GLOBAL CHRISTIANS
(1.55%)

*Rate = average annual growth rate, percent per year, between dates specified.

MISSIONS IN LATIN AMERICA
FROM ALL CHRISTIAN TRADITIONS

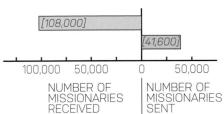

[108,000]

[41,600]

100,000   50,000   0   50,000

NUMBER OF
MISSIONARIES
RECEIVED

NUMBER OF
MISSIONARIES
SENT

1 MISSIONARY SENT
FOR EVERY **13,200** CHRISTIANS
IN LATIN AMERICA

1 MISSIONARY RECEIVED
FOR EVERY **5,500** PEOPLE
IN LATIN AMERICA

92 OF EVERY 100 NON-CHRISTIANS
PERSONALLY KNOW A CHRISTIAN
IN LATIN AMERICA

Source: *World Christian Database*, 2010 data

Christians and Evangelicals by country in Latin America, 2010

	POPULATION, 2010	CHRISTIANS, 2010	% CHRISTIAN, 2010	WCD EVANGELICALS, 2010	WCD % EVANGELICAL, 2010	OW EVANGELICALS, 2010	OW % EVANGELICAL, 2010
Anguilla	13,800	12,500	91.1%	1,900	14.0%	2,700	19.3%
Antigua & Barbuda	87,200	81,100	93.0%	19,400	22.2%	17,600	20.2%
Argentina	40,374,000	36,643,000	90.8%	1,589,000	3.9%	3,711,000	9.2%
Aruba	102,000	97,900	96.4%	5,700	5.7%	8,200	8.0%
Bahamas	360,000	336,000	93.2%	113,000	31.3%	124,000	34.4%
Barbados	280,000	267,000	95.2%	108,000	38.4%	87,600	31.2%
Belize	309,000	281,000	91.1%	37,600	12.2%	58,800	19.0%
Bolivia	10,157,000	9,391,000	92.5%	849,000	8.4%	1,628,000	16.0%
Brazil	195,210,000	177,577,000	91.0%	29,139,000	14.9%	51,334,000	26.3%
British Virgin Islands	27,200	22,300	82.0%	7,100	26.0%	6,400	23.3%
Caribbean Netherlands	17,600	16,600	94.1%	1,300	7.5%	1,700	9.4%
Cayman Islands	55,500	45,000	81.1%	6,400	11.5%	12,100	21.7%
Chile	17,151,000	15,201,000	88.6%	477,000	2.8%	3,158,000	18.4%
Colombia	46,445,000	44,449,000	95.7%	861,000	1.9%	3,461,000	7.5%
Costa Rica	4,670,000	4,474,000	95.8%	416,000	8.9%	689,000	14.7%
Cuba	11,282,000	6,681,000	59.2%	328,000	2.9%	981,000	8.7%
Curacao	148,000	138,000	93.5%	9,700	6.6%	13,800	9.3%
Dominica	71,200	67,200	94.4%	19,700	27.7%	11,100	15.7%
Dominican Republic	10,017,000	9,514,000	95.0%	459,000	4.6%	931,000	9.3%
Ecuador	15,001,000	14,362,000	95.7%	666,000	4.4%	1,170,000	7.8%
El Salvador	6,218,000	6,001,000	96.5%	641,000	10.3%	1,960,000	31.5%
Falkland Islands	3,000	2,500	82.9%	360	12.1%	330	10.9%

French Guiana	231,000	195,000	84.4%	6,300	2.7%	10,400	4.5%
Grenada	105,000	101,000	96.6%	13,500	12.9%	20,400	19.5%
Guadeloupe	459,000	440,000	95.9%	20,400	4.5%	20,500	4.5%
Guatemala	14,342,000	13,964,000	97.4%	1,991,000	13.9%	3,514,000	24.5%
Guyana	786,000	425,000	54.0%	109,000	13.8%	151,000	19.2%
Haiti	9,896,000	9,337,000	94.3%	1,155,000	11.7%	1,633,000	16.5%
Honduras	7,621,000	7,298,000	95.8%	768,000	10.1%	1,752,000	23.0%
Jamaica	2,741,000	2,318,000	84.5%	748,000	27.3%	765,000	27.9%
Martinique	401,000	387,000	96.5%	22,100	5.5%	24,900	6.2%
Mexico	117,886,000	113,110,000	95.9%	2,386,000	2.0%	9,166,000	7.8%
Montserrat	5,000	4,600	93.5%	1,400	27.5%	1,400	28.1%
Nicaragua	5,822,000	5,543,000	95.2%	820,000	14.1%	1,732,000	29.8%
Panama	3,678,000	3,328,000	90.5%	414,000	11.3%	677,000	18.4%
Paraguay	6,460,000	6,164,000	95.4%	219,000	3.4%	393,000	6.1%
Peru	29,263,000	28,225,000	96.5%	1,474,000	5.0%	3,427,000	11.7%
Puerto Rico	3,710,000	3,554,000	95.8%	367,000	9.9%	1,008,000	27.2%
Saint Kitts & Nevis	52,400	49,500	94.6%	8,500	16.2%	11,400	21.8%
Saint Lucia	177,000	170,000	95.9%	23,500	13.3%	25,300	14.3%
Saint Vincent	109,000	97,000	88.7%	32,600	29.8%	42,700	39.1%
Sint Maarten	42,500	38,700	90.9%	2,600	6.2%	970	2.3%
Suriname	525,000	268,000	51.0%	15,500	2.9%	72,200	13.8%
Trinidad & Tobago	1,328,000	842,000	63.4%	225,000	17.0%	272,000	20.4%
Turks & Caicos Is	31,000	28,500	92.1%	4,900	15.8%	10,700	34.5%
United States Virgin Is	106,000	101,000	94.8%	22,500	21.1%	26,100	24.5%
Uruguay	3,372,000	2,174,000	64.5%	74,200	2.2%	210,000	6.2%
Venezuela	29,043,000	26,924,000	92.7%	1,096,000	3.8%	3,147,000	10.8%

EVANGELICALS IN CENTRAL AMERICA AND THE CARIBBEAN

By Stephen C. Dove

Evangelicals comprise one of the fastest growing religious groups in Central America and the Caribbean. Though founded through foreign missionary efforts, through the twentieth century they became a decidedly domestic mass movement with a distinctive religious identity.

The integration of evangelical theology with local and national cultures is one of the defining elements of regional Evangelicalism. Across thirty-six independent countries and foreign territories, Charismatic worship, high levels of commitment, moral conservatism, the emergence of tight-knit communities, and the empowerment of local leaders are common evangelical characteristics.

Evangelicals have shared a recent history centered on a late twentieth-century growth boom that coincided with both a rise in Pentecostal practice and an increase in social and political participation.

Beyond these broad transcultural trends, making generalizations about Evangelicals in the area is difficult. This is true in part because of the social and cultural diversity of the region itself, which is home to more than one hundred European, indigenous, and Creole language and cultural groupings. Even in Spanish-speaking areas (some 80% of the area's population) cultural diversity, national differences, and the flourishing of ethnic subcultures are part of daily life.

Both between countries and within national borders, Evangelicals deal with significant variation both in levels of adherence and in daily practice. The most pronounced cultural divisions in the region flow from the historical legacy of European colonialism, which was divided between southern and northern Europe. In the former colonies of Spain and France where Catholicism remains the dominant religion in orthodox or syncretic forms, Evangelicalism is a relatively recent phenomenon. In Spanish-speaking countries, this history has produced a binary division of Christianity that has created a broader definition of Evangelicalism than the definition used the United States or Europe.

The Spanish term *evangélico* is thus a common self-referent for Protestants that carries a more inclusive meaning than the English "Evangelical," referring to a broad range of non-Catholic Christianities including historic denominationalism, fundamentalism, Pentecostalism, and Adventism. In Mexico, the term *cristiano* operates with a similar meaning. In French and Creole-speaking Haiti there is no parallel inclusive term, and the prevalence of Pentecostalism makes the Creole term *pankotis* (Pentecostal) a more useful category of analysis.

Former English and Dutch colonies account for less than 5% of the regional population (Pew Forum 2006). Most of these countries and territories have Protestant majorities with long but uneven traditions of Evangelicalism. In these areas, the term *Evangelical* usually describes a subset of Protestantism separate from historic denominations, one that takes a particularly high view of Scripture, emphasizes the importance of personal salvation, and encourages evangelism. Countries like Jamaica, Belize, and Curacao have participated alongside French- and Spanish-speaking countries in the Pentecostal boom of the last several decades, and labor migrations have also created religious connections that cross linguistic boundaries. These patterns have tended to link evangelical communities in the region despite national differences.

A study group meets in Jamaica
Photo: The Langham Partnership

Historical Roots of Evangelicalism

Historical Christian identities in the region date back to the Catholic evangelization of the fifteenth and sixteenth centuries. Although Catholicism quickly became the region's dominant religion, the first recorded Protestants were not far behind. Protestantism officially arrived with the establishment of the first English colony on Barbados in 1627. It is likely that unofficial Protestants arrived even earlier. Despite being illegal in Spanish territories, there were faint traces of Protestantism on mainland Central America as early as 1560 when the Inquisition in New Spain (modern Mexico and Central America) first held trials for accused Protestant heretics. In practice, though, neither the British nor Spanish cases represented intentional efforts to spread Protestantism among the general population in the region. Rather, they were national religious expressions of the colonial competitions of the era.

It was not until the first decade of the 1700s that the Church of England launched an evangelization effort among African slaves in the Caribbean. By midcentury, some slaves had also joined revival movements led by visiting Baptist, Wesleyan, and Moravian ministers. Building on this revivalist tradition, George Lisle, a former slave from Georgia, began the first black-led evangelization of Jamaica in 1783.

By the early 1800s planters were openly expressing concern about abolitionism among black and white Evangelicals, even though African-derived religions like Obeah and Myalism continued to wield greater influence among slave populations. Despite legal restrictions, British Protestantism also reached Spanish Central America in this period. In 1743, Anglicans evangelized the Miskito indigenous people on the Caribbean coast of modern Nicaragua as part of a larger British effort to create alliances against the Spanish. Despite the Church of England abandoning these efforts in 1785, the Miskito continued sending pupils to missionary schools in Jamaica. They maintain their Evangelical identity to the present.

In Spanish-speaking areas, the Miskito case was the exception rather than the rule for more than a century. New national constitutions in the 1800s finally guaranteed religious freedom, but these laws still did not match social norms. Official religious toleration was of little consequence to anyone other than foreign diplomats and a handful of insular immigrant communities, such as Mennonites. The earliest Protestants to use the legal opening for evangelization were British colporteurs (Bible salesmen) who, beginning in 1827, traveled sporadically through Mexico and Central America. American colporteurs also joined this missionary effort during the Mexican-American War (1846–1848). However, neither group approached evangelization in a systematic way, and neither established lasting institutions or communities.

It was not until permanent missionaries from US denominations arrived later in the nineteenth century that enduring Protestant congregations formed in the region's Spanish-speaking countries. Baptists established their first congregations in Mexico in 1864; Presbyterians pioneered work in Guatemala in 1882; and the dispensationalist Central American Mission founded churches in Costa Rica, El Salvador, Honduras, and Nicaragua between 1891 and 1900.

Despite the diverse denominational origins of these early Protestant missions, they shared several traits in common. First, each mission counted only a few hundred converts even after several decades of operation. Secondly, the majority of those converts came from the lower rungs of society and often described their conversion experience as a deliverance from problems like alcoholism or vagrancy. Lastly, most early missionaries established a paternalistic relationship with new converts that granted locals only a limited amount of leadership in their new churches.

There were a few notable exceptions to both the chronology and character of these early trends. As the earliest missionaries to the Panama Canal Zone focused their efforts on the English-speaking workers there, the first Spanish-language Protestant churches in Panama developed decades later than in the rest of Central America. And though Protestantism in Cuba followed a similar chronology to the mainland, the way that Protestantism arrived in the island nation was exceptional. Rather than emerging from foreign missionary efforts, the first Cuban Protestant churches formed in exile in the United States. Members of these congregations brought their new faith back to the island in the late 1870s at a time when foreign missionaries faced an effective ban, and these new churches operated under Cuban leadership until the Spanish-American War (1898) opened Cuba to US missionaries.

Throughout the region, until the first half of the twentieth century, foreign missionaries dominated Protestantism. Two changes, however, foreshadowed later trends that continue to mark Evangelicalism to the present day.

The first trend was the shift from denominational missions to faith missions: decentralized networks of churches and individuals which funded missionaries outside of traditional Protestant institutional structures. The most well-known and influential faith mission to emerge in this period was the Wycliffe Bible Translators. Wycliffe's origins lie in the highlands of Guatemala, where from 1917 to 1933 missionary Cameron Townsend (then part of the Central American Mission) worked with Kaqchikel Maya to produce one of the first translations of the New Testament into an indigenous language. From Guatemala, Townsend moved to Mexico where he partnered with the government of President Lázaro Cárdenas to undertake new translation projects, not only in Mexico but also around the globe.

The second significant change was the movement by local leaders to create churches and institutions independent of missionary control. Motivations for seeking autonomy ranged in scale (in the face of US neocolonialism) from broad social trends favoring nationalism to personality conflicts between missionaries and converts. There were, however, two commonalities in most movements. The first was that early to midcentury autonomy did not immediately lift Protestantism out of its status as a numerically and socially marginal movement. With some notable exceptions (for example, among supporters of the Mexican Revolution of 1910–1917), as late as 1960, Protestants in Spanish and French-speaking countries comprised less than 5% of the population, the vast majority of whom were either poor or socially displaced (Pew Forum 2006).

The second commonality was that, in most cases, national churches were more likely than their missionary cousins to embrace Pentecostalism. Beginning in the 1970s, this connection to Pentecostalism became increasingly important as the number of Evangelicals across the region rose dramatically. This growth was particularly pronounced in Central America where, by 1980, Evangelicals accounted for 13% of the population in Guatemala and 8% in Honduras, Nicaragua, and El Salvador (Dow and Sandstrom 2001). Most of this increase came from autonomous national Pentecostal groups. Pentecostal revivalism also permeated English-speaking areas in the Caribbean in this period, and by 1982, 25% of Jamaicans were Pentecostals. As was the case in large parts of Africa, Pentecostalism became an effective mode of Evangelical indigenization.

Now, in the twenty-first century, the surging growth of Evangelicals has moderated, but not disappeared. Instead, Evangelicalism has reached a period of maturity as a significant minority group with a legitimate claim to local identity. One marker of this growth has been a shift in the socioeconomic makeup of Evangelicalism. Certain sectors of Evangelicalism still draw heavily from populations that are poor and socially marginalized.

Alongside and often superseding the old pattern is a new normative narrative in which a rising generation of urban, socially aspirational Evangelicals have crafted theologies and practices that appeal to the middle class and embrace popular cultural trends. In this new era, Evangelicals still claim a common spiritual identity, but at the same time represent an economic and cultural diversity that disallows simple social classification of the movement.

Pentecostal Character

Pentecostals have been at the forefront of most of these late-twentieth and early twenty-first century Evangelical shifts, to the degree that the terms "Evangelical" and "Pentecostal" are merging.

In Guatemala, a 2006 Pew Forum report found that 85% of Evangelicals either self-identified as Pentecostal or spoke in tongues regularly. This correlation between Pentecostals and Evangelicals cannot be neatly transferred to every national context, but the Guatemalan case is indicative of the region generally. The most prominent exception is Mexico, where the 2010 national census found that only 25% of Evangelicals attend Pentecostal churches.

As with the term Evangelical, it is difficult to impose a single definition on regional Pentecostalism. Pentecostals reflect Evangelicalism's general diversity in terms of class, ethnicity, language, and geography. The main element that unites Pentecostals in Central America and the Caribbean (as it does elsewhere) is an emphasis on the personal action of the Holy Spirit in believers' lives, especially through speaking in tongues, healing, and prophecy. Regional Pentecostals also make heavy use of technology and media, employing everything from the near ubiquitous loudspeakers on local street corners to international broadcasts on radio, television, and the Internet.

Beginning in the 1910s, foreign missionaries were important for introducing Pentecostalism, but local actors and factors have driven the more recent Pentecostal growth. Although this growth is undoubtedly rooted in the spiritual gains for converts, Pentecostalism also has a social logic. For the poor, Pentecostalism offers an opportunity for physical healing and social transformation in locales where other institutions are absent or ineffective; its emphasis on personal holiness also provides a clear and coherent moral framework in the face of socially disorientating modernization. In countries affected by civil war in the twentieth century, such as Guatemala and El Salvador, Pentecostalism provided a transcendent option for social organization that was safely outside of the immanent ideological and political conflicts of the Cold War. In more recent years, Pentecostalism has also found new adherents among middle class, urban populations who use the church as a means for active political participation by redefining citizenship as a spiritual (rather than secular) duty.

Among Afro-Caribbean populations, Pentecostalism also arrived with missionaries in the 1910s and 1920s, and local leaders primarily drove the late twentieth-century growth phase. Its theological emphases on holiness and the personal experience of God are also similar to Pentecostalism in Spanish-speaking areas. However, Afro-Caribbean Pentecostalism differs from other versions because it participates in a long history of tension between Christian orthodoxy and such Creole religions as Obeah, Myalism, Santería, and Voodoo. This is not to say that Afro-Caribbean Pentecostalism is itself an inherently heterodox mixture of Christianity and Creole religions. Usually, it is not.

Due to its emphasis on spiritual warfare and the power of the Holy Spirit, however, Pentecostalism offers culturally resonant alternative to those non-Christian religions that rely heavily on rhetorics of sorcery and spirit control. In some societies, such as Haiti, Pentecostalism manifests as an absolute and hostile rejection of Creole religion, while in others cases, such as Jamaica, Pentecostal movements adapt certain elements of those religions as a means of laying claim to integral cultural beliefs long ignored by denominational Christianity. In both instances, the ability to offer a contextualized version of Christianity has been one of the biggest factors in Pentecostalism's success.

Political and Social Engagement

Evangelicals in Central America and the Caribbean do not only engage surrounding culture on a spiritual level. They also do so politically, and this engagement is a key and often-misunderstood aspect of their identity.

Contrary to popular perceptions, Evangelicals in the region are neither apolitical nor uniformly conservative. Instead, their relationship to politics is a complex mixture of identities. A significant number do choose to abstain from politics, mirroring secular trends of nonparticipation. But among the many who do participate, there is no clear alliance between Evangelicals and a particular political ideology. Public opinion polls routinely show Evangelicals split in their support for parties on the left and the right, with a slight majority usually favoring more conservative political groups.

Considering the historic connections between regional Evangelicals and US missionaries, some of the most surprising evangelical political activities in the twentieth century were in leftist revolutions. The most notable cooperation of Evangelicals with revolutionaries came in 1979 when Nicaragua's Evangelical Committee for Aid and Development (CEPAD), a coalition of leading denominations, announced that it would participate in the Sandinista government's social programs.

Even in Cuba, a number of Evangelicals supported revolution, notably Baptists and Presbyterians. Following the Revolution, the Castro regime suppressed most organized religion. After the easing of restrictions in the 1980s, however, Evangelicalism experienced a period of growth and public recognition, with a handful of Evangelicals even serving in the national assembly.

An equally visible group of Evangelicals actively supported right-wing political movements during this period. In Nicaragua, the National Committee of Evangelical Pastors (CNPEN) publicly opposed CEPAD's close relationship with the Sandinistas and allied itself with US foreign policy.

Most famously on the right, in 1982 evangelical army general Efraín Ríos Montt took power in Guatemala through a coup d'état. Ríos Montt's weekly Sunday sermons unequivocally mixed spiritual and religious rhetoric, and he relied on advisors from his church for governing advice. The most enduring legacy of Ríos Montt's presidency was a scorched earth campaign that resulted in the brutal killing of tens of thousands of indigenous Guatemalans; his willingness to mix Evangelicalism and politics, however, was also a landmark change. In 1991 Guatemalans democratically elected Jorge Seranno Elias as president, another conservative Evangelical. Ríos Montt and Serrano Elias remain the only two Evangelical heads of state in the history of Latin America. However, Evangelicals have successfully run for governorships and legislative posts elsewhere, and several denominations and pastors have begun taking public positions in elections.

Evangelical engagement in broader society also runs deeper than politics. On one level, this social engagement is a well-known phenomenon. Temperance was an early hallmark of missionaries, and deliverance from alcoholism remains an integral part of many converts' testimonies. However, as their numbers have increased, Evangelicals have added a focus on communal identity to their historical interest in personal regeneration.

In rural areas of Guatemala and Southern Mexico, several Maya communities have incorporated Evangelicalism into their ethnic identity, using it as an identity marker to counteract such disorienting forces as migration, modernization, and state-sponsored violence. In large urban areas, Evangelicalism offers an alternative to gang culture, which is both violent and pervasive in large Central American cities. In a broad sense, Evangelicalism serves as a substitute social network for those who do not want to join gangs, but in some cases, it is also one of the few legitimate ways to exit a gang without facing recriminatory violence.

Wider Influence

Evangelicalism's increasing demographic and social visibility in Central America and the Caribbean has also rippled outward. One of the first institutions to feel these ripples was the Catholic Church. In 1975, the Panamanian Bishops Conference became the first in Latin America to grant official recognition to the Catholic Charismatic Renewal (CCR). This Catholic movement has adopted some common evangelical practices both as a tool for spiritual revival and as a defense against evangelical proselytism. As demonstrated by the widespread approval of bishops across the region in the 1970s and 1980s, CCR is not a radical departure from Catholicism in favor of Evangelicalism; it reinforces orthodox Catholic doctrines such as Marian devotion.

However, it does so in unabashedly evangelical forms, ranging across seemingly superficial changes such as stadium crusades, television programs, and popular music styles. More substantive theological adjustments include emphases on the individual experience of the Holy Spirit and personal evangelism. Despite their similarities, Evangelicals and Catholic renewalists seldom worship together, and it is common for bishops to encourage CCR activities in strong Evangelical regions to serve as an inoculation against further shifts in religious demography. This general trend is most visible in Guatemala, where a 2006 Pew Forum survey found that 62% of Catholics considered themselves Charismatic.

The ripple effect of Central American and Caribbean Evangelicalism extends beyond the region itself. Thousands of foreign missionaries continue to lead evangelistic, relief, and development programs in the region, but Central American and Caribbean Evangelicals are also exporters of their versions of the faith. These missionaries populate mission fields throughout Asia, Africa, and the Middle East, but the top destinations are Europe and the United States, where vocational missionaries and immigrants-turned-pastors are returning to the historical cradles of Evangelicalism with the goal of reforming the religious landscapes of those countries both among fellow immigrants and beyond.

Dr. Stephen C. Dove is an assistant professor of History at Centre College in Danville, Kentucky. He earned his PhD from the University of Texas at Austin and his M.Div. from Fuller Theological Seminary. His current research project focuses on the local character of Protestantism in Guatemala during the late-nineteenth and early-twentieth centuries.

Bibliography and Further Reading

Austin-Broos, Diane J. *Jamaica Genesis: Religion and the Politics of Moral Orders*. Chicago: University of Chicago Press, 1997.

Bowen, Kurt. *Evangelism and Apostasy: The Evolution and Impact of Evangelicals in Modern Mexico*. Montreal: McGill-Queen's University Press, 1996.

Brennamean, Robert. *Homies and Hermanos: Gods and Gangs in Central America*. New York: Oxford University Press, 2011.

Corse, Theron Edward. *Protestants, Revolution, and the Cuba-U.S. Bond*. Gainesville: University Press of Florida, 2007.

Dow, James, and Alan R. Sandstrom, eds. *Holy Saints and Fiery Preachers: The Anthropology of Protestantism in Mexico and Central America*. Westport, CT: Praeger, 2001.

Garrard-Burnett, Virginia. *Protestantism in Guatemala: Living in the New Jerusalem*. Austin: University of Texas Press, 1998.

———. *Terror in the Land of the Holy Spirit: Guatemala under General Efraín Ríos Montt*, 1982–1983. New York: Oxford University Press, 2010.

Hartch, Todd. *Missionaries of the State: The Summer Institute of Linguistics, State Formation, and Indigenous Mexico, 1935–1985*. Tuscaloosa, AL: University of Alabama Press, 2006.

O'Neill, Kevin Lewis. *City of God: Christian Citizenship in Postwar Guatemala*. Berkeley, CA: University of California Press, 2010.

Pew Forum on Religion and Public Life. Spirit and Power: A 10-Country Survey of Pentecostals. Washington, D.C.: Pew Research Center, 2006. http://pewforum.org/Christian/Evangelical-Protestant-Churches/Spirit-and-Power.aspx

Samson, C. Mathews. *Re-enchanting the World: Maya Protestantism in the Guatemala Highlands*. Tuscaloosa: University of Alabama Press, 2007.

Smith, Calvin L. *Revolution, Revival, and Religious Conflict in Sandinista Nicaragua*. Religion in the Americas Series, v. 6. Leiden, The Netherlands: Brill, 2007.

Steigenga, Timothy J. *The Politics of the Spirit: The Political Implications of Pentecostalized Religion in Costa Rica and Guatemala*. Lanham: Lexington Books, 2001.

EVANGELICALS IN LATIN AMERICA

By Pablo A. Deiros

Despite numbering only 50,000 believers in 1900, the presence and testimony of evangelical churches in Latin America today is an unquestionable reality and an irreversible historical fact. In spite of the many conflicts and crises, which have shaped the continent's history, Evangelicals have won social visibility and notably grown in numbers. The multiplication of believers and churches has been steady and significant, though with identifiable take-off phases. By 1930, Evangelical numbers in Latin America as a whole had climbed to 1 million and to 5 million in 1950. This 5 million doubled to 10 by 1960, to 20 million in 1970, and to 50 million in 1980.

By the year 2000, Evangelical numbers in the vast ibero-indigenous-immigrant continent of South America had climbed to over 70 million, part of a Latin American total of approximately 120 million. The recent annual growth rate of over 10% (meaning that Evangelicals have been growing at almost three times the rate of the population in general) has been a key question for scholars of secularization and modernization. The highest concentration of Evangelicals is in Brazil (with 26.3% of the population, or 51 million adherents), and in Chile. Of all evangelical subgroups, Latino Pentecostals are the largest component, with Brazil, again, featuring the largest concentration of Pentecostals.

History

The nineteenth century represented a period of serious turbulence for the dominant Roman Catholic Church in Latin America. With independence from Spain and Portugal, the colonial church, which had existed since the time of the conquest, entered a period of crisis. By the end of the colonial period, the Catholic Church was weak both institutionally and politically.

It was in this context that Protestantism found a foothold on a continent from which it had been excluded for three centuries. Protestants did so in three ways. The first was by immigration. For ideological or economic reasons, many of the new nations opened their gates to Protestant migrants: investors, military and political advisors, scientists, and traders. Others, such as the Waldensians from the Pinerolo in Italy, were forced to migrate through politically and economically induced poverty, establishing themselves in Uruguay and Argentina (Río de la Plata). Yet others came first to the Caribbean or North America, before relocating with co-nationals and family members in the southern continent. Although these colonists were usually moved by economic motives, their beliefs were alive and few abandoned their faith to be absorbed by the religion of the majority.

Believing communities of this type contributed considerably to the economic and cultural development of the countries in which they resided. They were the founders of the major mainline or historic Protestant denominations with roots in Europe or North America. Their major early religious efforts were directed through the Bible societies—particularly the British and Foreign Bible Society and American Bible Society (ABS).

The second way Protestantism found a foothold on the continent was through the translation, printing, and distribution of the Bible, thus propagating the gospel. Andrew Milne, for example, was a Scots businessman converted at a meeting of the YMCA in London

> **Protestantism found a foothold on a continent from which it had been excluded for three centuries.**

in 1858. He came to Buenos Aires to manage fruit shipments in 1863 and worked for much of his life as a colporteur for the ABS until his death in 1907. Francisco Penzotti began as a pauper migrant sent to relatives in Uruguay (1864) where he was converted among Methodists, and became a Waldensian missionary in Uruguay (1879–1886), and then ABS agent in Peru (1888–1892), Central America and Panama (1892–1907), and La Plata (1907–1921) (Wosh 1994, 241). The close association of the Bible with the origins of Latin American Evangelicalism explains the love for the Scriptures so common in that region's evangelical movements.

The third way Protestantism was introduced to the continent was through the ministry of missionaries coming from Europe and North America. Most of the evangelical denominations developed in the Anglo-Saxon world were represented in Latin America through the work of modern mission societies or denominational boards. These forms of the Protestant faith had a rather slow development in the first half of the twentieth century. With the arrival of faith-missions by the middle of that century, proselytism increased. Churches, though, did not grow in significant numbers and were too much identified with the North Atlantic missionary metropolis and their culture. As with Penzotti, however, they played an important role in mediating the gospel to migrant groups, including the Swedes (such as Daniel Berg) and Italians (such as Luigi Francescon) who were converted in North America but found in Latin America their missionary calling.

With the emergence of Pentecostalism at the beginnings of the twentieth century, a new way of understanding the Christian faith and life began to develop. Latin American Pentecostalism belongs to that branch of Christianity that places the personal experience of the Holy Spirit as a sign of the condition of being a Christian. Resisted as a sect by most Evangelicals in the first half of the last century, it finally became a significant part of the evangelical family—and, by the second half of the century, its most influential expression. Its development has been particularly impressive in Chile, where it has been independent of external denominations since 1910 (and where it now comprises some 13% of the population) (Pew 2006); in Mexico, where it first overflowed among Latinos attending the Azusa Street revival (from 1909) and then was developed by missionaries from the United States (since 1921) (Navarro and Leatham 2004); and in Brazil, where Pentecostalism made its major advance thanks to both an autochthonous progressive growth (since 1911) and to missionary work (Campos 2011).

Character

Of all the manifestations of Latin American Protestantism, Pentecostalism has been the most deeply indigenizing. During the twentieth century, Pentecostalism experienced unprecedented growth in the continent, and in general is the fastest-growing Christian movement in Latin America.

Latin American Pentecostals share their testimony freely and widely and their commitment to their faith translates into a zeal for evangelism. This movement represents a very rich, often unique combination of independent Pentecostal strains that emerged from the historic evangelical denominations, and movements that originated in the missionary work of European and American Pentecostals in the first decades of the twentieth century. And its success is seen not only in its numbers, but in the fact that all evangelical denominations have moved to a more Pentecostal understanding of the Christian faith and practice. The acceptance of the actuality of the gifts of the Holy Spirit and a more enthusiastic way of expressing the Christian faith are now common attributes for most Evangelicals in Latin America.

A more recent development within broader Latin American Pentecostalism is the Charismatic Movement, which has drawn members from classic Pentecostalism as well as the historical (mainline Protestant) and missionary churches. This Charismatic renewal is distinct from its classical Pentecostal expression in its adaptability and willingness to include believers of different doctrinal and ecclesial persuasions, including Catholics.

In some countries, as Schultze demonstrates of Guatemala, this charismatization of the mainstream has been a mixed blessing to older church forms. Adoption of new wineskins for old doctrines legitimizes the new forms, and closes the distance for those who might transfer to the newer form (Schultze 1992). These issues have come to the fore in early media coverage surrounding the appointment of the first Latin American Pope, Francis I.

What Evangelicals Are Like

Most Evangelicals in Latin America are Pentecostal and/or Charismatics (80%). Even those who are not Pentecostal/Charismatics by membership or affiliation are so by conviction and practice. There is a growing Pentecostalization of Latin American Protestantism. This profile identifies Latin American Evangelicals not so much in interdenominational terms as by intra-denominational characteristics. This is made all the more evident in the current post-denominational culture which characterizes evangelical churches, wherein a new apostolic paradigm seems to prevail. In fact, Independent or nondenominational churches of a Charismatic orientation (such as the Igreja de Paz in Santarem, or the Evangelical Cathedral of Santiago), constitute the largest congregations in the Latin American continent. The mass of their constituency express certain common characteristics, outlined below.

A Popular Movement: The new social class of marginalized people, migrant workers produced by the migration from rural areas to the cities during the processes of development and industrialization characteristic of the middle of the last century, became the soil in which the evangelical growth was nurtured. Latin American Evangelicals have flourished among the popular social classes, even when its adherents have held to the values of the middle class or at least aspired to be part of it. Sociologically speaking, some researchers see it as a "Westernization" or "modernization" of the indigenous culture, others as a product of the transition between a traditional society and modernity, and even others as a need of a sociological identity in a massive society.

Since the 1960s, evangelical churches have been most successful in identifying themselves as the true churches of the disinherited. Unlike the historic or mainline Protestant churches with aspiration to reach the upper classes, evangelical churches are class-based organizations and often protest movements against the existing class structure. These churches have often been at variance with the surrounding social structure in terms of organizational rules and traditional symbols, which they consider as belonging to the upper classes. They refuse to accommodate themselves to traditional Latin American political and social values, a forthrightness which can also make its way into discussions with their brethren in North America.

Moreover, Latin American Evangelicals have flourished in places where there is rapid cultural change, in the alienation and aimless life of the urban areas, and in the rural districts where economic change has resulted in disturbance of traditional relationships. As Freston (1998) notes of Brazil's poorest suburbs:

> A . . . survey of evangelical institutions in Greater Rio de Janeiro discovered that, of the 52 largest denominations, 37 were of Brazilian origin, virtually all Pentecostal. While only 61 percent of all evangelical churches were pentecostal, 91 percent of those founded in the previous three years were.

Evangelical advances have usually been made among sectors of the working population of the lower strat —especially in areas or groups of marked social dislocation. In these circumstances Evangelicals have appeared as a lower-class solidarity movement or as a movement associated with the socio-economic aspirations of the dynamic lower-middle class sector.

A Latino Cultural Movement: Evangelicals in various forms have met with success in Latin America in part because they compare favorably among the lower and lower-middle classes and with both traditional Catholicism and mainline Protestantism.

Latin American Evangelicals inherited their liturgy, ecclesiology, and theology from European and North American missionaries. Their growth began, however, when they abandoned these traditional traits for a more contextualized theology and missiology. This represents a major change in the mind-set of the majority of Evangelicals: from the grammar of the faith to the emotional expression of it, from orthodoxy to orthopraxis; from hierarchical structures to more fluid organizations: from dispersion to integration; from a rationalist to relational approach to the gospel; from a sermon-centered service to a worship-centered service; and from the use of a hymnbook and organ in worship to rock'n roll and folk music.

Much has been written about the Latin American character, the traits of which include innate warmth and hospitality, resignation in the face of periodic natural calamities, a flexibility of spirit producing tolerance, enchantment with charismatic personalities, individualism, and a distinct turn to emotionalism and mysticism. Latin American Evangelicals have given these traits increasing channels of expression. In contrast with the evangelical type of service, the average meeting of mainline Protestant churches is often decried as colorless, tasteless, and boring. In place of the Catholic Church's technical-theological language, which only the clergy understands, Evangelicals have a highly significant system of communication. All may receive the gift of tongues (as most Evangelicals in Latin America have)—a more ecstatic experience than reciting the abstract phrases of a specialized language. Much of their liturgical dancing, clapping of hands, shoutings of Allelujahs, and group participation in prayer is a form of folk drama with high levels of participation.

While other Christian traditions embody the miraculous in texts or sacraments, Evangelicals offer a symbolic "incarnation" in the promise of miraculous healing, not only as the gift of God, but as proof of a measure of their faith and of the fact that God has responded to the people's attempt to communicate with Him. Great emphasis is placed upon group participation in prayer and singing, and the sermons are generally intellectually accessible with plenty of opportunities for response not only verbally but by signs of the indwelling of the Spirit as well. These sermons are expressed more in narrative terms than as logical and rational elaborations. Most evangelical preaching is of a testimonial character and highly emotional.

Evangelization has evolved to be more integral and holistic, and it refers to the proclamation of Jesus Christ not simply through words but also through Christian service, seeking justice and spontaneous worship. The preaching of the gospel involves the proclamation of Christ as Lord of the spirits, which results in spiritual warfare at all levels. The challenges of relating redemption to the problems of globalization, cultural identity, poverty, and oppression also remain critical.

A Social Uplifting Movement: Most converts to Latin American evangelical churches have been drawn from a rootless and disconnected subculture, from people whose extended family networks disintegrated in the rush to the cities and who therefore lost much of the social infrastructure needed to survive in the hostile urban environment. Sociologists have said that Evangelicals in Latin America find in their faith a sort of compensation for their social alienation.

An example of these trends is found in the growth of Pentecostal churches in northeastern Brazil. Common to all of them is that the followers constitute part of an underprivileged mass of people, many of them former Roman Catholics whose socioeconomic situation has made them receptive to the message of local preachers. The message invariably contains the promise of a better life predicated upon immediate conversion. Usually this involves the adoption of a more ascetic way of life.

Buoyed by emotional exaltation and messianic expectations, they are eager to proclaim their spiritual rebirth by engaging in forms of behavior intended to repudiate the weaknesses and sins of their former lives. The members of such churches have proved capable of remarkable success in redeeming their lives socially and, to some extent, economically. The pastors of local evangelical churches facilitate these personal and social transformations, often acting as public representatives of the unemployed and dispossessed seeking honest work (Vasquez 2009).

An Anti-intellectual Movement: The anti-intellectualism of certain segments of Latin American Evangelicalism is one expression of its pervasive anti-elitism. This is often a reaction against the higher learning of the elites in government and religion. Reason is set in unflattering contrast to revelation, and the arcane matters of modern science juxtaposed to the clear truths of the Bible.

In Chile, for example, higher formal education for both ministers and laity is frowned upon among some Pentecostal groups. Schisms have occurred in some denominations when some members have tried to introduce Bible schools. The preference for the poor and uneducated has wide and indisputable currency among the Chilean Pentecostal churches. Any kind of learning beyond the literacy needed to read the Bible can be frowned upon and educated members who show intellectual interests or ambitions are watched with considerable suspicion.

More recently, however, there has been increasing openness to credentials and formal education as churches and denominations have grown, bureaucratized, and entered the public sphere. More and more Evangelicals today are looking for wider opportunities for ministry training. The traditional feeling that the primary qualification is a good and pious character and that an intellectual pastor may actually be deficient in piety, fitted well when evangelical churches were defined by their retreat from the "world." However, Evangelicals have become less indifferent to social issues and political involvement.

By nature, Evangelicalism is strongly individualistic (in regard to social issues) and intensely emotional. As a result, its response to political and social issues has been mixed, and varies widely across the continent. As Paul Freston notes, "whether democratic or authoritarian, right-wing or left-wing, embracing existing parties or rejecting them, defending narrow corporatist projects or broader universalist ones, the political importance of this expanding religious movement increases daily" (Freston 2008, 4).

An Urban Movement: Evangelical expansion during the last three decades has mainly occurred in rapidly developing urban areas. In 1950, three-fourths of the population lived in cities of less than twenty thousand people, but by 1975 half the Latin American population was urban.

In 1960, only six or seven cities had more than half a million people. A decade later there were already thirty-six cities with more than five hundred thousand inhabitants. Declines in fertility rates have not offset much larger gains in life expectancy and action against infant mortality; as a result, the annual demographic growth rate has been above 3% (Wilhelm 2009). Combined with massive migration from rural areas to the cities and "about one-half of the population of the city of São Paulo . . . was not born there" (Wilheim 2009), has led to the growth of sprawling cities, often with extensive barrios, bajos, or favelas around their edges.

Rural-urban migrants have had to confront the social vacuum of great cities, marked by the absence of norms or social values, and the pressures of industrialization. As in nineteenth-century Europe, such conditions are a recipe for religious change. The weakening of traditional social controls and a situation of social instability and aimlessness—characteristics of modern urban life—favor the development of an acute crisis in personal identity in many of the urban migrants. This explains why many abandon their traditional Roman Catholic beliefs and practices to become Evangelicals.

A Diverse Movement: Latin American Evangelicals emerged from diverse backgrounds and in many places assumed quite different forms. Protestant immigration from Europe, missionary denominations, and faith missions from the United States, and Pentecostalism (both indigenous and with missionary origins in Europe and North America), combined with the new developments of Charismatics and neo-Pentecostalism, are all mixed in the melting pot of Latin American Evangelicalism.

All Latin American countries have seen the development of evangelical denominations and post-denominational groups regardless of their origin. Most of these groups were in fact very different from their classical North American denominational expressions in their adaptability and willingness to include believers of different doctrinal and ecclesial persuasions. As a separate movement or as a movement with scarce dependence from foreign missionary support, Latin American Evangelicalism has been characterized by its diversity, and its willingness to empower people across the boundaries of gender, race, and class.

Historical waves have produced three broad types of Evangelicals in Latin America. On the one side are those who could be named as classical or conservative Evangelicals, having their origins at the end of the nineteenth and the beginnings of the twentieth century. These have, within their denominations, reached a high level of ecclesiastical institutionalization and are intimately linked to the major evangelical denominations in Europe and North America. A second group, and probably not the most dynamic, is that of Evangelicals belonging to independent denominations or faith missions. Together with some expressions of traditional Pentecostalism, this group is more inclined to fundamentalist understandings of the Protestant faith.

The fastest-growing churches in Latin America today, however, belong to the third group of Pentecostal/Charismatic and nondenominational type of Evangelicals, particularly those belonging to what this author calls popular Pentecostalism or nondenominational Evangelicalism. These groups are inheritors of classic Pentecostalism and Evangelicalism, but they have acquired the traits proper to popularized religiosity. Some of them are borderline expressions of the Christian faith in its evangelical understanding mixed with elements of Pentecostalism. Others are the result of deep experiences of spiritual renewal in classic evangelical denominations, with a sound theology, a committed missiology, a flexible ecclesiology, and high levels of contextualization, that make their churches truly missional.

A Theologically Rich Movement: It is also possible to distinguish various theological Latin American evangelical traditions. There are those Evangelicals who, theologically, ecumenically, and sociopolitically, are strongly conservative. Although these Evangelicals have taken an important religious leap in accepting and integrating their respective ecclesial traditions to the evangelical experience, they maintain the theological tenets of classic fundamentalism. They keep a strong premillennial eschatology and biblical literalism along with an inerrancy view of the Scriptures. They also have rejected any form of relationship between Roman Catholics and Protestants and have supported a definite right-wing ideology in political matters.

On the other hand, there are those who can be described as open to interdenominational or ecumenical relationships. They are more open to progressive theological and sociopolitical currents. This group is not growing significantly due to their ambivalence with regard to committed evangelization.

Finally, there is a sector in Latin American Evangelicalism that, although identifying with Pentecostalism, keeps a critical attitude towards its theological conclusions, its worldview, and its sociocultural vision. This is the most influential expression of Evangelicalism today, and it is permeating the whole spectrum of evangelical churches with its influence. Their leaders are better trained and their churches are among the largest in the continent.

A Movement of Strong Leaders: In Latin American Evangelicalism, the Charismatic leader, unfettered by traditional ecclesiastical structures and drawing on the cultural resources of Hispanic societies, easily commands an enthusiastic band of followers (Matviuk 2002).

Individualism also finds fulfilment in the evangelical understanding of the Christian faith. At the top of the ecclesiastical structure in many evangelical churches is either a group of men or a single strong personality who dominates the group. The strength of this structure is, however, the full participation of almost everyone and a gradation which depends largely on function rather than background. (Since the 1970s, Latin America has been a significant exporter of Charismatic/Pentecostal styles of church organization, from Juan Carlos Ortiz through to contemporary styles of cell church organization).

Since members come largely from the same general socioeconomic class, there is not the tendency for the rich or well-educated to stifle the development of the more humble people, as is the case in many churches of the more historical or traditional denominations. There is a growing role for women in the fastest-growing evangelical churches, both as ordained or dedicated ministers and church leaders.

A Growing Movement: Pentecostals account for, on average, 75% of the Evangelical population in Latin America, to a point that today when one uses the term *evangélico*, it is almost synonymous with the term "Pentecostal," as it was traditionally the identification between Protestant and Evangelical.

It is also possible to distinguish various theological Latin American evangelical traditions.

In some countries the Pentecostal population consists of 90% of all non-Catholics, making them the most visible evangelical force in the subcontinent. (Matviuk 2002) There is a cluster of reasons for this growth. These include: spiritual factors (the free action of the Spirit); anthropological reasons (hunger for God); sociological elements (they provide a sure sense of shelter, security, identity, and community in the hostile world); pastoral methodology (strong leadership, lay participation); and psychological and cultural factors (freedom of worship and emotion, use of folk music and instruments).

Most evangelical churches are large, self-supporting, self-governed and self-multiplying churches, rooted among the poor or lower-middle-class urban populations. Evangelicals do not lack problems of leadership, education, division, and social alienation, but there is no doubt that they have a significant place in the present and future of Christianity in Latin America.

Dangers

The present situation of Evangelicals in Latin America is not homogeneous. Mainline Protestant churches and those of immigration origin are in decay. Though 80% of all *evangélicos* in Latin America today are involved in various Pentecostal/Charismatic groups, rapid numerical growth brings new dangers. Among them are triumphalism, the corruption of the Christian gospel for a gospel of prosperity, the concentration of power around Charismatic leaders, the lack of a deep process of discipleship for new believers, some imbalance between mind and heart that results in religious emotionalism and sentimentalism, and an increasing institutionalism that weakens the commitment to the kingdom of God.

Latin American Evangelicals love the Bible, but many are biblically illiterate. About 80% of all pastors lack a formal theological and ministerial training. Bible teaching in local communities is wanting, and the traditional evangelical zeal for Bible reading and attachment is disappearing. Unity continues to be a major challenge for Evangelicals. Efforts have been made—which proved to be successful—but the road to Christian unity to better fulfill the mission continues to be a prayer waiting for a response (John 17:21, 23).

Dr. Pablo Alberto Deiros is a pastor, teacher, and widely published writer, and has variously held such positions as vice-president, Seminario Internacional Teológico Bautista, Buenos Aires, Argentina, and cofounder of the Latin American Doctoral Program and of Latin American Christian Ministries, Inc.

Sources and Further Reading

Campos, Leonildo Silveira. "Pentecostalismo e Protestantismo "Histórico" no Brasil: um século de conflitos, assimilação e mudanças." *Horizonte* 9, no. 22 (Jul–Sep 2011): 504–533.

Freston, Paul. "Evangelicalism & Globalization: General Observations & some Latin American Dimensions," in *A Global Faith: Essays on Evangelicalism and Globalisation,* M. Hutchinson and O. Kalu, eds., Sydney: CSAC, 1998, 69–88.

———. *Evangelical Christianity and Democracy in Latin America.* New York: Oxford University Press, 2008.

Matviuk, Sergio. "Pentecostal Leadership Development and Church Growth in Latin America." *Asian Journal of Pentecostal Studies,* 5, no. 1 (2002): 155–172.

Navarro, Carlos Garma and Miguel C. Leatham. "Pentecostal Adaptations in Rural and Urban Mexico: An Anthropological Assessment." *Mexican Studies* 20, no. 1 (Winter 2004): 145–174.

Pew Trusts. "Historical Overview of Pentecostalism in Chile." October 5, 2006 and accessed January 2, 2014. http://www.pewforum.org/2006/10/05/historical-overview-of-pentecostalism-in-chile/

Rocca, Francis X. "Pope Francis discovers charismatic movement a gift to the whole church." Catholic News Service. August 9, 2013 and accessed January 3, 2013. http://www.catholicnews.com/data/stories/cns/1303443.htm

Schultze, Quentin. "Catholic vs. Protestant: Mass mediated legitimation of popular evangelicalism in Guate-mala." *Public Relations Review*, 18, no. 3 (1992): 257–263.

Vasquez, Miguel. "The Global Portability of Pneumatic Christianity: Comparing African and Latin American Pentecostalisms." *African Studies*, 68 no. 2 (August).

Wilheim, J. "Metropolises and the Far West in the Twenty-first Century." In *Brazil: A Century of Change*. Edited by I Sachs, J Wilheim, P. Pinheiro, and R Anderson. Chapel Hill, NC: University of North Carolina Press, 2009.

Wosh, Peter J. *Spreading the Word: The Bible Business in Nineteenth-Century America*. Ithaca, NY: Cornell University Press, 1994.

Evangelical Impact in Ibero-America:
One Meeting Launches Worldwide Mission Movement

It started as a coming together of Ibero-American (the Iberian Peninsula, Latin America, and Hispanics in the United States and Canada) mission agencies at a single meeting in 1987. It is now a mission movement with a worldwide scope.

In the early 1980s there was an awakening to mission work throughout Ibero-America, and many mission agencies and churches were involved. New agencies were established, and several events brought Evangelicals together to talk about what was happening.

As the movement spread, a group of evangelical leaders in the region decided to hold a gathering to encourage those involved in missions. The first Cooperación Misionera IberoAméricana (COMIBAM) congress, held in Brazil in 1987, established a point of reference that marked the mission movement in Ibero-America, says Decio de Carvalho, now the director of the organization that was established as a result of that gathering.

"That was the very beginnings of COMIBAM," he says of the 1987 meeting. In 1997 the second COMIBAM congress gave further guidance and stimulus to the national and other mission movements in the whole region.

Today an estimated fifteen thousand Ibero-American missionaries are serving through several hundred mission organizations in more than one hundred countries throughout the world. They are working primarily in cross-cultural settings, although some focus on reaching unreached groups within the region, including immigrants.

Over the years COMIBAM, which is headquartered in Puerto Rico, has grown to respond to the needs of new missionaries. Although there was a lot of enthusiasm in going out to share the gospel and build relationships, missionaries often lacked the tools to cope long-term in a cross-cultural environment. "People wanted to respond and go out," says de Carvalho, "but there were very few training and equipping opportunities." The result of inadequate training before going overseas? "There was a very high drop-out rate."

By the time a third congress was held in 2006 in Spain, research had revealed other needs. Many missionaries had inadequate health care, little vacation time, lack of pastoral care, and insufficient funds for retirement.

COMIBAM has been responding to those needs as well as pondering the bigger questions of the Great Commission. With about sixty million Ibero-American Evangelicals in the world, "we have not reached our full potential for blessing the nations," one document reads. Written a few years ago and called "Where Is Comibam International Heading?"[1] the document cites large multicultural cities, the re-evangelization of the West, being a testimony in a world of religious pluralism and among unreached people, being agents of reconciliation amid religious persecution and deep suffering in a world of violence, displacement, refugees, and immigrants as some of the other challenges. "What will our role be in sending missionaries from the region to other continents and to the West?" the document asks.

. http://globalmissionscott.blogspot.com/2008/05/where-is-comibam-international-heading.html/.

The training and support are now showing results. A denominational mission agency in Mexico has mobilized many of its one thousand churches to support missions in Central and South America, Central Africa, and Europe. In 2010 the churches held their own missions conference, which drew eight hundred participants.

COMIBAM also helps the younger mission movements in the regions, such as the one in Cuba, where it has offered guidance to a group of churches to establish an intercultural training center. And in 2011 the first COMIBAM youth event was held in Bogota, Colombia, ensuring a new generation of stronger, better prepared missionaries.

—Debra Fieguth

Evangelical Impact in Brazil: The Power of Mothers

At every level of Brazilian society, mothers, about eighty thousand of them, are praying for their children. Inspired by the leadership of the prophet Deborah in Judges 5 of the Bible, they are influencing not only their children but political leaders as well.

It began when pastors Marcelo Gualberto and Jeremias Pereira and his wife, Ana Maria, attended a Christian conference in Korea in 1995. As the meeting was coming to a close and missionaries were being sent out, the Korean leaders commented, "We have come to this point mostly due to the mothers."

The Brazilian leaders went home with a burden to start mobilizing mothers. They called the new movement, formed under the umbrella of Youth for Christ, WakeUp Deborah (*Desperta Debora* in Portuguese) because "Deborah saw the situation and the challenges the Israelites were going through," says participant Silvia Brynjolfson. Deborah called herself to "awaken" and be part of the solution.

Even when Ana Maria Pereira, the movement's first coordinator, struggled through treatment for terminal cancer, she continued to give powerful messages that mobilized mothers. Now coordinated by Helida Paixao, workers provide training for women in prison, speak out against violence against women and abortion, and find creative ways to minister.

In Manaus, a city on the Amazon known for its violence, murders were happening almost every day. The Deborahs began organizing themselves, walking around the city and praying. The violence decreased, and the mayor asked the women for a meeting.

One day a mother was waiting at a Manaus bus stop when a young man appeared, put a gun to her head, and demanded money. As she nervously searched her wallet for cash, the young man suddenly started shaking. He had noticed the WakeUp Deborah logo and slogan, "Mothers on their knees, children on their feet," emblazoned on her shoulder bag.

"Are you a Deborah?" he demanded. "Yes," she replied, "and I'm going to a prayer meeting."

The would-be mugger lowered his gun. "My mom and my grandmother are both Deborahs, and I know they are praying for me," he confessed. "That's why I don't want to continue doing this."

Stories like this abound among the Deborahs. Concerned about the high rate of rape and drug use at a Brazilian university, one group approached the principal to ask for use of the chapel for a presentation on respect and values. He agreed, and a large number of students showed up. The whole atmosphere of the university changed. Female students no longer lived in fear.

WakeUp Deborah is now a mature organization in Brazil and growing in many other countries, starting with Portuguese-speaking nations. In 2009 when Brynjolfson, who is originally from Argentina, attended a conference in Buenos Aires, "the Lord called me to start WakeUp Deborah in Canada." At the same time Saskia van Helden of the Netherlands felt led to start the movement in her country. Now it has spread through Europe, South Africa, Kenya, Mozambique, Chile, Bolivia, Argentina, and Mexico. In Ciudad Juarez, one of the most violent cities in the world, Deborahs have stood at traffic lights throughout the city holding signs saying "Pray for Your Children."

—Debra Fieguth

Evangelical Impact in Venezuela: Creating a Better World for Children

Red Nacional Cristiana de Servicios al Niño Venezolano (RENACSENIV) is a Christian interdenominational network that provides care and services to children in Venezuela with the goal of creating "a better world for the children." It was formed in 2002 as a nonprofit organization aimed at mobilizing churches and Evangelical Christian services agencies to rescue children between the ages of four and fourteen years old throughout the country.

Recognizing that the period from early childhood to age fourteen is a profoundly critical time in a child's development, RENACSENIV reaches out to children in the poor neighborhoods and barrios, primary and high schools, hospitals, prisons, garbage dumps, foster homes, and other places where children find themselves in difficult situations.

RENACSENIV is led by a national leadership team comprised of leaders from different churches and coordinated by Maritza Sibila, director of the Commission on Children of the Evangelical Council of Venezuela. The work is done through networks made up of families, churches, shelters, orphanages, and other Christian organizations that minister to at-risk children.

The ministry meets its goals through programs that focus on spiritual, educational, health, sports, and artistic areas, always sharing the knowledge of Jesus Christ with biblical, ethical, and social values.

RENACSENIV has grown much since its beginnings. During its first two years, eighteen civil associations were involved in the care of six thousand children, with the participation of more than six hundred volunteers, in the states of Anzoátegui, Vargas, Miranda, and the Capital District.

Now RENACSENIV is assisted by thirty-eight networks nationwide and over five thousand volunteers. More than five hundred thousand children and adolescents have been reached in 350 cities and towns in Venezuela. About 80 percent of the children are incorporated into local churches. The impact has been extensive, with an estimate of over one million families of children helped.

Volunteers from various churches and institutions are trained to participate in spiritual teaching programs as well as in the care of children and adolescents. Because they are working with at-risk children, staff and volunteers need to be able to address such issues as self-esteem, abuse, learning disabilities, and children's rights laws. The ministry has also established training programs for the families of the children. These activities have led to the need to design special programs that incorporate discipleship materials, publications, projects, and family guidance programs.

The ministry performs services in alliance with public and private organizations, both nationally and internationally. Accordingly, the ministry maintains relationships of mutual collaboration with international organizations like Viva: Together for the Children, Compassion International, and Samaritan's Purse. It also partners with the Evangelical Council of Venezuela, the National Association of Evangelical Christian Educators Venezuela, Athletes for Christ, Editorial Kerusso, Aglow International, Radio Trans Mundial (RTM) Venezuela, United Bible Societies, the Bible League, Pro Child Evangelism Association, Oansa (Awana), and others.

—Debra Fieguth

Evangelical Impact in Argentina: Equipping Pastors to Build the Church

The rapid growth of the Evangelical church, and especially the Pentecostal church, in Latin America during the last four decades of the twentieth century brought with it both joy and challenge.

There was joy that so many people were finding new life in Christ. But the challenge lay in how to equip pastors to teach and disciple all these believers. Theological education during those years seemed to take a step forward, a step back, and another step forward as the church worked through the best ways to provide training to pastors and lay people.

Norberto Saracco, an Argentine Pentecostal pastor and educator, helped steer the church along the path to providing appropriate pastoral education from the 1970s onward. The late 1970s "were very difficult days for Argentina," Saracco says. A military coup had taken power in 1976, and "everything was fear, repression, and death."

Theological education started small, with seventy-six pastors taking courses, many for the first time ever, over weekends in 1978. Then hundreds of students applied for extension courses. Education was decentralized, and seminaries were established in many cities, not just in Argentina but also in a number of South American countries.

During that era theological education was an instrument for church unity, says Saracco. Because of the political situation in Argentina, "society was divided and, therefore, so was the church." Seminary leadership would only work in a city if more than one church invited the seminaries in. As a result, churches became stronger and worked together.

By the 1990s an alliance of three organizations that had banded together was attracting more than twenty thousand students per year. But the success of that ambitious project was curtailed in 1994 due to personal and institutional conflicts.

Not one to give up, Saracco and other theological leaders decided to learn from what seemed to be failures and forge ahead with the strengths of previous programs. They developed a new program, Facultad Internacional de Educación Teólogica (FIET), or International Faculty of Theological Education. A decade later an average of one thousand eight hundred students were registering each year.

Still, challenges remained. A survey revealed 40 percent of the pastors in the city of Buenos Aires had no theological preparation whatsoever. Another 40 percent had some training, and only 20 percent had graduated from seminary. Thrust into ministry without training, many pastors had little time to take courses due to the demands and unpredictability of ministry work. In addition, the majority had to work at other jobs because they received no remuneration from the church. FIET responded by establishing a two-year diploma in pastoral care and spirituality, which required intensive training one Saturday a month and home study. FIET now offers bachelor's and master's degrees with university recognition.

With more established theological training, the church has begun to respond to a new phenomenon, prison ministry. An increase of violence and crime has led to prisons housing double the population they can handle. Corruption among penitentiary authorities has only made the problem worse. "Amidst this situation, the power of the gospel has begun to impact lives of prisoners and to affect the penitentiary system," says Saracco. In some jails more than 80 percent of the inmates have accepted Christ. "The environment within those institutions has changed, and corruption has diminished." Recidivism has also decreased. While 60 percent of the released prisoners will commit crimes again, only 5 percent in "Evangelical prisons" do so.

FIET has stepped in to provide a program for prison chaplains to minister to the congregations developing in Argentina's prisons. In some prisons, inmates hold three worship services a day, fast once a week, and tithe gifts of money they receive to help families in need outside the prison. Now courses are offered inside the prisons to equip inmates themselves to minister. Hundreds have taken the courses.

—Debra Fieguth

Norberto Saracco helped steer the church along the path to providing appropriate pastoral education from the 1970s onward.
Photo: Facultad Internacional de Educacion Teologic

NORTH AMERICA

POPULATION 346,501,000
MAJORITY RELIGION: CHRISTIANITY (78.7%)

NORTH AMERICA REPRESENTS

5.0% OF THE TOTAL
GLOBAL POPULATION

12.0% OF THE GLOBAL
CHRISTIAN POPULATION

1.6% OF THE GLOBAL
NON-CHRISTIAN POPULATION

9.9% OF THE GLOBAL
MISSIONARY FORCE RECEIVED

CHRISTIANITY IN NORTH AMERICA

POPULATION ■■■ CHRISTIAN ■■■ EVANGELICAL ■■■

CHRISTIAN & EVANGELICAL POPULATION

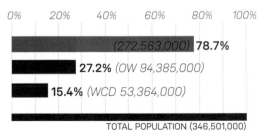

0%   20%   40%   60%   80%   100%

(272,563,000) **78.7%**

27.2% *(OW 94,385,000)*

15.4% *(WCD 53,364,000)*

TOTAL POPULATION (346,501,000)

GROWTH RATE* 1970–2010

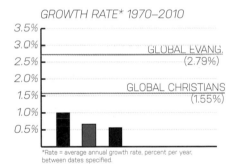

3.5%
3.0%
2.5% — GLOBAL EVANG. (2.79%)
2.0%
1.5% — GLOBAL CHRISTIANS (1.55%)
1.0%
0.5%

*Rate = average annual growth rate, percent per year, between dates specified.

MISSIONS IN NORTH AMERICA
FROM ALL CHRISTIAN TRADITIONS

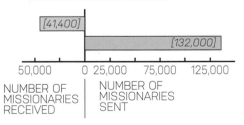

[41,400]

[132,000]

50,000   0 25,000   75,000   125,000

NUMBER OF
MISSIONARIES
RECEIVED

NUMBER OF
MISSIONARIES
SENT

1 MISSIONARY SENT
FOR EVERY **2,000** CHRISTIANS
IN NORTH AMERICA

1 MISSIONARY RECEIVED
FOR EVERY **8,400** PEOPLE
IN NORTH AMERICA

80 OF EVERY 100 NON-CHRISTIANS
PERSONALLY KNOW A CHRISTIAN
IN NORTH AMERICA

Source: *World Christian Database*, 2010 data

Christians and Evangelicals by country in North America, 2010

	POPULATION, 2010	CHRISTIANS, 2010	% CHRISTIAN, 2010	WCD EVANGELICALS, 2010	WCD % EVANGELICAL, 2010	OW EVANGELICALS, 2010	OW % EVANGELICAL, 2010
Bermuda	65,000	58,000	89.3%	8,400	13.0%	15,800	24.3%
Canada	34,126,000	23,662,000	69.3%	2,070,000	6.1%	2,602,000	7.6%
Greenland	56,500	54,300	96.1%	2,700	4.8%	2,700	4.7%
Saint Pierre & Miquelon	6,000	5,700	94.7%	11	0.2%	3	0.0%
United States	312,247,000	248,783,000	79.7%	51,283,000	16.4%	91,765,000	29.4%

EVANGELICALS IN NORTH AMERICA

By Larry Eskridge

Since the trans-Atlantic evangelical revivals in the mid-eighteenth century, North America (here defined as the United States and Canada) has played a key role in the development and history of the larger movement. Unlike most other nations and regions of the world, the arc of the Evangelical Movement is roughly contemporaneous with the comparatively short existence of these two nations birthed out of British overseas expansion. As a result, Evangelicalism has played a larger part in the history, culture, and politics of North America than in that of any other region of the world. This is particularly true in the United States where evangelical denominations and styles of religion not only claim large numbers of adherents but constitute a major component in the cultural identity of large swathes of the population.

Twinned with the region's enormous economic resources, North American Evangelicalism's numerical strength has made it a major factor in worldwide missions and evangelization. Denominational and independent mission boards, parachurch organizations, and relief agencies based in the United States and Canada have been instrumental in spreading the gospel and providing crucial resources to the rising church in the Majority World.[1]

While the burgeoning numbers and maturation of evangelical movements in Asia, Africa, and Latin America enhance their place within their own countries as well as the global evangelical spectrum, conservative Protestants in North America have reached something similar to a midlife crisis. Buffeted by secularization, ever-diversifying waves of immigration, and drift between segments of the movement, Evangelicals in Canada and the United States find themselves in complex and less accommodating cultures than was the case during the heady expansion of the mid and late twentieth century. North American Evangelicals have entered a pivotal period in terms both of their position within their own cultures and with regard to the nature of their relationship to the Evangelical Movement around the world.

Canada

Much of the story of Canadian Protestantism revolves around continuing influences from Britain and interchange with—and often resistance to, and differentiation from—its giant American neighbor to the south.

The first major evangelical revivals in Canada occurred in the Atlantic provinces in the 1770s and 1780s. An evangelical-style piety and revivalism suffused much of popular religious life in the Maritimes and appeared in the new settlements of Ontario in the early 1800s when a series of revivals swept Upper Canada. Through this period, interchange with American Evangelicals of various denominational stripes was relatively unhindered. This all changed with the War of 1812. That conflict not only cemented the primacy of a Loyalist Canadian identity separate from the United States, but it also erected barriers of suspicion and semi-separation between Evangelicals.

By the mid-nineteenth century, the focus of Canadian growth and settlement had pivoted to Ontario, as had the center of Canadian Protestantism. A strong Methodist movement vied for Evangelical leadership with the Presbyterians and Baptists, all arrayed against an Anglican power structure that was by no means without

---

1. The term "Majority World" is now commonly used to both counter the perceived negativity of older terms such as "Third World" or "Developing World," and to highlight the fact that these countries are indeed the majority of humankind.

Evangelical voices. That the contending interests of these parties did not break down into a war over establishment spoke to the reality of the growth of the evangelical groups, the challenges of building "civilization" in Ontario and the beckoning western expanses of Canada.

What emerged was a particularly Canadian evangelical expression that linked a desire for conversion with the duty to establish order and probity in the larger society. Canadian Evangelicals pursued their vision of a godly society through the establishment of colleges and seminaries as well as countless voluntary societies, promoting Sunday schools, Bible distribution, temperance, and the foreign missions.

The late nineteenth and early twentieth centuries appeared to vindicate this broad vision for a Canadian Protestant civilization. Presbyterians (1875) and Methodists (1884) constructed national denominations, and Baptists managed to form fairly strong provincial and regional associations. Discussions even began about the formation of a single united Canadian Protestant church. A decades-long series of debates and negotiations eventually issued in 1925 in the creation of the United Church of Canada, which took in nearly nine thousand Methodist, Presbyterian, Congregational, and Independent congregations. While this movement was underway, progress was made on the great temperance crusade; by 1914 prohibition was the law in every Canadian province.

The coming of the First World War shook Canadian society and revealed fault lines within Protestant ranks. Prohibition broke down rapidly and by the early 1920s it had been rolled back across most of the country. More serious was controversy surrounding Biblical criticism and liberal teaching in the pulpit, college, and seminary, connected to the fundamentalist movement that had begun to gain momentum in the United States. Toronto Baptist pastor T. T. Shields precipitated a cleavage among Ontario Baptists in the 1920s and became the leading figure in this Canadian movement.

Liberal Drift

Although Canadian fundamentalism never matched its American counterpart in size, influence, or rancor, it nonetheless formed a framework around which conservative Protestants from various small denominations and independent voluntary organizations could coalesce. While the increasingly liberal drift of the United Church would dominate Canadian Protestant life through its quasi-official cultural presence, conservative Evangelicals exhibited life and resilience through the World War II period.

Given the liberal control of the nation's denominational colleges and seminaries (which transitioned into a move toward outright secularization), conservative Canadian Protestants felt forced to seek other educational alternatives. Bible schools such as Ontario Bible College and the Prairie Bible Institute in Alberta proved a vital source of pastors, Christian workers, and missionaries. Over a hundred Bible schools and colleges were formed around the country, the bulk of them in Western Canada. Bringing additional revitalization on the nation's secular campuses was the InterVarsity Christian Fellowship, a British import which arrived in Canada in 1928, growing to become the springboard from which the organization began to spread to the United States and around the world. Its influence illustrated Canada's key role in mediating the various globalizations of the nineteenth and twentieth centuries.

The decades following World War II were a period of prosperity and growth, but also of rapid secularization, in Canada. Whereas in the United States the Baby Boom and the Cold War seemed to stimulate a desire for spiritual comfort and church-based community, the exact opposite seemed to occur in Canada. Church attendance and membership dropped by nearly half by the mid 1960s and the public Protestant presence of the United Church and the more liberal denominations in Canadian life eroded precipitously. Within that overarching context, Canadian Evangelicals emerged as the heart of religious life in the nation, not only holding their own but experiencing growth within their congregations, associations, and institutions.

Evangelicals Group Together

A group of Canadian Evangelicals, impressed with the role of the National Association of Evangelicals in the United States, sought to begin a similar organization for Canada. Founded in 1964, the Evangelical Fellowship of Canada (EFC) provided the beginnings of a more centralized voice for Evangelicals in the larger culture. Although support was slow to develop and finances were a problem for years, the EFC matured under the leadership of Brian Stiller (director 1983–1997). He revamped and refined the organization's magazine (*Thrust*, then *Faith Alive*, and later, *Faith Today*), and led the EFC as it sought to serve as an advocate for Evangelical positions in the media and to the government (Fieguth 2004).

Pentecostals proved a growing and important factor in this era. Not only was EFC head Stiller a Pentecostal, the premier Canadian evangelical media presence—100 Huntley Street (begun in 1977)—was also the creation of a Pentecostal, David Mainse. Canada's role within the World Pentecostal Movement was heightened by the major influence exerted by the so-called Toronto Blessing that began in early 1994 at the Toronto Airport Vineyard church led by John and Carol Arnott. Tens of thousands of visitors came from across the world to witness and experience the related phenomena and took the revival back to congregations all over the globe.

The latter decades of the twentieth and the beginning of the twenty-first century marked a Canadian Evangelicalism that had, to a degree, "arrived" but which found itself struggling against the counterweight of secularist trends in the larger society and the government. Just as it did in the United States, the megachurch model proved attractive in Canada. Congregations like Northview Community Church (Abbotsford, BC), Centre Street Church (Calgary, AB), and Springs Church (Winnipeg, MB) attracted thousands to their services in up-to-date, corporate-like campus settings.

Amid a Canadian educational system that made the establishment, support, and accreditation of religious-based colleges and universities much more difficult than was the situation to the south in the United States, institutions such as Regent College, Trinity Western University, and Tyndale University College grew in both reputation and constituent loyalty even as government meddling and financial challenges proved daunting.

Diversity and Evangelicals

Within the climate of secularism fostered by most sectors of the Canadian media, academy, and government, a wide berth for diversity is frequently perceived by Evangelicals as an edging out of Christian traditions, values, and morality. On the other side Evangelical resistance in connection with such issues as abortion, gender identity, and—especially—gay rights, is in turn frequently construed as bigotry and an attempt to return the country to the "bad old days" of white, male, Protestant hegemony. Inevitably, Evangelical involvement in the Conservative Party as well as the rise of groups such as the Canada Family Action Coalition, invite comparisons to the politicized elements of American Evangelicalism to the south (Stackhouse 2012, 3).

The challenges of negotiating and recalibrating the twenty-first-century vision of what it means to be a Canadian Christian within a diverse, secularized society will undoubtedly be a primary challenge in the years to come. Much of Canadian Evangelical history and activity has been typified by a larger shared goal of making Canada a shining model of Christian civilization for the rest of the world. As much as it differed in conception and implementation to the mind-set of their American Evangelical neighbors' "city upon a hill," there was indeed a core similarity. How the Canadian Church navigates this conundrum, particularly in the unparalleled absence of a Protestant mainstream, will have a great effect on Canada and could prove a beneficial guide to the more numerous and diversified brethren to the south.

The United States of America

From its creation in the 1770s into the mid-nineteenth century, the rapid territorial and economic expansion of the United States was paralleled by evangelical growth fueled by multiple revivals and a democratized religious marketplace of doctrine and ideas.

Within this dynamic cultural setting the Methodists, Baptists, and the rising Restorationist (Stone-Campbell) movement were ideally situated to take advantage of opportunities presented by westward development and challenges to hierarchical European traditions. Older Reformed bodies, congregationalist and Presbyterian, also grew within this context but were hampered by disputes over theology and technique. Meanwhile, the Anglican (Episcopal in the United States) Church, saddled with ties to the prerevolutionary order and largely adverse to revivalist measures, was eclipsed and, contrary to other English-speaking domains, was only a tangential player in the new Evangelical-dominated American context.

By the mid-nineteenth century, Evangelical Protestants had achieved a remarkable penetration into the nation's life and culture as churches and a welter of voluntary associations—denominational and interdenominational—promoted revival, reform, and good works. Prospects for any sort of golden American Evangelical Movement were shortly torpedoed by two major developments. First, waves of new immigrants from Western and Northern Europe brought large populations of Roman Catholics, Lutherans, and some Jews to the (mostly) northern United States.

Historic Evangelical Division

Secondly, strife and discord over slavery and the experience of the Civil War shook, and in some cases shattered, national ties within evangelical denominations and organizations. This latter event provided autonomy for the overwhelmingly evangelical African-American Church, such as the African Methodist Episcopal Church (formed in Philadelphia, 1816), and became the catalyst to the formation of numerous new black Baptist, Christian, and eventually, Holiness and Pentecostal denominations free from white control. For the older white evangelical denominations, however, the struggle left a legacy of sectional bitterness, separate cultural and theological trajectories, and flat-out division that took multiple decades to repair, and in some cases became a more-or-less permanent feature of the evangelical landscape.

By the beginning of the twentieth century, the United States' religious topography had undergone significant change. While revivalism thrived and Protestant denominations, organizations, and educational institutions proliferated and matured, ethnic and religious diversity challenged the old evangelical hegemony. The problems presented by industrialism and urbanization created a host of reactions and responses that ran the gamut from advocacy of temperance to the development of a Social Gospel that called on the church to ameliorate and correct the excesses of the capitalist order. Decades of accumulating developments in Biblical scholarship and science added to tensions that fueled both a secularist attack on Christianity as well as attempts to incorporate new ideas and understandings into theology, training, and church life.

Reaction to these multiple stresses created a rift between self-identified Liberals and traditionalists within evangelical churches and institutions. By the end of the First World War a full-blown Fundamentalist movement defending Biblical inerrancy was on the move to oust Modernist influence. Dovetailing as it did with larger cultural moves to battle alcohol (which resulted in the passage of Prohibition, 1919–1933), resist changing social mores and popular entertainment, and concern over the influence of non-Protestant immigrant groups (particularly embodied in a revivified new national version of the Ku Klux Klan), Fundamentalists were swept up in and labeled with perceived reactionary forces.

By the late 1920s it was clear that Fundamentalists had largely failed in their national cultural crusade and attempts to take back denominational and institutional machinery. They did prove remarkably effective in establishing and supporting a vast network of Bible-believing denominations and associations, parachurch organizations, publications, and training schools. Coupled with similar networks of denominations and institutions that had emerged from the nineteenth-century Holiness Movement and the Pentecostal revivals of the early twentieth century, there was clearly potential for a large-bloc conservative movement.

Associations Form

Dissatisfaction within these groups with their own cultural marginalization, isolationist mentality and—particularly among the fundamentalists—negative emphases, led to a call for greater cultural engagement and a reclamation of traditional Evangelical social engagement. This impetus led to the formation of the National Association of Evangelicals (NAE) in 1942, seeking the unity of conservative Protestantism. The new organization was broad-based in bringing together a disparate variety of traditions including various immigrant denominations (such as the Evangelical Free Church), holiness groups (such as the Church of God, Anderson, Indiana) and, most importantly, heretofore marginalized Pentecostal denominations such as the Assemblies of God and the Church of God, Cleveland, Tennessee.

However, the vision for a true equivalent to the more liberal Federal Council of Churches (later the National Council of Churches) failed to materialize as the NAE did not secure membership of major conservative denominations such as the Southern-based Presbyterian Church in the United States or the massive Southern Baptist Convention. Nonetheless, in tandem with the influential Youth for Christ Movement and the emergence of evangelist Billy Graham, the NAE provided a touch point and network for a less strident, more culturally-engaged, style of self-identified Evangelicalism that became the leading edge of conservative American Protestantism.

The 1950s and 1960s was a period of major expansion for the institutional and parachurch infrastructure of the nascent neo-evangelical movement. Postwar economic demand, suburbanization, and the "Baby Boom" fueled American prosperity more generally, but it also provided the wherewithal and optimism that produced a flurry of church planting, building programs, and the expansion and creation of evangelical organizations. Important ministries targeting youth and students such as Young Life, Campus Crusade for Christ, and the Fellowship of Christian Athletes were either started or hit their stride during this period. Building on distribution and funding strategies developed by radio preachers in earlier decades, Evangelicals, particularly Pentecostals, jumped on the opportunities presented by television. Evangelists such as Oral Roberts and Kathryn Kuhlman became household names. Meanwhile, the renewal of evangelical social concern saw the creation of groups like World Vision and Compassion International. Missions-oriented organizations, such as The Evangelical Alliance Mission (TEAM) and Wycliffe Bible Translators, grew dramatically and furthered visions of reaching the world.

The growth of the Evangelical Movement in the post-war decades was not, however, merely a matter of organization, demographics, and brick and mortar expansion. The experiences of World War II, the Cold War, and the rapid pace of change contributed to a significant, across-the-board surge in church attendance, membership, and interest in spiritual matters.

Charismatic Awakening

In terms of the evangelical dimension of this trend, the most important development came as a result of the widespread Charismatic awakening of the 1960s and 1970s. As mainline Protestant denominations of clergy and laypeople came into contact with Pentecostal broadcasts, ministries (such as the Full Gospel Businessmen's Fellowship International), and writings (David Wilkerson's *The Cross and the Switchblade* was particularly important), the revival spread into many Episcopal, Lutheran, Presbyterian, and Methodist congregations and eventually moved into the Roman Catholic Church. Although relations between old-line Pentecostals and the new Charismatics were not always smooth, the combined impact of these Spirit-fired groups made for a powerful presence within the larger evangelical church.

The Pivotal Figure of Billy Graham

During all the activity in this period, the figure of Billy Graham and the work of the Billy Graham Evangelistic Association (BGEA) played a central role. The half-joking statement that defined an Evangelical as someone who likes Billy Graham was in many ways an accurate gauge of the scope and orientation of the Evangelical Movement from the late 1940s into the early twenty-first century. Graham came as close as any one person could to symbolizing the Evangelical Movement. His evangelistic Crusades dominated the attention, headlines, and church life of the cities he visited, and reached nearly the entire nation through television.

Graham's supporting battery of ministries (such as *The Hour of Decision* radio program, *Decision* magazine, and Worldwide Pictures) and long string of best-selling books (including *Peace with God* [1953], *World Aflame* [1965], and *Angels: God's Secret Agents* [1975]) extended the reach of his ministry into the mainstream of American life. Often featured or quoted in secular magazine pieces and a frequent guest on late night television talk shows, Graham was the friend of several American presidents and was perennially near the top of annual "Most Admired Men" lists.

But Graham's influence went beyond his image. His efforts to create a "big tent" within his ministry and his willingness to work with those with whom he was not a perfect theological or stylistic match strengthened an already-existing tendency within the movement. Graham's irenic tendencies (as manifested in decisions like the move to reach out to mainline Protestants during the 1957 New York City Crusade) sometimes alienated former allies and reinvigorated a small group of separatist-inclined, self-identifying Fundamentalists. Much more frequently, however, Graham's generous inclinations won him new friends and reinforced the tone of cooperation and tolerance needed to hold together a burgeoning, but diverse, evangelical movement.

> By the mid-1970s American Evangelicals were riding high, so to speak, and had reached a peak season of success.

Riding High

By the mid-1970s American Evangelicals were riding high, so to speak, and had reached a peak season of success. The success of Graham, the expansion of parachurch groups like Campus Crusade and the Navigators, the ubiquitous presence of the "Electronic Church," the spread of the Charismatic revival, and the widespread publicity surrounding the youth-oriented Jesus People movement again catapulted Evangelicals into the public eye. Coupled with the declining numbers and influence of the old mainline Protestant churches, conservative Evangelicals had moved back into the center of American Protestantism. The presidential candidacy and subsequent election of avowedly born-again Southern Baptist Jimmy Carter seemed to validate *Newsweek* magazine's assertion that 1976 was "The Year of the Evangelicals" (Woodward 1976, 68–78).

Carter's ascension to the White House was a hopeful moment for those American Evangelicals who hoped to counteract what they viewed to be the harmful moral and cultural impact of the tumultuous 1960s. Carter, a Democrat, chose a middle-of-the-road course that did not sit well with many conservative Evangelicals who were looking to "reclaim" America. Independent Evangelical political organization grew quickly in the late seventies and aligned itself with the opposition Republican Party which had made great inroads among whites in the evangelically-oriented, and formerly Democratic, Southern regions of the United States. Groups like the Moral Majority and the Religious Roundtable led by prominent Southern television preachers like Jerry Falwell and James Robison agitated against abortion, pornography, the drug culture, the welfare state, and the overreach of the federal government (particularly regarding issues such as the banning of school prayer), while touting a strong anti-Communist line and support for Israel.

Ronald Reagan and Culture Wars

By the 1980 election cycle, dissatisfaction with Carter's policies and performance caused many Evangelicals to abandon him in favor of his conservative Republican, and much less-obviously pious opponent, Ronald Reagan. Evangelical political and cultural activism increased during the 1980s as the success of the "Reagan Revolution" convinced many conservative Evangelicals that they were in a position to win what came to be called the "Culture Wars." The growth in Evangelical cultural presence and political activism was hardly received with enthusiasm by more liberal, secularized segments of the American population. A sizeable portion of the American population perceived Evangelicals as pushing their values down others' throats and eroding the lines between church and state. A noticeable backlash arose in portions of the academy and in media portrayals, as well as in direct attempts to counter Evangelical political influence.

The extent and visibility of conservative Evangelical political and cultural activism masked the reality that a number of Evangelicals were more comfortable on the political center or left. Some groups, such as the Washington D.C.-based Sojourners Fellowship, were vociferous critics of capitalism and American policies in Central America, radical proponents of unilateral nuclear disarmament, and advocates for expanded government social programs. Few Evangelicals went that far, but it was clear that many conservative Protestants—such as those who joined the moderate left-of-center Evangelicals for Social Action (ESA)—were uncomfortable with the direction and tone of what they heard from the "Religious Right."

Mercy and Megachurches

The rise of ESA reflected the larger reality that, by the 1980s, there was a growing conviction among American Evangelicals that works of mercy and compassion were essential to the proclamation of the gospel. While charity efforts had always played a role, growing awareness of world poverty and the systemic factors that perpetuated such conditions fueled a growing effort to address these conditions.

Denominational relief departments grew and organizations like World Vision, Food for the Hungry, Samaritan's Purse, and NAE's World Relief expanded their programs and partnered with US government and foreign agencies. In the United States, new parachurch groups with large social ministry components, such as Prison Fellowship, sprang up. Even in many nonreligious organizations such as Habitat for Humanity, Evangelicals formed a substantial core of their active support.

One of the major changes of the 1980s and '90s was the "megachurch," a combination of the influence of the Church Growth Movement and the American penchant for bigger and better. Technically defined as a church with more than two thousand members, not all megachurches were Evangelical, but there were few that were not. With facilities that often resembled a public auditorium or corporate setting rather than a traditional church, the services usually featured casually-attired congregations singing upbeat praise music led by electronically-amplified worship teams.

Some of the megachurches, like Wooddale Church in Eden Prairie, Minnesota, were denominational (Baptist General Conference in this case), but many, like North Point Community Church (Alpharetta, Georgia) were an Independent congregation or, like Harvest Chapel (Riverside, California) or Canyon View Vineyard Church (Grand Junction, Colorado) loosely affiliated with the Calvary Chapel or Vineyard Movements. Probably the most influential of these megachurches was Willow Creek Community Church in South Barrington, Illinois, whose pastor, Bill Hybels, touted a seeker-sensitive attitude that sought to reach the "Unchurched Harry and Unchurched Mary" of America's suburbs. Willow Creek extended its reach through a roster of publications and seminars from its Willow Creek Association that impacted thousands of churches in North America and beyond. With roots in the area's nineteenth-century Lutheran and Reformed traditions, Hybels's approach seemed to provide a technology, that would even aid ailing traditional churches.

Despite the success of the megachurch and seeker-sensitive models, their growth revealed an undercurrent of dissatisfaction with the direction and content of the evangelical church. The overt politicization of sectors of the movement and the perceived near-total identification with the Republican Party was one of these problems. Others complained about the injudicious way in which Evangelicals had over-corrected for old strictures against entertainment and popular culture by embracing subpar, baptized Christian alternatives. The content of popular new evangelical worship styles and music also drew fire in a new set of "worship wars" as traditionalists lamented the disappearance of hymns and church organs in favor of worship choruses and contemporary bands. More problematic was a deep concern over what many deemed the shallow nature of evangelical theology and intellectual life as evidenced by the reception of historian Mark Noll's 1994 book, *The Scandal of the Evangelical Mind*.

These dissatisfactions manifested themselves in several ways. One was the growing attraction for many Evangelicals to the rigors of Reformed theology. In attracting adherents from other evangelical traditions, this occasionally led to a rejection of evangelical theology and identity. At other times, for example within the already troubled Southern Baptist Convention, it served to exacerbate existing tensions surrounding polity and doctrine. A second phenomenon was an increasing interest in liturgical worship and sacramental theology. The sources for this development were varied, including the influence of the broad-based Charismatic Movement, a general decrease in isolation and expanded educational opportunities and the largely posthumous impact of the writings of the English Anglican C. S. Lewis.

Generally, the attraction of the liturgical and sacramental seemed highest among the educated elite who found the traditions in which they had grown up lacking theological, emotional, and aesthetic sophistication. While a high church form of Anglicanism was the most popular option in this vein, there was also a small move into various strains of Orthodoxy and occasional conversions to Roman Catholicism.

Emerging Church

One of the catch-all repositories that channeled this sense of Evangelical dissatisfaction was the Emerging Church Movement. The emergents projected a decidedly left-leaning cultural sensibility, emphasized the arts and various strains of liturgical influence, and viewed a missional sense of praxis as Christians' main duty in the world. Intolerance for theological dogmatism was part and parcel of the movement's DNA and one of its main appeals, particularly for younger Evangelicals. Prominent leaders included such figures as Brian McLaren, Tony Jones, Shane Claiborne, and Rob Bell, who were often the targets for criticism from more traditional Evangelicals (McKnight 2014).

By the early years of the twenty-first century it seemed that American Evangelicalism had entered a less certain, less unified period. Major figures of the postwar revival passed away (Campus Crusade's Bill Bright, for example, who died in 2003), concluded their active ministry (Billy Graham preached his last crusade in 2005), and moved, or were moved, out of leadership positions (James Dobson, for example, who stepped down from his Focus on the Family ministry in 2010); a decades-long sense of stability was unraveling. While energy, a sense of mission, and a quest for cultural engagement remained hallmarks of the movement, there was less certainty about how Evangelicals should move forward with the unity, confidence, and commonly shared sense of authority.

One of the burning questions that faced the movement was the nature of its relationship to the political powers-that-be. Evangelicals' role in conservative and Republican politics had stimulated a reaction that moved

Bill Bright was one of the majo leaders of the postwar reviva
Photo © Bill Bright Media Foundatior

some to the other side of the political ledger in a manner that seemed as partisan on the Democratic side as the Republican boosterism they criticized. Many Evangelicals lamented having tied themselves too closely to any one party's political agenda and machinery in their quest for a more judicious and faithful interaction with the system. But there was also a palpable sense of political burnout that threatened a revival of the sort of political disengagement that had once been present among many conservative Protestants in the first half of the twentieth century.

Exacerbated by, and contributing to, the political rift that troubled Evangelicalism was the more ominous and enduring racial polarization that continued to ostrasize white Evangelicals from their African-American brethren. Disagreements over history, public policy, and political alignment meant that despite having broad doctrinal, moral, and cultural affinities through a shared evangelical heritage, there was only halting progress at best toward anything like a real unity in purpose and action. Larger questions about diversity within its own ranks—to say nothing of the larger culture—will be a major test facing the American Evangelical Church. One of the less publicized elements of the post-1965 change in immigration policies has been that a fair number of the newcomers from East and South Asia, Africa, Latin America, and Eastern Europe were also Evangelicals. The most noticeable dimension of this racial, ethnic, and cultural mix has been the growing Latino presence. The huge expansion of the overall Hispanic population in recent decades has led to a concurrent explosion in the number of Latino evangelical churches and organizations. How preceding waves of Evangelicals (white and black) relate to this swelling third force in their midst will be a telling key to the health of the overall movement in the years ahead.

Whatever direction American Evangelicals stake out under these circumstances, their vision for the Church, its role within society, and the global role to be played by the United States will impact America's direction, the development of the church abroad and, potentially, the future of the world itself. On a global scale the relationship of both segments of North American Evangelicalism—American and Canadian—to the rest of the world church will undoubtedly need to change from source and resource to partner and—it is likely—increasingly, mission field. In that regard, how North American Evangelicals manage their evolving relations with the church overseas may be as important for their own spiritual health as any impact they might hope to foster in other lands.

Dr. Larry Eskridge is associate director of the Institute for the Study of American Evangelicals (ISAE) at Wheaton College, Illinois. He is the author of *God's Forever Family: The Jesus People Movement in America*, and coeditor with Mark Noll of *More Money, More Ministry: Evangelicals and Money in Recent North American History*.

Sources and Further Reading

Carpenter, Joel A. *Revive Us Again: The Reawakening of American Fundamentalism*. New York: Oxford University Press, 1999.

Choquette, Robert. *Canada's Religions*. Ottawa: University of Ottawa Press, 2004.

DiGiacomo, Michael. "Pentecostal and Charismatic Christianity in Canada: Its Origins, Development and Distinct Culture." In *Canadian Pentecostalism: Transition and Transformation*. Edited by Michael Wilkinson, 15–38. Montreal & Kingston: McGill-Queens University Press, 2009.

Fieguth, Debra. "The EFC Holds True to Its Roots." *Faith Today* (September/October 2004) and accessed 21 January, 2014. http://www.evangelicalfellowship.ca/page.aspx?pid=286

Hankins, Barry J. *American Evangelicals: A Contemporary History of a Mainstream Religious Movement*. Lanham, MD: Rowman & Littlefield, 2009.

Hawkins, J. Russell and Phillip Luke Sintiere, eds. *Christians and the Color Line: Race and Religion after Divided by Faith*. New York: Oxford University Press, 2013.

Lindsay, D. Michael. *Faith in the Halls of Power: How Evangelicals Joined the American Elite*. New York: Oxford University Press, 2007.

McKnight, Scot. "Five Streams of the Emerging Church." *Christianity Today*. January 19, 2007 and accessed January 16, 2014. http://www.christianitytoday.com/ct/2007/february/11.35.html

Miller, Stephen P., *Billy Graham and the Rise of the Republican South*. Philadelphia: University of Pennsylvania Press, 2009.

Noll, Mark A. *A History of Christianity in the United States and Canada*. Grand Rapids: Eerdmans, 2009.

Stackhouse, John G., Jr. "Canadian Evangelicalism: Hanging On." *Evangelical Studies Bulletin*, no. 82 (Winter 2012): 1–4.

Woodward, Kenneth L. "Born Again! The Year of the Evangelicals." *Newsweek*, 25 (October 25, 1976): 68–78.

Worthen, Molly. *Apostles of Reason: The Crisis of Authority in American Evangelicalism*. New York: Oxford University Press, 2014.

Evangelical Impact in North America: Theological Training with a Difference

For years indigenous Evangelicals in North America have been trying to fit into the theological training offered by the dominant white culture. But since the establishment of the North American Institute for Indigenous Theological Studies (NAIITS) in 2003, they now have their own way of studying the Scriptures, led by indigenous scholars.

Indigenous peoples see things through a different set of lenses, says NAIITS cofounder Terry LeBlanc, a Mi'kmaq from the Canadian province of New Brunswick who now lives in Alberta. For example, the Western worldview is often dualistic, seeing the world as divided between the physical and the spiritual, while the indigenous worldview is more holistic. When Job tells his friends to consult the animals and the earth, for instance, "Westerners see it as a metaphor. We don't. We think that's real." Indigenous peoples from cultures around the world also tend to have more respect for elders and the wisdom they bring, LeBlanc points out.

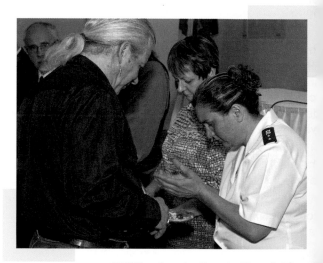

NAIITS cofounder Terry LeBlanc (left) say
the indigenous worldview is more holisti
compared to the Western view
Photo: NAIIT.

Instead of building an institution at a specific location, NAIITS partners with existing seminaries at several locations around North America, from California to Ontario. Faculty represent different indigenous groups: Mi'kmaq, Lakota, Métis, Cree, Carrier Sekani, Cherokee, Ojibway, Saulteaux, and Dene. "It's our energy, our efforts, and our people" doing the work of providing theological education, says LeBlanc.

(A member of the faculty until his death in 2013, NAIITS cofounder Richard Twiss, a Lakota–Sioux, was also the founder and president of Wiconi International. Based in Vancouver, Washington, Wiconi International ministers to First Nations people throughout North America.)

Unlike most educational institutions, which first offer undergraduate degrees, NAIITS began by providing master's and doctoral programs. It granted five doctoral and five master's degrees in its first decade, with growing number enrolled in master's programs. Now that a significant number of indigenous Christians have achieved high levels of education, the institute will begin offering bachelor's degrees. "We needed to have people at the top end who could teach people at the low end," LeBlanc explains.

Higher education in the theological arena not only helps with pastoral ministry and church planting but also with capacity building in the communities from which the leaders come. A robust indigenous theological education should provide Christian leaders with a more holistic approach to issues in their communities and how they interact with the dominant culture.

—Debra Fieguth

Evangelical Impact in the Media: Taking Jesus and the Bible to the Big Screen

Successful television producer Mark Burnett—known in North America for *The Voice*, the *Survivor* series, and other reality TV shows—and his actress wife, Roma Downey—perhaps best known for her role in the long-running television series *Touched by an Angel*—have many accomplishments and awards between them.

A common love for God's Word led them to launch their most ambitious project ever, a ten-hour television miniseries called simply *The Bible*. "We love [the Bible's] stories of love and redemption, and God's heart and hope for his people," explains Downey.

The Bible was an enormous but vital undertaking. "The Bible is the most read book of all time," Burnett points out. "It has touched the lives of billions of people across the planet and has significantly shaped history, culture, literature, art, politics, and human behavior." And yet many people are no longer familiar with the text.

For Burnett and Downey it was a labor of love to draw together a team of scholars, theologians, and pastors to serve on an advisory board, as well as a carefully chosen cast. Downey herself played the emotionally demanding role of the mother of Jesus. The series was shot largely in Morocco, where the terrain is similar to what it might have been like in biblical times.

Although many movies and TV shows over the years have depicted biblical themes, perhaps none has told the metanarrative in such a detailed way as *The Bible* does. The miniseries "paints the grand narrative of God's love for all of us," says Burnett.

The series aired on the US-based History channel in the spring of 2013, garnering more than thirteen million viewers for the first episode. Close to one hundred million people in total watched the series. Later in the same year it was aired in several other countries, including Australia and the United Kingdom.

Expressing God's love through history was a key part of the project. "I hope they go to the Bible itself and drink in the actual text," says Downey, "because it is a book that changes lives."

The producers of an earlier movie, *JESUS*, know just how much the Bible can change lives. Since 1979, when Campus Crusade for Christ first launched the film, more than two hundred million people have viewed its dramatized story of Jesus based on the Gospel of Luke. The movie has been translated into well over a thousand languages, with new ones being added every month. Viewers in some two hundred countries have seen the Jesus film in villages, in homes, and in makeshift outdoor theatres, with countless numbers coming to know Christ as a result. Technology has allowed the reach to extend even further. Viewers can now get an app to watch the Jesus film in selected languages on their mobile phones.

—Debra Fieguth

ASIA

POPULATION 4,165,440,000
MAJORITY RELIGION: ISLAM (25.9%)

ASIA REPRESENTS

60.2% OF THE TOTAL
GLOBAL POPULATION

15.1% OF THE GLOBAL
CHRISTIAN POPULATION

82.3% OF THE GLOBAL
NON-CHRISTIAN POPULATION

13.8% OF THE GLOBAL
MISSIONARY FORCE RECEIVED

CHRISTIANITY IN ASIA

POPULATION ▬ CHRISTIAN ▬ EVANGELICAL ▬

CHRISTIAN & EVANGELICAL POPULATION

0%   20%   40%   60%   80%   100%

8.3% (344,142,000)

3.5% (OW 146,853,000)

1.3% (WCD 54,987,000)

TOTAL POPULATION (4,165,440,000)

GROWTH RATE* 1970–2010

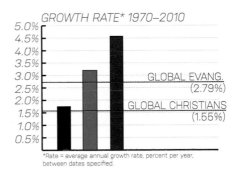

GLOBAL EVANG.
(2.79%)

GLOBAL CHRISTIANS
(1.55%)

*Rate = average annual growth rate, percent per year,
between dates specified.

MISSIONS IN ASIA
FROM ALL CHRISTIAN TRADITIONS

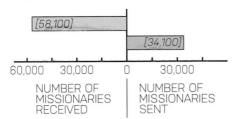

[58,100]

[34,100]

60,000   30,000   0   30,000

NUMBER OF
MISSIONARIES
RECEIVED

NUMBER OF
MISSIONARIES
SENT

1 MISSIONARY SENT
FOR EVERY **10,000** CHRISTIANS
IN ASIA

1 MISSIONARY RECEIVED
FOR EVERY **71,700** PEOPLE
IN ASIA

13 OF EVERY 100 NON-CHRISTIANS
PERSONALLY KNOW A CHRISTIAN
IN ASIA

Source: *World Christian Database*, 2010 data

Christians and Evangelicals by country in Asia, 2010

	POPULATION, 2010	CHRISTIANS, 2010	% CHRISTIAN, 2010	WCD EVANGELICALS, 2010	WCD % EVANGELICAL, 2010	OW EVANGELICALS, 2010	OW % EVANGELICAL, 2010
Afghanistan	28,398,000	29,300	0.1%	5,200	0.0%	8,400	0.0%
Armenia	2,963,000	2,770,000	93.5%	24,000	0.8%	268,000	9.0%
Azerbaijan	9,095,000	301,000	3.3%	3,000	0.0%	18,500	0.2%
Bahrain	1,252,000	163,000	13.0%	4,200	0.3%	23,600	1.9%
Bangladesh	151,125,000	751,000	0.5%	137,000	0.1%	633,000	0.4%
Bhutan	717,000	6,700	0.9%	880	0.1%	13,000	1.8%
Brunei	401,000	55,000	13.7%	6,500	1.6%	24,700	6.2%
Cambodia	14,365,000	349,000	2.4%	211,000	1.5%	240,000	1.7%
China	1,359,821,000	107,956,000	7.9%	15,246,000	1.1%	75,399,000	5.5%
Cyprus	1,104,000	793,000	71.8%	4,700	0.4%	6,600	0.6%
Georgia	4,389,000	3,734,000	85.1%	25,000	0.6%	65,200	1.5%.
Hong Kong	7,050,000	956,000	13.6%	230,000	3.3%	434,000	6.2%
India	1,205,625,000	56,383,000	4.7%	9,310,000	0.8%	26,290,000	2.2%
Indonesia	240,676,000	29,186,000	12.1%	7,707,000	3.2%	13,011,000	5.4%
Iran	74,462,000	272,000	0.4%	21,300	0.0%	118,000	0.2%
Iraq	30,962,000	478,000	1.5%	23,700	0.1%	53,400	0.2%
Israel	7,420,000	180,000	2.4%	15,500	0.2%	31,000	0.4%
Japan	127,353,000	2,618,000	2.1%	335,000	0.3%	596,000	0.5%
Jordan	6,455,000	172,000	2.7%	10,100	0.2%	19,100	0.3%
Kazakhstan	15,921,000	4,222,000	26.5%	37,800	0.2%	105,000	0.7%
Kuwait	2,992,000	264,000	8.8%	5,700	0.2%	46,400	1.6%
Kyrgyzstan	5,334,000	412,000	7.7%	2,200	0.0%	40,200	0.8%
Laos	6,396,000	187,000	2.9%	141,000	2.2%	170,000	2.7%
Lebanon	4,341,000	1,544,000	35.6%	19,400	0.4%	21,400	0.5%
Macau	535,000	38,700	7.2%	3,900	0.7%	8,500	1.6%
Malaysia	28,276,000	2,517,000	8.9%	603,000	2.1%	1,208,000	4.3%

Country							
Maldives	326,000	1,500	0.4%	170	0.1%	230	0.1%
Mongolia	2,713,000	45,300	1.7%	5,300	0.2%	33,500	1.2%
Myanmar	51,931,000	4,063,000	7.8%	1,482,000	2.9%	2,517,000	4.8%
Nepal	26,846,000	906,000	3.4%	420,000	1.6%	838,000	3.1%
North Korea	24,501,000	205,000	0.8%	10,300	0.0%	246,000	1.0%
Oman	2,803,000	121,000	4.3%	3,900	0.1%	24,000	0.9%
Pakistan	173,149,000	3,774,000	2.2%	945,000	0.5%	1,141,000	0.7%
Palestine	4,013,000	74,600	1.9%	5,800	0.1%	4,100	0.1%
Philippines	93,444,000	84,909,000	90.9%	3,006,000	3.2%	11,558,000	12.4%
Qatar	1,750,000	168,000	9.6%	3,930	0.2%	14,600	0.8%
Saudi Arabia	27,258,000	1,193,000	4.4%	26,830	0.1%	38,600	0.3%
Singapore	5,079,000	963,000	19.0%	266,000	5.2%	377,000	7.4%
South Korea	48,454,000	15,960,000	32.9%	12,580,000	26.0%	8,165,000	16.9%
Sri Lanka	20,759,000	1,832,000	8.8%	195,000	0.9%	243,000	1.2%
Syria	21,533,000	1,119,000	5.2%	12,900	0.1%	23,700	0.1%
Taiwan	23,146,000	1,390,000	6.0%	197,000	0.8%	649,000	2.8%
Tajikistan	7,627,000	97,100	1.3%	1,800	0.0%	7,000	0.1%
Thailand	66,402,000	812,000	1.2%	379,000	0.6%	307,000	0.5%
Timor-Leste	1,079,000	923,000	85.5%	22,400	2.1%	27,100	2.5%
Turkey	72,138,000	194,000	0.3%	9,400	0.0%	7,300	0.0%
Turkmenistan	5,042,000	77,400	1.5%	690	0.0%	1,700	0.0%
United Arab Emirates	8,442,000	1,061,000	12.6%	8,200	0.1%	60,800	0.7%
Uzbekistan	27,769,000	348,000	1.3%	8,300	0.0%	85,000	0.3%
Viet Nam	89,047,000	7,532,000	8.5%	1,260,000	1.4%	1,577,000	1.8%
Yemen	22,763,000	39,200	0.2%	4,100	0.0%	4,300	0.0%

EVANGELICALS IN RUSSIA AND CENTRAL ASIA

By William Yoder

Evangelicals across the entire breadth of the great land mass once known as the Soviet Union continue to share values and concerns. Within the Commonwealth of Independent States (CIS), which includes all of the former USSR except for the three Baltic states, "traditional" religious faiths confront the least public resistance. The Russian Orthodox, Sunni Muslims, Jews, Buddhists, and Animists have been present longest. Turkic-Muslim influence reaches almost to the gates of Moscow. Kazan, seven hundred kilometers to the east of Moscow, remains a center of Muslim life in Russia. Its Kremlin (of which Russia still has eleven) features both a mosque and an Orthodox cathedral. About 6.5 % of Russia's population is Muslim (Elliott 2014).

Only in nationalistic south Russian hotspots such as Dagestan and Chechnya are Muslims known for their radicalism. Elsewhere (for example, in the wide expanses of Tatarstan), Muslims have been a stabilizing force for centuries. Kazakhstan, the world's largest landlocked country, remains in many respects a secular society. In great contrast to Western Europe, headscarves on Muslim women (a key identity sign in countries where Muslims are in the minority) are rare in that country.

Though Roman Catholics and Lutherans were not included among the privileged, traditional faiths defined by the controversial Russian legislation of 1997, they too enjoy broad public recognition. Their high acceptance levels are undoubtedly related to their lack of mission activity across ethnic boundaries. Traditionally, religion is equated with nationality. Catholics have therefore been viewed as Poles or Baltic peoples, and Lutherans as Germans or Scandinavians. These historic denominations have little to fear as long as they restrict their work to members of their own ethnic minority.

The Baptist Union of Kazakhstan has traditionally been a very conservative federation and states that it attempts to avoid contact with Pentecostal and Calvinist circles. Yet by force of events, its president, Franz Tissen, has proven in his statements to be an apostle of religious liberty. The facade of a Baptist chapel in Aktas near Karaganda expresses a Baptist conviction well: "A House of Prayer for All Nations." That sentence runs counter to national practice and places Baptists and Pentecostals in the vanguard of the struggle for religious liberty. In Central Asia, the presence of multiethnic Protestant communities jumble and confuse the tacit (but essentially official) division of labor, which assumes that the Imam is responsible for ethnic Asians and the Orthodox priest for ethnic Europeans.

Repression

In all of these countries (except perhaps for Ukraine) Evangelicals experience some form of repression. On the continuum, the Orthodox, Lutherans, and registered Baptists are perceived by the state as most loyal—or at least most subdued. The Evangelicals thought of as troublemakers tend to be the Charismatics, the Pentecostals, the unregistered Baptists, and "sects" such as the Jehovah's Witnesses. A study by the Oslo-based Forum 18 news service lists 146 fines issued in Kazakhstan for "illegal religious activities" during the first eleven months of 2013. These included 83 fines for unregistered Baptists, 28 for Jehovah's Witnesses and 17 for Pentecostals. No Catholics, Orthodox or Lutherans were fined, and only 1 fine was issued to a registered Baptist. Such movements draw on deep histories both within Protestant independency and spiritual Christian tendencies in Russian history.

The unregistered Baptists or Initiativniki, which were founded in 1961 and are now named the International Union of Churches of Evangelical Christians-Baptists (IUCECB), have no more than 1,000 adult members in all of Kazakhstan. It is important to note that, even in the post-Communist era, the IUCECB congregations have refused to register and become legal religious entities when given the opportunity. Consequently, their church buildings remain the legal property of private individuals. The IUCECB reports a global membership of 78,015; roughly 20,000 of them still residing on Russian soil. During its heyday (1966), this Church claimed as many as 55,000 adherents.

Very much in contrast to the Charismatics, the tightly-knit IUCECB remains on the fringe of public society. Not all Protestants welcomed perestroika; recently, the leader of a nonregistered, Mennonite congregation in Western Siberia, for instance, spoke of a "tsunami of evil and debauchery" inundating Russian Protestants in 1990–1991 (Yoder 2014). The IUCECB's wariness regarding outsiders makes it nearly immune to Western theological and cultural influence.

Until it disintegrated into its Baptist, Evangelical-Christian, Pentecostal, Adventist, Reformed and Mennonite factions in 1991, the Soviet-era All-Union Council of Evangelical Christians-Baptists featured no less than a million members. That union's legal successor, the Union of Evangelical Christians-Baptists (RUECB), presently only claims seventy-two thousand adult members in Russia, though almost twice that in Ukraine.

Many autonomous groups, both registered and unregistered, exist apart from the RUECB and IUCECB. Baptist-oriented believers may still total 200,000 in Russia. The Charismatic-oriented Associated Russian Union of Christians of Evangelical-Pentecostal Faith (ROSKhVE) led by Bishop Sergey Ryakhovsky claims twice that number. Though commonly available, public estimates list only 300,000 Protestants and 140,000 Catholics for Russia; the number of active Protestants could be as high as 800,000—still considerably less than 1% of the population. Estimates of the Orthodox population in Russia range between 40 and 75% (Elliott 2014).

Throughout the former USSR, converts to Evangelicalism must reckon with a cultural resistance, which varies across the region. That cultural jolt is weakest in pluralist, pro-Western Ukraine and strongest in a setting such as Turkmenistan. It can also be claimed that Asian Muslim culture impedes religious freedom more than government; the state commonly proclaims that it is merely following majority wishes. As one Kazakh pastor has stated: "Our biggest problem is the persecution of believers by their families" (in Yoder 2014). In Central Asia, a convert to Christianity is excluded from community identity activities; one cannot, for example, expect to be buried in a traditional graveyard. For Christian converts, the loss of family and nationality is a common price.

Evangelical mission is often confrontational in Eastern Europe. Yet Alexander Fedichkin, a Baptist pastor in Moscow and president of Russia's Evangelical Alliance, cautions that all systems of faith "possess their own internal logic. Attempts by outside forces to destroy that logic leads to serious conflict." He compares confrontational evangelism to an attack on someone's family. In such an instance, the father—or bishop—feels called "to resist that which is threatening to destroy his family and its values." Fedichkin also describes Orthodoxy and the Baptists as "two old confessions in need of adaptation." In the Orthodox realm, dissident Orthodox splinter groups (apart from the conservative-Orthodox Old Believers, who broke with the Moscow patriarchy in 1666 and remain a trusted historico-national entity) are repressed by the majority, state-supported Moscow Patriarchy.

Ethnic Mix

Noticeable among the Evangelicals of Russia and Central Asia are the workers and missionaries of Korean ethnicity. These missionaries can be from South Korea or the United States and are mostly from Presbyterian, Methodist, or Charismatic churches. Russian Presbyterianism is thus profoundly decentralized; South Korea has roughly 120 independent Presbyterian denominations, most of whom (in a post-Colonial reflex) have sent missionaries to the former USSR bloc, which in its imperial and Communist phases played a significant role in Korean history.

The expulsion of German and Baltic Russians eastward after Hitler's attack on the Soviet Union in June 194
was accompanied by an expulsion westward of Koreans from the Russian Far East. The refugees from West and
East then became acquainted in Siberia and Central Asia. Vladimir Li, president of the fledgling Presbyterian
General Assembly, and Methodist bishop Eduard Khegay, are both Moscow-based Russians of Korean ethnicit
raised in Kazakhstan. A consequence of Korean Presbyterian fissiparousness, however, is that no one—including
Vladimir Li—has a thorough overview of Korean activities in Russia.

Charismatic Presence

Despite minimal training and resources, Pentecostal and Charismatic/Pentecostal groups have achieved
significant success among young people, particularly those suffering from substance abuse. Indeed, the Char
ismatic denomination Izkhod (Exodus) was founded to serve those recovering from drug addiction. The New
Life rehabilitation center near Kingiseppe and the Estonian border has served as a home to as many as four hun
dred addicts at a time. The rehab programs of traditional Baptist congregations have also done well. An article
published in 2010 expressed concern that Russia's Baptist congregations would be overrun by ex-addicts at th
expense of higher-level social groups. Indeed, a large percentage of students in its seminaries are ex-addict
from a non-Christian background.

Differences Everywhere

Present nearly everywhere throughout the former USSR are tensions between Evangelical and Cha
ismatic circles. In Russia, the Pentecostal Movement is represented largely by the historical Russian Churc
of Christians of Evangelical Faith (RTsKhVE) and the 1997-founded Associated Russian Union of Christians o
Evangelical-Pentecostal Faith (ROSKhVE). Though its head bishop Sergey Ryakhovsky stems from the unregis
tered Pentecostal Movement, ROSKhVE is known for its willingness to engage with government and Orthodo
circles. It is not only President Putin who offers public condolences when disasters occur; Ryakhovsky frequentl
also does so.

At ROSKhVE's national conferences, the Russian national anthem is frequently played. When the Russia
government recognized the breakaway Georgian regions of South Ossetia and Abkhasia as independent state
in August 2008, ROSKhVE and two smaller denominations rapidly expressed support. This posture stands i
sharp contrast to "Charismatic" (a term rejected by most of Russia's "neo-Pentecostals") positioning in Belaru
and Ukraine, where the movement usually strikes a decidedly anti-Russian pose. ROSKhVE places great stock i
the fact that Bishop Ryakhovsky is a member of Russia's Public Council for the Cooperation with Religious Orga
nizations at the Seat of the Russian President. Since Alexander Semchenko (now an Evangelical Christian) exite
from the RUECB in 2009, Baptists are no longer represented on that level.

A case can be made for describing contemporary church Pentecostals (or Charismatics) as the ex-USSR
most liberal and progressive Christian movement. In considering issues such as contemporary forms of wo
ship, the counseling of troubled pastors, divorce and remarriage, women's ordination and openness for yout
culture, Charismatic and Pentecostal work is certainly considered liberal. Methodists could also be described a
liberal, as the majority of their pastors are women, yet they have no more than 2,400 members within Russia.

In contrast, the New Testament congregation pastored by RTsKhVE-President Eduard Grabovenko in Perr
(Ural) now has 4,500 members and owns the city's most prominent ex-Soviet House of Culture. Its visibilit
causes uneasiness in Orthodox and government circles. Moscow's largest Protestant congregation is also Pente
costal: the 4,000-member Word of Life congregation pastored by the Norwegian Mats-Ola Ishoel. It belongs t
the ROSKhVE and was founded by Ulf Ekman from Sweden's Word of Life Movement in 1995.

Rick Renner's large Good News congregation in Moscow offers highly-choreographed and televise
church services featuring carefully prepared twenty-minute sermons (with only brief slots for "glossolalia

or "speaking in tongues") to approximately two thousand attendees each week, and to thousands of others through targeted outreach functions (Renner 2013). Renner's polished, high-volume music and push for health-and-wealth do not sit well with those accustomed to traditional evangelical fare, yet these new forms of worship and theology are not without their adherents in Russia and Ukraine. Renner, who hails from Oklahoma, has enjoyed strong support from Texan Charismatic Kenneth Copeland. Despite their many shortcomings, Charismatic and Pentecostal communities clearly represent the most dynamic, growth-oriented segment of Russian and Ukrainian Protestantism.

The Charismatic, Kiev-based "Invictory" is the Protestant world's strongest Russian-language news service—its nearest competitors are located in North America. The most prominent Protestant service in Russia, Semchenko's Evangelical-Christian news service *Protestant*, is visible but struggling financially. Baptist and Lutheran news services are even further behind. Baptist strength is located in a very different sphere: continuity and tradition. Its remaining membership does not depend on transfer growth and suffers comparatively little year-to-year attrition.

Evangelical Mistrust

Some developments in Ukraine over the past decade have strengthened the stereotype of Charismatics as businesspeople looking for easy profits. In 2010, Sunday Adeleja, the Nigerian-born founder of Kiev's Embassy of God megachurch, was found guilty of involvement in a pyramid, money-making scheme and barely escaped jail time. That significantly hindered the growth of his movement both in Ukraine and internationally. Pentecostal leaders such as Renner, who also has a congregation in Kiev, distanced themselves from him. Very much in contrast to Russia's ROSKhVE, Ukrainian Charismatics—including Adelaja—had close ties to the pro-Western Orange Revolution Movement of 2004–2005. There is a body of opinion that links this political stance and regional xenophobia to the judicial outcomes in the case.

Alexey Ledyaev, a Riga-based Ukrainian Charismatic from Kazakhstan, has attained acclaim as a leader of the anti-gay Watchmen on the Walls Movement based in Latvia and the Pacific Northwest, United States. More controversial was his 2002 book, *The New World Order*, which borrows heavily from the Christian Reconstructionist thinking of R. J. Rushdoony (1916–2001) and calls for the creation of an elitist, Christian, and clerical society. The book led to a break with Ryakhovsky: Ledyaev is presently also barred from entering Russia. His international New Generation denomination nevertheless remains active in Russia and Ukraine. The New Generation has split in Russia, and the larger wing is now under the ROSKhVE umbrella.

The Charismatic Maxim Maximov is founder and director of CNL, the world's leading Russian-language Christian television network. Its headquarters in Almaty, Kazakhstan, might be considered unusual, as is its status within the federation in general. On a recent trip to that country, the author could not locate a single Baptist or Lutheran pastor willing to speak positively of Maximov's work. CNL is seen as a highly-independent, foreign-funded, non-native entity, which has attracted criticism of heightening tension with Kazakhstan's rulers.

The globalization of media and of migration inevitably leads to external divisions being replicated in the former USSR. Cessationist Evangelicals, those who believe that healing and other gifts of the Spirit ceased with the death of the last of the original apostles, also draw upon support from abroad. Strange Fire, a conference branding the Charismatic Movement as "un-Christian," was held at John MacArthur's Master's Seminary at Sun Valley, California, in October 2013. That conference was streamed to a well-known Baptist preacher's school in Samara/Volga. The Southern Baptist International Mission Board (IMB) has often hired only cessationist missionaries, yet John MacArthur wields considerably more influence in the ex-Soviet realm. Some traditionalist Baptist circles, which have virtually always been Arminian and pacifist in orientation, are resisting this imported form of Calvinist teaching.

Worth noting is the considerable influence which émigré Slavic communities have in the ex-USSR. Émigré congregations located in Germany are often very traditional and may have ties to the IUCECB. Contrastingly, the United States also has a strong Charismatic, Slavic movement. In his blog, Russell Korets, a Ukrainian pastor in Seattle, Washington, reports that Slavic congregations are inundated by visiting pastors from the ex-USSR hoping to raise funds for projects in the home country. Inevitably, those who control the finances wield influence. The Internet offers expatriates broad opportunities for involvement in church politics back home. The Russian-language website, Heresy—No! based in Alberta and Oregon, attempts to warn Evangelicals half a globe away of the dangers of Charismatic and Calvinist teaching.

Areas of Cooperation

Despite their many differences, Pentecostals, Charismatics, and Evangelicals do cooperate on a few projects. Moscow's Slavic Centre for Law and Justice, an official branch of Washington DC's American Center for Law and Justice (ACLJ), has earned the respect of virtually all Protestant groups due to its legal work on their behalf. ACLJ is part of the ministry of the television evangelist Pat Robertson. Though its activities are largely confined to single annual events, the National Prayer Breakfast Movement has been present in Russia for two decades and holds an annual conference in Moscow's most prestigious hotel (The President). The National Prayer Breakfast Movement also holds events in roughly ten other Russian cities.

The Moscow-based Advisory Council for the Heads of the Protestant Churches of Russia has during the past decade-and-a-half played a role as a single voice of Protestantism vis-à-vis government and society. But currently its influence is dwindling due to lack of unity. Lutherans and Baptists resist the desire of Pentecostals/Charismatics to address society in the name of all Protestants.

The situation is certainly different within the Christian Inter-Confessional Advisory Committee for the CIS-Countries and Baltics (KhMKK in Russian). The only Protestant on the three-man ruling committee is a Baptist: Vitaly Vlasenko, director of the RUECB's Department for External Church Relations. Since the Moscow Patriarchy is no longer an active member of the Geneva-based World Council of Churches, it has at times pushed the KhMKK as a Moscow-based, inter-confessional alternative. Orthodox reluctance to strengthen the legitimacy of its Protestant rivals, however, has delayed its growth. One of its rare, larger-scale meetings was held in St Petersburg in February 2014. Support for family issues—which is connected with an internationalized struggle against the recognition of same-sex unions—is regarded as one ground upon which Russian Christians can demonstrate unity.

In regards to charity work, Protestants have also tended to display unity. Adoption programs such as Ukraine (or Russia) without Orphans enjoy wide Protestant support. If the drug rehab centers of one denomination come under government surveillance, all will tend to offer support. Protestants will usually close ranks when attacked from outside. The Moscow Patriarchy has occasionally made overtures to the RUECB. Even though Baptists do not enjoy the legal status of a traditional Russian faith, in a speech in Odessa on July 22, 2010, Patriarch Kirill went so far as to stress the Slavic character of the Russian and Ukrainian Baptist Movement. The Baptist leadership interpreted these overtures as an attempt to divide the Protestant community; Orthodoxy sided with the Baptists and Lutherans as they formed a joint front resisting the powerful Pentecostal and Charismatic Movement.

Common Grounds Within the Slavic Countries

Over the past ten years, a type of Westward-pointed messianic spirit has arisen among the Protestants of Russia and Ukraine. The rising prevalence of pornography, screen violence, human trafficking, and the rights of sexual minorities in the West has reawakened the old Slavic belief in the moral superiority of their own culture. In citing Western legislation on homosexuality, Ryakhovsky claimed in 2012 "Russian government legislation has never promoted immorality." At the WCC's Tenth Assembly in Busan, South Korea in November 2013, Metropolitan Hilarion (Alfeyev), chairman for the Department of External Relations for the Moscow Patriarchy, concluded

"In the past 50 years, the course of the Protestant churches has distanced themselves much further from Orthodoxy than was ever the case in the first 400 years since the Reformation" (in Yoder 2013).

Protestants—and not only the Orthodox—have resented the fact that joining the European Union would give Western liberals and humanists the right to impose their worldview on the faithful of Eastern Europe. In Moldova and Ukraine, Protestants have been demanding that their countries remain exempt from EU requirements regarding equal rights for sexual minorities.

Ukraine's role as a beacon of Western-style religious liberty is related closely to the fact that no Orthodox denomination is capable of achieving a monopoly. In contrast to Russia and Belarus, the Moscow Patriarchy here faces stiff competition from autonomous, national Orthodox denominations as well as the liturgically Orthodox Ukrainian Greek Catholic Church loyal to the Vatican. Within Russia itself, the Moscow Patriarchy's monopoly over Christians is most under threat in regions of the thinly populated Far East, where on Sundays the number of Protestant worshippers may outnumber the Orthodox ones.

Common Ground Within Central Asia

The republics of Central Asia demonstrate significant differences. The population of Uzbekistan (30.2 million) outstrips the geographically much larger Kazakhstan. The total population of Central Asia (if excluding Mongolia) is roughly 67 million. Tadzikistan is unique among the five republics, for it is the only one which has a majority Persian, non-Turkic populace. Its non-Turkic language, Farsi or Persian, is spoken by 75 million people between Afghanistan and Iraq and is used for some Protestant mission work in Russia.

In the five Muslim-majority countries of Central Asia, Evangelicals are doubly impacted by migration flows. They must come to grips with departures not only to the West, but also to Russia and Ukraine. Until 1990, Kazakhstan was home to a million ethnic Germans; that number has since shriveled to no more than 100,000. Today, active Kazakh Lutherans number only 2,000. Since 1987, the number of Kyrgyz Baptists has collapsed from 13,000 to 3,000. Only a fraction of Kyrgyzstan's ethnic Koreans remain: roughly 15,000. The Lutheran World Federation lists seventeen Lutheran congregations and 1,000 members in Kyrgyzstan; Uzbekistan (home to 45% of the population of Central Asia) has only 500 Lutherans in three congregations. Turkmenistan is reported to have 1,000 Baptists and Tajikistan to have 400. Virtually every Evangelical family in Central Asia is split, with some of its members living outside the country.

Work migration is also a major issue in Central Asia. Due to the destruction of local industry and agriculture, entire villages are left without working-age men. The phenomenon of fathers leaving their families for extended periods has ravaged family life. Moscow's unofficial population of 16 million includes more than two million semi-legal and illegal workers from Central Asia, often suffering under dismal living and working conditions. Evangelical mission efforts are attempting to reach these migrants. Though contacts with the churches of China are minimal even in Central Asia, Moscow does feature a mission effort among immigrant Chinese.

The German pastor Manfred Brockman from Vladivostok, head of the Lutheran church in the Russian Far East, agrees heartily with the assessment of his Beijing colleague, Pastor Karl-Heinz Schell: "The Christianization of China can no longer be stopped." Brockmann pointed out that China may already have as many as 130 million Christians—compared to Russia's 143 million inhabitants.

Thanks to the emigration of ethnic Europeans from Central Asia, the percentage of Evangelicals among the remaining Christians is on

In the five Muslim-majority countries of Central Asia, Evangelicals are doubly impacted by migration flows.

the increase. In Kyrgyzstan, for example, most Evangelicals are Russians with a smattering of Russian-Germans and Koreans. Koreans, both those born there as well as those who have arrived as lay missionaries, are known as high achievers in business and professions and exhibit an importance far beyond their actual numbers.

This emigration, however, has resulted in a serious "brain drain" from Central Asia. Once, 45% of Kyrgyzstan's population was Russian; that number is now down to 9.1%. Previously multicultural societies are becoming monolithic. This out-migration of ethnic Europeans from the countries is accompanied by the return of Muslim peoples to their traditional homelands. After serious unrest in the Kyrgyz region surrounding Osh in 2010, thousands of ethnic-Uzbeks fled across the border to Uzbekistan. Thanks in part to governments efforts, ethnic Kazakhs (the Oralman) have been repatriated from Mongolia, China, and Russia back to Kazakhstan.

Kazakhstan remains the center of evangelical activity in Central Asia, hosting conferences and youth gatherings intended to benefit the entire region. The distribution of Evangelicals is highly uneven: Turkmenistan and Tajikistan are without any registered Lutheran congregations. Much as in Soviet times, lay Lutheran grandmothers are still being forced to "marry and bury" in the remote corners of Central Asia and the Russian Far East. By way of contrast, the Evangelical presence is by far most dense in Ukraine. Though Kazakh Lutherans believe they can grow even when restricting their mission efforts to national minorities (which make up 35% of the population), the consensus among Central Asian Evangelicals is that their churches will only flourish by evangelizing the Muslim majority. This type of activity is relished least by government authorities.

In Kazakhstan, evangelization efforts among Muslims have met with some success. Franz Tissen states that membership in his Baptist union never exceeded seventeen thousand—its membership now stands at twelve thousand. He reports that during one calendar year in the early 1990s when his Union lost one hundred members through emigration, baptisms topped 160: some 80% of his Union's members were not raised in Protestant families. No ethnic-Kyrgyz Christian has been a believer for more than two decades, though 20% of the country's Baptists are Kyrgyz.

Repression in Central Asia

All five Central Asian governments claim to be secular, committed (in a necessary carrot to foreign investment) to combating Muslim extremism and terrorism. But their rulings on Islam also repress Protestants. The state-allied Orthodox churches of Central Asia thus persecute Protestants jointly with Muslims. In Turkmenistan, for example, religious books without the stamp and signature of a Muslim imam or an Orthodox priest are considered illegal. Protestant-government tensions appear strongest in Tajikistan and Turkmenistan with Uzbekistan coming in a close third.

Tough registration requirements and curbs on educating children are planned as a means of limiting Protestant growth. Kazakh laws introduced in November 2011 decree that only congregations of more than fifty members may be officially registered. Lutheran bishop Yuri Novgorodov calls the measures a bureaucratic nightmare and hopes to overcome the hurdles by combining smaller congregations into a single church meeting in multiple locations. In Kyrgyzstan, the minimum membership is two hundred. Political unrest and instability have kept these governments occupied with issues more pressing than the registration of small Protestant denominations. Turkmenistan's head Baptist, Vassily Korobov, claimed in 2012: "These are not the worst of times. Communist rule was significantly more trying and yet the church survived. We live from the expectation of the ages that the Lord will protect his children" (in Yoder 2012).

Role of the Evangelical Alliance

Though the Evangelical Alliance has many contacts in Kazakhstan, a Central Asian office is active only in Kyrgyzstan. Its role in Kyrgyzstan is unique. Founded in 2006, it can be understood as the administrative arm o an even broader Association. The Alliance enjoys the services of a professional lawyer and defends the rights of Protestants as needed.

Ukraine's Alliance is based in Kiev and Odessa and was only founded officially in 2011. The reluctance of its large Baptist union (125,000 members) to become a member has deterred growth. Belarus does not officially have an Alliance, but its Baptist union has nearly 14,000 members.

The Russian Evangelical Alliance was founded in April 2003. Virtually all Protestant denominations are members; the most active ones include the Seventh-Day Adventists, Baptists, Evangelical-Christians, Presbyterians, and Methodists. But top-level participation is limited and most efforts are sustained by grass-roots support. An annual conference is held in February or March around Moscow. The Alliance's general-secretary, the Evangelical Moscow pastor Sergey Vdovin, sees the Alliance as vitally important for the well-being of Russian Protestantism:

> **The spirit of independence is very strong among us . . . A church will often regard itself as independent, even if it belongs to a union. We attempt to protect ourselves from others. So it is the Alliance which helps release our believers from this bondage. The Alliance brings fresh air; it is our bridge to the world Protestant community. Through it we have access to the expertise of international churches older and larger than our own. They are a voice to us from the universal body of Christ.**

Dr. William (Bill) Yoder has worked in Russia since 2002, commuting to Moscow from Orsha, Belarus, since 2010. He grew up as a Conservative Mennonite in Florida and has spent his years in Europe since 1971 as a church worker and journalist. He was active in East Germany and Poland during the 1970s and 1980s and received a PhD in political science from Berlin's Free University in 1991.

Sources and Further Reading

Basse, Ottokar, and Gerhard Stricker. *Religionen in der UdSSR: Unbekannte Vielfalt in Geschichte und Gegenwart*. Zollikon: G2W-Verlag, 1989.

Elliott, Mark, ed. East-West Church and Ministry Report. 1993–2014. *http://www.eastwestreport.org*

Kube, Stefan, and Regula Zwahlen, eds. *Religion und Gesellschaft in Ost und West*. Glaube in der 2. Welt, 2012. http://g2w.sui@bluewin.ch and http://www.g2w.eu

Mandryk, Jason, and Molly Wall. *Operation World*, 7th ed., Downers Grove: InterVarsity Press, 2012. http://www.operationworld.org

Mojzes, Paul. *Religious Liberty in Eastern Europe and the USSR: Before and After the Great Transformation*. New York: Columbia University Press, 1992.

Mojzes, Paul, and Walter Sawatsky, eds. *Religion in Eastern Europe and earlier: Occasional Papers on Religion in Eastern Europe, 1981–2012*.

Renner, Rick. Renner Ministries: Report to Partners 2013, 2013 and accessed January 5, 2014. http://www.renner.org/wp-content/uploads/2013/12/2013-Partner-Annual-Report.pdf

Sawatsky, Walter. *Soviet Evangelicals since World War II*, Scottdale: Herald Press, 1981, and Eugene: Wipf and Stock Publishers, 2007.

Yoder, William. Protestants in the ex-USSR, 2007–2014. http://rea-moskva.org and http://www.baptistrelations.org

EVANGELICALS IN EASTERN ASIA

By Xiyi Yao

This entry will deal with countries historically referred to as mainland China, Hong Kong, Macau, Taiwan, North Korea, South Korea, Japan, and Mongolia. The beginning of the Evangelical Movement in these countries can be traced back to the early nineteenth century when Protestant missionaries from the West first arrived there. By the late twentieth century, these Evangelicals had become the dominant force in the Protestant family in East Asia.

Mainland China

Very much like India and other fields, the Protestant mission in China was started as a result of the evangelical revivals in the Anglo-Saxon world in the later eighteenth century. After the arrival in 1808 of the first Protestant missionary, Robert Morrison (1782–1834) of the London Missionary Society, the Western missionary presence in the Chinese society remained very limited until the mid-nineteenth century when, in the wake of the Chinese defeat at the hands of the Western powers, the entire country opened up. The last four decades of the nineteenth century witnessed a major expansion of missionary movements in China. From 1860 to 1905 the total number of Protestant missionaries increased from about 100 to 3,500 (Bays 2012, 68).

Throughout the nineteenth century Protestant missionary enterprises were largely organized through a "Protestant Missionary Consensus" (Patterson 1998) despite increasing denominationalism and the emergence of a progressive, cultural reform-focused mission approach advocated by British Baptist missionary Timothy Richard (1845–1919).

Echoing contemporary Evangelicalism in the West, this consensus put evangelism at the center of mission but acknowledged necessary and supplementary roles for social services. Quickly rising as the largest mission agency in China, J. Hudson Taylor (1832–1905) and his China Inland Mission embraced this consensus within its more conservative outlook and identity.

Hudson Taylor's eschatological theology (a branch of theology that considers final events in history), almost single-minded emphasis on evangelism, and uncompromising stance on non-Christian religions were not only shared by the majority of the Protestant missionaries of his times but also exerted a shaping influence upon the embryonic Chinese Protestant Church. The nineteenth-century missions also left rich legacies for the future church in China: cultural and political engagement, a Three-Self (Self Governing, Self Supporting, and Self Propagating) ecclesiastical vision, and the fruits of the Taiping Rebellion (1850–1864).

Soon after the collapse of the Qing Dynasty in 1911, it became clear that the overall mission scene—now featuring new and considerable efforts especially in the areas of educational, medical and other social services and related institution building—was becoming much more diverse. Even more significant was the diversification of the theological outlook of the missionaries. As liberal or modernist theologies found their audience among China missionaries, the supernatural aspects of the gospels were questioned. Old missionary emphases and methods were challenged, and various social gospels and religious relativism were promoted as the future path of the missionary movement. As these debates fed back to the respective sending countries, it did not take long for conservative missionaries to rally for the inerrancy of the scriptures, the centrality of evangelism, and the uniqueness of the missionary message. Consequently the modernist-fundamentalist controversy raged on through much of the 1920s and 1930s, fatally undermining the missionary consensus from the previous century.

The Chinese Church Comes of Age

The early decades of the twentieth century also witnessed the coming-of-age of the Chinese church. The missionary tutelage of the nineteenth century ended, and a new generation of Chinese Christians began to take up leadership roles. Parallel to broader Chinese nationalist developments in politics and culture, the movement for a more independent Chinese church gained momentum. As the Chinese church began to develop its own character and explore its own future orientation, it immediately found itself at the center of a theological storm which divided it from very early on. While liberals were entrenched in such urban institutions as the YMCA and the National Christian Council, the conservative or Evangelical Movements were prominent in the revivals sweeping across the country in the 1920s and 1930s.

Starting from the 1907 Manchurian Revival, waves of evangelical revival defined the emergence and developments of a uniquely native evangelical tradition. A generation of evangelical church leaders emerged— such as Wang Mingdao (1900–1991), Watchman Nee (Ni Tusheng, 1903–1972), and John Song (Song Shangjie, 1901–1944)—and indigenous church groups and movements such as the Jesus Family, the True Jesus Church, and the Bethel Band were born. While sharing all the fundamental evangelical convictions, the Chinese Evangelicals also diverged significantly over their responses to the Reformed tradition and to new movements such as Pentecostalism. Though related to Western missionaries, they were largely quite independent from missionary support and control. Their emphasis on the holiness of personal life and certain practices of spiritual gifts resonated with elements of the Confucian (and other indigenous) moral traditions. In comparison to the liberal wing of contemporary Protestantism, Evangelicals contributed most to evangelism and church planting in the country, and thus shaped the character of the Chinese church. And in spite of all the wars and revolutions of the 1930s and 1940s, Chinese Evangelicals were able to launch a wide range of ministry and mission endeavours in such areas as campus evangelism and mission outreach to Muslims.

After the regime change in 1949, church-state relations became a decisive factor in the life of the Protestant church in China. Granting religious tolerance, the new Communist authority aimed to contain and control religious communities and foreign/Western influence. From 1950 to 1954, with official backing, the Three-Self Patriotic Movement (TSPM) was launched and established as the only national organ of the Protestant church. While some evangelical leaders and groups decided to join, others, such as Wang Mingdao, refused to do so, and boycotted the TSPM as a modernist enterprise. Many evangelical church leaders were jailed for a range of crimes, including participation in unregistered organizations, illegal business activities, suspicion of conspiracy, and the like.

As the wider social context hardened throughout the 1950s and 1960s, Christian communities struggled for survival, and some of them were even forced to go underground. That was the beginning of what is now commonly known as the House Church Movement. When the atheistic fanaticism of the Cultural Revolution (1966–1976) was unleashed, even the TSPM was shut down, and clandestine house churches became the only way for the Church to continue to meet and worship.

Soon after the end of the Cultural Revolution, the Communist Party initiated a massive campaign of economic reform, including a return to religious tolerance. As a result, the TSPM was rehabilitated, and a new China Christian Council (CCC) founded as the official organ of the Protestant church in the early 1980s. From the 1980s to early 1990s, TSPM/CCC contributed significantly to the resurrection of the church, especially via Bible printing, the reopening of churches and theological education. In these years, the churches under TSPM/CCC experienced impressive growth, to the point where they currently number about twenty-four million members (Johnson et. al. 2013).

While liberal theology continues to be influential to some extent among TSPM/CCC national leadership and top theological educational institutions, the majority of its local congregations and pastors are Evangelical. In the recent decades the TSPM/CCC began to face a number of major challenges: a remarkable growth of house churches, the increasing assertiveness of local TSPM/CCC centers and a continuing shortage of clergy.

House Church Growth

In the wake of the Cultural Revolution, likewise, house churches reemerged and grew quickly. To the mid-1990s, they were strongest in rural areas and among marginal social groups. However, more recently the highest growth rate has been among house churches in urban areas and among social elites. Since the 1990s, house churches have been the fastest growing sector of Protestantism in China, currently claiming about seventy million members (Johnson et. al. 2013). Of course, defining any movement as disparate as house churches is tricky. Another common term for them is unregistered church. In any case, the defining factor is that house churches shared discomfort with the more Erastian TSPM/CCC—viewed by them as being too closely tied to authority—and a desire to maintain their independence.

Geoff Tunnicliffe of the WEA meeting with Minister of Religion in Forbidden City, Beijing.

Just like their evangelical forefathers, the contemporary house churches demonstrate certain well-known features; they are theologically evangelical, indigenized, heavily reliant on lay involvement and leadership, and very enthusiastic for evangelism. In fact, house churches have been a major missionary force in the Chinese society over the past decades and increasingly embrace the vision of world mission.

The well-known tensions between the TSPM/CCC and house churches, in fact, have more to do with historical and political factors than theological differences. The differences between them at the top level may be deep-rooted but at the grassroots there is considerable cooperation between the TSPM/CCC and house church congregations. Given the structural and psychological barriers, however, it will take time for reconciliation to take place at the national level.

Hong Kong, Macau, and Taiwan

In the nineteenth century, Macau and Hong Kong served as the beachhead and springboard for Christianity's entry to and expansion in mainland China. Macau was a primarily Catholic hub with a tiny Protestant community and Hong Kong a largely Protestant base.

Due to the efforts of the Western missionaries and several waves of emigration from mainland China, major Protestant denominations were established in Hong Kong. Until the early twentieth century, however, Hong Kong itself did not become the focus of most of missionary agencies but was always considered a mission field under a larger south China region. The Revolution and ensuing regime change in mainland China in the 1940s brought in a huge influx of refugees. Even as missionaries withdrew, new indigenous churches spread rapidly. As these new people and churches were integrated into the local society, and Hong Kong's cultural and religious ties with mainland China were severed, a genuinely native Christian movement began to take shape.

Since then the Church in Hong Kong has experienced slow growth, its current four hundred thousand members accounting for about 4% of the population. As with its mainland Chinese counterpart, the mainstream of the church in Hong Kong is Evangelical and has a disproportionately large presence in local educational and social service systems. Since its return to Chinese rule in 1997, Hong Kong has resumed its historic role as a base for the evangelization of mainland China and has strengthened its ties with the church in China. Despite Catholicism's long-term influence, by way of contrast, Macau remains predominantly a Buddhist society. The Evangelical Protestant presence is much smaller than is the case in Hong Kong.

Taiwan's Christian story began when Dutch arrived in 1624, but the presence of the Dutch Reformed Church ended in 1662 with their expulsion by the Ming Koxinga regime. The last three decades of the nineteenth century witnessed new waves of Catholic and Protestant missionary endeavors. Presbyterians were the most successful in their missions and church planting, a consolidation that continued under Japanese rule (1895–1945). In the wake of World War II and the beginning of the new KMT regime, the Protestant scene quickly diversified under pressure from the arrival of numerous mainline denominations and indigenous groups from mainland China. Throughout the 1960s, church growth was impressive but plateaued around 1970. The only exceptions are some indigenous and Charismatic groups. Christians currently make up about 4.5% of the population, about half of whom are Protestants.

Korea

Korea's first encounter with Protestantism did not happen until the 1860s. From 1865–1866, a Welsh Congregationalist missionary made attempts to enter Korea but died in tragic circumstances. In the 1870s, the Ross brothers from the Scottish Presbyterian mission stationed in Chinese Manchuria translated the Scriptures into Korean with the help of a few converted Korean merchants. These Christian merchants were instrumental in bringing the Bible to Korea and in founding the earliest congregation inside Korea.

The arrival in 1884 of American Presbyterian missionary Horace N. Allen (1858–1932) marked the beginning of persistent Protestant missionary endeavor. The next year Presbyterian Horace G. Underwood (1859–1916) and Methodist Henry G. Appenzeller (1858–1902) arrived. The remaining years of the nineteenth century witnessed the impressive growth of a missionary force and ministry not only focused on evangelism, but which also encompassed medical and educational work.

The missions in the city of Pyongyang and its surrounding region seemed most fruitful, and the city quickly became a stronghold of the Northern Presbyterian Mission (USA). At the end of the century the famous "Nevius Plan" (proposed by John L. Nevius [1829–1893], a Presbyterian missionary to China) was adopted by the Presbyterian missions in Korea. With its emphasis on building (in Henry Venn's famous words) "self-governing, self-supporting, and self-propagating" indigenous churches, this plan played a pivotal role in the emergence of an independent, robust Evangelical community in the country.

In the wake of Japanese victories over China (1895) and Russia (1905), Japan progressively established and consolidated its dominance in Korea. From 1910 to 1945 Korea was ruled as a colony of Japan. As the national crisis deepened, a revival commenced in Pyongyang in 1907, and quickly swept across the Church in the country. Marked by emotional confession, repentance, and prayers, the Great Revival of 1907 shaped the character of the Korean Church.

Soon the Korean Christians found themselves confronted with mounting pressure from the Japanese colonial regime and the rise of the nationalist movement. In this struggle, the Christian missionaries and church as a whole not only stood with the nationalist cause, but even played leading roles in such patriotic campaigns as the March First Movement of 1919. As Japanese authorities began to "Japanize" Korean culture and society, missionary institutions and the church became key defenders of native language and culture. The Japanese effort to force Korean people to worship at Shinto shrines also triggered intense and lasting debates and divisions among the missionaries and Korean Christians over the compatibility of Shinto practice with Christian beliefs. It produced fallout which continued to haunt the Korean church even into the post-war years. During these decades of Japanese occupation, the Korean Christians went through much trial and suffering. When the Japanese occupation ended in 1945, the Korea peninsula was immediately divided into the Communist North and capitalist South and was later devastated by the Korean War (1950–1953). The church too went through some very turbulent decades.

Internally, the church struggled with the tension and disputes between the resisters and collaborators from the Japanese colonial era and between the Korean believers and returning missionaries over such issues as church leadership and property ownership.

Externally, former Christian strongholds in the North were ruined by massive Communist persecution, resulting in the flight of a large number of Christians to the South. The arrival of fundamentalist North Korean Christians reinforced the conservative orientation of the church in the South; the bitter experience of Korean believers under Communism profoundly shaped their political outlook and contributed to their deeply rooted anti-Communism.

From the 1960s to the 1980s, economic expansion transformed South Korea into an industrial power. These decades also witnessed exponential church growth. Massive revival events featuring such international evangelists as Billy Graham attracted thousands to come to the Christian faith. As a result, some of the largest megachurches in the world took shape in South Korea.

The church's ministries and institutions such as seminaries and hospitals also expanded considerably. Overall, the mainstream of the Protestant community in South Korea remained theologically evangelical and politically conservative. In the campaigns against military dictatorship and social injustice, it was the more progressive and liberal wings of the church that spoke out, fought and, developed such contextualized theologies as Minjung Theology. The Korean Church began to send missionaries overseas even before World War II. But it was in late decades of the twentieth century when the church in South Korea emerged as a major force in worldwide mission.

In the early 1990s signs began to point to a slow-down in church growth in South Korea. In the first decade of the twenty-first century the total number of Protestants even dropped slightly (Park 2012). The number of new overseas missionaries from South Korea was also in decline (Moon 2012). The church is confronted with such issues as the corrosive influence of materialism, and divisions over the prosperity gospel, social justice and equality for the marginalized, national unification, women's roles in the church, and so on.

The twenty-first century is full of challenges as well as opportunities for the evangelical churches in South Korea. In the officially atheist state of North Korea, by way of contrast, there remains only a tiny Protestant minority.

Japan

Like its neighbors China and Korea, Japan under the Tokugawa Shogunate chose to seal its borders until an American fleet forced it to open up in 1853. Soon after the signing of the treaty between Japan and the United States, Episcopal, Presbyterian, and American Dutch Reformed churches began to send their missionaries to three treaty ports. It was not until 1873 that the official ban on Christianity was fully lifted. As a result, an increasing number of new mission agencies and denominations arrived in a short period of time.

After a slow start in mission work, the first Protestant church was established in 1872. Among the early Japanese converts were a significant number of social elites: samurai and intellectuals. Japanese Protestants took the initiative to organize several regional evangelistic bands and revival meetings. Throughout the 1880s the Protestant church made strides in total numbers of new members and ministries. Toward the end of the nineteenth century, liberal theology made its way from Europe through missionary networks and Japanese students studying abroad, gaining influence among Japanese Protestants. Consequently, the Protestant community here too became polarized into liberal and fundamentalist camps. Some conservatives who were open to the critical methods of liberalism were also identified as "neo-Evangelicals" (Fujiwara 2012). As the Meiji Regime began to promote State Shinto as an official ideology and strengthen state authority in the late nineteenth century, Japanese Christians found themselves under mounting pressure to conform to state beliefs and practices. The deteriorating social environment also contributed to a rapid curtailment in church growth.

The first two decades of the twentieth century witnessed the deepening of Japanese Protestant involvement in social services and the ecumenical movement, and the rise of German-inspired scholarly theologizing (particularly Neo-Orthodoxy). As Japanese government and society of the late 1920s was increasingly militarized, Christians came under even heavier pressure to identify with rising nationalism.

With few exceptions, the majority of the Protestant churches in Japan decided to conform. The result was the merging of almost all churches into one single United Church of Japan, and the collaboration of the churches with the Japanese government in World War II.

After the war ended, the United Church of Japan survived, but many denominations disaffiliated. The post-war Protestant community also witnessed a short-lived boom. A large number of American missionaries commenced work, resulting in a significant number of evangelistic campaigns through the 1950s. This church grew significantly.

However, as Japanese society was transformed by economic take-off, the United Church stagnated. Today, it remains a tiny minority. Throughout the 1950s and 1960s, the United Church as a whole played a more active role in social movements (such as antiwar protests) than in the pre-World War II era. Since the 1970s, Japanese Christians have been facing a not-so-new challenge: rising nationalism. Today, while the largest Protestant bodies are affiliated with the World Council of Churches, more conservative churches (attached to the Japan Evangelical Association) are affiliated with the World Evangelical Alliance.

Mongolia

Mongolia's encounter with Protestantism came in 1870, when James Gilmour (1843–1891) of the London Missionary Society arrived in the field. After about two decades of hard work, Gilmour managed to produce only a tiny flock of converts. The Mongolian Protestant community remained very small through the early twentieth century, reduced almost to extinction when the country became a satellite state of Soviet Russia.

The democratization of Mongolia from 1990 to 1992, however, has ushered in unprecedented church revival and growth. Various Protestant evangelical missions—including those indigenous to Asia—were quickly launched in the ensuing years. The results were an exponential increase of numbers both of churches and in believers. To train pastors for these rapidly growing churches, Union Bible Theological College was founded in 1995. Today most of Mongolian churches are represented by the Mongolian Evangelical Alliance.

Dr. Kevin Xiyi Yao is associate professor of World Christianity and Asian Study at Gordon-Conwell Theological Seminary. He was educated in China and America in the 1980s and 1990s, and earned a Doctor of Theology from Boston University in 2000. From 2003 to 2011 he taught at the China Graduate School of Theology, Hong Kong. He has numerous publications in the area of mission history in China.

Sources and Further Reading

Bays, Daniel H. *A New History of Christianity in China.* Malden, MA: Wiley-Blackwell.

Fujiwara, Atsuyoshi. *Theology of Culture in a Japanese Context: A Believers' Church Perspective.* Eugene, OR: Pickwick, 2012.

Johnson, Todd, ed. World Christian Database, Leiden: Brill, 2007 (et. seq.).

Kim, Soo. *History of Christianity in Korea.* Qumran Publishing House, 2011.

Moffett, Samuel Hugh. *A History of Christianity in Asia, Vol II: 1500-1900,* Maryknoll, NY: Orbis, 2005.

Moon, Steve Sang-cheol. "Mission from Korea 2012: Slowdown and Maturation." *International Bulleting of Missionary Research,* 36, no. 2 (April 2012), http://krim.org/files/Missions%20from%20Korea%202012.pdf, accessed 27 June 2014.

Mullins, Mark R., ed. *Handbook of Christianity in Japan.* Leiden, The Netherlands: Brill, 2003.

Park, Joon-sik. "Korean Protestant Christianity: A Missiological Reflection." *International Bulleting of Missionary Research*, 36:2 (April 2012), 59–62.

Patterson, James Alan. "The Loss of a Protestant Missionary Consensus, Foreign Missions and the Fundamentalist-Modernist Conflict." In *Earthen Vessels, American Evangelicals and Foreign Missions, 1880–1980*. Edited by J. Carpenter and W. Shenk. Grand Rapids: Eerdmans, 73–91, 1990.

Evangelical Impact in China: Vibrant Church Grows

In the days of the Cultural Revolution (1966–76) the church in China was forced underground. Meetings had to be secret. Bibles were banned. Conversion was illegal.

The revolution failed to stamp out Christianity, however, and after Mao Tse-tung's death in 1979, when churches started reopening, the Christian faith not only took root but mushroomed. "To say [growth] is spectacular is an understatement," says scholar David Reed, a student of the Chinese church for many years.

While observers disagree on the number of Christians in China now—estimates range from 40 million to 130 million—there is no disputing that the church in the most populous country of the world is a large and vibrant one. Several recent studies estimate between 60 and 80 million Chinese Christians. Another puts the number at 106 million Chinese Christians in 2010.[1]

The difficulty in determining the numbers is that because of China's long history of persecution, some churches are registered with the government, and some are not. Within six major movements there are thousands of unregistered churches. In Shanghai, for example, there are at least a thousand house churches, many of them consisting of thirty to sixty people, but some much larger. House church networks now send missionaries and evangelists throughout China.

The True Jesus Church, for example, was started by Chinese Christians in 1917.

An estimated seven hundred thousand Christians lived in China in 1949. Due to persecution and hardship, that number had dropped to five hundred thousand by 1980. Despite greater official tolerance since the 1990s, persecution still exits, albeit sporadically and mostly by local officials. Some Christians reported an increase in persecution prior to the 2008 Beijing Olympic Games, and again in 2012. But it is encouraging to note that today many unregistered churches are allowed to worship openly.

Most of those attending registered churches are Evangelicals, as are those within the house churches. A significant number are Charismatic or Pentecostal believers.[2] Today government officials assigned to monitor church life encounter Christian faith in their assignments.

Worship style has begun to include contemporary praise and worship, a combination of indigenous music along with songs imported from Taiwan and Singapore. These expressions are gradually replacing traditional Protestant worship, which was largely made up of older hymns introduced by Western missionaries.

No doubt access to the Bible has had an impact on Christian faith. By 2012 China's Amity Press, the official publisher of the Chinese Bible, had printed an amazing one hundred million Bibles in thirty-five years. It is predicted this number might double within ten years.

—Debra Fieguth

> **Even before 1949, when foreigners, including missionaries, were expelled from China, there were strong indigenous churches.**

---

1. Center for the Study of Global Christianity, "Christianity in Its Global Context, 1970–2020: Society, Religion, and Mission," (South Hamilton, MA: Gordon-Conwell Theological Seminary, 2013).

2. Luke Wesley, *The Church in China: Persecuted, Pentecostal, and Powerful* (AJPS Books, 2004).

Evangelical Impact in South Korea: Prayer Defines World's Largest Church

Throughout the evangelical world Christians are accustomed to participating in midweek prayer meetings. Perhaps a handful of faithful people—a dozen, or even a hundred—might gather to pray for the church and for the world.

The folks at Yoido Full Gospel Church in Seoul out-pray the rest. Up to 10,000 people, as well as a 500-hundred voice choir, gather regularly on Wednesday evenings for prayer. With 830,000 worshippers at its peak in 2007, Yoido is known as the world's largest church. At special prayer meetings held at four o'clock in the morning, up to three hundred thousand people meet together.

Of course it didn't start out this way. In 1958 only six people met together at the home of Pastor Ja-shil Choi for the first service. In addition to the other pastor, David Yonggi Cho, were Choi's three daughters (one of whom later married Yonggi Cho) and an elderly woman who wanted shelter from the rain.

Undaunted, Yonggi Cho and Choi began knocking on doors, inviting people to the new church, which soon outgrew Choi's living room and migrated to a tent in her backyard. The two pastors prayed for the sick and offered humanitarian assistance to the poor. In just three years the church had grown to one thousand members and finally purchased land for its own building.

In 1967 Yonggi Cho restructured the ever-growing congregation, dividing the city of Seoul into zones and appointing leaders to oversee cell churches that met for Bible study and prayer during the week and gathered corporately on Sundays. The new growth happened through multiplication of these cells: every time a cell reached a certain size, it split in two. That form of multiplication has been adopted by churches in many other countries.

There were 125 cells in 1967; now there are several thousand throughout Seoul, and the church has planted satellite congregations in different parts of the city. With several worship services throughout the day on Sunday, the Yoido site on Yoi Island still draws some six hundred thousand worshippers. Another million and a half visitors pass through its doors every year. Yoido also sends missionaries to other parts of Korea and around the world.

Since the beginning, Yoido's ministries have included compassionate and practical outreach in addition to spiritual. They help when disasters like the 2011 Japanese tsunami strike. They care for the elderly and the sick through palliative care and health services, for children through various ministries, and for the unemployed through a training center. A current project is to establish a heart hospital in Pyongyang, North Korea.

Yoido is also involved in teaching, through its own university and seminary, and in communications, through its own newspapers and television network.

Yonggi Cho retired in 2008 after fifty years as lead pastor, turning over the reins to Lee Young-Hoon.

—Debra Fieguth

Evangelical Impact in Japan: Ministry for Disasters

For a year after the March 2011 tsunami devastated coastal Japan, children at Hakusai Nozomi Preschool in Fukushima were not allowed to play outside. But when volunteers built a bamboo park with radiation-free bamboo, the simple climbing structure provided healing to both the children and the builders.

"People involved were being slowly rejuvenated by the experience," says Yoshinobu Akashi, pastor of Jo-ban Church and headmaster of the nursery school. (The church building itself was destroyed.) When the playground was ready, "we were blown away by the energy of the children."

The bamboo park was only one of many creative ways volunteers and staff from Christian Relief, Assistance, Support, and Hope (CRASH) Japan responded after the disaster that claimed some twenty thousand lives, destroyed hundreds of thousands of buildings, and left untold numbers of people homeless.

CRASH Japan was started in 2005 as a ministry to prepare for natural disasters in Japan. They provide things like child trauma camps during the 2004 tsunami and Typhoon Haiyan in the Philippines in 2013.
Photo: CRASH Japan

High on the list of nations prone to natural disasters, Japan frequently deals with earthquakes and other calamities. But the earthquake, tsunami, and nuclear fallout in 2011 were "probably a couple of magnitudes higher than anything else we've had to deal with," says Jonathan Wilson, founder and president of CRASH Japan.

The ministry was started in 2005 to prepare for such disasters, explains Wilson, a longtime missionary to Japan who works with Japanese churches. He is an American expatriate, while most of the staff and volunteers are Japanese.

Workers use Japanese customs and resources to help people deal with the trauma of losing so much. In Soma City, where many people are still living in temporary housing, a volunteer arranged a traditional Japanese tea ceremony. For one woman, who had not been outside since the disaster, participation made all the difference. "She helped out and served everyone," says organizer Miyuki Takemura. "And she had a big smile." In the tea ceremony, the server wears a towel around her waist, just as Jesus did when he was washing the feet of his disciples. The ceremony symbolizes servanthood and humility. "The aim is to connect with the heart of the recipient."

Discouraged and depressed by the loss of their homes and all their belongings, many residents of temporary housing have shut themselves up and cut themselves off from others. Some have considered suicide. But volunteer teams visiting these displaced residents and showing them Christian love and compassion have made the difference, bringing joy and hope to those who thought they had none.

At less than 1 percent of Japan's population, Christians often feel isolated and churches tend not to get involved in their communities. But since the tsunami there has been a shift, both in how churches respond to the community and how the communities see the church. Many have become more open to the gospel, and churches are being planted. In one area, recognizing that most of the organizations helping them were Christian-based, town officials remarked, "We know whom we can trust."

Even in towns hit hard by radiation, "many of the pastors have chosen to stay," says Wilson. Although some families with young children have left for safety reasons, "others are moving in to minister."

—Debra Fieguth

EVANGELICALS IN SOUTHERN ASIA

By Wessly Lukose

With a few exceptions such as India and Pakistan, Evangelical Christianity in South Asia remains relatively unresearched. Although South Asian Christianity is diverse in its historical origin, establishment, and expressions, it is as old as Christianity itself. Indeed, with the exception of Bangladesh, Bhutan, Maldives and Nepal, Christianity here largely has non-Western origins. The fact that Evangelical Christianity was not making much progress in the region, perhaps gave rise to the perception that South Asia has been a particularly difficult region for the Christian Gospel.

Christians are still a tiny minority in this region. It is the heartland of many world religions. India and Nepal are Hindu-dominant nations. Afghanistan, Bangladesh, Iran, Maldives, and Pakistan are Islamic nations. Bhutan and Sri Lanka are predominantly Buddhist countries. Nevertheless, substantial growth of Christianity is taking place in most of these countries.

The real impetus of this growth is the coming of Pentecostalism. Evangelicalism has become the prevailing form of Christianity in South Asia because of the impact of Pentecostalism, and it has led to significant growth among the marginalized and poor in most Asian countries (Shah 2009, xi). Pentecostal emphasis on Holy Spirit experiences such as healing, miracles, exorcism, visions, and deliverance from other evil forces are among the chief reasons for such a growth. While there is a general Evangelical consensus, there is also substantial diversity with multiple expressions of Evangelicalism seen throughout South Asia.

Nations with Long Christian History

Most South Asian nations, including India, Pakistan, Sri Lanka, Iran, and Afghanistan have a long history of Christianity. There exist strong and ancient traditions among Christians in India, Pakistan, and Sri Lanka, because they came under the influence of the message of Jesus long before Westerners reached the subcontinent.

Rajendra Prasad, first president of an independent India, made a remarkable comment during his address at the St. Thomas Day celebration in New Delhi on December 18, 1955:

> **Remember, St. Thomas came to India when many of the countries of Europe had not yet become Christian, and so those Indians who trace their Christianity to him have a longer history and a higher ancestry than that of Christians of many of the European countries. And it is really a matter of pride to us that it so happened. (in Mundadan, 1984, 1)**

Among the South Asian nations, India has the most well-established of ancient Christian traditions, holding that St. Thomas, one of the twelve disciples of Jesus Christ, came to South India in AD 52, and preached the gospel even to the high caste Brahmins. As a result, seven churches were formed.

The local Christian communities (St. Thomas Christians) have their own oral and literary traditions and other well-structured documents that mention the apostle Thomas's arrival, preaching and martyrdom in India. There is also a north Indian tradition that St. Thomas also preached in northwest India (the current Pakistan) in the Punjab, leading to the conversion of King Gundophorus or Goduphar. Legends connect the origin of Evangelical Christianity in Sri Lanka to St. Thomas, and some archaeological evidence supports the existence of a significant Christian community there in the sixth and seventh centuries, which later declined. If these traditions are taken into consideration, we can convincingly conclude that it is the evangelical form of Christianity that was originally introduced in South Asia.

India is the largest country in South Asia, and it is a land of pluralism in terms of culture, language, religion and race. It is the most ethnically diverse nation on earth, with more than 2,500 distinct people groups. There are 325 languages and more than 700 dialects spoken in India. There are many religious groups: Hindus (82 %), Muslims (12.12 %), Christians (2.34 %), Sikhs (1.94 %), Buddhists (0.76 %), Jains (0.40 %) and others (0.44 %) (Johnson and Ross 2009).

Evangelical Christianity was solidly established in India in the eighteenth century, with the arrival of several missionaries from the West. The most remarkable contribution of the Germans, Bartholomaeus Ziegenbalg and Heinrich Pluetschau of the Danish-Halle Mission (the first Protestant missionaries to India) was perhaps the translation of the New Testament into the Tamil language.

The Moravian Missions were involved in forming small cells within the churches to enrich the spiritual life of the congregations through Bible study, prayer, and evangelism. The works of the Society for the Propagation of Christian Knowledge (SPCK), the Church Missionary Society (CMS), and the London Missionary Society (LMS) further accelerated evangelical work in India as they established a number of centers in South India in the nineteenth century. Additionally, the coming of the Baptist missionary William Carey in 1793 and the establishment of Serampore Mission stimulated rapid growth with its contribution towards literature, education, and evangelism.

The availability of the Scriptures in indigenous languages was another important factor for maintaining evangelical fervour in India. The missionary organizations in India created a missionary zeal and passion among the indigenous Christians for a rapid evangelization of India, a passion that paved the way for religious awakening and the subsequent growth of Christianity.

Evangelical Christianity is growing significantly in both urban and rural areas. There are numerous independent local missionaries working in the Indian villages, and consequently there is an unprecedented growth. There are a number of mega churches in the Indian metropolitan cities with thousands of members. The vibrant form of Evangelical Christianity, blended with the Charismatic experience, appeals to Indian masses, drawing hundreds to Christ every day. There is an increasing concern among Christians that the percent of Christianity is much higher than the official data. Most evangelical scholars agree that perhaps as much as 5% of the total population (as opposed to an official figure of around 2%) is Christian (Johnson and Ross 2009).

Indian Evangelicals are the most established Christians in South Asia. The Evangelical Fellowship of India (EFI), the national alliance of Evangelical Christians and churches, was formed in 1951, soon after India gained Independence. It has a membership of eighty-two denominations and 148 related organizations and thousands of individual Christians.

EFI has taken a number of valuable initiatives, including a monthly magazine, *AIM*, training programs for both clergy and laity, a Commission on Emergency and Relief, Urban Network, Legal Association for Christians, and a Council for Financial Accountability. It is a charter member of the Asia Evangelical Alliance and World Evangelical Alliance.

Although Pakistan's Muslim majority obtained separate nationhood during India's independence in 1947, it officially became the Islamic Republic of Pakistan only in 1973. The population consists of South Asian people groups (81.4%) including Urdu Muslims, Jat, Sindhi, Punjabi, Bengali Rajasthani, Kashmiri, and Indo-Iranian groups (18.1%) such as the Pashtun and Baloch. Although the majority of the population is Muslim (95%), Hindus

A Langham Partnership cluster group meets in India
Photo: The Langham Partnership

(1.5%) and Christians (2.5%) are not an insignificant element of the total population. Of the fifty-seven countries of the Organization of Islamic Cooperation, Pakistan has the second largest Christian population after Indonesia. The official language of Pakistan is Urdu, but the majority of the population understand or speak Punjabi as well (Lukose 2013).

In 1580, and again in 1597, the Jesuits were invited by Akbar to Lahore. Lahore had a fairly large church comprising Portuguese, Armenians, and Hindustanis. Although there was initial toleration, churches were suppressed gradually. Later under British rule, missionary work was allowed after 1833. Due to the tireless efforts of Henry Martyn, the New Testament was translated into Urdu, Persian, Hindi, and Arabic, a significant step for the work of Evangelical Christianity in Pakistan.

Many missions, including American and United Presbyterian missions (now the Presbyterian Church of Pakistan), CMS, and the Church of Scotland, began to work in the Punjab. There was a great response to the Christian message from the depressed and lower Hindu castes such as the Megs and Chuhras, and thousands started turning to Christ. By 1859, this was a mass movement of conversion among the Chuhra.

In 1970, the Anglican Church of Pakistan, the Pakistan Lutheran Church and the Sialkot Church Council joined to become the Church of Pakistan (CoP), now the second largest denomination in the country. Most members of CoP are descendants of those converted during the Chuhra Movement between 1880 and 1930. According to the 1999 census, 80% of all Christians reside in the Punjab (Lukose 2013). There are other evangelical churches like the Presbyterian Church of Pakistan, Associate Reformed Presbyterian Church, Free Gospel Assemblies, United Pentecostal Church, and the Brethren Churches as well as para church organizations like Operation Mobilization, Scripture Union, and Pakistan Fellowship of Evangelical Students. Many of these run schools, medical institutions, clinics, dispensaries, the Open Theological seminary (theological education by Distance Learning), and Bible Training institutes.

Although a majority of Christians are from a non-Muslim background, there is an increasing number of Muslims coming to faith in Jesus today, through media such as literature, radio, and television. Charismatic experiences such as dreams and visions play a significant role in the conversion of many Pakistani Muslims. Pakistan is the world's second largest concentration of unengaged and unevangelized nation and the second largest Muslim country on earth.

The present form of Evangelicalism in Sri Lanka entered through the Dutch Presbyterian and Reformed churches in the seventeenth century. The translation of the Bible in Tamil and Sinhalese in the eighteenth century was a turning point in the growth of Evangelicalism in Sri Lanka. The coming of other missionary bodies, such as the Baptists (1812), Wesleyan Methodists (1814), American Board of Commissioners for Foreign Missions (1816), and Church Missionary Society (1818), and their engagement in social domains like education, medicine, and printing, further fostered evangelical growth. The Assemblies of God (1923) and the Ceylon Pentecostal Mission (CPM, now the Pentecostal Mission) were the major Pentecostal missions in the pre-independent twentieth-century Sri Lanka.

The CPM (founded in 1924) is a Sri Lankan Pentecostal mission which has followed the Sri Lankan diaspora to found churches in America, France, England, India, and Malaysia. With the coming of Pentecostals and charismatics in the 1970s, there has been a proliferation of Independent churches. They have taken Evangelical Christianity to many rural and urban sectors in Sri Lanka as they make inroads into the mainstream population, engaging Buddhists, Muslims, intellectuals, and ordinary people.

Afghanistan

The first entry of Christians into this region is in the fourth century. A Bishop of Herat attended the Council of Seleucia in AD 424. However, the advancement of Islam in the country eradicated most Christians by the early fifteenth century. There are reports of a Georgian Bishop in Kabul and a Jesuit mission in the region in the fifteenth or sixteenth century and also the reports of itinerant Protestants from Iran and India.

One of the first evangelical missions established in the region was the Afghan Mission of the CMS in 1853. It was started in Peshawar (now Pakistan) among the ethnic Afghans. A chain of mission stations was developed along the borders of Afghanistan, in India and Iran, providing hospitals, clinics, schools and churches. A number of people were converted, but at the same time many were martyred, and many church buildings were demolished by the government. However, the government allowed a number of social projects, mainly medical, by Christians in the 1960s under the International Afghan Mission (now known as International Assistance Mission). The Assemblies of God started mission work among the Afghan refugees in Delhi and Uttar Pradesh, under the leadership of Ezekiel Joshua. A few of them went back to Afghanistan as missionaries, and many of them were imprisoned.

As the Taliban regime was defeated by the United States and Northern Alliance, many Afghan refugees who had become Christians returned from countries like Pakistan and India and formed a largely underground national church. Although the size of this group is not known, some claim it to be several thousand, and growing. They cannot meet publicly, and even the timing and location of their meetings is secret.

Iran

Although Christians were present in Iran from the earliest centuries, Christianity has always been a minority religion, less than 1% of the total population. Zoroastrianism was the state religion before the Islamic invasion. Christians in Iran were mainly Armenian Orthodox, Assyrian Church adherents, and Chaldean Catholics.

Evangelical missions begun in Iran in the nineteenth century achieved no great success; with the coming of Pentecostal and Independent churches in the recent years, however, here too Christianity is growing (Bhakiaraj in Johnson and Ross 2009, 143). The main evangelical churches are the Assyrian Evangelical Church, Assyrian Pentecostal Church, Iranian Assemblies of God, and the Anglican Diocese of Iran. There are reports claiming that underground church multiplication is a remarkable feature of Evangelical Christianity in Iran, which is said to be the result of Spirit experiences like signs and wonders, dreams, and visions. Christian satellite-television broadcasts and Christian websites in the official language of the country, Farsi and the increasing availability of Scriptures, may be conditioners of this growth.

Nations of Recent Christian Experience

Some South Asian countries, such as Bangladesh, Bhutan, Nepal, and the Maldives, have a comparatively recent experience of Christian contact. Christianity entered into most of these nations in the sixteenth century through Portuguese missionaries and became more established through the mission movements of the eighteenth and nineteenth centuries.

Bhutan is one of the least responsive South Asian nations to the Christian message. It has maintained its Tibeto-Buddhist heritage as the world's last Mahayana Buddhist Kingdom. Lamaistic Buddhism is its official religion with full state support. Ngalongs, Sharchops, and Nepalese are the three largest ethnic groups in the country. Christianity is yet to make an inroad into the mainstream population.

Although there was no further established Christian engagement, Bhutan's first contact with Christianity was during the visit of two Portuguese Jesuit fathers (Cacella and Cabral) en route to Tibet in 1626. They were followed by William Carey and a friend. It was the native Nepali-Lepcha church of Kalimpong that made the first Evangelistic expeditions into Bhutan after forming their own mission (Kalimpong Pardeshiyon ka Mission) in 1891. With the coming and settling of Dr. Craig (a Scottish missionary from Eastern Himalayan Mission) in the 1960s, several other missions followed, including the Leprosy Mission, the Norwegian Santal Mission, and Medical Mission Fellowship. However, since the mid-1980s the government began to nationalize the hospitals and other social projects and to expel foreign missionaries.

Evangelical Christianity has been growing more among the Nepalese than the Tibeto-Buddhist Bhutanese, as Nepalese were the most responsive groups in Bhutan. Nepalese are the third largest group in Bhutan. Small house churches were formed in several places, while the largest church was formed in the capital of Thimphu, drawing a predominantly Nepali and Lepcha congregation. As open evangelistic activities are not allowed, there has been less church growth among the native Bhutanese. The major Christian work has been done through personal witness and testimony of Nepali, Lepcha Bhutia, and other Indian Christian professionals, laborers, and settlers. However, the natives who are converted exercise a strong and vibrant Christian faith even in the midst of persecution.

Bangladesh is another country of restricted expanse, though with a teeming population of 120 million. It is one of the poorest nations on earth; life expectancy and literacy rate are also very low. Although the constitution guarantees religious freedom, it states that Islam is the state religion of the nation. After Muslims (86%), Hindus (12%) and Buddhists (0.6%) also constitute the total population. Bengalis (94.3%) and Urdu Muslims are the major people groups in the country (Lukose 2013).

Christianity first arrived in 1576 through Portuguese merchants from Goa. The first Protestant church in Bangladesh was a Baptist church founded at Dinajpur by the Serampore Mission in 1806. It later became one of the largest churches in the entire northern part of South Asia. During the nineteenth century, Baptists were the virtual pioneers of popular education in most towns. The missionaries of the Baptist Missionary Society (BMS) also pioneered English education in Dhaka. CMS missionaries planted a number of churches in the districts of Meherpur Kushtia in the 1830s. The activities of BMS and CMS encouraged other British missions, who were already operating in other parts of South Asia, to expand their works into these widely separated areas.

The Assemblies of God mission came to Bangladesh in 1945. All-One-in Christ Church (Fellowship Church) is the oldest indigenous church, founded in 1947. After Bangladesh became an independent nation in 1971, many new evangelical churches including Bible Medical Missionary Fellowship, Presbyterian Church Mission, Church of God Mission, Canadian Baptists' Overseas Mission, Korean Methodist Mission, New Apostolic Church, and World Missionary Evangelism, entered Bangladesh. Recently, a number of indigenous churches, such as the Masihee Jamat, Isa-I-Jamat, Talitha Kumi Evangelical Church, Evangelical Holiness Church, and the Bangladesh Christian Church, have come into existence. Today, the majority of Christians are indigenous tribal people mostly living along the Indian border. Ecumenical initiatives among various Christian denominations are on the rise. Although Christians are still a relatively small community, Evangelical Christianity is vibrant and increasingly local in Bangladesh.

The Himalayan Kingdom of Nepal became a Republic only recently, in May 2008. It lies in between two large nations, China and India, and is one of the poorest countries of the world. Its geographical location makes it difficult to build roads or develop economically. Although officially a Hindu kingdom, Nepal has diverse cultures, languages, ethnic groups and religious practices. According to the Government religious statistics, there are Hindus (89%), Buddhists (7%) and Muslims (3.5%) (Johnson and Ross 2009).

The first recorded Christian contact in Nepal was through the Jesuit missionaries in the 1620s, while they were seeking a more convenient way to Tibet. In the early 1700s, Capuchin missionaries followed the same path, and later established a mission in the Valley of Nepal. The work was extended to Kathmandu, Bhadgaon, and Patan over the next fifty years. However, with the expulsion of Christians under the young king Prithivi Narayan Shah, Nepal was firmly closed to Christianity for two centuries, until 1951 (Boopalan 2012, 101).

However, many Nepalis came into contact with Western as well as Indian missionaries across the border in India, especially in the northeast, north, and northwest parts, and many became Christians. Meanwhile, the Bible was also translated into Nepali, and many Nepali movements were established, including the Assemblies of God, the Nepali Evangelistic Band (later International known as Nepal Fellowship, or INF), and the United Mission to Nepal, or UMM. Taking advantage of Nepal's cautious opening to the outside world in 1951, the new Nepali converts in India began to move to Nepal and engage in evangelistic activities in the country, and subsequently many turned to Christian faith. The Nepali government allowed even a few Western missions to become involved—though with restrictions—in development activities although they have never received visas for church-related works.

A significant development was the formation of Nepal Christian Fellowship (NCF), a fellowship of local Christians and churches. It provided a sense of solidarity in the face of growing persecution through the 1960s. NCF (now called National Churches Fellowship of Nepal, or NCFN) is a member of the Evangelical Fellowship of Asia and of the World Evangelical Alliance. NCFN has set a goal of establishing at least eight thousand churches across the nation in partnership with all local churches and mission organizations. Besides NCFN, other major evangelical churches are the Assemblies of God Nepal, the Agape Fellowship, the Evangelical Christian Fellowship of Nepal, and the Evangelical Christian Alliance of Nepal.

Until the advent of democracy in 1990, conversion to what was considered a foreign religion, such as Christianity or Islam, was exclusively forbidden by law. However, in 1990, the law was revised and consequently all Christians who were imprisoned for their faith were released. Christians began to experience greater freedom and engaged in ever-expanding Christian activities including large public meetings broadcasting of Christian radio and television programs, which resulted in the growth of churches.

In stark contrast to the landlocked, mountainous Nepal, the island-based Republic of the Maldives is the smallest South Asian nation in both population and land area. The entire population is officially Muslim. More than 99% of the country is in the Indian Ocean, consisting of over a thousand tiny islands. Archaeological evidence indicates that both Hinduism and Buddhism flourished in the islands prior to the invasion of Islam in twelfth century. Although the ruling Sultan Hasan IX became a Christian in 1552, and Portuguese later ruled the islands for a period of about fifteen to seventeen years, the natives of Maldives did not renounce their religious allegiance.

The first recorded Protestant Christian effort for Maldives took place in the nineteenth century. John Leyden was commissioned to translate the four Gospels into the Dhivehi language. He had engaged in this project in Calcutta with the assistance of a Maldivian, Hasan bin Adham. In the early 1960s, when English medium education was introduced for males in the Islands, many resident teachers from abroad (mainly Sri Lanka) came to the Maldives. Some of them were Evangelical Christians. Gradually Christian witness and small group prayer meetings were formed. Later, President Ibrahim Nasir (1968–1978) sold airtime on the national radio station Voice of Maldives, for the broadcast of American Christian Evangelistic broadcasts. There has been increased openness to foreign investment and development since the 1980s. As a result, Evangelical Christian professionals from several nations began to come, and they joined the existing Sri Lankan Christian witness. In 1995, the Dhivehi Gospel of Luke was finally published, which further strengthened Evangelical Christian mission in the islands.

Concerns, Challenges and Future

Although poverty, social unrest, and the feeble socioeconomic status of the church are burning issues for Evangelical Christians in South Asia, the chief concern is the identity issue and the religious intolerance. Although South Asia has a non-Western origin of Christianity, the impact of colonization in most nations is so great that Christianity is mistakenly identified with colonization and is misrepresented as a religion of the West. Consequently, Christians have little voice in the chief domains of society.

The island-based Republic of the Maldives is the smallest South Asian nation in both population and land area.
Photo: www.designpics.com

As most of the region was under the British regime in the beginning of the twentieth century, even the local Christians were often suspected as agents of foreign/imperial power. In the contemporary South Asian scenario, the quest for authentic religious identity is one of the most daunting challenges facing South Asian Christianity. The intricate relationship between the social, religious, and political aspects of society is a major reason for this (Lukose 2013, 15–18).

People belonging to Tribal Communities and Scheduled Castes suffer as their official privileges and welfares are denied when they become Christians. Similarly, the Afghan Christians are not officially recognized as Christians but as expatriates. Subsequently they face adverse reactions from the militant religious groups in most of the region. More than in any other regions, Christians in South Asia are in constant and close contact with people of other faiths: Muslim, Hindu, Buddhist, Sikh, and others. Therefore, it is expected that this will potentially intensify both conflicts and dialogue.

Generally speaking, religious freedom across the region is heavily restricted. In most nations there are legal restrictions for open evangelistic activities. Although the Indian Constitution advocates religious freedom, many individual states have anti-conversion laws in effect, which significantly curtail Evangelical Christian activities.

In Pakistan, the minorities are not free to profess and practice their religion. The voice of the minorities goes unheard. The doors to government jobs or to the army, air force, and/or navy, are closed to Christians. There is no provision for Christian students in government schools to receive religious instruction, while Islamyat and Pakistan studies are compulsory for all. Counter to the United Nations guidelines on Human Rights, apostasy from Islam carries a death sentence.

There is not a single church building in Afghanistan and to become a Christian is to invite the death penalty. In Bhutan, as Christianity has been considered a threat to Buddhism, open evangelistic activities are also not allowed. Many Bhutanese Christians have been deprived of their jobs as well as their homes, and a few Christians have been imprisoned and harassed by local officials. Since 1989, with the introduction of the government policy of expulsion of non-nationals, many Nepali Christians have been expelled.

Hindu and Islamic militant religious groups pose a threat to Christians in the region. Thousands of Christians have been harassed, made homeless, and their churches burned, often after incitement by either Hindu nationalists or by Maost guerillas. A 2014 attack on Christian churches by extremist Buddhist monks in Sri Lanka serves as an example of rising religious tensions in a nation which, until recently, has been relatively peaceful. It is no wonder, then, that South Asian Christians seek to minimize any indicator that they are less than fully and authentically indigenous to their cultures.

In spite of these concerns, the reality is that the future of Christianity and its center of gravity continue to move south. Evangelical Christianity has become an emerging force in South Asia today because of its active lay participation, native leadership, and Charismatic nature. Asia is home to 60% of the total population of the world and the number of Christians in Asia doubled in the twentieth century. The second half of the twentieth century saw a gradual and steady growth of Evangelical Christianity in Asia. According to Boopalan, although Asian churches were seriously affected by the Second World War, a mature Evangelicalism emerged, and from the 1960s onwards, Asian Protestant Christianity took a turn which by the end of the twentieth century was largely Pentecostal in form (Boopalan 2012, 101).

Many South Asian nations have witnessed the fastest decadal Christian growth anywhere in the world. Afghanistan and Nepal have the fastest growth of Christianity in the region (Nepal, 4.66% and Afghanistan, 9.05%), while Iran and Sri Lanka have the least growth. However, Sri Lanka has the highest percentage of Christians (8.8% of the total population) (Johnson and Ross 2009).

More than any other religious group, Evangelical Christianity has experienced a dynamic, sustained and extensive expansion across South Asia. The most important factor in recent Christian growth has been its Charismatic expression.

If the current growth is sustained, Evangelical Christianity may well become an active force in the chief domains of South Asian societies. The predominant form of Christianity in the twenty-first century will be Pentecostal and Charismatic. The recent growth of Pentecostalism and its impact in Asian countries cause Sebastian Kim to observes, "with the exception of Islamic nations, this trend seems to be set to continue" (Kim, in Johnson and Ross 2009, 135).

Dr. Wessly Lukose is a principal lecturer in Missiology and registrar at Filadelfia Bible College, Udaipur, India, and closely associated with church planting there and in Birmingham, England. He took his PhD at the University of Birmingham on a contextualized Spirit missiology, built around the indigenous nature of Rajasthani pentecostalism. His thesis was published in 2013 under the title *Contextual Missiology of the Spirit: Pentecostalism in Rajasthan, India.*

Sources and Further Reading

Budijanto, Bambang, ed. *Emerging Missions Movements: Voices of Asia*. Colorado Springs: Compassion International & Asia Evangelical Alliance, 2010.

Bhakiaraj, Paul Joshua. "Christianity in South-Central Asia, 1910–2010." In *Atlas of Global Christianity*. Edited by Johnson and Ross, 2009.

Boopalan, Sunder John. "Pentecostalism in Asia." In *Asian Theology on the Way: Christianity, Culture and Context*. Edited by Peniel Jesudasan and Rufus, Rajkumar. London: SPCL, 2012.

Clive, Calver. "Our Evangelical Heritage." In *Global Crossroads: Focusing the Strength of Local Churches*. Edited by W. Harold Fuller. Metro Manila: World Evangelical Fellowship.

England, John C. *The Hidden History of Christianity in India*. Delhi: ISPCK, 1998.

Evers, George. *The Churches in Asia*. Delhi: ISPCK, 2005.

Frykenberg, Robert Eric. "Christianity in India: From Beginnings to the Present," *Oxford History of the Christian Church*. Edited by Henry and Owen Chaddwick. Oxford: OUP, 2010.

Hedlund, Roger, ed. *Oxford Encyclopaedia of South Asian Christianity*. Vols 1–2. New Delhi: OUP, 2012.

Hoke, Donald E. *The Church in Asia*. Chicago: Moody Press, 1975.

Johnson, Todd M. and Kenneth R. Ross, eds. *Atlas of Global Christianity*. Edinburgh: Edinburgh University Press, 2009.

Johnstone, Patrick. *The Future of the Global Church: History, Trends and Possibilities*. Milton Keynes: Authentic Media, 2011.

Kim, Sebastian "Christianity in Asia, 1910–2010." In Johnson and Ross, 2009 (above).

Lukose, Wessly. *Contextual Missiology of the Spirit: Pentecostalism in Rajasthan, India*, Oxford: Regnum, 2013.

Shah, Timothy Samuel. "Preface." In *Evangelical Christianity and Democracy in Asia*. Edited by David H Lumsdaine. Oxford: OUP, 2009.

Mandryk, Jason. *Operation World: The Definitive Prayer Guide to Every Nation*. Colorado Springs: Biblica Publishing, 2010.

Moffett, Samuel Hugh. *A History of Christianity in Asia*, 2 vols, Maryknoll, NY: Orbis, 2005.

Mundadan, A. Mathias. *History of Christianity in India: From the Beginning up to the Middle of the Sixteenth Century, up to 1542*. Bangalore: Theological Publications in India, 1984.

Phan, C. Peter, ed. *Christianities in Asia. The Global Christianities Series*. West Sussex: Wiley-Blackwell, 2011.

Sunquist, Scott W., ed. *A Dictionary of Asian Christianity*. Grand Rapids: Eerdmans, 2001.

Evangelical Impact in India: An Umbrella for Missions

With more than a billion people, India is a close second to China in population. India is colorful, complicated, and religious, with Hindus, Muslims, Sikhs, Christians, and others all jostling for space and a voice the way the country's pedestrians do on its crowded city streets.

Although the disciple Thomas brought the gospel to India in the first century, Christianity has remained a minority religion there. Missionary work in the last decades has been done primarily by indigenous organizations because foreign missionaries were asked to leave in the mid-twentieth century.

Under the umbrella of the India Missions Association (IMA), established in 1977, some 250 agencies labor to bring the gospel of Jesus to the people, many of whom have never even heard his name. One mission director noted that when the question, "Do you know Jesus?" is asked, many people reply simply, "He doesn't live in my village."

IMA, with some sixty thousand Christian workers within India and beyond, is primarily concerned with cross-cultural missions, says IMA general secretary, Susanta Patra. Its goals are ambitious: to reach every level of the stratified Indian society and all its people groups with the gospel. From the elite and affluent, to the middle class, to the poor and marginalized, "everyone is reachable," Patra asserts.

Member agencies range from small to large. Take, for example, Nagaland, a small northeastern state that received the gospel through American Baptist missionaries in the nineteenth century and is now more than 90 percent Christian. The Nagaland Missionary Movement, begun in 1985, reaches across the border to neighboring Bhutan and Nepal, where it currently focuses on medical needs.

Central India Christian Mission (CICM) is a large organization that does church planting, leadership and vocational training, medical work, and outreach to children. "Children's ministry has always been a significant part of ministry in India," says Ajai Lall, CICM's founder and director, noting that both his grandfathers grew up in Christian orphanages.

In India there are millions of hungry and homeless children. Workers talk of finding babies abandoned by desperate mothers in garbage heaps and toilets and on train tracks. One baby boy was found in a plastic bag, barely breathing, at the side of a village trail, his umbilical cord still attached. He was brought to one of the CICM's children's homes and is now a thriving six-year-old.

Tiharu was a child whose impoverished father sold him into slavery for a fifty-kilogram sack of rice. "I felt as if I didn't have a choice," the father said. As a child laborer, Tiharu worked twelve hours a day and was beaten and tortured regularly. He was rescued by CICM, and now he is a pastor who has planted five churches, baptized three thousand believers, and rescued 150 children himself.

Vocational training has given women a livelihood making and selling eyeglasses; provided solar lights so village children can study in the evening without electricity, thus improving their test scores; and empowered men and women to achieve a higher economic level as well as new confidence.

—Debra Fieguth

EVANGELICALS IN SOUTHEAST ASIA

By Violet James

Southeast Asia is made up of eleven countries (Brunei Darussalam, Cambodia, Indonesia, Lao Peoples' Republic, Malaysia, Myanmar, Singapore, Philippines, Thailand, Timor-Leste, and Viet Nam). The *euangelion* (Greek for "good news") came to Southeast Asia first in the sixteenth century with traders and colonizers and has been dispersed by progressive waves of cyclical migration and mission.

Evangelical values and beliefs with regard to mission and evangelism are now present in most of the traditions of the Christian faith in the region—Protestant, Roman Catholic, Greek Orthodox, Pentecostal-Charismatic, Independent, and even some marginal groups. As the missionary movements entered the Majority World in the nineteenth and twentieth centuries, becoming more prominent in the twenty-first century, Evangelicalism proper has further evolved, embracing social concern for the poor and the marginalized. The Lausanne Covenant of 1974 brought the various Protestant denominations, especially from the Majority World, to reconsider the mission of the Church. Representatives from the various evangelical traditions combined the Great Commission (Matt. 28:19–20) with the Great Commandment (Matt. 22:37–39) in crafting the Covenant, highlighting the importance of both Word and deed in fulfilling Christ's mission to the lost. The social reality presented by Southeast Asia—particularly in the Philippines—played a significant role in bringing about this repositioning of classical Evangelical thought.

History

Long before the arrival of European missionaries and merchants, Southeast Asia was heavily influenced by Indic and Chinese cultures. Since the eighth century, Arab traders brought Islam to the maritime islands. The European powers (the Portuguese first, followed by the Spanish, Dutch, French, and British) came from the sixteenth century and by the nineteenth century had extended their rule over many parts of Southeast Asia. The Portuguese, Spanish, and French introduced Roman Catholicism to Timor Leste, the Philippines, Cambodia, Laos, and Vietnam (Indo-China), while the Dutch and British brought Protestantism to Indonesia, Myanmar, Malaya (Malaysia), Singapore, and Brunei. Thailand alone was never colonized, though it had evangelical missionary exposure in the nineteenth century, during the "open door" policy of Kings Mongkut (1804–1868) and Chulalongkhorn (1853–1911). Christianity was slow to take root and, despite signs of a quickening tempo, Evangelicals currently constitute less than 1% of the population.

Colonialism created a favorable environment for missionaries to pioneer and establish churches. The colonial powers did not openly encourage conversions to Christianity and in some areas actively dissuaded missionary access, but their political presence nevertheless provided both infrastructure and a form of credibility to Western culture as a bridge towards modernization. Christianity took root, usually as a minority religion, the exceptions being the large Roman Catholic presence in the Philippines and Timor Leste.

Colonialism spread the seeds of its own destruction, introducing colonial elites to modern ideas, and providing the prompt towards national identities. The maturation and eventual independence of these countries, however, was not without bloodshed and deep animosity towards their colonial masters. The proliferation of nationalist movements in the interwar period found its opportunity through the aggressive expansion of the Japanese Empire, which expelled European administrations and provided the organizing point and even model for independence movements. After World War II, the colonial masters returned only to find themselves often unwanted. Southeast Asia became a key point of experimentation and contestation in the Cold War between aligned and nonaligned countries, with some nations embracing Communism as an extension of nationalist movements for liberation from foreign oppression. Ho Chi Minh, the Vietnamese leader, galvanized his people and successfully liberated the North from the French in 1954, laying the basis for reunification of the country in 1975. Laos and Cambodia also became Communist, and there was deep fear of a domino effect over the whole of Southeast Asia. Communism did make inroads into Indonesia, Malaysia, Singapore and even Thailand, but was eventually contained or suppressed—albeit at a cost which (as in Indonesia's case, for example) produced sometimes-grievous religious reactions.

Current Composition

Today there are 594 million people in Southeast Asia, of whom 129.7 million are Christian. Of this number, some 14.6m (2.5%) are Evangelicals. Philippines is the largest Christian nation in Asia, with 90% of the population Roman Catholic and 8–9% Evangelical. The Timor Leste population is over 90% Roman Catholic, with about 3% Evangelicals (Johnson and Ross 2009).

In the rest of Asia, Christianity is a minority faith. The majority of Indonesians and Malaysians are Muslim, with a Christian population of about 10% of the population. Approximately 10% of Indonesians (or 2.4 million) are Evangelical, however, compared to 4.5% of Malaysians. (Some estimates of rapidly growing Pentecostal and Charismatic churches alone put that population at over 3 million, and the country's capital features significant churches, such as Stephen Tong's Messiah Cathedral).

Thailand, Cambodia, Laos, Myanmar and Vietnam are primarily Buddhist, and the Evangelical population is very small (1.4% in Thailand, 2.4% in Cambodia, and 3.4% in Laos), with the exception of Myanmar and Vietnam, where they number 7% and 9% respectively. The church in Cambodia suffered near destruction after the advent of the Khmer Rouge regime in 1979 and it was only in 1990 that it could be legally registered. Even in this short time, however, it has grown significantly, with a 7.28% per annum increase in the last ten years. Singapore is a multicultural and multiethnic nation: despite the large Buddhist-Taoist-Confucian presence, 18.1% are Christians and more than two thirds of these are Evangelicals (12.6%) (Johnson and Ross 2009).

Challenges from the Start

Despite their association with colonialism, European Protestantism and Catholicism were challenged from the start by the culturally ingrained high religions of Buddhism and Islam. Christianity made particular inroads in what contemporaries called "low religious cultures" prevalent among tribal peoples, such as the Karen and Chin in Myanmar, the Batak in Indonesia, the Lisu in Thailand, and the Dayak and Iban in Malaysia. Though constantly challenged by self-consciously nationalist high religions, Christianity found a warm reception among these animistic tribal peoples, many of whom were ready and waiting for the message of peace and reconciliation from the Great High God.

There were mass tribal conversions to evangelical faith in Myanmar, Indonesia, and Malaysia and to Roman Catholicism, especially in the Philippines, where some peoples developed unique practices by blending indigenous beliefs with Catholicism. With the exception of the Philippines and Timor Leste, Evangelical Christianity has been disadvantaged for several reasons: its exclusive nature alienates it from others; its overt conversionism makes Evangelicalism unpopular with other faiths; and its status as a minority makes Evangelicalism the target of persecution by majority faiths, such as Buddhism or Islam, who in democratic settings are able to redefine communal rights through the ballot box. In later years, the emergence of large, energetic Charismatic churches has re-elicited this sort of undesirable product of identity politics.

Political independence took diverse forms. Cambodia, Laos, and Vietnam adopted forms of Communism under which all religions were suppressed. Singapore and Malaysia had a one-party democratic government, and Thailand and the Philippines had liberal democratic governments that promised religious toleration to minority groups. Thailand continues to regard its monarch as a god-king and believes that to be a Thai is to be a Buddhist. The King (Bhumibol Adulyadej or Rama IX) has repeatedly reaffirmed Buddhism as the nation's religion.

In the Communist sphere, there has been some relaxation of controls. In 1986, for example, Vietnam began to relax its control over the church and liaised with the Vatican over the appointment of leadership for the Catholic Church. The evangelical churches, which had grown to some size under the influence of the Christian and Missionary Alliance and other denominations, refused to come under the control of the State and went underground. These churches continue to come under state scrutiny and often face harassment and persecution.

The situation is more intense again for those tribal Christians who were associated with the American military during the Second Indochinese War and who have been discovered to have links with foreign missionaries. Some tribes in Myanmar are also under surveillance because of their involvement in politics, their resistance to the military government, and their lack of nationalist compliance. In Laos, continuing low-level movements for autonomy (among the Hmong people, for example) justify state restrictions on expatriate involvement, evangelism, and the building of new churches. As a matter of law, therefore, all Protestant churches are required to join the Laos Evangelical Church.

In most of these countries, conversion to Christianity and interreligious marriage are officially permitted. In reality, however, there remain many challenges. In Brunei, Indonesia, and Malaysia, both the civil and the shari'a courts can be applied in any given situation; in most cases, Islam prevails and conversions to Christianity are prohibited. A Muslim can never convert to Christianity and if he or she chooses to marry someone of another faith, that individual must first convert to Islam. The Religious Harmony Bill was passed in Singapore in 1990. It is mandatory for all Singaporeans to exercise sensitivity and respect for others in that multireligious community, avoiding disharmony and animosity at any cost. This has had implications for the propagation of the gospel for the Evangelical Church. There has been some judicial activity, and state interest in churches. Nevertheless, Singapore's commercial elites, particularly from the ethnic Chinese community, have played a significant role in extending Evangelicalism in surrounding countries and in funding global missions.

Prime Concerns and Issues

Almost all Southeast Asian nations have long experiences with colonialism, stretching back, in many cases, over hundreds of years. The stamp left by each colonizing power guided the subsequent growth of indigenou religious movements. In the Philippines, for instance, the Spanish favored Roman Catholicism and resisted Protestant attempts at penetrating the islands. It was only with the American ascendancy from 1898 that Protestant churches obtained a wider liberty of action. Present before the influx of Islam, the Spanish supported conversion, and skillfully managed to contain the Muslims in the island of Mindanao. Thus Roman Catholicism thrived in the Philippines, eventually making it the largest Christian nation in Southeast Asia.

The situation in Indonesia was quite different. The Reformed Protestant Dutch administration was less interested in evangelization than in economic gain from the rich spices that gave the islands their name. At the same time, they tried to keep Roman Catholicism at bay by providing chaplaincies for their own people. The crescent here preceded the Cross, and so Islam became the dominant religion in what is today the largest Muslim nation in the world. Local identity politics, joined more latterly by Caliphatism and the overflow of extremism from conflicts in the Middle East, have fueled violence and persecution of Christians among Islami fringe groups. In more general politics, minority-baiting (not only against Christians, but against minorities such as Ahmaddiya Muslims) has become a mechanism for mobilizing Islamist popular support.

A century of British colonialism in Myanmar, Malaysia, Singapore, and Brunei also brought with it a variet of Protestant denominations. However, it was American Protestant missionaries who made the great break though among the people in Myanmar. Active missionary work began with Adoniram Judson, the first Ame ican-Baptist missionary to set foot in Myanmar. Animist tribal peoples living in fear of spirits experienced a movement of the Holy Spirit which resulted in thousands turning to Christ, especially among the Karen, Chin, Lisu, and Lahu peoples. The transformation and dynamic ministry of former robber and murderer Ko Thy Byu, for example, brought thousands of Karen to Christ and energized indigenous missions to other tribes as well. Some tribes had preconditioning stories of redemptive capacity which laid the basis for indigenization. Among the Lahu, for example, a sorcerer declared that it was futile for them to search for the true God because at the right time, God himself would seek them out. But they needed to wait for a sign—"white people on white horses, would bring white teaching" (Sunquist 2001). When the Protestant missionaries came and preached the good news, thousands were converted. Today, though struggling with all the normal issues of intergenerational nominalism, the Baptists are the largest denomination in Myanmar.

The former combined British territory of Malaya (Malaysia and Singapore) gained independence in 1957, with the latter becoming a separate nation in 1965 due to its recognition that its Chinese majority would have been at a significant disadvantage in an Islamic and Malay-dominated country. The London Missionary Society (LMS) first entered these two countries seeking a base for the evangelization of China.

When the doors of China were temporarily closed, the mission moved to Singapore, setting up a printing press to translate Bible portions and the whole Bible into Chinese vernacular. After 1842, when China's doors were reopened, the LMS relocated to Hong Kong and all the missionaries left, except for one, Benjamin Keasberry, who resigned from LMS in order to work among the Malays in Singapore. He started a school for Malay boys and also a Malay chapel. While the school did not last and the Malay conversions were few, the chapel became a lasting center for Peranakan Christians, Chinese who had adopted the Malay culture. Keasberry was also instrumental in helping establish a Chinese church that is active till today. He was followed by many more missionaries from different Protestant evangelical missions and denominations, leading to a proliferation of schools for boys and girls, medical clinics, hospitals, and churches. While the main ethnic groups were represented, political restrictions meant that it was never an easy task to evangelize the Malays.

In the 1950s many evangelical organizations established works in Southeast Asia. Youth for Christ, Scripture Union, Navigators, and Campus Crusade for Christ worked among students in the schools and universities. This was a period (1960s–1990s) of significant evangelical expansion among students, and of an expanded consciousness of evangelical teachings even among non-converts.

East Malaysia (Sabah and Sarawak) has seen greater growth in Evangelical numbers, in part because the presence of tribal people (Dayak, Iban, and others) laid the basis for mass conversions. Another reason for a strong Christian presence here was the large migration of Chinese Methodist Christians from Southern China. Today, Sabah is more than 33% Christian, and Sarawak more than 38% Christian (Johnson and Ross 2009).

In West Malaysia, where Islam has been the official religion since 1957, Christianity remains a minority faith, primarily among the Chinese and Indians. Evangelical Christians are unafraid to address issues, such as the use of the term Allah for "God" in translations of the Bible, and to speak against unjust laws and marginalization of the Christian faith. In January 2013, the National Evangelical Christian Fellowship (NECF), established in 1983, addressed the issue of Allah by declaring that Christians should be given:

> [T]he right to profess, practice and manage their religious affairs including the use of "Alkitab", the Bible in "Bahasa Malaysia" and the native languages of Sabah and Sarawak which also use "Allah" both in the private and public spheres of life which includes Church and home. (NECF Malaysia)

A recent ruling that "Allah" can only be used by Muslims, except in Sabah and Sarawak, demonstrates the interconnection of religion and public order in such countries.

In Brunei, evangelical faith experienced a breakthrough because of the presence of British, Australian, and other European missionaries who invested their lives in the establishment of schools, hospitals, and churches. In the past few years, however, the Sultan of Brunei has adopted a platform known as MIB ("Melayu, Islam Berjaya") indicating that Brunei is Malay in culture, Islamic in religion, and a monarchy (with the king as the head of the country). MIB has become compulsory in all schools, and every student regardless of race or religion must go through this indoctrination. The intended outcome is the conversion of students to Islam. The few mission schools started by the Anglican Church are under threat of losing their distinction; the term *Allah* is forbidden for use by all non-Muslim peoples, and Christian symbols (even in mission schools) have been denounced as offensive to the Muslims. Despite these challenges, Brunei today has approximately thirty-two thousand Evangelicals (7.8%) (Johnson and Ross 2009).

European missions to Cambodia, Laos, and Vietnam were largely Roman Catholic until the twentieth century, creating a demographic reality that affected both French and American involvement in the subsequent wars. When the Christian and Missionary Alliance (CMA) entered Vietnam in 1911, it established the Evangelical Church of Indo-China, rendering it the only regional Protestant evangelical mission-denomination for the next fifty years.

After the ravaging of the three countries through the wars which spilled out of Vietnam, the withdrawal of American forces resulted in low morale among the missionary population. Eventually the North reunified the country, all the foreign missionaries left and the church went underground. Remarkably, however, there are about 8,524,000 Evangelical Christians (8%) in Vietnam, who continue to labor under significant disadvantages.

> **After the ravaging of the three countries through the wars which spilled out of Vietnam, the withdrawal of American forces resulted in low morale among the missionary population.**

The genocide in Cambodia in 1975–1979 came close to wiping out the church. When it was legalized and reopened in 1990, however, the church grew rapidly and is considered one of the fastest-growing churches in the region. Today there are approximately 366,000 Evangelical Christians (2.4%) (Johnson and Ross 2009).

In 1900, the whole of Southeast Asia had 381,000 Evangelical Christians (0.4%) but by 2010 the number had soared to 14,648,000 (2.5%). The presence of the many overseas evangelical organizations such as Campus Crusade for Christ, Operation Mobilization, and the Overseas Missionary Fellowship assisted in widespread indigenization of the faith among ethnic minorities, creating bridges for engagement with the emerging global culture. Some groups, such as the International Fellowship of Evangelical Students (1934) were actively engaged in university evangelism from the 1960s to the 1990s and established evangelical churches. The Asia Evangelistic Fellowship (1960) and the Billy Graham Association organized city-wide crusades around the region with thousands of conversions (Goh 2005).

Many international organizations such as the World Evangelical Alliance (formerly World Evangelical Fellowship) made their headquarters in Singapore because of that city-state's political stability and strategic location in Southeast Asia. Such groups have been particularly adept at using media and popular culture to spread the faith. Here, as in other parts of the world, Evangelicals used the printing press to produce gospel literature and translate the Bible into the vernacular languages of the peoples through Wycliffe Bible Translators (1934) and the United Bible Societies (1946). In 1945, the Far East Broadcasting company was established by returning US soldiers, John Broger and Bob Bowman. It would grow into a significant regional work, with broadcasting stations in Saipan and the Philippines reaching millions of listeners in more than 130 languages. Low-cost media such as radio has since been expanded into television, and more recently into social media (Internet broadcasting).

Future

The evangelical Church in Southeast Asia reflects the unity of its oneness in the Bible and the finished work of Christ on the cross but, for cultural and historical reasons, it is also very diverse. It has taken a life of its own, becoming a vibrant and dynamic community with a potential for greater growth and diversity.

Despite all these complexities, evangelical churches are growing rapidly, in parts of Southeast Asia (such as Singapore) far outstripping the older, liberalized mainstream. There is continuous migration of peoples and the sociological and demographic features are constantly evolving. One can find in a single congregation in Singapore numerous cultures and people of different ethnic groups: Singaporean Indians, Singaporean Chinese, Malaysian Chinese, or people from the Republic of China sitting beside Filipinos, Indonesians, Vietnamese, and Indians from India. Singapore Bible College, for example, includes an interesting composition of students and faculty from approximately twenty-eight different countries, primarily from Southeast Asia.

Commencing as an offshoot of Western Evangelicalism, and replicating many mainline denominations in Southeast Asia, Asian Evangelicalism is today an important contributor to the global Church. This arm of the Church has evolved to become Charismatic, Independent, dynamic, and diverse. The question thus arises as to how one recognizes the edges of Evangelicalism when it may look very different from the traditional denominations. This is a particular challenge for the Western church as it seeks to partner with Asian Evangelicals without importing enculturated definitions of the faith.

Dr. Violet James is dean of students and professor of Church History at Singapore Bible College. Her PhD dissertation (Aberdeen University) was on "American Protestant Missions and the Vietnam War." She has published widely on Asian Christianity, including recent entries in the *Atlas of Global Christianity*, and a centennial history of the Christian Church in Vietnam (*Vietnam: God's Sovereign Work in His Church*, 2010).

Sources and Further Reading

BBC News. "Malaysia "Allah" court ruling: PM Najib speaks out." BBC News. October 22, 2013 and accessed December 28, 2013. http://www.bbc.co.uk/news/world-asia-24621992

Goh, Robbie B. H., *Christianity in Southeast Asia*, Singapore: ISEAS Publications, 2005.

Harris, Brian. "Beyond Bebbington: the Quest for Evangelical Identity in a Postmodern Era." *Churchman* 122, no. 3 (2008), 201–219.

Hefele, Peter & Andreas Dittrich. "The Situation in North East Asia & South East Asia." *KAS International Reports*, June 2011.

Hitchen, John M. "What It Means to Be an Evangelical Today—An Antipodean Perspective." *Evangelical Quarterly* 76, no. 1 (2004), 99–115.

Jenkins, Philip. "The clash that wasn't." *The Christian Century* 129, no. 14 (Jul 11, 2012): 37.

Johnson, Todd M. & Kenneth R. Ross, eds. *Atlas of Global Asian Christianity, 1910–2010*. Edinburgh: University of Edinburgh Press, 2009.

Sng, Bobby E. K. *In His Good Time*. Singapore: Graduate Christian Fellowship, 2003.

Sunquist, Scott, ed. *A Dictionary of Asian Christianity*. Grand Rapids: Eerdmans, 2001.

Walls, A. F. "The Evangelical Revival, The Missionary Movement & Africa." *Evangelicalism Comparative Studies of Popular Protestantism in North America, the British Isles, and Beyond*, 1700–1990. Mark A. Noll, David Bebbington and George A. Rawlyk (eds), New York: Oxford University Press, 1994.

Evangelical Impact in the Philippines: Microfinancing Leads to Macro Change

Compassion to serve and facilitate transformation is what motivates a Christian microfinancing program aimed at helping impoverished women.

Kabalikat para sa Maunlad na Buhay (KMBI) started in 1986 with just 37 clients and has grown into one of the largest and most successful microfinancing organizations in the Philippines. Now some 257,000 women are helped by 1,300 staff members in seventy-one branches all over the country.

KMBI typically works with groups of thirty to forty women who meet regularly for encouragement and accountability. The women mutually guarantee each other's loans and provide emotional support for one another.

When Edisa's rug-making business got a boost from KMBI, not only her finances changed. "My social and spiritual life flourished," she says. Because she is now a leader of other businesswomen she has learned new skills, including how "to show compassion the way I never did before." She notes that KMBI has taught women to be good stewards of the resources given to them. The things she has learned, such as respect and discipline, she now teaches to the other women in her group.

The organization also supports the women's spiritual growth, believing this is how people can be genuinely transformed. A personal relationship with Jesus keeps the women "rooted in his teachings," which they can then apply in business, childrearing, relationships with their husbands, and care of the environment. A ripple effect means the family and the whole community can be transformed.

Using the three-pronged approach of building capital, capacity, and character, KMBI's staff participates in devotions and retreats, leadership training, outreach projects, and ministry opportunities.

KMBI has helped many women pull themselves out of poverty. For example, Cina's enterprise of juice drink production received a boost in capital so she can now supply drinks to local schools and shops. Lydia, a mother of eight with fifteen employees, processes eight tons of *nata de coco* (a type of coconut jelly) every week. The giant fruit company Dole is her biggest client.

—Debra Fieguth

Evangelical Impact in Indonesia: Church Planting Like No Other

Undeterred by challenges in a country that is made up of 250 million people spread across six thousand inhabited islands, many of them difficult to reach, Christian pioneers in Indonesia are managing to carry out one of the most rigorous and effective church-planting plans in the world.

It all started in the late 1970s when Chris Marantika, a young Indonesian who had graduated from Dallas Theological Seminary in the United States, had a vision to plant churches in his homeland. He called it Vision Indonesia 1:1:1, meaning one church was to be planted in each village in one generation. Marantika founded the Evangelical Theological Seminary of Indonesia (ETSI) in Yogyakarta, training students in both theological studies and church-planting methods.

Planting a church in a village that does not yet have one is an ETSI graduation requirement. And in order for a church to be considered established, there must be at least thirty baptized believers meeting together.

Some three decades later, four thousand five hundred new churches have been planted by ETSI graduates as well as thirty branch seminaries throughout the islands, training even more pastors. Still, half the country's sixty-seven thousand villages do not have a church.

Although Indonesia has the highest population of Muslims in the world, Christians there are legally free to practice their faith. In fact, Christianity is one of five recognized national religions. Life can be dificult, though, fo those who convert from Islam and, in some regions, even life threatening. Despite the law's support of religious freedom, construction of new church buildings often faces stiff opposition from hardline groups. Even established churches sometimes face the threat of closure.

At times, tension between religious communities in certain regions results in violence and death. Several years ago, during one of the worst religious conflicts, a pastor and a student returning home from church one Sunday afternoon were murdered. Although Christians were angry and grieving, Marantika wrote a letter to the Christian community asking them not to retaliate because the deaths were an opportunity to be a testimony.

Then there is the sheer remoteness of some villages. One trip to reach an animistic group involved a twelve-hour motorbike ride on dirt roads, followed by several hours of boat travel. But the effort was "richly rewarded by the mass of people hearing the gospel for the first time, demon-possessed people freed by the name of Jesus, and people receiving Jesus as their Lord and Savior," says Marantika.

Some of the branch seminaries have taken new initiatives to include training in community development skills, such as agriculture and microcredit.

"I continue to praise and thank God for the zeal of the students and faculty in ETSI year in, year out to press on with Vision 1:1:1, despite the challenges they have to face," says Marantika.

The impact of ETSI has been felt in other arenas besides the church. There is now a Christian university as well as a Christian high school. A gradual democratization of Indonesia has led to more freedom of the press, including allowance for Christian broadcasting and participation by Christians in politics.

In the beginning, funding for ETSI came from Partners International, a North American organization that assists ministries in developing nations. Gradually the Indonesian church began contributing to the funding, and today about a third of the seminary's budget comes from the indigenous church.

—Debra Fieguth

Evangelical Impact in Cambodia:
A Church Rising from the Ashes

When the Khmer Rouge took over Cambodia in 1975, people were ready for peace. Cambodians had suffered through years of civil war complicated by the larger Vietnam War. But the Khmer Rouge brought more violence, killing the elite, the educated, the urban, the wealthy—anyone who did not fit a narrow definition of what the ideal person should be. The genocide went on for four years.

Many Christians were among the two million or more who lost their lives through executions, starvation, and forced labor in the Cambodian Killing Fields. "The church was pretty much wiped out in the revolution," says Brian McConaghy, the Canadian founder of Ratanak International, a ministry that works solely in Cambodia.

Many of the Christians who did survive managed to make it across the border into Thailand. Although missionaries had been expelled from Cambodia, some, particularly those with the Christian and Missionary Alliance (CAMA), followed the Cambodian people to the Thai refugee camps, where, bereft of everything—family, homes, and material possessions—they were hungry to hear about the love of Christ. Then, when the displaced Cambodians were forcibly repatriated in the early 1990s, the fledgling Christian population moved back into every province of the country. CAMA returned to Cambodia with them.

McConaghy, then a member of the Royal Canadian Mounted Police (RCMP), learned about the immense needs in those early years and began shipping medical supplies to CAMA for the resident missionaries to use and distribute. He named his new organization Ratanak after a Cambodian baby girl who had died for lack of medical care.

Over the years Ratanak has participated in development projects focusing on water supply and agriculture. But its focus widened when, in his role as a police officer, McConaghy followed a pedophile to Asia and

Thousands of women and children are forced into sexual exploitation in Cambodia.
Photo: Ratanak International

learned just how deeply exploited young Cambodians, especially girls, had become. In a country where poverty is a never-ending struggle, young children and teens are extremely vulnerable to sex trafficking and exploitation.

Ratanak has partnered with other organizations in rescuing and rehabilitating some of these young girls, establishing a home and a skills-training program to help them build a better life. Ratanak-funded projects work during the day with hundreds of children, primarily in the capital city of Phnom Penh, who have not yet been rescued from brothels and are sold at night. Cambodian Christians staff the programs, using their own cultural background and experiences to minister in the Khmer language to those damaged by trauma.

Reaksa Himm, a survivor of the bloody Khmer Rouge regime who as a boy witnessed his family being slaughtered, has provided psychological training for those working directly with victims. Now a Canadian citizen, Himm has returned to Cambodia as a Christian missionary.

Survivors of exploitation pray together before performing a traditional Cambodian dance
Photo: Ratanak International

Another Cambodian Christian (and former soldier in the civil war), Yeng Ros, heads a Ratanak-funded training program in the villages to help people identify sex predators. Working with the organization Chab Dai (Khmer for "joining hands"), Yeng and his team have trained some thirty thousand villagers to protect their children from exploitation.

A generation after the genocide, the needs are still great. "The entire society was significantly influenced by trauma," McConaghy points out. But with help, the church is growing and maturing.

—Debra Fieguth

Children play together near one of Ratanak's ministry locations in Cambodia.
Photo: Ratanak International

EVANGELICALS IN WESTERN ASIA: GREATER SYRIA (ISRAEL, PALESTINE, SYRIA, AND LEBANON), JORDAN, AND IRAQ

By Azar Ajaj

The Holy Land has long attracted the attention of Evangelicals, who have shared the common Christian interest in the persons and events recorded in the Bible. The geopolitical decline of the Ottoman Empire in the nineteenth century and the location of the region at the nexus of Africa, Asia, and Europe have drawn the attention of others. The rise of millenarianism and dispensationalism—as popularized by figures like Darby and Scofield—further heightened its status as a focus of religious and political interest. This was absorbed into high imperial thought in such movements as British Israelism.

One important millenarian movement, for instance, interpreted Romans 9–11 to mean that a substantial number of Jews would convert to Christianity prior to the bodily return of Jesus Christ. The London Jews Society (LJS, today known as the Church's Ministry to the Jews or CMJ) was established in 1809 and had a profound impact on the shape of Evangelical and Protestant Christianity in what was then Greater Syria, a governorate of the Ottoman Empire administered from Damascus. The LJS coordinated the missionary work of various evangelical missionaries, mainly Anglicans and Lutherans. The Dane Hans Nicolayson and his family were the first Protestants/Evangelicals to settle in the city of Jerusalem in 1826, then an unsanitary and sometimes dangerous walled city where the gates were still locked at night.

Other missionaries soon joined him, and in 1841, Michael Solomon Alexander, the first Protestant bishop of Jerusalem, was ordained in London. Alexander, whose episcopate only lasted four years, had been a rabbi but had come to believe that Jesus was the Messiah promised in the Tanakh. Alexander and other believing Jewish people of the time called themselves Hebrew Christians. (The term messianic Jew did not then exist, and these believers had no qualms about identifying themselves clearly as members of the one, holy, Catholic, and apostolic church mentioned in the creeds.) Christ Church in the Jaffa Gate of the Old City today is the fruit of his labor.

The mission of the CMJ in relation to Jerusalem was to establish a Hebrew congregation on Mount Zion, and in this they were, barely, successful. The prayer book was translated into Hebrew, and Hebrews were baptized, confirmed, married, buried, and in a few cases ordained to the diaconate and presbytery (Crombie 2006). The LJS also witnessed about Jesus the Messiah to Jewish people in such other centers as Istanbul, Baghdad, Haifa, Tiberias, and Tunis. It was a time productive of fascinating figures such as Joseph Wolfe, whose missionary adventures are recounted in a number of volumes. Wolfe, a Jewish man, converted to Catholic Christianity and was baptized by the local bishop, then became a Protestant cleric. One of Wolfe's main goals was to find the lost tribes of Israel and identify the "kings of the east" who would cross the Euphrates at the time of the great eschatological battle between good and evil mentioned in Revelation 16:2.

Samuel Gobat, the Swiss French evangelical missionary, succeeded Alexander as the Protestant bishop in Jerusalem. In 1855 Gobat invited the Church Mission Society (CMS) to open Palestine as a mission field. Unlike the LJS, CMS missionaries were open to welcoming Christians from the ancient, local churches into the Protestant fold (Orthodox, Maronite, Coptic, Greek Catholic). Gobat and the CMS tended to see the spirituality of the ancient churches as hopelessly compromised and found little value in them. Under Gobat's bishopric, an arabophone group of congregations came into being in cities like Nazareth (Miller 2012), Nablus, Haifa, Jerusalem, and eventually on the East Bank of the Jordan in Salt (White 2012).

While the missions of the Anglicans and Lutherans in the Transjordan and the Presbyterian and Congregationalists in Syria-Lebanon were the largest and most important missions, other groups would arrive later and, usually, in smaller numbers. In the twentieth century new arrivals to Lebanon and Syria included the Brethren, the Assemblies of God, and the Baptists, among others.

Israel/Palestine

Other evangelical churches also started their mission to the region. The Christian and Missionary Alliance (CMA) established their first church in the Middle East in Jerusalem in 1890 (UCCI 2009, 48). Shukri Musa, a Palestinian from Safed, decided after being baptized by George Truett at the First Baptist Church in Dallas, to return home and share the gospel with his people. He arrived in 1911, began in Zefat (or Safed), and later in the same year founded the first Baptist church in the Holy Land in Nazareth (Baker 1961).

In the 1920s, with increased political stability under the British Mandate, several missions started to work in the area. The Church of the Nazarene started ministry in Jerusalem in 1920 among Armenian refugees (Smith, 1937, 178). The Assemblies of God mission had also shown interest in the Holy Land and started its official work in the

> **Evangelical churches in Israel are formed almost entirely of converts from other forms of Christianity.**

country in 1926. The Open Brethren Church began at the same time, although several individuals had ministered in the country since the end of the eighteenth century. Nothing was formally established until 1926, when Bet Hassda Assembly was founded in Haifa. Later assemblies were founded in Jaffa and Jerusalem, and then in Nazareth (Tatford 1982, 100–113). The Closed Brethren ministry began in the land in the 1940s through a Druze convert from Syria, establishing the first church in a small Galilean village of Kufer Yasif.

Most of the evangelical churches in Israel/Palestine are rooted in these missions in one way or another. The number of the Arabic-speaking evangelical congregations in Israel is approximately thirty-five, with an estimated membership of five thousand. Most of these churches are located in the north of the country. In 2005 these churches (with the exception of the Closed Brethren) came together to form the Convention of the Evangelical Churches in Israel (CECI). In addition to these churches, there are also more than one hundred Messianic fellowships (whether established congregations or small home meetings) spread through Israel, with roughly fifteen thousand members. Jewish churches have chosen to remain distinct to emphasise the Jewishness of their identity to other Jewish Israelis. They distance themselves from Christian cultural markers, particularly in light of the church's history of anti-Semitism. They also desire to emphasize their continuity with the Jewish people. However, in the fundamental issues of faith, there are no differences between Messianic Jews and Christians (Kjaer-Hansen and Skjott 1999).

Evangelical churches in Israel are formed almost entirely of converts from other forms of Christianity, though occasionally one will find a convert from Druze, Judaism, or Islam. A handful of congregations scattered throughout the country are formed primarily of Christians from a Muslim background. In Israel, Muslims have the freedom to convert legally to Christianity, something which is not the case in the West Bank and Gaza, where the Islamic shari'a is a key source for legislation.

In the Palestinian Authority areas of Jerusalem and Gaza, there are approximately eleven evangelical churches with membership around one thousand. In 1998, most of these churches formed the Council of Local Evangelical Churches in the Holy Land (now the World Evangelical Alliance member body for this region). It is important to note that in both countries, evangelical churches are not state-recognized denominations. The conventions are, however, with the WEA's assistance, seeking recognition from the State of Israel and the Palestinian Authority.

Syria and Lebanon

In what is known now as Lebanon and Syria, the Congregationalist and Presbyterian missionaries from the American Board of Commissioners of Foreign Missionaries (ABCFM, or simply American Board) arrived in the area in the 1820s (Makdisi 2009, 2). Eventually, in 1850, the Sublime Porte (the Ottoman imperial government) recognized the legal existence and autonomy of a distinct Protestant millet (Turkish) or dhimmi (Arabic). Converts trickled in from other churches, Maronite, Armenian, and Greek and Syriac Orthodox, but converts from Islam were few in number. In 1848 the first Congregationalist and Presbyterian church in this area was founded in Beirut, and in the next decades, other churches were founded in Lebanon and Syria (Diab 2009, 111–12).

In 1920, the National Evangelical Synod of Syria and Lebanon was formed, and by 1959 the National Synod took responsibility from the American Mission, representing the thirty-eight evangelical churches then existing as well as the medical and educational services of the American Presbyterian mission (National Evangelical Synod of Syria and Lebanon 2012).

The CMA was the next evangelical mission, arriving in Syria in 1921, and eventually planting churches in Damascus and Homs. The Church of the Nazarene soon followed. Other groups, such as the Assemblies of God and the Baptists, arrived in Syria later. In 1963, all the expatriate clergy were asked to leave the country, leaving ministry in the hands of the local pastors and leaders (Barret, Kurian, and Johnson 2001, 721). Until tensions rose in 2011, resulting in civil war, Syrian Christians enjoyed a great amount of religious freedom.

In Lebanon, the Baptists were the next to start an evangelical ministry. The first known Baptist church in Lebanon was constituted at Beirut in 1895 by Said Jureidini, a Lebanese who had embraced evangelical faith in an American Baptist church (McRae 1969, 38–39). Other denominations followed; Assemblies of God missionaries arrived in Lebanon in 1912 and established their ministry a few years after that in Beirut. After the 1948 war, the Church of the Nazarene founded a center in Jordan and in 1952 started a ministry in Beirut. Today there are at least twelve denominations: Presbyterians, National Evangelical Church, Adventist, Baptist, Church of God, Church of the Nazarene, CMA, AOG, Brethren, Quakers, Free Evangelicals, and Armenian Evangelicals. These churches have about fifty thousand members who are officially registered with the government. In 1937 the Higher Evangelical Convention in Syria and Lebanon was founded, and today represents all these churches in both countries (Diab 2009, 113–14).

The Evangelical community in Lebanon is active in reaching out to its own people through education. Almost thirty schools spread throughout the country are run by denominations and individual Evangelicals. Several denominational seminaries serve the Evangelical community in Lebanon, Syria, and other Arab countries. Lebanese denominations also offer medical and cultural services.

Jordan

Protestant missions were active in the Levant from the 1820s, yet we do not find any evidence of interest in the work in Jordan until the second half of the nineteenth century, when the CMS became active on the East Bank of the Jordan River. Some of the earliest figures, such as Frederick Augustus Klein, a native of Strasbourg who was active in the Transjordan and later Egypt, had joint interests in science and archaeology. Klein is best remembered today for his discovery of the Moabite Stone in 1868, which gave a qualified affirmation to Biblical material from the book of Kings.

The East Bank was also an arena for indigenous leaders in which to minister and flourish. Khalil al Jamal, a non-ordained catechist and native of Nazareth, was active in Al Salt. While he did not found the work there, it was after his arrival in 1879 that the Protestant community there "began to enjoy a measure of stability" (Rogan 2002, 129). The church in Salt would later send members to conduct home meetings in Amman, twenty miles away, and the Church of the Redeemer was officially organized there in 1927 (Miller 2007, 405). Michael Qa'war, Serpahim Boutaji, and Naser Oude were other early Anglican Arab evangelical leaders in the Transjordan—and sometimes Egypt. John Zeller encouraged and trained this group of Arab leaders. Zeller ministered in Palestine for approximately forty years and was instrumental in establishing Nazareth as a center for Arab Evangelicalism in the region. Zeller actively supported training indigenous leadership, (Ben Artzi 1988, 89), some of whom would go on to minister east of the Jordan.

Interestingly, the evangelical work in Jordan began as a result of an internal quarrel in one of the Christian clans (Al Fawakhri) in the town of Salt in 1926. Since the Orthodox priest was a member of one of the two groups, the other decided to leave the denomination. They approached Laura Radford, a missionary from the Assemblies of God mission in Jerusalem and asked her to open a mission in Salt. Having no one from her mission at that time to send, she encouraged a young man by the name of Roy Whitman to take up the task.

Whitman was staying at the mission building and studying Arabic in Jerusalem. He accepted the offer, and traveled there without knowing that a quarrel lay behind the invitation. Whitman's move to Salt was a major milestone of the evangelical work in Jordan (Dalleh 1987, 145), and his ministry is often considered as the beginning of the Assemblies of God ministry there.

Ironically, Whitman himself did not belong to the Assemblies of God, so a church presence with an ongoing link to the Assemblies did not emerge in Jordan until the 1960s (Habash 2011, 1). Whitman carried on with his ministry, establishing the Free Evangelical Church in 1941, an independent local ministry influenced by open Brethren theology. Although this denomination was small and local, its contribution to the Evangelical community in Jordan is notable. Many pastors and leaders from other denominations were touched by Whitman's ministry.

The Church of the Nazarene was the next to come to Jordan, beginning in Amman in 1948, then expanding to Zarqa a year later. The church opened a school there and established its first church in 1954. Baptist work in Jordan began in the same period, when the Southern Baptist missionaries came to Ajloon in 1951. They took over Ajloon Baptist Hospital, originally founded by the CMS, and a school, both of which still function. Two years later, originating from the ministries of the hospital and the school, the first Baptist Church in Jordan was established (Ayoub). The Baptist work in Amman began with the Baptist Bookshop, which was to lay the groundwork for the emergence of the Baptist churches currently present in the capital city (Habash 2011, 3). Seventh Day Adventists and the Christian Missionary Alliance were also active in the country.

In 1998 the five evangelical denominations in Jordan formed the High Evangelical Convention of Jordan, a WEA member body, which helps to coordinate ministries and represents the churches when they attempt to receive official recognition from the government. Although there are no official statistics for evangelical church membership, the estimated number is around eight thousand (between official members and attendance), with approximately sixty congregations. The churches serve the local community through social ministries, mainly through schools, bookshops, and theological education institutions. They also supply health services through hospitals and clinics.

Iraq

Protestant mission to Iraq began in the 1820s when the LJS's Joseph Wolff visited the area. He met with Jewish people, Syrian Catholics, and Yazides. He was followed in 1829 by Anthony Groves, a former dentist who became a leading closed Brethren missiologist. Groves remained in Bagdad for four years (Genymeh 1998, 50–51). Organized ministry began in 1839 when the American Board sent its first missionaries to Mossel and Kurdistan. Out of this mission work, the National Evangelical Protestant Denomination (Presbyterian in practice) was established, with churches in Mossel, Bagdad, Kirkuk, and Basra. The Evangelical Protestant Assyrian Denomination also has its roots in the American Board's mission, yet it was officially established in 1921 in Bagdad. The Seventh Day Adventist mission found its way to Iraq in 1923 in major cities like Bagdad, Mossel, and Kirkuk (Genymeh 1998, 181–85).

The CMS began ministry in Bagdad in 1883. Five years later they established the Arabic Turkish Mission, an independent ministry with a focus on education and medical service. An Anglican church grew out of this and was built in Bagdad and dedicated in 1937. This building was used also by other small evangelical groups in Iraq. In the second half of the twentieth century, other evangelical groups such as the Armenian Evangelical Brethren, Assemblies of God, and Brethren also started their ministries in Iraq (Genymeh 1998, 186–208).

Challenges Facing the Christians in the Middle East

Declining numbers form the main challenge for Christians in the Middle East, Evangelical or otherwise. The emigration of Christians leaves the Land of the Bible with no, or in the best case only a marginalized, Christian witness (Belt 2009). Political instability, tension, the rise of political Islamic parties, wars, and civil wars that sadly characterize this area all contribute to the emigration.

Protestant mission to Iraq began in the 1820s when the LJS's Joseph Wolff visited the area.
Photo: Public Domain

Christians were not the only people who left for the West, but because of the nonviolent, pacifist stance of many, Christians' emigration rate has been higher than other groups. The growth of Islamic fundamentalism in the last thirty years also feeds into the emigration of at-risk minority Christians, who suffer from diminishing religious freedom. In most of these countries, Christians are allowed to convert to Islam, but it is illegal for Muslims to convert to Christianity. The Christian birth rate is relatively low in comparison to the Muslim community, thus contributing to the decline of Christians in the Middle East.

Economic instability in various countries of the Middle East makes life, let alone institution building, difficult. The underperformance of economies in the Middle East cannot be reduced to any single factor, like the Israeli occupation of the West Bank or the rise of extremism or globalization, though these factors are significant. Unemployment and the rising cost of living, in conjunction with social, cultural, and religious tensions, has also been a significant factor contributing to Christian emigration.

These factors affect all Christians, not just Evangelicals. Growth in the Evangelical Church typically comes from historical churches and not from other religions, presenting the problem of declining sources of growth. Evangelical churches and parachurches in the Middle East share the Gospel with their surrounding religious and ethnic context. In each of these countries local ministries can be found, where Evangelicals try to build bridges and meet the needs of their own people. The support of international agencies, such as IFES and CCC, which work among university students and are well established in many of these countries, has been essential. The United Bible Society has been active in the region since the first half of the nineteenth century, translating and distributing Bibles in several languages.

In a time of great challenges for Evangelicals in the Holy Land, it is necessary that Evangelicals understand their important role in keeping the Christian witness alive.

Azar Ajaj is president of Nazareth Evangelical Theological Seminary, where he also lectures. He has been an ordained minister to his Arab Israeli community for over twenty years. He holds a BA in Biblical Studies from Bethlehem Bible College and an MTh from International Baptist Theological Seminary in Prague. He is now working on his PhD with Spurgeon's College, doing research on the history of the Baptists in Israel.

Sources and Further Reading

Ayoub, Jamal. Baptists in Jordan. Accessed October 6, 2013. http://history.jordanbaptist.org/baptistsonstage

Baker, Dwight L. *Baptist Golden Jubilee, 50 Years in Palestine-Israel*. Baptist Village, Israel: Baptist Convention in Israel, 1961.

Barret, David, George Kurian, Todd Johnson. Syria. Vol. 1, in *World Christian Encyclopedia*, 719–721. New York: Oxford University Press, 2001.

Belt, Don. "The Forgotten Faithful." *National Geographic*. June 2009 and accessed May 22, 2013. http://ngm.nationalgeographic.com/2009/06/arab-christians/belt-text/1

Ben Artzi, Yossi. "John Zeller—Missionary to Nazareth and the Holy Land." *Katedra* 50 (1988): 73–97.

Crombie, Kelvin. *A Jewish bishop in Jerusalem: the life story of Michael Solomon Alexander*. Jerusalem: Nicolayson's, 2006.

Dalleh, Geryis. *The Revival*. Masouriat Al-Meten, Lebanon: Baptist Publishing House, 1987.

Diab, Issa. *Introduction to the History and Theology of the Evangelical Churches* (Arabic). Beirut: Daar Manha-lAl-Hayat, 2009.

Genymeh, Hareth. *Protestant and Evangelicals in Iraq* (Arabic). Bagdad: Al-Naasher Al-Maktabi, 1988.

Habash, Jiries O. "Evangelical Churches in Jordan." MEATE Journal: 1–15, 2011.

Kjaer-Hansen, Kai, and Bodil F. Skjott. *Facts & Myths about the Messianic Congregations in Israel*. Jerusalem: UCCI, 1999.

Makdisi, Ussama. *Artillery of Heaven*. Ithaca, NY: Cornell University Press, 2009.

McRae, Jane Carroll. *Photographer in Lebanon, The Story of Said Jureidini*. Nashville, Tennessee: Broadman Press, 1969.

Miller, Duane Alexander. "Christ Church (Anglican) in Nazareth: A brief history with Photographs." *St Francis Magazine* 8, no. 5 (October 2012), 696–703.

———. "Morning Prayer, Low Style, in the Anglican Diocese of Jerusalem: Church of the Redeemer, Amman, Jordan." In *Anglican and Episcopal History* 76, no. 3 (September 2007): 404–8.

Rogan, Eugene. *Frontiers of the State in the Late Ottoman Empire: Transjordan, 1850–1921*. Cambridge: Cambridge University Press, 2002.

Smith, Roy E. *A History of Missions of the Church of Nazarene*. Kansas City, MO: Nazarene Publishing House, 1937.

Tatford, Fredk. *The Restless Middle East*. Bath, UK: Echoes of Service, 1982.

The National Evangelical Synod of Syria and Lebanon. 2012 and accessed July 2, 2013. http://www.synod-sl.org/?page_id=38

White, Malcolm. "Anglican Pioneers of the Ottoman Period: Sketches from the CMS Archives of some Arab lives connected with the Early Days of the Diocese of Jerusalem." *St Francis Magazine* 8 (April 2012): 283–314.

Evangelical Impact in Israel and Palestine: Reconciliation Is Key

Salim Munayer, an Evangelical Palestinian, and Evan Thomas, a Messianic Jew, started Musalaha (Arabic for "reconciliation") during the middle of the first intifada, a land-related uprising of Palestinians against Israelis that lasted from 1987 to 1993.

A Musalaha youth group. *Photo: Musalaha Ministry of Reconciliation*

"Jesus, in his last words, prayed that [the church] would be one," says Munayer. He is the Jerusalem-based director of Musalaha, and Thomas is chair of its board. They have been working on unity between Palestinian and Messianic believers ever since the founding of the organization.

Believing that reconciliation is best done at the grassroots level, Musalaha takes mixed groups of young people to the desert—the Negev in Israel, the Sinai in Egypt, or the Wadi Rum in Jordan—for an intense period of getting to know and understand each other.

Shadia Qubti, a Palestinian Baptist from Nazareth, went on a desert encounter in Jordan after high school, knowing only that it was a Christian conference. "It was the first time I had met Messianic Jews. I didn't know someone could be Jewish and also believe in Jesus."

During the encounter Qubti became close friends with a young Messianic Jewish woman. As the two deepened their friendship, they began to understand much more of each other's story. Once afraid of Israeli soldiers, Qubti was surprised to find her new friend had been in the Israeli army. (All young Israelis, male and female, must serve in the army for a term). At her friend's wedding, Qubti was a bridesmaid.

Qubti now leads the children and youth section of Musalaha. Children from Israel and Palestine come together for summer camps, taking part in Bible studies and singing in both Hebrew and Arabic. "We have had children not willing to touch each other, or refusing to stay in the same room with the other side," says Qubti. "This is why we do camp."

When two children, an Israeli and a Palestinian, once refused to stay with each other, "we asked why, and they didn't know." When camp leaders explained to them Jesus wants them to love each other, "five or ten minutes later they were convinced."

Hedva Haymov moved to Israel from New York as a young Messianic believer. In America, Haymov says, Messianic congregations "taught us that the Jews needed to come back to Israel." But a desert encounter changed her perspective. Now she heads the Musalaha women's ministry.

"It's our primary target to get women from both sides together," Haymov explains; it is a task that is more difficult with adults than it is with children. It starts with gathering the Palestinian Christian women together "well before we get them to meet with Israelis." Palestinian women, Haymov notes, often don't know their own history and lack the freedom and self-confidence of many Israeli women. A group of Palestinian Christian and Palestinian Muslim women also meets, but extending that relationship to include Muslims and Jews will take more time.

Although reconciliation is always challenging and difficult, Musalaha is growing and having an effect. About three thousand people go through the program every year, according to Munayer. Now there is also a curriculum for reconciliation, with materials being used in Rwanda, Burundi, Nigeria, and other parts of the Middle East.

—Debra Fieguth

EUROPE

POPULATION 740,308,000
MAJORITY RELIGION: CHRISTIANITY (78.4%)

EUROPE REPRESENTS

10.7% OF THE TOTAL
GLOBAL POPULATION

25.5% OF THE GLOBAL
CHRISTIAN POPULATION

3.4% OF THE GLOBAL
NON-CHRISTIAN POPULATION

25.2% OF THE GLOBAL
MISSIONARY FORCE RECEIVED

CHRISTIANITY IN EUROPE

POPULATION ▰▰▰ CHRISTIAN ▰▰ EVANGELICAL ▰▰▰

CHRISTIAN & EVANGELICAL POPULATION

0%   20%   40%   60%   80%   100%

(22,715,000) **78.4%**

2.5% *(OW 18,306,000)*

3.1% *(WCD 22,715,000)*

TOTAL POPULATION (740,308,000)

GROWTH RATE* 1970–2010

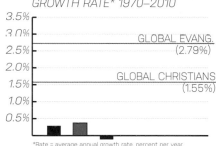

3.5%
3.0%
2.5%   GLOBAL EVANG.
         (2.79%)
2.0%
1.5%   GLOBAL CHRISTIANS
         (1.55%)
1.0%
0.5%

*Rate = average annual growth rate, percent per year,
between dates specified.

MISSIONS IN EUROPE
FROM ALL CHRISTIAN TRADITIONS

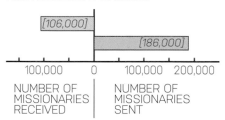

[106,000]

[186,000]

100,000   0   100,000   200,000

NUMBER OF   NUMBER OF
MISSIONARIES   MISSIONARIES
RECEIVED   SENT

1 MISSIONARY SENT
FOR EVERY **3,100** CHRISTIANS
IN EUROPE

1 MISSIONARY RECEIVED
FOR EVERY **6,900** PEOPLE
IN EUROPE

73 OF EVERY 100 NON-CHRISTIANS
PERSONALLY KNOW A CHRISTIAN
IN EUROPE

Source: *World Christian Database*, 2010 data

Christians and Evangelicals by country in Europe, 2010

	POPULATION, 2010	CHRISTIANS, 2010	% CHRISTIAN, 2010	WCD EVANGELICALS, 2010	WCD % EVANGELICAL, 2010	OW EVANGELICALS, 2010	OW % EVANGELICAL, 2010
Albania	3,150,000	1,027,000	32.6%	9,700	0.3%	14,500	0.5%
Andorra	77,900	71,500	91.8%	55	0.1%	310	0.4%
Austria	8,402,000	6,514,000	77.5%	47,700	0.6%	40,500	0.5%
Belarus	9,491,000	7,012,000	73.9%	146,000	1.5%	123,000	1.3%
Belgium	10,941,000	7,667,000	70.1%	40,900	0.4%	133,000	1.2%
Bosnia-Herzegovina	3,846,000	1,858,000	48.3%	2,100	0.1%	2,200	0.1%
Bulgaria	7,389,000	6,172,000	83.5%	136,000	1.8%	146,000	2.0%
Channel Islands	160,000	136,000	85.2%	25,800	16.2%	16,600	10.4%
Croatia	4,338,000	4,056,000	93.5%	17,300	0.4%	19,400	0.4%
Czech Republic	10,554,000	5,844,000	55.4%	135,000	1.3%	72,900	0.7%
Denmark	5,551,000	4,647,000	83.7%	282,000	5.1%	193,000	3.5%
Estonia	1,299,000	570,000	43.9%	118,000	9.1%	65,700	5.1%
Faeroe Islands	49,600	48,600	98.0%	8,700	17.6%	14,400	29.1%
Finland	5,368,000	4,336,000	80.8%	531,000	9.9%	649,000	12.1%
France	63,231,000	41,685,000	65.9%	674,000	1.1%	603,000	1.0%
Germany	83,017,000	58,091,000	70.0%	1,296,000	1.6%	1,741,000	2.1%
Gibraltar	29,300	25,800	88.3%	360	1.2%	900	3.1%
Greece	11,110,000	10,173,000	91.6%	18,800	0.2%	41,400	0.4%
Holy See	800	800	100.0%	16	2.0%	20	2.5%
Hungary	10,015,000	8,724,000	87.1%	421,000	4.2%	282,000	2.8%
Iceland	318,000	301,000	94.7%	7,900	2.5%	12,600	4.0%
Ireland	4,468,000	4,202,000	94.1%	151,000	3.4%	71,100	1.6%
Isle of Man	84,000	70,600	84.1%	23,100	27.5%	8,600	10.3%
Italy	60,509,000	48,787,000	80.6%	309,000	0.5%	633,000	1.0%
Kosovo	2,084,000	122,000	5.9%	1,300	0.1%	810	0.0%
Latvia	2,091,000	1,549,000	74.1%	87,100	4.2%	157,000	7.5%

Country							
Liechtenstein	0.5%	190	0.7%	240	89.4%	32,300	36,100
Lithuania	1.2%	35,900	0.3%	8,300	88.8%	2,724,000	3,068,000
Luxembourg	0.5%	2,600	0.2%	1,100	82.4%	418,000	508,000
Macedonia	0.2%	4,300	0.2%	4,800	63.1%	1,326,000	2,102,000
Malta	1.2%	5,200	0.2%	1,000	98.0%	416,000	425,000
Moldova	3.7%	132,000	0.6%	20,300	96.7%	3,454,000	3,573,000
Monaco	1.0%	380	0.2%	57	86.0%	31,700	36,800
Montenegro	0.0%	290	1.4%	8,400	77.3%	479,000	620,000
Netherlands	4.3%	717,000	3.7%	610,000	63.3%	10,516,000	16,615,000
Norway	8.4%	410,000	11.0%	537,000	89.7%	4,387,000	4,891,000
Poland	0.2%	95,400	0.3%	101,000	95.4%	36,439,000	38,199,000
Portugal	3.0%	319,000	1.2%	123,000	91.1%	9,650,000	10,590,000
Romania	5.3%	1,150,000	6.8%	1,486,000	98.5%	21,531,000	21,861,000
Russia	1.1%	1,637,000	0.6%	899,000	80.7%	115,942,000	143,618,000
San Marino	0.0%	4	0.0%	0	91.9%	28,400	30,900
Serbia	0.6%	44,800	0.3%	23,800	89.2%	6,747,000	7,563,000
Slovakia	1.2%	67,200	1.8%	98,600	85.6%	4,650,000	5,433,000
Slovenia	0.1%	1,800	0.4%	7,400	87.7%	1,801,000	2,054,000
Spain	1.0%	462,000	0.3%	142,000	88.3%	40,778,000	46,182,000
Sweden	6.8%	642,000	7.6%	717,000	63.4%	5,952,000	9,382,000
Switzerland	4.3%	336,000	3.9%	307,000	80.3%	6,289,000	7,831,000
Ukraine	3.8%	1,737,000	2.5%	1,130,000	83.6%	38,489,000	46,050,000
United Kingdom	8.8%	5,465,000	19.3%	11,999,000	72.3%	44,886,000	62,066,000

EVANGELICALS IN EASTERN EUROPE

By Scott Klingsmith

Until 1989, the term Eastern Europe carried a meaning that was generally understood. It meant the Union of Soviet Socialist Republics (USSR) and those Communist countries dominated by it, plus Yugoslavia and Albania. Today, the definition is more challenging. Sometimes commentators refer to the Russian Federation and the western countries pertaining to the Commonwealth of Independent States (CIS) and the Baltics are included, but sometimes not. Those countries in the western part of the region prefer to see themselves as Central European, rather than Eastern. For the purposes of this article, we refer to the formerly Communist Central European countries (minus the former East Germany) and the countries of former Yugoslavia. Today, with the exception of some of the smaller states of former Yugoslavia, all these countries are members of the European Union.

In Communist times there was a tendency for those outside the region to see all these countries monolithically, as though Communist governments made them all the same. But each country is distinct, with different languages, ethnicities, histories, church situations, and spiritual conditions. With the exception of Romania and Moldova, it is a region where Evangelicals are a very small presence. They represent between 0.1 and 1% of the respective national populations, even though there are strong Roman Catholic and Orthodox traditions. At least five of the thirty countries in the world with the smallest percentage of Evangelicals are in this region, ahead of such countries as Libya, Saudi Arabia, and Bangladesh. At the same time, churches are growing, despite slow or even negative general population growth, with seven of the top twenty countries in greatest population decline in this region (Grudzinska-Gross 2014).

Evangelicals in Eastern Europe have always been an opposed and at times persecuted minority. Even before Communist times, Evangelicals were viewed very negatively by the majority church, condemned as sectarians, foreigners, and sheep stealers. To a certain extent, and in varying degrees around the region, the fall of Communism reinforced the centrality of traditional socioreligious identities and so reawakened this hostility to what were considered foreign traditions. Where there is opposition today it is as likely to come from leaders of the majority church as from government officials (Perica 2004).

Evangelicals of an older generation have been profoundly shaped by their experiences under Communist rule. They grew up in conditions where the churches were severely restricted, facing opposition and perhaps persecution for actively expressing their faith. In many instances Evangelicals were restricted in their choice of profession and were denied access to higher education. A number of pastors, particularly in Romania, spent time in prison. Lutheran pastor Richard Wurmbrand, who was imprisoned for fourteen years, is perhaps the best known among many. As a result, Evangelicals were often in a survival mode, building barriers between themselves and the society around them with clear rules for behavior and thought, which would protect them from contamination or opposition. This often was true also for their relationship with other Christians. Evangelicals were opposed by the majority Church and generally had a great distrust of other denominations. Baptists and Pentecostals in many countries were deeply suspicious of each other (Volf 1996).

Red Square, Moscow

The younger generation of Evangelicals has had a completely different experience. They have little or no memory of Communist times. They have lived through both growing prosperity and real economic uncertainty and have experienced the growing pains of the move toward democracy. They are usually better educated, have traveled more and have a greater understanding of the world. They are also influenced by broad societal trends and have rebelled to some extent against the legalism of their parents. At the same time, they are members of churches that make up very small minorities in their countries, which often makes them reticent to be engaged in public witness. Despite this, evangelical churches around the region are growing, and some at a significant rate (Wachsmuth 2014).

History

Evangelical roots in Central Europe begin with the Reformation. Bohemia, today's Czech Republic, was the home of Jan Hus, a fifteenth-century predecessor of Luther. Later the Moravian Brethren, forced from their homeland by the Hapsburgs in the eighteenth century, found refuge on the estate of Count Nicholas von Zinzendorf in what is now eastern Germany. They became a major early missionary movement. Poland and Slovakia were heavily influenced by Lutheranism and, to a lesser extent, Calvinism, but during the Counter-Reformation were re-won by the Catholic Church. Hungary was most touched by Calvinism and remained the most Protestant of all the Eastern European countries. This was also true for the Hungarian population of Transylvania, the western part of Romania. The Orthodox countries never experienced reformation and therefore have a very different character (Kool 1993).

The more recent evangelical presence in the region traces its origin to Baptist initiatives from Germany in the nineteenth century. Johann Gerhard Oncken sent traveling evangelists to German communities in Austria, Hungary, Poland, and Romania starting in the 1840s and 1850s. The first Baptist church in Poland was established in 1844, in Hungary in 1846, and in Romania in 1863. Oncken's motto was "Every Baptist a missionary," and this propelled Baptists to evangelize all over Eastern Europe. The movement toward the indigenous populations primarily began in the years leading up to World War I and experienced rapid growth in the following years. The first Romanian Baptist church was formed in 1912 (Klingsmith 2012).

Pentecostals, who in most of the countries make up the largest proportion of Evangelicals, began in the early twentieth century. These churches were often started by repatriates from the United States who had been influenced by the Azusa Street Revival (from 1906). The Charismatic movement has been a mostly post-revolution phenomenon.

There are Evangelicals within the historic churches, but they are often hard to identify. In addition, a number of smaller denominations, such as the Brethren and the Seventh-Day Adventists, are active.

Current Composition

The countries in this region can be grouped in a variety of ways, all of which are unsatisfactory to a certain extent. For our purposes, we will look at them according to the majority Christian expressions in the country. The countries to the west and north are traditionally Roman Catholic, and those in the Balkans, to the southeast, are Orthodox.

Catholic Central Europe

The Czech Republic, although one of the birthplaces of the Reformation, is now one of the most secular countries in the world (according to a recent poll, only 16% say they believe in God), with only 0.7% Evangelical. In fact, government statistics show the dominant Catholic Church now claiming only about 10% of the population. The Evangelical Church of the Czech Brethren is the largest group. Slovakia, separated from the Czech

Republic in 1993, seems considerably more religious, with an Evangelical population a bit over 1%. In both countries, groups such as Josiah Venture and newer style local churches have been attracting young people. Although small, Evangelical and Charismatic churches are alive and growing (Wachsmuth 2014).

The Catholic Church in Poland under the Communists was a rallying point for nationalism; particularly after Polish cardinal Karol Józef Wojtyla became Pope John Paul II. It has lost considerable status and influence in the years since the revolution, but still claims a large majority of the population. Protestants are a very small minority, but the inclusion of those influenced by renewal movements within the Catholic Church may indicate more Evangelical presence than just those in the Protestant denominations. Nevertheless, recent research indicates that the commonly accepted figure of 0.3% may in fact be too large by half, and the true figure should be .15% (Wachsmuth 2014).

In 1600, Hungary was 90% Protestant, and although the Counter-Reformation reclaimed many, a significant number of people remained either Reformed or Lutheran—far more than in any other country in the region. Today Evangelicals are around 3%, although it is difficult to determine the numbers within the historic churches who would identify as Evangelical. The Charismatic Faith Church is the largest church in Hungary and one of the largest megachurches in Europe. It claims a membership of more than seventy thousand and nonmember supporters in the hundreds of thousands, both in Hungary and in neighboring countries. There are increasing restrictions on churches and Christians. A 2011 church law removed church status from sixty-six religious communities, and official status as a church can now be granted only with a two-thirds majority of Parliament. In addition, far right-wing political parties are strongly anti-Evangelical as well as virulently anti-Semitic and anti-Roma (Kool 1993; Klingsmith 2012).

Orthodox Balkans

Somewhat ironically, Romania, which had one of the most repressive regimes in the region, and was the only one whose revolution in 1989 was violent, also has the largest Evangelical presence in the region, with over 5%. Many large and active Pentecostal and Baptist churches are here, particularly in Transylvania in the northwest. A spiritual awakening in the early 1970s led to significant church growth, despite pretty severe persecution. Romanian Christians have been on the forefront of internal church planting and external mission efforts.

One unique feature of Romanian church life is the existence of the Lord's Army (*Oastea Domnului*), a temperance and renewal movement within the Orthodox Church. Estimates of how many of these would be considered Evangelical vary; some of the fellowships are very integrated into Orthodox churches, while others are only marginally connected to the Orthodox Church and essentially have an independent, more Evangelical identity (Klingsmith 2012). Historically and ethnically related to Romania is Moldova, which has the second largest Evangelical presence in the region (3.7%), and now also has a growing missions movement. (It is the only country covered in this article that was part of the old Soviet Union.)

In the past thirty years Evangelicals in Bulgaria have nearly quadrupled, from 0.4 to 1.9%, even though life and ministry for them has been challenging. The number of long-term missionaries is relatively small, and many have not stayed for more than a few years. A significant number of national missionaries, meaning those working in local outreach, are helping churches build bridges to non-Christians (Klingsmith 2012).

The countries of former Yugoslavia are divided between historically Roman Catholic (Slovenia and Croatia), Orthodox (Serbia, Montenegro, and Macedonia) and Muslim (Bosnia and Kosovo). Under the firm grip of the Communist government, ethnic and religious identity was suppressed, which gave the impression that the tensions between the different groups had disappeared. However, with the end of Communist rule, these identities reasserted themselves, often violently. Religion and ethnic identity became fused, and historical animosities broke out into civil war and ethnic cleansing in the mid-1990s. Evangelicals are about the only group that has avoided these divisions, as they are not identified with any ethnic or national group. Seen with suspicion by all other parties, they are nevertheless a strong witness to the power of the gospel to heal and bring reconciliation

Evangelical churches are the only places where interethnic harmony and love are demonstrated. Ethnic identities seem largely irrelevant in these fellowships.

Evangelicals have been active socially and have consequently been accused of proselytism and of using material benefits to attract converts. They have had to be careful not to tie aid to religious expression and have had to clearly show that their concern for the poor and the marginalized (especially for the Roma), is simply an expression of the gospel, not a strategy for growth. Although they have been the primary suppliers of aid following the wars and the boycott of Serbia, Evangelicals are not acknowledged in the media, and so their efforts are largely unknown.

Serbia is the largest of the former Yugoslav states. Evangelicals make up only about 0.6% (although some observers find this estimate inflated), and only around one-third of these are ethnically Serb, the others primarily Slovak, Hungarian, and Romanian. They face severe opposition from the Orthodox Church, the government and the national media. There are regular instances of violence against church building and pastors (although this seems to be gradually decreasing), and they endure long delays in getting any kind of official recognition or permissions. The smaller states Montenegro, with only a few hundred believers, and Macedonia (0.2%) have been closely related to Serbia, although both are now independent. There are no known believers among the large ethnic Albanian population in the former "Greater Serbia."

Bosnia and Herzegovina is still suffering the consequences of the 1991–1995 war with Serbia. It is the place where the term ethnic cleansing was first formulated, and the results of that war can still be seen in bullet-riddled walls and destroyed buildings throughout the country. It has a Muslim majority and a very small Evangelical presence (0.1%). Both the government and the religious authorities make Christian existence difficult. Much social work has been carried on by Christians, but they are still seen with wide suspicion. Europe's newest country (although not recognized by all), Kosovo, with its Muslim Albanian majority, has a tiny Evangelical population of around thirty-five churches with two thousand believers. Slovenia, with .1% Evangelical, is, along with Croatia, historically Catholic. Evangelicals are an insignificant, divided, and struggling presence (Klingsmith 2012).

Special mention needs to be made of the Roma (traditionally called gypsies), an ethnic group spread throughout the region. Universally despised, often even by Christians, they are the most marginalized group of society. Poverty, lack of education, and unemployment are all much higher among the Roma than in the general population. They make up between 5 and 10% of the populations of Slovakia (9.3%), Hungary (7.7%), Bulgaria (4.7%), Romania (officially 3.8%, but could be as high as 10%), and Macedonia (5.2%). Despite their lack of status in society, or perhaps because of it, the Roma are among the most responsive peoples to the gospel. Thriving Roma churches exist in Romania, Ukraine, Bulgaria (more than twenty thousand believers) and elsewhere in Europe (Klingsmith 2012).

Mission

Mission from outside

During Communist times several mission agencies (among them Navigators, Slavic Gospel Association, Open Doors) carried out clandestine activity, primarily in Bible smuggling and discipleship efforts. Started in 1979, Biblical Education by Extension (BEE, now called Entrust) was a cooperative effort between a number of Western agencies which delivered church-based theological education for pastors and church leaders who had little or no access to biblical training.

With the fall of Communism came a major influx of Western missionaries, many of whom had little knowledge of, or sympathy for, the established churches, both historic and evangelical. Many of these efforts didn't last long. Those organizations that are still present have by and large developed more sensitive partnerships with national believers.

Internal outreach

Since 1989 a number of church planting efforts have been initiated, some through the efforts of outside missionaries and others by leaders within various countries. In Romania, hundreds of new churches were planted, led by the United World Mission following a strategy of Saturation Church Planting. In Serbia the Antioch Mission and the Union of Baptist Churches in Serbia developed a strategy to plant new churches in cities and towns where there was no evangelical witness (Klingsmith 2012).

Theological education and leadership training have been strong priorities around the region. Both through non-formal education programs as well as through the development of many Bible colleges and seminaries, leaders for churches and mission are being trained.

Evangelicals have also been socially active. In Romania, dozens of orphanages were built to respond to the desperate situation of orphans. In Bosnia homes for boys, farms, many relief efforts, provision of food and school supplies for students and English lessons have been areas of activity. In Moldova orphanages have been started, and youth camps are a common form of outreach. And in Macedonia, Christian businesses attempt to demonstrate ethical business practices, provide jobs and witness to the gospel (Wachsmuth 2014).

Cross-cultural mission initiatives

Mission from the region has mostly been recent. Although there were a few missionary impulses before and during Communist times, mission was essentially destroyed under the Communists. The Romanian Baptists had a small mission society between World War I and World War II, and the Hungarian Lutherans and Reformed had some clandestine missions involvement under Communism. But for most Evangelicals, mission was something that Westerners did. Travel restrictions and opposition from the State made anything external seem impossible. From 1990 on, some church leaders began to travel and experience more of the world and saw that their churches, because of their experience of faithfulness under persecution, had something to offer the rest of the world. They began to challenge their churches to engage in mission beyond their own borders. In addition, several Western missionaries brought a concern to see churches throughout the region sending missionaries.

At first through short-term mission trips, and later through long-term missionary commitments, churches throughout the region were awakened to see their own responsibility to reach out to the world. In the early days following the revolutions, a number of small, indigenous efforts were begun, from Poland, Hungary, and Romania, and, to a lesser extent, from the Czech Republic. Soon, international agencies like Youth With A Mission (YWAM), Operation Mobilization (OM), Wycliffe Bible Translators, and others were recruiting young people from these countries (Klingsmith 2012).

Although accurate numbers of missionaries sent from these countries today are difficult to ascertain, Romania, Poland, Czech Republic, and Moldova have active sending movements. The seventh edition of Operation World lists 28 missionaries from Czech Republic, 60 from Hungary, and 230 from Romania. A lack of agreement on definitions of missionary makes numbers difficult to compare.

Romanians have developed a variety of mission structures, ranging from the initiatives of a single local church to a country-wide cooperative initiative. An early effort, Romanian International Mission (MIR), began with great enthusiasm, but soon foundered because of lack of clarity of purpose and personal rivalries and agendas. More recently, a successful umbrella organization, Partners in Mission (PIM), has developed with the goal of assisting denominations and mission agencies fulfill their vision of missionary sending. PIM's first working group focused on member care issues. Romanian missions have focused on two main areas. The first is the intentional sending of missionaries, either through denominational structures or through international agencies. The second is through motivating and equipping migrant workers going to Western Europe, helping them take their fervent brand of Evangelicalism with them to encourage churches in the countries where they are working.

In Poland, the effort and expense of getting government recognition caused two new mission agencies—Mission to the East and Wycliffe Poland—to join together in the Biblical Mission Association (BMA), a cooperative effort. Several smaller partners joined in ensuing years. Ministry in Central Asia, translation work in Africa, and evangelistic and relief work among the Roma in Ukraine are some of their primary ministries.

In addition to the ministry of OM, Wycliffe, and a couple of local churches, a major emphasis in Hungary is on missionary training and scholarship. The Protestant Institute for Mission Studies (later the Central and Eastern European Institute for Mission Studies—since closed) was a valuable place of motivation for and the study of missions, first in Hungary but also regionally.

The New Mission Movement Network (NMMN) was a region-wide initiative designed to encourage the development of emerging missions and associated with the European Evangelical Missionary Association. It became the Central and Eastern European Missions Forum (CEEMF) in 2009, when mission leaders in the region stated "we are no longer emerging; we have emerged." Following three successive American missionaries, in 2012 a Romanian mission leader became the coordinator.

One final network, focused on the study of mission in the region, is the Central and Eastern European Association for Mission Studies (CEEAMS). Although intentionally ecumenical, with mainline, Orthodox, Catholic, and Evangelical membership, Evangelical missiologists are in the forefront and are the most active.

Mission efforts face a number of challenges. One is the struggle to financially support the missionaries who are sent out. As costs have risen, partnerships with Western churches have been necessary to meet needs. A second challenge is a lack of commitment from many pastors and church leaders, who see the needs in their own countries as too great to release young people to cross-cultural ministry. In addition, missionaries often have a lower status in the churches than pastors do and thus often receive less support. A further challenge is to develop appropriate sending structures, as well as adequate preparation and member care for missionaries (Klingsmith 2012).

Looking to the Future

Evangelicals in Central and Eastern Europe face a variety of challenges. Their tiny size and history of division makes it difficult for them to gain constructive social attention. Because of persecution they were often forced to meet in secret and to build strong walls to protect themselves from the government and society. This has made some reluctant to be publicly active in evangelism and outreach. The societies they are trying to reach still have hangovers from Communist times and a materialist regime now also increasingly marked by secularization and materialism.

At the same time Evangelicals have had to deal with a resurgent power of the majority church, whether Catholic or Orthodox, which often brands them as sects or cults and accuses them of fishing in their neighbor's pond. While there have been some cooperative efforts, particularly in the areas of Bible translation and social work, in general relationships with the majority Church are still strained. While religious freedom has increased in some countries, several others still limit religious expression as it relates to official recognition as religious organizations, the right to construct church buildings, and to openly evangelize (Klingsmith 2012, Wachsmuth 2014).

Many opportunities exist. The possibility exists for mature partnerships with Western and non-Western missionaries. No longer seen merely as the weak younger sister of Western churches, they can define relationships that are mutually beneficial for all parties.

While the increase of secularism presents a challenge for the gospel, growing disillusionment with materialism is leading to a renewed search for meaning and interest in spirituality on the part of many people. Evangelicals have the chance to demonstrate through their humility and contentment that faith in Jesus offers satisfaction and fulfillment in life.

Finally, while the missionary movements are still quite small, they offer the possibility of sending missionaries to places restricted to Westerners, and where their cultural adaptability, historical relationships, modest lifestyle and relative political weakness open doors to effective witness.

The year 2014 marked the twenty-fifth anniversary of the fall of Communism. It was an occasion for many churches, schools, and mission agencies to reflect on the past two and a half decades and to see where they have come from, what they have experienced and learned, and where God might be leading them in the years ahead.

Dr. Scott Klingsmith is Assistant Professor, Intercultural Studies and Missiologist-in-Residence at Denver Seminary, in Colorado, and editor of *Acta Missiologiae*. He was educated at Trinity International University (PhD), Denver Seminary (MDiv), Colorado State University (BA). Before joining Denver Seminary, he served with WorldVenture in Vienna, Austria from 1985–2008, and has had extensive teaching experience around the world, including in the Czech Republic, Ukraine, Bosnia, Germany, Hungary, Romania, India, and the United States Scott is a member of the Central and Eastern European Association for Mission Studies, the American Society of Missiology, the World Evangelical Alliance Missions Commission, and the Evangelical Missiological Society.

Bibliography and Further Reading

Acta Missiologiae: A Journal for Reflection on Missiological Issues and Mission Practice in Central and Eastern Europe

Grudzinska-Gross, Irena, *Eastern Europe,* Frankfurt: Peter Lang GmbH, Internationaler Verlag der Wissenschaften, 2014.

Klingsmith, Scott. *Missions Beyond the Wall: Factors in the Rise of Missionary Sending Movements in East-Central Europe.* Nürnberg: VTR Publications. 2012.

Kool, Anne-Marie, *God Moves in a Mysterious Way: The Hungarian Protest Foreign Mission Movement (1756–1951).* Zoetermeer: Uitgeverij Boekencentrum, 1993.

Perica, Vjekoslav, *Balkan Idols: Religion and Nationalism in Yugoslav States*, Oxford: Oxford University Press, 2004

Volf, Miroslav, *Exclusion and Embrace: A Theological Exploration of Identity, Otherness, and Reconciliation*. Abingdon, 1996.

Wachsmuth, Melody, ed. Between Nation and Religion: Christian Witness in Southeastern Europe, *Evangelical Interfaith Dialogue*, Spring 2014. http://cms.fuller.edu/EIFD/issues/Spring_2014/Spring_2014.aspx

Evangelical Impact in Bulgaria:
From a Secret Institute to a Society Shaper

A theological training institute that taught students in secret during the Communist era has found a new focus in preparing professionals to minister in the marketplace.

The Bulgarian Biblical Academy–Logos secretly trained Evangelicals for ministry between 1979 and 1989 explains Nikolay Nedelchev, one of the academy's founders, who is also president of the Bulgarian Evangelical Alliance.

But the interdenominational institute's roots go back even further. The original seminary, the only one in the country, began during Turkish rule, operating from 1863 to 1944. When the Communists came to power they shut it down until Nedelchev and his colleagues quietly prepared the way for the establishment of a new institute, the United Theological Faculty (UTF), in 1999.

In 2012 the name was changed from United Theological Faculty to Saint Trivelius Christian Institute after Khan Tervel, a Bulgarian Christian leader from the eighth century known to all branches of Christianity. The

A class graduation at Trivelius Institute.
Photo: Krasimira Dimitrova

same year Saint Trivelius formed a partnership with the New Bulgarian University at that university's request. The partnership benefits both sides, says Nedelchev. Saint Trivelius students can get a degree from the university, and the university's professors "can learn from our professors. They can see the Christian way of life."

The evangelical church in Bulgaria flourished in the decade following the fall of communism, growing from two hundred churches in 1989 to almost one thousand three hundred churches in 1999. The need for training pastors was great during those ten years. But in more recent years, as more Bulgarian Christians enter various professions, they want to be theologically equipped to minister in the work setting. Put simply, "they want to serve where they are professionals," explains Nedelchev.

Even though the name of the institute changed over the years, the goal remained the same: training people to serve God in their contemporary context.

Lawyers, accountants, musicians, teachers—people from all walks of life—have studied at Saint Trivelius. One board member is on the Supreme Court. Besides undergraduate and master's degree programs, Saint Trivelius also trains chaplains for hospitals, prisons, and the military.

The evangelical church in Bulgaria still lives with challenges, even now that the persecution of the Communist era is no longer a threat. "In the beginning the challenge was to learn to live with freedom. Now the challenge is how to live with materialism."

A growing Muslim population, mainly from Turkey, is also a challenge. "But we are learning how to use this opportunity and become friends," Nedelchev says. Through sharing the love of Christ with Turkish Muslims, the church has seen many converts. The school has trained approximately sixty Muslim converts to Christianity, and many have gone back to Turkey to work among their own people.

Saint Trivelius Christian Institute has also built bridges with the Orthodox Church, whose mostly nominal members make up 80 percent of the country's population of 7.5 million. The school offers joint seminars with Orthodox theological faculty and draws on Orthodox professors to teach Hebrew and biblical archaeology.

—Debra Fieguth

Study group in Sandanski, Bulgaria.
Photo: Krasimira Dimitrova © Trivelius Institute

EVANGELICALS IN NORTHERN EUROPE

By Mark Hutchinson

The stereotypes of Northern Europe are many: technologically advanced, but also inheritors of a brutal pagan past; first to take up the Reformation but also first to ride the waves of secularization, peaceful social democrats, and fearsome religious warriors.

Most of the region received one or another of the major traditions to emerge from the Reformation, with Danish, Swedish, Norwegian, and Finnish identities becoming closely associated with their national Lutheran churches. In Denmark, state Lutheranism emerged via virtual royal coup d'état, later followed by absorption of the church into an absolutist state (Petersen and Petersen, 2013). In Finland, on the other hand, Orthodox Finns were classified as ethnic Karels while under Russian rule. While now one of the most peaceful, advanced regions in the world, from 1100 onwards, the border or buffer states (Norway and Finland in particular, but in the nineteenth century also Schleswig Holstein in the context of rising Prussian militarism) were dominated by contesting alliances between the Danish, Swedish, German, and Russian crowns, ensuring continued popular differentiation of languages and religious traditions as a means of defending national identity.

Of the Scandinavian countries, only Norway remains outside the European Union. Denmark was an early member, Finland and Sweden joined only after the collapse of the Soviet Union (enabling them to protect against the future, but also avoid entanglement in the present), and Iceland is in the process of applying. Norway's population narrowly rejected two referenda, largely due to the potential impact of centralized government on sovereignty and the fishing industry. The staggered entry dates are a broader reflection of the variegated reactions in northern cultures and churches, to centralism, bureaucracy, and external pressures on community and group identities.

Scandinavia

Sharing in the Reformed magisterial traditions, Scandinavian countries were also touched by the Moravian and Hallensian pietism, which had reshaped German Evangelicalism; this was in part imported by Swedish POWs repatriated after the Great Northern War (1700–1721), and through the presence of migrant Moravian communities. As in Germany, one result was the development of Scandinavian missionary societies, including the Swedish Evangelical Mission (SEM) (1856), the Swedish Mission Bible-True Friends (SMBV), the Norwegian Lutheran Mission (NLM), for example, and independent revivalist traditions.

The Lutheran state churches, while on the one hand a vehicle for pietism, also fell victim to the increasing rationalism and indifferentism of the ruling classes. Freemasonry and enlightenment mysticism became "the wet-nurse of all the confused mysticism which the enlightenment professed to discard" (Hovde 1948, 306). The evangelical basis of Scandinavian churches was undermined from the early 1700s by such movements as natural religion, mesmerism, and the mystico-rationalist unitarianism of Swedenborg. "It was as if," notes Nicholas Hope, "in the inclement climate of economic individualism, enlightened parish clergy (in office until c. 1840) were in the end too zealous with the use of reasonable speech." On the other hand, "awakened parishioners . . . preferred the hymns, devotional books, and homily of an earlier age" (Hope 1995, 355).

From 1796 the revivalism of Hans Nielsen Hauge "directed [his] barbs primarily at the prevailing uninspired orthodoxy" and "the indolence, gaiety, and uppishness of the official clergy" (Hovde 1948, 317). His personal ministry and many followers produced a form of Haugean revivalism, which had a significant impact on both

Norwegian religion and industry. While Hauge's followers had some influence in Sweden and Denmark, the movement emerged in a time of considerable tension between the three major Scandinavian countries, limiting his direct influence.

Instead, Sweden had a less coherent läsarne movement (Pietist/nonconformist), and the loss of Norway by Denmark in 1814 opened space for questioning of the spiritual effectiveness of the official church, leading to a reframing of Danish national spirituality under deeply held Lutheranism of (the early) N. F. S. Grundtvig. Popular revival movements emerged (in Jutland from 1799, for example), often from among rural populations as protests "against the bone-dry, devitalized spirit of the orthodox and the rationalistic clergy alike" (Hovde 1948, 308). These movements were heavily shaped by the European expansion of the Bible Society, which flooded Scandinavian rural towns and parishes with Bibles and hymnaries.

Scandinavians were also heavily exposed to the growing global shipping industry and tended to bring back influences from overseas. Successful movements sought ways of connecting to the nationalist feeling of the time; not to do so could be dangerous. The importation of Baptist teaching by a sailor in 1839 led to stringent official repression, while Scottish Wesleyan George Scott barely escaped with his life in 1842 when it was rumored that he had made disparaging remarks about Swedes. Nevertheless, these movements connected with popular revivalism, producing an energetic and increasingly coherent form of Scandinavian Evangelicalism gathered, for instance, around the National Evangelical Foundation and its journal *Budbäraren*.

The revival movements in the nineteenth century marked the National churches in different ways: in Sweden 6% of the population was organized into free churches. In Norway and Iceland the corresponding figure was 4% and in Denmark and Finland, where revivals were kept within the National church, only 1% (Sjöström 2011, 12).

It was a dynamic influence, however, taken abroad with extensive Scandinavian emigration, to Brazil and the United States, for instance. Scandinavian migration to the United States had a powerful influence. This was part of the even larger great European migration which went out into the world in the nineteenth and twentieth centuries, carrying with it some 1.3 million Swedes and more than 800,000 Norwegians attracted by low cost, high quality farmland and metropolitan factory work in the upper Midwest. Chicago and Minneapolis were the urban centers for this wave and a natural focus for the emergence of evangelical movements that would later feed influences back to Scandinavia. Their churches would contribute to various streams of American Evangelicalism, to the foundation of the Mission Covenant Church of Norway, to the spread of Pentecostalism to South America through Daniel Berg and Gunnar Vingren, or to the internationalization of Billy Graham's revivalism through the Evangelical Free contributions to Youth for Christ. In turn, post-War migration and evangelical expansion would bring these influences back, producing new waves of awakening.

By 1870, the Methodist Episcopal Church in Chicago had sufficient members to organize separate Swedish and Danish Conferences around the world with their own campgrounds at Des Plaines, Illinois, their own theological seminary based at Northwestern University, and their own missionary networks, such as the Scandinavian Alliance. It was out of this latter, founded by energetic missions motivator, Swedish-born Fredrik Franson, that TEAM was formed in the United States, and multiple other missionary agencies in Europe. In a sense, the international space was a necessary alternative to the ambivalent position of Scandinavian Evangelicals at home. Not only did "modern theology . . . serve to strengthen [the] gap between parish clergy and their poor flock," it led to the institutionalization of state churches.

Scandinavians were also heavily exposed to the growing global shipping industry and tended to bring back influences from overseas.

A shift towards the social gospel and ecumenism likewise left the spirituality of individual salvation unengaged. Just as the nineteenth century Scandinavian countries sought political unity in Scandinavism against the rising power of France and Prussia, so the powerful impact of the Student Christian Movement, internationalization and two world wars led them into a long-running search for regional and global ecumenism. Such emphases not only tended to operate at a level well above the average parishioner, but, particularly after World War II, national churches such as the Church of Norway found it difficult to maintain the popularity it had enjoyed during the anti-Nazi struggle, in a post-war period "dominated by materialism and non-Christian Humanism," and the political rise of socialism (Sjöström 2011, 23, 50).

Despite relatively high levels of public trust in religious institutions (Manchin 2004), weekly church attendance in all Scandinavian countries has trended sharply down in the post-war period, settling at between 2% (Norway) and 5% (Sweden), despite nominal membership ranging between 60 to 80%. This trend now seems to be reaching a "lowest level" in Finland, "the most Lutheran country in the world" (Pickel and Muller 2009, 50). For example, the actual number of regular churchgoers has not decreased, though the percentage of the population affiliated to a movement continues to do so.

The collapse of popular spiritualities in general has proceeded more slowly, with a reemergence (particularly in Iceland) of formal pagan movements and more general lingering superstitions, as noted in the telling article entitled "Estonians desert Church but pay to 'commune' with angels" (Reigas 2007). All countries include a large percentage of their populations that maintains that they are "religious in their own way" (Pickel and Muller 2009, 104). Revivalist influences from the English-speaking world have joined these pagan movements. With the evangelical language of the Lutheran churches acting as sort of cultural vocabulary, many disconnected Evangelicals were open to revivalism. Even when they joined the World Council of Churches, Norwegian ecumenists insisted on inserting "according to the Scriptures" in the WCC theological basis.

After the Azusa Street revival (see above), Methodist Thomas Ball Barratt in Oslo and Baptist Lewis Pethrus in Stockholm planted and led powerful national Pentecostal movements that made Scandinavia a center for the re-evangelicalization of other parts of Europe and of mission into India and China. These movements originated in or drew upon traditional Evangelicalism and were particularly held together by their extensive newspaper and publishing activities. While they believed in the common apostolic faith and signs, they differed in their international reference points. The Swedish Baptist origins of Pethrus, for example, naturally also drew upon Baptistic influences such as that of Chicago's William Durham.

After World War II another Baptist, Billy Graham, drew some fifty thousand people to a crusade in Stockholm. As was a standard approach for the Billy Graham Organization, a broad net was cast, stirring a response among both the national church and among laity. John Olav Larssen (Norway's Billy Graham) commenced a ministry that would touch hundreds of thousands of people, both in Norway and abroad. Scandinavian-born Evangelicals in the United States heavily shaped the sort of Protestant revivalism which filtered back to Europe. Joseph Mattson-Boze's Philadelphia Church in Chicago, for example, acted as a funnel for Latter Rain and Word Faith preaching, particularly that of William Branham, to spread back to Sweden and through their missions efforts, to Africa and South America. These influences interacted with Pethrus's more traditional Evangelicalism to spark local revivals.

The global concerns that fueled state church ecumenism also continued to feed Scandinavian interest in missions. In 1965, for example, Aril Snorre Edvardsen founded the organization Troens Bevis Verdens Evangelisering, which grew to support around one thousand native missionaries around the world and supported reconciliation between Christianity and Islam. At the same time, "many of the so-called 'Faith ministers' owe a lot to Edvardsen who as early as 1961 actively promoted the most prominent advocates of the post-World War II healing movement (1946–59)" (Lie 2000).

Some of these organizations drew their energy and personnel from the 1950s Charismatic renewal, which spread among Scandinavians (in Sweden through the Förnyelseväckelsen, or "renewal revival"), led by young evangelists and songwriters such as Nils Olof Algot Niklasson and Georg Johansson. (The connections between the evangelist-led Charismatic renewal and a remnant of Lutheran pietism can be seen in the case of Hans-Jacob Frøen, who—at the resurgence of Charismatic phenomena in Norway in 1970—asserted that he had experienced such energy as early as 1938). This wave created new organizational forms, such as the Oase summer camps and the Oase Foundation, which brought together people from various traditions. These later became the basis for extended influence by the Word Faith Movement, including among its numbers some of the region's largest churches, such as Oslo Kristne Senter or OKS, founded by Åge Åleskjær in 1985, or Livets Ord, founded by Ulf Ekman in Uppsala in 1983.

As Geir Lie has noted, the Charismatic Movement was a many-headed, and many-footed movement: "'The movement' reflects a multitude of traditions from which the various groups trace their origin" (Lie 2000). Pentecostalism, the Charismatic Movement and the Faith Movement combine and separate in different locations and times, making identification of a particular theological culture difficult. Such difficulties, however, also reflect the highly mobile nature of Scandinavians in the post-War period. Åleskjær, for example, studied at Kenneth Hagin's Rhema Bible Training Center in Tulsa, Oklahoma, an influence which connected him to the extensive American Charismatic church scene, and which continues to influence his preaching on grace and faith. From the 1980s, Norway in particular saw "an almost explosive mushrooming of new and independent churches" (Lie 2000). More recently, the large Scandinavian presence among students at Hillsong College, Sydney, Australia, has likewise brought back variant influences, leading to the establishment of Hillsong Churches in Stockholm and Copenhagen.

It has not escaped popular notice that a large proportion of attendees in Sweden's evangelical churches are foreign born, where English services can provide a cushion to the shock of Scandinavian language and culture. On the other hand, most of the growing churches are Hillsong-like: Hillsong itself (Stockholm), Connect (Gothenburg), and Södermalm (Stockholm). This global influence has also provided a renewal of older churches, such as Daniel Norburg's Immanuel Church (Malmo).

The Baltic States

Historically, the Baltic countries have been defined by their location on the religious "fault line" separating the Catholic West from the Orthodox East, a line across which a great deal of blood has been spilled (be it by Teutonic knights, Mongol invaders, or Russian armies). The territorial principle of Orthodox and Catholic churches created pseudo-state churches even when (as under Communism) no such arrangement existed; these churches also formed close associations with nationalist movements, some of which verge on the xenophobic. There are regular tensions between the Moscow Patriarchate and Catholic communities over what the former considers its "canonical territory."

After the decline of Communism, the rapid transition of the Baltic States into the European Community has generally seen a rapid rise in living standards and in increased mobility—both in terms of employment migration and vertical social mobility—among the relatively small populations of these countries. There are traditional links between the Baltic States and Scandinavia, with the Danish (twelfth and sixteenth centuries) and Swedish (seventeenth century) Empires ruling over parts of the region at various times. The region has always had a Russian population, one which swelled massively in the twentieth century due to a deliberate Russification program under Stalinist occupation, through to 1989.

It has not escaped popular notice that a large proportion of attendees in Sweden's evangelical churches are foreign born.

In order to maintain stability, minorities can be granted cultural autonomy status, a designation which also has religious consequences, identifying the proper orbit of a particular religion with a region's constituent ethnicities. The largest religious denomination in Estonia and Latvia is Evangelical Lutheranism (about 14%), while in Lithuania it is Roman Catholicism (over 80%). Estonia is known as the most irreligious country in Europe, with only 16% of its population expressing any belief in the existence of God, though the proportion of its population which expresses evangelical views (4%) is fairly average. In Lithuania, traditional Protestant communities (about 1% of the population) were heavily impacted by deportation and oppression under Russian occupation, with the result that post-war Evangelicalism (now about 1%) has had little tradition within which to work (Manchin 2004).

These crossflows can be seen in the emergence of transnational churches, such as the Jaunâ Paaudze (New Generation) Movement of Kazakhstan-born Alexei Ledyaev. When this ethnically Russian Baptist and later Pentecostal "apostle" was banned from using a local Lutheran church, Ledyaev attracted support from Norway, which in turn enabled him to run city-wide campaigns and expand his local church to over five thousand and to plant internationally. In later years, Ledyaev associated more closely with American apostolic groups, attracting hate mail from both Latvian nationalists (who dislike his presumed Russophonism) and social progressives (who dislike his activities with right-wing groups such as Watchmen on the Walls) and decry his support of the conservative Latvia's First Party.

Concerns

Nordic societies gravitate toward big government and pervasive welfare states. Inevitably, this inclination means that education or charity or health care (all traditional locations for Christian action) are often funded from the center and often come with intrusive government regulation. Arguments for an evangelical-like movement toward more independence from the State thus have a strong historic basis (Petersen and Petersen 2013). Alarm was registered in 2009, for example, when the Swedish National Agency for Higher Education tied accreditation of theological institutions to its insistence that they shift resources toward general religious studies rather than theology, threatening degree-granting status and student funding. Christians, along with those of other traditions, can found faith-based schools, but the fear that such developments threaten the public ideology "that science and secularism could build a model society" has provoked both public protest and government intervention (Hansen 2009; Petersen and Petersen 2013). In a 2002 survey of religious attitudes across Europe, Denmark was rated as the most intolerant of "religions that take themselves too seriously" (Copenhagen Post 2003); the Jyllands-Posten cartoon controversy of 2005 reflects deeply seated secularist skepticism of the role of religion.

Other legislative threats have emerged against preaching in public; hate crimes relating to expressions of belief about homosexuality, and even the printing of the traditional text of the Bible. Some churches have accepted de-registration rather than being forced to perform marriages outside their theological understandings. Even though many state churches, such as that of Sweden, were formally disestablished through the 1980s–2000s, the traditional tie between State and Church has left in the mainstream church a cultural suspicion of evangelical enthusiasm and separatism. As Thomas Dixon noted in 2001, "Evangelical Lutheran pastors are all but locked out of senior positions in the Church of Sweden."

Those standing against cultural relativism in such churches are sometimes the object of media-driven attacks: the non-separationist Bishop of Gothenberg, Bertil Gärtner, for example, became "the symbol, figurehead, even hate object, of all those who were in favour of" women's ordination (Olofsson 2009). In 2008, the Latvian Evangelical Lutheran Church chose to divide from its Swedish equivalent, and attach itself to The Lutheran Church—Missouri Synod in the United States, over the same issue. The association of evangelical groups in Northern Europe with American equivalents, the Word of Faith Movement, Missouri Synod, Restorationism and the like, internationalizes the domestic politics associated with American Evangelicalism. Therefore, it is often easier for these organizations to live in international and expatriate spaces than it is to put down roots into local cultures.

For their part, the Baltic states are still drawn into tensions within their large ex-Soviet neighbor over the activities of foreign nationals. When seeking to cross boundaries, pastors such as Ledyaev have been refused visas or planning permissions and exposed to administrative harassment and even arrested for various causes. In some cases, nationalism and the remnants of the old Soviet empire have seen Russian officials exiling Russian-born and speaking evangelists back to the Baltic states, or vice versa, with no reference to their rights as citizens. Such actions take place in the context of continuing sensitivity within the Baltic national consciousness of Stalinist crimes against humanity, and of Russian threat. At the time of writing, with Russia in the Crimea, it is a cultural reaction which the rest of Europe is now taking seriously.

Sources and Further Reading

Copenhagen Post. "Religion not for us, Danes say." October 3, 2002.

Dixon, Tomas. "Sweden: Locked out." *Christianity Today*, August 1, 2001.

Fagan, Geraldine. *Believing in Russia—Religious Policy After Communism.* London: Routledge, 2012.

Halldorf, Joel. "Algot Niklasson och förnyelseväckelsen inom pingströrelsen 1950–51." Centrum för teologi och religionsvetenskap.Lunds Universitet, 2004.

Hansen, Collin. "Seminaries in Peril: Government evaluation threatens training of Swedish pastors." *Christianity Today*, July 27, 2009.

Hope, Nicholas. *German and Scandinavian Protestantism*, 1700–1918. Gloucestershire, United Kingdom: Clarendon Press, 1995.

Hovde, B. J. *The Scandinavian Countries, 1720–1865: The Rise of the Middle Classes.* Vol. 1. Cornell University Press, 1948.

Kostlevy, William. *Holy Jumpers: evangelicals and radicals in Progressive Era America.* New York: Oxford University Press, 2010.

Lembke, Judy. "Expats flock to Sweden's evangelical churches." The Local: Sweden's news in English, March 27, 2013.

Lie, Geir. "The Charismatic/Pentecostal Movement in Norway: The Last 30 Years." Cyberjournal for Pentecostal-Charismatic Research. February 2000 and accessed October 17, 2013. http://www.pctii.org/cyberj/cyber7.html

Manchin, Robert. "Religion in Europe: Trust not filling the pews." Worldwide Religious News. Sept 21, 2004 and accessed October 17, 2013. http://wwrn.org/articles/6292/?&place=eu

Olofsson, Folke T. "Bishop Bertil Gärtner in memoriam." 2009 and accessed March 26, 2014. http://kalin.nu/english/olofsson2.htm

Petersen, Klaus and Jorn Henrik Petersen. "The Good, the Bad or the Godless Society?: Danish 'Church People' and the Modern Welfare State." *Church History.* 82, no. 4 (December 2013): 904–940.

Pickel, Gert and Olaf Müller. *Church and Religion in Contemporary Europe*, Wiesbaden: Springer Fachmedien, 2009.

Reigas, Anneli. "Estonians desert Church but pay to 'commune' with angels." Worldwide Religious News. wwrn.org/articles/25072/

Sjöström, Lennart. "The Quest for a Nordic Church Fellowship Challenged by the Formation of the Nordic Ecumenical Institute/ Council." MThesis, University of Uppsala, 2011.

Torjesen, Edvard P. *Fredrik Franson: A Model for Worldwide Evangelism*, Pasadena: William Carey Library, 1983.

EVANGELICALS IN SOUTHERN EUROPE

By Mark Hutchinson

Evangelicals in southern Europe (Albania, Andorra, Croatia, Gibraltar, Greece, Holy See, Italy, Malta, Portugal, San Marino, Spain) are an often-overlooked but dynamic element of the world-wide Evangelical community. Classical evangelical denominations (the English and American Baptist and Methodist churches, and so forth) and societies (the Bible Society and the Salvation Army, in particular) have supported workers and causes in the region for well over a century. In almost all cases, Anglo-Americans have met cultural resistance due to their homeland being associated with imperialism. The exception is when the foreign input attaches to a movement from below (the preference of the poor and/or marginalized), or taps into a movement for change, which then gets caught up in an emerging ethnic, regional, or national identity.

All southern European countries have long histories of established state churches heavily shaped by their national or community identities. As Perica (for the Balkans) and Viroli (for Italy) have noted, these are not so much matters of theology as myths of national origin which co-opt for the nation what it means to be "Christian" (Perica 2004, 5; Viroli 2009).

State applications of the theoretical freedoms of religion vary considerably; evangelical churches are often treated as foreign sects, raising the social cost of conversion among those who would retain self-identification as Maltese, Italian, etc., believers. As a result, the majority of southern European Evangelicals, after a long history of incubation in small mainline movements, now belong to high energy/identity communities centered on Pentecostal or Charismatic churches. The various waves of evangelical formation have also occurred over a lengthy period of time, leaving a legacy of tension and suspicion between the various denominational forms. Finally, many countries in the region are heavily affected by their location on the "refugee highway" from the Global South to the employment centers of Europe.

Iberia: The Empires Strike Back

A nominally secular country, Portugal is dominated by cultural Catholicism (88% of Portuguese consider themselves "religious," compared to 86% of Italians, 80% of Greeks, and 61% of Spanish citizens), for which a renewed Concordat (2004) provides continued special status. Prior to 1974, Evangelicalism was legally proscribed and leaked into the country through its reliance on British trade, from its former colonies, and through diplomatic ties (Hutchinson and Wolffe 2012). The Brazilian Baptist Mission Board sent its first missionary there as early as 1911. Freedom of religious practice was not legalized until after the Carnation Revolution (1974). Attainment of registered status is now relatively simple, though attaining entrenched status (permitting incorporation, marriage celebrancy, and so forth) is more difficult, and cultural Catholicism in local government still impedes the spread of Protestant churches.

The Portuguese Evangelical Alliance (PEA) obtained entrenched status with the Ministry of Justice in 2006 and continues to press for greater actualization of constitutional protections. After stabilization in the 1980s, Evangelicalism in Portugal began to grow relatively rapidly, growing from around 45,000 to somewhere between 150,000–200,000 members. While core evangelical churches, such as the Assembleias de Deus em Portugal, grew between 1 and 2% per year, the most rapid growth occurred after the "missiological turn" of Latin American churches (COMIBAM I Sao Paolo, 1987). The result was also a rapid fragmentation of the evangelical scene as some older forms were charismaticized, and the country saw a rapid expansion of new—particularly

Brazilian-initiated, and more recently African-initiated—churches. This growth, and the financial and media-orientation of some new churches (such as the Igreja Evangélica Cristã Maná) inevitably draw legal attention in a country with a total population of only 10.5 million. At the more enthusiastic end of estimates, DAWN (Discipling a Whole Nation) Europe suggests that there are now as many as two thousand evangelical churches in Portugal; the Portuguese Evangelical Alliance (PEA) is following a strategy to double that number by 2015.

Revolution, division, and secularism also typify Spain. The Spanish Civil War, on the tail of centuries of Inquisition, Fascism, and state absorption of the church's functions have left Spain even more anticlerical than most southern European countries. Up until the 1960s, therefore, the largest evangelical churches in Spain largely catered for the floating international population (drawn by work, military operations, holiday, retirement, or onward missionization into, for example, North Africa).

From 2008, Spain was also deeply influenced by a general economic crisis in southern Europe. As a closed country, radio was a tool used by early evangelical missionaries, such as in the work of Paul Freed from Morocco from 1954. Since that time, significant migration and re-migration from Latin America—the source of over a quarter of Spain's foreign born population—and the Philippines has provided rich soil for overseas-initiated evangelical churches. For instance, Movimiento Misionero Mundial (Iglesia Cristiana Pentecostes de España) was founded in Puerto Rico in 1963 but now claims more than six thousand congregations in sixty countries, including twenty in Spain. While sharing a common language, regional dialects, the ethnic and class-assumptions of *castellano*, and assumptions about the resources needed to sustain a work in Spain have presented real problems for many Latino missionaries. Since the early 2000s, there has also been a sharp increase of boat-borne sub-Saharan refugees. The Canary Islands received more than thirty thousand in 2006 alone.

There are now more than six hundred thousand Africans in Spain, among whom early signs of indigenous churches are forming. Evangelical churches are involved in refugee care and evangelism among the migrants. In 1986, the Federación de Entidades Religiosas Evangélicas de España replaced the older Comisión de Defensa Evangélica in order to act as a point of common address to the state. It currently claims a total constituency of around four hundred thousand.

The largest evangelical church in the country is also not among the mainstream Spanish population but among the Gitanos. While connected to the French Gypsy revival of the 1950s, conversion among Gitanos has a number of differences to the Gypsy Church elsewhere in Europe. Spread largely among non-nomadic, Spanish-speaking gypsies, evangelical conversion has been an important means of resisting identity threats (Catholicism, absorption by the Spanish state, urban drift, and so forth) and the impact of illicit drugs on youth and extended families. In the face of their challenges, the Iglesia Evangélica de Filadelfia, founded around the work of Brother Emiliano, runs extensive detoxification programs, among its some one thousand communities scattered through Spain and another two hundred in Portugal. Nearly half of Spanish Gitanos identify as Evangelicals, suggesting that there may be as many as two hundred thousand around the country. In the words of Manuela Cantón Delgado, in their evangelical churches "they are the leaders, the pastors like them are gitanos, while in the Catholic Church they feel marginalized" (Delgado 2010). Its success is the result of a "strategic and intentional mobilization of ethnicity."

In the Shadow of St. Peter's

Unlike the above mentioned countries, in the Waldensian (valdese) tradition, Italy's evangelical tradition stretches back before the Reformation. Hounded out of the rest of Europe, the valdesi maintained a precarious existence by paying close attention to theological trends, training in leadership, adopting a strategic though minor part in the Great Game of European politics, and developing an indigenous military tradition. Though ultimately liberalized, the long valdese resistance to cultural genocide won it a place in Italian politics and culture; because of this, Italian Evangelicalism's success is due to this resolute people. Waldensian churches, colleges, and schools were central to the rise of Italian liberal institutions, as well as to foundational institutions and leaders—Guglielmina Malan, Alfredo Del Rosso, Teofilo Gay, Luigi Francescon—of early Italian Evangelicalism. They remain important spokespeople for religious rights, and are actively supportive of Baptist, Methodist, or Pentecostal churches.

The Fascist regime shattered the gains made by reformed and revivalist evangelical denominations under the earlier 1848 Albertine concession of civil and political rights. All Protestant churches were identified as foreign imports, and, by the 1929 Concordat, Catholicism was linked even more closely with racist/essentialist ideas of Italian nationalism. While many of these communities were subsequently broken up under Fascist legislation, which remained in force until 1955, their emphasis on the miraculous, on literal Biblicism, and their independence of trained and paid ministry saw Evangelicals and Pentecostals disperse into underground groups which continued to grow.

After 1943, the leaders of these scattered works, such as Umberto Gorietti, sought international support. The American Assemblies of God provided recognition and the basis for a formal *intesa* (understanding or contract) between the Italian Assemblies of God (ADI) and the state. Despite continuing local resistance to property ownership, public testimony and conversion, this organizational ability—providing property security, training, and stable ministerial incomes, and a channel for foreign support—has led to the majority of evangelical churches in Italy growing within one or another of the Pentecostal traditions, particularly the ADI. Over the longer run, the ADI's sectarianism (originally a strength) and its succession pattern have made it subject to institutionalization, opening space for later waves of international influence to give rise to new denominations and movements.

In more recent years, those networks which did not join the ADI, such as the Congregazioni Cristiane Pentecostali and many Independent churches, drew together in a loose network under the title of the Federazione delle Chiese Pentecostali (FCP), mainly as a means of obtaining corporate representation with the State. The birthplace of the ADI, in anticlerical, independent-minded and high-migration Sicily, remains the heart of Evangelicalism in Italy. Not only does Sicily feature the nation's largest church (Lirio Porello's Chiesa Cristiana Evangelica Parola della Grazia, Palermo), but about a quarter of all Italian Evangelicals live on the island and often act (be it in the north, or abroad) as a migrant core for church planting.

By way of contrast, most foreign evangelical missionary activity is in the north, where it is assumed that higher incomes and cultural levels will produce greater cultural impact. The fruit of this has been historically important, but numerically inconclusive; Italy hosts only thirty thousand or so non-Pentecostal Evangelicals, with CESNUR estimating the Pentecostal community at ten times that size (313,000). And while less than 1% of the Italian population is Pentecostal, some 4% of immigrants are. With a declining indigenous Italian population, the growth of Latin American and African churches has become important. As 52% of immigrants are Orthodox or Muslim, however, it is unlikely that Evangelicals will grow as a proportion of population (Introvigne 2012).

Latin American leadership is central among the Independent Pentecostal churches, such as the Independent Ministero Sabaoth, or the Elim Missione Cristiana Vida y Poder, both in provincia di Milano, or MxG in Roma. The theological variety implied by this sort of migration, and the nearby influence of Britain and the United States, is everywhere to be seen in Italian evangelical media, particularly in the extensive network of locally run evangelical radio stations, and TCI's heavily American-influenced Christian television broadcast. Parachurch ministries and ecumenical events, such as Atleti di Cristo, Gruppi Biblici Universitari, or the March for Religious Liberty, provide ways into a public sphere dominated by politics, economics, and Catholicism.

Heretics, Etymologically So

For Greek Evangelicals, the identification of nationality with the majority religious tradition was further reinforced by the lack of a Greek experience of the Reformation, by the close identification of Greekness with Orthodoxy as a result of centuries of Turkish occupation, by the country's continued existence on Europe's traditional divisions with Islamic and Slavic spheres, and by a historic self-consciousness as the tradition that gave the world the New Testament. To be fully Greek, one needed to profess Orthodoxy; heresy was—and in some circles still is—regarded as treachery.

Up until the 1970s, this religious ethnocentrism received favored treatment from Western Protestants (particularly Anglicans), who either saw Orthodoxy as a direct line to the apostolic legitimacy denied them by Catholic primacy or participated in the sort of romantic classicism which had seen Lord Byron and his generation champion the cause of Greek independence. The European Union originated in 1961 but was frozen under the Greek Military Junta; nevertheless, Greek adherence to the European Union has gradually increased international criticism of Orthodox and nationalist oppression of religious minorities. There is a history of infringement of individual and group human rights. The Orthodox Church is constitutionally established as the prevailing religion, proselytism is banned and only known religions are recognized. Treatment of Evangelicals and other minorities has seen a gradual improvement, though there are continued "administrative obstacles or legal restrictions on religious practices" (US State Department).

Evangelicalism in Greece has four major sources: an autochthonous reformed Greek Evangelical Church, established by medical doctor Mikhalis Kalopothakis in 1858; refugees from Greek-speaking evangelical communities in Asia Minor after the fiasco of the Greco-Turkish War (1919–1922); return migration (from the 1920s onwards) of Greeks converted to Pentecostalism abroad; and direct foreign missionary activity, to a lesser extent among ethnic Greeks and to a larger extent among the growing non-Greek ethnic and asylum-seeking groups in the country, such as Turks, Roma, Albanians, and so forth. Estimates of evangelical affiliation range from twenty thousand to forty thousand out of a total Greek population of 11.4 million. Burgess's (2001) enthusiastic figure for "Charismatic" Christians of more than one hundred thousand is difficult to substantiate. The drift of Evangelicals to Orthodoxy through the 1990s (for example, neo-Charismatics such as Kallistos Ware) has created links in the West but has left Greece itself largely untouched.

Smaller Countries

All the smaller countries in the region have populations which make Evangelical minorities difficult to sustain. Andorra (87,000), Monaco (35,000), and San Marino (31,000) are such small populations as to be insignificant in terms of Evangelicalism. Malta (420,000), Croatia (4.5 million), and Albania (3.2 million) all have extensive global diasporas which feed evangelical influences back into what are majority non-evangelical communities (Catholic in the former two, or Orthodox and Muslim in the case of Albania) (US Department of State 2007; and Hutchinson and Wolffe 2012).

Malta has a long, symbolic Christian past, as the landing place of St. Paul and as the center for the Hospitaller Order until the end of the eighteenth century; the Catholic Church is recognized in the Constitution as "the religion of Malta." Centrally located in the Mediterranean, however, the islands have long attracted international visitors; British occupying forces and seamen prior to independence (1964), international tourism and retirement resettlement afterwards.

As early as 1822, Malta began to act as a neutral location for the administrative offices of Anglican, Evangelical, and (more recently) Pentecostal outreach into the Middle East and North Africa. Despite this, the number of evangelical churches is small; the first Maltese evangelical churches were founded in the early 1970s and the formation of a national Evangelical Alliance (TEAM) was a late occurrence (2007). The number of members is estimated to be lower than three thousand. As a small, principled community, evangelical churches have occasionally found themselves squeezed between politicized Maltese social reformists and Catholic traditionalism. (TEAM 2013)

Ever since St. Paul was shipwrecked here, Malta has had a long, symbolic Christian past.

On the Other Side of the Adriatic

The Albanian Evangelicalism which had begun to flourish under national leaders such as Gjerasim Qiriazi and Konstandin Kristoforidhi in the nineteenth century was virtually annihilated under the officially atheistic post-World War II Communist regime. However, almost immediately after the collapse of totalitarianism in 1991, missionaries such as John and Lynne Quanrud (Icthus Fellowship and Seattle's University Presbyterian Church) shifted from their work among ethnic Albanians across the border to commence meetings within Albania itself.

Missionary agencies established cooperative works such as the Albanian Encouragement Project, which helped develop the small but important cadre of secret Christians and had developed by the sharing of literature or by listening to Christian radio from across the border. John Butterworth's story of Berti Dosti's conversion, leading to the foundation of the church in Lushnje, is exemplary of this (Butterworth 2010). The Quanruds themselves established Emmanuel Church, opening the first new Protestant building in Tirana in 1998 and rebuilding the foundations of an authentic Albanian Evangelical identity.

> **Dependency Christianity remains an issue in a country with over 70% unemployment, and flooded by wealthy overseas sects.**

This rebuilding requires great tact, as historical interpretation remains fraught; Muslim Albanians object to a religious census which might undermine claims to normativity, while traditional Christians have criticized Turkish representatives over the "violent Islamisation" of Albania under the Ottomans. In 1998, it was estimated that there were eight thousand Evangelicals in Albania, organized in 154 churches throughout the country. Dependency Christianity remains an issue in a country with over 70% unemployment, and flooded by wealthy overseas sects. Meanwhile, Evangelicals have been visibly active in responding to social issues, especially the Kosovan refugee crisis, the spread of prostitution, drug-use and AIDS in Albanian society, and food aid to the isolated, poor and mountainous hinterland. There are now perhaps twenty thousand Evangelicals in Albania, leading the Albanian government to sign a formal agreement with the Evangelical Brotherhood of Albania (VUSH) in 2010 despite occasional outbreaks of official intolerance.

Of the approximated nine thousand Protestants in Croatia, some seven thousand are Evangelicals, the bulk of which are divided more or less equally between the Evangelical Pentecostal Church and the Baptist Union, with others attached to smaller groupings such as the Union of Pentecostal Churches of Christ, the Brethren, the Church of God, and Word of Life. With strong American and English ties, the Evangelical Theological Seminary in Osijek has been a key institution for over forty years, not only for Croatia, but also for much of Eastern Europe. Contrastingly, the Teološki fakultet "Matija Vlačić Ilirik" in Zagreb founded 1976, looks northwards to the historic, reformational German influence, and serves the Baptist and Lutheran churches. Countering the fragmentation that arose after the end of the civil war (1991-1995), the Croatian Evangelical Alliance (PEV, est. 1992) has acted as a force for unity against a continuing tendency towards splintering. The after effects of war and ethnic division are healing, but continue to be a concern in the community building efforts of evangelical churches.

Prime Concerns and Issues

The prime common concern of Evangelicals in almost all southern European countries is the protection and extension of religious freedoms, often entrenched in constitutions but denied in practice. Led by theologians such as Leonardo De Chirico, the various national branches of the Evangelical Alliance are active in pointing out abuses of law or process. Almost as common, due to their position on the porous maritime borders of Europe, is concern for the rights of asylum seekers. Many local churches facilitate services for diasporic communities, both religious and social/legal. Scores of church-based NGOs also now exist to support this work and related social work both in the host country and abroad, such as Progetto Africa based in CC Emanuel, Ragusa.

While not universal, local church and denominational missions to Romania, Albania, and other parts of Eastern Europe are quite common. Moreover, while some evangelical communities are quite large, the difficulties of achieving registration in their home countries and their dispersion across a wide range of denominational structures often means that sustaining indigenous training for new generations of ministers, church planters, and other ministries is difficult.

There are, for example, only three permanent degree-granting evangelical Bible colleges in Italy, two of which rely on external accreditation. Many movements send their candidates abroad or depend upon local unaccredited options. Among the consequences are problems of generational succession and theological fragmentation both within and between various evangelical movements. The rate of change in European communities is a society-wide cause of concern—the radicalization of secular, nationalist, and Islamic bodies, for example, has a tendency to catch Evangelicals in the middle. At the western end of the Mediterranean, local government opposition tends to be the major expression of this, while at the other end, it can take the form of violence against Evangelical converts in Orthodox and Muslim majority communities.

Sources and Further Reading

Butterworth, John. *God's Secret Listener: The Albanian Army Captain Who Risked Everything*. Oxford: Lion Hudson PLC, 2010.

COMIBAM, "Que es Comibam?" http://www.comibam.org/que-es-comibam/, accessed 27 June 2014.

Delgado, M. "Gypsy Pentecostalism: Ethnopolitical Uses and Construction of Belonging in the South of Spain." *Social Compass* 57, no. 2 (2010): 253–267.

Gallagher, Anna Marie, José Riera, and Maria Riiskjaer. Refugee protection and international migration: a review of UNHCR's role in the Canary Islands, Spain, Geneva: UNHCR, 2009.

Gay y Blasco, Paloma. "The politics of evangelism: Masculinity and religious conversion among Gitanos." *Romani Studies* 5, 10, No. 1 (2000): 1–22.

Hutchinson, M. and J. Wolffe. *A Short History of Global Evangelicalism*. Cambridge: CUP, 2012.

Iatrides, John O. "Evangelicals." In *Minorities in Greece: Aspects of a Plural Society*. Edited by Richard Clogg. London: Hurst, 2002.

Introvigne, M. and PierLuigi Zoccatelli, Le Religioni in Italia, Torino: CESNUR, 2012. http://www.cesnur.org/religioni_italia/default.htm

Perica, Vjekoslav. *Balkan Idols: Religion and Nationalism in Yugoslav States*. Oxford: OUP, 2004.

Pettifer, James and Mentor Nazarko. *Strengthening Religious Tolerance for a Secure Civil Society in Albania and the Southern Balkans*. Amsterdam; Washington, DC: IOS Press, 2007.

TEAM (The Evangelical Alliance in Malta), http://teammalta.org/, accessed 27 June 2014.

U.S. Department of State. Country Reports on Human Rights Practices. Washington: U.S. Department of State, 2007.

Viroli, Maurizio. *Come se Dio ci fosse: Religione e Libertà nella storia d'Italia*, Milano: Einaudi, 2009.

Evangelical Impact in Spain: The News Goes Digital

It may be small in number but its influence is big. About eight years ago, seeking to offer a Christian perspective on the news, Alianza Evangélica Espanola, a national evangelical alliance based in Barcelona, created a news and opinion website called Protestante Digital (http://www.protestantedigital.com) that now has hundreds of thousands of readers.

"We were looking for a way to have news with a Christian perspective that can influence society from a Christian point of view," explains Jaume Llenas, general secretary of Alianza. Its president, Pedro Tarquis, started the website.

Spain is an ideologically divided country. On one side are the "very secular," who "reject everything that has even a little smell of spirituality, especially Christian spirituality," says Llenas, while on the other side are very conservative Roman Catholics.

Protestante Digital strives to show a third side, a view that is neither secular nor Catholic, but biblical. "We think the kingdom of God is for everybody," Llenas says.

Opinions are shared on the website in three ways: an official statement from Alianza, a personal opinion from an Alianza leader like Llenas or Tarquis, or a blog from any of the Protestante Digital's writers.

Protestante Digital has weighed in on such topics as taxes, gambling, and abortion. For example, in Spain people have the option of diverting some tax money to the Roman Catholic Church. When the government raised the possibility of including other religions as recipients of diverted tax money, Alianza, through Protestante Digital, disagreed. "The best thing is that the government not give money to religions just for being religions," says Llenas. "They should give it for being good for society. We do not want to receive government money."

When a large American company wanted to build a gambling complex, purportedly to help Spain reduce taxes, Protestante Digital protested out of concern for the social problems associated with gambling.

Protestante Digital has also suggested that women who seek abortions should receive information about the risks of the procedure as well as about what it might be like to keep the baby.

With only about four hundred thousand Evangelicals, half of them immigrants, in a country of forty-seven million, the voice of Evangelicals is being heard. Polls show Protestante Digital has two hundred thousand new visitors a month, reading an aggregate of three million pages of content. About a third of them are non-Evangelicals, and an increasing number of hits come from Latin America and the United States.

Political parties have taken notice of Protestante Digital and used the arguments they have read on it. The minister of justice, who is also responsible for religious matters, reads the website every day.

Besides providing perspectives on daily news stories, Protestante Digital also includes special sections for Roma readers (a large proportion of Evangelical churchgoers are from that group), families, and young people.

Reader response on the website and through Facebook is mostly positive, says Llenas. "Usually they perceive us as balanced."

—Debra Fieguth

EVANGELICALS IN WESTERN EUROPE

By Mark Hutchinson

Western Europe is home both to many of the historic birthplaces of Evangelicalism and also to the great global empires of the eighteenth and nineteenth centuries. Evangelicalism has been fundamentally shaped by tensions between nonconformism and Establishment, minority and majority status, indigeneity and migration. Each European cultural and linguistic bloc, centered on Germany, Britain, the Netherlands and France, developed its own ecclesial forms, liturgical and preaching styles, social work, relationships with power, and global networks. The projection of religious forms, colporteurs of the British and Foreign Bible Society, German Lutheran and Moravian missionaries, Dutch merchants, or French religious orders, was inevitably influenced by the expansion of these imperial cultures. Yet as their empires collapsed at the edges and the effects of World War II and the Cold War pushed them into the European Union as members of the new international order, the cultural, economical, and linguistic inheritance of Empire continued to trickle back via migration and refugee flows.

In all three cultural and four linguistic zones, the result has been the rise of religious plurality at the same time that the nation states themselves have been secularizing. Western Europe therefore presents the picture of, at one level, advanced high modern secularization, and on the other, the increasing diversity and assertiveness of minority religious cultures. The clashes between individual and community rights, and national, transnational and global communities, fill the news headlines about Western Europe around the world. From jihadi imams in London to French courtroom clashes over Scientology and burqas, Western Europe's core crises reflect the collapse of established, former imperial Christianity and the rising tide of vibrant, experiential faiths supported by migration flows.

One result is the growth of Evangelicalism in most constituencies, both as a proportion of Christian constituencies, and in terms of overall numbers. Attending this has been a long-running debate among scholars as to what all of this means for the hard secularization thesis.

While all agree that Christianity as a whole is heading for minority status right across Europe (displaced by a combination of Islam or local equivalents of the no-religion category), at the same time, European Christianity is now more open to the rest of the world, adaptive, and energetic than it has been for more than a century. Much of that energy comes from growing evangelical congregations, the presence of which continues to trouble the European secular elites who have adopted European secularizing exceptionalism as part of their identities. Underpinning secular Europe, as Grace Davie has pointed out, has been a social shift (matching the increasing European engagement with global markets) from "a culture of obligation . . . to a culture of consumption or choice" (Davie 2013).

Anglophone Western Europe

Evangelical Christianity as a religious form emerged from the combined flow of English and German speaking peoples to and fro across the Atlantic to the New World. The First Great Awakening emerged amid migrant Scots, Dutch, German, and English speaking communities in New Jersey, Massachusetts, and other northeastern colonies and in their Old World home communities. It was through these flows and events of the 1730s and 1740s that the First Great Awakening birthed the post-Puritan form of reformed Christianity that we now know as Evangelical Christianity. It embedded itself in both the established churches (Anglicanism and Presbyterianism), in the nonconformist traditions (Congregationalism, the Baptists, even elements of the Quaker tradition), and in new, often unstable synthetic traditions such as Methodism. Among the former, it could take the shape of a church party and among the latter groups that of a preaching and revivalist tradition. Its ability to mobilize the working classes to infiltrate new organizational forms (such as the great voluntary societies), address the great issues of the time (such as slavery), and to finesse access to the organs of British imperial power (spreading revival, education, and evangelism among the military and administrative strata from Canada to Tasmania) ensured its spread all over the world.

In the process, anglophone Evangelicalism became almost synonymous with Victorian moralism and

Methodist revival meetings spread throughout Britain and North America in the eighteenth century.
Image: North Wind Picture Archives

reformism, profiting even from the steady disestablishment of the Established churches. Through schools, orphanages, hospitals, and rescue missions the world over, British Evangelicals created a life which was at once public and, through Holiness conventions, dedicated journals and acronymic associations, intensely and spiritually private. The high point of this fusion, even as disestablishment began to bite, was the emergence of the mass evangelism which, from H. G. Guinness through to Billy Graham, was the shape of third phase, globalizing Evangelicalism until the late 1950s. An example was Alexander Somerville, Free Kirk divine, baronial heir, and peripatetic preacher "of Christ wherever the English language is spoken." Intimate of Robert Murray McCheyne, and the brothers Bonar, he shared their fiery sermonizing and their end-times Zionism, his biographer (George Smith) declaring him an "apostle for modern times," producing converts, "ministers and missionaries, students and artisans, rich and poor, men, women, and children, of all nationalities and of all lands" (Smith 1890).

The events of World War II, the collapse of Empire, and the rise of the consumer society and the sexual revolution, steadily vitiated the moral consensus which gave Evangelicals their voice at home and with post-Bandung anticolonialism, and the expulsion of missionaries from China, their impact abroad. The broader religious crisis of the 1960s which McLeod calls "the final crisis of Christendom" seemed to imply that the general downturn which applied to the mainstream churches also applied across the board to Evangelicalism (McLeod 2007; Brown 2010). As Brown notes, however, the evangelical elements of major churches tended to remain relatively solid, while variant evangelical forms—the youth revival of the 1960s, the Charismatic renewal of the 1960s and 1970s, and the emergence of globalizing megachurches in the 1980s—grew rapidly. As Village notes, change in liturgical practice does not affect the coherency or theological commitments of Evangelicals to the extent that it does, say, Anglo-Catholics (Village and Francis 2010).

Within traditional churches (such as the Anglican Communion), this meant that Evangelicals became both proportionately larger and more influential than ever, an influence reinforced by evangelical voices from the Majority World. This was at the cost of fragmentation and charismatization/privatization; however, as Patrick Mitchel shows with regard to Northern Ireland, Evangelicals diverged in terms of their attitude towards national and public issues. On the one hand, there remained a strong conservative antilibertarian streak of the older Festival of Light and Orange Lodge ilk, which Brown notes acts as a public stereotype of negative evangelical moralism. On the other hand, there have developed a wide range of attitudes towards moral and social reform among evangelical constituencies. A similar division occurred within evangelical ranks over whether believers should stay with their "mixed" denominations. The arguments were theological, but the contextual driver was, as the position of public religion declined, the growing irrelevance of historic forms (Randall 2004).

British Evangelicals, as David Bebbington has shown, remain activists, as well as Biblicists and crucicentrists. Their pragmatic approaches have seen a variegation of missional forms (house churches, new missional movements, a leading role in the emerging church), responding to societal change by embracing social reform, empowering women and young people, adopting forms of symbolic public presence, through, for example, the Jesus March, and shifting liturgical practices, in particular the rising use of Charismatic practices (raised hands, tongues, gentle forms of prophecy) even in non-Charismatic denominations.

> The growth of charismatic phenomena was propagated by a succession of agencies: the Fountain Trust, Dales Week, John Wimber and his Vineyard churches. Perhaps most influential, however, was Spring Harvest, a week-long training conference that from 1979 brought together Charismatics and non-Charismatics. It ensured that styles of worship associated with renewal penetrated far beyond the movement's immediate constituency. (Bebbington 2007, 17)

This shift towards a spirituality of personal authenticity within evangelical churches—as opposed to a spirituality of the objectified Word—created a natural bridge for the acceptance and growth of migrant-based megachurches in Britain. As John Wolffe explained in 2011, church decline has slowed or even reversed in high migration centers such as London. The top ten largest churches in the city are largely forms of either reverse mission or migrant churches: Matthew Ashimolowo's largely West African Kingsway International Christian Centre (KICC), the Australian-based Hillsong London Church, and globalized Holy Trinity Brompton, all draw heavily on migrations from the old Empire (Hutchinson and Wolffe 2012; Clarke 2010). Centered in what remains one of the world's great financial capitals, these networks have globalized. The British government, for example, remains vocal with regard to the persecution of minority Christians while British Evangelical NGOs (such as TEAR Fund) work around the world.

On the home front, Evangelicals and their postmodern children have adapted to the crisis of secularization of the long 1960s. Theologically evangelical but organizationally and liturgically diverse movements pick through the heritage of Christianity and adopt worship forms considered contextually apposite. From twenty-four hour prayer movements to new forms of Christian community to emerging church models such as the ikon and Zero28 networks based in Northern Ireland, Evangelicalism has developed both relatively strong core institutions (The Evangelical Alliance, TEAR Fund, Soul Survivor, and the like) and a dizzying variety of grassroots organizations. As a whole, this has been without the fighting fundamentalism tone of American evangelical churches, possibly because the smaller British evangelical population, within the broader cultural meliorism established by formerly dominant Anglicanism, provides fewer rewards for public competition.

Germanophone Western Europe

The decline in church attendance found in Britain is also found in the home of the Reformation: Germany. Shockingly, the Protestant tradition there is constitutive of German identity in ways that Anglicanism is not for Britons. After all, the union of the German nation came late, leaving German nationalism to be long dependent on the fruits of the Reformation; both the second and third Reichs were not merely reorganizations of the State, but also of the constituent church identities. The collapse of the unity between confession and national identity, first with the divisions led by the confessing church against Hitler, and then the organized, passive resistance of the federated Evangelische Kirche in Deutschland (EKD) to the East German state through the 1970s, provided the cultural space for younger Germans to choose more secular lifestyles.

The linguistic struggle over the meaning of the word *evangelical* (traditionally *evangelisch*) thus reflected larger divisions in the regionalized historic churches. By the nineteenth century, the original Reformation gospel orientation of the word had come to mean simply those churches which were non-Catholic. The religious awakening which swept through Lutheran Europe in the mid-nineteenth century, described by Nicholas Hope as a significant "reaction against the successful application of enlightened principles in government, in consistories, in university law and theology faculties, and in vicarages" (1995, 355) was effectively a popular rejection of the mere absorption of the spiritual life of Germans into the ritual life of the deified State. It left pietist Germans with no word for the sort of energetic American-style Evangelicalism which came into prominence at the formation of the Evangelical Alliance and later through the 1960s. A new word (*evangelikal*) was then appropriated and propagated by the organs of the Evangelical Alliance (Geldbach 1998).

This increasing distinction between the old Evangelicalism and the new took place through a progression of crises. The *evangelische* response to the rising Pentecostal movement, for example, was in 1909 to declare it (in the *Berliner Erklärung*) as "not from above, but from below" (Simpson 2011). The neo-Orthodox inspired Barmen Declaration (1934) divided the Confessing Church from the Nazi-supported "German Christians" over the issue of the state control and the subordination of the Word and Spirit to the Church. Though in "the mid-1980s, the EKD churches in East Germany (organized as a separate national confederation, the BEK) consistently represented the major ideological and political alternative to the Communist Party and the socialist state," the union of East and West saw the collapse of the State church's politico-cultural distinctiveness (Geldbach 1998).

Mobile, disillusioned, and wealthy youth, pushing to detach themselves from the generation, which had lived through the war, were happy to abandon the official churches. The scale of this abandonment, linked to an ever decreasing income stream from church taxes as Germans removed their names from denominational rolls, can be seen in the gradual denuding of many German communities of church architecture. In 2013, *Der Spiegel* reported an EKD spokesman as saying, "Between 1990 and 2010 we closed 340 churches, and of those 46 were demolished . . . [and] it may be necessary to give up an additional 1,000 buildings" (Schulz 2103). Even so, the EKD is still by far the largest denominational stream in Germany, and contains many people who would consider themselves Evangelical (one estimate suggests 1.5 million of the EKD's 24 million members).

Outside the EKD, there is a variety of much smaller free evangelical movements, which (not unlike the Moravians) have in various cases made more impact through their external missions programs than in their own country. Two movements which organize their evangelical origins around the Book of Concord are the Evangelical Lutheran Free Church (1,500 members) spread across Germany and Austria, and the Independent Evangelical-Lutheran Church (35,000 members). Baptist Churches, which include many Evangelicals, together count some 82,000 members.

In the other majority German-speaking country in the region (Austria), the historic dominance of Catholicism has left little public space for the growth of alternative forms of Christianity. Here Evangelicals constitute perhaps 0.5% of the population, between fifty thousand and eighty thousand. The Free Churches still often need to explain their distinctiveness from state Protestantism. In order to further distinguish themselves, church representatives (from the Baptist churches, the Federation of Evangelical communities, the Charismatic Elaea Christian communities, the Free Christian Church, Pentecostal Church in Austria, various Independents and the Mennonite Free Church of Austria) met in the early twenty-first century to commence a process of gaining common recognition from the state. In 2013, the Freikirchen in Österreich, including 160 congregations, was recognized as a formal denomination.

The decline of profession and church attendance among Catholics has largely been taken up by non-Christian migration or the no-religion category. The status of Vienna at the center of European finance and tourism, however, has seen quite a number of church plants by or among expatriates living in the country (for example, by the European Christian Mission or by Gianni Gaeta's Lifechurch network) in addition to the activity of evangelical outreach agencies among migrant workers, women and youth. Once the frontier between Christendom and the Ottoman Empire, crossroads cities like Linz and Vienna are served by organizations such as Herzwerk, which works among victims of human trafficking, drugs and prostitution, particularly from Eastern Europe and Nigeria.

Mobile, disillusioned, and wealthy youth were happy to abandon the official churches.

The Netherlands

In the Netherlands, historical oscillations between Catholic and Protestant regimes have marked the country deeply. The south of the country (particularly Noord-Brabant and Limburg) has a higher Catholic constituency, while the north tends to be more mainline Protestant and secularized: in neither place does weekly church attendance exceed 4% of the population. The confessional communities associated with waves of pietist renewal in the eighteenth and nineteenth centuries, however, tended to withdraw into the center, forming an identifiable Bible belt (*Bijbelgordel*) which stretches north-northeast through the country, from Zeeland, through the West-Betuwe and Veluwe, to the northern parts of the Overijssel. It was in this area that church attendance and evangelical conviction have tended to remain high. Therefore, the majority tradition of the Netherlands, as well as the minority actualities, has significant evangelical traditions to draw upon.

In the Netherlands, historical oscillations between Catholic and Protestant regimes have marked the country deeply.
Photo: www.designpics.com

As with the other European empires, trade and migration (more than conquest) took the Dutch Reformed tradition all over the world, among the best known being Jan van Riebeeck's establishment of the Dutch Reformed Church (DRC) of South Africa in 1652. Dutch Reformed traditions have also acted as an intellectual core for broader evangelical communities. Dutch Reformed migrants to various parts of the world have been powerful influences in the global evangelical publishing, bookselling, and education sectors, an influence which echoed back into the Netherlands through the neo-Calvinist revival among leading Dutch thinkers such as Abraham Kuyper, Herman Bavinck, and Louis Berkhof. Their influence continues to be important in global Evangelicalism, particularly through their emphasis on the Lordship of Christ over all of life and philosophical categories such as worldview.

With the Bible Belt to draw upon, evangelical Christian Democratic traditions thus retained public influence longer than in other parts of Europe. Kuyper's insistence on adherence to the Canons of Dort and on championing the equality of secular and Christian education in parliament were part of a platform which eventually saw him both establish the Free University and serve as Prime Minister (1901–1905). Dutch Evangelicals continue to play an energetic part in Dutch politics, particularly in Christian Democratic parties (Noll, 2007). In 2002, for instance, Free University graduate Jan Peter Balkenende was elected Prime Minister for the Christian Democratic Appeal party, serving until 2010.

This persistent rump of evangelical conviction in the Netherlands has meant continued pressure for renewal in the old Reformed traditions, essential in the Netherlands, where the fastest growing religion is Islam (5% of the population), and where no grouping of Protestant churches except the reformed traditions embrace more than 1% of the population. The sense of crisis which has come across these reformed traditions as affiliation has collapsed, moreover, provides opportunities for evangelical growth. The Netherlands entered the twenty-first century as one of the most secular countries in Western Europe (with fewer than 39% of the population declaring a religious affiliation). In response to its free-falling numbers, in 2004 the Dutch Reformed Church, the Reformed Churches, and the Evangelical Lutheran Church combined to form the Protestantse Kerk in Nederland (PKN). Those Evangelicals who remained in this pluralist arrangement tended to gather into the Evangelisch Werkwerband (formed in 1995 around the *Evangelisch Manifest*), founding growth groups (Gemeente Groei Groepen), restarting or planting new churches, and seeking to expand outreach to the increasingly detached under-thirty-year-old cohort in Dutch society. Others disagreed with what was seen as unconfessional pluralism or with lowest common denominator stances on issues of public concern. Numerous people in congregations left to join other reformed churches, while some forty thousand people in 120 local congregations left to form the Restored Reformed Church.

The fragmentation of the historic religious settlement in the Netherlands presents challenges and opportunities for other types of Evangelicalism to find traction in a country which has had an ambivalent relationship with Arminianism, a school of theology based on the teachings of Jacob Arminius, a Dutch theologian. As Kuyper later wrote, Methodism for the Dutch "was at best an emergency means to lead a temporarily sleeping church out of its slumber" (Beardsall 2003). This is no longer the case. Among the approximately 3.5 million first and second-generation immigrants—out of a total population of seventeen million people—there is a growing Evangelical presence.

One of those migrants to return from the former Dutch East Indies (now Indonesia), for example, was Peter Sleebos, who is now head of the Verenigde Pinkster-en Evangeliegemeenten (VPE), the local affiliate of the worldwide Assemblies of God. Sleebos has brought missionary experience to reformulation of domestic church planting approaches, helping a traditionally gridlocked European Pentecostal Movement begin once more to grow. Assisted by American missionaries (through, for example, Azusa Theological Seminary), this largest of nontraditional churches in the Netherlands now supports missions in other parts of Europe and overseas. Due (until 2009) to a relatively long running and liberal immigration policy, the Netherlands features significant evangelical communities from Africa and Asia, particularly among the large Ghanaian community.

Ironically, growth of these churches has been encouraged by a broader cultural turn against migration, allocating to churches the role of maintaining, justifying, and making bearable racial and cultural marginalization. Their connection to the Pentecostal community is strengthened by common practices such as tongues, prophecy, and healing (the key exponents of which, such as the healing evangelists Jan Zijlstra and Johan Maas Bach, owe much to the visits of T. L. Osborn in the 1950s and 1960s).

While migration provides growth, however, the Evangelical role in peacemaking has necessarily been strained in the face of rising cultural and religious conflict and violence. To many Dutch Evangelicals, this state of affairs indicates that the liberal experiment has collapsed and that the litany of failed reforms supported by both the political left and the political right now calls for a more robust, gospel-based public response.

Francophone Western Europe

France is, after the Scandinavian countries, the model most often used by scholars to demonstrate European secularisation/exceptionalism. The entry of France into nationalist modernity was marked by violent revolution, specifically targeting the fusion of church and state under the *ancien régime*. French public life through the twentieth century was thus marked by "la guerre des deux Frances," Catholic and *laïque* (Davie 2013).

There is, therefore, a continuing public suspicion of religious communities, whether they be Catholic, Muslim, cultic, or Evangelical. Despite being the country which gave the world (among others) the Waldensians, Calvin, the Huguenots, and the *Reveil*, it is largely due to the degree to which modernity in the West benchmarks itself against "les lumieres" (the Enlightenment), the French Catholic/secular debate which dominates most writing about the country.

French Evangelicalism (based in both France and francophone Switzerland), however, had a significant impact in the nineteenth and twentieth centuries, as organizations such as the Société des missions évangéliques de Paris (1822–1971) spread out into imperial francophone regions (particularly in Africa and Oceania) with the Bible and its reformed traditions of preaching. French evangelical churches have also provided important alternative views for mainline anglophone Evangelicalism, in francophone Canada, for example, and through the influence of leaders such as William Booth's daughter Kate (the Maréchale). French networks were also important in the reestablishment of post-war evangelical university student networks in Europe; in 1943, the Groupes Bibliques Universitaires were founded by the Swiss Rene Pache (1904–1979) while the International InterVarsity Movement came to be headquartered in francophone Switzerland (Fath 2005). Finally, for twentieth-century Evangelicals, any strategic map for campaigns in declining, secularizing Europe always included Paris, that brilliant jewel of fashion and intellectual life. As part of his own post-War evangelical form of NATO, Billy Graham accepted invitations to tour a resistant France, even while bypassing a much more welcoming Italy. As the *Time* reporter covering the event noted, most Frenchmen thought they knew who Graham was:

> **As Billy Graham arrived in Paris to begin a five-day evangelical crusade, a phalanx of welcomers broke through a line of gendarmes at the railway station, shouting 'Beelee! Beelee! Beelee!' 'Beelee? Who is this Beelee?' asked a harassed official. Said a bystander in surprise: 'Why, monsieur, do you not know Beelee Graham, the American clairvoyant?'**

This might be considered fair repayment for running a crusade in a country which had invented the art some 860 years before. Reception of Evangelicals is, however, a continuing problem for a country which greeted Salvation Army lasses in the 1890s with brickbats, bans, and street violence. There is little cultural understanding of the difference between Evangelicals and syncretistic cults (such as the Order of the Solar Temple), a problem which has been compounded in more recent times by the strength of Evangelicalism among francophone non-white migrants from France's old empire. In a settlement that Resnik (2010) refers to as "catho-laique," cultural Catholic norming (through anti-cult organizations such as UNADFI), xenophobic right wing reaction and organized left wing atheism do not leave a lot of public space for orthodox Christian resurgence. As Palmer notes, France is "remarkable" among Western countries for "its unique and paradoxical form of intolerance toward religious minorities" (Palmer 2011).

The bases for evangelical growth in France were laid by such significant figures as Andre Thobois (Chair of the Free Faculty of Protestant Theology of Vaux-sur-Seine, 1984–1994, and long-serving pastor in the Avenue Du Main Baptist Church, Paris), and began to pick up pace from the 1970s. It is a growth which, in turn, questions the presuppositions of much secularisation theory, as Fath notes, a more refined approach might be to speak of recomposition rather than straight religious decline.

Much of the growth in French Evangelicalism has been through lay evangelism by Pentecostal believers. By the early twenty-first century, Fath notes that 60% of French evangelical growth since World War II had been of this type. "Significantly, almost 100% of this development can be credited to French lay preachers, with no US help" (Fath 2005). In 2012, the French National Council of Evangelical Churches (CNEF) reported that, "of the nation's 1.6 million Protestants, 460,000 now identify as evangelicals."

Three major contributing streams point to the enabling changes in French society: increased migration from struggling former imperial dependencies, revival among France-based Rom/Gypsy communities, and the planting of new churches. All three are related to labor migration, though at different levels and with differing relationships to globalization. On the one hand, some estimates suggest that Paris is served by more than three hundred Afro-French churches, drawing on the 43% of francophone majority world labor migration to France which originates in Africa, and the "500,000 people of Antillean descent [who] live in metropolitan France" (Dobie 2004). Such churches, gathered in organizations such as the "Communauté des Eglises d'Expression Africaine de France" (CEAF), see the spiritual vacuum created by the Enlightenment as an opportunity for mission. "Might the global and holistic vision of the churches of African expression," asks Majagira Bulangalire of CEAF, "which leads them to involvement in all areas of life, be one of the most interesting examples of adaptation to be studied?" (Bulangalire 2006).

Another migration, that of French Gypsies, has likewise found a more French identity in Protestantism. During the mass deportations of eastern European Rom under the Sarkozy regime, French Protestant Gypsies who had converted in the Life and Light Movement (begun in an Assemblies of God Church in a series of healing experiences in the 1950s), became an important moderator of French opinion. This evangelical revival has now seen some 145,000 of the 425,000 Gypsies in France converted: "Their tight organization, work and family ethic, regard for civil law, and stress on education has made them the 'go-to' Gypsy group for French authorities" (Marquand 2010). The result is a growing pastorate, a dedicated Gypsy seminary, and international missions through

Gypsy networks. At the other end of the economic scale is the modern take on a very traditional practice, church planting from abroad among the international communities in major French cities. Anglican churches, of course, had been present since the sixteenth century, beginning with the private chapels of English Ambassadors. The rise of an Evangelical *via media* in the nineteenth century resulted in the expansion of missionary enterprises in Europe, particularly after the rise of American Evangelicalism in the 1950s. By the 1970s, Robert Vajko recorded, forty-eight American missions (or societies) established themselves in France with a workforce of 378 missionaries (Fath 2005). The planting of a branch of the Hillsong Church in Paris, originally among Anglo expatriates, but with increasing success among the African and Antillean diaspora, is an indicator that Paris remains a powerful cultural and political node of global culture. It joins longer-established churches, such as the Assemblée Evangélique de Pentecôte (Saint Denis), which draw multicultural audiences in their hundreds every Sunday, while also catering for wandering Australasian and South African Christian tourists seeking a home away from home.

There are always problems. In high resettlement cities in much of Europe, space costs are a significant problem. The proliferation of churches renders some evangelical activities (particularly among poor migrants) illegal. A downward swing in supply, constrained by poor relationships with traditional churches, and the closing of many former church sites in France, have met an upswing in demand. The CNEF reports that the number of churches nearly tripled in 2011, from 769 to 2,068, as local ethnic communities and the "compensators" related to pastoral office in marginalized settlements resulted in a proliferation of new congregations. In such circumstances, ethnic Pentecostal churches can fall out of favor with culturally oblique municipal councils and planners (Althoff 2012). Likewise, Biblically-literalist ethnic churches have drawn criticism for their involvement in practices such as exorcism: a breakaway Adventist group made international news in such a case in 2013, being brought to trial for "kidnapping, acts of torture and barbarism" (AFP 2013). Ultimately, however, the evangelical churches are well established in France, and look likely to be able to ride the roller coster of French public concern over "les sects."

Sources and Further Reading

AFP. "French torture trial over crucifixion-style exorcism." October 7, 2013. http://en.starafrica.com/news/french-torture-trial-over-crucifixion-style-exorcism.html.

Althoff, Allison J. "Paris problem churches multiply but lack space." *Christianity Today* 56, no. 9 (October 2012): 15.

Beardsall, Sandra. "John Wesley and the Netherlands." *Anglican Theological Review* 85, no. 3 (Summer 2003): 570.

Bebbington, David W. "Evangelicals and public worship, 1965–2005." *Evangelical Quarterly* 79, no. 1 (2007): 1–22.

Brown, C. "What was the religious crisis of the 1960s." *Journal of Religious History*. 34, no. 4 (December 2010), 468–79.

Bulangalire, Majagira. "The consequences of the enlightenment—a point of view from the churches of African expression in France." *International Review of Mission* 95, no. 378–379 (July–October 2006): 293–8.

Clarke, Clifton R. "Old Wine and New Wine Skins: West Indian and the New West African Pentecostal Churches in Britain and the Challenge of Renewal." *Journal of Pentecostal Theology*, 19, no. 1 (April 2010): 143–54.

Davie, Grace. "Religion in 21st-Century Europe: Framing the Debate." *Irish Theological Quarterly* 78, no. 3 (2013): 279–93.

Dobie, Madeleine. "Invisible Exodus: The Cultural Effacement of Antillean Migration." *Diaspora: A Journal of Transnational Studies* 13, no. 2 (2004): 149–183.

Fath, Sebastian. "Evangelical Protestantism in France: an example of Denominational Recomposition?" *Sociology of Religion* 66, no. 4 (2005): 399–418.

Francis, Leslie J. and Carol Roberts. "Growth or Decline in the Church of England during the Decade of Evangelism: Did the Churchmanship of the Bishop Matter?" *Journal of Contemporary Religion* 24, no. 1 (2009), 67–81.

Geldbach, Erich. "'Evangelisch,' 'Evangelikal' & Pietism: Some Remarks on Early Evangelicalism & Globalization from a German Perspective." In *A Global Faith: Essays on Evangelicalism and Globalisation.* Edited by M. Hutchinson and O Kalu. Sydney: CSAC, 1998.

Hope, Nicholas. *German and Scandinavian Protestantism*, 1700–1918. Oxford: Clarendon Press, 1995.

Hudson, Alexandra. "Seeking security, Dutch turn to Bible Belt." Reuters. March 12, 2007 and accessed January 6, 2014. ncls.org.au/default.aspx?sitemapid=2106

Hutchinson, Mark and John Wolffe. *Cambridge Short History of Global Evangelicalism*. Cambridge: Cambridge University Press, 2012.

Marquand, Robert. "In France, an Evangelical Gypsy Group Shakes Up the Immigration Debate." September 3, 2010 and accessed January 6, 2013. *Christian Science Monitor.*

McLeod, H. *The Religious Crisis of the 1960s*. Oxford: Oxford University Press, 2007.

Mitchel, Patrick. *Evangelicalism and National Identity in Ulster, 1921–1998*. Oxford and New York: Oxford University Press, 2003.

Noll, Mark. "Protestant evangelicals and recent American politics." *Journal of American and Canadian Studies* 25 (2007), 3–18.

Palmer, Susan J. *The New Heretics of France: Minority Religions, la République, and the Government-Sponsored "War on Sects."* New York: Oxford University Press, 2011.

Randall, Ian. "Evangelicals, Ecumenism and Unity: A Case Study of the Evangelical Alliance." *Evangel* 22, no. 3 (Autumn 2004): 62–71.

Resnik, Julia. "Integration without assimilation? Ethno-nationalism in Israel and universal laïcité in France." *International Studies in Sociology of Education* 20, no. 3 (2010): 201–224.

Schulz, Matthias. "The Last Supper: Germany's Great Church Sell-Off." *Spiegel* Online, February 14, 2013.

"Religion: Billy Graham in Paris." *Time Magazine.* June 20, 1955 and accessed January 6, 2013. http://content.time.com/time/magazine/article/0,9171,861605,00.html#ixzz2pa2sjUTK

Simpson, C A., "A critical evaluation of the contribution of Jonathan Paul to the development of the German Pentecostal movement," University of Wales, Bangor (United Kingdom), ProQuest, UMI Dissertations Publishing, 2011.

Village, Andrew and Leslie J. Francis. "An Anatomy of Change: Profiling Cohort Difference in Beliefs and Attitudes among Anglicans in England." *Journal of Anglican Studies* 8, no. 1: 59–81.

Wolffe, John. "Building on History: The Church in London." 2011 and accessed January 16, 2014. http://www.open.ac.uk/Arts/building-on-history-project/index.html

Evangelical Impact in Great Britain:
The Course That Changes Lives

What started as a small program to introduce new Christians to the basics of their faith has grown into a worldwide movement. More than twenty million people in 169 countries have participated in the Alpha Course, which began in 1977 at Holy Trinity Brompton (HTB), an Anglican church in London. "We needed something that was going to introduce the Christian faith to those who were new to it," explains Mark Elsdon-Dew, Alpha's communications director.

More than one million people in the United Kingdom have taken an Alpha course. Nicky Gumbel leads one of the classes at Holy Trinity Brompton in London.
Photos: Alpha International

When Nicky Gumbel took over the Alpha Course at HTB in 1990, he discovered participants in the ten-week course who were not Christians at the beginning but became Christians during the series. Gumbel, now HTB's vicar, decided to change the way Alpha was marketed. He advertised it for those who wanted to investigate the Christian faith and had questions that could be answered in an informal setting.

It took off. Hundreds of people responded by taking courses at HTB, and many churches began asking how they could run the program themselves. "We've been training people ever since," in Britain and around the world, says Elsdon-Dew.

To date, more than one million people in the United Kingdom have taken an Alpha course. "In this country you're within ten minutes of an Alpha course wherever you go!" according to Elsdon-Dew. There are Alpha groups for seniors, students, and youth; Alpha for the workplace; Alpha for the armed forces; and Alpha for people whose first language is not English. Alpha is also run in about 80 percent of the country's prisons. A related charity cares for ex-offenders, and among them the recidivism rate is far lower than the national average.

The Alpha Course is good news for the church in London. While church membership is declining in parts of Great Britain, especially among young people, it is increasing in London and some of the other cities in the country.

HTB still offers the Alpha Course four times a year, with up to a thousand people attending each course. The average age of the participants is twenty-seven. "Many of these young people have no Christian upbringing or background at all," Elsdon-Dew notes. "But they're fascinated by spirituality of any kind and asking the big questions: What's the meaning of life? What happens when I die? What about forgiveness, suffering, other religions?"

In the Alpha Course they can ask all the questions they want.

—Debra Fieguth

OCEANIA

POPULATION 36,659,000
MAJORITY RELIGION: CHRISTIANITY (74.4%)

OCEANIA REPRESENTS

0.5% OF THE TOTAL
GLOBAL POPULATION

1.2% OF THE GLOBAL
CHRISTIAN POPULATION

0.2% OF THE GLOBAL
NON-CHRISTIAN POPULATION

3.7% OF THE GLOBAL
MISSIONARY FORCE RECEIVED

CHRISTIANITY IN OCEANIA

POPULATION ▬ CHRISTIAN ▬ EVANGELICAL ▬

CHRISTIAN & EVANGELICAL POPULATION

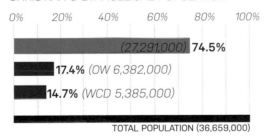

0%   20%   40%   60%   80%   100%

(27,291,000) **74.5%**

17.4% (OW 6,382,000)

14.7% (WCD 5,385,000)

TOTAL POPULATION (36,659,000)

GROWTH RATE* 1970–2010

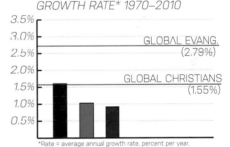

3.5%
3.0%
2.5%   GLOBAL EVANG.
2.0%   (2.79%)
1.5%   GLOBAL CHRISTIANS
1.0%   (1.55%)
0.5%

*Rate = average annual growth rate, percent per year,
between dates specified.

MISSIONS IN OCEANIA
FROM ALL CHRISTIAN TRADITIONS

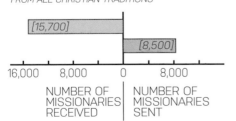

[15,700]

[8,500]

16,000   8,000   0   8,000

NUMBER OF
MISSIONARIES
RECEIVED

NUMBER OF
MISSIONARIES
SENT

1 MISSIONARY SENT
FOR EVERY **3,200** CHRISTIANS
IN OCEANIA

1 MISSIONARY RECEIVED
FOR EVERY **2,300** PEOPLE
IN OCEANIA

75 OF EVERY 100 NON-CHRISTIANS
PERSONALLY KNOW A CHRISTIAN
IN OCEANIA

Source: *World Christian Database*, 2010 data

395

Christians and Evangelicals by country in Oceania, 2010

	POPULATION, 2010	CHRISTIANS, 2010	% CHRISTIAN, 2010	WCD EVANGELICALS, 2010	WCD % EVANGELICAL, 2010	OW EVANGELICALS, 2010	OW % EVANGELICAL, 2010
American Samoa	55,600	54,700	98.3%	12,500	22.5%	14,600	26.2%
Australia	22,404,000	15,542,000	69.4%	2,543,000	11.4%	3,108,000	13.9%
Cook Islands	20,300	19,600	96.6%	1,400	7.0%	2,500	12.4%
Fiji	861,000	550,000	63.9%	163,000	18.9%	215,000	25.0%
French Polynesia	268,000	252,000	94.0%	6,700	2.5%	19,700	7.4%
Guam	159,000	150,000	94.2%	10,300	6.5%	25,600	16.1%
Kiribati	97,700	94,700	96.9%	6,600	6.7%	7,200	7.3%
Marshall Islands	52,400	50,100	95.5%	26,400	50.4%	28,200	53.8%
Micronesia	104,000	98,200	94.8%	20,200	19.5%	27,000	26.1%
Nauru	10,000	7,500	75.0%	730	7.3%	1,200	12.4%
New Caledonia	246,000	210,000	85.2%	15,600	6.3%	17,600	7.2%
New Zealand	4,368,000	2,666,000	61.0%	615,000	14.1%	784,000	17.9%
Niue	1,500	1,400	97.6%	43	3.0%	120	7.8%
Northern Mariana Is	53,900	43,800	81.3%	5,100	9.5%	11,300	20.9%
Palau	20,500	19,000	92.7%	4,900	24.0%	4,900	24.0%
Papua New Guinea	6,859,000	6,503,000	94.8%	1,684,000	24.5%	1,773,000	25.9%
Samoa	186,000	184,000	98.8%	19,400	10.4%	32,300	17.3%
Solomon Islands	526,000	502,000	95.3%	146,000	27.8%	179,000	33.9%
Tokelau Islands	1,100	1,100	94.6%	70	6.2%	41	3.6%
Tonga	104,000	99,700	95.8%	9,400	9.1%	16,100	15.5%
Tuvalu	9,800	9,300	94.4%	590	6.0%	1,800	18.1%
Vanuatu	236,000	221,000	93.5%	94,700	40.1%	113,000	47.8%
Wallis & Futuna Islands	13,600	13,200	97.4%	29	0.2%	150	1.1%

EVANGELICALS IN AUSTRALIA AND NEW ZEALAND

By Mark Hutchinson

While historically and politically embedded in Oceania, Australia, and New Zealand (ANZ) stand out as the largest and most Europeanized of the Pacific nations. The product of similar, and often the same colonial impulses, their national histories have also varied due to geography, contact history, economic resources, migration patterns, and constitutional history. The imbalances in the relationship between the two countries also cause them to variously conflict, converge, and exchange influences. Religiously, they have often acted as a single region of exchange for ideas, members, and ministerial labor. Their churches have been, and remain, important to one another, to the extent that this give and take receives—like the large New Zealand-born migrant community in Australia—remarkably little attention. Both have strong Anglican and Catholic religious cultural defaults, and both demonstrate the secularizing patterns (evident in large "no religion" categories in their census figures) seen in most late modern countries of European settlement. Religious sectarianism has not been as marked in either country as in the originating countries of migration, an observation which has often misled observers to think that religion has either not been present or has at least been unimportant. The historical literature, however, indicates otherwise.

Among the forms of Christianity that successfully globalized through the nineteenth century, evangelical traditions treated Australia and New Zealand as the last two stations on a globe-spanning religious railway. Missionaries and evangelists from Samuel Marsden to Billy Graham came to ANZ after first visiting the transplanted British cultures or growing number of American commercial outposts in India, China, Malaya, even Japan, all of which were considered (in Europe and North America) more missiologically important than the island dominions. After the high period of chartered migration companies and pauper migration (1840s), migrants too developed an international track to Australasia, often via South Africa, or Canada. The forms of Evangelicalism which arrived in the country tended to be shaped depending on the period in which people migrated, the point of colonial development, and the strength of the existing "pull" cultures and organizations.

Australia

Despite early disestablishment (after the collapse of early preferential land-based schemes), Anglicans remained the single largest religious community in both countries. In Australia this was rapidly challenged by the scale of Irish migration, transplanting to the southern continent Ireland's majority Catholicism and minority (but important) Anglo-Irish and Presbyterian forms. The Anglo-Irish filled many of the colonies' professional, medical and legal strata, while the Presbyterian influence played an important part in the development of education—including the early emergence of public education—business cultures, and science.

More importantly, the emotions swirling around the disestablishment of the Church of Ireland, World War I conscription, and Home Rule, and their impact on the identity of the Protestant British empire ensured that Irish Evangelicals had a disproportionate influence on Evangelicalism in both Anglican and Presbyterian churches. The commitment of Evangelicals to the Imperial cause could be measured, as Robert D. Linder has shown, by their high rates of volunteering in World War I. Voluntary political organizations, such as the Orange Institution and Australian Protestant Defence Association, moved from (in the early twentieth century) a central position in evangelical life to being essentially irrelevant by the end. Evangelicals themselves were increasingly marginal to the developing welfare state across the twentieth century and decreasingly present in the declining mainstream churches, even as evangelical moral assumptions decamped from the public sphere.

The two significant exceptions to this were the continued strength of revivalist Christianity among Aboriginal and Torres Strait Island Australians in the Uniting Church and the dominant reformed Evangelical party in Sydney Anglicanism. Despite an important organizing role in the Australian Christian Lobby and a few other more marginal organizations (such as the Christian Democratic Party), by the end of the 2010s, public Evangelicalism was a mere shadow of the constituency which had exerted considerable influence through such bodies as the Local Option League at the end of the nineteenth century and the Festival of Light through to the middle of the 1980s. The huge crowds of the 1959 Billy Graham Crusade proved to be a peak, rather than the forerunner, of an incoming evangelical tide.

At the same time, evangelical spirituality has remained vibrant within those bodies with less immediate connection to the secularizing public sphere. Baptist churches, for example, which had long (as a matter of belief) refused government support, grew steadily through to the end of the 1990s, while Pentecostal churches (after a long hiatus) exploded in the late 1970s (in part on the back of growth and fragmentation in the mainstream Charismatic Movement).

By 2006, Pentecostal churches were the second largest Christian constituency by attendance in the country, drawing more than 250,000 attendees on any given Sunday morning. While Pentecostal growth continued through the 2000s, after the initial energy provided by the Charismatic Movement had faded, the greater part of that growth was in churches larger than 2,000, particularly in the rapidly globalizing Hillsong church network which emerged in the 1980s out of the work of New Zealand father and son team, Frank and Brian Houston. Unlike the United States, Australian megachurches are predominantly Pentecostal and Charismatic in expression.

New Zealand

Compared to nineteenth century missions among indigenous Australians (which, except for Moravian efforts, Richard Broome famously typified as like writing on sand), the Maori inhabitants of New Zealand responded rapidly, in places enthusiastically, to the coming of the Christian gospel. By 1838, as the Ngāti Rarawa chief Nopera Pana-kareao traveled between villages with his New Testament in his hand, Maori were evangelizing themselves: the great baptism period had begun which would see over 50% of Maori in church on any given Sunday.

It was not to be a straightforward or bloodless cultural contact. Traditional, as well as land-focused and imperialist wars between 1845 and 1872, succeeded the deadly Musket Wars (1807–1842). Detaching gospel-orientation from imperialism was also not straightforward. Evangelicals were divided on adapting the faith to Maori communalism, to a theology in which belief in the miraculous went beyond mere affirmation of the text, and where tapu and mana became important ecclesial organizing principles. Ringat and Ratana churches remain evidence of these original movements, and some of the structures of modern movements, such as Destiny Church, are evidence of their continuing importance. Hoverd reports a forty-year growth trend, 1966–2006, among Maori forms of Christianity, with Evangelicals and Ratana/Ringatu tending to gather in similar socioeconomic strata.

The Anglican and Catholic Churches, which played an important role both in evangelizing the islands and representing significant pakeha constituencies, remain significant in New Zealand, despite decline and ageing in their core constituencies. In the Methodist and Anglican constituencies, the Polynesian membership of churches is almost always more Evangelical than the broader Pakeha (Caucasian) constituency.

New Zealand Evangelicals remain an absolute minority across the nation, though growing steadily as a proportion of the whole body of church attenders. Between 2001 and 2006, census returns suggest that "Evangelical, Born Again and Fundamentalist" categories increased by 25.6%, and affiliation with Pentecostal churches increased by 17.8% (Hoverd and Sibley 2010).

Retaining this distinctive, by, for instance, dedicated ministry formation, is not without its challenges. The universities dominate the post-secondary sector, and there are few evangelical options among the colleges associated with a state institution. The largest independent evangelical provider has been the Bible College of New Zealand (originally the Bible Training Institute, now Laidlaw College), with around one thousand students in various modes of offer. Within the Anglican Church, evangelical parishes, and the more evangelically oriented Diocese of Nelson, often sent its ordinands abroad for training—from 2006, it established Bishopdale Theological College, offering programs through Laidlaw.

New Zealand has long demonstrated a receptivity to religious innovation and energetic forms of faith, from Norman McLeod's globe circling "pure and uncorrupted gospel" (in Hutchinson and Wolffe 2012), to healers such as J.A. Dowie, the restorationists of the Latter Rain Movement and the charismaticized Pentecostalism of the Hillsong and CCC movements. Its position at the "end of the world" has attracted millenarian and exclusivist movements, including strong and often controversial Exclusive Brethren communities with which are associated some five thousand of the twenty thousand self-described Brethren in New Zealand. The church scene also continues to interact with the migrant nature of New Zealand society. High levels of in-migration ensure that those traditions which are dominant in the two-thirds world (Pentecostalism and Charismatic forms among them) are well-represented in non-European populations, while high levels of labor out-migration has ensured that even pakeha New Zealanders have encountered religious variety. A large proportion of the largest Pentecostal denomination (the Assemblies of God in New Zealand), for example, are of Tongan, Samoan, Fijian, Indian or Korean extraction, ensuring it is a lively movement experiencing the usual pluralist cultural negotiations.

While present in New Zealand since the early 1900s, Pentecostalism emerged as a significant part of New Zealand Evangelicalism through the 1960s, when a nationally significant Charismatic renewal among university students and mainline attenders expanded Pentecostal congregations and produced new forms of church-planting and evangelism. New Zealand ministries, such as Scripture in Song, had a global impact. Successive waves of charismaticized New Zealanders pushed out into the region, creating a significant impact not only on Australia, but through missionary organization and sending on to East Africa and Southeast Asia.

As well as producing energetic missions and ecclesial movements, New Zealand has also produced a strong evangelical thought tradition, particularly in the reformed tradition. Prominent writers and teachers have included William Orange in Christchurch, the ancient historian Edwin A. Judge, classicist E. M. Blaiklock, businessman R. A. Laidlaw and missionary and Bible teacher J. Graham Miller. For many of these, the British ISCF/Crusaders/InterVarsity tradition was important. Orange, for example, was early involved in Tyndale House.

As evangelical growth has stalled among Pakeha, New Zealand has also become a significant source of post-evangelical emerging church thought. The Prodigal Project and Mt Eden Baptist Church (later renamed Cityside) were examples of how antipodean (Australian and New Zealand) thought could have more than a merely local impact. New Zealand thought and church practice has continuing links with and ties to many churches in Asia and the United Kingdom.

Challenges and New Modes of Mission

Evangelicals in Australia and New Zealand, regardless of whether they are members of magisterial or one of the Free Church traditions, experience a common set of challenges. The major contextual challenge is the fact that the early causes of evangelical social effectiveness, which linked conviction to social practice via nineteenth century morality, have broken down. Despite the fact that evangelical nongovernmental organizations, for example, are still highly visible in the two countries, their ability to impact upon public policy and to act in an explicitly faith-based manner are significantly diminished. Those agencies which were previously evangelical in nature, such as the Salvation Army or the traditions which in Australia fused in 1977 to form the Uniting Church, have also become decreasingly so.

Those that retain a significant Evangelical presence, such as Sydney's Anglicare and Hammondcare agencies, face either internal divisions over the proper role of public religion or, on the other hand, external opposition from a variety of interest-based lobby groups. An instance of this pressure on Evangelicals to absent themselves from the public sphere arose in 2010 in the midst of debate over Anglicare's opposition to proposed legislation authorising adoption by gay couples. Though Anglicare's CEO Peter Kell was in fact protesting not the legislation itself so much as the impact on religious conscience of an ideologically-fuelled drive to change the status quo, the case was misreported in the press under the misleading title "Churches push gay adoption ban" (SMH 2010). The dominance of church agencies in the Welfare sector (over 50% of service delivery, and almost all the largest nongovernment bodies) was in part the problem; the fact that Anglicare was the major provider of adoption services in Sydney made it a key target for its opponents. The fact that legislation would coerce religious conscience would push Anglicare out of the service, warned Kell, and spark a crisis in an already strained sector.

This is the daily reality of secularization and the power of organized secularism (Peter Hitchens' "tyranny" of secularist "tolerance-speak") in Australia and New Zealand. Against this, the individualist, Bible-based anti-speculative traditions of evangelical thought influential in Australia have shown themselves inadequately equipped. In New Zealand and Australia tolerance is extended to minorities while they remain minorities within defined communal walls. Religion is permissible when it can be construed as a form of ethnicity (and so quaint), but not when it claims its own status as specifically religious, i.e., supernatural. Such religion is subjected to a variety of social restraints, ranging from opprobrium (where such beliefs are seen as ridiculous) to legal penalties (for allegedly dangerous idiosyncratic ministries such as Catch the Fire, which saw a pastor jailed for resisting a judicial ruling under the Racial and Religious Tolerance Act) and even, very occasionally, church burning or physical violence.

The hidden mechanisms of social control were identified by ABC journalist James Valentine when speaking about Australian "permissible bigotry." In Australia Christians and Hillsong members rank alongside other stereotypes such as "fiery redheads" and "bottom-feeder lawyers" as legitimate targets. If, in the words of historian Russell Ward, the nineteenth century Australian was "a good bloke, a mate . . . though not religious in the conventional sense of the word" (in Reardon 2003), by the end of the twentieth century evangelical conviction was no part of the idealized Australian make-up at all.

Steering a way forward in these non-neutral highly mediatized, libertarian communities, which at the same time authorize strong lobby and caucus-driven traditions to infringe upon the rights of particular groups, is the central challenge for evangelical public faith. Out of this flows the daily fare of politics, marriage equality campaigns, the pitching of religious traditions against one another, moral panics about the influence of Australia's vanishingly small fundamentalist subculture or opinions expressed by the Australian Christian Lobby, or even Hillsong's alleged involvement in "rigging" the music charts or reality TV talent shows. This in an industry defined by precisely that. At the same time, core Evangelicalism is facing a slow collapse of its traditional constituency, and a shift to new, quite culturally different constituencies. At the time of this writing, the largest evangelical church attending constituency in Australia is the Assemblies of God, an innovation in terms of the historic Anglican dominance of Australian Protestantism.

At least half of those who consider themselves Christians with evangelical-like value sets attend no church. In New Zealand, Alan Jamieson suggests, a growing "churchless faith" is increasingly the norm. This softening (and in some cases, collapse) of the center has a direct impact on institutions (such as the old Bible College Movement), relationships, and mission. It has, for example, been unusual in the past for major NGOs to approach Pentecostal constituencies for support. At the same time as World Vision Australia was looking for new partners however, there has been a significant shift towards social engagement by megachurches in Australia and New Zealand. What had at one time been quite a critical relationship has in recent years become one of relatively warm, public mutual respect. On the downside, many independent Bible colleges have merged or collapsed and significant numbers of mainline former parishes have of necessity been conflated or closed. This has left evangelical congregations in the position of having to re-evangelize their own denominations and develop programs such as over plant-ing (where new congregations are commenced in a building or par-ish while continuing older, more traditional ministries) in order to consolidate their presence in Australian and New Zealand suburban settings. Other churches have developed new mechanisms for ur-ban missions. Evangelical congregations and movements thus find themselves, on the English model, less a party within a larger move-ment than isolated and distinct communities of faith. There is a nec-essary impact on ecclesiologies (nature, function and constitution of a church), in part explaining the prominence of post-evangelical and emerging church models among younger and former Evangelicals.

What is different is the consciousness not just of being in the church, but the deliberative way of actually being the church to the world.

Due to the relatively small size of the Christian constituencies in Australia and New Zealand, and the unique shape of the reformed and Charismatic revivals of the 1960s and 70s, conflict between re-formed and Charismatic movements has been inevitable. Until the turn of the twenty-first century, there was comparatively little en-gagement between Sydney Anglicanism, for example, and the developing megachurch movements. With the dominance of the Reformed Evangelical party in the former, and the increasing institu-tionalization of the latter, however, there has been increasing reasons for common cause in recent years. Students at Sydney's Evangelical Anglican bastion, Moore College, for instance, now regularly study Pentecostal churches, and there is an observable movement of members between the various churches in any particular city. The largest challenges in both countries, however, relate to pluralization and globalization. New Zealand in particular is open to migration from the Pacific Islands, India, and China, creating significant cultural diversity in any particular evangelical movement.

Internal tensions are inevitable, such as the lengthy court case between the Samoan and national Assem-blies of God movements through the early twenty-first century. European congregations find themselves of-ten challenged by the co-location of an ethnic congregation in the same building, particularly one that may be more internationally connected than linked to the local church presbytery or parish. Gaining a reputation as a Chinese, Filipino, or African church can become a self-fulfilling prophecy and alter the ability of a church or college or school to engage the plural setting in which it finds itself.

In this setting, the understanding not merely of a group of coexisting congregations, but of groups of churches within and across denominations, as a system involved in the same larger mission becomes pressing. It is not surprising, therefore, that it is not only Pentecostal and Charismatic churches in Australia and New Zea-land that have spawned global networks of churches. Hillsong is the example normally noted, as it has churches on four continents, but the Christian City Churches have more than three hundred churches worldwide, the CRC Movement is present in Asia and the Pacific, and churches such as Planetshakers and Paradise Community Church even use simulcasting technology. Sydney Anglicanism too has been touted by its more liberal coreli-gionists as a threat to world Anglicanism, through the funding of ministry training, ties with conservative local church groups, influence in the Global Anglican Future Conference (GAFCON), the InterVarsity Movement, and cross-boundary direct church planting.

Most of this is not new, given the extended missionary history of Australian and New Zealand evangelical churches. What is different is the consciousness not just of being in the church, but the deliberative way of ac-tually being the church to the world.

Sources and Further Reading

Gilling, Bryan, ed. *"Be Ye Separate": Fundamentalism and the New Zealand Experience.* Hamilton: University of Waikato & Colcom Press, 1992.

Glover, R. "For a Happy Marriage, try the Submissionary Position." *Sydney Morning Herald*, September 1, 2012.

Guest, Mathew and Steve Taylor. "The post-evangelical emerging church: Innovations in New Zealand and the UK." *International Journal for the Study of the Christian Church* 6, no. 1 (March 2006): 49 –64.

Hoverd, William James and Chris G. Sibley. "Religious and Denominational Diversity in New Zealand 2009." *New Zealand Sociology*, 25, no. 2 (2010): 59–87.

Hutchinson, Mark. 'Truth and Jest: Evangelicalism in Contemporary Australia." *Evangelical Studies Bulletin* no. 79. Chicago, USA: ISAE, 2011.

Jamieson, Alan. *A Churchless Faith: Faith Journeys Beyond the Churches.* London: SPCK Publishing, 2002.

Lange, Stuart M. *A Rising Tide: Evangelical Christianity in New Zealand 1930–65.* Dunedin: Otago University Press, 2013.

Lineham, Peter. "The Fundamentalist Agenda and Its Chances." *Stimulus* 14, no. 3 (2006): 2–14.

Morrison, Hugh, Lachy Peterson, Brett Knowles, Murray Rae, and Lachy Paterson, eds. *Mana Māori and Christianity.* Wellington, N.Z.: Huia, 2012.

Porter, Muriel. "Sydney Anglicans and the threat to world Anglicanism." Religion & Ethics, Australian Broadcasting Corporation, 2013 and accessed May 1. http://www.abc.net.au/religion/articles/2011/08/29/3304954.htm

Reardon, Judith, The Development of the discourses of mateship in Australia with special reference to the period 1885–1925, PhD Thesis, James Cook University, 2003.

Roxborogh, John. "Mapping the Evangelical Landscape in New Zealand." *Mapping the Landscape: Essays in Australian and New Zealand Christianity. Festschrift in Honour of Professor Ian Breward. Susan & William W. Emilsen.* New York: Peter Lang (2000): 318–331.

Evangelical Impact in Australia: Standing with Those in Need

Meeting both practical and spiritual needs of Australians is at the center of one of the largest community organizations in the country. Mission Australia (MA), with three thousand employees helping some three hundred thousand people, has a vast reach, assisting the needy in employment, housing, education, and many other areas.

While the gospel message is not always overt, "Everything we do is represented in God's love for people," says Paul Molyneux, MA's national chaplain. The organization's founding purpose—"Inspired by Jesus Christ, Mission Australia exists to meet human need and to spread the knowledge of the love of God"—is based on 1 John 3:16.

MA's roots go way back. In 1859 a city mission modeled after London City Mission was established in Brisbane, shortly followed by one in Sydney. Meant primarily to meet the needs of homeless men, but also to minister to women and orphans, city missions were soon springing up in every capital city in Australia.

It was only in 2000, however, that the city missions, along with other agencies, merged to form MA, a nationwide organization that works in towns and rural communities as well as in cities.

MA has a special focus on reconciliation with indigenous peoples: Aboriginal people and Torres Strait Islanders. "We believe the issues our indigenous people face are significant ones," says Molyneux. There is a large gap in living standards between the indigenous peoples and other Australians, for example. This gap shows up in life expectancy, education, substance abuse, alcoholism, homelessness, and unemployment, particularly among young people.

The detailed Reconciliation Action Plan (RAP) developed by MA attempts to address these issues with a commitment to four main areas: building relationships with indigenous peoples and organizations, respecting indigenous peoples and their cultures, fostering cultural appreciation through awareness training, and participating in celebratory events with indigenous peoples.

"We long for the healing of our national soul," states the RAP summary, "as we see Aboriginal and Torres Strait Islander cultures fully valued, broken relationships restored, and social inequalities eradicated." Because the issues are so big, progress is slow, says Molyneux, but there is hope.

Many of the MA staff deal primarily with the practical work of helping people get on their feet. Some of the ways in which this is accomplished are through

- employment agency and job support with 140 sites throughout the country;
- early learning and child care;
- training in automotive technology, business, care for the elderly, children's services, construction, English language and adult literacy, horticulture, hospitality, retail, and youth work;
- housing; and
- research and advocacy on social policy.

MA also conducts the largest annual youth survey in Australia, giving thousands of teenagers the opportunity to share their priorities and concerns. The top issues—such as family finances, drugs and alcohol, the environment, and employment—vary from one year to the next. The results give government agencies, the media, and communities insight into youth culture and help them to respond more effectively.

Twelve chaplains who work across Australia under Molyneux's leadership provide spiritual assistance to the staff working directly with clients. "Chaplains are also part of maintaining the Christian ethos and conversation," Molyneux notes. And that is where the spiritual and the practical come together. Recently, a young man struggling with addictions approached an MA chaplain who was conducting a Bible study at a drug rehabilitation center. In the conversations that followed, the young man realized his spiritual need and committed his life to Christ.

With the country's large influx of refugees, MA has also found ministry opportunities with newcomers. Molyneux cites the example of a refugee who found a job through one of MA's employment centers. The employer commented that the refugee was the best worker he had on the floor of his factory. Now members of four refugee families are working in the same place. Not only are they providing good work for the employer, they are also enjoying the best salaries they have ever had.

—Debra Fieguth

EVANGELICALS IN MELANESIA & MICRONESIA

By Mark Hutchinson

The Way(s) of the Sea

While often overlooked by scholars, Oceania is home to a higher proportion of Christians than most parts of the world. Like the region's landmasses, however, religion is highly diversified, spanning thousands of dialects—more than seven hundred dialects and discrete languages in Papua New Guinea (PNG) alone and one thousand three hundred in Melanesia—and producing over a quarter of the world's distinct religious traditions.

The dominant geographical fact is the makeup of the island, and the connecting canoe/sailing links. Only PNG, which hosts nearly three-quarters of the combined Melanesian/Micronesian population, might be considered a mainland. Tribal life prior to globalization is thus traditionally oriented around tight definition of permissible kinship exchanges, relationship to land, sea, and climate, and the fragility of food supplies and shelter in small spaces. Food staples, such as pandanus on Kiribati or breadfruit in the eastern Carolines, shaped regional religions in some areas. However, Palau and Yap, where taboos are more important, are exceptions to this. Though there is wide variation, there are common themes. For example, the sky and hero pantheons, ancestral spirits and ghosts, shamanic possession and trance for divination, common trickster gods such as Olofat share in these themes (Dobbin 2011).

With the impact of globalization, both traditional and indigenized religions interact heavily with traditional and modern authority structures, often resulting in instability or intercommunal friction. Language and religion are inevitably taken together, as language provides not only the symbolic universe for traditional religions, but in many cases has determined the spread and success of various forms of Christianity and the varying success in attempts to move from tribal communities to nation states. Traditional religion also remains a live issue. As Guiart (2005) notes, Although the inhabitants of the Loyalty Islands "have been Christians for a century and a half (twice as long as the natives of New Caledonia proper) sacred groves still exist there, the old deities are remembered, and the cult of the dead continues to surface from time to time." When, as in PNG, intractable diseases (such as AIDS) are faced by inadequate health and education systems, reversion to traditional cures, folk magic, and puri puri is common.

Among the Melanesian religions, animism, symbolic totemism, and belief in continuous communication with the dead are common, beliefs which are entrenched in Orpheus-like fables of journeys in the land of the dead. All genealogies commence with family myths of intercourse between the divine and the human, providing chieftainly families with significant power. This is reinforced in those areas where priestly lineages died out, as many were in the process of doing even prior to the advent of missionaries, causing chiefly families to take on increased religious potency. In some of the literature, the drivers for continuance in the region's traditional religions (entrenched cor-

> **The dominant geographical fact is the makeup of the island, and the connecting canoe/sailing links.**

ruption, the rise of casino capitalism, the need for translocal imagined communities, anticolonialism and social protest) have been seen as the drivers for the rapid growth of Pentecostal and Charismatic forms of faith.

Religion in a Time of Change

Early missionaries often mistook some parts of the region (particularly Micronesia) as having no religion, due to the relative lack of architectural expression. The mythical character of Pacific religions, however, ensured relatively rapid adoption of the Christian story often through mass conversion, the Biblical narrative providing a flexible framework into which local authority, power, and symbolic structures could be knit.

Expansion was facilitated by the travel of local people by canoe and sail between islands—Fijian travel to Samoa in 1815, for example—and by indigenous missionary work prior to the arrival of Europeans in a particular place. The timing of the opening up of the Pacific meant that Protestant missionaries tended to arrive first, with the first wave from 1797, when the London Missionary Society (LMS) opened a sporadically successful work on Tahiti. They quickly began to cooperate, carving up regions into comity relationships that avoided overlap and competition. The related martyrdoms fed evangelical missionary zeal for decades. LMS then expanded to the Cook Islands, Samoa, the Loyalty Islands, western and eastern Papua, and the Torres Strait Islands. The Wesleyan Missionary Society, which was founded in 1814, worked in Tonga, Fiji, the Solomon Islands, and New Zealand; the Anglican Church in northern Vanuatu and the eastern Solomon Islands. Later the Queensland-based South Seas Evangelical Mission worked in the central Solomons.

From the 1820s, the American Board of Commissioners for Foreign Missions was active in the parts of Micronesia not already converted under Iberian Roman Catholic influences. The pre-World War I German influence in PNG made Lutheranism and German Catholic missions significant, while Catholic missions that were primarily French expanded into most of the Pacific after the advent of the Marists in 1818.

The longitudinal, multi-linguistic and multi-origin nature of Protestantism in the Pacific means that the term *evangelical* is open to multiple uses. In the former French sphere of influence, for instance, there are evangelical churches which have more in common with European traditional Protestantism than with the English understanding of the term. Evangelicals in traditional Protestant denominations are thus in some tension with those in later waves of evangelisation, which from 1960s took advantage of the association of mainline religions with majority ethnic cultures or classes. Most Pacific nations were profoundly affected by World War II and subsequent globalization. Some of these nations, particularly Nauru, experienced exploitation, disease and colonial labor migration which date back well into the nineteenth century, leaving legacies which still impact on contemporary social and political life.

These islands thus face stresses relating to shifts into monetary economies from subsistence economies, population growth, and internal and external ecological challenges. In addition, resource rich areas are subject to incursions by development projects and the effects of cyclical tourism that often increase such social pathologies as land alienation, urban drift, use of intoxicants, intergroup violence, and public corruption. One might see the 2014 riots in the Australian-run refugee camp on PNG's Manus Island in this light. Climate change is a region-wide concern. Rising ocean levels and increased storm activity decreases community autonomy and threatens the disappearance of some island nations. In other settings, decreasing crop yields and increasing scarcity of timber and other resources threatens traditional lifestyles.

In countries other than those with soft passports, such as PNG, these pressures have given rise to extensive Pacific diasporas among nations and across the wider former colonial networks in the wider world. Such people movements are intrinsically interconnected with the spiritual economies of the Pacific, which have been transformed by the insertion of Christian beliefs into the Pacific cosmos (Scott 2005). In the words of Fazeya, "Churches play an important role in maintaining social cohesion in communities and directing communal activities" (2001), but in order to keep doing so, churches need to focus on holistic well-being approaches.

From Fiji to the Solomons

Dominated by the British during the nineteenth century, Fiji consists of 322 islands, of which about 110 are inhabited. Nearly half the population are Indo-Fijians, among whom the majority religion is Hinduism. In Fiji, as in Tonga, from which many of the islands were evangelized, one of the great evangelical traditions (Methodism) achieved virtual state church status. Its general acceptance by the indigenous chieftainly class has ensured both indigenization and also tension with the ruling classes. Lotu—worship or Christianity—is paired with vanua (place, or land), meaning that indigenous Fijian Christian identity is often starkly marked off from that of Indo-Fijians, many of whom were originally Hindu (Tomlinson).

This attitude to land and people draws heavily on Old Testament metaphors. Fijian Christians are ambivalent about certain traditional elements of vanua—the drinking of kava in its traditional religious sense. Methodist churches have also been on both sides of the various exertions of military power in the repeated coups after 1987. As Fraenkel notes, by 2011 "The Great Council of Chiefs had been disbanded, and the fourteen Fijian provincial councils were each either deeply split or overtly pro-Bainimarama." Such conflicts regularly see the invocation of Biblical texts or even prophecy in public discourse. Civil agencies transform with the appropriation by the Fiji Police Force of "spiritual warfare" language into "charismatic" institutions (Trnka in Fraenkel, 2011).

While the language and methods of the schismatic and officially preferred New Methodist Church (crusades, public parades, conversion, Biblical preaching, and so forth) are recognizably evangelical, their erastianism (belief that the state is superior to the Church in matters of ecclesiology) and submission to authority would have seemed odd to their nineteenth century forebears. On the other hand, traditional Methodists (more than three hundred thousand members) are concerned about the spread of what they see as American fundamentalism, in particular among Pentecostal churches.

Rootlessness due to landlessness, and urban drift are pointed to as major causes. As Ernst has noted, the Assemblies of God through the 1990s grew at a remarkable 27% per year, in part due to its ability to break the nexus between Fijian ethnicity and Christianity. Up to one-quarter of AGF churches in northern Fiji are Indo-Fijian. While that growth has now slowed, approximately one quarter of the Methodist tally to 8% of the rest of the population; 170,000 people gathered in churches such as the Baptist Union, Assemblies of God, Christian Mission Fellowship, and the Christian Outreach Centres might be considered evangelical in Bebbington's terms.

Many of these churches also maintain a presence in the significant Fijian and Indian diasporas, such as Joseph and Martha Suren's Agape Revival Centre Church which has Hindi and English language centers in Lautoka and Auckland, and a "mission" in Andra Pradesh. Suliasi Kurolo's Word Faith is connected to Christian Mission Fellowship, which runs an extensive missions network in addition to churches and school in Fiji, and daughter churches in Queensland and Victoria. Many Australian and New Zealand megachurches have outreaches or relationships with Fijian locations. There are seven Sydney-originated C3 churches in Fiji.

As befits the major French colony in the region, the majority religion in New Caledonia (or Kanaky) is Roman Catholicism. The population of the "mandated collegiate" French state, however, is made up of a highly diverse population across which religious traditions are spread unevenly. The European population (33%) is largely Catholic, while the indigenous population (Kanak, 44%) has a prominent broad Protestant tradition (largely gathered in the Evangelical and Free Evangelical Churches, originally founded by the London and Paris Evangelical Missionary Societies), with Kanak indigenizations, as well as more recent Baptist and Pentecostal forms of Evangelicalism.

Other religious traditions, such as the Muslim Javanese, arrived as a result of colonial plantation labor transfer or as Samoan and Vanuatan labor migrants seeking work in New Caledonia's mining or tourism industries. Rapid growth in Pentecostalism occurred after American (the Killingbecks) and French (the Ledrus) AG missionaries joined forces and began work among English-speaking Vanuatuan migrant workers, who were isolated by their language from mainstream society. Returning francophone migrants to France, many of whom had to travel there to complete compulsory military service, brought with them the influence of French evangelical churches, founding dedicated organizations such as Mission du Pacifique (2002), which saw the expansion of evangelical works to places further afield, such as the Wallis and Futuna Islands. YWAM and Operation Mobilisation have local works, such as the Club Biblique Street children's work, Discipleship Training, and a Bible School for the Nations. The strength of these religious traditions makes the Kanaky nationalist cause important to all churches.

Vanuatu holds a special place in the religious iconography of the Pacific. It is the landing place of the Portuguese explorer in the service of Spain, Pedro Fernandes de Queirós, who came looking for the Great Southland of the Holy Spirit and left the name "Espiritu Santo" on one of its eighty-plus volcanic islands. Canadian and Australian Presbyterian mission churches are now about one-third of the population. They are featured strongly in the history of these islands. The extension of British and French rule through a Condominium arrangement until independence in 1980 also left strong Roman Catholic and Anglican traditions, making up a combined 30% of the population and promoting a national form of Pidgin (Bislama) as a mechanism for bridging indigenous, francophone, and anglophone communities. While nearly 97% of the population is Christian, and the national politics essentially emerged from church colleges and communities, traditional practices and syncretic cargo cults (particularly the John Frum Movement, strong on Tanna) remain a focus of anticolonial religious protest. In the words of one former participant, "I'm now a Christian, but like most people on Tanna, I still have John Frum in my heart" (Raffaele 2006).

Traditional practices, such as bride price marriages, belief in sorcery, and the like remain a point of frustration for Christian churches, particularly when they spark societal violence between de-territorialised tribal groups in, for instance, the squatter camps around Port Vila. Up to a third of the population in Port Vila attends a Pentecostal church (some two thirds of which are indigenous in origin), while Charismatic prayer and worship is also common in Presbyterian, Anglican, and Catholic congregations. Rapid change with the growth of tourism income and its consequent increase in inequalities, predatory capital, and land alienation, preference such empowerment models of church, providing mechanisms for dealing with change, an implicit critique of colonialism, and a means of compromising with kastom. Eriksen (2009) provides examples—in the Renewal Church (Santo) and the Healing Ministry (Nguna)—of how traditional spiritualities are absorbed and transformed through rupture in the indigenous appropriation of healing and Charismatic Christianity.

As in Vanuatu, the Solomon Islands were subject to European incursions in search of indentured labor and resources. Even when the islands came under British and German protection, the only advantage to indigenous peoples as a whole was access to missionaries, particularly from the LMS and the South Seas Evangelical Mission (SSEM). The islands that make up the country are divided by politics (with pre-World War I German influence in Bougainville and Buka), language (Papuan versus Austronesian language groups), and culture (with significant Polynesian outliers). While cargo cults were relatively rare in the Solomons, the literal appropriation of the biblical text (such as neo-Israelite movements that seek the ancient sites of the Lost Tribe of Israel in the Malaita bush) and its priestly, ritual application (for example, by the Melanesian Brotherhood, an indigenous Anglican missionary movement) indicates that indigenous appropriation of Christianity is strong.

The reflex impact of Solomons Christianity on, for example, the early Australian Charismatic Movement, has been the cause of some tension in reformed Evangelical circles. The island state has been the site of considerable turmoil, requiring external military and policing support, over inter-island tensions (particularly between Guadalcanal and Malaita). "There is a distinct lack of organic unity or shared values between state and society, and a limited commitment to the introduced system of government" with religion (including Islam on Malaita) and kastom competing with more satisfying local identities to fill the gaps (Dinnen 2009; McDougall 2009). The proliferation and contestation among Christian groups and the judgmental interiority of perpetual sinfulness implicit in reformational Christianities are two among a number of catalysts for the proliferation of new Pentecostal forms and of smaller groups among migrant communities.

Highlands and Islands: Papua and Its Archipelagos

With more than 10% of the distinct languages on the planet is the largest island in the region, shared by Papua New Guinea and West Irian. PNG, whose population is more than seven million inhabitants, should be the superpower of the region, but its mountainous interior and highly divided and intensely tribal demography drive its politics, which in turn has significant problems with public corruption due to the lack of a tradition of disinterested service. Potentially a wealthy country with vast mineral and fossil fuel resources, the income is unevenly distributed. Some 85% of people still live by subsistence farming, and infant and maternal mortality rates are among the highest in the region. This has led to significant social violence. Neither Western nor Asian investors have brought with them the sort of ethical, sustainable investment which creates stable socioeconomic conditions.

While nation-making in Indonesia (camped on PNG's border in Irian Jaya) informs PNG public discourse as both inspiration and threat, the ethical implications of Malaysian timber and resource companies fuels Christian-Muslim tensions, particularly when repression of West Papuan nationalism in Irian Jaya flares up. In the absence of working public institutions, religious identities have taken deep root, with over 95% of the population associated with a Christian Church, and a small but increasing rate of Muslim conversion.

About half of all education and health care in the country is run by church-based agencies (more in some sectors, such as Teacher Education). The entanglement of Christian churches with a corrupt public sector has contributed to this latter, as has the connection between cargo cult spirituality and the arrival of prosperity-driven fundamentalism. Dealing with the underlying traditional religious attitudes and *kastom* has made PNG a major laboratory for modern Christian missiology, and ironically (through the work of scholars such as Alan Tippett), a source for the thought which has underpinned much evangelical church planting in the West.

Indigenizing the faith without triggering cargo responses or appropriations of the spirits which are not recognizably Christian has remained a significant issue in the extension of various denominations. Belief and practice of witchcraft is still common, even in Christian communities, and this, rather than more naturalistic causes, are often blamed for deaths in a community. The appropriation by missions of communal or inter-tribal buffer lands also continues to create conflict. Nevertheless, the long history of mission churches in many parts of PNG has resulted in a rationalization of religious life, with many "traditions that were in open conflict with these authorities . . . simply no longer practiced." Given the interconnectedness of Melanesian subsistence/exchange economies with traditional ritual, such rationalisation has socioeconomic as well as religious impacts. As Schram notes of the Auhelawa people, most Papuans "incorporate their Christian belief into bwabwale with prayers, blessings and songs" (Schram 2007).

The 1.3 million Evangelicals on the island, by way of contrast, have been more wary of *kastom*, and many define themselves more by its absence than its presence. These communities have been particularly influenced by missions originating in New Zealand, Australia, and the Pacific Islands. The importance of indigenous missionaries from the Loyalty Islands, the Cook and Solomon Islands, and Samoa has been explored by Crocombe and others, and points to the deeper interconnectedness of Pacific communities, prior to, but in an expanding fashion after the development of European interisland trading and labor flows.

Pan-denominational growth was particularly visible from the late 1970s, both by expansion into un-evangelized areas, and by the Evangelicalization/Charismaticization of existing traditions. The Amalgamated Full Gospel Church Outreach Centre Association is an example which divided from the United Church. The Assemblies of God, another example, was largely initiated by Australian missionaries, and at more than three hundred thousand members is now larger than its parent body. In addition, Foursquare, Apostolic, Christian Revival Crusade, and Christian Outreach Centres all have significant constituencies in PNG, as do the Baptist Churches, Swiss Evangelical Brotherhood, South Seas Evangelical Mission, Nazarene, Apostolic, the New Tribes Mission, the (Swedish) Philadelphia Church and the like. While there is significant interaction between most traditions, there are furious local debates, for example, over the reality of periodic spiritual renewal movements which impact most traditions.

Micronesia

Dominated by Spain (as the Spanish East Indies) until after the Spanish American War (1898), Micronesia has a relatively small population. Land and water are often in short supply. Almost all Micronesian countries suffer from the effects of climate change, particularly drought, salination, and rising sea levels, aspects which affect their participation in international politics, such as the Whaling Commission, trade relations with China, and so forth. The government of Kiribati (which though geographically dispersed over 3.5 million square kilometres of ocean, contains only 811 square kilometers of land), in particular, has been active internationally, seeking solutions for climate-related crises. Guamand Nauru, with a once significant superphosphate export industry, are possibly the most Westernized of the islands.

As a consequence, events elsewhere (Australian concerns with refugee detention for example, or American downsizing of the military presence on Guam) can have significant local effects, with impacts on local peoples, such as the Chamoru, described by Rapadas (2007), as "a sad, dispirited people." With some exceptions, Micronesia has had relatively few of the nativist movements which have seen returns to indigenous religious practice in parts of Melanesia. Its symbolic universe is thus highly Christianized, leading its crisis politics to be drafted as evidence by academic secularists in the West.

While there has been much literature on the problem of religious conviction in the face of climate change (Kuruppu 2009). However, there is growing attention to the contribution that spiritual capital can make to threatened societies. Not only does Christian identity support community identities faced with being spread out in deterritorialised diasporas or permanent refugee status in the case of nations threatened by inundation, a fate already modeled by the Banaban people, expropriated by phosphate mining after World War II. But it provides mechanisms for engaging with global issues, and dealing with the necessary heavy reliance on larger nations, such as Japan, Australia, and the UK). The people of God metaphor is a powerful one, inspiring both indigenous Pacific missions, such as the Deep Sea Canoe Mission, a Pacific version of China's Back to Jerusalem Movement, and evangelically inspired politics, such as Micronesia's willingness to vote against the majority of the UN General Assembly in support of Israel.

Sources and Further Reading

Barden, Kenneth E. "Land's End: Can an Island Nation Survive Without Its Islands?" *World Policy Journal* 28:2 (2011): 49–55.

Bouma, Gary D., Rodney Ling and Douglas Pratt. *Religious Diversity in Southeast Asia and the Pacific: National Case Studies*, Google e-book: Springer, 2010.

Crocombe, Marjorie Tuainekore, ed. *Polynesian missions in Melanesia: from Samoa, Cook Islands and Tonga to Papua New Guinea and New Caledonia*. Suva: Institute of Pacific Studies, University of the South Pacific, 1982.

Dobbin, Jay. *Summoning the Powers beyond: Traditional Religions in Micronesia*. University of Hawai'i Press, 2011.

Ernst, Manfred, ed. *Globalization and the re-shaping of Christianity in the Pacific Islands*. Suva: Pacific Theological College, 2006.

Fraenkel, Jon. "Fiji." *The Contemporary Pacific* 23, no. 2 (Fall 2011): 456–76.

Gunson, Niel. *Messengers of grace: evangelical missionaries in the South Seas 1797–1860*. Oxford: Oxford University Press, 1978.

McDougall, Debra. "Becoming Sinless: Converting to Islam in the Christian Solomon Islands." *American Anthropologist* 111, no. 4 (December 2009): 480–491.

Raffaele, Paul. "In John We Trust." *Smithsonian Magazine*, February 2006. http://www.smithsonianmag.com/people-places/john.html#ixzz2DeIjE38n

Scott, Michael. "'I Was Like Abraham': notes on the anthropology of Christianity from the Solomon Islands." *Ethnos: Journal of Anthropology* 70, no. 1 (2005): 101–125.

Tomlinson, Matt. "Sacred Soil in Kadavu, Fiji." *Oceania* 72 no. 4 (June 2002), 237–257.

Trnka, Susanna. "Re-mythologizing the state: public security, 'the Jesus Strategy' and the Fiji Police." *Oceania* 81, no. 1 (March 2011): 72–87.

US Department of State. *Country Reports on Human Rights Practices*. Vol. 1–2. Washington, (2007): 1040ff.

EVANGELICALS IN POLYNESIA

By Peter Lineham

The conversion of Polynesia to Christianity was a profoundly significant event, the story of which has been made very familiar both in the history of missions and in the narratives of the Pacific islands. Out of the evangelical awakening, the first of the broad evangelical missionary societies (which became known as the London Missionary Society, or LMS) sent its initial mission to the Pacific.

It was a team of twenty-nine men, including four ministers, although most of the others were artisans. Most were sent to the Society Islands (Tahiti), with smaller groups sent to the Marquesan Islands and to Tonga. The mission quickly fell into disarray, and by 1803 only four missionaries were left. However, after the conversion of the high chief Pomare in 1812, and the latter's supremacy over the whole island group of Tahiti in 1816, Christianity was in a position to become the national religion.

In 1817 John Williams arrived in Polynesia, and in 1823 he extended the LMS mission to Rarotonga in the Cook Islands, eventually using his boat the Messenger of Peace to evangelize many Polynesian islands. Williams was killed and eaten on Eromanga (New Hebrides) while extending the mission into Melanesia in 1839.

The missions rapidly expanded but became denominationalized and nationalized. The American Board of Commissioners (Congregational) established a mission in Hawaii in 1820, in collaboration with one of the Tahitian converts, and here too it became the state religion. With the formation of Church Missionary Society (CMS, 1799) by Anglican Evangelicals, and a separate Wesleyan Methodist Missionary Society (WMMS, 1815), the LMS became in effect a Congregational Mission. The CMS developed a mission in New Zealand from 1814, and in 1822 the WMMS sent Walter Lawry to lead a mission to Tonga, later extended by John Thomas and John Hutchinson. In 1830 the leading chief of Tonga was converted. The WMMS and the LMS competed for influence in Samoa, seeing the island group become predominantly congregational, while the WMMS extended into Fiji.

A feature of the Christianization of the islands was the ministry of indigenous Pacific missionaries, beginning with islanders from Raiatea. Pre-existing trading and family connections—such as those that connected Tonga to many locations in the Fiji group—for example, became important pathways for evangelism. Renowned for their navigational skills, indigenous teachers such as Taharaa, Faaruea, and Hatai took Christianity all over the Pacific, making an impact on Hawaii, Fiji, Samoa, and even New Guinea.

On the tail of Spanish and French exploration, Catholic missions expanded throughout the Pacific later in the century. Today, Catholicism is overall the largest denomination in the region, though individual islands all have a specific Protestant dominating tradition, often as a result of sponsorship by a dominating ruler. Revivals gave the Protestantism of the Pacific an evangelical face, though its heart was often focused on communal and national commitment rather than individual salvation. Christianity was remarkably successful in becoming accepted as part of the essence of island culture.

The Protestant missionary organizations were still there until 1961 in Samoa and until 1963 in French Polynesia. The Free Wesleyan Church of Tonga broke away from Australian Methodist control in 1885, helping to preserve Tonga's political independence. Elsewhere Methodists remained under the supervision of the Australian Methodist Church until 1963. In practice, though, churches had indigenous ministers and leadership long before this.

> **Today, Catholicism is overall the largest denomination in the region.**

Current Composition

In recent times Polynesia has been profoundly affected by migration. New Zealand, Hawaii, and Tahiti, once the heartlands of Polynesia, now have a minority of people with Polynesian ethnicity. Meanwhile, the metropolitan centers in New Zealand, Australia, and the West Coast of the United States are now the home of more than half of Polynesians; Auckland has more Samoans than Samoa. Hawaii represents a special case; 10% of Hawaiians have pure Polynesian ethnicity while another 13% are Polynesian to some degree, though this may not be Hawaiian but Samoan or Tahitian. One-third of Polynesians in Hawaii are from other parts of the Pacific. Hawaii is at once an island and a metropolitan destination.

Each island has its own distinctive religious balance and emphases, but a pervasive Polynesian pattern can be identified. Polynesian migrants retain close links with their islands of origin. Emigrants generally retain their childhood religion, and the Church in Auckland or Los Angeles often functions as a surrogate village, complete with family and authority structures. Even second-generation New Zealanders, Australians, or Americans often fervently adhere to local branches of their churches.

Congregationalism is particularly strong in Polynesia, although this is a congregationalism which embraces state links with the church and a hierarchical social structure. In French Polynesia the Evangelical (Maohi) Protestant Church is the strongest, although its polity today is essentially Presbyterian rather than Congregational. In Samoa the Congregational Christian Church in Samoa (Ekalesia Fa'apotopotoga Kerisinao I Samoa) is dominant while in American Samoa the Congregational Christian Church is also very strong. The Cook Islands Christian Church and the Congregational Christian Church of Niue (Ekalesia Niue) are from the same tradition. These churches might best be described as conservative, rather than evangelical. Although there are significant evangelical voices within them, there are equally some liberal influences calling for an indigenization of the church and redefinition of the Christian message. In the metropolitan centers, Congregationalists who arrived in New Zealand from the Cook Islands in the 1950s did not fit well into the small and liberal denomination in New Zealand, and in 1969 their Pacific Islands Congregational Church was handed over to the Presbyterians. Subsequently, some islanders (especially from Samoa) have preferred to form separatist congregational churches. A similar pattern is evident in other metropolitan centers.

The Methodist tradition is particularly strong in Tonga, Fiji, and to a lesser extent, Samoa and Fiji. The Free Wesleyan Church of Tonga (Siasi Uesiliana Tau'ataina 'o Tonga) split from Australasian Wesleyan control in 1885. The split was partially healed in 1924 but Methodist here remains disputative. There is a single Methodist Church for both Samoas. Methodists in Australia are part of the Uniting Church and here as elsewhere some Methodists have preferred to affiliate with their island denomination.

Some smaller evangelical churches have been planted in the Pacific, but rarely with great success. Open Brethren assemblies were planted in Samoa in 1954, with links to Maori and Fijian equivalent bodies. The Salvation Army came to Tonga only in 1986. Various branches of the Churches of Christ have established themselves in Tonga, American Samoa, and other places since 1960. "Regular" Baptists are not common in the Pacific, but various independent Baptist churches have established themselves, including the Bible Baptists in Tonga (1994), and the Happy Valley Baptist Church in American Samoa (1976). Independent evangelical churches emerged in French Polynesia among dissentients from the main Protestant church, including the Keretitiano Church, the Autonomous Church, the Pain de Vie Church in western Tahiti, and other churches in Pueu in Tahiti and in Raiatea. The growing liberal and hierarchical character of the main Protestant church was the fundamental reason for these evangelical schisms.

Adventists in the Pacific look back to a significant group of Pitcairn Islanders who adopted this faith in 1886. They were planted in the French Society Islands in 1890, and in Niue in 1915; other foundations are similarly quite early but their activities were less successful in Polynesia than in Melanesia. They are particularly active in Samoa, American Samoa, and Tonga, though their numbers are rather small. The Church of the Nazarene planted a number of congregations in Samoa in the 1970s, including one in American Samoa.

Pentecostal churches have developed a significant presence in most of the islands since 1970, although origins go back earlier than that in the case of specific Europeans and Chinese in the islands. Pacific islanders in Australia, New Zealand, and the western seaboard of the United States were quite attracted to Pentecostalism, especially when disillusioned about their traditional churches. When all the different Pentecostals are counted there is evidence of remarkable growth, although Mormons (The Church of Jesus Christ of Latter-day Saints) and Jehovah's Witnesses have generally grown even more quickly.

Most Pentecostal churches are more obviously branches of international bodies. The most successful of these is the Assemblies of God. They were first planted in American Samoa in 1926 by Hermann and Frances Winkelman but did not grow significantly until a revival in 1952. At that time a branch was planted in Western Samoa. Huge growth has taken place among AOG churches since the 1970s. By 2002 there were sixty-four churches, a Bible school, a radio station, and a significant youth ministry. In Samoa, they are now the fifth largest denomination with 28,200 adherents (6.6% of the population in 2006) plus 12,000 in American Samoa. There are a number of schismatic groups from the same family. There are also significant branches of the island AOGs in New Zealand, United States, and Australia. The New Zealand Samoan Assemblies of God split from the New Zealand AOG in 2005, taking with it some 40,000 members and 125 congregations. Because Assemblies of God are independent movements, there are many other schisms from the AOG throughout the Pacific, including the Peace Chapel in Samoa, the Bible Study Fellowship of Samoa (founded in 1976 by Max Rasmussen), a French Polynesian group which split away in the 1980s and the Church on the Rock, established in Tonga in 1991. In French Polynesia, the AOG were reshaped by Chinese prophetic influences associated with Kong Duen Yee in the 1960s, and this group appeals especially to the Chinese diaspora which is widely spread in commercial circles through the Pacific.

The New Life Church of New Zealand planted a branch in Tonga in 1975. The Apostolic Church on the Rock was founded in Niue in the 1980s with links to the Apostolic Church in New Zealand. The New Apostolic Church (an originally German offshoot of the nineteenth-century Catholic Apostolic Movement) arrived in Tonga in 1978. The Tonga Fellowship for Revival was established in 1994 and the United Pentecostal Church of Tonga in 1974. The Word of Life Outreach Centre and the Word of Life Christian Fellowship were both founded in American Samoa around 2000. Some of these churches can draw on overseas support, but this does not ensure their long-term success.

The Tokaikolo Christian Fellowship of Tonga is a striking example of how effective an indigenous Pentecostal church can be. Senituli Koloi (whose full name, after the year of his birth, literally means "century of the arrival of Christianity") was a minister of the Free Church working under the authority of the interdenominational evangelical body Scripture Union. Koloi later took a more Independent and Charismatic direction creating a movement called Maamafo'ou (New Light). Although he died in 1980, the movement continues and promotes extensive evangelical activities. Similarly in Samoa, Pastor Viliame Mafoe, a former Methodist lay preacher, established the Worship Centre in 1997 and it grew rapidly, absorbing some other Independent churches.

Life and Aspects

Evangelicalism in many respects was the common characteristic of all the forms of Protestantism planted in the Pacific in the early years of the nineteenth century. After a period of liberalization and institutionalization, since World War II, it has become resurgent. The deep rifts between the main Protestant church and the separatist churches, however, make it difficult to establish a common definition of *evangelical,* and therefore to establish how many Evangelicals there might be. This chapter asserts that a section of each main Protestant church should be included, but acknowledges that consequently statistical analysis is extremely conjectural.

The resurgence of Evangelicalism has much to do with the increasing accessibility of the Pacific to international visitors, and the opportunities and economic necessities which lead Polynesians to seek to improve their lives abroad. The image of the Pacific as an untarnished edenic setting may bring a trail of people and cruise ships to the Pacific, but it does not aid these tiny nations, many of whom are among the poorest states in the world, increasingly afflicted by the instability and political volatility that such economic conditions breed.

The rise of new religious traditions, Christian and non-Christian, is much influenced by these circumstances. Churches with strong international connections appeal as a way out of the economic malaise. Typically such churches are less concerned with community needs, although they generally reinforce traditional family structures and give a sense of confidence in uncertain times. In recent years apocalyptic expectations have flourished among some of the new churches.

Typically, Pentecostals are much less respectful of traditional Pacific customs than the established churches. These churches are often highly conservative in their Biblical interpretation, and inclined to defend the Christianized state, which is under severe pressure in the contemporary world. They can act as unreflective vehicles of globalized forms of American culture, which they employ with little discernment. On the other hand, they are vibrant and emotional in their music and worship style, and thus often feel more akin to some aspects of island culture.

Prime Concerns and Issues

Mission

Many of the church congregations that are distinctively evangelical have come into existence in reaction to forms of state church Protestantism which inhibit a strong sense of mission. Yet the very mission which is so strongly a focus is often negated by the constant splits and personality troubles in these communities and ethical concerns about the conduct of ministry and the use of money. Many of these aspects are also vividly apparent in the Pasifika churches of Australia, New Zealand, and the western part of North America (including Hawaii), where many Polynesian churches are branches of island churches. The place of materiality, communal ownership, and mana in these churches causes these churches, as well, to suffer from leadership disputes and disputes over money and property. The largest numbers of the Polynesian churches on the mainlands are in association with one or another of the local denominations: in Australia, the Uniting Church, in New Zealand the Pacific Island Church of the Presbyterian Church of Aotearoa-New Zealand, and the Methodist Church of New Zealand. Most of these denominations have developed independent structures for the Polynesian congregations, but frequently the membership is large enough to receive significant attention and support from the sponsoring denomination. The fact that there are high levels of Evangelical commitment within the Pasifika wings of these mainstream Protestant churches means that they have had a significant impact on the host denominations.

In addition to denominational forms, there are a range of evangelical ministries very active in the Pacific. These are of various styles and approaches. The Bible Society's work uses a ship, while Scripture Union employs indigenous staff. Youth for Christ has established offices in Fiji and Samoa, while Youth with a Mission (YWAM) uses all of these and a variety of community forms besides. There are evangelical radio stations in most nations. Promise Keepers has a presence in some places. Evangelical coordinating bodies exist in several Polynesian states, including the Tonga Evangelical Union.

Pentecostal nondenominational bodies include Ambassadors for Christ, established in 1992. Trinity Broadcasting Network established a branch in Samoa in 2002 with great success. YWAM has been very active in Hawaii, forming the University of the Nations, and has also made an impact sporadically in other parts of the Pacific, and from the 1970s its volunteers and its ships visited centers of population in the Pacific. The focus of such short-term mission approaches often raises the issue of cultural sensitivity.

Future

The trend towards decline in the state-linked Protestant churches is the most significant trend in the region. In the process it seems likely that evangelical elements in these denominations across the region will have more opportunities. At the same time, the rise of new denominations includes a significant proportion of Pentecostal believers, in particular, although Mormons and other sectarian groups are growing more quickly, and Catholicism offers more common threads. The tendency of Evangelical and Pentecostal communities to divide and innovate means that their long term impact is difficult to detect. Much energy is lost in disputes and failures, though at the same time they are a source of energy for those confronted by the effects of globalization. As students of American exceptionalism have noted with regard to that part of the world, strident competition may increase short-term impact but over the longer term undermine the credibility of the Christian community.

Dr. Peter Lineham is professor of History at the Auckland campus of Massey University. He has published widely on Australian, New Zealand, and Pacific religious history. His most recent book is *Destiny: The Life and Times of a Self-Made Apostle.* He is frequently called upon by the media to explain religious issues.

Sources and Further Reading

Ernst Max, ed. *Globalization and the Re-Shaping of Christianity in the Pacific Islands.* Suva, Fiji: Pacific Theological College, 2006.

Ernst, Manfred. *Winds of Change: Rapidly Growing Religious Groups in the Pacific Islands.* Suva, Fiji: Pacific Conference of Churches, 1994.

Forman, Charles W. *Island Churches: Challenge and Change.* Suva: Institute of Pacific Studies of the University of the South Pacific, 1992.

———. *The Island Churches of the South Pacific: Emergence in the Twentieth Century.* Maryknoll, NY: Orbis, 1982.

Garrett, John. *Footsteps in the Sea: Christianity in Oceania to World War II.* Suva and Geneva: Institute of Pacific Studies, University of the South Pacific in association with World Council of Churches, 1992.

———. *To Live among the Stars: Christian Origins in Oceania.* Suva and Geneva: Institute of Pacific Studies, University of the South Pacific in association with World Council of Churches, 1982.

———. *Where Nets Were Cast: Christianity in Oceania since World War II.* Suva and Geneva: Institute of Pacific Studies, University of the South Pacific & World Council of Churches, 1997.

Gunson, Niel. *Messengers of Grace: Evangelical Missionaries in the South Seas, 1797–1860.* Melbourne: Oxford University Press, 1978.

Herda, Phyllis, Michael Reilly and David Hilliard, eds. *Vision and Reality in Pacific Religion: Essays in Honour of Niel Gunson.* Christchurch and Canberrra: Macmillan Brown Centre for Pacific Studies and Pandanus Books, 2005.

Hinton, Vaughan. *Tides of Change: Pacific Christians Review Their Problems and Hopes.* Melbourne: Commission for World Mission of the Uniting Church of Australia, and Joint Board of Christian Education, 1981.

CONTRIBUTORS

Evangelicalism and Evangelism

Dr. Frances S. Adeney is the William A. Benfield Jr. Professor of Evangelism and Global Mission at Louisville Presbyterian Theological Seminary in Kentucky. She is currently working on a book about women and Christian mission.

Evangelicals and Other Religions

Dr. Miriam Adeney is an anthropologist and missiologist at Seattle Pacific University in Washington, United States, and Regent College in Vancouver, Canada. She is the author of *Kingdom Without Borders: The Untold Story of Global Christianity, Daughters of Islam: Building Bridges with Muslim Women, God's Foreign Policy: Practical Ways to Help the World's Poor, How to Write: A Christian Writer's Guide*, and *A Time for Risking: Priorities for Women*. She has served as the president of the American Society of Missiology and is on the board for Christianity Today International, as well as task forces for the World Evangelical Alliance and the Lausanne Committee for World Evangelization. She has received the Lifetime Achievement Award from Christians for Biblical Equality.

Pentecostals: Their Rise and Role in the Evangelical Community

Dr. Allan Heaton Anderson is a professor of Mission and Pentecostal studies in the Department of Theology and Religion at the University of Birmingham, United Kingdom.

Evangelicals in the City

Dr. Ash Barker founded Urban Neighbours of Hope (www.unoh.org) in Melbourne, Australia, in 1993. The organization has grown into numerous neighborhood-based teams in Thailand, Australia, and New Zealand. In 2002 Barker moved with his family to the largest slum in Bangkok, Thailand, where they have lived since then. Barker is now the convener for the newly formed International Society for Urban Mission (www.newurbanword.org).

The Future of the Evangelical Movement

Dr. Paul Joshua Bhakiaraj is a professor at the South Asia Institute of Advanced Christian Studies (SAIACS), Bangalore, India. Among other affiliations he is an associate of the Missions Commission of the World Evangelical Alliance (WEAMC); a member of the Lausanne Theology Working Group; and a member of the International Networking Team of International Fellowship of Mission as Transformation (INFEMIT).

Evangelicals in Mainline Denominations

Dr. John Bowen is the director of the Institute of Evangelism at Wycliffe College in Toronto. He is the editor of *Green Shoots Out of Dry Ground: Growing a New Future for the Church in Canada* (Eugene, OR: Wipf & Stock, 2013) and the author of several books.

Evangelicals and Politics

Tim Costello is the chief executive officer of World Vision Australia, a Baptist minister, and a global leader on social justice issues.

Evangelicals and the Lausanne Movement [and] The Challenge of Evangelical Diversity

Rose Dowsett is a founding member of the Evangelical Alliance Scotland and served as missiological adviser to the Evangelical Alliance-UK, and as vice-chair of the World Evangelical Alliance's Mission Commission. She was a member of the Lausanne Theology Working Group and of the small international team that drew up the Cape Town Commitment.

What Evangelicals Believe

Dr. C. Rosalee Velloso Ewell is the executive director of the Theological Commission for the World Evangelical Alliance. She is a Brazilian Baptist theologian from São Paulo with a PhD in theological ethics from Duke University in Durham, North Carolina. She also serves as the New Testament editor for the forthcoming *Latin American Bible Commentary* and is the author and editor of various books and articles.

Ministry Profiles

Debra Fieguth is a freelance journalist in Kingston, Ontario, Canada, and the author of *Keepers of the Faith*, and *The Door is Open: Glimpses of Hospitality in the Kingdom of God*.

Evangelicals and the Arts

John Franklin is executive director of Imago (www.imago-arts.org), a Toronto-based initiative designed to support Christians in the arts in Canada. He is chair of the Arts in Mission Task Force for the WEA Mission Commission, was a member (with an arts focus) of the program team for Cape Town 2010: The Third Lausanne Congress on World Evangelization, and serves as chair of Lausanne Canada.

Evangelicals and Roman Catholics

Dr. Timothy George is dean of Beeson Divinity School of Samford University in Birmingham, Alabama, and general editor of the *Reformation Commentary on Scripture.*

Evangelicals and Bible Translation

Dr. Gilles Gravelle is the director of research and innovation at The Seed Company. His forthcoming book, *The Age of Global Giving* (William Carey Library, Pasadena) discusses the critical changes taking place in mission finance.

Dr. Roy L. Peterson is president of the American Bible Society and former president and CEO of The Seed Company, a Wycliffe Bible Translators affiliate. Earlier in his career, He served in Ecuador and Guatemala, also for Wycliffe organizations.

Evangelicals and Environmental Stewardship

Dr. Ken Gnanakan is an educator, environmentalist, and theologian based in Bangalore, India. He is the founder and chancellor of the ACTS Group, chair of the International Council for Higher Education, and chair of Theological Book Trust.

Evangelical Engagement with Ethnodoxology

Dr. Robin P. Harris is president of the International Council of Ethnodoxologists (ICE). She is an assistant professor and Director of the Center for Excellence in World Arts at GIAL in Dallas, Texas. She has served for decades in cross-cultural contexts, including ten years in Russia, and helped launch the Arts in Mission task force of the WEA Mission Commission.

200 Events in Evangelical History
Evangelicals You Would Want To Know

Albert W. Hickman is Senior Research Associate at the Center for the Study of Global Christianity and an associate editor of the *Atlas of Global Christianity*. He focuses on collecting and analyzing denominational statistics for the World Christian Database. He also serves as a liaison to groups such as Finishing the Task.

Evangelicals and Ecumenism

Dr. Rolf Hille is director of ecumenical affairs of the World Evangelical Alliance, Germany, and former chair of the Theological Commission of the World Evangelical Alliance.

Evangelicals and Theological Education

Dr. Riad Kassis is the program director for Langham Scholars (Langham Partnership), the international director for International Council for Evangelical Theological Education, and a theological educator and writer based in Lebanon. The writer would like to acknowledge the input of Chris Wright, Evan Hunter, Scott Cunningham, and Melody Mazuk.

Evangelicals and Science

Dr. Harry Lee Poe is a theologian, author, and the Charles Colson Chair of Faith and Culture at Union University in Jackson, Tennessee.

The Story of the World Evangelical Alliance

Dr. Ian Randall is a senior research fellow at the International Baptist Theological Seminary in Prague and Spurgeon's College in London. He is the author of a number of books on evangelical history.

Evangelicals and Social Justice

Dr. Ron Sider is the Senior Distinguished Professor of Theology, Holistic Ministry, and Public Policy at Eastern University's Palmer Theological Seminary in King of Prussia, Pennsylvania. He has published more than thirty books, including *Rich Christians in an Age of Hunger*, lauded by *Christianity Today* as being among the top one hundred most influential books in religion in the twentieth century.

Evangelicals and Gender

Dr. Aída Besançon Spencer is professor of New Testament at Gordon-Conwell Theological Seminary in South Hamilton, Massachusetts, and an ordained minister in the Presbyterian Church (USA).

Evangelicals and the Marketplace

Dr. R. Paul Stevens is professor emeritus of Marketplace Theology at Regent College in Vancouver, Canada. He is a marketplace ministry mentor and author and coauthor of numerous books, including *Work Matters: Lessons from Scripture*, *Taking Your Soul to Work*, and *Entrepreneurial Leadership*.

Evangelicals in the Middle East

Dr. Wafik Wahba is professor of Global Christianity at Tyndale University College and Seminary in Toronto, Canada. He has taught theology and intercultural studies in the United States, the Middle East, Africa, Asia, and South America. He co-led the unit on theological education for mission at the Lausanne 2004 Forum for World

Evangelization in Pattaya, Thailand, and is one of the authors of "Effective Theological Education for World Evangelization," Lausanne Occasional Paper No. 57 (May 2005). Dr. Wahba serves on the board of directors for several international Christian organizations.

Evangelicals and Prayer

Molly Wall is a researcher, editor, and program manager with Operation World in the United Kingdom. She has served as a researcher and curriculum developer with the U.S. Center for World Mission in Pasadena, California.

Evangelicals and Religious Liberty

Roshini Wickremesinhe is the director of the Colombo office of the International Institute for Religious Freedom.

Godfrey Yogarajah is the executive director of the Religious Liberty Commission of the World Evangelical Alliance.

Who Are Evangelicals? A History

Dr. John Wolffe is professor of Religious History at The Open University based in Milton Keynes, United Kingdom. He is the author of many works, including *The Protestant Crusade in Great Britain, 1829–1860*; *God and Greater Britain: Religion and National Life in Britain and Ireland, 1843–1945*; *Evangelical Faith and Public Zeal: Evangelicals and Society in Britain, 1780–1990*, edited with introduction, and *The Expansion of Evangelicalism: The Age of Wilberforce, More, Chalmers and Finney*.

Evangelicals and Missions

Dr. Allen Yeh is associate professor of Intercultural Studies and Missiology at Biola University in La Mirada, California. He Is the coauthor of *Routes and Radishes and Other Things to Talk About at the Evangelical Crossroads*, and coeditor of *Expect Great Things, Attempt Great Things: William Carey and Adoniram Judson, Missionary Pioneers*.

Demographics of Global Evangelicalism

Gina A. Zurlo is assistant director of the Center for the Study of Global Christianity in South Hamilton, Massachusetts, as well as a PhD candidate at Boston University School of Theology in Boston, Massachusetts.

Regional Essays

Western Asia

Azar Ajaj is president of Nazareth Evangelical Theological Seminary where he also lectures. He has been an ordained minister to his Arab Israeli community for over twenty years. He holds a BA in Biblical Studies from Bethlehem Bible College and an MTh from International Baptist Theological Seminary in Prague. He is now working on his PhD with Spurgeon's College, doing research on the history of the Baptists in Israel.

Eastern Africa

Dr. Girma Bekele is adjunct professor of Missions and Development Studies at Wycliffe College in the University of Toronto, Canada, and visiting professor of Global Mission, Covenant Theological Seminary, St. Louis, Missouri. He has worked in relief and development both as practitioner and consultant, and currently resides in Toronto, where he worships and ministers at the Ethiopian Evangelical Church in Toronto.

Latin America

Dr. Pablo Alberto Deiros is a pastor, teacher, and widely-published writer, and has variously held such positions as vice-president, Seminario Internacional Teológico Bautista, Buenos Aires, Argentina and cofounder of the Latin American Doctoral Program and of Latin American Christian Ministries Inc.

Central America and the Caribbean

Dr. Stephen C. Dove is an assistant professor of History at Centre College in Danville, Kentucky. He earned his PhD from the University of Texas at Austin and his M.Div. from Fuller Theological Seminary. His current research project focuses on the local character of Protestantism in Guatemala during the late-nineteenth and early-twentieth centuries.

North America

Dr. Larry Eskridge is associate director of the Institute for the Study of American Evangelicals (ISAE) at Wheaton College, Illinois. He is the author of *God's Forever Family: The Jesus People Movement in America*, and coeditor with Mark Noll of *More Money, More Ministry: Evangelicals and Money in Recent North American History*.

Western Africa, Northern Europe, Southern Europe, Western Europe, Australia and New Zealand, Melanesia, and Micronesia

Dr. Mark Hutchinson is a social and cultural historian attached to the University of Western Sydney and The Scots College, where he is director of academic programs. He has written eleven books and more than ninety articles and papers. His recent works include *Cambridge Short History of Global Evangelicalism* (with John Wolffe, 2012) and *A University of the People* (2013).

South-Eastern Asia

Dr. Violet James is dean of students and professor of Church History at Singapore Bible College. Her PhD dissertation (Aberdeen University) was on "American Protestant Missions and the Vietnam War." She has published widely on Asian Christianity, including recent entries in the *Atlas of Global Christianity*, and a centennial history of the Christian Church in Vietnam (*Vietnam: God's Sovereign Work in His Church, 2010*).

Africa

Dr. John Charles Kerr has served at Trans-Africa Theological College in Kitwe, Zambia for eighteen years. He and his wife, Ruth, combine teaching and administration with ministry to all corners of Zambia. He is involved in sponsoring orphan care and community schools, conservation agriculture, and skills training. His book, *Hidden Riches Among the Poor*, chronicles highlights of his Africa experience.

Eastern Europe

Dr. Scott Klingsmith is assistant professor, Intercultural Studies and Missiologist-in-Residence at Denver Seminary, in Colorado and editor of *Acta Missiologiae*. He served with WorldVenture in Vienna, Austria, from 1985–2008, and has had extensive teaching experience around the world, including in the Czech Republic, Ukraine, Bosnia, Germany, Hungary, Romania, India, and the United States.

Polynesia

Dr. Peter Lineham is professor of History at the Auckland campus of Massey University. He has published widely on Australian, New Zealand, and Pacific religious history. His most recent book is *Destiny: The Life and Times of a Self-Made Apostle.* He is frequently called upon by the media to explain religious issues.

Southern Asia

Dr. Wessly Lukose is a principal lecturer in Missiology and registrar at Filadelfia Bible College, Udaipur, India, and closely associated with church planting there and in Birmingham, England. Wessly took his PhD at the University of Birmingham on a contextualized Spirit missiology, built around the indigenous nature of Rajasthani Pentecostalism. His thesis was published in 2013 under the title *Contextual Missiology of the Spirit: Pentecostalism in Rajasthan, India.*

Northern Africa and Egypt

Dr. Duane Alexander Miller serves on the faculty of both Nazareth Evangelical Theological Seminary in Nazareth, Israel, and Saint Mary's University in San Antonio, Texas. His PhD dissertation was "Living among the Breakage: Theology-making and ex-Muslim Christians" (Edinburgh, 2013). His main areas of interest are religious conversion from Islam to Christianity and the history of Protestant missions in the Middle East.

Eastern Asia

Dr. Kevin Xiyi Yao is associate professor of World Christianity and Asian Study at Gordon-Conwell Theological Seminary. He was educated in China and America in the 1980s and 1990s, and earned a Doctor of Theology from Boston University in 2000. From 2003 to 2011 he taught at the China Graduate School of Theology, Hong Kong. He has numerous publications in the area of mission history in China.

Russia and Central Asia

Dr. William (Bill) Yoder has worked in Russia since 2002, commuting to Moscow from Orsha, Belarus, since 2010. He grew up as a Conservative Mennonite in Florida and has spent his years in Europe since 1971 as a church worker and journalist. He was active in East Germany and Poland during the 1970s and 1980s and received a PhD in political science from Berlin's Free University in 1991.

Photo Editor

Rob Robotham is a freelance graphic designer who lives in Toronto.

The Editorial Team

General Editor Dr. Brian C. Stiller is Global Ambassador for the World Evangelical Alliance, author of twelve books and served as President of Tyndale University College & Seminary in Toronto. Stiller also served as president of The Evangelical Fellowship of Canada and chaired the Lausanne's Younger Leadership Conference—Singapore '87.

Associate Editor Dr. Todd M. Johnson is Associate Professor of Global Christianity and Director of the Center for the Study of Global Christianity at Gordon-Conwell Theological Seminary. Johnson is visiting Research Fellow at Boston University's Institute for Culture, Religion and World Affairs leading a research project on international religious demography. He is coauthor of *The World's Religions in Figures* (Wiley-Blackwell), coeditor of the *Atlas of Global Christianity* (Edinburgh University Press), and coauthor of the *World Christian Encyclopedia* (Oxford University Press, 2nd ed.). He is editor of the World Christian Database (Brill).

Area Editor Dr. Mark Hutchinson is a social and cultural historian attached to the University of Western Sydney and The Scots College, where he is Director, Strategy, Partnerships and Research. He has written eleven books and more than ninety articles and papers. His recent works include *Cambridge Short History of Global Evangelicalism* (with John Wolffe, 2012) and *A University of the People* (2013).

Managing Editor Karen Stiller is a senior editor with *Faith Today* magazine, a publication of The Evangelical Fellowship of Canada, and a partner with the Canadian Christian New Service. She is author of *Going Missional: Conversations with 13 Canadian Churches who Have Embraced Missional Life* and coauthor of *Shifting Stats Shaking the Church: 40 Canadian Churches Respond* (World Vision, 2015). Stiller is also a freelance journalist and editor.

NOTES

NOTES

NOTES

NOTES

NOTES

NOTES